12.00

Boundary of Holy Roman Empire

Lands of direct rule by Austrian Habsburgs

D1033981

)km

0   50   100   200 miles

Vistula

Warsaw

P O L A N D

Breslau (Wrocław, Vratislav)

Brieg

UPPER

SILESIA

Cracow

Olomouc (Olmütz)

Troppau (Opava)

MORAVIA

Brno (Brünn)

au)

ER

Vienna

Nagyszombat (Trnava)

Tisza

TRANSYLVANIA

A

Pressburg (Pozsony, Bratisláva)

r

lt

z

Raab (Győr)

Esztergom (Gran)

Buda (Ofen)

H U N G A R Y

Maros

Pécs

(Fünfkirchen)

O T T O M A N

E M P I R E

Danube

about 1600

A History of East Central Europe

VOLUMES IN THE SERIES

VOLUME VI

The Peoples of the Eastern Habsburg Lands,
1526–1918

A HISTORY OF EAST CENTRAL EUROPE

VOLUME VI

EDITORS

PETER F. SUGAR
University of Washington

DONALD W. TREADGOLD
University of Washington

The Peoples of the Eastern Habsburg Lands, 1526–1918

BY ROBERT A. KANN and ZDENĚK V. DAVID

UNIVERSITY OF WASHINGTON PRESS
Seattle and London

Endpaper maps: (front) *from R. J. W. Evans,* Rudolf II and His World: A Study in Intellectual History, 1576–1612 *(Oxford: Clarendon Press, 1973)*; (back) *from Robert A. Kann,* A History of the Habsburg Empire, 1526–1918 *(Berkeley: University of California Press, 1974).*

Copyright © 1984 by the University of Washington Press
Printed in the United States of America

All rights reserved. No part of this publication may be reproduced or transmitted in any form or by any means, electronic or mechanical, including photocopy, recording, or any information storage or retrieval system, without permission in writing from the publisher.

Library of Congress Cataloging in Publication Data

Kann, Robert A., 1906–1981
    The peoples of the Eastern Habsburg Lands, 1526–1918.

    (History of East Central Europe; v. 6)
    Bibliography: p.
    Includes index.
    1. Europe, Eastern—History. 2. Central Europe—History.
I. David, Zdeněk V. II. Title. III. Series.
DJK4.S93 vol. 6 [DJK38] 949s [949] 83-21629
ISBN 0-295-96095-7 (alk. paper)

This book was published with the assistance of a grant from the National Endowment for the Humanities.

Foreword

The systematic study of the history of East Central Europe outside the region itself began only in the last generation or two. For the most part historians in the region have preferred to write about the past of only their own countries. Hitherto no comprehensive history of the area as a whole has appeared in any language.

This series was conceived as a means of providing the scholar who does not specialize in East Central European history and the student who is considering such specialization with an introduction to the subject and a survey of knowledge deriving from previous publications. In some cases it has been necessary to carry out new research simply to be able to survey certain topics and periods. Common objectives and the procedures appropriate to attain them have been discussed by the authors of the individual volumes and by the coeditors. It is hoped that a certain commensurability will be the result, so that the eleven volumes will constitute a unit and not merely an assemblage of writings. However, matters of interpretation and point of view have remained entirely the responsibility of the individual authors.

No volume deals with a single country. The aim has been to identify geographical or political units that were significant during the period in question, rather than to interpret the past in accordance with latter-day sentiments or aspirations.

The limits of "East Central Europe," for the purposes of this series, are the eastern linguistic frontier of German- and Italian-speaking peoples on the west, and the political borders of Russia/the USSR on the east. Those limits are not precise, even within the period covered by any given volume of the series. The appropriateness of including the Finns, Estonians, Latvians, Lithuanians, Belorussians, and Ukrainians was considered, and it was decided not to attempt to cover them systematically, though they appear repeatedly in these books. Treated in depth are the Poles, Czecho-Slovaks, Hungarians, Romanians, Yugoslav peoples, Albanians, Bulgarians, and Greeks.

There has been an effort to apportion attention equitably among regions and periods. Three volumes deal with the area north of the Danube-Sava line, three with the area south of it, and four with both areas. Four treat premodern history, six modern times. The eleventh consists of an historical atlas and a bibliography of the entire subject. Each volume is supplied with a bibliographical essay of its own, but we all have attempted to keep the scholarly apparatus at a minimum in order to make the text of the volumes more readable and accessible to the broader audience sought.

The coeditors wish to express their thanks to the Ford Foundation for the financial support it gave this venture, and to the Henry M. Jackson School of International Studies (formerly Far Eastern and Russian Institute) and its four successive directors, George E. Taylor, George M. Beckmann, Herbert J. Ellison, and Kenneth Pyle, under whose encouragement the project has moved close to being realized.

The whole undertaking has been longer in the making than originally planned. Two of the original list of projected authors died before they could finish their volumes and have been replaced. Volumes of the series are being published as the manuscripts are received. We hope that the usefulness of the series justifies the long agony of its conception and birth, that it will increase knowledge of and interest in the rich past and the many-sided present of East Central Europe among those everywhere who read English, and that it will serve to stimulate further study and research on the numerous aspects of this area's history that still await scholarly investigators.

PETER F. SUGAR
DONALD W. TREADGOLD

Robert A. Kann

Robert A. Kann was a world-renowned historian of the Habsburg empire. Beginning with his magisterial two-volume *Multinational Empire: Nationalism and National Reform in the Habsburg Monarchy, 1848–1918* (New York: Columbia University Press, 1950), his scholarly reputation was firmly established on both sides of the Atlantic. He taught and conducted research in Europe, as well as in the United States. His American and European colleagues and former students dedicated to him a collection of essays for his seventieth birthday (Stanley B. Winters and Joseph Held, eds., *Intellectual and Social Developments in the Habsburg Empire from Maria Theresa to World War I;* Boulder, Colo.: East European Quarterly, 1975). He was similarly honored on the occasion of his seventy-fifth birthday (Stanley B. Winters, ed., *Economic Growth and the Impact of the Dual Alliance in the Habsburg Monarchy,* in a special issue of *East Central Europe,* 7 [1980], no. 2). Bibliographies of Professor Kann's publications included in these two volumes reflect the impressive range of his scholarly contributions. Above all, these tributes attest to the high regard in which he was held both professionally and personally.

My association with Professor Kann began in the early seventies in Princeton, New Jersey, where he resided when teaching at Rutgers University. As Slavic bibliographer and history lecturer at Princeton University, I became acquainted with him during the final stages in the writing of his *History of the Habsburg Empire, 1526–1918* (Berkeley: University of California Press, 1974). Our collaboration on the present volume started in the summer of 1973, and continued after my relocation to Washington, D.C., in 1974 and his appointment to the University of Vienna in 1976. The manuscript was essentially completed in February 1980. At the time of his sudden death in August 1981, we had carried out a substantial part of revisions suggested by the manuscript readers

and editors, and had reached agreement on the rest. It was a rare fortune to have had the opportunity of working closely with Professor Kann
in the course of our joint authorship of this volume.

Washington, D.C.   ZDENĚK V. DAVID
April 22, 1983

Preface

This volume surveys the history of the peoples of the Eastern Habsburg lands from 1526–27 to 1918, that is from the union of the Austro-German Alpine Hereditary Lands with those of the Bohemian and Hungaro-Croatian crowns. It discusses this history, however, only insofar as it has not been covered, for that period, in other volumes of this series. This means that, listed in alphabetical order, the Croats, Czechs, Magyars, Serbs, Slovaks, and Slovenes will be reviewed in full; of the Romanians only those settled in the Bukovina; and of the Ruthenians only those in Transcarpathia and the Bukovina; the Poles in their domestic history are not discussed at all. Concerning the Poles and the majority of the Romanians (in Transylvania, the Crişana-Maramureş area, and the Banat) and Ruthenians (in eastern Galicia) not surveyed in this volume we refer to volumes V, VII, and VIII.

Inasmuch as the Austro-Germans and Italians are definitely to be counted as Western peoples under Habsburg rule, they naturally are not discussed in this volume. A word of explanation may be in order in regard to the Czechs and Slovenes, who in a geographic sense have to be counted as Western Habsburg peoples but in an ethnic and predominantly a historic sense as Eastern. This problem and others that arise in the complex concept of Eastern peoples in the Habsburg lands are treated in the first chapter of this study. There, as well as—in a different context—in the last chapter, the issue will have to be raised to what extent problems of the Habsburg empire as a whole belong to the topic of this volume. To put it another way: can the history of the better part of the empire's peoples be separated from the history of the empire itself?

While, in our opinion, overall empire problems in foreign and domestic relations, in the socioeconomic as well as the cultural field, cannot be part of our subject matter, we are of course conscious that empire-wide issues in all these respects provide the background for our analysis. Accordingly they will be surveyed not only in the introductory and concluding chapters but, as to specific matters, frequently also in the analysis of the individual ethnic groups, which is the main purpose of this study.

Every one of them, therefore, has to be perceived on a threefold level: by itself, within the Eastern parts of the Habsburg empire, and more briefly as part of this even wider entity. We hope that this rather novel approach to our subject will serve its purpose of penetrating a composite phenomenon of East Central European history in space and time.

In the spelling of names of places and persons this volume complies with the rules accepted by the editors and authors of the series.

Among those who helped during the preparation of this volume, several must receive special acknowledgment. John W. Brennan commented on several sections of the manuscript. Vlad Georgescu advised on Romanian-language titles for the history of Bukovina. Paul Robert Magocsi provided copies of rare literature on Transcarpathian Ruthenia. Ivan Berend, Carl-Ludwig Holtfrerich, and Franklyn D. Holzman clarified several points of economic history. The series editors, Peter F. Sugar and Donald W. Treadgold, provided valuable guidance, as well as advice on the arrangement and format of this volume. Katherine O'Leary McQuie typed much of the manuscript. Eleanor Miller Coombs suggested stylistic improvements. Among the libraries used, Státní a Universitní Knihovna in Prague, Nacionalna i Sveučilišna Biblioteka in Zagreb, and especially the Library of Congress in Washington, D.C., proved most helpful.

Finally, Zdeněk V. David wishes to express a deep appreciation to his teacher, James H. Billington, for his constant help and encouragement, and to acknowledge an indebtedness to his parents, JUDr Václav David and Julie Davidová, as well as to the late Georges Florovsky (1893–1979) for their inspirational example.

ROBERT A. KANN
ZDENĚK V. DAVID

Contents

The Peoples of the Eastern Habsburg Lands,
1526–1918

CHAPTER 1

The Habsburgs and the Eastern Habsburg Lands, 1526–1918

Any considerations of this relationship, and in a wider sense the topic of this volume, revolve around two preliminary questions. What do we understand by the term Eastern Habsburg lands? And to what extent —if any—are we justified in conceiving of a bond among the Eastern Habsburg lands beyond the strictly legal one of subordination under the rule of a dynasty? As to the first issue, two conflicting answers are possible, one focused on geographic criteria, the other on ethnic and historical factors.

We will take the Habsburg empire[1] roughly within the boundaries it had from the peace of Karlowitz (Sremski Karlovci, Karlócza) of 1699 to 1918 (exclusive of the not yet annexed territory of Bosnia-Herzegovina), and will draw an imaginary line from the northernmost to the southernmost point. The area west of this line, including the contiguous territories of the indisputably Western Habsburg peoples (Austro-Germans, Italians), would also comprise the major part of Bohemia and a slice of Moravia—that is, the overwhelming majority of the Czechs. Also to the west of the imaginary line we would find almost all the Slovenes and a major portion of Croatian areas of settlement. The Mag-

---

1. The term "Habsburg empire," which was legally valid only between 1804 and 1867, will be used as a historical but not legal-political concept throughout this study. See R. A. Kann, *The Multinational Empire: Nationalism and National Reform in the Habsburg Monarchy, 1848–1918,* 2 vols. (4th reprint ed.; New York: Columbia University Press–Octagon Press, 1977), 2:3–28, 345–55. See also, by the same author, *A History of the Habsburg Empire, 1526–1918* (Berkeley: University of California Press, 1974), pp. x–xiii, 1–4. It will be made clear at the appropriate places whenever the term "empire" does not refer to the Habsburg monarchy but to the Holy Roman Empire.

yar, Romanian, Serb, Slovak,[2] and subsequently the Polish and Ruthenian territories would almost in their entirety be to the east of the north-south line.

If we turn to the ethnic and gradually evolving historical concept, we have to disregard the north-south line as the criterion of what is east and west, and perceive the Czechs, together with all the other Slav peoples in the Habsburg realms, as Eastern people. That is even more obvious in the case of the Slovenes, the only other Slav people located almost totally to the west of the imaginary north-south line. Because of their ethnic or historic affiliation with other South Slav peoples, their Eastern association was even less challengeable than that of the Czechs.

Within the Eastern area we would also have to place one fully non-Slav group and one that is primarily non-Slav, the Magyars and the Romanians. As to the latter, a significant ethnic relationship between Romanians and Slavs had been brought about by many centuries of intermarriage. An ethnic mixture to that degree was lacking between Magyars on the one side and Slavs and Romanians on the other. Where, before 1918, intermarriage of Slavs and Romanians with Magyars did exist, the price to be paid for such a mixture was complete Magyarization as a consequence of the dominant Magyar political position in the Danube valley. Thus a continuous conflict runs through the better part of the modern history of Magyars versus nationally conscious Slavs and Romanians. It is true that most Slavic peoples, and indeed Germanic and Romance peoples, had conflicts with some of their neighbors at times; the Magyars had trouble with all of them most of the time. The understandable feeling of ethnic isolation among the Magyars was largely responsible for this peculiar relationship. To be sure, this does not void the geographical facts, but it certainly interferes with the assumption of a common link between the Eastern peoples in the Habsburg lands. What kind of union is indeed conceivable that would include peoples in continuous struggle with each other—not only Magyars with Slavs but Slavs with other Slavs, the conflict between Poles and Ruthenians to wit?

Before we attempt to answer this question, obviously a far more complex one than the problem of the imaginary geographic dividing line between Eastern and Western peoples in the Habsburg lands, it would be helpful to arrive at a clear understanding of what is meant by the distinction between Eastern and Western Habsburg peoples.

Concerning the division between East and West, the answer will of necessity have to be based on a compromise. It is natural for a historical study to put greater emphasis on ethnic factors and cultural and social

2. Following the practice of the official Austrian nationality statistics, the Slovaks outside of Hungary—that is, those in the former Lands of the Bohemian Crown—were perceived as Czechs.

evolution of peoples than on geographical data and political history. This means that we will perceive all Slavic peoples, including the westernmost ones (Czechs, Slovenes, and Croats), as Eastern peoples. This Eastern concept naturally also includes the Romanians. Beyond this— the major divergences between Magyars, Slavs, and Romanians notwithstanding—the fact remains that Magyar history has been to a greater extent and for a longer period part of Eastern rather than Western History.

This kind of determination—and here the compromise comes in— requires exceptions, and major exceptions at that. Geographic factors do, of course, greatly influence historical developments. There can be no question, for instance, that the Czech Reformation as precondition for the rise of Lutheranism in Germany has much closer spiritual and political ties to the West than to the East. In this sense, Czech history in the sixteenth century and even in the early seventeenth century was indeed part of the history of the Western Habsburg lands, although not in all spheres of human activity. Magyar history after the Austro-Hungarian Compromise (*Ausgleich*) of 1867, and in particular after conclusion of the Austro-German alliance of 1879–1918, had much more in common with the interests and objectives of the Austro-Germans than with those of Slavic peoples. At least to this extent—though not to it alone—Magyar political history for a limited time must be considered to be part of Western history.[3] Finally, Western affiliations, in particular to the Republic of Venice, played an important role in the late medieval and early modern history of Croatia. These, however, are only some very obvious examples of specific qualifications that have to be made to modify our basic East-West distinction. They do not obviate the Eastern affiliation of these ethnic groups for the best part of their history.

It could be said in general that all major ethnic groups under Habsburg rule[4] shared the great experiences of Renaissance, Reformation, Counter Reformation, and the Thirty Years' War; and along with the Poles and Ruthenians they shared the Enlightenment, French Revolution and Napoleonic wars, Restoration era, Revolution of 1848, and Neo-Absolutism until 1859. Therupon national life of the Habsburg peoples branched out in more diffuse ways and summarization becomes more problematical.

With the exception of Hungary under King Matthias I Corvinus (1458– 90), the Renaissance was of declining significance as we move from the

---

3. It may well be argued that the same applies to the first two decades after the reconquest of Buda by imperial forces in 1686 and to the era from the death of Leopold II in 1792 to the Congress of Vienna in 1814–15.

4. In alphabetical order: Croats, Czechs, Germans, Italians, Magyars, Poles, Romanians, Ruthenians, Serbs, Slovaks, Slovenes.

German-Italian West to the Transylvania East. To establish here a straight Western concept compared with an Eastern one would be difficult, inasmuch as decided Eastern influences heralding from the Polish kingdom also are notable in this period. Anyhow, in terms of this study the onset of the Renaissance precedes even the political union of the Habsburg lands brought about in 1526–27.

Concerning the Reformation on the European continent and not merely within the Habsburg realms, the Czechs were unquestionably the leading nation. Inasmuch as the Protestant Reformation—except for relatively brief phases of Slovene and Magyar history, especially east of the Tisza (Theiss, Tisa) River—had a much greater impact on West European than on East European lands, the Czechs have to be comprehended in this connection as Western Habsburg people to the end of the Bohemian phase of the Thirty Years' War.

The Counter Reformation, with its consequences of cultural delay,[5] unquestionably originated in the West, but it had an equally significant impact on the East. The major difference was in timing. When the Counter Reformation began to make its full impact felt in the East— that is, even before the reconquest of Buda by imperial armies in the war against the Turks in 1686—it had spent its most aggressive tendencies in Austro-German, Slovene, and Czech territories. Only then were its full political and cultural consequences felt by the Eastern peoples, for a time still mainly by the Magyars. A major result of the Counter Reformation in the context of our study was undoubtedly that it strengthened the position of the Austro-German Hereditary Lands against the Lands of the Hungarian and Bohemian Crown, which in the course of the sixteenth and seventeenth centuries were either ravaged by the Ottoman forces from the east or subjugated by imperial armies from the south.

The Thirty Years' War, which overlaps with the era of the Counter Reformation, reveals in full clarity the gradual transition from ideological conflict to the even more complex social and national struggle. Without doubt it was accompanied by far greater suffering for the West than for the East. This, of course, had largely geopolitical, strategic reasons. In this context, the Czechs, who as much as the Germans or more bore the brunt of fighting and devastation, must be counted with the West.

Yet a general observation holds true for the Counter Reformation as well as the Thirty Years' War. Conflicts that could still be reconciled in political or religious terms became irreconcilable when they broadened into social or inter-nationalities' conflicts. As such they became truly

---

5. The Counter Reformation is understood here primarily as a political movement, as distinguished from the Catholic Reformation as a spiritual one with rich cultural achievements.

insoluble.[6] That is as true of the fate of the Czechs after the battle of the White Mountain in 1620 as of the Magyars at the time of the Rákóczi insurrections and the so-called peace of Szatmár of 1711 between emperor and Magyar rebels.

Late Baroque and early Enlightenment overlapped in the first half of the eighteenth century in the Habsburg lands. The former was of steadily declining momentum, the latter had as yet made little impact on the contemporary scene. Late Enlightenment and the era of the French Revolution had a much greater immediate influence on the Western than on the Eastern Habsburg lands—in purely political terms, that is, and politics here means mainly foreign policy. Change in domestic policies, on the other hand, while more often than not originating in the West, affected all Habsburg lands deeply. In matters cultural, the influence of the Enlightenment was far reaching in all Habsburg lands, though perhaps somewhat greater in the West than in the East. The revolutionary era was, however, of far less importance in all Habsburg lands, West and East alike, than in the Germanies to the north and west and the Italian states to the south.

The great impact of the Napoleonic wars before 1809 extended again far more markedly to the traditional Western Austro-German and Italian national groups, and only since the peace of Schönbrunn of 1809 distinctly to the western fringe of the South Slavs, the Croats and Slovenes.

The reactionary Restoration era from 1814 to the Revolution of 1848, and Neo-Absolutism after the revolution, oppressed all Habsburg peoples roughly to the same degree—with one exception, the Magyars. With brief interruptions, Hungarian autonomy dominated by the Magyars was on the whole respected until 1848; but after their defeat in the revolution and the War of Independence in 1849, the same Magyars were more brutally oppressed than any other people. This held true for the entire Neo-Absolutist era.

The distinction between East and West became more complex when constitutional government was on the rise and the political life of the Eastern peoples developed more fully. Beginning with the era of constitutional government in the Western part of the empire after 1867, a concept of Slavic solidarity, though by no means unity, developed haltingly. It had become apparent briefly already at the Slav Congress in Prague in the spring of 1848. Yet this solidarity, which must be confused neither with a Russian-inspired political Panslavism nor with the Slavic Renaissance in the cultural field, not only united but to a degree divided the eastern peoples of the Habsburg empire. The Panslav Con-

6. The term "inter-nationalities' conflict" as used here refers to collisions between peoples who usually represented not entire nations but fractions of them, in other words national groups or nationalities. See Kann, *The Multinational Empire*, 1:29–33.

gress of 1867 in Moscow brought the conflict between the Catholic Poles and the other—Orthodox—Slav peoples of the empire into the open; and the same can be said for the long-smoldering enmity between Poles and Ruthenians, after a kind of Galician autonomy was granted practically to the Poles alone in 1868. In either case the religious factor was merely a symptom of ethnopolitical differences that had existed between Magyars and surrounding Slavs and Romanians for centuries.

From now on the Czechs and all South Slavs in the empire, whatever their geographic situation, have to be counted with the East. But following the Compromise of 1867, the Magyars joined the Germans as part of a Western alliance in terms of joint dominance in foreign and domestic policies. The Romanians, on the other hand, supported the Eastern Slavic peoples on the grounds of common opposition to the oppressive Magyar nationality policy. The Croats, owing to the existence of an imperial military border district on their ethnic territory and as a consequence of their struggle against Magyar claims for supremacy, had particularly close ties with the Austro-German imperial West as the main seat of executive power. But they too gradually became involved in the struggle for South Slav unionism, and their continuing aspirations for South Slav leadership must not be confused with pro-Western political affiliation. Like the Slovenes farther to the west, they eventually amalgamated fully with the Eastern sphere of the Habsburg monarchy. The Italians under Habsburg rule remained closely tied to the West during this era; but in their case "West" has to be understood increasingly as alignments and loyalties transcending the western and southern borders of the Habsburg empire.

Altogether if we review the situation just before the outbreak of World War I, only the German-Magyar axis remained closely tied to Germany as a matter of interest as well as principle. If one separates the two factors, one might add to this axis the Poles and Slovenes, both Catholic ethnic groups whose loyalty was, however, qualified: it would last as long as adherence to the Habsburg monarchy, represented by the German-Magyar axis, served their interests better than an association of Russia with the West European powers. In any case, the distinction between Western and Eastern interests became ever more clearly accentuated.

The World War itself does not provide a very useful yardstick for measuring developments between 1914 and 1918. The idea of separation from the empire was now increasingly linked to the fortunes of the war and to the geopolitical situation of individual ethnic groups, favoring those settled at the fringes of the empire against those in a more central position, such as the Czechs, Slovenes, and Croats. The greater chance of cooperation with those ethnic groups that had conationals across the border became a decisive factor. One might perhaps distinguish now between the following groups: first, the German-Magyar axis, within which a liberal Magyar opposition attached to the values of Franco-British limited democracy, became increasingly discernible; second, there was a group of Slav ethnic bodies—Poles, Croats, Slovenes, and Slovaks—whose long-range interests lay with the East but the more immediate ones with the Habsburg West (in the case of the Poles, after the dissolution of the Habsburg empire, for two decades the Atlantic West); third, a group—consisting of Czechs, Ruthenians, Serbs, and Romanians—was committed to the East either sooner or more firmly than the second group; and this was true even though Romanian cultural values were predominantly pro-French and the Czech geopolitical position would tend to make the nation a natural member of the middle group. Nevertheless, political, cultural, and ethnic interests in the case of Czechs, Ruthenians, and Serbs, and geopolitical ones in the case of the Romanians, transformed these four ethnic bodies into the spearhead of Eastern concerns against the preservation of the Habsburg empire.

Thus, quite apart from the entirely separate position of the Magyars, the East did not represent a uniform entity through the war years.

Concerning the common experience and interests of the peoples under Habsburg rule from 1526 to 1918 in foreign relations, the following facts stand out. In the sixteenth-century wars between the Habsburg powers and France, the involvement of the German Habsburg realms, compared with the leading role of the Spanish power, was secondary. The interests of the Eastern Habsburg lands were affected only insofar as the Franco-Turkish alliance of 1536 at least indirectly strengthened Protestantism in eastern Hungary and Transylvania, whereas Emperor Charles V's efforts in the Schmalkaldic war in Germany against the Protestant princes led ultimately only to a meager compromise. The leading role of the Czechs within the Protestant Reformation was, of course, touched by these developments but as yet neither decidedly weakened nor strengthened.

Of far greater immediate significance for the evolution of West-East relations were, of course, the Turkish wars. Taking a large-scale view, here and only here can one speak of a solidarity of interests between Western and Eastern Habsburg peoples in an era still dominated by the notion of common Christian values in defense against the onslaught of the Mohammedan Turkish power. This was on the whole true only for the sixteenth century. The concept of Christian defense was steadily undermined by several forces. One was the never-to-be-healed rift between Catholicism and Protestantism, which became increasingly apparent when in the seventeenth century the wars against the Turks shifted, first intermittently and then steadily, from defense to offensive warfare. There was also the fact that a military command in these wars gave the Germans unchallengeable predominance, a fact resented in particular by the Magyars but also to some degree by the Czechs throughout the era of the Counter Reformation. The Habsburg peoples naturally were affected very unevenly by the Turkish wars. Only Magyars, Serbs, Romanians, and eastern Croats suffered directly from Turkish occupation; Austro-Germans experienced only occasional forays into their territories. The decisive role the West played after the lifting of the siege of Vienna in 1683 and the ensuing great imperial offensive in Hungary is, on the other hand, somewhat overrated. Unlike the onslaught under Süleyman the Magnificent a century and a half earlier, the Turks would presumably have been stopped in southern Germany even if they had succeeded in taking Vienna in 1683.[7] An Ottoman Empire in decline, made manifest by the reconquest of Hungary in barely four years (1683–87), could undertake relatively brief campaigns against the West, but it was no longer in a position to expand permanently in that direction. All things considered, the Turkish wars hurt the West primarily in political and military aspects; they hurt the East in the ethnic, ecological, and cultural spheres as well.

The wars of succession of the eighteenth century fought by the Habsburgs (the Wars of the Spanish Succession, the Polish Succession, the Austrian Succession, and the Bavarian Succession) represented a not entirely successful attempt to supplant ideological warfare with wars resulting from contrived legal issues. Thus it was believed that a genuine rationalization for the justness of war had been found. With the only partial exception of the minor War of the Polish Succession, all these wars were fought over issues of main concern to the Western Habsburg lands. The conquests or barter of territory in the Spanish Netherlands, Milan, Naples, Sicily, and Sardinia, during and after the War of the Spanish Succession, the claims of France, Bavaria, Saxony, Piedmont, and above all Prussia in the War of the Austrian Succession, concerned primarily the West, as did, of course, Joseph II's efforts to join Bavaria to the Habsburg lands a generation later. Even the War of the Polish Succession, with the ensuing installation of a former Polish king as duke of Lorraine under French tutelage, represented really as much—if not more—of a conflict between Habsburgs and Bourbons as between Bourbons and Romanovs. It should be added that the Habsburgs in general throughout the eighteenth and nineteenth centuries considered even the smallest territorial gains in the West, illustrated by the conflict about small Italian principalities, to be far more important than potentially large territorial conquests in the East. The comprehensive plans of Eugene of Savoy in the Balkans served only as a sub-

---

7. The first Turkish siege of Vienna took place in 1529.

stitute for more direct Habsburg aims to secure the succession in Italian secundo- and tertio-genitures. In this sense, the occupation and finally annexation of Bosnia-Herzegovina under Francis Joseph represented chiefly a mere substitute for the loss of Lombardy and Venetia. No doubt Habsburg foreign policy in the eighteenth century was Western oriented, and the shift in that respect brought about by the conflicts with Russia and the Balkan countries under Francis Joseph after the middle of the nineteenth century derived primarily from the fact that the roads to the west and north became blocked for good.

Disregard for the interests of the Eastern Habsburg peoples in the prolonged succession struggle resulted in their indifference to the German-oriented foreign policy of Joseph II. This is one of the major reasons why it failed completely.

The Austro-Prussian conflict and Italian unification dominated the next phase of foreign relations. One of the major consequences of the three Silesian wars between 1740 and 1763, quite apart from the rise of Prussia to great power rank under Frederick II, was the weakening of the predominant German position in the Habsburg lands. It resulted less from the loss of Silesia directly than from this loss in conjunction with the acquisition of Galicia-Bukovina, which, in turn, served as model for the likewise compensatory occupation of Bosnia-Herzegovina a century later. Here we face the gradual shift to a situation that gave the East far greater weight in the Habsburg lands, though still not equal weight. The loss in Habsburg power due to the cession of Silesia was undeniable; the gain through the acquisition of the Carpathian provinces and later of Bosnia-Herzegovina became increasingly problematical.[8] Whether under different conditions of European great power relations this increased importance secured by the Eastern part of the Habsburg empire could have had a salutary effect on the stability of the Danube monarchy is one of the questions of historical "might have been" that will never be answered.

As matters actually stood, another interpretation is far more suggestive. Notwithstanding the prestige factor, the loss of the Italian provinces in the wars of 1859 and 1866 was by no means as detrimental to Habsburg power as the loss of Silesia a century before. Now it was at least belatedly recognized that it no longer made sense to defend untenable positions in the West. The occupation and subsequent annexation of Bosnia-Herzegovina, on the other hand, decisively weakened and endangered the Habsburg empire. It embroiled Austria-Hungary in a continuing crisis in the Balkans and, far more important, led to an inevitable collision course with Russian interests. The contests of the Habsburg empire in the West had not imperiled its true life lines. The

8. Between 1786 and 1849 the Bukovina was administered jointly with Galicia.

crisis in the East did just that. While Eastern interests in the dual monarchy thus grew in strength and Western interests correspondingly weakened further, both became more unmanageable.

Of great importance in this respect was the attraction Pan-Germanism had in the German-controlled West of the empire and Panslavism had for the majority of its Eastern peoples. It may be debated whether the centrifugal force of one or the other was stronger in the domestic field. Yet it is not debatable that the German Empire wanted to control Austria-Hungary's foreign policy not through dissident Pan-German Ultras in the German *Reichstag* and in the Austrian *Reichsrat* but by cooperation with the leading German and Magyar parties in Vienna and Budapest. The tsarist government, presumably against the will of the tsars themselves, who were still wedded to the idea of monarchic solidarity, had to accept fully the Panslav ideology in foreign relations. This was the only popular policy compatible, at least for a time, with tsarist rule.

Largely for this reason the ominous expansion policy in the Balkans was an ill-chosen response to more important setbacks in the West. The decisive victory of Prussia in the struggle for German supremacy led almost straight to the Compromise of 1867 and with it to the necessity for the Austro-Germans to share power with the Magyars. A further consequence of this state of affairs was an Austro-German–Magyar directed foreign policy based on close alliance with the new German empire, as against the differing interests of all the Slavic peoples under Habsburg rule and eventually those of the Romanians as well. In regard to the Romanians, it is true, common interests with the Slavic peoples on main issues of foreign policy may have been few until the early twentieth century. In the end the Romanians took a decisive turn toward the Russian East, which they did not love more but feared more than the Habsburg power.

All things considered, it would be an oversimplification to speak of a clearcut pro-Russian attitude on the part of the Habsburg Eastern peoples in matters of foreign relations. Complex distinctions have to be made between the various national groups. Yet, in general it can be stated that the East did not share the interests represented by the Austro-German–Magyar foreign policy. It saw no reason for a confrontation with France and Great Britain, and feared and rejected one with Russia.

In the World War period, of course, these distinctions became ever clearer. Apart from common concerns for defense of the homeland against foreign invasions, all official war objectives of the dual Habsburg monarchy transcending defensive interests were chiefly those of Austro-Germans and Magyars and not those of the Eastern peoples.

Here an increasingly sharp difference between Eastern and Western interests became apparent.

Distinctions between West and East are just as clear if we turn from foreign relations to domestic policies, in particular to the administration of the Habsburg lands from the union of 1526–27 to the disintegration of the empire in 1918. Here, however, one has to be clear about the semantics of the problem. Well into the second half of the nineteenth century the Habsburg monarchy was not thought of as a multinational empire at all. We speak of straight centralism on the one hand and of the development of Metternich's concept of a decentralized unitary state (various kinds of autonomies for some regions or peoples) on the other. Inasmuch as these autonomous institutions, which became increasingly important in the course of the second half of the nineteenth century, never pertained to all Habsburg lands, and after the Compromise of 1867 not even to all the Lands in the Western or Eastern part of the empire, one cannot even speak of semifederalist tendencies that would be based on an equal relationship of the component parts of an empire to the central government. What is certain, however, is that centralism until 1867 stood unequivocally for German dominance in the Habsburg monarchy, though not necessarily for conscious German nationalism. Not until 1867 was this system converted into the previously noted kind of condominum of joint German and Magyar predominance. Yet, even after 1867, increasing Magyar power notwithstanding, the imperial tradition and the tradition of the unitary state and the efforts to preserve or restore it were still focused on Vienna and not Budapest. It is therefore fair to say that centralism represented the desired state concept of the Western part of the empire. The diverse built-in autonomies for various peoples, Eastern peoples all of them, with the exception of the Italians, stood for limited concessions made by necessity only to some highly selective interests. Yet by no means can it be said that the decentralized unitary state represented any kind of state program for the East. It was at best a substitute for such a program, no more and probably even less.

The key figure in creating the administrative structure of the Habsburg empire was Ferdinand I (1526–64),[9] as the first regent of the territories of the Alpine Hereditary Lands in conjunction with those of the Bohemian and the Hungarian and Croatian crowns. His sovereignty was limited. The best part of Hungary was, up to the ninth decade of the seventeenth century, under direct or indirect Turkish control, except for short intermissions. Only the small strip of Hungarian territory in the west and northwest and the western part of Croatia

9. As emperor of the Holy Roman Empire, 1556–64.

were in substance under Habsburg rule. Furthermore, until his election as emperor in his own right in 1556, Ferdinand as regent of the Hereditary Lands remained in principle subordinated to his imperial brother, Charles V. Accordingly he was just as much concerned with the relationship of the Hereditary Lands to the Holy Roman Empire as to the Eastern crowns. One of the ablest rulers in the long history of the Habsburg monarchy, Ferdinand introduced several new institutions, such as the Secret Council (*Geheime Rat*) entrusted with the handling of foreign affairs and the Aulic Council (*Hofrat*) for administrative and judicial matters which dealt primarily with agenda resulting from the affiliation of the Hereditary Lands with the Holy Roman Empire. Yet in the first part of his administration Ferdinand appointed Hungarian and Bohemian members to the Aulic Council and later also to the Aulic War Council (*Hofkriegsrat*). He went further than that in the establishment of the administrative body that dealt with the financial affairs of his realms, the Court Chamber (*Hofkammer*). Four such agencies were created—in Prague, Pozsony (Pressburg, Bratislava), Innsbruck, and Vienna. In a loose way all these chambers were subordinated to the one at the seat of Ferdinand's residence; nevertheless a considerable measure of autonomy was for the first time recognized for Eastern lands.

One has to add that the Estates in the Lands of the Bohemian Crown held a far stronger position than those in the Hereditary Lands, inasmuch as the Bohemian Crown had been traditionally far more independent of imperial interference than the Hereditary Lands.[10] Even in Hungary, as far as it remained free from Turkish sway, the nobility represented as *curia* in the diet were more powerful than in the Hereditary Lands. Because the Turkish occupation practically freed Croatia from the overlordship of Hungary and subjected only eastern Croatia to Turkish rule, the power of the *banus*—the head of government who combined in his office the direction of supreme administrative, judicial, and military functions—increased considerably. On the other hand, Transylvania, the principality in the Hungarian East, was under Ferdinand's control for only a few years in the 1550s. Otherwise it remained until the end of the seventeenth century under various princes who made their peace with the Ottoman Empire, the Polish crown, and—last and least—with the faraway emperor in Vienna.

The strong position of Bohemia within the Habsburg lands was de-

10. Concerning the historical relationship between the Bohemian Crown and the Holy Roman Empire before the union of 1526, see Alfons Huber and Alfons Dopsch, *Österreichische Reichsgeschichte* (2d ed.; Vienna: F. Tempsky, 1901), pp. 95–101. See also Richard Plaschka, "Das böhmische Staatsrecht in tschechischer Sicht," in Ernst Birke and Kurt Oberdorffer, eds., *Das böhmische Staatsrecht* (Marburg/Lahn: Elwert, 1960), pp. 5–7; and K. J. Dillon, *Kings and Estates in the Bohemian Lands, 1526–1564* (Brussels: Les Éditions de la Librairie Encyclopédique, 1976), passim.

stroyed as a consequence of the battle of the White Mountain in 1620, in which nationalism and Protestantism alike had to succumb to the force of the victorious Counter Reformation. The new Bohemian constitution of 1627 did not do away with the estates system, but it weakened, if not paralyzed, its activities by the advance of centralization. Indeed, centralization had its longest, relatively unchallenged day in the era from the accession of Ferdinand II as Holy Roman emperor in 1619 to the last years of the reign of Leopold I (1657–1705).

Limited change occurred with the reconquest of Hungary in the 1680s. The Counter Reformation, with its belated but all the stronger impact on prostrate Hungary, forced the Magyars at the diet (*Reichstag*) of Pozsony, 1687–88, to surrender the free election of the king and the nobles' right of resistance against violations of the constitution by the sovereign. Two decades of social and political Magyar unrest followed. As a very limited counterweight to the force of the disloyal Magyars, Leopold I granted limited autonomy to the Hungarian Serbs and a fartherreaching autonomy to the three-nation state of Transylvania (Magyars, Szekels, Germans), which included the establishment of a separate Court Chancellery of this principality in Vienna.

The issuance of the Pragmatic Sanction, the adoption of a universal order of succession for all the Habsburg lands between 1712 and 1725, was again a step toward centralization, somewhat modified by the fact that the estates, including those of Hungary, Bohemia, and Transylvania, were asked to confirm it. With the proclamation of the Pragmatic Sanction, an "invisible Habsburg empire"—as it has been called, since it existed in fact but not yet in name—became a political reality after the War of the Spanish Succession and the victorious peace of Passarowitz (Požarevac) of 1718 in the East. This new entity, now a genuine great power in its own right, pushed the Holy Roman Empire into the background, although it was to be dissolved formally only at Napoleon's behest in 1806 and an Austrian empire was not to be proclaimed until 1804.

In the center of the period from the introduction of the Pragmatic Sanction to the proclamation of a substitute (so to speak) Austrian empire, we face the Maria Theresan and Josephin reform era. Both rulers moved further in the direction of the unitary state, although the process of transformation was handled with much greater prudence and skill under the empress and her advisers than under her older son. A joint Bohemian-Austrian (i.e., Austrian Hereditary Lands) Chancellery lost supreme jurisdiction in judicial affairs. On the other hand, Transylvanian autonomy remained intact and was formally strengthened by the adoption of the title of grand prince of Transylvania by the sovereign.

A separate administrative agency with limited autonomy was created

for the Banat (roughly southeastern Hungary), Transylvania, and Illyria (as part of the western South Slav orbit), though only the Transylvanian autonomy survived until 1848. As to the other territories, the
empress yielded to Magyar opposition and her innate fear of too far-
reaching concessions to demands for full autonomy. On the other hand,
the institution of the so-called military borders, first established by Ferdinand I on Croatian soil as fortified territory in which the settlers were
bound to form a kind of semimilitary organization, had been expanded
in the course of a century and a half across southern Hungary. While
part of the Slavonian Military Border was incorporated under Maria
Theresa into Croatia as a concession to the Magyars, other military border districts survived as late as 1881.[11] The net result, though not necessarily the objective, was that some Hungarian national groups—Serbs,
Romanians (in Transylvania referred to as Vlakhs), but also substantial
numbers of Croats within the military borders—had secured a better
chance to preserve and strengthen their national identity.

The overall effect of the Maria Theresan reforms in the context of
the problem of Eastern and Western Habsburg empire concepts remains, however, the radical reduction of estates' powers outside of
Hungary and the complete merger of the administrations of the Hereditary Lands and the Lands of the Bohemian Crown. The Croatian
Military Border served as model for the institution in general, which
spread along the south of Hungary from Croatia to Transylvania.

The more radical Josephin centralization and Germanization efforts
that followed the Maria Theresan reforms were, taking a short-range
view, in the purely political sphere. They were perhaps not quite as
important in themselves as they seemed to contemporaries, since most
of them were voided even before the emperor died. Their impact on
the later evolution of Austrian centralism and liberalism is another matter. In our context of East-West relations a most important consequence
of the reforms was the accentuation of Magyar and at least indirectly
also Croatian nationalism, resulting from the imperial challenge, and
of Romanian nationalism in Transylvania as directly furthered by Joseph II. Actually the emperor not only infringed on Magyar rights by
the highly controversial Germanization decrees in the language question; it is less well known that he also strengthened Magyar jurisdiction
in financial and economic matters. He did so, it is true, by scrapping
the Transylvanian autonomy of the three-nation state, or rather three
privileged nations state, but at the same time he laid a kind of corner-

---

11. On the Croatian Military Border see the two studies by Gunther E. Rothenberg,
The Austrian Military Border in Croatia, 1522–1747 (Urbana: University of Illinois Press,
1960) and *The Military Border in Croatia, 1740–1881* (Chicago: University of Chicago Press,
1966). The Croatian Military Border may serve as model for the institution in general,
which spread along the south of Hungary from Croatia to Transylvania.

stone for its future extension and transformation by recognizing for the first time a limited autonomy of the underprivileged Romanians in Transylvania. All things considered, the emperor's administrative policy in Hungary was perhaps more subtle and complex, though not more successful, than is commonly assumed.

His successor, Leopold II, voided the infringement on Magyar rights insofar as he restored Transylvanian autonomy and created an Illyrian Court Chancellery. It was meant to take care of the educational and religious needs of the Hungarian Serbs. Somewhat similar to the situation under Leopold I, this concession was designed to serve as counterweight against Magyar claims for restoration and extension of their state rights beyond those existing under the Maria Theresan reforms. The Illyrian Court Chancellery was abolished under Leopold II's son Francis I (II).

No radical changes in the administrative system took place during the long reign of this unimaginative and unenlightened emperor and his mentally incapacitated son Ferdinand, dubbed the Benign. One might speak of a continuation of the trends toward the unitary state, with Hungary and the Lombardo-Venetian Kingdom as the then major exceptions. It should be added that, such exceptions notwithstanding, the decentralized unitary state was on the whole inefficiently administered from 1792 to 1848. This was worse in the first part of Francis's reign until 1815 than in the second, even more reactionary but less confused phase.

Like the Josephin radical reforms, the innovations brought about by the Revolution of 1848 were far more important in their longer range, indirect consequences than in their transitory immediate results. The lessons of incipient liberalism could be suppressed but not forgotten. Those of nationalism, especially the nationalism of the Slavic peoples expressed so vividly in the Slav Congress of Prague in late spring of 1848, survived and expanded vigorously but had not the slightest repercussion in permanent administrative changes. The strange exception was the incorporation of Transylvania into Hungary in 1848. Although voided under the counter- and postrevolutionary regime of Neo-Absolutism, it became permanent in 1867 as part of the Austrian Compromise with Hungary. In effect this meant that the union between Hungary and Transylvania, brought about under the flag of the revolution as social protest against Habsburg rule, was restored as a Habsburg concession to an antirevolutionary Magyar government in Hungary.

The constitutional experiments from 1860 to the conclusion of the Austro-Hungarian Compromise of 1867 attempted first a semifederalist solution of the empire's domestic crisis. After it had failed, mainly but not exclusively because of Magyar resistance, the way to conclusion of the Compromise was open. As noted, it was made acceptable to the Austro-German establishment only by the decisive defeat in the Austro-Prussian war of 1866, which toppled the Habsburg monarchy's position in Germany for good. True, conclusion of the Austro-German alliance of 1879 revived the monarchy's relationship with the second German empire in a limited way in the sphere of foreign policy, but only at the price of acceptance of a secondary role in this alliance.

The main provisions of the Austro-Hungarian Compromise in extent and intent are well known. They affiliated the two states by the common agenda of foreign affairs, defense, and joint expenditures for these agenda, as well as various economic matters to be renegotiated every ten years. One sovereign was to govern both states in the dual capacity of emperor in the West and king in the East. This complex system could not even serve as an imperfect model for Western and Eastern state concepts anchored in the ethnic and historic rights of the peoples under Habsburg rule. The ever more assertive role of Magyar-dominated Hungary in the half-century-long history of the Compromise was not based on the position of the Magyars as the politically dominant Eastern nation per se. It was embedded in Magyar acceptance of Western principles of foreign policy and defense needs. The Hungarian constitutional laws, more ancient but also more restrictive than the new Austrian Cisleithanian ones of December 1867, remained untouched by this development.

Eastern interests were taken care of only to a limited degree in the system. Apart from a never enforced, fairly liberal Hungarian nationality law of 1868, the only important concession to Eastern national interests was the Hungaro-Croatian Compromise of 1868, an agreement unlike the Austro-Hungarian Compromise concluded not between political equals but unequals. Actually this arrangement merely recognized a limited Croatian autonomy in legislative and executive agenda. While the Western, that is Austrian,[12] nationality legislation was superior to the Hungarian not in its wording but in its administration and interpretation by the courts, the semiautonomy granted in this system to the Galician administration in 1868 was even more restrictive than the provisions of the Hungaro-Croatian Compromise.[13] Furthermore,

12.   The official term for the western half of the monarchy between 1867 and 1917 was "the kingdoms and lands represented in the [Austrian] parliament." This cumbersome terminology was generally bypassed and the term "Austria" substituted for it. It should be noted and will be made clear in this study in the appropriate places that the term "Austria" is also frequently used for the Habsburg empire as a whole.

13.   Surveys of administrative developments are to be found in Huber and Dopsch, *Österreichische Reichsgeschichte;* Ernst C. Hellbling, *Österreichische Verfassungs- und Verwaltungsgeschichte* (Vienna: Springer, 1956); Friedrich Walter, *Österreichische Verfassungs- und Verwaltungsgeschichte von 1500–1955* (Vienna and Cologne: Böhlaus Nachf., 1972). See also J. Ulbrich, *Das österreichische Staatsrecht* (Tübingen: Mohr [Siebeck], 1909) and Henrik Marczali, *Ungarische Verfassungsgeschichte* (Tübingen: Mohr [Siebeck], 1910).

it was not anchored in constitutional law but in substance in administrative decrees.

A major attempt was made by the cabinet of Count Karl Hohenwart, in 1871, to grant the Czech people in the Lands of the Bohemian Crown a general joint diet with broad legislative functions. They would have overlapped largely with the legislative powers of the Cisleithanian Austrian parliament. Actually, though not by the letter of the law, these reforms would have meant the conversion of the Habsburg monarchy into a kind of semitrialistic system in lieu of the dualistic empire structure. Magyar opposition and veiled threats from Germany that adoption of the plan of Hohenwart's cabinet might endanger German interests in Austria, the potential ally of the future, proved to be effective. The Hohenwart plan, which included also a fair settlement of Czech and German claims in the language conflict, fell through. It had at least been introduced in parliament, while future concepts of a trialistic empire structure, comprising the Austrian and Hungarian South Slavs as equal force with Germans and Magyars, never went beyond preliminary planning. Not even the formal annexation of Bosnia-Herzegovina in 1908, which followed the occupation of 1878, could change this. The severely restrictive constitution granted to Bosnia-Herzegovina by the emperor-king in 1910 did not lead to any change in the direction of trialism.

To sum up: Even a brief and sketchy survey shows clearly that homogeneous concepts of Eastern versus Western administrative systems simply did not exist.

Admittedly it could be argued that before the Compromise of 1867 the German dominated West of the Habsburg empire represented by approximation a kind of semiunitary, semicentralized state concept. Yet it has to be denied that, with the major exception of the Magyars, the mostly rudimentary autonomous rights granted to Eastern peoples stood for any kind of truly unified interests.

Does the situation look different in the cultural orbit? We have noted that with the exception of the era of Corvinian Hungary, the Renaissance had declined in significance on its route from West to East within the confines of the Habsburg lands. We have further recognized that the Reformation had the greatest impact on Czech history, in particular in its influence on developments in Germany. Apart from conditions in sixteenth- and seventeenth-century eastern Hungary and Transylvania and the sixteenth-century Slovene territories, the weight of the Reformation was again greater in the West than in the East, depending of course on the assumption that the Czechs in this specific context have to be comprehended as part of the West. This in turn helped to shape the future impact of German nationalism on the Czechs. But the Czech Reformation codetermined Western intellectual history well beyond

Germany far more than that of the East. It is still reflected in the long-range influence of Comenius's Humanism, to refer to only one illustrious pattern-forming example.

In cultural terms, the era of the Counter Reformation coincided with the prevalence of the Baroque style in the formative arts, literature, and music. Here we note again a predominant share of Germans, Slovenes, and Czechs, for the Hungarian territories under Turkish occupation were not able to participate before the end of the seventeenth century. The exception—a limited exception according to its results—would be western Croatia.

Unquestionably the Enlightenment came from the West, but because of the somewhat backward, predominantly agrarian structure of the Habsburg lands, it did not generally have the same cultural influence on any of them, including the Hereditary Lands, as on countries west of the Habsburg empire. The impact of this great intellectual movement during the reigns of Joseph II and his brother, which germinated later changes, must certainly not be taken lightly. Yet its immediate consequences, very notable as they were, do not fully compare with those of the Baroque and its predominantly conservative spirit.

When we turn to the era of Biedermeier and romanticism, roughly from the Josephin reign (1780–90) to the Revolution of 1848, the situation changes. This is the time of the Slavic Renaissance, which had its beginning in the late Enlightenment. Now the impact of new thought is more conspicuous among the Eastern peoples, including the Magyars, and the national revolution of the Romanians than in the German-Italian West. This conclusion is not an attempt to compare Eastern and Western achievements. Value judgments are largely a matter of individual preference. Respect for tradition and search for originality of thought existed in West and East alike. But inasmuch as this period of awakening conscious nationalism is of greater significance for the East than for the West—in many respects a *beatus possidens* already—involvement of the masses steadily increased on its eastward route. By the mid-nineteenth century the handicap of cultural delay in Eastern development, brought about largely by the Turkish invasions, had been overcome for all practical purposes. The new intellectual and artistic currents—historicism, realism, impressionism, and expressionism—affected all peoples under Habsburg rule, though not necessarily at the same time or to the same degree. The Slavic Renaissance remained the one and only movement in which we can acknowledge the existence of a kind of unified Eastern concept, although this acknowledgment will have to be qualified.

What do such findings add up to in our search for an answer to the question whether a unitary concept of the Eastern Habsburg lands has ever existed? Let us first determine whether one can speak of a genuine unitary concept of all the Habsburg lands, East and West together. The answer is no. This does not mean that the union of 1526–27 showed intrinsic signs of decay. The Habsburg union, squeezed in between Turkish aggression from the East, the divisive influence of the Reformation, and later French expansionism from the West, evolved as a genuine great power by the early eighteenth century. As such it appeared no less vigorous than any other major European country. Yet, inasmuch as this Habsburg empire could never become a national state like countries to the West and East, it could not create that common sphere of interests of even the upper strata of society in the union, let alone that of the majority of the people, which more fortunate countries could develop in the course of the centuries from the Reformation to the French Revolution. This common sphere of interest did not even represent rudimentary features of democracy as in the instances of Russia, prerevolutionary France, Spain, or Prussia; but it did represent a potentially greater involvement in issues of the public domain. In regard to the West, the Habsburg empire could not remain in step when the transition from feudal to bourgeois society came into full swing. In regard to the East, no unifying substitute for the concept of Panslavism in its full strength existed in the Habsburg lands. It was indeed predictable that the end of the Habsburg empire was bound to come before the era of nationalism would end.

Considering the failure to create this common spiritual bond between the Habsburg lands, sometimes referred to in too pretentious language as the Austrian state idea, it appears clear that the decentralized unitary state had to fail. Wide divergences not only between East and West but also within Eastern and Western ways of thought became manifest.

If we look first at the union idea in the West, four basic concepts come to mind. In the first place, we think of the tradition of the Holy Roman Empire of which the Western Habsburg lands formed part. With the failure to accomplish the union, the *grossdeutsch* ideology in Austria developing after the Congress of Vienna may be considered a substitute continuation of the Holy Roman Empire idea. Second, there is the German nationalist concept of a German cultural, if not political, mission in the East with the objective of establishing German predominance between the Little Carpathians and the Black Sea. Third, well into the eighteenth century the mission of the Habsburg lands as a bulwark of Christian civilization against the Turks was very much alive. Finally, at least for the sixteenth century, the universal empire idea under Charles V, in which the sun never set, had a certain reality. None of these broad concepts had at best more than halfway temporary success. All of them had failed prior to the dissolution of the Habsburg empire. Still they all represent fairly clear union concepts in a historical framework, and they all perceived the East as a mere appendix to Habsburg power.

How about this East? None of these four Western concepts, except to a very limited degree the Turkish danger concept, was ever shared by the East. Numerous historical, ecological, and perhaps above all linguistic factors help us understand that the East did not possess a unity idea comparable to that of the West. It may be suggestive to adduce Panslavism as a counterargument. Its great emotional stimulus should not be denied. Yet romantic Panslavism, as represented foremost by Ján Kollár in East Central Europe, lacked any chance of future realization in political terms. Political Panslavism, at least in the shape of Pan-Russism, had far less impact on the Slavic peoples of the Habsburg monarchy in peacetime than is commonly assumed.

There is, of course, the notion of the Slavic Renaissance as a powerful, all-embracing cultural bond of all the Slavic peoples in East Central Europe in general and specifically within the Habsburg empire. This thought is correct as far as the overall challenge of the Slavic Renaissance goes; it is misleading if it induces us to press the Eastern Habsburg peoples into an artificial union scheme. The West with its German predominance represented genuine political concepts, although they were frequently repugnant to other peoples. The East stood for diversity of individual development of each Slavic people under the auspices of the new cultural awakening, generalized under the caption "Slavic Renaissance." The stimulus of the Slavic Renaissance was indeed general, but its application to each Slavic nation was very specific. The West thus stood for some kind of unity, the Slavic East for diversity and individuality, surely a development fully equal in value to that of the West.

How about other East Central European peoples in the Habsburg empire; how about the Magyars and Romanians, to return therewith to our previously noted qualification of an Eastern union concept? To deal with this question we have to do away with clichés and abstractions such as the notion that the national groups in Hungary had an identical response to the Turkish occupation. This is erroneous in political, economic, and religious terms. The same holds true for the assumption that the non-Magyar Hungarian national groups responded in the same way to the oppressive Magyar nationality policy between 1848 and 1918. Yet, from the standpoint of historical truth the most detrimental cliché is the belief that the nationality conflict in the confines of the Habsburg empire was insoluble because the Habsburg empire failed to solve it. This deduction is not convincing. Whether a solution of this problem in democratic, nontotalitarian terms might be feasible in East Central Europe—that is, outside of the political framework and geographic confines of the bygone Habsburg empire—has of course never been proved and cannot be tested for the foreseeable future. In any case, the future of the union concept has to be separated from the history of the efforts to preserve a venerable but doomed empire structure.

CHAPTER 2

Government by the Estates, 1526–1620

The Czechs

By the time the Habsburgs ascended the throne of Bohemia in 1526, the Bohemian state—essentially the political body of the Czechs—had been in existence for half a millennium. Its basic core of Bohemia and Moravia was consolidated in the High Middle Ages by the Přemyslids, building on the tradition of the semilegendary duke Saint Wenceslas (died c. 935). In the fourteenth century under the Luxemburg dynasty—including the illustrious Charles IV (1346–78)—the realm was augmented by the Lands of Silesia and by Upper and Lower Lusatia. The newly added territories were heavily Germanized, although with substantial minorities of Poles and Czechs in Silesia and Sorbs in the Lusatias. Threatened with disintegration in the aftermath of social and religious upheavals of the Hussite wars (1420–36), the entire state was reassembled by the Jagiellonians (1471–1526), who moreover linked it in a personal union with the Kingdom of Hungary. This linkage continued under the Habsburgs after 1526 and was supplemented by a similar tie with the Austrian Hereditary Lands. In addition, unlike Hungary or Poland, the Bohemian Kingdom was loosely linked from the mid-tenth century with the Holy Roman Empire, in which the Bohemian king exercised the role of the first elector according to the Golden Bull of 1212.

CENTRAL ADMINISTRATION

The Concept of the Bohemian State

From the fourteenth century the term "Bohemian Crown" was customarily used, partly in a geographic sense to denote Bohemia proper as well as the other four Lands (Moravia, Silesia, and the two Lusatias), and partly in the juridical sense to denote the entire Bohemian state as a political body. In the second sense, the Bohemian Crown was viewed as superior to both the king and the estates, who were its organs, and thus it resembled the contemporary Polish or Hungarian concept of statehood rather than the more purely feudal one prevalent in the Holy Roman Empire. The Bohemian state was a loose confederation of five Lands linked together (1) by the king and some of his agencies, (2) by a common organ of the estates, the General Diet, and (3) by common concerns: defense, foreign relations, and the right of residence (*inkolát*). The estates of the Land of Bohemia proper held a special position in the state, serving as guardians of the unity of the Crown, electing or accepting a new king, and controlling certain organs common to the entire Crown: the Royal Council, the Bohemian Chancellery, and two judicial bodies—the Aulic Court (*dvorský soud*) and the Chamber Court (*komorní soud*).

Ferdinand I's accession to the throne in 1526 was an important landmark in Bohemia's internal political development. As an adherent to the Spanish absolutist model of royal authority, he inevitably resented the Polish pattern of the estates' supremacy, entrenched in Bohemia most conspicuously under the two Jagiellonian kings. Ferdinand I did strengthen royal power significantly, especially in the wake of the unsuccessful uprising of the estates in 1547, although under his weaker successors the estates regained some of the lost ground. On the whole, and in contrast to the situation in neighboring Hungary, the Habsburgs were more successful during the sixteenth century in limiting the estates' autonomy at the local level—particularly in the counties or circuits (*kraje*)—than at the central administrative level of the Lands. The contest was to climax early in the next century (1618–19) when the estates boldly attempted to create an oligarchical republic with a figurehead king, but the issue of the battle of the White Mountain (1620) finally favored royal absolutism.

Until the Thirty Years' War (1618–48), the Habsburgs preserved the territorial integrity of the Lands of the Bohemian Crown, which had been threatened in the fifteenth century by the designs of Brandenburg, Saxony, and Poland especially on Silesia and the Lusatias. In addition, the cohesiveness of the individual Lands increased. Thus the westernmost region of Cheb (Eger) was more clearly attached to Bohemia and the ecclesiastical principality of Olomouc with Moravia. In Silesia several of the duchies fell under immediate royal rule with the extinction of local dynasties, and in the remaining so-called mediate duchies, the powers of the ruling princes, already excluded from foreign relations, were further limited in internal affairs. The formation of common political and administrative organs for the whole Land of Silesia was accelerated.

The King and His Agencies

Although he became king by a free election of the Bohemian diet in 1526, Ferdinand I (1526–64), in his search to affirm royal authority, was able by the midpoint of his reign (in 1545) to secure admission of hereditary succession in the Habsburg dynasty. His successors were, in fact, accepted by the diet during the lifetime of the preceding monarchs. Not until 1619 did the Bohemian diet once more assert the right of free royal election to choose Frederick V, the Elector Palatine, generally known as the Winter King (1619–20).

A formidable task facing Ferdinand I was to create new agencies of direct royal power within the Bohemian state. Under the Jagiellonians virtually all organs of government responsible solely to the king had vanished. The existing government agencies had to be staffed with the consent of the estates and were responsible to them. Ferdinand I established in 1527 a new agency of royal power, the Bohemian Chamber (*česká komora*), staffed by bureaucrats appointed directly by the king and responsible to him. Among other functions, it administered royal properties, estates, the regalia and towns, and royal debts, and prepared financial propositions for the diet. Originally its immediate jurisdiction covered the whole state, but in the mid-sixteenth century subordinate offices emerged in the Lands outside of Bohemia: master of rents (*rentmistr*) in Moravia, the Silesian Chamber in Silesia, and the captains of the Land in the two Lusatias. The Bohemian Chamber acquired control over preexisting royal officials, whose functions were of significance for the entire Bohemian Crown: (1) the king's procurator, who represented the king as a party in judicial proceedings, (2) master of coinage (*mincmistr*), supervisor of minting and mining, and (3) the captain of German fiefs (*hejtman německých lén*), the chief administrator and judge of smaller fiefs of the Bohemian Crown scattered in Bavaria, Saxony, and Brandenburg. In addition to the Bohemian Chamber, Ferdinand I established in 1548 another specifically royal agency, partly staffed by professional officials, the Council on Appeals (*rada nad apelacemi*). He wished that appeals from all courts in the Bohemian Crown, which otherwise were under the estates' exclusive control, should be discussed in the Council. The courts of royal towns eventually submitted to this arrangement; of the courts of nobility, however, only those of the Lusatias and some of the Silesian duchies did.

While these organs, despite some negative features, tended at least to strengthen the unity of the political body of the Bohemian Crown, the central agencies, established by Ferdinand I in Vienna, had on the contrary—from the standpoint of Bohemia's independence—a detrimental tendency to merge the Bohemian state into a new, larger state including the Alpine Hereditary Lands and Hungary. The impact of some of these agencies was more significant than that of others. In regard to the Bohemian Lands the influence of the Court Chancellery (*Hofkanzlei*) was greatly weakened by the operations of the Bohemian Chancellery. The Aulic War Council (*Hofkriegsrat*) remained ineffectual because the estates of the Bohemian Crown retained full control over the military establishment. More serious was the direct ascendancy of the Court Chamber (*Hofkammer*) over the Bohemian Chamber, which, despite the protests of the estates, was even tightened in 1568. The most ominous role was played by the Secret Council (*Geheime Rat*), which dealt not only with foreign affairs but also important internal matters, such as petitions of the highest organs of the Bohemian Crown. Its decisions were formally presented as those of the king, but ordinarily the king simply accepted its advice.

The king was expected to reside in Prague, but only Rudolf II actually did so regularly from 1583 to 1612. From 1539, when the king was absent from the city, the administration of Bohemia was usually entrusted to the highest officials of the Land under the chairmanship of the supreme count palatine (*nejvyšší purkrabí, Oberst Burggraf*). Each such provision, considered temporary, ended with the presence of the king in the Land. The king's permanent deputy or lieutenant officiated in each of the other Lands; he was called captain of the Land (*zemský hejtman*) in Moravia, chief captain (*vrchní hejtman*) in Silesia, and *fojt* (*Vogt, advocatus*) in each of the Lusatias.[1]

Organs of the Estates: The Diets

The basic vehicle of the power of the estates was the diets (*sněmy*). Their organization differed somewhat in each Land. In Bohemia the Hussite wars ended the clergy's representation. The nobility formed the first two colleges (*curiae*) of the barons (*páni*) and the knights (*rytíři*). About fourteen hundred noble families were entitled to representation in 1600. While the barons usually could afford to attend the diet in person, the less affluent knights traditionally held congresses in the cir-

---

1. In addition to representing the king, the captain or the *fojt* was the chief of the estates. He exercised his administrative, military, and judicial powers in the name of both the king and the estates.

cuits (*kraje, Kreise*) to elect two to six representatives to the diet from each circuit. The kings since Ferdinand I, however, had sought to suppress the *kraj* assemblies and thus interfered with the regular representation of the knights. Each royal town had a single vote in the third college, into which it sent two or three representatives elected by the town council. In Moravia, in addition to the barons, knights, and towns, the estate of prelates survived, although for the purposes of voting in the diet, it formed a single college with the towns. The situation in the princely diet of Silesia and the Lusatias varied slightly.[2]

The diet's presiding officer in Bohemia was the supreme count palatine, in Moravia the captain of the Land, in Silesia the chief captain, and in the Lusatias the *fojt*. In the plenary sessions of the diets each college had one vote, and a unanimous vote of the colleges was required to adopt a measure. The basic powers of the diets were to approve taxes and provide soldiers. Their legislative functions included approving new legal codes, considering religious affairs and domestic police measures, and regulating royal rights such as mining and minting. The Bohemian diet moreover performed functions affecting the entire Crown, particularly electing or accepting a new king, and had to confirm any foreign treaty that concerned royal succession or the boundaries of the state.

The kings since Ferdinand I had wished to restrict the freedom of the diets. They insisted successfully that only the king could convoke the diets, and that (except in Moravia) the diets' decisions required a royal sanction for their validity. Ferdinand I assaulted the estates' right of legislative initiative, demanding that royal propositions be considered first and dissolving the diets as soon as the propositions were accepted. The estates retaliated successfully by refusing to vote taxes before their own petitions had been presented.

Occasionally the diets elected commissions to deal with special problems, or to govern in the absence of a recognized king, as in Moravia in 1608 after the renunciation of allegiance to Rudolf II, or during the uprising of 1618–19 when the diets in Bohemia and Moravia each chose thirty directors from the three principal estates. In both Lusatias and in some Silesian duchies the diets regularly elected a group of elders of the Land to exercise the powers of the estates between the diet sessions. In Bohemia and Moravia this function was performed by the "highest officials" of the Land.

A special organ of the estates of the entire Crown was the General Diet, composed either of delegations from each Land or of the entire Bohemian Diet together with delegations from the other Lands. Each

2. The princely diet of Silesia, acting for the entire Land, consisted of three colleges representing respectively (1) the reigning princes, (2) the barons, prelates, and knights of the "immediate" duchies, and (3) the towns of the "immediate" duchies. In addition, the individual duchies had their own diets.

Land had one vote and only those Lands that approved a measure were bound by it. These diets convened either to witness royal coronations or to consider questions of internal security, religion, or defense. In the sixteenth century the kings convoked them most often—eleven times between 1530 and 1595—to grant money or soldiers for the Turkish wars.

In pursuit of his centralist goals, Ferdinand I desired common congresses of the Bohemian estates with those of the Alpine Hereditary Lands and Hungary. He failed largely because the Bohemian, and even more the Hungarian, estates objected to meetings outside their own territories. Early in the seventeenth century the estates themselves sought mutual contacts to resist Habsburg absolutism and religious,encroachments. In 1608 the estates of Moravia concluded a confederation with their Austrian and Hungarian counterparts against Rudolf II. In 1619–20 the estates of all the Lands of the Bohemian Crown negotiated another confederation with the estates of Austria and Hungary. The ties established by these agreements amounted to close military alliances.

Organs of the Estates: The "Highest Officials"

The top administrators and judges in each Land, called the "highest officials" (*nejvyšší úředníci zemští*) in Bohemia and Moravia, represented primarily the estates whose consent was required for their appointment or removal by the king. The twelve officials of the Land in Bohemia and the six in Moravia enjoyed particular prominence. Most of them exercised judicial functions. The Court of the Land (*zemský soud*) in Bohemia included the supreme count palatine, the judge of the Land (*zemský sudí, iudex terrae*), the chamberlain (*komorník, camerarius*), and the notary (*písař zemský, notarius terrae*). They were assisted by assessors: eight barons and five knights. This court, with minor exceptions, had jurisdiction over both civil and criminal cases involving the nobility. In Moravia the judges of the Court of the Land included all the highest officials of the Land.[3] In both Bohemia and Moravia the subchamberlain served as the chief liaison between the Land and the royal towns.

All the officials of the Land together with the assessors of the Court of the Land formed the Royal Council in Bohemia and the Council of the Land (*zemská rada*) in Moravia. The Bohemian Council maintained the traditional claim that any royal decision concerning the Bohemian state required its consent. As noted earlier, however, Ferdinand I began to rely primarily on the advice of his personal council (*Geheime Rat*). He did invite the estates to provide him with Bohemian councilors in Vienna, but they declined for reasons of economy. As a result, in practice,

3. The captain, the chamberlain, the judge of the Land, the aulic judge (*hofrychtéř, iudex curiae*), the subchamberlain (*podkomoří, subcamerarius*), and the notary.

the operations of the Royal Council were largely confined to Bohemia proper, where it supervised the administration and appointed lower officials as well as implemented the diet's decisions, especially with regard to taxation and defense. The Council of the Land in Moravia played a similar role. In Silesia the chief captain remained the sole official of the Land.

Of exceptional importance was the office of the Bohemian chancellor, whose jurisdiction surpassed that of the other eleven highest officials of the Land in Bohemia. Through him the Bohemian estates could wield influence in the other Lands of the Bohemian Crown and guard against a unilateral exercise of royal authority. The chancellor was the keeper of the great seal, which had to be affixed on all major royal documents. His signature attested their constitutionality and consistency with the existing laws. Ferdinand I attempted to eliminate this check on his power, first by transferring the great seal to his court in Vienna, and then by authorizing in 1527 the Bohemian Chamber in Prague to issue major documents without reference to the chancellor. Remonstrances of the Bohemian diet, however, forced the king to restore the great seal to the chancellor in 1529, and to restrict the Chamber in 1530 to issuing documents of lesser importance and limited to the finances of royal properties. Subsequently, particularist demands of the individual Lands challenged the integrity of the power of the chancellor, who continued to reside in Prague. Because in the Lusatias and in Silesia (except for Upper Silesia) the official language was German, a special German section operated in the Bohemian Chancellery under a vice-chancellor who was appointed by, and subordinate to, the chancellor. At the request of the Silesian estates, the German section was temporarily (1611–16) withdrawn from the jurisdiction of the Bohemian chancellor and constituted as an independent Silesian-Lusatian Chancellery with residence in Wrocław.[4]

The Status of Language and Religion

The position of strength which the Czech language had gained in public life in the wake of the Hussite wars continued, though with certain setbacks, during the sixteenth century. Czech remained the official language of government in both Bohemia and Moravia, with the notable exception of the German section of the Bohemian Chancellery, as well as in all of Upper Silesia. German was the official language in both Lusatias, the duchies of Lower Silesia, and in the central agencies of

---

4. Under the arrangement of 1611–16 the king appointed the vice-chancellor from nominees selected by Silesian and Lusatian estates. In 1616 the German section was fully restored to the Bohemian Chancellery in Prague. A special subdivision operated within the German section to process Czech documents for Upper Silesia.

Silesia as a whole. The languages of the Lusatian Sorbs and the Silesian Poles were not in official use except in certain local courts.

The advance of German in Bohemia and Moravia was due partly to demographic factors: the influx of German artisans into towns, and penetration of German peasants into the frontier areas, particularly in northern Bohemia. Another factor was the spread of Lutheranism, which introduced foreign preachers and bestowed on the German language a status akin to that of Latin in the Catholic Church. Finally, there was the influence of the Habsburg kings. While their Jagiellonian predecessors had used Czech freely, the Habsburgs with the exception of Maximilian II (1564–76) had only vague knowledge of this language, and their councilors were almost exclusively German. Under the royal influence the position of Czech as the sole official language in Bohemia began to weaken. In particular the two royal agencies established by Ferdinand I in Prague, the Bohemian Chamber in 1527 and the Council on Appeals in 1548, were officially bilingual in their external contacts, and the former even had German as its exclusive internal language. German towns in Bohemia and Moravia used their language in internal affairs, although in official contacts with other towns or with agencies of the Land they had to employ Czech and thus maintained Czech notaries.

In the early seventeenth century the powerful surge of Germanization caused the Bohemian diet to insist in a resolution of 1615 that only Czech could be used in the courts, parishes, and schools, that the knowledge of Czech was a prerequisite for the right of domicile, and that only natives of at least three generations could hold offices in towns and in the Land. These provisions remained as ineffectual as the earlier stipulation of 1609 by the Moravian diet that children of domiciled foreigners could inherit real estate only if they knew Czech. One area in which the use of Czech almost disappeared in the sixteenth century was diplomatic correspondence, where it had been widely employed before 1526 in contacts with Hungary, Poland, Lithuania, and even with Saxony, Bavaria, and Brandenburg.

The efforts of the Habsburgs to promote Catholicism in the Bohemian state were even less successful before the Thirty Years' War than their aspirations to political absolutism. The freedom of the Hussites— generally known as Utraquists in the sixteenth century—to receive communion in both kinds was protected under the Compacts of Prague, which had been the law of the land since 1485 and acknowledged as such by Ferdinand I. The Lutherans initially sought protection under the compacts, calling themselves Neo-Utraquists, but they gradually realized that the conservative tenor of the compacts, closer to Catholicism than to Protestantism, could in fact be used against them. Seeking more secure protection, they succeeded in obtaining from the sympathetic Maximilian II in 1575 an oral approval of the Bohemian Confession, which covered not only the Lutherans but also—an innovation—the more radical Bohemian Brethren. With the persistence of substantial minorities of Catholics, Bohemia and Moravia were revealing remarkable religious diversity by the latter part of the sixteenth century. In Silesia and the Lusatias the predominant majorities were Lutherans.

Under Rudolf II (1576–1611) pressure against Protestantism intensified, but in the end the king needed the Protestant estates' political support and had to issue for Bohemia a Letter of Majesty in 1609 approving the Bohemian Confession and granting freedom to both Lutherans and Bohemian Brethren. The Lutherans of Silesia received a similar guarantee in the same year. Oral assurances of religious freedom were given to both Lutherans and Brethren in Moravia by 1608, and to Lutherans only in the Lusatias in 1611, by King Matthias (1611–17).

LOCAL ADMINISTRATION

The Circuits (Kraje)

The intermediate territorial jurisdictions in Bohemia between the Land and the noble manor were represented by fourteen circuits (*kraje, Kreise*). Since 1528 the king had appointed in each circuit two captains (*hejtmané*), a baron and a knight, both resident within the circuit. After 1549 their tenure was limited to one year. The circuit captains were primarily police and administrative officials, charged with arresting criminals, suppressing disorders, controlling the vagabonds, taking measures against counterfeiting, regulating hunting and fishing, enforcing wage rates, and protecting the rights of employees. They also assisted with tax collection and the organization of the military levy. A major success of the Habsburg policy of centralization was the elimination of the circuits in Bohemia as centers of local autonomy and as strongholds of the political influence of the estates, particularly the lower nobility. The key to this was the virtual suppression of the circuit assemblies (*krajské sjezdy*) of the local estates, which had met regularly under the Jagiellonians to prepare materials for the diet, to implement its decisions, and even to elect the circuit captains. At the circuit assemblies, the knights also elected delegates to represent them in the diet. As early as 1528 Ferdinand I had decreed that the circuit assemblies could not be held without specific royal authorization, and moreover that they could not deal with any political issues. In 1547 an unauthorized convocation of the circuit assemblies became punishable by death.[5] The resulting absence of organized noble communities in the Bohemian circuits contrasted strikingly with the situation in the Hungarian counties, and helped to account for the weakness of the lower nobility in Bohemia compared with Hungary.

In Moravia the intermediate administrative echelon was even weaker than in Bohemia. Not until 1529 was the Land divided into four quarters (*čtvrti*), for purposes of anti-Turkish defense. In 1569 these divisions stabilized into five circuits. In time of need the Diet elected for each circuit two captains (a baron and a knight), whose functions were primarily military (command of the levy) rather than administrative. In Silesia, administrative subdivisions were not needed because of the existence of the duchies. They were, however, established in the Lusatias.

The administration of justice in the Lands of the Bohemian Crown also illustrated the weakness of the organizational structure between the Land as a whole and the local manor. The old courts at the circuit (or comparable) levels, which had tried cases of the nobility and had heard peasants' appeals from seigneurial courts, disappeared in the period from the Hussite wars to the mid-sixteenth century, first in Bohemia and Moravia, then in Upper Silesia and the Lusatias. Thus, with certain exceptions in Lower Silesia, justice over nobles became entirely concentrated in the central Courts of the Land, while justice over the peasantry was fully exercised in the manors.

The Towns

The most important municipalities in the Bohemian Lands were the royal free towns, entitled to representation in the diets and not subject to any local seigneur. They numbered forty in Bohemia, six each in Moravia and Upper Lusatia, and four in Lower Lusatia. In Silesia royal towns properly speaking existed only in the "immediate" duchies.

In the beginning of Ferdinand I's reign the royal towns were still free of appointed royal officials, as had been the case since the mid-fifteenth century. Power rested with an oligarchy of several patrician families. The head of the town government was the mayor (*purkmistr, magister civium*), whose office was held in succession by the individual councilors for terms between four weeks and a quarter of a year. The retiring councilors elected their own successors in a procedure known as "free election." The new council was confirmed by an appropriate official of the Land, in Bohemia and Moravia by the subchamberlain. In many

5. Subsequently, until the Bohemian uprising of 1618, the circuit assemblies were permitted on rare occasions for the specific purpose of electing the knights' delegates to the diet.

towns special nationality or religious requirements were stipulated for the post of councilor. For instance, the candidate had to be a Czech and Utraquist in most Bohemian towns, a Catholic in Plzeň (Pilsen), and a Catholic German in Olomouc. Financial management was entrusted to the First Councilor (*primas*) and overseen by a group of town elders (*obecní starší, cives seniores*), selected from retiring councilors. Gatherings of all the burghers in a town, called the "great communities" (*velká obec, communitas, universitas*), were held rarely. In fact, Ferdinand I in 1528 stipulated that convocations of such assemblies required special royal permission.

Having curbed the power of lower nobility by restricting the circuit assemblies, Ferdinand I took advantage of the abortive uprising of the estates in 1547 to limit the autonomy of royal towns as well. Particularly affected were the towns of Upper Lusatia and Bohemia, except for Budějovice, Plzeň, and Ústí, which had remained loyal to the king. Aside from other penalties, royal judges (*královští rychtáři*), as well as royal captains in case of the towns of Prague, were imposed on the towns. Appointed by the Bohemian Chamber, they sat with the councils and town courts and supervised their activities. Moreover, the town councilors were henceforth selected, without participation of the townsmen, by royal officials. Subsequently these measures were somewhat modified. Silesian royal towns suffered lesser penalties, and Moravian and Lower Lusatian ones that had not participated in the uprising of 1547 remained unaffected.

In the judicial area, the royal towns were endowed with both the lower and the higher jurisdictions. The former was exercised by the town judge (*rychtář* or *fojt*), a simple town employee in charge also of police work, who tried less serious cases. More serious civil and criminal cases, including capital offenses, were tried before a court (*iudicium bannitum*) consisting of the mayor and the councilors. In Bohemian and Upper Lusatian towns after 1547 the royal judge also took part in the proceedings. The custom of appeals to foreign town courts, especially to Magdeburg, was proscribed in 1532. After 1548 recourse from the town courts was to be solely to the royal Council on Appeals in Prague.

The cameral towns (*komorní města*) occupied an intermediate status between the royal free and the subject towns. Their numbers increased in Bohemia and Moravia as subject towns purchased their freedom from the control of local seigneurs. They came under the jurisdiction of the Bohemian Chamber, and were not entitled to representation in the diets. The subject towns varied widely in size. While the smaller ones resembled villages, the larger ones often had governmental structures similar to those of royal free towns. The seigneurs, however, preserved varying degrees of control over the selection of councilors and town elders.

The Manors

The peasant population in the Lands of the Bohemian Crown was generally under the jurisdiction of the local seigneurs. In Bohemia and Moravia the transfer of full governmental authority to the noble land-lords had occurred before the Hussite wars, in Silesia during the fif-teenth century, and in the Lusatias by the middle of the sixteenth. On his manor the seigneur exercised judicial, police, and executive au-thority on behalf of the Land. These functions were usually performed for the seigneur by his representative, entitled variously as sub-cham-berlain, captain, or simply "official" (*Amtmann*). On larger manors this functionary was usually drawn from the ranks of lower nobility. Par-ticularly concerned with justice, tax collection, and military matters, he visited, as the need arose, various parts of the manor and convened meetings at which he held court, appointed village judges and coun-cilors, monitored village affairs, and updated official records and reg-isters. The village judge, who also headed the village, was usually called *rychtář* or *fojt* in Bohemia and Moravia, and was appointed by the sei-gneur. In Silesia his title was *Schultheis* (*šoltys*) and in the Lusatias *Richter* (*wjesny sudnik*), and the office was often hereditary. The judge was as-sisted by councilors, appointed by seigneurial officials for one year in Bohemia and Moravia, and usually for life in Silesia and the Lusatias. The village judge and the councilors were not agents of local autonomy, but rather of seigneurial authority and interest.

The courts of the manor exercised both the higher and the lower jurisdictions over the peasants. The village judge and the councilors tried minor cases in the individual villages. Major criminal and civil cases were tried before the seigneur, or more likely his official, and assessors chosen usually from the village judges.

FISCAL AND MILITARY AFFAIRS

Ordinary and Extraordinary Taxes

Ferdinand I found regular royal income in the Bohemian Crown greatly diminished because of the weakness of royal authority during the preceding century. His main fiscal objectives were (1) to increase the so-called ordinary income and (2) to regularize the "extraordinary" income, which depended on the grant of taxes by the diets.

The ordinary income collected by the Bohemian Chamber came from various sources, such as royal estates, royal towns, and ecclesiastical es-tates. Ferdinand I increased the number of royal estates in Bohemia in

1547 by confiscating properties of the insurgent towns. While royal towns traditionally contributed semiannual fees to the Chamber, an additional royal tax on brewed and imported beer was imposed on the towns of Bohemia, Upper Lusatia, and Silesia as yet another punishment for the 1547 uprising. Ferdinand I and his successors until 1611 regarded ecclesiastical estates as part of the Chamber's domain, and often appropriated their income.

Another category of ordinary income derived from the so-called regalian rights applied to mining, the sale of salt, customs, and minting. Ferdinand I initiated royal control over the sale of salt, imported into Bohemia and Moravia from Austria and into the Lusatias and Silesia from the Baltic region. By the 1570s the entire salt trade was to become a royal monopoly. The royal income from customs had suffered before 1526 because many customhouses had been appropriated by private seigneurs. Ferdinand I corrected the situation, at least in Bohemia proper, by prohibiting private customhouses in 1549, and subsequently by regularizing the tariff system for all the Bohemian Lands.

As for the "extraordinary" taxes, before 1526 the diets had rarely granted them and the kings were expected to cover the expenses of the state from "ordinary" income. Ferdinand I was notably successful in obtaining regular grants of these taxes. As during the late Jagiellonian period, the basis of the extraordinary taxation was the declared value of certain properties or incomes, or both. Initially the nobility paid the tax on real property and on income from feudal dues; the townsmen—enjoying a relative advantage—paid on real property only, not on income. From 1542 the tax was levied also on the income and real property of subject peasants. Under Maximilian II the nobles scored a major victory in 1567 when (in Bohemia and Moravia) the houses of seigneurial subjects in villages and towns, and houses in royal towns, became a new base for extraordinary taxation. The nobles paid nothing unless they owned houses in royal towns. This tax system proved inadequate and it was supplemented in 1569–75 by a sales tax of one-thirtieth of the value of the goods sold. Before the end of the century the nobles once more paid taxes, this time on the number of subject peasant households. Other taxes followed, especially on chimneys, shops, and beer. The yield of the extraordinary taxes in Bohemia more than doubled during Ferdinand I's reign, and was ten times larger in 1600 than in the 1520s. Silesia retained the original (as of 1526) basis for extraordinary taxation. In the Lusatias a tax by chimneys took its place.

The extraordinary tax was collected by the estates themselves, not by a royal organ such as the Bohemian Chamber. Moreover, the estates retained the important power—which the contemporary Hungarian diet had lost—of disbursing the proceeds of the tax for their stated purpose, usually to maintain troops in Hungary against the Turks. In Bohemia the diet elected three tax collectors of the Land (*berníci zemští*), one from each estate.[6]

Royal income from both the ordinary and extraordinary taxation defrayed expenses of the royal court, diplomacy, royal officials, interest on the royal debt, and the military establishment in Hungary. From 1541 the Bohemian Lands annually contributed twice as much revenue as the Alpine Lands. Of their contribution only one-twentieth was spent on the territory of the Bohemian state in the sixteenth century.

The Bohemian Army and Foreign Policy

In the fifteenth century, and especially during the Hussite wars, the traditional military levy of nobles, townsmen, and peasants had fought zealously and effectively. Subsequently, it was outmoded by changes in military techniques and was rarely used. When the levy was called in the sixteenth century, the towns and manors tended to supply their quota of soldiers in the form of mercenaries, or more often the diet instead of a levy directly granted a certain number of mercenaries.

The army was controlled by the estates, which raised, paid, and administered it with their officials. It could not be deployed outside the Bohemian state without the estates' permission. Thus the use of Bohemian troops in Hungary depended on special agreements, such as the undertaking by the estates to defend the Hungarian frontier at Komárno (Komárom) in 1577. Ferdinand I failed in his efforts to subordinate the Bohemian contingents to the *Hofkriegsrat*.

The basic unit of mercenary troops was the regiment, headed by a colonel who was its master, commander, and supreme judge. He hired the troops and concluded agreements with the estates to enter their service. The numbers of mercenary troops were relatively large. In 1542 the Bohemian Lands raised 10,000 soldiers of cavalry and 14,000 of infantry. During the uprising of 1618–20, when the Bohemian army acted for the last time as an independent body, it consisted of about 25,000 mercenaries by 1619.

While the estates safeguarded the independence of the Bohemian army until the Thirty Years' War, distinct Bohemian foreign relations largely ended with the accession of the Habsburgs. The kings conducted a single foreign policy for all their domains. Their position as Holy Roman emperor played, of course, an important role here. Only minor international agreements with Poland, Brandenburg, the Pala-

---

6. They received the tax money either from the Circuit tax collectors (*krajští berníci*), specially elected by the diet, or (as in 1556–95) from the regular circuit administrators, the captains. The diet also elected a paymaster (*colmistr, Zahlmeister*) to pay the troops in Hungary.

tinate, and Saxony, such as those concerning foreign fiefs of the Bohemian Crown, were concluded by the Habsburgs in their distinctive role as Bohemian king. During the conflict between Rudolf II and his brother Matthias, the estates of Bohemia and Moravia tried to regain a direct role in foreign affairs. In 1608 the Moravians were promised that questions of war and peace would be decided only with the concurrence of the diet. In the Bohemian Confederation of 1619 such power was granted to the General Diet.

ECONOMIC LIFE[7]

Agriculture

From the early sixteenth century the noble seigneurs in the Bohemian Lands increasingly involved themselves in direct operation of agricultural enterprises instead of relying primarily on income from peasant dues. Among the reasons for the change in seigneurial economic policy were the rise of mercenary armies, freeing the nobles from military preoccupations; the increasing prosperity of towns, inspiring the seigneurs to emulate the burghers in acquiring wealth; and the declining value of money, diminishing the worth of the fixed peasant dues. Early in the century the entrepreneurial activity of the seigneurs focused substantially on construction of ponds for pisciculture. Ponds became especially numerous in southern and eastern Bohemia, as well as in western Moravia. Eventually about 78,000 of them dotted the Bohemian countryside. By the mid-sixteenth century, seigneurial breweries acquired special importance. Brewing light beer out of wheat and engaging in large-scale production (often several hundred hectoliters a year), they overshadowed the older, smaller enterprises in seigneurial towns, which specialized in dark beer made with barley. As a result of these trends the breakdown of the sources of income of a typical manor (Jindřichův Hradec, for instance) showed in 1559–60 that the yield of peasant dues declined from its earlier preponderance to less than 38 percent of the total income, while the rest came from other sources: 30 percent each from ponds and breweries, 1.5 percent from forests, and 1 percent from the demesne estates.

The end of the sixteenth century and the beginning of the seven-

7. Economic data in this section are derived from *Přehled československých dějin* (Prague: Československá akademie věd, 1958), 1:315–59; František Kavka and Josef Válka, *Dějiny Československa. 2. 1437–1781,* 2d ed. (Prague: SPN, [1970]), pp. 94–150; Jan Kapras, *Právní dějiny zemí koruny české* (Prague: Česká Grafická Unie, 1913), 2:377–87; Josef Petráň, "Středoevropské zemědělství a obchod v 16. a na počátku 17. století," *Československý Časopis Historický* 19 (1971): 355–80; Josef Janáček, "České soukenictví v 16. století," ibid., 4 (1956): 553–90; *Přehled dějin Československa* (Prague: Academia, 1982), I/2:23–40.

teenth witnessed a notable increase in the importance of the demesne estates as a special focus of seigneurial entrepreneurship. The main stimulus for the seigneurs' direct involvement in crop and animal production was the marked rise in agricultural prices. Owing to this price revolution, the cost of bread and beer (reflecting the cost of barley, rye, and wheat), as well as the value of cattle, began to increase in the 1570s. In Prague between 1576 and 1615 the price of beer rose by 62 percent, and that of cattle by 66 percent. The price of bread doubled in Bohemia from the 1580s to 1620. The expansion of the demesne estates and of their production resulted in another shift in the typical breakdown of the sources of manorial income. Early in the seventeenth century the yield from the demesne estates ordinarily constituted the largest source of seigneurial revenue, breweries the second, ponds or forests the third, and peasant dues the fourth.

In the period of agricultural prosperity—the late sixteenth and early seventeenth centuries—rye was the grain mainly involved in long-distance trade and export. Oats and barley were largely consumed by the producers, and local breweries used up two-thirds of the wheat output. In Bohemia the chief grain exporting area lay between the Ohře and Labe (Elbe) rivers north of Prague, with Litoměřice as the trade center and Saxony as the land of destination. On the whole, however, grain exports from the Bohemian Lands did not compare in size with those from contemporary Poland or eastern Germany. Thus in Moravia around 1600 only 5 percent of grain production was marketed outside the manor of origin. Though more localized, wine production was of major significance. In Bohemia the vineyards, owned mostly by townsmen, were concentrated in the area of Prague, Litoměřice, Louny, and Libochovice, and in the sixteenth century produced up to 340,000 hectoliters of wine annually. Wine exports, largely from the region of Litoměřice, were directed to Saxony. In Moravia, nobles' estates in the southern region accounted for most of the output, while Bohemia and Hungary received most of the exports. With the growth of beer production, the cultivation of hops spread, especially in central Bohemia and southern Moravia. The areas around Rakovník and Žatec acquired an excellent reputation in this field.

Although manors in general received significant income from the sale of cattle, sheep, dairy products, eggs, and feathers, animal breeding was not highly developed in the Bohemian Lands, except in northeastern Moravia and the Silesian county of Těšín, where the raising of sheep and goats, as well as cattle, flourished. Meat consumption, particularly in Prague, could not be satisfied from domestic sources. In the late sixteenth century the Slovak area was a major supplier of cattle. After the outbreak of disturbances in northern Hungary it was eclipsed by Poland, especially the Poznań area, in the early seventeenth century.

The rise of seigneurial entrepreneurship created new demands, causing the peasants of the Bohemian Lands—like those of other areas of East Central Europe—to pass through the stage of second serfdom or neo-serfdom.[8] The pressure to enlarge the demesne estates could not be satisfied by the absorption of abandoned peasant homesteads. It led to forcible acquisition of peasant lands, a practice either subject to ineffectual legal limitations (as in Bohemia after 1548) or openly sanctioned (in Silesia after 1562). As a result of this process, the remaining peasant households had to pay higher taxes because the land incorporated into the demesnes became tax exempt.

A major source of the peasants' hardship was the seigneurs' need for more labor on the enlarged demesnes. Some seigneurs exacted more than the traditional amount of unpaid labor (the so-called *robota*) in exchange for favors (such as loans in times of distress), but many resorted to arbitrary increases of the *robota*. Although this practice was often held illegal (for instance, in 1528 in Silesia), it was facilitated in the Bohemian Lands by the peasants' loss of the right to seek redress beyond the manorial courts. In the areas where no customary limit of the *robota* had existed, the seigneurs were free simply to raise their demands to meet the needs of the enlarged demesnes. Another way to ease the labor shortage was to require peasants' children to work on the demesnes, a practice sanctioned by law in Upper Lusatia (1539) and Silesia (1565), and gradually by custom in Bohemia and Moravia. To prevent the peasants from escaping the reinstituted serfdom, the noble landlords sought to limit the right of migration. A law, dating to 1487 in Bohemia, that required peasants to obtain their seigneur's permission before moving acquired a new significance, and a similar measure was enacted in Silesia in 1528.

Crafts, Industry, and Mining

With few exceptions, artisan production in the sixteenth-century Bohemian Lands was conducted on a small scale by guild craftsmen and was destined for local markets. The quality of crafts was improving,

8. The concept of "neo-serfdom" or "second serfdom" refers mainly to the phenomenon, limited to Eastern Europe, of increasing reliance on serf labor by the feudal landlords during the sixteenth and seventeenth centuries compared with alternate forms of feudal exactions, especially dues in money or in kind. The specific forms of this phenomenon varied among the national areas of East Central Europe. For a general discussion of the concept see "Symposium" in *Slavic Review* 34 (1975): 225–78, especially László Makkai, "Neo-Serfdom: Its Origin and Nature in East Central Europe," pp. 225–38; see also "Serfdom in Central and Eastern Europe," *Cambridge Economic History of Europe* (Cambridge: Cambridge University Press, 1977), 5:113–23; and Henry Kamen, *The Iron Century: Social Changes in Europe, 1550–1660* (New York and Washington: Praeger, 1971), pp. 199–228.

mainly under Ferdinand I (1526–64) and Rudolf II (1576–1611) with the influx of foreign (German and Italian) artisans whose advanced techniques were adopted locally. Reaching its peak in the sixteenth century, guild organization exhibited great diversity. Simple guilds combined craftsmen of one kind in a single town, complex ones amalgamated craftsmen of different types, and so-called intercity ones combined artisans from several towns. There were even guilds of the Land, those in the capitals (Prague, Olomouc, Wrocław), which either supervised corresponding guilds in other localities (such as, the guild of tanners in Prague) or were open to individual craftsmen in various towns (like the guilds of goldsmiths or painters). Although they were decreasing, restrictions on guild membership based on religion or nationality were still common. In Bohemia, guild members had to be Catholics in Catholic towns, but analogous provisions were dropped in Utraquist towns after 1526. During the sixteenth century the Czechs became eligible for guild membership in Moravia and Upper Silesia, but the original German monopoly persisted in Lower Silesia.

The guilds were increasingly subject to regulation, not only by the town governments but also by the diets. Sensitive to inflation, the Bohemian diet was eager to control both prices and wages, stipulating maximum rates in 1547 with revisions in 1578 and 1605. The rural seigneurs also encroached on the rights and privileges of the town guilds. Thus some Lands (Bohemia in 1517, Lusatia in 1547) lifted the traditional prohibitions on artisan activities within a mile of each town, enabling the seigneurs to maintain craftsmen in their villages.

Textile production tended to break the constraints of guilds and achieve higher volume, as well as more advanced organization. Above all, the output of linen grew dramatically, stimulated by demand for light clothing in the newly discovered tropical territories overseas. Linen production became highly developed in the northern tier of the Bohemian Lands (Upper Lusatia, Silesia, and northern Bohemia), and was marketed initially through Leipzig. By the last quarter of the sixteenth century much of the output was organized by south German merchant houses (above all from Nuremberg) on the basis of the putting-out system. A merchant wholesaler contracted for the delivery within a year of a certain amount of linen from either guilds or—particularly in Silesia—domestic producers, to whom in turn he advanced money or raw materials. Linen production reached its peak in the north of the Bohemian state in the late sixteenth and early seventeenth centuries. A more limited production of woolen cloth was concentrated in several towns of southern Moravia and northeast Bohemia with markets respectively in Austria and Poland. It was dominated by several wholesalers through the putting-out system, with the chief center in Jihlava (Iglau), where an early attempt was made to establish a manufactory.[9] In the late sixteenth century, high production costs caused a decline in demand for Bohemian woolen cloth, especially on the Polish market.

Ironworks and glassworks traditionally developed outside the framework of the guilds. Throughout most of the sixteenth century, iron was still produced in primitive ovens, and water-propelled hammers for crushing the ore constituted the most important mechanical equipment of the ironworks. Owned usually by noble landlords, the widely scattered ironworks were either operated by the manor or (more often) leased to outside entrepreneurs. As a major technological advance, in the 1590s high furnaces were first introduced, still fueled by charcoal, but enabling continuous operation. On the whole, however, iron production in the Bohemian Lands failed to satisfy the local needs. In particular, better iron products, such as steel and wire, were supplied from Styria. Implements, such as knives, and virtually all armaments were also imported. In comparison, glass increasingly became an article of export during the sixteenth century. Of the thirty-four known glassworks most were located in the border mountains of Bohemia and Moravia; but a few were in the interior regions, as around Beroun and Zbiroh, where wood and silica were plentiful.

Mining of precious metals had a tradition in Bohemia, reaching deep into the Middle Ages. In the first half of the sixteenth century the older silver producing regions were overshadowed by a new center, developed in Jáchymov (Joachimsthal) by the noble Šlik family in 1518. Although other nobles opened mines in the Ore Mountains (Krušné Hory) of the northeast, the second most important area of silver mining was newly developed at Rudolfov in southern Bohemia. Ferdinand I's partial expropriation of the Šliks' mines in 1528 dampened private initiative in metal extraction until 1534, when the king guaranteed the nobles' right to mines on their own land. However, he seized the mines of royal towns in 1547.

In the second half of the sixteenth century, Jáchymov and Rudolfov, producing 750 and 600 kilograms of silver per annum respectively, declined in importance, and the older centers, Kutná Hora (3,000 kg of silver annually) and Příbram (1,500 kg), once more took the lead. Still the entire Bohemian silver production remained modest, barely equaling a single Slovak center, Banská Štiavnica. Moreover, mining operations were losing profitability because of the influx of American silver to Europe.

---

9. Throughout this volume the term "manufactory" refers to the locus of large-scale production based on division of labor (in contrast to the artisan workshop), but not yet employing mechanization and/or steam power (in distinction from modern factory). The term "protofactory" has been sometimes used to designate this type of enterprise.

In the extraction of tin, however, Bohemia was outstanding during the sixteenth century. The total output from 1500 through 1620 is estimated at 34,000 tons, yielding an annual average of 283 tons. For the sixteenth century the Bohemian production probably represented somewhat over two-thirds of the European total, except for England. Mined under the direction of the Bohemian Chamber in Krupka, Cínovec, and Horní Slavkov, tin was exported to Austria and Italy.

Trade

The disruption of long-distance commerce, dating to the turmoil of the Hussite wars, was yet repaired in the first half of the sixteenth century. The important international trade routes avoided the Bohemian Lands, except for the highway from Leipzig into Poland via Wrocław. Foreign trade was mediated by the neighboring German cities, especially Nuremberg, Augsburg, and Leipzig, whose commercial houses had representatives in the Bohemian Lands. The dependence on foreigners for organizing external trade went hand in hand with the lack of sophistication in domestic commercial institutions. Commercial companies were rarely formed and, if so, only for specific ventures, not as continuing enterprises. Attempts to unify the currency were made by Ferdinand I, who hoped to establish the thaler minted in Jáchymov as the standard unit of money. The Diet's effort in 1544 to define the relative values of other circulating currencies signaled the failure of standardization. An attempt to unify weights and measures in 1549 also failed. Modern credit methods, common in the West, made only slow advances. Although, by midcentury, bills of exchange were available in Wrocław (as well as in Prague) for Leipzig, they could not be obtained in Wrocław for Nuremberg.

While the attainments of the Bohemian Lands in the higher commercial sphere were not distinguished, there was a solid achievement in the humbler sphere of local markets. Unlike their confreres in Poland or Hungary, the Bohemian seigneurs by the sixteenth century had developed their subject towns into commercial centers. The flourishing state of towns, such as Český Krumlov, Třeboň, Jindřichův Hradec, Pardubice, and Jičín, attested to the success of these endeavors.

In the long run the aloofness from the arteries of international trade, combined with the growing ascendancy of the noble estates, was causing the Bohemian Lands to fall behind the economically advancing countries of Western Europe. In the short run it helped to cushion them from the adverse effect—experienced by the adjacent German areas— of the shift of the main commercial routes from the Mediterranean to the Atlantic in the late sixteenth century. The shift increased the commercial significance of the rivers Labe (Elbe) and Odra (Oder). The navigability of the Odra was extended upstream from Wrocław to Racibórz, and the merchants of Leipzig failed in their efforts to interrupt the northward passage of Bohemian trade on the Labe.

When Prague became the residence of the emperor under Rudolf II (1583–1611), the German cities, such as Nuremberg, had to share their role in the external trade of the Bohemian Lands with Linz, Vienna, and cities of northern Italy. Occasionally English and Dutch merchants also appeared in Prague, reflecting the growing importance of the Atlantic routes. Imports involved mainly overseas goods, luxury products, iron implements, and cattle; export articles included, above all, linen and woolen cloth, tin, and agricultural products (grain, wine, and hops). International transit trade through Prague, especially from Hungary to Nuremberg, and from Leipzig to Vienna, had only minor significance.

From the time of Ferdinand I, both import and export duties had been paid at the border in Silesia and the Lusatias. In Bohemia and Moravia only export duties were so paid, while a tax on imported (as well as domestic) goods, called *Ungelt,* was collected at warehouses located in designated towns. Under Rudolf II the Lands of the Bohemian Crown moved toward a customs union through provisions that (1) domestic goods imported or exported from one Land to another paid lower tariffs compared with foreign goods, and (2) foreign goods on which customs were paid in one Land were duty free if reexported into another Land.

The Slovenes

Virtually the entire area inhabited by the Slovenes was under the rule of the Habsburgs in the early sixteenth century: Styria since 1282, Carniola and Carinthia since 1335. The Slovenes lived in southern Carinthia and southeastern Styria, and had a majority in Carniola. They also were the major group in Gorizia, which Emperor Maximilian I had gained between 1500 and 1509. When Ferdinand I accepted the Crown of Saint Stephen in 1526, he acquired in addition a small Slovene area of southwestern Hungary, the Prekmurje, between the rivers Mura (Mur) and Rába (Raab) in Zala and Vas counties. Only two Slovene groups lived as yet outside the Habsburg territories, one northwest of Gorizia (the so-called Venetian Slovenia), the other in northwest ("Venetian") Istria. After 1521 the border between the Habsburg monarchy and Venetia remained stable until the demise of the latter in 1797. The boundaries of the Slovene-inhabited Habsburg Lands had become essentially fixed by 1526 with the exception of Carniola, which included Trieste (till 1550),

Rijeka (till 1570), and the Pazin Duchy in northeast ("Austrian") Istria (till 1809).

The Slovene ethnic area stabilized by the mid-fifteenth century after Germanization had caused it to contract in the north for five hundred years. In the countryside most of the German colonists were assimilated. The towns were predominantly Slovene in population except those on the coast, Milje (Muggia), Koper (Capo d'Istria), Izola (Isola), and Piran (Pirano), which were mostly Italian. Although the towns in the interior had a Germanic appearance, this merely reflected the character of the relatively narrow upper socioeconomic class. The nobility was largely German even in the purely Slovene territory, to a much lesser extent Italian on the western fringes. Because of the non-Slav character of the upper classes, the Slovene language did not enjoy the widespread use in public life as did Czech in contemporary Bohemia and Moravia; instead it occupied a subordinate status, like Polish in Silesia or Lusatian Sorbs in the Lusatias.

THE ADMINISTRATIVE SYSTEM UNDER FERDINAND I (1522–64)

The Power of the Prince

The political power of the estates had flourished in the fifteenth century and received regular institutional expression in the individual Lands. Annual sessions of the diets had become common since the 1440s, with the increasing demands of the emperor—in his role as the prince of these Lands—for "extraordinary" taxes. The diets were divided into four colleges (curiae) representing the prelates, the higher nobility, the lower nobility, and the towns. Although admitted in the fifteenth century, the towns did not secure formal recognition of their right to sit in the diets until the second half of the sixteenth century, when the nobility came to view them as desirable allies in a common struggle for Protestantism and against the prince. Each diet elected a committee to represent the estates between the sessions of the diets. By the early sixteenth century each committee had at its disposal a permanent staff of paid officials.

The estates of Carniola, Carinthia, and Styria tended to keep in close touch. In particular, their estates committees began to meet jointly by the mid-fifteenth century to discuss matters of mutual interest, such as defense against the Turks. These contacts foreshadowed more substantive ties within the area known as Inner Austria, which was soon to acquire a formal administrative identity. This grouping of Lands, partly Slavic and partly Germanic, offered a curious parallel to the Lands of the Bohemian Crown, although the Slavic element was numerically weaker and politically powerless in Inner Austria.

Ferdinand I on assuming power in the Austrian Lands in 1522, following the Compact of Brussels with his elder brother Charles V, proceeded to strengthen princely authority to counterbalance the power of the estates. In the Lands including Slovene populations he did not have to start virtually afresh as he had to do in the Bohemian state. Instead, he had the precedents set by his grandfather Maximilian I (1493–1519), who had already confronted and modified the situation of almost unchecked estates' power, resembling Bohemian conditions under the Jagiellonians. Then the sole agent of direct princely power in each of the Lands (Carniola, Styria, Carinthia) had been the *vicedom*, largely restricted to the administration of the prince's estates and regalian rights. Inspired by his experiences in the Duchy of Burgundy, Maximilian I proceeded to create new official bodies with jurisdiction over whole groups of Lands. In 1493 he established in Vienna the *Regiment*, an agency to represent princely authority in an area then officially called Lower Austria, including in addition to three Lands with Slovene populations (Carniola, Carinthia, Styria), also Austria above and below the Enns (ordinarily known as Upper and Lower Austria). It was a counterpart of the *Regiment* in Innsbruck, the jurisdiction of which covered what was then officially called Upper Austria, namely the Tyrol, Voralberg, and small southwestern German fiefs, known as the Forelands (*Vorderoesterreich*). Shortly afterward, Maximilian entrusted financial matters for Lower Austria to the Chamber, newly created in Vienna, and restricted the *Regiment* to administrative and judicial affairs. The new official apparatus sought to gain ascendancy, among other means, by building up an appellate jurisdiction for the individual Lands, not hesitating to make use of the peasants' dissatisfaction with the manorial courts. Inevitably, the estates bitterly opposed such efforts, and on Maximilian's death in 1519 they succeeded in obtaining an almost complete dissolution of the new agencies.

Ferdinand I resolutely overrode the estates' objections and soon restored the two *Regiments* and financial Chambers. Moreover, by 1527 he had proceeded to subordinate even these institutions to the new tier of organs, established in Vienna to cover matters concerning all his realms: the *Geheime Rat*, the *Hofrat*, the *Hofkanzlei*, and the *Hofkammer*. The final element added in 1556, the *Hofkriegsrat*, restricted the previous autonomy of the *Regiment* in military matters. Otherwise Ferdinand I employed two principal means of strengthening the princely authority. One was the standardization of administrative norms. Between 1542 and 1552 he introduced a standard set of "police regulations" in each of the Inner Austrian Lands. These were followed by sets of mining regulations, amplifying the prince's regalian rights. Uniform procedures before the princely courts were also instituted (for Carniola in 1535). The other approach used by Ferdinand I to check the estates' power was to stabilize the assessment and collection of the "extraordinary" tax, although its grant still depended on an annual approval by the diets. In the early 1540s the estates agreed on the basic measure of the tax: the amount of dues received by the noble from his peasant subjects. For the purposes of tax assessment, special registers of income from property (*Gültbücher*) were established in the individual Lands at midcentury. After their introduction the tax yielded 5,632 pounds in Gorizia, 22,000 in Carniola, 34,824 in Carinthia, and 72,248 in Styria. The amount doubled during the 1550s and tripled or quadrupled by the end of the century, finally stablilizing at the quadruple level at the time of the Thirty Years' War (1618–48). Inflation accounted for much of the increase. Although measured by the value of the noble's dues from his subject peasantry, the tax after 1557 was in fact largely paid by the peasants themselves. The nobles contributed a small portion of this tax only in certain periods, thus 5 to 19 percent in 1575–77 and 1587–92, and 25 to 30 percent in 1594–1605.

Ferdinand I's reforms represented a high point in the efforts to strengthen princely authority in the Slovene Lands. After his death the estates' power was to be once more on the rise. In the first place, they were able to influence the composition of the new administrative bodies, and thus they could dilute their bureaucratic substance and compromise their character as instruments of purely princely authority, particularly in the case of the *Regiment* and the *Hofkriegsrat*. In the second place, because of the greater proximity of the Turkish threat, the estates of the Slovene Lands, even more effectively than the Bohemian estates, could turn the ruler's financial dependence into an instrument of power. Since the ruler's assured "ordinary" income was barely sufficient to cover the cost of civil administration, he continued to depend increasingly on the diets for the grant of "extraordinary" taxes for military expenditures. The estates had not only retained their power of annual approval of the amount of the tax but also could insist on the control of its expenditure.

The Institutions of the Estates

The internal administration of the Lands within the Slovene territory remained entirely under the control of the diets and the estates. The principal administrator in each Land (Carniola, Carinthia, Styria, Gorizia) was the chief of the estates, the captain of the Land (*Landeshauptmann*). Nominated by the estates, and appointed by the prince, he swore an oath of fidelity to both. He was assisted by the Committee of the Land, elected by the diets. In Carniola, for instance, in 1531 the Committee of the Land could assemble in one of two variants. A Narrow Committee consisted of seven members including a representative of the towns, namely the mayor of Ljubljana (Laibach). In more serious matters, this group convoked the Great Committee with ten additional members. The decisions of the diets and the committees of the Lands were implemented by chancelleries and an apparatus of officials, paid by and responsible to the estates. These officials primarily supervised collection and expenditure of taxes, preservation of public order, maintenance of forts, and construction of roads.

A striking sign of the estates' ability to challenge the princely authority was a widespread adoption of Protestantism. The Reformation appealed first to the townsmen; after 1540 the nobility assumed its leadership. Protected by the diets, the Lutheran Church subsequently developed its own organization under superintendents, with churches and schools conducting religious services in the vernacular (mainly Slovene in Carniola, German in Styria and Carinthia).

The estates were also largely in charge of the local governments (in the manors and towns), as well as of the judicial system. In the manors, public authority was exercised by seigneurial officials, in towns by judges and councils. These functionaries collected taxes, provided police protection, and—except in Gorizia and the Pazin Duchy—dispensed the civil and lower criminal justice. Higher criminal justice—for individual criminal judicial circuits—was vested in the courts of certain manors and towns, exercising the *Blutbann* (jurisdiction concerning capital crimes).

Ordinarily the peasants were subject to the patrimonial courts, but there were some significant exceptions. Disputes concerning vineyards were tried by special peasant courts, directed by the seigneur, and guided by the *Bergrechtsordnung* (the Vineyard Ordinance), which from 1582 existed also in a Slovene translation under the title *Gorske Bukve*. In the Pazin Duchy the peasants had their own elected courts. In Gorizia only a few manors had their own courts; most of the area was directly under the Court of the Land, headed by the captain of the Land, and justice was dispensed by circuit Judges of the Land. In all the Lands, appeals from the manorial and town courts went to the captain of the Land, and from the courts of the prince's estates to the *vicedom*.

The nobility in both civil and criminal cases was under the jurisdiction of the Courts of the Land, called in Carniola the *Landschrannengericht*. These courts consisted of the captain of the Land and several assessors (twelve in Carniola, for instance) elected by the nobility. When the Court of the Land determined that an extremely serious crime had been committed, the accused could be deprived of his noble status and transferred for punishment to an ordinary court of higher justice. Only cases of high treason were tried by the *Regiment*.

The Military Organization

The Turkish threat increased during the sixteenth century when the border of the Ottoman Empire advanced within 15 kilometers of the

Slovene area. Between 1522 and 1532 major Turkish incursions into the Slovene Lands averaged five per year. The Turkish advances against Vienna in 1529 and 1532 were especially devastating. Although such invasions later subsided, minor raids represented a constant danger. Most important, to keep the Turks from the immediate border, the Inner Austrian estates assumed increasing responsibility for the defense of the shrinking remains of the neighboring Kingdom of Croatia.

The military organization in the Slovene area was still essentially of the feudal type. Each noble was obliged to supply one rider and a certain number of foot soldiers for every one or two hundred pounds of income from his estate, and maintain them for three to six months. Responsible for their own defense, the towns also had to provide foot soldiers. The free peasants, found still in Gorizia and the Pazin Duchy, were to serve personally as infantrymen. The largest host was raised by the "insurrection" or a levy of peasants. For that purpose all able-bodied peasants were registered, and in case of need every thirtieth, twentieth, tenth, or fifth registered man could be called up—in Carniola in the mid-sixteenth century even every third one. After 1527 the estates also employed mercenary troops. In addition, they could mobilize the Christian refugees from the Turkish territory, the Uskoks, who were settled in Carniola around the towns of Žumberak, Metlika, and Kočevje in the late 1530s. The entire military organization was in the hands of the estates. All the officers had to be local nobles. The estates were even entitled to appoint their own officers or commissioners to command the prince's mercenaries while passing through their Lands.

For defense, fortifications (tabori) were erected on hillocks, usually around churches. Guards, stationed on hills from the border into the interior, signaled the Turks' approach. Begun in 1522, this warning network eventually covered all of Carniola, Styria, and Gorizia. To strengthen the defense organization, Carniola was divided in 1536 into five military districts or quarters (Viertel), each under a captain of the quarter who called out the "insurrection" in cases of danger. Styria received a similar military organization in 1541.

The involvement of the Slovene area with the defense of the Croatian and the Slavonian military borders steadily increased. Starting with seven fortresses in 1522, the Inner Austrian estates were to be responsible for sixty within the borders in 1572. By the mid-sixteenth century Styria bore most of the expenses of the Slavonian Border, and Carniola with Carinthia those of the Croatian Border.[10] Used to defray the costs of soldiers' pay, military construction, weapons, and other supplies, the outlays mounted sharply from some 10,000 florins in the 1520s to 300,000

10. Concerning the organization of the Slavonian and Croatian military borders see the section Croats, 1526–1620, especially pp. 90–91, 96–97.

by midcentury, and stabilized by 1578 at 550,000 florins. In addition to money, the Slovene Lands furnished other assistance. In times of special danger, as in 1558, 1563, and 1565, a peasant "insurrection" was called up to assist the borders. Compulsory peasant labor from Carniola and Carinthia was used to erect fortifications, in particular the fortress Karlovac begun in 1579.

UNDER A JUNIOR BRANCH OF THE DYNASTY, 1564–1619

New Institutions

After the death of Ferdinand I in 1564 the Slovene area was separated from the main body of Habsburg possessions and placed together with all of Inner Austria (Carniola, Carinthia, Styria, Gorizia, Trieste) under a junior branch of the Habsburg family beginning with Archduke Charles (1564–90), Ferdinand's youngest son. He established in Graz a set of central governmental agencies on the model of the Viennese ones, namely the *Geheime Rat,* the *Hofrat,* the *Hofkanzlei,* the *Hofkammer,* the *Regiment,* and finally in 1578 the *Hofkriegsrat.* Within the new framework the contest between the princely authority and the power of the estates continued. Until the late 1570s the situation definitely favored the estates because the archduke found himself in great need of financial assistance, in part to maintain the new administrative apparatus in Graz and in part to cover the mounting outlays for the defense of the Croatian and Slavonian military borders. Therefore, he had to conciliate the estates, even to the point of officially granting religious freedom to the Protestant nobles and their subjects in Styria in 1572, and in Carniola and Carinthia in 1578.

At the same time Charles was seeking ways to lessen his dependence on the estates. In the first place, he endeavored to increase his financial freedom. He introduced new indirect taxes, and he took over the collection and raised the rates of tolls and customs. South German merchants provided him with loans against the expected yield of future "extraordinary" taxes. The diets were induced to grant extraordinary taxes for more than one year. Carniola, for instance, approved the tax for eleven years in 1570, and Styria for five in 1572. In the second place, Charles sought to dilute the estates' power in military affairs by augmenting his own mercenary troops and by strengthening the authority of the *Hofkriegsrat* in Graz. Finally he found new ways of spreading his influence within the noble class itself. Thus he favored certain elements within the nobility, especially its lower stratum, for appointments within the new central agencies. Above all, he created a large number of new dependent nobles, the *Briefadel* (nobility of letter). By the middle of the next century 50 percent of Inner Austrian nobles were to belong to this group.

The defense relationship with the military borders was not affected in 1564, when the Lands of Inner Austria came under the rule of Archduke Charles and Croatia remained under the immediate jurisdiction of the emperor. In fact, in 1578 Rudolf II transferred the direction of Croatia's defense to the archduke, whose *Hofkriegsrat* in Graz became the chief military agency not only for Inner Austria but for Croatia as well. Under this arrangement the peasant "insurrection" in the Slovene Lands was closely coordinated with the garrisoning of the forts in the military borders. The captain of every quarter (*Viertel*) in the Slovene Lands became responsible for maintaining, on a rotation basis, a certain quota of peasant soldiers in the borders.

Religious Oppression and Decline of the Estates

By the early 1580s Archduke Charles felt strong enough to undertake a limited action against Protestantism. His main target was the towns that—with a few individual exceptions—were not included in the grants of religious freedom given to the nobility and its subjects in 1572 and 1578. Moreover, the time seemed propitious, since the towns, for economic reasons, were losing the nobility's support.[11] While Protestantism was not completely proscribed, all Protestant clergy were ordered to leave the towns. Other measures followed after 1582, including dismissals of Protestants from the central agencies in Graz, and a campaign to stamp out the Reformation on ecclesiastical estates, as well as in all of Gorizia, a Land unprotected by pledges of religious freedom.

The pressure lessened during the regency of Archdukes Ernest (1591–93) and Maximilian (1593–96), following the death of Charles. The respite ended with the assumption of power in 1596 of Charles's son Ferdinand, the most dedicated champion of the traditional twin objectives of the Habsburgs, absolutism and Catholicism. He hastened to complete the work of the Counter Reformation in the towns of Inner Austria. In 1598 he reaffirmed the order banishing all Protestant ministers and teachers. A year later all townsmen were ordered to adopt the Catholic faith or emigrate. Special itinerant commissions enforced these measures in 1599–1601 under the direction of Bishop Tomaž Hren in Carniola and Bishop Martin Brenner in Styria and Carinthia. They met little resistance, and Slovene urban Protestantism survived only in the Prekmurje region thanks to the grant of religious freedom in Hungary in 1606. With the victory of the Counter Reformation in the towns of

---

11. The sharpened competition of the towns with the seigneurs and their serfs is discussed on pp. 51–52.

Inner Austria, attempts were made to strengthen the influence of townsmen in the diets and the administration of the Lands. The influence of the prelates' estate also increased.

After 1600 only the nobility could publicly profess Protestantism and show a measure of independence toward Archduke Ferdinand. However, the zenith of its power had passed irreversibly in the late sixteenth century, and its self-confidence and readiness for self-assertion steadily diminished. Factors contributing to its docility were the fear of internal unrest (between 1573 and 1628 some twenty local peasant rebellions took place) and the fear of external enemies, the Ottoman Empire and Venice. Also, its inner solidarity was shaken by the emergence of a substantial Catholic faction, which owed its rise partly to the influence of Jesuit schools, above all the University of Graz. Increasingly reluctant to resist the annual demands for the "extraordinary" tax by Ferdinand, the nobles suffered a crippling setback to their power and influence: loss of control over the military forces. After 1606 the traditional military organization based on the feudal concept of service by nobles, and the peasant "insurrection," became largely obsolete. As early as the Second Venetian War (1615–17), fought mainly in Gorizia and Istria, the principal role was played by the archduke's mercenary troops. At the outbreak of the Thirty Years' War, Ferdinand relied almost entirely on mercenaries hired independently of the estates. The nobles of Inner Austria, conscious of their weakness, declined in 1618 to join their Bohemian confreres in the anti-Habsburg revolt, although they still felt strong enough a year later to refuse Ferdinand—by this time the main ruler of the Habsburg possessions and soon to be emperor as Ferdinand II (1619–37)—aid against the Bohemian insurrection.

ECONOMIC LIFE[12]

Agriculture

In the course of the sixteenth century the peasant population was placed under increasing strain with the growth of the tax burden required to defray the expenses of the Turkish warfare. An increasing involvement in trade brought some relief as it helped the peasants to raise more money. At the same time it precipitated a clash with the

12. Economic data in this section are derived from *Historija naroda Jugoslavije* (Zagreb: Školska knjiga, 1959), 2:339–55; Bogo Grafenauer, *Zgodovina slovenskega naroda* (Ljubljana: Kmečka knjiga, 1956–1961), 3:9–37, 4:15–18; Ferdo Gestrin, "Économie et société en Slovénie au XVIe siècle," *Annales: Économies, Sociétés, Civilizations*, 17 (1962): 663–90; *Ljubljanska obrt od srednjega veka do začetka 18. stoletja*, ed. Vlado Valenčič (Ljubljana, 1972) [Razprave Mestnega arhiva ljubljanskega, zv. 3]; *Zgodovina Slovencev* (Ljubljana: Cankarjeva založba, 1979), pp. 227–39, 302–4.

urban merchants. Thus in Carniola in 1552 the towns attempted to exclude the peasantry from commercial pursuits. The seigneurs initially also opposed peasant trading, and in 1535 the higher nobility in Carniola sought to obtain a monopoly on trade in cattle and grain. Gradually, however, the nobles adjusted to commercial cooperation with their serfs to the point of forming joint trade associations with them. By 1578 they even helped their peasants to secure additional commercial rights; the latter could now sell not only agricultural products but also manufactured ones, such as cloth, boots, and gunpowder. The trade in wine grew especially fast, since the competing wine-producing areas of Hungary had been lost to the Turks. Viticulture was more profitable than grain growing. Owing to the general European price revolution, however, the price of grain was also rising in the Slovene area—some 300 to 400 percent during the sixteenth century. Although most of the rise was due to inflation, some real gain in relation to artisan products was registered.

Commercial opportunities acted as stimuli for agricultural development. In mid-sixteenth century the conventional three-field system was occasionally replaced by a four-field one, partly thanks to the planting of buckwheat on the fallow. Buckwheat in turn favored bee-keeping, and an active trade in honey and wax developed toward the north and the coastal towns. Horse raising for draft intensified to meet transportation requirements. In Carniola alone at mid-century between four and six thousand horses were engaged in commercial haulage of goods.

Income from commerce, however, provided only a limited relief for the hard-pressed peasantry, because trade itself became subject to new imposts by both the prince and the estates. Above all, additional customs lines were drawn, and rates raised at others. Thus a new tariff was imposed in 1544 on cattle transported from Carniola to Gorizia. In the second half of the century the rate at this boundary was doubled on all articles except grain (unless exported to Venetia). At this time cattle transported from Ptuj (Pettau) to Trieste paid customs at fourteen different points. Moreover, after the victory of the Counter Reformation in towns, the prince limited the peasant trading rights in Carniola by 1602, and even more severely in Styria in 1604.

Another new fee was extracted from the peasants by the mid-sixteenth century, mainly on the prince's estates, for conversion of their homestead tenures from a lease to a hereditary basis. A commission assisted in carrying out this reform in Styria in 1545–70, and similar bodies were established in Carniola and Carinthia around 1570. The levies most resented by the population were those newly introduced by the estates to cover the prince's demands for increases in the military contribution. Thus the estates in Carniola, in addition to imposing new customs, levied in 1570 a high fee on wine production. To impress the peasants with the need for the fee, the odious decree appeared in a Slovene translation—the first known official document in the Slovene language. Because of animated resistance, the tax was eventually restricted to wine sold in taverns.

In addition to the burdens imposed by taxation, during the sixteenth century the nobles were increasing demands on the subject peasantry in connection with organizing their estates for market production. The demesnes were growing through absorption of peasant lands abandoned during wars, especially the Turkish ones, and through cancellation of peasant leases, seizure of common pastures, and clearing of virgin lands. The exaction of compulsory labor from the serfs grew accordingly. While in the mid-fifteenth century the labor dues had been down to twelve days per year, or not enforced at all, a century later they rose commonly to three days per week (including compulsory labor on anti-Turkish fortifications). The peasants' right of migration was restricted as well.

Although the regime of second serfdom was and remained milder in Inner Austria than in any other Eastern Habsburg lands, peasant grievances over mounting exactions were severe. They helped to fuel the uprising that broke out among the serf population in southern Styria in early 1573. It occurred in conjunction with a massive peasant revolt in the adjacent areas of Croatia under the leadership of Matija Gubec.[13] Several local peasant rebellions followed.

Crafts, Industry, and Mining

During the sixteenth century, urban crafts constituted the main basis of nonagricultural output, although they experienced significant competition from peasant craftsmen and from importers of foreign goods. In this period crafts were becoming increasingly specialized. Thus by 1610 Ljubljana had 167 artisans representing 34 different crafts. The guilds normally embraced the craftsmen of a single town, but in some cases guilds in a given town, such as Ljubljana, attracted membership of artisans from other towns as well.

Aside from artisan production, mining and smelting, which had originated in the fifteenth century, continued to develop in the sixteenth. Metallurgy in the Slovene area embraced the traditional output of iron and lead, as well as the more recent one of mercury and copper. Important technical improvements affected iron production. Larger furnaces were erected that were capable, toward the end of the sixteenth century, of producing one-third to one-half a ton of raw iron in twelve to twenty-four hours. Also, greater use was made of water power for

13. See pp. 92–93.

crushing the ore, driving the bellows, and lifting the hammers. By 1570 there were twenty-two smelters in Carniola with a combined average annual production of about 2,000 tons of cast and wrought iron and steel. Fewer smelters existed in Gorizia and the Slovene parts of Styria and Carinthia. The production of mercury in Idrija, begun by 1493 with a heavy involvement of capital from Venetia, passed into local ownership in the 1520s, and the output reached 50 tons annually. The Idrija mine achieved particular prosperity in 1539–73 with the exceptional demand for mercury due to a new method of purifying precious metals, combined with disruption of the Spanish mercury production at Almadén. Slovene mercury then dominated the European market, with about 1,600 tons produced in Idrija.

The sixteenth century was marked in the Slovene area by a reassertion of the regalian rights in mining, largely dormant in the previous century. New mining statutes were promulgated for individual regions and entire Lands. Ore deposits and forests (as sources of charcoal for smelting) were declared the prince's property, and mining personnel placed under the cameral authorities. Smelting also came under the supervision of the prince, who now shared in the profits from the sale of metals.

Relatively large enterprises emerged in the field of metal processing for armaments output. The production of cannonballs was concentrated in Fužine near Ljubljana in the 1520s. A major cannon foundry was added in the beginning of the sixteenth century to the copper refinery, founded earlier by the Fuggers at Podklošter in southern Carinthia. In 1522 another large gun foundry was established in Celje.

While the enterprises in smelting and metal processing were acquiring at least in part the character of manufactories, other new lines of production still employed artisan methods. The demand for paper—generated by Protestant publishing activities—stimulated the emergence of paper mills in Fužine and in Šentvid (St. Veit) and Šentrupert (St. Ruprecht) in Carinthia. By the mid-sixteenth century, glassworks were established in Ljubljana and Radgona, as well as several breweries in Styria and Carinthia. All these enterprises were operated by skilled craftsmen.

Trade

The Turkish conquests in Hungary and Croatia severely disrupted the trade of the Slovene area. The loss of commercial contacts in the East could be repaired in part by increased trade, some of transit character, with the towns of southern Germany, as well as with Venice and Italy in general.

The traditional exports of iron and mercury became supplemented by shipments of cattle and grain, especially to the coastal cities. Imports consisted mainly of luxury articles, armaments, colonial goods, and textiles, such as silk and velvet. Long-distance trade continued to cross Slovene territories. Among its routes, the oldest one from Italy through Villach to Vienna maintained its importance. The route from Trieste via Ljubljana to Graz was of lesser significance.

Within a broader context, the transfer of major commercial routes from the Mediterranean to the Atlantic was causing a slowdown in the development of Slovene manufacturing and to some extent of mining and smelting toward the end of the sixteenth century. The effect was to be even more pronounced in the seventeenth.

The Magyars

When Ferdinand I became the ruler of Hungary[14] in 1526, the Hungarian state (like the Bohemian Kingdom) had already been in existence for half a millennium. The Magyars, originally nomadic invaders of Ural-Altaic origin, had consolidated their state in the Carpathian basin by the end of the eleventh century after the adoption of Western Christianity under king Saint Stephen (c. 974–1038). Subsequent efforts to expand into the Balkans resulted in the permanent attachment of Croatia to the Hungarian state (by 1102). The extinction of the native dynasty of Árpád (in 1301) was followed in the fourteenth century by progressive internal reforms and renewed attempts at southeastward expansion under the Anjou line of kings. The fifteenth century began with efforts—under Sigismund of Luxemburg (1387–1437)—to strengthen royal authority by balancing off the interests of the lower nobility against those of the magnates. The brilliant King Matthias I Corvinus (1458–90) resumed this policy and turned his might to ephemeral conquests at the expense of Bohemia and Austria. After his death, royal power suffered an abysmal decline under the Jagiellonian rulers (1490–1526), whom Hungary shared with Bohemia and indirectly with Poland. The political weakness, combined with intense social hatreds (epitomized by the peasant rebellion of 1514), led to the catastrophic defeat of the Hungarian army by the advancing Turkish power at Mohács in August 1526.

14.   The sections on the Magyars deal with general problems of Habsburg-controlled Hungary and with issues concerning Magyar-inhabited areas in particular. The specific developments of the Slovak, Ruthenian, and Serb areas of Hungary are covered in sections on these particular national groups.

CENTRAL ADMINISTRATION

The Crown and the King

Facing the reduction of royal power, Ferdinand I—the conflict with the Magyar counter king John Zápolyai (1526–40) notwithstanding—succeeded in reasserting limited authority over the central administrative institutions in Hungary. His task was facilitated to some degree by the fact that he held only part of the country. For its defense the king depended on outside help. The shape of Ferdinand's share of Hungary was delineated during 1526–38. After initial victory over John Zápolyai, he suffered a drastic reversal when the latter enlisted Turkish aid in 1529. Ferdinand I was left with strips of western and northern Hungary, the former containing large German minorities within the Magyar population, the latter inhabited by Slovaks and Ruthenians, as well as by Magyars. In addition he controlled the western part of Croatia. The peace of Nagyvárad (Oradea) confirmed this division in 1538. With Buda lost, Pozsony (Bratislava, Pressburg) became the administrative capital of Habsburg-ruled Hungary. After Zápolyai's death, the Turks by 1541 annexed central Hungary (including Buda), and left his son and heir, John Sigismund, in charge of Transylvania, as a vassal state of the Ottoman Empire. The resultant division of historic Hungary into three parts was to continue for a century and a half.

During intermittent warfare with the Turks in the late sixteenth and into the seventeenth century, the Habsburg territory suffered further diminutions in both western and northern Hungary. Moreover, early in the seventeenth century the Habsburgs met reversals in their conflicts with Transylvania. Failing to annex the principality in 1600–1605, Rudolf II was forced by the insurgent Translyvanian prince István Bocskai to yield temporarily the counties of Ugocsa, Bereg, and Szatmár in the treaty of Vienna in 1606. Early in the Thirty Years' War another Transylvanian prince, Gábor Bethlen, taking advantage of Ferdinand II's preoccupation in Bohemia, grained, aside from the three counties ceded to Bocskai, also Abaúj, Zemplén, Borsod, and Szabolcs, through the treaty of Mikulov (Nikolsburg) in January 1622. The most significant and lasting consequence of the victories of the Transylvanian princes was a reversal, in Habsburg Hungary, of the trend toward royal absolutism, as well as Counter Reformation, and a corresponding rise of self-confidence among the Hungarian nobles. The precedent was set at Vienna in 1606, when the Habsburgs promised both toleration of Protestantism and partial restoration of the estates' influence in the central administration of their part of the Hungarian Kingdom. The Hungarian diet enacted these provisions in 1608 and King Matthias II (as Holy Roman emperor, Matthias I) sanctioned them. Unlike in Bohemia and the Slovene areas, in Hungary the gains for the estates' power and religious freedom were not lost, but rather confirmed, during the Thirty Years' War, thereby strengthening the country's ability to challenge royal absolutism in the future.

Despite the strength of the estates, the Hungarian constitutional tradition preserved a high regard for the state as transcending both the king and the estates. This idea, embodied in the concept of the Holy Crown, developed mainly in the fourteenth century, in part under the impact of Neapolitan tenets imported by the Angevin dynasty. It differed from constitutional thought prevalent in contemporary Germany, which still viewed the state more or less as a conglomeration of private dominions held together by the feudal rights of the ruler.

At the accession of Ferdinand I the Hungarian estates insisted, as those in Bohemia had, that with the extinction of a reigning dynasty the diet had the right of free election of a new king. Once a dynasty was established, according to Hungarian constitutional practice, new kings were chosen from its male members. The diet, however, stubbornly refused to acknowledge the principal of automatic succession based on primogeniture. The Hungarian Crown remained in theory elective until 1687, but in practice the diet was committed to the election of a Habsburg ever after 1526.

The Diet and the Estates

The Hungarian diet (*országgyűlés, Reichstag*) from the beginning of the sixteenth century consisted of two chambers. The higher nobility represented a separate estate. Its members, often called the magnates, together with the highest ecclesiastics (bishops and abbots), formed a special chamber of the diet, known as the Table of Magnates (*tabula superior, felső tábla*). When in 1608 the distinctive character of the estates was legally defined, the right of the magnates to attend the diet in person was affirmed. The very numerous lower nobility was not entitled to personal attendance at the diet. It participated through elected representatives who sat in the Lower Chamber, or Table (*tabula inferior, alsó tábla*). The lower nobles' representation through delegates was in effect throughout the sixteenth century. While followed intermittently in the fourteenth and fifteenth century, this practice too received formal legislative sanction only in 1608.

The estate of the lower nobility consisted of several strata, each with different rights and duties, as well as styles of life. At the top was the stratum of "propertied nobles" (*nobiles bene possessionati*), who could in fact fully enjoy the rights and bear the duties of this estate. Obliged to attend county assemblies and, if elected, to hold county offices, they normally dominated the assemblies in which votes were "weighed" according to wealth and corresponding prestige rather than counted. Although the line separating the "propertied nobles" from the rest was flexible, the approximate criterion was the dominion over at least twenty serfs. At the other end of the spectrum within the lower nobility were the "one-hide nobles" (*nobiles unius possessionis*), who had no serfs, and thus worked the land themselves and could not really live in the style of a noble. Unlike other nobles, they were obliged to pay taxes, having no serfs on whom to pass the burden. This obligation was repeatedly affirmed in the sixteenth and seventeenth centuries. Moreover, they were expected to contribute occasionally to labor on public works.

Between the nobles and peasants was an intermediate class, the *praediales,* who entered the service of a magnate to perform military duties. Exempt from servile labor, they received a hereditary piece of land (*praedium*). By the sixteenth century most frequently they served ecclesiastical magnates and were known as *praediales praelatorum.* A special category consisted of personal nobles, such as Catholic priests. Finally there were those who enjoyed the status of nobility only in their own locality.[15]

In 1514 Stephen Werbőczi, royal protonotary, listed among the prerogatives of the nobles the direct subordination to the Crown without any intermediate jurisdiction, freedom from servile work and (except for the one-hide nobles) from taxation, and the "right to resist," granted by the Golden Bull of Andrew II in 1222 and applicable if the king violated the constitution or other laws. To this must be added the seigneurial power, namely the exercise of public authority over the peasants settled on the noble's manor.

The free royal towns formed the third estate. As collective units but not as individuals they enjoyed noble status. Free royal towns had been entitled since 1405 to regular participation in the diet, where their representatives did not form a separate college but sat with the deputies of the lower nobility in the Lower Table, in which all the towns had only one vote jointly. Thus they carried little political weight in the Hungarian diet compared with the role of towns in the contemporary diets in the Bohemian Lands or the Slovene-inhabited Lands of Inner Austria. Within the town the burghers had the same rights that the nobles enjoyed in the entire country. In principle, they were exempt from the seigneurial and county jurisdiction, and placed directly under the king and his officials. Unlike the nobles, however, the free royal towns were subject to taxation.

The Hungarian diet had been recognized as the regular organ of legislative power since the reign of King Sigismund. The king was still authorized to issue ordinances, dealing with minor matters or imple-

15. For instance, the Fusiliers of Szentgál in the county of Veszprém.

menting existing legislation, but he could not promulgate general laws (*decreta generalia*) without the diet. The "extraordinary" tax could not be collected without the approval of the diet, although under the Habsburgs the estates lost the power to control the expenditure of the proceeds of this tax, a power they had possessed under the Jagiellonians and which the diets of the Bohemian Lands still enjoyed. The diet's other powers included approval of treaties involving changes in the boundaries of the state; the election, or acceptance, of a new king; and election of the *palatin* (*nádor*), ordinarily the chief official of the state.

The convocation of the diet was normally the right of the king. After 1608, if he failed to fill the office of the *palatin* for more than a year, the judge of the court (*iudex curiae, országbíró*) or the *tavernicus* (chamberlain) could convoke the diet to elect a new *palatin*. After 1618 the *palatin* himself could assemble the diet, if the country was attacked and the king absent. Under the Habsburgs the diet met irregularly, and the estates asked in vain, for instance in 1563, for a return to annual sessions, which had been the norm under the Jagiellonians. With Buda in Turkish hands, the sessions were usually held in Pozsony. Legislative initiative belonged to both the king and the diet. The former submitted his "propositions" for consideration first to the magnates then to the Lower Table; the diet formulated legislative proposals as "petitions" and submitted them for the king's sanction. Although the final text of legislation was in Latin, the diet debated mostly in Magyar. In each chamber the more influential rather than the more numerous section determined the adoption of a measure; votes were not counted but "weighed." As a special feature of the voting procedure in the Lower Table, the deputies from the counties were bound by instructions from the county assemblies that had elected them. If new, unscheduled matters were introduced in the diet, the deputies had to refer back to the counties for additional directives. Customarily they also reported to the counties on the diet proceedings both during and after sessions. The tight control of the counties over their deputies profoundly affected the country's public life, shifting its focus to a considerable extent from the diet to the county assemblies.

The laws adopted in a session of the diet were not promulgated separately but incorporated as individual "articles" into a single law or decree (*decretum*). The king provided the decree with a preface, a conclusion, and a seal as the sign of his approval or sanction. Early in the Habsburg period the diet wished to advance the codification of Hungarian law. The existing code, the *Tripartitum opus iuris consuetudinarii inclyti regni Hungariae,* had been completed in 1514 by Werbőczi and printed in Vienna in 1517. This document in general was accepted as authoritative, although it lacked the full force of law, since it had not received full royal sanction. A revision of the code, ordered by the diet

and completed in 1553, failed to secure the king's approval. The diet
again took up the cause of revision in 1608 and 1609, but still in vain.[16]
Werbőczi's skillfully designed legal compilation was and remained the
Magna Charta, certainly not of the liberties of the Hungarian nation,
but of the privileges of the national nobility, higher and lower alike.

Executive and Judicial Officials

The greatest advance of royal authority under Ferdinand I was reflected in the change of the kingdom's central administrative institutions, over which—compared with the contemporary situation in Bohemia—he asserted a higher degree of royal ascendancy. The situation was only partially reversed in the wake of the Bocskai uprising
(1606–8).

Under the Jagiellonians the main administrative and judicial organ
of the country—which also served as the king's chief advisory body—
the royal council, had been controlled by the estates, which selected,
paid, and held responsible the councilors. This body was also known as
the "narrow" council, to distinguish it from the "great" council, which
by the sixteenth century had developed into the Table of Magnates.
Under Ferdinand I the "narrow" council, now usually called the Council of the Lieutenancy (consilium locumtenentiale, Statthaltereirat), lost its
main function to the Viennese Geheime Rat, which became in fact the
king's principal advisory group on Hungarian foreign and domestic affairs. With respect to its other functions, the council (located in Pozsony) turned from an instrument of the estates into an organ of royal
power. Its members, though still drawn from the Hungarian nobility,
were appointed and paid by the king, as well as responsible to him.
The Hungarian diet in vain asked for restoration of its former control
over the council, and of its power to elect the councilors. These requests
were not heeded even at the time of the major concessions that the new
King Matthias II was forced to grant to the estates prior to his election
in 1608.

The office of the palatin, the highest official of the realm, was highly
respected by the estates. He was traditionally chosen for life by the diet,
and the estates saw in him the principal defender of their rights and
privileges. After the death of Palatin István Báthory in 1530, Ferdinand I
did not permit the position to be filled, and instead created the office
of royal lieutenant (locumtenens regius), who became the chief official of

---

16.   The failure of official codification was offset to a large extent by unofficial efforts,
particularly Zacharias Mossóczi's and Nicholas Telegdi's Decreta, constitutiones et articuli
regum inclyti regni Hungariae, published in Trnava (Nagyszombat, Tyrnau) in 1584. This
compendium, in turn, provided the basis for subsequent authoritative, though unofficial,
compilations, called since the late seventeenth century Corpus Iuris Hungarici.

the kingdom, the king's representative, and chairman of the Lieutenancy Council. Pressed by the diet, Ferdinand I permitted in 1543 the election of a palatial lieutenant (*locumtenens palatinalis*), who was, however, subordinate to the royal lieutenant and restricted to certain judicial functions. The royal lieutenant still performed the main duties of the *palatin's* office.

Not until 1608, after the Bocskai uprising, was the post of the *palatin* restored, and the king promised not to let the office remain vacant for more than one year. Under the new rules, the diet made the selection from four candidates, two Catholics and two Protestants, nominated by the king. With the restoration of the *palatin*, the offices of both the royal lieutenant and the palatial lieutenant were allowed to lapse.

Under Ferdinand I the supreme judicial functions, which had previously been performed by the king in person, by the *palatin*, or by the "narrow" council, became vested in the royal lieutenant and the Lieutenancy Council. As early as the 1540s a body, distinct from the council and called the Court of the Lieutenancy (*iudicium locumtenentis*), began to emerge to perform these functions. The royal lieutenant likewise acquired the power to hear appeals from all the courts in the country.[17] He exercised the appellate jurisdiction in conjunction with a judicial body, the membership of which was defined precisely in 1582 as consisting of the palatial lieutenant, three bishops, and three secular magnates. This in essence created the court which later became known as the Table of Seven or Septemviral Table (*tabula septemviralis*). With the restoration of the office of the *palatin* in 1608, the functions of the royal lieutenant as the "prime judge" (*primarius iudex*) also passed on to him.

A role superior, in fact, to that of the Lieutenancy Council belonged in the Hungarian administration to the Hungarian Chancellery, which was transferred by Ferdinand I to Vienna in 1529.[18] It was through this agency that the king exercised his power to issue executive ordinances, while the Lieutenancy Council had the task of enforcing them. The Hungarian estates objected to the emergent dependence of the Hungarian Chancellery on the Austrian Court Chancellery (*Hofkanzlei*), and maintained from 1559 on that no ordinances issued through the "cancellaria germanica" could be valid in Hungary.

Another major function, withdrawn from the estates' control under

17. According to fifteenth-century usage, appeals from the county courts and certain royal town courts were to go, in the first instance, to a royal judge entitled *personalis* (short for *personalis praesentiae regiae in iudiciis locumtenens*), from the other royal town courts to the *tavernicus*.

18. Its antecedent within the previous Hungarian governmental structure was the Major Chancellery (*cancellaria maior*), which had existed since 1320 side by side with the Minor Chancellery (*cancellaria minor*), a body handling special judicial cases. After 1526 the Minor Chancellery lost its independence and turned into an ancillary agency to the Lieutenancy Council, specifically to its incipient judicial branch.

Ferdinand I, was the management of royal finances. A new bureaucratic institution, the Hungarian Chamber, was established for that purpose in 1528 and staffed by officials paid by the king. After 1531 the
Chamber was located in Pozsony, with a branch for the collection of
income from the northeastern counties first in the castle of Šariš and
from 1567 in Košice (Kassa). The Chamber's head, the president (*praeses
camerae*), was assisted initially by five, later more, councilors (*camerarii*).
Its jurisdiction covered taxes, customs, and tolls, the "thirtieth" (an export and import duty), and the regalian income primarily from mining
and minting. In 1548 the Chamber was explicitly declared independent
of the Lieutenancy Council and became increasingly subordinated to
the Viennese *Hofkammer*. Despite protests of the Hungarian estates, in
1569 this dependence was not only tightened, but also royal mines and
certain customs offices were placed directly under the *Hofkammer*. The
only concession the Hungarian estates could extract in 1606 was the
promise that the Hungarian Chamber would be limited to financial affairs and not intervene in other matters.

The estates did preserve a major role in the collection of the annual
"extraordinary" tax, also called the war tax (*subsidium, dica, contributio*),
which, as noted earlier, required approval by the diet. The collection
was directed by officials (usually called *thesaurarii*, later *perceptores gen-
erales*), elected by the diet. In a further attempt to curb the estates' fiscal
autonomy the king insisted in 1547 that a representative of the Hungarian Chamber work with the diet officials. The Chamber was in charge
of disbursing the proceeds of the tax.

Hungarian and Imperial Armies

The traditional Hungarian military organization consisted of the so-
called banderial system, established in 1435 under King Sigismund. The
banderium was an armed unit fighting under a single banner, and several were maintained more or less permanently in the sixteenth century. First among them was the royal *banderium* of one thousand cavalrymen, financed by the king from royal income and proceeds of his
estates. Prelates and religious corporations, receiving tithes, were obliged
to furnish *banderia*, which by 1555 were permanently stationed in the
border castles, designed for anti-Turkish defense. Secular magnates were
required to raise full (four hundred cavalrymen) or partial *banderia*,
depending on their income, and station them either on their own manors or in the border fortresses. To help defray their expenses, the magnates could retain the proceeds of the war tax collected on their manors, instead of turning them over to the county officials.

In cases of special emergency the *banderia* of the king, the prelates,
and the magnates were supplemented by the general levy or "insur-

rection" (*exercitus generalis, insurrectio generalis*). Additional troops were organized under the banners of the counties (*banderia comitatum*). They consisted of "propertied" nobles, who lacked their own *banderia,* and the poor ("one-hide") nobles. The former also furnished one cavalry-man for every twenty subject homesteads (*portae*). Finally, every five peasants sent one infantryman into the county *banderium,* even though this requirement clashed with the law of 1514 prohibiting the peasants to bear arms. The general levy likewise included the *banderia civitatum,* furnished by the royal free towns, the size of which depended on the number of burgher houses in a town. In addition, the towns bore a special responsibility for the supply of cannons and powder to the army. In the absence of a *palatin,* the nominal commander of the Hungarian army was the supreme captain of the Land appointed by the king.

Under the exigencies of the pressing needs of anti-Turkish defense, the actual powers of the king-emperor overrode in practice the theo-retical control of the military establishment by the estates. Thus main-tenance of the essential border fortresses did not really fit the pattern of the "banderial" system. Even the troops of the magnates and the prelates, which were permanently stationed in the border castles, were not commanded by their nominal masters, but by royal officers, and were integrated with the rest of the royal host. The latter consisted largely of foreign mercenaries, whom the diet permitted the king to station on Hungarian soil in 1546. In 1547 the territory of Hungary under Habsburg control was divided for the purposes of defense into two Captaincies-General, one on each side of the Danube. By 1555 the northern one was subdivided into the Captaincy of the Mining Towns and the Captaincy of Upper Hungary;[19] the southern one into the Cap-taincies of Danube-Balaton and Balaton-Drava. The officers of the royal army from the captains-general to the vice-captains (commanding smaller districts and individual castles) were Hungarians. The supreme com-mand, however, was not exercised by a Hungarian institution like the Lieutenancy Council, but by the Viennese *Hofkriegsrat.*

LOCAL ADMINISTRATION

County Officials

The Hungarian counties (*comitatus, megye*) had been strong units of provincial self-government since the reign of Sigismund (1387–1437), when the exercise of administrative, judicial, and military powers in each county devolved from royal officials to the local nobility. As royal au-

---

19. The boundary between the two Captaincies followed approximately the dividing line between central and eastern Slovakia.

thority expanded within the central administration at the expense of
the estates from 1526 to 1605, the county governments—on the contrary—maintained and even increased their significance as power bases
of the estates, especially the lower nobility. Nothing comparable was
occurring in the Bohemian or the Inner Austrian Lands. Because of
the role of the Hungarian county governments in the power relationship between the king and the estates, their organization and functions
merit particular attention.

The self-government in each county was restricted to the community
of nobles, and was exercised primarily through the county assemblies.
Although in theory organs of the entire nobility, the assemblies were,
in practice, dominated by the upper stratum of the lower nobility (*nobiles bene possessionati*). General meetings of county assemblies (*congre-
gatio comitatu generalis*) occurred usually once every three months. In
the interim, special assemblies were held, attended primarily by county
officials to deal with emergencies and current administrative matters.
Extraordinary assemblies, called "restorations," elected county officials.
The officials were accountable to the assemblies.

The chief county official in theory, though not necessarily in practice,
was the *főispán (supremus comes, Obergespan)*, who alone preserved char-
acteristics of a royal agent. Except in the counties where the office was
hereditary, he was appointed by the king as a representative of the king's
power and interests. In actuality, the royal power of appointment was
seriously restricted by the requirement that the appointee be a resident
and property holder, as well as a *persona grata,* in the county. Moreover,
before assuming office, the *főispán* had to swear to observe the county's
autonomous rights, and a delay in the oath could void the appointment.
Early in the seventeenth century, the counties even required a written
affirmation of the appointee's oath. In addition, the county assembly
could hold the *főispán* responsible for misuse of power.

An inherent ambiguity affected the *főispán's* office, since he was to
represent the interests of both the central state authority and the local
county autonomy; and to assure harmonious functioning of central
administration and local self-government. Thus the *főispán* played two
roles, one as an administrator on his own initiative, the other as an
executor of royal ordinances in the name of the king. In this last respect
the prompt delivery of royal revenue was particularly important. In
regard to county agencies the *főispán* usually convoked and presided
over the county assembly and the county court. He also supplied leadership in the "restoration" assemblies.

A unique position, in some respects more important than the *főispán's*,
was occupied by the *alispán (vicecomes, Vicegespan)*. Originally an assist-
ant of the *főispán* who appointed him, from 1504 the *alispán* could be
appointed only with the consent of the county assembly. The outcome

of the continuing struggle over the control of this office represented a historical landmark in the development of county autonomy. From 1548 on the *alispán* was elected by the county assembly, and the *főispán* merely confirmed the election. Thus the *alispán* turned from a mere deputy of the *főispán* into the first official of the county self-government with an independent power base. His functions included, in certain cases, the convocation of the county assembly; and he presided, in lieu of the *főispán*, over the county court. A special duty was the supervision of peasant migration among seigneurial jurisdictions. In recognition of his importance, an *alispán* often served as a delegate to the diet, or as a member of other missions representing the counties. Like the *főispán*, the *alispán* was held accountable by the assembly for his official conduct. In larger counties more than one *alispán* could be elected.

The next echelon of county government consisted of the county judges (*iudices nobilium, Stuhlrichter*). Each county, regardless of size, had four of them, and they were elected by the county assembly from among the propertied nobles. Before the emergence, in 1548, of the *alispán* in his new role, they had been the chief defenders of county autonomy. A nobleman elected to this office was obliged to serve for at least one year. Each judge had special jurisdiction in one of the four districts (*járások*) making up each county. Their main judicial function involved participation in the sessions of the county court chaired by the *főispán* or *alispán*. Their nonjudicial functions included assistance with military registration and raising the levy, with assessment and collection of taxes, and with supervision of peasant migration.

The county judges were, in turn, aided chiefly by the jurors or assessors (*iurati nobiles, assessores*). The custom to elect them dated from the early fifteenth century, and their number for a county had been fixed at twelve since 1514. By the second half of the sixteenth century the jurors functioned as regular salaried county officials, who, in addition to their original duties as members of the county court, assisted with judicial investigations and with administrative tasks. Another important official of the county was the notary, whose main responsibility was to record the proceedings of the county court. He also carried out administrative functions, especially tax collection.

County Functions

Most functions of the county governments involved activities on behalf of the central administration. This role in particular enabled the counties to serve as bastions of the estates' power in relation to the royal authority. The most important task was the management of the war tax, which was paid in the sixteenth century by all homesteads (*portae*) of subject peasants, in amounts varying over the years. Nominally the process of assessment and collection was directed in a county by a royal tax collector (*dicator*), an employee of the Hungarian Chamber. Actually he could not act without authorization by the county assembly and co-operation of county officials. Sanctions against tax evaders were also administered solely by the county governments. The fines for nonpayment had to be authorized by the assemblies, and collected by the *al-ispán* and the county judges. Toward the end of the sixteenth century, counties often dispensed with the *dicator* altogether.[20]

County governments performed essential functions in the organization of the Hungarian army under the "banderial" system. The county judges, assisted by the jurors, prepared lists of subject peasants, and on the basis of the established quotas determined the number of soldiers supplied by each noble. They also granted exemptions from military duty. When the military levy was proclaimed, the soldiers from each county were commanded by the *főispán*, or by a special commander elected by the county assembly.

The counties also had a major part in directing and controlling the country's legislative processes. This role was based on the right of each county assembly to elect two to four delegates (*electi nobiles, nuntii*) to the diet, and especially on its right to bind the delegates with detailed instructions concerning every measure proposed at the diet session. The counties also became guardians against unconstitutional exercise of legislative power by the central government. A decree of the diet in 1545 openly prohibited the *főispán* and *alispán* from obeying any orders or edicts of the king or the royal lieutenant if issued in an unlawful manner. The resistance of the counties, in the first instance, could take the form of either oral (through deputations) or written remonstrances. If this approach failed, the county officials could resort to the *vis inertiae*—an extreme procrastination in implementing the objectionable edict. The ultimate resort was a refusal to collect taxes.

Aside from the crucial interaction with the central administration, the counties operated as agents of local self-government. Since 1486 they had been authorized to levy local taxes to help defray expenses of their diet delegates. By the 1530s the right to tax was extended to cover all local public needs, including salaries for county officials, hitherto compensated by fees for certain official acts. The basic revenue was then the house tax, collected not only from the peasants but also from the nobles, as well as from the royal free towns on estates owned in the county. With the *alispán* serving as the collector, the proceeds were deposited in the county treasury. In addition, after 1543 the county could retain part of the war tax for internal administrative expenses. As organs of local self-government the county assemblies had the right to

---

20. Instead, they elected a tax collector (*exactor*) from their own midst, or the *alispán* directed the tax collection himself.

adopt local ordinances (*ius statuendi*). Initially restricted to matters of county police and judicial procedure, these statutes in the course of the sixteenth century began to cover all concerns of local administration. The diet had the power to invalidate those county ordinances that did not conform to the valid general laws. Finally, the county's judicial autonomy was exercised through the county court (*sedes iudiciaria nobilium*). The court held wide jurisdiction over both nobles and commoners in criminal and civil matters, but certain cases were reserved to the Crown—above all, litigations over possession of noble estates and suits involving values of more than one hundred florins.

Towns

The towns never approached the position of importance enjoyed in public life by the counties. Part of the reason was that the king, relying on the Hungarian Chamber, asserted his authority, particularly in fiscal matters, more effectively in towns than in the counties. Moreover, within Hungarian internal politics, even the royal free towns (*liberae et regiae civitates*) carried little weight, since their delegates in the diet held only a single vote jointly. In any case, the royal free towns were few. Of the approximately fifteen in the early sixteenth century, only eight remained in the Habsburg part of Hungary: one (Sopron) in western Hungary, the other seven in the Slovak area in the north. The rest had been lost to the Turks.

Aside from representation in the diet, the status of the royal free towns was marked by exemption from county jurisdiction and direct subordination to royal officials, the *tavernicus* or the *personalis*. While contributing their share to the general war tax (*dica*) voted by the diet, such towns also paid a special tax to the king.

Other royal towns (*regiae civitates*) were not entitled to send delegates to the diet. They were, however, exempted from county jurisdiction, subordinated directly to royal officials, and required to pay the town tax to the king. A special subgroup was the royal mining towns (*regiae et montanae civitates*), concentrated in the central and eastern Slovak area. Some of the royal towns eventually advance to the status of "free" towns with the right of representation in the diet.

The third category of towns was the market towns (*oppida privilegiata, liberae villae*). They enjoyed certain freedoms, especially varying degrees of self-government, bestowed by royal or seigneurial grants. Their autonomy, however, was limited, and they remained basically under the jurisdiction of both the noble seigneurs and the counties. The market towns obtained formal legal recognition as a distinct category in 1608.

A prolonged struggle within the towns during the sixteenth century was over the status of resident nobles, who resented subordination to

the urban authorities and the obligation to pay local taxes. The issue
was only partly resolved in 1608 when the diet guaranteed the nobles'
right to acquire real estate in royal towns and share in other rights and
freedoms of the burghers, but obliged the resident nobles to pay local
taxes and carry other public burdens.

Ethnic inequalities were another source of conflict. The Germans,
who traditionally constituted the most influential groups in many towns,
in the sixteenth century often resorted to drastic measures, such as excluding other nationalities from municipal governments, in order to
preserve their own privileged position. Finally, in 1608 the diet intervened with a decree that stipulated equal access to public office in royal
towns by all nationalities, and prescribed a regular rotation by Germans, Magyars, and Slovaks in each major office.[21]

The main organ of town self-government was the council, composed
of the judge (*iudex*) and the sworn burghers (*iurati cives*), usually twelve.
Hungarian royal towns—unlike their Bohemian counterparts since
1547—remained internally free of appointed royal officials. The councils made decisions in a collegiate manner and had jurisdiction over
both administration and judiciary. Originally, a gathering of all burghers, the so-called whole community (*tota communitas*) annually elected
the judge and the councilors. By the sixteenth century this function had
been largely assumed by a narrower elite, the Elected Community (*electa
communitas*), consisting of fifty to one hundred members (*electi cives*). In
Pozsony, for instance, there were sixty. This essentially oligarchic group
elected town officials, impeached and tried them for malfeasance, and
audited the accounts of departing councils. The town council, like the
county assemblies, had the right to issue ordinances concerning internal
police and other matters. The town court, composed of the judge and
the councilors, had complete civil and criminal jurisdiction over the
burghers, including the right of capital punishment (*ius gladii*). Resident
nobles generally resisted the jurisdiction of town courts. The burghers
outside of towns, however, were subject to either the seigneurial or county
courts.

Seigneurs and Peasants

The peasant population of Hungary was administratively and judi-
cially subject, in the first instance, to the seigneurs and, in the second,
to the counties. This principle was originally enunciated in 1381 and
reconfirmed in 1608. In addition, the peasants owed their seigneurs
free labor, as well as dues in money (*terragium*, *census*) and in kind. Aside
from periodic "gifts" of foodstuffs (*munera*), the dues in kind had con-

21. Concerning these conflicts, particularly important for the Slovak national development, see pp. 79–81.

sisted since 1531 mainly of the *nona*, one-ninth of wine and grain produced by a peasant. The peasants, of course, also paid the war tax to the king, the house tax to the county, and the tithes to the church. Special disabilities were imposed on the rural population in the wake of the great uprising led by György Dózsa in 1514. As a result, the peasant could not leave the manor without his seigneur's consent. He was also barred from bearing arms and from holding a higher ecclesiastical office.

The rise in the agricultural activity on the demesnes had led since the 1530s to increasing exactions of unpaid labor (*servitia rusticalia, robot*) from the serfs. In opposition to the lower nobility, the magnates also wished to attract more peasants to their estates. The freedom of peasant migration was, in fact, restored temporarily in 1547, and permanently in 1556, with the proviso that a new seigneur was ready to accept a migrant. It was reconfirmed in 1596. Thus, unlike the peasants elsewhere in East Central Europe (including the Bohemian and the Inner Austrian lands), those of Hungary regained in the sixteenth century the legal right to change their seigneurs. This freedom, which was often more illusory than real, benefited mostly the magnates who could offer inducements (especially temporary relief from dues) to attract new serfs and possessed adequate powers of coercion to retain them. The lower nobility felt disadvantaged. In 1608 the responsibility for regulating peasant migration shifted from the central administration to individual county assemblies, where the determination became a test of strength between the magnates and other nobles.

Although all peasants were equally under the jurisdiction of the seigneurs, their economic status differentiated them into three classes: homesteaders who possessed at least one quarter of a hide (*coloni*), cottagers who owned only a house or a garden (*inquilini*), and renters who did not even have a house (*subinquilini*). In every manor the seigneur had jurisdiction over all civil and minor criminal matters. Only some seigneurs possessed the right of higher justice covering serious crimes (*ius gladii*). The manorial court (*sedes dominalis*) was chaired by the seigneur or his representative (*officinalis, villicus,* or *castellanus*), and otherwise consisted of assessors, chosen by the seigneur from the subject peasantry of the manor. Appeals from manorial courts went to the county courts. The seigneur could delegate some of his authority to peasant villages, which then elected their own judge (*biró*) (usually from three candidates nominated by the seigneur), as well as jurors. The office of the village judge could also be granted as a hereditary right to a particular family. In such cases the judge was usually called *scultetus* (*soltesz, Schultheis*). The competence of the village judge was usually restricted to civil matters, and his judicial activities were closely monitored by a manorial official.

ECONOMIC LIFE[22]

Agriculture

Despite the continuous warfare of the sixteenth century, Hungarian agriculture experienced a period of rising prosperity. The main reason was the increase in agricultural prices. As exemplified particularly by the market of Sopron in western Hungary, the increase was steep for wine from the beginning of the century, also steep for grain and more moderate for cattle from the midcentury. This rise, in turn, reflected an increased demand for agricultural products in Western Europe and it affected Hungarian prices not only for the products exported (like wine and cattle) but also for those destined primarily for the internal market (grain). Grain production increased on both the seigneurs' demesnes and the peasants' homesteads. Extensive cattle raising spread in the lowlands depopulated because of the Turkish warfare. Thus peasants residing in towns rented deserted village lands for pastures. Wine production received additional impetus in the mid-sixteenth century from the invention of a new method for producing the sweet wine of Tokay. Favored by the particularly advantageous price relationship, viticulture by the end of the century, in certain areas, entirely replaced other forms of crop raising.

As in the Bohemian Lands and elsewhere in East Central Europe, in Hungary a major organizational change in agriculture was sparked in the sixteenth century by a basic shift in the seigneurs' economic orientation. A new preoccupation with entrepreneurial activities supplemented the former reliance on peasant dues as the principal source of manorial income. The seigneurs were particularly eager to increase grain production on their demesne estates. These estates grew by absorbing abandoned peasant lands, parts of existing peasant homesteads, or entire peasant homesteads from which the former users were moved to previously uncultivated areas. As elsewhere in East Central Europe, in Hungary the seigneurs' interest in increased production led also to greater need for compulsory peasant labor, and ushered in the era of so-called second serfdom or neo-serfdom. The labor dues, hitherto often ig-

22. Economic data in this section are derived from Ervin Pamlényi, ed., *A History of Hungary* (London: Collet's, 1975), pp. 135–43; *Istoriia Vengrii* (Moscow: Nauka, 1971), 1:302–5; L. Makkai, "Die Hauptzüge der wirtschaftlich-sozialen Entwicklung Ungarns im 15.–17. Jahrhundert," in *La Renaissance et la Réformation en Pologne et en Hongrie* (Budapest: Akadémiai Kiadó, 1963), pp. 35–46; J. Szűcs, "Das Städtewesen in Ungarn im 15.–17. Jahrhundert," ibid., pp. 129–64; V. Zimányi, "Mouvement des prix hongrois et l'évolution européenne, XVIe–XVIIIe s.," *Acta Historica* 19 (1973): 305–33; and by the same author, "Les problèmes principaux du commerce extérieur de la Hongrie à partir du milieu du XVIe jusqu'au milieu du XVIIe siècle," in *La Pologne et la Hongrie aux XVIe–XVIIIe siècles* (Budapest: Akadémiai Kiadó, 1981), pp. 25–43.

nored, became regularly exacted from the peasants as early as the 1530s. By midcentury the legal limit of one day per week was no longer sufficient, and the serfs were commonly required to work on the demesne two or three days per week. Some seigneurs observed no limit at all. The mounting exploitation caused peasant disturbances in the 1570s.

Aside from the operation of the demesne estates, the seigneurs extensively engaged in trade. Selling not only the products of the demesnes, they also traded in articles that they acquired by obligatory sales from their serfs, a practice specifically sanctioned by the diet in the middle of the sixteenth century. The seigneurs profited particularly by the sale of wine both outside their manors and locally in the seigneurial taverns. Other entrepreneurial activities of the noble landlords included forestry, raising fish, and flour milling.

Crafts, Industry, and Mining

The relative prosperity of agriculture was accompanied in the sixteenth century by a crisis in the production of artisan goods. The key to this crisis was Hungary's failure to keep up with its western neighbors in the development of the putting-out system, which lowered the cost of artisan products by tapping large reservoirs of cheap labor: the underemployed and impoverished peasantry. Confined to the guild system, Hungary's urban craftsmen were unable to decrease production costs to compensate for the higher cost of raw materials, caused by the price revolution in agriculture. They found it difficult to compete with imported articles, fabricated more efficiently under a more advanced system of production. Concerned about inflation, the Hungarian diet intervened and worsened the plight of urban artisans by fixing prices, enforced by county ordinances, at levels that did not yield adequate profits to the craftsmen.

Competition, damaging to the urban crafts, originated not only abroad but also in the countryside. The seigneurs encouraged on their manors production by unskilled rural artisans, who sold their rudimentary wares at low prices. As a result, the urban craftsmen suffered losses of demand among the peasant consumers, who preferred the rural artisans' cheaper goods, albeit of inferior quality.

The rural artisans' production could not substitute adequately for the operation of the putting-out system, or a well-developed network of urban crafts. Thus the domestic output in Hungary failed to satisfy the internal need for most of the basic artisan goods. Such articles as cloth, metal implements (knives, scythes, and locks), arms, glass, and pottery had to be imported from abroad.

Industrial enterprises, above the level of artisan workshops, were represented in sixteenth-century Hungary by mines and smelters producing copper, silver, gold, and iron. Almost all the mining and metallurgical activities were concentrated in the Slovak territory.

Trade

While suffering a decline in craft production, large towns in sixteenth-century Hungary also lost their importance as trading centers. With the diminution of commerce in artisan goods, the larger towns were also losing the trade in agricultural products (above all, cattle) to the rural towns and marketplaces. The royal towns found it difficult even to purchase sufficient food supplies, and began to rely on their own subject villages to provide them with foodstuffs in the form of feudal dues.

The structure of external trade reflected the growing ascendancy of agriculture over crafts. Available statistics indicate that in the mid-sixteenth century agricultural products and metals constituted 99 percent of exports. Agricultural products predominated, among them cattle, which accounted for 80 percent of all exports. The competition of cheaper American gold and silver caused a marked decline in the share of metals compared with the fifteenth century. The decline in copper exports was less significant.

Finished industrial goods made up 90 percent of imports. Since their prices declined in relation to agricultural ones, the volume of their imports increased during the sixteenth century, considerably damaging (as noted earlier) the domestic craft production. Cloth came from Germany, the Bohemian Lands, and—to a lesser extent—England; metal implements and armaments from Bavaria and Styria; pottery and glass from England, Italy, and Germany. The Ottoman Empire, as well as Western Europe, furnished luxury goods, such as spices, furniture, fine cloth, and rugs. Preserved registers from 1542 indicate that cloth and linen represented 51 percent of the value of imports, articles of clothing 15 percent, iron and other metal implements 10 percent. The rest was made up of leather, fur, and wooden products.

The Slovaks

The Slovak ethnic territory of northern Hungary experienced serious disruptions during the first century of Habsburg rule. It was the scene of major battles between Ferdinand I and John Zápolyai in 1526–38. After 1541 it was exposed to encroachments by the Ottoman power established in central Hungary. The fierce struggles of Hungarian nobility against Habsburg absolutism under the leadership of István Bocskai (1600–1605) and Gábor Bethlen (1619–26) also took place primarily in northern Hungary. A major consequence of the Turkish conquests was the marked advancement of the Magyar influence on the Slovak territory. The central institutions of the Hungarian state were transferred there; Pozsony became the seat of the Lieutenancy Council and the usual meeting place of the diet. The archbishop-primate moved his residence to Trnava (Nagyszombat) in 1543 after the fall of Esztergom to the Turks. Magyar nobles escaping Ottoman power contributed, partly through intermarriage, to the increasing Magyarization of the lower gentry of northern Hungary, which had been largely Slovak. Magyar peasants also sought refuge from the Turks, and as a result in the late sixteenth and early seventeenth centuries the Magyar-Slovak ethnic frontier, especially in southwestern Slovakia, shifted as far north as it had ever been or would be.

ADMINISTRATIVE AND MILITARY AFFAIRS

Central Administration

The crucial instrument of the new royal administration for Hungary, the Hungarian Chamber, was also located in the Slovak area in Pozsony after 1531. When it was supplemented around 1539 by the Chamber of Spiš, which exercised jurisdiction east of the line of Liptov-Zvolen, the seat of this second Chamber was first the castle of Šariš, then Košice (Kassa). As far as the Slovaks were concerned, this administrative division—likewise observed by the imperial military establishment—had a detrimental effect on the possibility of their national consolidation. It introduced a jurisdictional barrier between two parts of the Slovak ethnic territory and tied each part closely with the adjacent Magyar areas. Western Slovakia was combined with the Magyar counties of western Hungary (Transdanubia) within the territorial jurisdiction of the Pozsony Chamber, known as Lower Hungary (*Nieder-Ungarn*). Central and eastern Slovakia was joined with the Magyar counties of the Tisza region into the jurisdictional area of the Spiš Chamber, known as Upper Hungary (*Ober-Ungarn*).

In the Slovak area the two chambers soon began to extend their official apparatus into lower administrative levels, creating subordinate agencies and courts, especially after 1546 when the crown became more deeply involved in mining and metallurgical operations. The system stabilized by 1573 with the issuance of a new mining ordinance by Maximillian II. The principal functionaries of the central bureacratic system in the Slovak territory were then the Chamber count in Banská Štiavnica, the vice-count in Kremnica, and the administrator in Banská Bystrica. These agents of royal power, often charged with functions other than industrial management and tax collection, tended to clash with the municipal officials in those towns in which they exercised jurisdiction. As instruments of direct royal authority the Chamber officials were also deeply resented by the nobility.

The Towns

The older royal towns, which preserved their political rights in the sixteenth century, included the *tavernicus* towns of Pozsony, Košice, Trnava, Prešov (Eperjes), Bardejov (Bártfa), and Sabinov, as well as the seven mining towns, the most important of which were Banská Štiavnica, Kremnica, and Banská Bystrica. A few towns, engaged in viticulture, enjoyed new prosperity, profiting from the elimination of competition from the wine-producing regions of central Hungary. They gained the status of royal free towns: Skalica in 1577, and Modra, Sv. Jur, and Pezinok in 1598. Sixteen towns of the Spiš area, mortgaged to Poland, were administered by the Polish captain (*starosta*) from Stará L'ubovňa. About 150 towns and marketplaces on the Slovak territory remained under seigneurial jurisdiction.

Many lesser nobles, escaping from the Turks, sought refuge in the towns of the Slovak area, mainly between 1540 and 1563, and proved a mixed blessing. Wishing to stand under the protection of the county authorities, they were reluctant to obey the town governments or to pay taxes. Yet, resentful of the magnates (the usual seigneurs of subject towns), they tended to support the towns' efforts to obtain royal free status.

Having to bear heavy burdens, the towns of the Slovak territory experienced a developmental slowdown in contrast to the vigorous growth of the preceding century. The various warring factions, as well as the Turks, practiced outright extortion by the imposition of ransoms. The towns spent heavily on maintaining garrisons at their own expense. In addition, they were taxed severely to support the royal mercenaries, drawn from Austria, Saxony, Spain, and Belgium. Thus in the second half of the sixteenth century the mining towns contributed 200,000 florins, while the Chamber officials in some of these towns, such as Kremnica, Banská Bystrica, and Banská Štiavnica, raised another 600,000 florins.

The ravages of warfare initially caused prices in royal towns to rise steeply, above all for foodstuffs; the increase ranged between 200 and 400 percent from 1525 to 1535. Subsequently, high prices persisted, as the noble seigneurs preferred to market their produce not in royal towns but in their own subject towns, in the border fortresses, or abroad. In the free towns and the mining towns the inflation imposed extraordinary hardships on the wage laborers, whose incomes initially rose only 25 to 50 percent. The resulting social discontent erupted most dramatically in the miners' rebellions in Banská Bystrica in 1537, and again in 1566. The effects of inflation became once more acute in the opening years of the seventeenth century, and a new wave of disorders broke out among Slovak miners. They were centered in Banská Štiavnica and began in 1606 and culminated in 1610.

The Manors

The living conditions of the Slovak peasantry also worsened during the sixteenth century. Although this was true of the peasants in much of East Central Europe with the emergence of the so-called second serfdom or neo-serfdom, the exactions were exceptionally onerous in Slovakia because of aggravating factors. The peasantry bore much of the expenditure of the constant struggle against the Turks, and suffered from pillage and destruction during the conflicts between the king and the estates in the first half of the sixteenth century and in the early seventeenth. Another oppressive factor was the extreme concentration of nobility on the Slovak territory, driven there by the Turkish conquest.[23] The overabundance of nobles caused the peasants to bear an increased tax burden (to compensate for the tax-exempt nobility), and to support more elaborate county governments, while having at their disposal less land outside the demesnes than the peasantry elsewhere in Hungary. The prevalence of mountainous terrain intensified the scarcity of agricultural land. By the end of the sixteenth century, and especially in the seventeenth, there were often five, and sometimes as many as ten, homesteads on one hide of land in the Slovak area.

A long-term aggravation of the peasants' condition was the expansion of the demesnes by the seigneurs, which was fairly rapid in the second half of the sixteenth century. Because the larger demesne estates required an increase in peasant labor (*robota*), the limit of the *robota*, established by the Hungarian diet at fifty-two days per year for each hide of peasant land, was in practice greatly exceeded, particularly on the manors of western and central Slovakia. The increased demand for *robota* led to the tightening of personal bondage to ensure a permanent labor supply. Even inhabitants of certain subject towns became obliged to perform free labor on their seigneurs' demesne estates in the late sixteenth century, in addition to the traditional monetary dues. The greater development of the internal market also brought new burdens for the subject peasants, who were required to transport for sale the seigneurs' produce, mostly grain and wine. The work counted toward

23. The effects of the influx could be felt for a long time. After the peace of Szatmár in 1720, for instance, the Slovak area would still contain 55 percent of all the noble population of Hungary (without Transylvania and Croatia), while constituting only 20 percent of the Hungarian territory.

the prescribed labor time, but the serfs had to cover all the costs, sometimes even the tolls.

The Turkish Warfare

After the fall of central Hungary to the Turks in 1540–41, almost
the entire southern edge of the Slovak territory was exposed to direct
Turkish pressure. With the conquest of Esztergom and Nógrád in 1543–
44 the Ottoman forces were poised for an invasion of Slovakia. Although a formal truce between the emporer and the sultan prevailed
from 1547 to 1593, local Turkish commanders pursued further conquests with the strategic objective of seizing the central mining towns.
They were most successful in 1552–54, establishing a solid bridgehead
on Slovak territory with the conquest of the fortresses of Šáhy and
Fil'akovo. The defense line then came to rest on the forts of Komárno,
Nitra, Levice, Modrý Kameň, Divín, Hajnačka, and Eger. The Turks
advanced even closer to the mining towns in the early 1570s, seizing
Hajnačka (1571), Divín, and Modrý Kameň (both in 1575). These were
their last successes before the major war of 1593–1606, the so-called
Fifteen Years' War.

The Turkish-ruled Slovak territory became part of the Paşalik of Buda,
which was subdivided into sancaks, each headed by a *bey* (*beğ*). The valley of Šáhy was incorporated into the sancak of Esztergom, while Fil'akovo
formed the center of a separate sancak with its own *bey*. All the land
belonged to the sultan, who assigned it in fiefs to lower Turkish nobility, the *sipahi*. The sancaks were further subdivided into districts (*na-
hiya*), each encompassing several towns and villages. The judge (*kadi*)
and tax collector (*defterdar*) administered towns and larger villages. The
exactions of the Turkish authorities were not limited to the territories
under their full control. By threats of pillage they coerced payment of
regular taxes from localities lying as far as 40 kilometers beyond the
frontier line. The affected population had to assume the burden in addition to taxes, tithes, and other dues to the Hungarian authorities.

Within the defense zone certain trends resembled those characteristic
of the Croatian and Slavonian military borders.[24] By the middle of the
sixteenth century, several thousand South Slav refugees from Turkish
rule had reached Slovak territory. Most were Croats from Slavonia, who
settled near Pozsony and on Žitný Ostrov; a group of Serbs found refuge in the area of Komárno. As in Croatia and Slavonia, the imperial
commanders in Slovakia sought direct administrative jurisdiction in the
border area. Becoming, in fact, the seigneurs of such fortress towns as
Krupina, Nitra, and Zvolen, they began to expand their authority into

24. On the military, administrative, and social organization of the Slavonian and Croatian
military borders see pp. 90–91, 93–94, 96–97.

rural areas, taking over feudal dues from the villages to pay their mercenaries. Unlike the Croatian *Sabor*, the Hungarian diet, however, was
successful (in 1578) in checking the imperial officers' assumption of a
quasi-seigneurial status over the peasantry.

As the Inner Austrian estates were required to finance the Croatian
and Slavonian military borders, the estates of the Bohemian Lands became financially responsible for the defense of the Slovak border. From
the mid-sixteenth century they bore most of the expenses for its western sector, centered in Komárno. Toward the end of the century their
responsibility was extended to cover the newly organized "mining frontier" (*banská hranica, Bergstädtische Grenze*) in the central sector. Even the
eastern segment of the defense line at Košice was financed largely by
the Silesian Chamber.

Several factors help to account for the fact that, despite developmental similarities, no separate entity resembling the Croatian and Slavonian military borders appeared on the southern edge of Slovakia.
Instead of forming distinct military communities, the South Slav refugees assimilated fairly rapidly with neighboring Slovak or Magyar
peasantry. The Hungarian diet, as a more powerful body than the
Croatian *Sabor*, was more effective in averting the establishment of territorial administration by the imperial commanders. While bearing the
financial burden of defense, the Bohemian estates did not obtain an
independent responsibility for military command in the Slovak defense
zone, such as the Inner Austrian estates enjoyed (in conjunction with
the Graz *Hofkriegsrat*) in the Croatian and Slavonian military borders.

The long Turkish war of 1593–1606 resulted in a significant diminution of Slovak territory under direct Turkish rule. In 1593–94 the
imperial troops conquered the sancak of Fil'akovo, as well as the neighboring sancaks of Szécsény and Nógrád in the Magyar area to the
southwest. The Turks, however, resumed the initiative, and seizing the
pivotal fortress of Eger in 1596 they sought to recover their losses in
the entire central sector of the Slovak frontier. Eger became the capital
of a newly formed paşalik, and from this center, relying largely on the
fierce military prowess of the Crimean Tatars, the Ottoman authorities
regained in 1599–1600 the submission of parts of the three lost sancaks. Pressed simultaneously by the Bocskai insurrection, the emperor
confirmed this state of affairs in the treaty of Zsitvatorok, which concluded the protracted war in 1606. The new Paşalik of Eger included
the eastern section of the sancak of Fil'akovo, while its western part
together with the fortress of Fil'akovo remained in the hands of the
imperial army. The *bey* and other administrators of Fil'akovo sancak
henceforth resided in Eger. The Paşalik included three other sancaks
strung along to the south: Hatvan, Szolnok, and Szeged. Relying on
intimidation, the Turks continued to collect taxes from much of the

Slovak territory (including the large town of Rímavská Sobota), which had escaped their direct rule by the treaty of Zsitvatorok.

THE SLOVAKS AND THEIR NEIGHBORS

Slovak Ethnic Identity

The military turmoil, combined with the administrative segmentation and ethnic diversity of the Slovak territory, had an unfavorable effect on the consolidation of the Slovak nationality, which had not yet acquired a definite designation prior to the sixteenth century. The usual term applied to the Slovaks in the preceding three centuries was "Sclavi" or "Slavi," rendered in the native tongue as "Slovienin." The term "Slovák" was of Czech origin, and initially (and sometimes still in the sixteenth and early seventeenth centuries) it was used to designate the Slavs in general. The adjectival form *slovenský*, also of Czech origin, could refer to the Slovenes or the inhabitants of Slavonia as well. From the mid-sixteenth century, however, the words "Slovák" and *slovenský* were used in Czech most frequently to refer to the Slav inhabitants of northern Hungary. The first use of the designation inside Slovak territory is found in a report from 1456 that the town of Bardejov employed two captains, one a Czech and the other a "Slowak." The Germans in the sixteenth century often referred to the area as "slowakische Land," though they tended to call the inhabitants "Wenden" or "Winden." Moreover, the Germans and Magyars often confused the Slovaks with Czechs, speaking of them as "Bohemi." Otherwise in the sixteenth century the Magyars called the Slovak area "Tótország," and the Turks "Tot Viyalet."

Recent Slovak historians have emphasized the beneficial effect of the Czech language among the Slovaks as a bond of cultural unity and a shield against Magyarization. The use of Czech proliferated in the fifteenth century under the impact of the Hussite penetrations into northern Hungary, as well as the patronage of the language by King Matthias I Corvinus, motivated by his designs on the Bohemian Lands. As early as the fifteenth century most royal towns employed Czech notaries. The town of Žilina in the 1470s acquired a Czech translation of the Magdeburg Laws used extensively by Bohemian as well as Hungarian towns. The town officials in Trenčín took their oath of office in Czech. In the sixteenth century Czech became used even more widely and also began to undergo various degrees of "Slovakization," initially because of uncertainty about standard grammatical norms, and then later, in the following century, intentionally. The use of Czech was not limited to towns, where it often functioned as the official language of municipal councils and artisans' guilds; it was also employed in county assemblies and manorial offices. Even certain powerful magnates used it in both official and private correspondence. Among the sixteenth-century composers of historical songs, two members of the gentry wrote in "Slovakized" Czech: Martin Bošňák, captain of the castle of Babolcsa, and Štefan Komodický, captain of Ónod. Other gentry poets, such as the famous Bálint Balassi and John Rimay, wrote verses in this language as well as in Magyar.

Relations with the Germans and Magyars

The Slovaks found themselves in an active relationship with the Germans and to a lesser extent with the Magyars, particularly in towns that had been traditionally dominated by German patrician classes. In the second and the third quarters of the sixteenth century the position of the Slovaks in towns in relation to the German patriciates was generally improving by the effect of three diverse factors: (1) the struggle of John Zápolyai against Ferdinand I, (2) the migration of Magyar nobles into towns, and (3) the conflict between the Chamber officials and the German patriciates in the central mining towns.

John Zápolyai and his partisans, during the struggle with Ferdinand I in 1526–38, favored the Slovak element in the towns of eastern and central Slovakia, viewing the German burghers as partisans of the Habsburg cause. In fact, the noble followers of Ferdinand I in western Slovakia called Zápolyai derisively the "Slovak" or "Slavic" king (*tót király*).

The migration of the Magyar nobles into the towns of Slovakia helped to weaken the position of the Germans and improve that of the Slovaks in two ways. In the first place, the nobles tended to bring along large retinues of servants, mostly Slovaks, and thus increase the numerical proportion of the Slovaks in the towns of their refuge. This was a major factor in a development which in the second half of the sixteenth century led to Slovak majorities in Banská Bystrica, Pukanec, Nová Baňa, L'ubietová, and Skalica, and near majorities in Trnava, Prešov, Bardejov, Banská Štiavnica, Kremnica, Jur, Modra, and Pezinok. In the second place, the Magyar nobles directly challenged the power monopoly of the German patricians within the towns. Most notably their protestations induced Ferdinand I to issue the famous *Privilegium* of 1551, a precedent-setting decision that provided that in the town of Trnava the Germans had to share municipal power equally with the Slovaks and Magyars. The three nationalities were to rotate in the offices of the town judge and the captain, and receive parity on the town council.

Confronted with the German patriciates' increasing hostility against their interference in municipal affairs, the Chamber officials by the midsixteenth century began to favor Slovaks over Germans for lower managerial and supervisory positions in the mines and allied industrial plants, particularly in the towns of central Slovakia. The resulting tension between the Germans and the Slovaks became so pronounced that it aroused the interest of the Turks, who wished to infiltrate the central mining towns. Resorting to psychological warfare, they tried to gain the Slovaks' favor by issuing anti-German proclamations.

During the last three decades of the sixteenth century, the situation in the towns of Slovakia became more stable. The Habsburg kings did not wish to undermine further the power of the German patricians, because they regarded them, in the final analysis, as more loyal than the other ethnic groups. Moreover, the Magyar nobles did not press for further changes in this period. The German elites, in fact, fortified their power by using the guild regulations to restrict the Slovaks' influence and to stem their migration into towns. Thus in 1573 the cabinetmakers in Prešov limited guild membership to German masters. In 1554 the shoemakers of Banská Štiavnica, in addition to such a limitation, proscribed the acceptance of Slovaks even as apprentices. Similar regulations were passed by guilds in Pozsony, Levoča, and Košice. The Slovaks, in turn, in the rarer instances of their own ascendancy, adopted similar tactics to protect their dominance. Thus in Trenčín the tailors' guild admitted in its meetings the use of Slovak or "Moravian," but not Hungarian. The Slovaks of Skalica protested the diet's decision of 1563 granting Magyar nobles the right to purchase houses freely in the towns.

In the early seventeenth century the Slovaks advanced their cause by allying with the Hungarian estates against the king. During the uprising of 1600–1606, led by István Bocskai, the prince of Transylvania, the urban Slovaks generally favored the insurgents and facilitated—especially in the mining regions—the passing of the towns to Bocskai's side against the German opposition. In return, the insurgents' diet of Košice adopted a guarantee of national equality in town governments. This provision became a part of the treaty of Vienna in 1606 and was enacted by the diet of Pozsony in 1608. Essentially applying the *Privilegium* of Trnava (1551) to all Hungarian royal towns, it gave Slovaks a share of municipal power equal to that of the Germans or the Magyars. Moreover, in 1609 the diet established a fine of two thousand florins for violating this law. The enactments of 1608–9 caused conflict between the *palatin*, who sought to enforce them, and the king, who wished to protect the German patriciates. In 1610 the *palatin* was able to apply the law in Krupina in response to joint complaints by Slovak and Magyar burghers. The crucial case was that of Banská Bystrica. Responding to the Slovaks' appeal of 1611 for representation on the town council, the *palatin* imposed the statutory fine on the recalcitrant German government. The king, in turn, intervened to confirm the traditional privileges of the Germans and to countermand explicitly the *palatin's* orders. Furthermore, future complaints against the Germans' privileges had to be tried by a court of the six mining towns, with the right of final appeal to the king. This decision jeopardized further advances of Slovak power in towns.

The Slovak cause, however, suffered a more serious setback on the eve of the Thirty Years' War because of a basic realignment of political interests. It involved a shift of the German burghers' sympathies from the Habsburg dynasty to the Hungarian estates, largely because of the increasing Habsburg support for the Counter Reformation. Carried out mainly by the Chamber officials, the anti-Protestant campaign evoked intense resentments, culminating in 1617 in a serious clash over an ecclesiastical appointment in Banská Bystrica. Combined with their earlier grievances against the Habsburg bureaucracy (the Chamber officialdom), this assault on their religious convictions inclined the German burghers toward an anti-Habsburg alliance with the *palatin* and the Hungarian nobility. By the time of the Bethlen uprising (1619–22) the German patriciates no longer sided with Vienna and the king, but supported the insurgent Hungarian estates. The Magyar rebels were, in turn, anxious to consolidate the new alliance with the German burghers, assuring them steady material support from the mining towns. Under these circumstances, abetting Slovak interests in relation to the German elites appeared not only unnecessary but counterproductive. Unlike the Bocskai rebellion, that of Bethlen did not benefit the urban Slovaks.

Contacts with the Czechs

The Protestant Reformation increased contacts between Slovakia and the Bohemian Lands. Lutheranism began at first to spread among the urban Slovaks; by the midsixteenth century it had also reached the Slovak peasantry, after the Hungarian nobility had overcome its distrust of the new religion as a "German" import. The lack of Slovak clergy had to be remedied, and the towns, as well as the seigneurs, actively solicited preachers from the Bohemian Lands, especially Moravia and Silesia. In the second quarter of the century many Czech ministers served in the Slovak area, particularly in Trenčín and Nitra counties and in the mining towns of central Slovakia. They brought Czech liturgical books, and Czech became accepted as the language of religious services among Slovak Lutherans. This acceptance strengthened the function of Czech as a bond of cultural unity among the Slovaks. Paradoxically, while among the Czechs Lutheranism tended to lessen national distinctiveness (promoting Germanization), among the Slovaks it helped to affirm an ethnic identity and to raise national awareness. More remarkably, the Slovak Calvinists also adopted Czech as their liturgical language despite their physical proximity to, and spiritual kinship with, the Magyar milieu in southern and eastern Slovakia.

The Slovak Protestants acquired a formal religious organization only after the successes of the Bocskai uprising. In 1610 a Protestant synod, which met in Žilina, organized three superintendencies in the counties of western and central Slovakia. A similar synod, meeting in Spišské Podhradie in 1614, created two superintendencies for eastern Slovakia. The supervisory bodies established by the synod of Žilina were dominated by Slovaks, and their official language was Czech.

The Slovak Humanist culture emerging in the second half of the sixteenth century was also closely linked with the cultural milieu of the Bohemian Lands. The scarcity of clergy and others with higher education, which had marked the first half of the century, was definitely overcome in the second half thanks to the development of educational interests and institutions (both Protestant and Catholic) stimulated by the Reformation. In fact, a surplus of Slovak intelligentsia sought employment in the Czech regions. Many Slovak students who attended the Prague University remained in the Bohemian Lands to pursue careers as educators, clergymen, and even public functionaries. Other Slovaks who had not studied there became active in Czech areas, particularly as ministers and teachers in Moravia.

Intensified cultural and religious contacts were only one aspect of closer relations between Slovakia and the Bohemian Lands in the century after 1526.[25] The effect of a common sovereign, which lessened the significance of the Bohemian-Hungarian border, was strengthened by the need of the vestigial strips of Hungary (left after the Turkish conquests) for a broader hinterland, which could be provided by adjacent Habsburg possessions. Thus the close relations that developed between Croatia and Inner Austria were paralleled to some extent by those between Slovakia and the Bohemian Lands, mostly Moravia and Silesia.

A major manifestation of the close relations was the acquisition of estates by the nobility on either side of the border. Nobles from Slovakia were drawn to Moravia by the more advanced economy, as well as greater security from the Turks. Bohemian nobles came to Slovakia for military reasons, and had as early as the struggle between Ferdinand I and Zápolyai acquired estates there in recompense for military service. Subsequently, sizable Bohemian contingents garrisoned the Slovak border defenses against the Turks, and some of the noble commanders settled in the area permanently. A notable example was Jan z Pernštejna, the captain of Moravia, who through marriage to a noble widow became the master of the castle and the manor of Hlohov. At the other end of the social spectrum, peasants migrated across the bor-

25. For more detailed discussion of Slovak Humanism see p. 449; on commercial contacts between Slovakia and the Bohemian Lands, p. 85; on the Czech contribution to Slovakia's military defense, p. 77.

der as well. The harsh laws following the Dózsa peasant rebellion of 1514 induced Slovak peasants to emigrate, defying the Hungarian diet's efforts to reclaim the escapees. Many settled in southeast Moravia in the vicinity of Stráni and Hrozenkov; and the area of Valašsko in eastern Moravia was colonized in the sixteenth century largely by Slovak shepherds and peasants. Peasant colonists from Moravia, in turn, penetrated into Pozsony and Nitra counties. So many Moravians settled in the neighborhood of Skalica that by 1548 it aroused the Hungarian diet's fear of the area's alienation.

ECONOMIC LIFE[26]

Agriculture

The main impetus for nobles to enlarge their demesnes (noted earlier) and intensify production in the second half of the sixteenth century stemmed less from the requirements of foreign trade than from the demands of the internal market. The Slovak territory, on the whole less fertile than the areas of central Hungary lost to the Turks, was put under heavy pressure by a heightened demand for agricultural products, above all for grain and meat, the production of which rose substantially. The demand was generated partly by the presence of a large number of foreign mercenary troops and partly by the intensification of the mining operations in central Slovakia, where the number of laborers mounted to between five and six thousand during the sixteenth century. The widespread European price revolution favoring agricultural goods, which affected the Slovak area in the second half of the sixteenth century, acted as an added stimulant to increasing production. During this period the nominal price increased 200 percent for grain, 100 percent for wine, and 150 percent for cattle. Grain growing occupied a dominant position in Slovak agriculture. The leading crop was wheat, followed by rye, barley, and oats. Viticulture was second in importance, spread particularly in the counties of Pozsony, Nitra, Tekov, and Hont. Cattle raising ranked third.

The seigneurs enlarged their demesne estates or established new ones— on lands cleared of forests, or appropriated from the church with the

26. Economic data in this section are derived from *Dejiny Slovenska*, ed. L'udevít Holotík (Bratislava: Slovenská akadémia vied, 1961), 1:273–77; *Přehled československých dějin* (Prague: Československá akademie věd, 1958), 1:368–74; František Janek, *Upevňovanie vzťahov Čechov a Slovákov pri vyučovaní dejepisu* (Bratislava: Slovenské pedagogické nakl., 1961), pp. 50–56; Pavel Horváth, "Poddanská otázka na Slovensku v období tzv. druhého nevoľníctva," *Historické Štúdie* 10 (1965), pp. 12–18; Peter Ratkoš, Pavel Horváth, Anton Špiesz, and others, *Materiál z vedeckého sympózia o charaktere feudalizmu na Slovensku v 16.–18. storočí*, published as *Historické Štúdie*, XVII (1972); Josef Macůrek and Miloš Rejnuš, *České země a Slovensko ve století před Bílou Horou* (Prague: Státní pedagogické nakl., 1958), pp. 1–146; *Přehled dějin Československa* (Prague: Academia, 1982), I/2:133–41.

advance of Reformation, or deserted by the peasants, such as during the warfare between Ferdinand I and Zápolyai. Sometimes the deserted homesteads were flooded to create ponds for pisciculture. There were cases of direct expropriation of peasant lands, such as in the wine producing regions of western and southeastern Slovakia. In the less fertile mountain valleys of the north, virgin soil was put under cultivation. The enlarged demesne estates diversified and improved production through the introduction, though still on a modest scale, of gardens and orchards, barns for cattle and horses, and extensive raising of sheep (to meet the greater demand for wool, meat, and cheese). Although less significant as a source of income than in the Bohemian Lands, seigneurial breweries sprang up together with the supporting hops cultivation.

Mining, Industry, and Crafts

In nonagricultural production the greatest importance in the Slovak territory belonged to mining and metallurgy. The first place was occupied by copper, which was the leading export article next to cattle and wine. The largest smelter, in Banská Bystrica, was operated by the Augsburg merchant firm of the Fuggers until 1546, then directly by the Chamber, which channeled the exports primarily to Silesia and Germany. Between 1526 and 1539 the Fuggers produced on the average 1,064 tons of copper annually. The secondary copper production of the Spiš area (averaging in 1541–45 92 tons per year at Smolník) was exported to Poland, with the merchants of Levoča serving as middlemen. Mining of precious metals, used mostly for coinage, was concentrated in the Slovak Ore Mountains (Rudohorie) and the Spiš region, which in the second half of the sixteenth century produced together around 400 kilograms of gold and 7,000 of silver annually. Gemer county led in iron production with forty-one furnaces at midcentury, followed by Spiš and Zvolen counties. Salt mines near Prešov were also of major significance.

Artisan production on the Slovak territory was largely confined to urban guilds during the sixteenth century. Requirements of foreign mercenaries, stationed in the border fortresses, led to a moderate expansion of output, mainly in armaments, clothing, and footwear. The restriction of the guild masters to two or three journeymen, which prevented enlargement of workshops, favored increasing specialization of individual crafts. For instance, as the century progressed, the armorers became divided into five different guilds. While until midcentury the crafts were concentrated mainly in the royal free towns, subsequently they spread into the subject towns, and the emergence of guilds followed there, particularly from the 1570s.

Nevertheless, toward the end of the century the largest number of crafts were still in the royal free towns. Košice added twenty new guilds to the fifteen medieval ones; then followed Levoča (with twenty-eight), Trnava, Bardejov, Pozsony and Prešov. In smaller towns, masters of different crafts could combine. Thus in 1551 clothmakers, butchers, tailors, and bakers formed a complex guild in the Spiš towns mortgaged to Poland. Intercity guilds also appeared, such as the guild of stone-cutters and masons that represented the seven mining towns from 1570. With the constant danger of attacks by foreign and domestic foes, the artisans were closely associated with the defense of their towns. Usually each guild assumed responsibility for a specific section of the town walls.

Trade

During the sixteenth century substantial trade relationships existed between the Slovak area and the Bohemian Lands. The evidence is provided by commercial correspondence found in the town archives of both western (Trnava, Žilina, Trenčín, Skalica, Pozsony) and central Slovakia (Banská Bystrica and Banská Štiavnica). Another source is the registers of import and export duties, the so-called "thirtieth." Those of Žilina, preserved for the years 1529–33 and 1537, record the flow of trade particularly from Silesia to northern Slovakia. The commerce of Czech areas with southwest Slovakia can be traced from the registers at Trnava, Skalica, and Holíč (preserved for 1541), and with the mining and other towns of central Slovakia from the registers at Trenčín (for 1557–62). Imports into Slovakia primarily included goods of artisan production, such as clothing (cloth, linen, hats, leather, processed fur), metal products (weapons, knives, scythes, sickles) and glassware; exports into the Bohemian Lands consisted mostly of raw materials (copper, lime) and agricultural products (cattle, horses, rawhides, raw wool, wine, fruit). Merchants and artisans also migrated between the Slovak and Czech areas. In particular, Czech artisans were welcomed into Slovak guilds, and skilled Czech craftsmen helped to construct anti-Turkish forts. The closeness of the commercial ties is indicated by the fact that in 1548 the Hungarian diet ordered the acceptance of Bohemian currency everywhere in Hungary, while proscribing the circulation of Polish money.

The overall external trade of the Slovak area did not suffer from the Turkish occupation of central Hungary and Transylvania compared with the fifteenth century. Although copper production at Banská Bystrica declined with the Fuggers' departure, Slovak copper virtually monopolized the European and overseas markets until the outbreak of the Thirty Years' War. In addition to the flourishing wine exports to the adjacent regions from southwestern Slovakia, wine was newly exported to Poland from eastern Slovakia. Southwestern lowlands provided cattle for shipment to the west, and local towns served also as transit centers for cattle exports from central Hungary and the Danubian Principalities. Eastern Slovak towns acted as intermediaries for Transylvania's commerce with Poland and Western Europe.

The Croats

In the early sixteenth century the Habsburgs ascended the throne of Croatia, a transaction that in its external aspects paralleled their assumption of power in Hungary, with which the Croatian state was associated. The Croatian Kingdom, established in the tenth century, included originally not only the territories of modern Croatia but also large western sections of Bosnia and Herzegovina. The tie with Hungary, costing Croatia its external independence while preserving a considerable degree of internal autonomy, originated in 1102 with the election of Hungarian rulers as kings. Under the Hungarian dynasties, Croatian territory became the object of encroachments by the Republic of Venice, which permanently seized southern Istria in the thirteenth century and most of the Dalmatian coast with the adjacent islands by 1420. Internally, since the midthirteenth century, the Croatian Kingdom had been subdivided into two large units with separate diets and administrative systems: Slavonia in the north and Croatia (in the narrower sense) with Dalmatia in the south, with the chain of the Gvozd Mountains serving as the line of division. It became customary to refer to the entire realm as the Triune Kingdom of Dalmatia, Croatia, and Slavonia, even after most of Dalmatia was lost in the early fifteenth century and the kingdom became, in fact, limited mainly to Slavonia and Croatia proper.

CENTRAL ADMINISTRATION

The King and the Hungarian Crown

Despite the association of the Kingdom of Croatia-Slavonia with the Kingdom of Hungary, the estates of Croatia-Slavonia asserted and exercised separately in 1527 their rights to select a new king after the extinction of the Jagiellonian dynasty. As in Hungary, in Croatia-Slavonia the presence of two rival candidates precipitated a cleavage. The magnates favored Ferdinand I, the lower nobility John Zápolyai. The former was initially elected by an assembly of Croatian nobility on New Year's Day of 1527 and recognized in the south. To the north the Slavonian nobility elected John Zápolyai a week later. Not until 1538 did

Ferdinand I succeed in eliminating the influence of his rival from the kingdom, which had in the meantime greatly diminished because of the advance of Turkish power. The Turks continued to conquer more territory until 1594, when the area of the kingdom controlled by the Habsburgs shrank to 16,000 square kilometers from the original 50,000 in 1526. In the second half of the sixteenth century, writers spoke of "the remnants of the remnants of the once glorious Kingdom of Croatia." Thus only part of the Croatian population lived under Habsburg rule, with an increasingly large proportion falling under Turkish domination. A third segment of Croats—in Dalmatia, the coastal islands, and southern Istria—remained under the rule of Venice.

Within the Habsburg territory after 1526 the dividing line between Croatia and Slavonia shifted considerably. The area of Croatia advanced north from a relatively narrow coastal strip up to the river Kupa, while the territory designated as Slavonia correspondingly decreased to the area between the Kupa and the Drava. At the same time the political significance of the division began to fade as the Croatian nobility, escaping north and west from the Turkish advance, started to merge with the Slavonian nobility. With the traditional Dalmatia lost to Venice, the designation "Dalmatia" was sometimes applied to the Croatian littoral from Trsat (just east of Rijeka) to Senj.

The tie between the Croatian Kingdom and Hungary further weakened during the sixteenth century. Stronger links developed with the Slovene areas of Inner Austria, on which Croatia increasingly depended for defense against the Turks from 1522. This led (as will be discussed later) to the establishment of the fortified imperial "military borders," which eventually eluded Croatian authority.

The Croatian Kingdom continued to share certain common institutions with Hungary, above all the Hungarian diet, and two royal agencies: the Hungarian Chancellery and the Hungarian Chamber. By the end of the sixteenth century, however, the connection with Hungary became almost entirely nominal, while real power rested in Graz with the *Hofkriegsrat*, and particularly in Vienna, where the *Geheime Rat* and the *Hofkammer* asserted ascendancy respectively over the Hungarian Chancellery and the Hungarian Chamber.

Banus and Banovac

The chief official in Croatia, the representative of the king as well as the leader of the estates, was the *banus* (*Regnorum Dalmatiae, Croatiae et Sclavoniae Banus*), sometimes referred to as viceroy (*prorex*). The intermediary institution between the *banus* and the king was the Hungarian Chancellery. The Habsburgs continued to fill the office of *banus* during virtually the entire sixteenth century.[27] Usually a single *banus* held office. Ferdinand I in 1526–39 and Maximilian II in 1567–76, however, maintained two *bani* simultaneously. In the latter instance, one was a magnate, the other a prelate (the bishop of Zagreb). They shared a single seal and performed jointly judicial and administrative functions, but the magnate alone was in charge of military affairs. In a major assault on the substance of the office of *banus* in 1595, Rudolf II appointed two officials, but merely as *banal* administrators, who were limited to judicial and administrative functions and barred from military command. This direct attempt to downgrade the office failed. The following year the two administrators were raised to the status of regular *bani*, and shortly afterward the tradition of a single *banus* resumed. Nevertheless, the power of the *banus* suffered a gradual erosion in the latter part of the sixteenth century when—after 1578—the archduke, governing Inner Austria from Graz, and his *Hofkriegsrat* asserted their claims for control over the military activities of the *banus*. Even more serious was the full-fledged development of the military borders after 1595 as a separate territorial jurisdiction exempt from the authority of the *banus*.

The deputy of the *banus* appointed by him was the *banovac* (*vicebanus*, *podban*). While the *banus* was chosen by the king from the magnates or prelates, the *banovac* served also as the chief representative of the estate of lower nobility. A new office introduced under the Habsburgs was that of the *banal* lieutenant (*locumtenens banalis*, *banski namjesnik*). This official, the first one of whom was appointed by Ferdinand I in 1531, was to exercise interim power between the departure from office of a *banus* and the appointment of his successor by the king.[28]

The Diet (Sabor)

During the period 1527–36, when John Zápolyai controlled Slavonia, separate Croatian and Slavonian diets were held. A common diet met only once in 1533 (*conventus regnicolarum regnorum Croatiae et Sclavoniae*). After 1536 a single diet (*Sabor*) was the rule, with one exception in 1558. The common *Sabor* met under the chairmanship of the *banus* or his deputy two or three times a year for one or two days most often in Zagreb or Varaždin. It assembled usually before and after the sessions of the Hungarian diet, but also on other occasions, the most important of which were the installation of a new *banus*, conclusion of peace, dec-

27. This contrasted with the situation in Hungary, where the office of the *palatin* was left vacant by the Habsburgs in the sixteenth century.
28. In 1581 an attempt was made to appoint a *banal* lieutenant during the absence of the *banus* from the country, but the *Sabor* successfully insisted that the *banovac* should represent the *banus* in such instances.

laration of a general military levy (*insurrectio*), and consideration of royal propositions. A major issue bearing on the estates' power, as to whether only the king, or the *banus* also, had the right to convoke the diet, was resolved in 1567: the *banus* could convene the *Sabor*, but had to inform the king first.

All the adult male members of the magnate families could attend the diet in person. The same held true for the bishops, in addition to representatives from cathedral chapters and religious orders. The lower nobility was customarily represented by the *banovac*, the protonotary, the vice-protonotary, and the officials of the counties (*županije*), as well as by two deputies elected in each *županija*. Finally, each royal free town could send two deputies. The total number of participants was probably around fifty.

The diet possessed a wide competence. In the legislative sphere it dealt with royal propositions presented by the king's orators (most often on religious, fiscal, or military matters) in addition to proposals of the *banus* and petitions of the estates submitted either by individuals or the estates collectively. The *Sabor* maintained control over the executive power by electing several officials of the Land, in particular the protonotary, the vice-protonotary, and, on occasion, the captain of the kingdom, as well as certain officials (the *podžupan* and the noble judges) of the *županije* of Zagreb and Križevci. It also chose two or three deputies to the Hungarian diet and prepared their written instructions. Among the *Sabor*'s administrative functions the most important were the assessment of dues and taxes and matters of military defense. Active also in the judicial sphere, the diet elected certain judges and occasionally conducted trials.

The *Sabor*'s decisions were often unanimous, but at times sharp disagreements arose, especially between the higher and lower nobility. In 1579 at a session in Varaždin the disputes became so acrimonious that the diet had to be dissolved. The *Sabor*'s proceedings were recorded in Latin, but speakers often used Croatian, German, and even Italian. The decisions or "articles" of the diet (or at least the more important ones) were submitted to the king and, on receiving his sanction, were authenticated by the seal of the kingdom.

In addition to the instructed deputies (*nuncii regni*) elected by the *Sabor*, the Hungarian diet could be attended by all the Croatian magnates and prelates entitled to personal participation in the *Sabor*. The latter were free agents, not bound by any instructions. At the Hungarian diet the Croatian representatives took an active part in the coronation proceedings of a new king. The most significant recurrent function of the diet from the Croatian point of view was the grant of the war tax. To be valid in the Croatian Kingdom, the tax, however, required approval and promulgation by the *Sabor*. In the latter part of the sixteenth century the Croatian estates hoped to enlist the Hungar-

ian diet's aid against the growing ascendancy of Inner Austria, especially the Graz *Hofkriegsrat* and its subordinate commanders in the affairs of Croatia. This expectation had its disadvantages, however, because
it encouraged the Hungarian diet to deal with Croatian matters, over
which it had had no previous jurisdiction.

The Judiciary

The legal system of Croatia-Slavonia was greatly influenced by Hungarian law, especially as interpreted in the *Tripartitum* of Werbőczi, written in 1514. A Croatian translation by Ivan Pergošić, a judge in Varaždin,
appeared in 1574. Another outstanding Croatian legal scholar, Ivan Ki-
tonić (1561–1619), attempted to modify certain aspects of Werbőczi's
work. The supreme court of Croatia-Slavonia was the *Banus'* Octaval
Court (*iudicia octavalia*). It had existed since the fifteenth century and
was composed, in addition to the *banus*, *banovac*, and protonotary, of
assessors especially elected by the *Sabor*. During the sixteenth century
there was considerable concern that because of the disorders of the times
this court, which gradually became known also as the *Banus'* Table (*tabula banalis*), was not sitting as regularly as its importance required. According to a custom, developed in the previous century, it held two
different types of sessions. The General Court (*iudicium generale*), usually conducted by the *banus*, was concerned mostly with important state
actions and issues concerning the privileges of the nobility; the Brief
Court (*iudicium breve*), directed by the *banovac* and the vice-protonotary,
mainly tried ordinary cases of civil and criminal law. A key official in
the judicial system was also the protonotary, who was elected by the
Sabor, which jealously guarded this right from usurpation by the *banus*.
The protonotary by himself tried cases in a special probate court, *iud-
icatus et forum protonotariale*.

LOCAL ADMINISTRATION

Civil Croatia and the Military Borders

The territory of the Croatian Kingdom under Habsburg rule was
subject to further subdivision during the sixteenth century. Although
the process was not completed until the 1590s, an increasingly clearer
distinction emerged between the "civil" part, in which the *banus* and the
Sabor maintained power, and the area of the military borders, which
became to an ever greater degree governed by officers of the imperial
army, directed from the Austrian Lands. The military borders had their
origins in the Jagiellonian period in 1522, when King Louis II permitted the troops of the Austrian Habsburgs to help guard the Turkish

frontier. After 1526, several military districts, or captaincies, garrisoned by imperial mercenaries, were gradually organized in the areas facing the Turks. The imperial commanders expanded their power within these districts from military to administrative and judicial spheres. Their position was further strengthened in 1578 when Rudolf II entrusted the supreme command in the military borders to the ruler of Inner Austria, Archduke Charles in Graz. In the 1590s the distinctiveness of the borders began to increase, with the arrival of new peasant immigrants, the so-called Vlakhs. This development is discussed in a subsequent section.

Between 1526 and 1568 a single commander, the high captain (*supremus capitaneus ad confinia Croatiae Sclavoniaeque*), headed the entire military border. In 1568 two independent commands were created, one for the Slavonian Border, the other for the Croatian Border, each headed by a general captain, or general. The former had its headquarters in Varaždin, the latter after 1579 in Karlovac (Karlstadt). Between the Croatian Border and the Slavonian Border lay the *Banus'* Border (*confinia banalia*), formally established by Rudolf II in 1583, and centered in Petrinja on the lower Kupa River, for the defense of which the *banus* and the *Sabor* were responsible. The Croatian and Slavonian military borders were divided further into captaincies. At the next lower level were the castellans, located in small towns. Most of these officers were nobles from the Lands of Inner Austria. After 1578 the *Hofkriegsrat* in Graz coordinated the command of the two borders.

The territory outside the military borders, that of "civil" Croatia and Slavonia, was divided into three counties or *županije* (Zagreb, Varaždin, Križevci), and three duchies or *knezije* (Vinodol, Modruše, Moslavina). The *županije* merit particular attention since their governmental structures, representing the local nobility, resembled those of the Hungarian counties, and they could serve a similar function in defending the estates' prerogatives against absolutist claims of royal authority. The chief officials of the *županija* were the *veliki župan* (*supremus comes*) and his deputy the *podžupan* (*vicecomes*). Either one could preside over the assembly (*skupština*) of the *županija* and the court of the *županija*. Other important officials were the notary and four noble judges (*iudices nobilium*). A *županija* was subdivided into four districts (*processus, kotar*), each headed by one of the noble judges, who exercised both administrative and judicial functions.

Seigneurs and Peasants

The local level of government, except in the royal free towns, was in the hands of the nobles, more specifically the magnates and the upper stratum of the lower nobility. Among the magnates in the sixteenth century the oldest and most distinguished families were the Zrinskis (Zrínyi) and the Frankopans (Frangipan). Of the families that newly arose to prominence, the Erdedis (Erdődy) received the title of count in 1565, and the Draškovićes that of baron in 1567. By 1604 the Keglevićes, Pathews, Ratkajs (Rathkay), and Thuroczys had joined the estate of the magnates. The lower nobility was subdivided into the "propertied" nobles (*nobiles bene possessionati*), who had peasant subjects, and the one-hide nobles (*nobiles unius possessionis*), who were without serfs. Unlike the one-hide nobles of Hungary proper, those of Croatia were traditionally exempted from the payment of the war tax (*dica*) and other extraordinary imposts. This privilege was reconfirmed by Ferdinand I in 1548, and by Rudolf II in 1602 and 1608. Finally, in 1610 the *Sabor* itself affirmed their immunity from both taxes and servile labor. The *praediales* and the *libertini* formed an intermediate stratum between the nobles and the peasants. Attached to the estates of ecclesiastical prelates and secular magnates respectively, both groups were personally free and exempted from taxation and labor obligations, but had to perform military service for their lords.

The peasants were entirely under the jurisdiction of their seigneur. He, or his representative, was their judge, and they owed him dues in money and kind, as well as uncompensated labor. In addition, the seigneurs passed on to their serfs the payment of several taxes: the tithes to the church, the *dimnica* to the estates, and the war tax to the king. There was a gradation among the peasants according to the amount of property they held.

As elsewhere in East Central Europe, in Croatia in the sixteenth century the nobles sought to enlarge their estates, and their dependence on peasant servile labor grew correspondingly. As a result, considerable attention was paid to peasant migration. In 1538 the right to move, denied since 1514, was restored to check unauthorized escapes of the serfs. In 1557 the *Sabor* approved for Croatia the complex rules governing peasant migration that the Hungarian diet had adopted a year earlier. While in the fifteenth century unpaid labor on the demesnes had involved no more than thirty or forty days a year per peasant homestead, by the mid-sixteenth century it amounted to two or three days a week. It was a specific feature of Croatian feudalism that the seigneurs were increasing the dues in kind during the sixteenth century. The oppression of the "second serfdom" was added to other burdens peculiar to the Croatian situation, such as compulsory work on fortifications and carting of military supplies, and produced profound discontent. In the 1550s entire villages were found to prefer Turkish rule over the oppressive treatment of their Christian seigneurs. In 1573 the accumulated resentment burst out into a major uprising centered around Zagreb. Some 12,000 peasants took part under the leadership

of Matija Gubec, and 3,000 perished in the final battle against the seigneurs' troops.

Imperial Commanders and the Vlakhs

The pattern of seigneurial jurisdiction was seriously disrupted in the
military borders toward the turn of the sixteenth century with far-
reaching consequences for the internal government of the Croatian
Kingdom. The great Turkish war of 1593–1606 stimulated a mass influx of Christian refugees from Turkish territories, called the Vlakhs,
most of whom were Orthodox and probably Serbian. While the previous refugees, known as Uskoks, had been settled in the 1530s largely
in the Slovene Lands, especially Carniola, the new migrants received
land in the depopulated zone between the forts and the frontline in the
military borders. Moreover, by an edict of Archduke Ferdinand of Inner Austria (the later Emperor Ferdinand II) in his role as the supreme
commander of the military borders, most of the new settlers were freed
from feudal dues in 1597. The Croatian estates initially acquiesced, since
previously empty lands were involved. Soon, however, it became clear
that by virtue of exemption from feudal dues the Vlakhs were simultaneously withdrawn from the system of seigneurial jurisdiction and
placed instead under the administrative and judicial authority of the
imperial commanders and their headquarters in Graz. In fact, not only
the noble seigneurs but also the *banus* and the *Sabor* lost jurisdiction
over the area. This marked the final step in the emergence of the military borders as a distinct administrative territory, and their full separation from civil Croatia.

Beginning in 1604 the *Sabor* repeatedly demanded the subordination
of the Vlakhs to the noble landowners, and a full restoration of the
power of the *banus* over the entire territory of the kingdom. These efforts were largely unsuccessful during the first two decades of the seventeenth century. The position of the Vlakhs was especially strong in
the Slavonian Border, where they had settled in large numbers. They
also enjoyed firm support from the imperial officers who were drawn
mostly from the Styrian nobility and eager to preserve their power in
the border. Finally, the Vlakhs there were always ready to resist any
encroachments on their rights.

The Vlakhs' position was considerably weaker in the Croatian Border. Their numbers were smaller, and many of the imperial officers
there were Croatian noblemen, who naturally sympathized with the *Sabor*'s demands. Moreover, the estates of Carniola and Carinthia, which
primarily financed the Croatian Border, tended to favor the Croatian
nobles and fear the Vlakhs. Engaged as they were from 1600 to 1620
in the final contest with Archduke Ferdinand for the preservation of

their political power,[29] the estates of Carniola in particular viewed the Croatian estates as potential allies against the prince, while the Vlakhs in the Croatian Border appeared as likely instruments of the archduke's military power. Thus the nobles of Carniola not only opposed granting privileges and immunities to the Vlakhs but even advocated their removal into Hungary or the Slavonian Border.

The Towns

The towns occupied a special place in the system of local government. Those of the first rank, the royal free towns, included Zagreb, Gradec, Varaždin, Koprivnica, and Križevci in Slavonia, and Senj and—until 1592—Bihać in Croatia. They were entitled to elect and send deputies not only to the *Sabor* but also to the Hungarian diet. By the late sixteenth century the burghers were regarded as the fourth estate, following the prelates, magnates, and the lesser nobles. Enjoying a high degree of autonomy, the royal towns chose their own councils headed by a judge, adopted their own ordinances, and were not subordinated to the *banus* but directly to the king, who was represented for that purpose by the Hungarian officials—the *tavernicus* and the *personalis*. The town court was conducted by the town judge, assisted by elected assessors, with appeals going to the Hungarian *tavernicus*. Aside from the judge (*iudex civitatis*) and the assessors (*iurati cives*), the town council consisted of twenty councilors (*consiliarii, viri communes*). The requirement that the membership of the council be changed annually prevented in general the formation of oligarchic governments, which had prevailed in the royal towns of Austria, Bohemia, and Hungary.

The towns of the second rank were those subjected to the jurisdiction of an ecclesiastical or secular seigneur. The degree of self-government depended on the will of their lord, and they were not represented in the *Sabor*. The subject towns in Croatia for the most part enjoyed more autonomy than those in Slavonia.

FISCAL AND MILITARY AFFAIRS

The King's and the Estates' Taxes

A major source of the king's revenues in the Croatian Kingdom was the war tax (*dica, subsidium, contributio*). Since Croatia proper was exempted from its payment, the *dica* was collected only in the three *županije* of Slavonia, where it customarily amounted to half the rate authorized

29. See p. 51.

by the Hungarian diet for Hungary. The king appointed a special official (*dicator*) who prepared a register of all chimneys (*fumus, dim*) subjected to the tax. For the actual collection of the tax, the king, however, had to depend on the good will of the agents of the estates, the officials of the *županije*. The royal free towns also paid the *dica*. The money was eventually sent to the Hungarian Chamber in Pozsony.

Because of a drastic decline of the taxable chimneys in the three *županije*, from 10,645 in 1543 to 4,648 in 1554, the Hungarian Chamber attempted unsuccessfully to subject to the war tax certain exempted groups, such as the one-hide nobles or the officials of the Land and of the *županije*. By 1578 the number of chimneys sank to 3,800. Only toward the end of the century did the yield of the *dica* increase substantially when the house (*domus*) was substituted for the chimney as the unit of taxation. Since a single hearth was often shared by several houses of related peasants, the number of taxable units increased sharply. In the three *županije* 11,957 houses were registered in 1598. After ten years of ardent resentment, however, the old system of assessment by chimneys was reinstituted. Another royal tax flowing from Croatia-Slavonia into the Hungarian Chamber was the "thirtieth" (*tricesima, harmica*), a customs duty on imported and exported goods.

In addition to the taxes collected on behalf of the king, the estates also needed a revenue for the internal administration of the kingdom. Thus a new regular tax developed in the first half of the sixteenth century, the *dimnica* (*pecuniae fumales*), the proceeds of which were retained and expended by the Croatian estates and their officials. Since 1538 the *dimnica* had been collected on the basis of registers compiled for the war tax (*dica*). It defrayed the salaries of various public officials,[30] but the largest proportion was spent on a special contingent of troops, the *haramije*, maintained by the estates. Hence the tax itself became known as *pecuniae haramiales*.

Croatian and Imperial Armies

The military organization of civil Croatia-Slavonia consisted of the regular and the extraordinary forces. The former had two components: the *Banus' Banderium* and the *haramije*. The *Banus' Banderium*, also known as Royal *Banderium*, was financed by a royal subsidy granted to the *banus*. It was to consist of six hundred cavalrymen and four hundred infantrymen, but the *bani* often had difficulty in obtaining the subsidy, particularly between 1590 and 1607, when Rudolf II intended to eliminate the *Banderium* altogether. The main function of the *Banus' Banderium* was to defend the *Banus'* Border on the Kupa River. The *haramije*, a

---

30. Such as emissaries to the royal court, assessors of the Octaval Court, and deputies to the Hungarian diet.

corps of three hundred infantrymen, was established in 1539 and financed by the *Sabor*. Initially it was designated for service in the interior, but later a part of the corps was stationed at the frontline on the Kupa, and even on the Drava.

The extraordinary military forces of civil Croatia-Slavonia consisted of the *banderia* of the magnates and prelates, and ultimately of the general levy (*insurrectio, generalis expeditio, exercituatio generalis*). If the kingdom was endangered, the *banus* could request the great secular and ecclesiastical lords to lead their *banderia* into the field. Owing to the enormous loss of subjects and property by the mid-sixteenth century, however, none could raise a full *banderium* of four hundred cavalrymen, except the Zrinskis, who also had estates in Hungary. In case of extreme danger the *Sabor*, following the precedent of 1478, could call up the general levy. According to the *Sabor*'s regulations of 1528, every able-bodied noble and every tenth peasant were required to serve. Moreover, every noble supplied and equipped one cavalryman for every twenty peasant subjects. Commanded by the *banovac*, these riders were to shield the borders of Carniola against Turkish penetration. A new law in 1592 stipulated that, in case of a general levy, also the poor nobles (*armales nobiles impossessionati*) and the burghers of royal free towns with their dependents had to serve. Foreign merchants had the choice of serving personally or dispatching one cavalryman for every five hundred florins' worth of property.

The entire armed force of civil Croatia-Slavonia was headed by the *banus* together with the captain of the kingdom (*capitaneus regni*), who was elected by the *Sabor* and specifically in charge of defending with the *haramije* the forts along the Kupa.[31]

The contribution of the imperial armed forces in the military borders to the defense of Croatia-Slavonia against the Turks greatly overshadowed the domestic military efforts. Since the 1530s the Lands of Inner Austria had borne the main financial burden, with Styria supporting the Slavonian Border, and Carniola with Carinthia the Croatian Border. The yield of the Croatian war tax (*dica*) covered only a minute fraction of the annual expense of the two borders. Inner Austria contributed over 500,000 florins annually after 1578, and by 1594 the total had reached the impressive figure of some 21,000,000 florins. Sizable aid since the 1530s had also come from other parts of the Holy Roman Empire. Channeled through Graz, it amounted to two and a quarter million florins between 1576 and 1613. The number of soldiers in the military borders fluctuated between four and five thousand. In 1577, for instance, the total was 4,729 mercenaries, with 1,972 in the Slavonian Border, and 2,757 in the Croatian Border.

---

31. Occasionally the *banus* himself was elected captain.

When Archduke Charles of Inner Austria assumed the supreme command in 1578, the military borders contained sixty fortresses on a 300 kilometer front in Croatia, and twenty-eight on a 100 kilometer front in Slavonia. The archduke elaborated precise instructions for the *Hofkriegsrat* in Graz, entrusted with paying and supplying the troops. Simultaneously he issued sets of regulations (*Kriegsordnung*) for the infantry and cavalry in the borders. The fortifications consisted of stone castles and wooden forts (*palanka*), connected by chains of watchtowers (*čadak*). A major addition to the defense system was the large fortress of Karlovac, the construction of which began in 1579.

ECONOMIC LIFE [32]

Agriculture

Crop raising was traditionally the chief agricultural activity in the parts of Croatia that remained under Habsburg rule. Agriculture, however, encountered severe obstacles and setbacks in the sixteenth century. The territory near the Turkish frontier suffered frequent devastation. Desolate tracts lay in all three parts of the military border. There was a chronic shortage of peasant labor. Some peasants were abducted by the Turks, others escaped not only to seek security from Turkish danger but also to avoid the harsh consequences of the incipient "second serfdom," being imposed by the seigneurs. The work of the remaining peasantry suffered from disruptions by special requirements, such as compulsory labor on fortifications and deliveries of supplies into the fortresses, and by exposure to Turkish raids while working in the open fields. Natural disasters, mainly floods, also interfered with the tilling of soil. Above all, the Sava periodically flooded extensive agricultural areas.

Despite the adverse circumstances, enough grain was raised in the years of normal harvests not only to feed the local population and to satisfy the needs of the military borders but also to yield a surplus for export. In need of more cash to cover rising prices and taxes, the seigneurs were particularly eager to increase production on their enlarged demesnes. Years of poor harvest, however, could cause famines, as happened in 1527, 1570, and 1587. Wheat was the most valuable crop destined mainly for sale. In quantity of production it was exceeded only

32. The economic data in this section are derived from *Historija naroda Jugoslavije* (Zagreb: Školska knjiga, 1959), 2:414–16, 425–33, 452; Vjekoslav Klaić, *Povjest Hrvata* (Zagreb: Matica Hrvatska, 1973), 5:701–9; *Dějiny Jugoslávie,* ed. Václav Žáček (Prague: Svoboda, 1970), p. 171; Kveta Kučerová, *Chorváti a Srbi v strednej Európe* (Bratislava: Veda, 1976), pp. 289–94; Josip Adamček, *Agrarni odnosi u Hrvatskoj od sredine XV do kraja XVII stoljeća* (Zagreb: Sveučilišna Naklada Liber, 1980), pp. 229–493.

by millet which served as the basic foodstuff for the peasantry. Besides the growing of grain, viticulture was important, particularly on peasant lands in all parts of Croatia and Slavonia. The *Sabor* sought to open export outlets for wine in Hungary, although most of the output was consumed internally, especially by the foreign mercenaries in the military borders.

Animal raising was greatly strengthened with the arrival of the Serbian refugees (the Vlakhs) in the 1590s. The Vlakhs brought with them herds of cattle and other livestock, reaching ratios of up to five animals to one person. Initially, they shunned crop production. Pig raising, however, had a long local tradition in Croatia dating at least to the fifteenth century.

Crafts and Mining

Despite economic disruptions due to virtually continuous warfare, craft production was actually stimulated in sixteenth-century Croatia by the presence of the mercenary soldiers, who required a considerable supply of handmade articles. Crafts were strong in the royal free towns, as well as some others, such as Krapina, Samobor, Jastrebarsko, and Sisak. Certain artisans had been organized in guilds since the fifteenth century (shoemakers, furriers, bridle makers, and saddlers), others only since the beginning of the sixteenth.

Guilds sought to protect their members from competition of artisans from other towns. If an outside master was apprehended selling goods in a town, his wares were subject to confiscation. Guilds also strove to limit internal competition, and to ensure access to raw materials for all masters. Each master was restricted to two journeymen and two apprentices, unless there was an exceptionally high demand for certain goods combined with an abundant supply of labor. Heavy fines were meted out to masters who offered special enticements to customers. In addition, town governments shared in regulating artisan activities. An entire guild could lose its charter if its members violated the official price schedule. Every master took an oath before the town authorities, pledging to observe restrictions on the accumulation of goods and capital.

Despite their best efforts, however, the guilds could not shield the urban craftsmen from the competition of peasant artisans. The village craftsmen were supported and protected by the noble seigneurs, who exempted some of their serfs from monetary dues in lieu of supplying them with handmade articles, such as barrels, arrows, bowls, troughs, and sieves. Other serfs were encouraged to work as craftsmen (carpenters, cabinetmakers, etc.) in the manor houses and on the demesnes, as well as in the seigneurs' subject towns.

The only industrial activities outside the crafts were mining and metallurgy. In the sixteenth century the silver production in Gvozdansko was most important. The mine belonged to the Zrinski family, which also managed a mint in Gvozdansko, where between 1527 and 1534 silver groschen with the image of Ferdinand I were coined. Estimated income from the mine and the mint amounted to 30,000 ducats annually. After a Turkish attack in 1540 damaged the mine and foundry, operations were restored in 1549. In 1578 the Turks occupied the area permanently and destroyed the mine.

The other important activity was copper mining in Rude near Samobor. Employing mostly German workmen, the mine was owned by a German noble family until 1578, then by Croatian magnates. For the sixteenth and early seventeenth centuries there is also evidence for the mining of salt and other minerals in the area of Zagreb.

Trade

Despite dislocations caused by Turkish conquests and disruptions of warfare, lively trade relations prevailed in sixteenth-century Croatia, stimulated largely by the demand of the mercenaries in the military borders. The merchants in towns failed to safeguard a monopoly of trade in the face of powerful incentives of both nobles and peasants to engage in commerce. The seigneurs' increased need for income has already been mentioned. The peasants also had to sell a portion of their products to raise cash for taxes and feudal dues. The nobles held special advantages in trade over both the peasants and the townsmen, enjoying an exemption from the "thirtieth" and the tolls on goods grown on their demesnes, or purchased for their own use.

In the era of inflationary pressures, the estates tried to restore a measure of stability. The *Sabor* decreed maximum prices on a large number of goods in 1528 and 1538, and a comprehensive set of price regulations in 1603. Speculation, involving purchase and resale of goods, caused concern in the second half of the sixteenth century. In 1560, royal commissioners complained that imperial soldiers paid the nobles or townsmen from two to six times more for foodstuffs than they would in purchases directly from the peasants. The *Sabor*, in turn, remonstrated in 1588 with the military authorities that the mercenaries resold goods purchased from the peasants at prices two or three times higher.

Weekly fairs played a crucial role in the marketing of goods. In addition, larger towns enjoyed the privilege of holding large or annual fairs, the most prominent of which (in Gradec and Zagreb) attracted merchants, nobles, and peasants not only from Croatia and Slavonia but from the Slovene Lands and more remote areas. Late in the sixteenth century the right to hold fairs, originally confined to towns, was

gradually extended to larger villages, in a process reflecting the seigneurs' eagerness to promote trade. The right of compulsory sale (*ius
depositionis*), which forced merchants passing through to sell their goods
in certain localities, was originally rare, but by 1605 it applied to several
towns. Subsequently, with a recognition of its harmfulness to the flow
of trade, the tendency was to eliminate this requirement.

Turkish conquests severed the traditional direct routes to the Adriatic. Moreover, the *Sabor* in 1528 and again in 1538 strictly prohibited
any trade on the Sava and Drava with the Turkish-occupied territories.
Instead, most external trade was now passing through the Slovene Lands,
following roads to Metlika, Novo Mesto, and Ljubljana in Carniola, as
well as to Ptuj and Radgona in Styria. These routes also channeled supplies to the military borders, and the *Sabor* in the late sixteenth and
early seventeenth centuries importuned the seigneurs to maintain the
connecting roads through their manors under the threat of forfeiting
the right to collect tolls.

The main articles of Croatian external trade were grain, salt, and
cattle. Grain was usually exported, except in years of poor harvest, when
the deficit was covered by imports from Italy or Hungary. Most salt
used in Croatia was imported, and the grain exports largely balanced
the salt imports. Grain and salt passing through the port of Bakar (Buc-
cari) were valued at ten thousand florins annually in the second half
of the sixteenth century. Cattle, amounting to about 80,000 head per
year in the late sixteenth century, accounted for the most voluminous
export item. They were usually driven through Ptuj to the Adriatic ports.
Aside from salt, imports (coming mainly from Italy) involved primarily
fine textiles and overseas goods. Like domestic trade, external commerce became the object of regulatory concern by public authorities.
After 1560, royal commissioners insisted on reductions in grain exports
to assure adequate supplies for the military borders. The Croatian estates usually favored unhampered exports of grain as well as wine as a
means of safeguarding supplies of salt, and also of money for peasants'
dues and taxes. Nevertheless, the *Sabor* occasionally did restrict exports
of both grain and cattle in order to keep domestic prices from rising.

The Ruthenians

In the first phase of their reign in Hungary after 1526 the Habsburgs
failed to gain control over the four principal Ruthenian counties of
northeast Hungary (Ung, Bereg, Ugocsa, and Máramaros). The treaty
of 1538 assigned the area to John Zápolyai. In 1551–55 the entire territory was temporarily held by Ferdinand I together with all of Transylvania, but it was only in the 1560s that the Habsburgs definitely ac-

quired Ung, Bereg, and Ugocsa, while Máramaros remained attached to Transylvania. Even then the Habsburgs as kings of Hungary had difficulties in their part of Transcarpathia in maintaining authority over local nobles. The latter generally Protestant and sympathetic to Transylvania, tended to disregard the directives of the officials of the Chamber of Spiš, the main channel of royal authority available in the area. This was particularly true of the manor of Mukacheve (Munkács, Mukachevo), covering most of Bereg county, which belonged to the powerful Protestant Rákóczi family from 1588 to 1606. Conversely, Habsburg power in Ung county increased greatly in 1605 when the Drugeths, the masters of Uzhhorod (Ungvár) manor, converted to Catholicism. Under the treaty of Vienna in 1606 Bereg and Ugocsa counties passed briefly under the sovereignty of Transylvania under István Bocskai, who was elected prince of Transylvania by the Protestant estates in 1605. He died the following year.

In order to strengthen their authority against the largely Protestant and Magyar (or Magyarized) seigneurs, the Habsburg rulers sought amicable relations with the Orthodox Church, the religious organization of the Ruthenian peasantry. The Orthodox Church in Transcarpathia was governed by the bishops of Mukacheve, whose hierarchical superiors were the metropolitans of Moldavia. Liturgical books were imported from Kiev. The bishops of Mukacheve received royal patents of protection, directed primarily against the masters of Mukacheve manor, from Ferdinand I in 1551, Maximilian II in 1569, and Rudolf II in 1597. Wishing to exclude the Mukacheve bishops' authority from their territory, the Transylvanian princes from 1600 made sporadic efforts to found a new Orthodox bishopric for Máramaros, the part of Transcarpathia still under their sovereignty.

After the devastation caused by warfare in the first half of the sixteenth century, agricultural prosperity set in under the relatively stable Habsburg rule.[33] New peasant populations were attracted to Transcarpathia, often by promises of temporary exemptions from dues and services to the seigneurs. Much of the migration originated in Galicia, where seigneurial exactions were particularly onerous. On the Nevice manor in Ung county, for instance, the number of villages increased from forty-five in 1559 to sixty-six in 1582. As early as 1570, an imperial commission under Count Nicholas Salm reported relative abundance, especially of cattle and money, among Ruthenian peasants of western Transcarpathia.

Urban craftsmen, particularly numerous in Uzhhorod and Mukach-

---

33. Economic data in this section are derived from Ivan G. Kolomiets, *Ocherki po istorii Zakarpat'ia* (Tomsk: Izd-vo Tomskogo universiteta, 1953–59), 1:15–61; 2:88–89; Michael Lacko, *The Union of Užhorod* (Cleveland: Slovak Institute, 1966), p. 70; *Zakarpats'ka oblast'* (Kiev: Ukr. Rad. Entsyklopediia, 1969), p. 78.

eve, consisted mainly of descendants of foreign artisans invited by the Hungarian kings between the thirteenth and early sixteenth centuries. In the second half of the sixteenth century the membership in artisan guilds was mostly German, and the guild rules in effect barred Ruthenians by excluding persons of serf origin or Orthodox faith. The bar against the admission of the Orthodox was not lifted until 1608. In the area of mining the ranking enterprise on Transcarpathian territory was the salt mines near Khust in Máramaros county under the sovereignty of the Transylvanian princes. German colonist miners carried on the operations in open pits.

CHAPTER 3

Royal Absolutism and Administration
by the Estates, 1620–1740

The Czechs

At the end of the Thirty Years' War the Bohemian state still represented the largest entity among the Habsburg possessions, owing to the Turkish occupation of most of Hungary. It had lost Upper and Lower Lusatia, ceded by Ferdinand II (1617–37) to his ally the Elector of Saxony temporarily in 1623, and permanently by the Peace of Prague in 1635. Even so, its territory covered 129,000 square kilometers compared with 107,000 for the German Alpine Lands, and 67,000 for Hungary and Croatia actually under Habsburg rule. The balance was to shift in favor of Hungary only with the reconquest of lost territories from the Turks in 1683–99, and even further after 1740 with the loss of most of Silesia by the Bohemian state to Prussia.

ROYAL POWER

Absolutism and Counter Reformation

Nevertheless, the outcome of the battle of the White Mountain on November 8, 1620, which ended the Bohemian uprising of 1618, abruptly altered the balance of power between the king and the estates in both Bohemia and Moravia. The previous dualism of state power shifted drastically in the king's favor in all the major branches of government: executive, legislative, and judicial. The changes were defined primarily in the Renewed Land Ordinances, issued by the king for Bohemia in 1627 and for Moravia a year later without consultation with or approval by the estates. Establishing an automatic process of royal succession, the ordinances eliminated opportunities for the estates to exact concessions as a prerequisite for the "acceptance" of a new king. The Pragmatic Sanction, submitted to and adopted by the Bohemian and Moravian diets in 1720, was to extend further the principle of preestablished hereditary succession by applying it to heirs in female lines.

Despite the absolute power, which the king had acquired in the seventeenth century, he could not entirely dispense with the cooperation of the estates, since he lacked an adequate bureaucratic apparatus of his own. The estates could no longer seriously challenge him, but he still depended for the exercise of his authority on a governmental machinery that was to a large degree staffed and operated by the estates. The nobility was by now purged of Protestants and in fact of anybody faintly suspected of heterodoxy, which was viewed as evidence of disloyalty to Habsburg rule. It is, therefore, not surprising that the victorious Ferdinand II could assure Bohemian nobles by a special Letter of Majesty in 1627 of their retention of all privileges, grants, and immunities that were not contrary to the Renewed Land Ordinance. A similar letter to the Moravian nobility in 1628 even enumerated the privileges that remained valid.

In Silesia the constitutional changes were not so abrupt or far reaching as in Bohemia or Moravia. This Land surrendered, after the battle of the White Mountain in 1621, not directly to Ferdinand II but to his ally the elector of Saxony on the basis of so-called Saxon Accord. On taking over Silesia, Ferdinand II had to recognize this treaty, which granted general amnesty for all insurgents, as well as perpetuation of the existing liberties. Subsequently, the Habsburgs remained more circumspect in the application of absolute government here than in the other Lands of the Bohemian state.

Following the battle of the White Mountain, the Counter Reformation in Bohemia and Moravia was even more abrupt and drastic than the political reorganization. The clergy of the Bohemian Brethren and the Calvinists, as well as all Anabaptists in Moravia, were expatriated as early as 1621. The banishment of Lutheran ministers was delayed until 1622–24 to pacify Ferdinand II's ally, the elector of Saxony. In 1622 the Jesuits were authorized to supervise education and censor books; the feast day of John Hus was abolished as a public holiday; and communion under two kinds was proscribed for the laity. A campaign to reconvert townsmen and peasants took place in 1623–24, with the result that Bohemia and Moravia acquired a superficial Catholic appearance. Actually many Protestants remained. Thus special missions, supported by military detachments and directed by "Reformation"

Commissions, had to continue their work for many years. Many Protestants emigrated, not only from areas bordering Saxony, Silesia, and Hungary, but also from towns deep in the interior. The suppression of Protestantism was formally legalized in 1627, when the Letter of Majesty of 1609, granting religious freedom, was explicitly abrogated and the Renewed Land Ordinances declared the Roman Catholic religion the only admissible one. The main thrust of the Counter Reformation then turned against the nobles, who so far had been spared. Those who did not wish to conform had to leave the country. Protestant hopes engendered during the rest of the Thirty Years' War by periodic military or political successes of the Saxons or the Swedes were completely extinguished in October 1648 by the Treaty of Westphalia, which gave the Habsburgs full freedom to settle religious affairs in both Bohemia and Moravia. The Counter Reformation gradually prevailed, with only small communities of secret Protestants surviving into the eighteenth century. These recalcitrants could face severe penalties, since heterodoxy became equated with treason.

The Counter Reformation's force was significantly curtailed in Silesia. The Saxon Accord of 1621 gave protection to the Lutherans, though not to the Brethren or the Calvinists. After its expiration, the Treaty of Westphalia stipulated freedom for Lutheranism in four duchies—Oleśnica (Oels), Brzeg (Brieg), Legnica (Liegnitz), and Wołow (Wohlau)—and preservation of three specific churches in other parts of the Land. The Treaty of Altranstaedt with Sweden in 1707 not only revived these provisions but also authorized establishment of fifteen additional Lutheran churches, one of them in Těšín (Teschen).

Germanization

The most important consequence of the battle of the White Mountain from the standpoint of the Czechs' survival as a distinct ethnic group was the precipitous decline in the public use of the Czech language. It resulted largely from an intensification of pressures already operating in the sixteenth century: German immigration and the impact of the Habsburg government. German immigrants to a large extent filled the population gaps caused in towns and the countryside by the Thirty Years' War. Among the foreign nobles who acquired estates of the banished Protestants, some were of Italian or Spanish extraction, but most were German. Also the remaining Czech noble families became essentially Germanized by the beginning of the eighteenth century. Artisans and peasants, immigrating mainly from Austria, Bavaria, and Swabia, widened the border belts of German settlement and enlarged the German islands in the interior. Influential German minorities, favored by political circumstances, also sprang up in the towns of otherwise Czech areas. This was especially evident in Moravia, where the decimation of local urban populations had been particularly severe. As a result, this Land appeared externally even more Germanic than Bohemia.

A major setback for the use of Czech in public life was its demotion from the status of sole official language in Bohemia and Moravia to a position of theoretical equality with, but a practical subordination to, German. Characteristically, only the German version of the Renewed Land Ordinances, which enunciated this novel linguistic equality, was considered authentic, and a Czech version of the ordinance for Moravia never appeared in print. The new regime carefully safeguarded the rights of German. For instance, when the Moravian Court of the Land continued to render judgments exclusively in Czech, it was ordered in 1654 to issue decisions in the language of the original petition. Before long, the presumption was that the principle of equality applied only to the agencies' external contacts with outside parties, and not to internal transactions within the agencies themselves. Thus the Moravian Tribunal in 1639 and the Prague Council on Appeals in 1644 were directed to adopt German as their internal official language.

On the whole, the public use of Czech persisted in Bohemia more than in Moravia for the rest of the seventeenth century, and even into the eighteenth. Almost all Bohemian manors prepared their land registers in Czech in 1654, as well as revisions of these records in 1670–82, while in Moravia most of them filled their tax reports in German by 1667. The Bohemian Council of the Lieutenancy corresponded with the Bohemian Chancellery in Czech, at least concerning such matters as the appointment of circuit (*kraj*) captains; its Moravian counterpart, the Tribunal, always wrote in German. The Chancellery issued certain documents for Bohemia in Czech, all documents for Moravia in German. In Moravia, Czech disappeared from the records of the Court of the Land in 1690 and from the register of noble estates (Tables of the Land) in 1730, while in Bohemia the corresponding institutions to some extent continued to use Czech.

Although most of the royal patents or ordinances for the Bohemian Lands, emanating from Vienna, were also issued in Czech translation, the agencies of the Viennese government generally fostered Germanization, as did the imperial army, which under Leopold I (1657–1705) made fluent knowledge of German obligatory for every army officer. Czech was losing ground even in those institutions that the estates still dominated. Thus in 1720 the Bohemian diet published its accession to the Pragmatic Sanction exclusively in German. The position of Czech remained strong only in town governments. In fact, German towns, such as Brno (Brünn), corresponded with Czech towns in Czech.

In Silesia the Slav element gained some strength after the Thirty Years' War because most of the religious emigrants were German. Above all, certain ecclesiastical institutions, such as monasteries, were Polonized. Still, German continued as the official language of the central administration and of the duchies of Lower Silesia. In the duchies and towns of Upper Silesia, Czech persisted, despite some impediments, as the official language until the annexation of most of the area by Prussia in 1742.

Most Czech historians, from František Palacký to Josef Pekař and Kamil Krofta, have viewed the consequences of the battle of the White Mountain as an unmitigated disaster from the standpoint of Czech national survival. A minority, however, has maintained that a victory of the Protestant estates would have caused an even more pervasive Germanization, since it would have drawn Bohemia and Moravia most intimately into the politics and culture of Germany. The Habsburg victory, on the contrary, isolated the Czech area from the main body of Germandom and preserved Czech ethnicity in a semidormant state until it was ready to revive once more. While the latter view has naturally appealed to Catholic historians from Václav Tomek to Bohdan Chudoba, it was also advanced by the French Protestant, Ernst Denis in his celebrated *La Bohême depuis la Montagne-Blanche*.[1] The post-World War II Marxist historiography deplores the outcome of the battle of the White Mountain as a reversal for the "progressive" bourgeois forces in favor of the "reactionary" feudal order, and for its destructiveness of Czech cultural values, but remains optimistic about the survival of Czech ethnicity, under almost any circumstances, within the oppressed peasant masses.[2]

Administrative Agencies

The ascendancy of royal power over the authority of the estates was evident in the administrative as well as judicial agencies of the Bohemian Lands, inasmuch as the "highest officials" became primarily agents of the king. This process of "royalization" of the chief administrators and judges reversed the fifteenth-century development by which royal officials had turned into creatures of the estates. The king was now able to appoint officials, and even create new agencies, without the approval of, or consultation with, the diets or the estates. The highest officials no longer swore allegiance to the estates, but only to the king. He fur-

1. (Paris: E. Leroux, 1903), 1:179–80.
2. For a discussion of the historiography of the Bohemian uprising of 1618 and its consequences see František Kavka, *Bílá Hora a české dějiny* (Prague: Státní nakl. politické literatury, 1962), pp. 5–16; Francis Dvornik, *The Slavs in European History and Civilization* (New Brunswick, N.J.: Rutgers University Press, 1962), p. 464, n. 14, for a judicious comment on the older controversy; and most recently, Victor S. Mamatey, "The Battle of the White Mountain as Myth in Czech History," *East European Quarterly* 15 (1981): 335–45.

ther safeguarded their loyalty by appointing them not for life as hitherto, but only for a five-year term which could be extended at his pleasure. Thus the highest administrative agencies of the Land came to resemble the specifically royal agencies, such as the Bohemian Chamber or the Prague Council on Appeals, established by Ferdinand I and maintained since the sixteenth century. The one basis on which the estates could still to some extent influence the officials of the Land was the requirement that the latter had to be appointed from domiciled nobles and members of the diet. The effect of even this provision was weakened by the king's newly acquired power to be the sole grantor of the right of domicile (*inkolát*).

Among the agencies of the Bohemian Lands, the Bohemian Court Chancellery continued to hold a special position, but only as a shadow of its former self. In a formal sense it perpetuated the principle of the unity of the Bohemian state, because its jurisdiction covered specifically all the three Lands of the Bohemian Crown. At the same time, it symbolized the autonomy of the Bohemian state, since the central agencies of the Viennese government did not usually operate in the Bohemian Lands directly but issued their instructions through the Bohemian Chancellery. The substantive character of the Chancellery as an agency of specifically Bohemian state interests, however, was eroded by the royal political absolutism, which largely insulated it from the influence of the Bohemian estates. In addition to the transformation of the supreme chancellor into a royal official, the Chancellery itself was transferred to Vienna in 1624, and the Bohemian officials of the Land—other than the chancellor—were explicitly barred from participating in its work. Moreover, because its personnel (seven members toward the end of the seventeenth century) was insufficient to conduct its business, it borrowed officials from other governmental agencies in Vienna, such as the *Hofrat*, most of whom naturally were not Bohemian nobles. Only during the reign of Charles VI (1711–40) in 1719 was the staff of the Bohemian Chancellery enlarged to eleven to perform adequately its prescribed functions. At the same time, it was divided into a *senatus publicus* for administration and *senatus iudicialis* for the judiciary.

The highest administrative body in Bohemia proper was the Council of the Lieutenancy (*místodržitelská rada*), created in 1623 after the restoration of the highest officials of the Land. Like its predecessor, the Royal Council, it consisted of the highest officials and judges of the Land, as well as additional nobles appointed by the king, and was headed by the supreme count palatine. It differed from the earlier body not only because of the "royalization" of its membership but because it lacked even a theoretical mandate to serve as the king's chief advisory body on Bohemian affairs. That role was taken over by the Bohemian Chancellery in Vienna. The distribution of authority now resembled that in sixteenth-century Hungary between the Council of the Lieutenancy in Pozsony and the Hungarian Chancellery in Vienna. Under the direction of the Bohemian Chancellery, the Council had jurisdiction over all aspects of public administration, as well as certain military affairs. In addition, it exercised limited judicial functions, mostly supplementing the Court of the Land. It operated through three sections: Czech, German, and military.

As for Moravia, Cardinal Francis Dietrichstein administered this Land, with the title of *gubernator*, until 1636. After his death in that year, a new administrative body was created, the Royal Tribunal, also known as the Captaincy of the Land (*zemské hejtmanství*), which became the successor of the Council of the Land existing before the battle of the White Mountain. The Tribunal differed from its Bohemian counterpart, the Council of the Lieutenancy, by its more extensive judicial functions, and by its strongly bureaucratic character. Except for the captain of the Land, who served as its chairman, the highest officials of the Land were initially excluded from participation. Instead, its membership consisted of paid professional bureaucrats: two councilors, a Czech and a German secretary, as well as auxiliary personnel. The highest officials of the Land were not permitted to participate until 1726. A new supreme administrative body, the Chief Office (*Oberamt*), was created in Silesia in 1629 under the chairmanship of the chief captain, who was drawn from among the Silesian princes. With its extensive judicial functions and membership of paid professional royal officials, the *Oberamt* resembled more the Moravian Tribunal than the Bohemian Lieutenancy Council.

The Bohemian Chamber, which had functioned as an avowedly royal agency since 1527, grew in importance up to the end of the seventeenth century with the expansion of indirect taxation, which it largely administered. In disregard of the autonomy of the Lands of the Bohemian Crown, it received orders directly from the Viennese *Hofkammer*, rather than through the Bohemian Chancellery. Attempts to remedy the situation, particularly in the 1680s, were ineffectual. In a similar deviation, the *Hofkammer* maintained direct relations with the master of rents in Moravia and the Silesian Chamber, royal agencies, which in their respective Lands performed functions analogous to those of the Bohemian Chamber in Bohemia proper. In disregard of the unity of the Lands of the Bohemian Crown, by the mid-seventeenth century neither agency was dependent on the Bohemian Chamber.

Judicial Agencies

The assertion of royal power became evident during the century after the battle of the White Mountain also in the judiciary. The king and his designated agents—rather than the estates and their organs—assumed the authority of ultimate decisions in judicial proceedings. Above all, the Bohemian Chancellery, in addition to its other duties, was assigned crucial judicial functions, which in effect made it operate as a supreme court for the Bohemian Lands. The Renewed Land Ordinances bestowed upon it appellate jurisdiction from the Bohemian and Moravian Courts of the Land, which had previously defended the finality of their judgments with intense obstinacy. Shortly thereafter, the Chancellery was empowered to accept appeals from the Prague Council on Appeals, and—in a particularly sweeping measure—to review sentences of any court in the Bohemian Lands when capital punishment was involved. At the next lower echelon, the Prague Council on Appeals—clearly an organ of royal power—added a general supervisory role over town courts in all the Bohemian Lands to its earlier appellate jurisdiction over them. An important new departure, originating in 1644, was the gradual expansion of the Council's supervisory role to include manorial courts, an expansion that reflected the slowly evolving royal concern for the subject peasants.

The Bohemian and Moravian Courts of the Land, still strongholds of the estates, were not only placed under the appellate jurisdiction of the Bohemian Chancellery but also faced the rise of competing judicial authority in the "royalized" Lieutenancy Council in Bohemia and the Royal Tribunal in Moravia. In Silesia the general rule in this period was that appeals from the courts of the individual duchies went to the Prague Council on Appeals in criminal cases and to the Bohemian Chancellery in civil matters.

FUNCTIONS OF THE ESTATES

The Diets

The diets of the individual Lands remained the chief instruments of the estates' political influence, although they retained a mere fraction of the power they had enjoyed in the past two centuries. According to the Renewed Land Ordinances (1627–28) the convocation of the diets was reserved to the king under the penalty of death. The king's agents, the royal commissioners, henceforth controlled the diets' proceedings. The ordinances denied the Bohemian estates the right of legislative initiative entirely, while the Moravian ones could exercise it only in minor—mostly police—matters. Subsequently the royal *declaratoria* of 1640 restored legislative initiative to the Bohemian diet, but likewise only in minor matters. The diets could not reject royal propositions, but only consider the manner of their implementation. As a major concession, the Renewed Land Ordinances still recognized the estates' right to approve all new taxes, although the exercise of this right was again circumscribed: it could not serve as an occasion for imposing "improper" conditions encroaching on the king's authority, or exacting new rights or privileges for the estates.

The composition of the Bohemian diet was altered by the addition of the *curia* of the prelates (Catholic bishops, provosts, and abbots), who became the first estate. In the Moravian diet the prelates rose to the first rank from a lowly third place. The weight of the lower nobility (*rytíři*) declined catastrophically, further differentiating the sociopolitical structure of the Bohemian Lands from that of Hungary or Poland. Compared with 1,128 families belonging to this estate before the battle of the White Mountain, only 238 were left by the end of the seventeenth century. Aside from punitive actions following the Habsburg victory, the decline of the *rytíři* was due to economics: their inability to compete with the latifundia of the higher nobles (*páni*) during the agricultural depression following the Thirty Years' War. The political power of the towns was also drastically curtailed. Only six towns were entitled to full participation in the Bohemian diet after 1627. The number was gradually reduced by 1709 to the three towns of Prague. In Moravia representatives of all the seven royal towns could attend the diet, but until 1711 they had to stand during the proceedings. The most serious setback was the reduction in both diets of the town representatives to a single joint vote, so that the weight of the entire estate of towns equaled that of a single baron or knight. Although most discussions occurred in the four *curiae* meeting separately, voting in this period took place in joint sessions. As a result of these changes and reforms, the Bohemian and Moravian diets were clearly dominated by the higher nobles and the prelates.

In Silesia the princely or central diet was not subjected to immediate reforms after 1620. Gradually, however, its legislative initiative was curtailed, and by 1726 it was virtually reduced to considering royal propositions.

The diets' legislative activity still ranged widely, covering commercial and other economic regulations, public works, police measures, and public health. Taxation remained the most important area. The kings still sought the diets' consent for the direct "extraordinary" tax, which became known as the Contribution and constituted the main revenue of the state. During most of the seventeenth century, the kings also usually sought the approval of the diets for new types of taxes. The diets' consent was by no means automatic. The estates engaged in negotiations with the king or his commissioners, and often granted less than the royal proposition asked for. For instance, in 1631 instead of the requested 360,000 florins in military Contribution, the Bohemian diet granted only half of that sum. The estates tended to oppose, in particular, requests for sales taxes, partly because they affected the nobility as much as the commoners, and partly because the kings were likely to convert them after a time into permanent revenue without any further reference to the diets (the so-called *incameration*). Thus the Bohemian diet successfully resisted the imposition of an array of indirect taxes on flour, beverages, meat, and leather in the late 1670s. Characteristically, the estates no longer adopted the methods of direct refusal, but rather a more cautious one of evasion and procrastination.

Not until the end of the seventeenth century did the king proceed to introduce certain taxes without consulting the diets. After the archbishop of Prague had challenged this practice in the Bohemian diet in 1692, a royal rescript of 1694 declared that the diets' role in fiscal affairs was a matter of royal favor, and not of inherent right. The king thus proclaimed imposition of taxes a part of his absolute power. Nevertheless, the diets' consent was still requested for the most important direct tax (the Contribution) and some of the older indirect taxes. The estates' power in the fiscal field, though further weakened, had not yet vanished in the opening decades of the eighteenth century.

The Committees of the Land

The estates attempted with some success to use their political influence in the diet, and particularly their role in the fiscal field, to recreate and maintain an administrative apparatus of their own that would partly compensate them for the "royalization" of the traditional administrative organs of the Lands. In Bohemia they had a nucleus of such an agency in the four tax collectors of the Land, one chosen from each estate, who managed the collection of the Contribution. In addition, in 1654 the diet created a permanent Chief Commission of twelve members, which functioned between its sessions mostly to prepare a new land register (*berní role*). After the commission's termination in 1674, the estates could create merely ad hoc special commissions. Not until 1714 did the king allow them to form a new permanent organ to assure administrative continuity between legislative sessions. Known as the Committee of the Land (*zemský výbor*), this body took over the collection of the Contribution, whereupon the tax collectors' office was abolished. The Moravian estates initially lacked any administrative organs of their own. Even the Contribution was collected by the royal master of rents. After 1656 the estates assumed control over their fiscal responsibilities through periodically elected deputations, which directed collectors in each circuit. Finally, as early as 1686, the diet received permission to establish a permanent Committee of the Land.

While in Silesia the Contribution remained based on the traditional principle of declared value of certain properties, in Bohemia and Moravia it assumed the form of a tax on land. New land registers were prepared, the Tax Roll (*berní role*) in Bohemia in 1654 and the *cadaster* in Moravia in 1664. The diets voted lump sums, which were then pro-rated according to the number of taxation units in each Land. Initially only the peasants and the townsmen paid, while the nobles were ex-empted. The tax was divided according to use into three parts: for mil-itary purposes (*militare*), for the king personally (*camerale*), and—by far the smallest amount—for the estates' administrative needs (*domesticale*, later called the Domestic Fund). As early as the 1660s the yield of the tax proved insufficient. It was then supplemented in Moravia by a tax on houses and chimneys, and in 1697 the nobility began to contribute according to the hides and chimneys of subject peasants. The Bohe-mian nobility had started to pay a portion of the tax already in 1667, and its share became known in 1706 as the "extraordinary" Contribu-tion, while the peasants paid the larger "ordinary" Contribution.

It Bohemia the military share of the Contribution remained under 1,000,000 florins in the seventeenth century, then rose rapidly to 3,000,000 in the 1730s. In Moravia it increased correspondingly from 300,000 to 900,000 florins. At times, the estates preferred to furnish and equip recruits, in which case a certain amount was subtracted from the Contribution for each recruit. At other times, the king himself re-quested directly a number of recruits. The Bohemian diet, for instance, was asked for 3,900 men in 1683, and for 6,500 in 1704. Although the Bohemian Lands supported considerable contingents, the latter were dispersed throughout a single "imperial" army, and thus the Bohemian state had no distinctive military force of its own.

Early in the eighteenth century the Bohemian and Moravian estates had an opportunity to express their political aspirations through the work of two commissions, one in each Land, appointed to revise the Renewed Land Ordinances. Active mainly in 1709–10 and the early 1720s, the commissions aimed at a codification of laws, merging the ordinances with subsequent legislation, above all the edicts of the Bo-hemian Chancellery. Out of the planned nine sections of the new code, they eventually drafted only one, concerned with constitutional law (*ius publicum*). The draft sought to eliminate humiliating references to the uprising of 1618, and to stress the rights and privileges of the estates, as well as the powers of the diets. The *elaboratum Bohemicum* (the pro-posals of the Bohemian commission) dwelt on the unification of Bo-hemian and Moravian laws, and on the traditional symbols of the unity of the Bohemian Lands, such as the institution of the occasional Gen-eral Diet, which had fallen into disuse after the battle of the White Mountain. This unfinished work of legal codification evoked the clear-est public assertion of the traditional rights of the estates, and of the integrity of the Bohemian state, between the imposition of royal absolutism in the 1620s and the resistance to Joseph II's reforms late in the eighteenth century.

Circuits (Kraje) and Towns

The circuit (kraj) became firmly established in the seventeenth century as a unit of district administration in the Bohemian Lands except in Silesia, where the territorial organization of the individual duchies obviated the need for such subdivisions. There were fourteen to fifteen kraje in Bohemia before 1714, twelve afterward. Two captains, a baron and a knight, continued to head each kraj; except for emergencies, they were to make decisions jointly. Their terms of office ran for a year with frequent reappointments until 1685, when a five-year term became customary. They maintained their offices on their own manors, so that the kraj had no permanent center. While earlier the kraj captains had functioned primarily as agents of the estates, after 1620 they came under joint control of the king and the estates. Although still drawn from the nobility domiciled in the kraj, they were appointed by the king and made responsible to the Lieutenancy Council. During the seventeenth century the instructions defining their responsibilities were issued by the estates; after the turn of the century only by the king. In Moravia the earlier rudimentary kraj organization disappeared in 1621–28, but in 1637 five kraje were reestablished on the Bohemian model, and their number was raised to six by the reform of 1714. A single captain, usually a baron, headed each kraj, and was, in turn, responsible to the Royal Tribunal.

The kraj captains performed similar functions in both Bohemia and Moravia. Their instructions assigned them police duties, including suppression of heterodoxy and conspiracies against the king, as well as safeguarding of public health, roads, weights and measures, and coins. As a reflection of new social policy, they became responsible, on behalf of the king, for the protection of subject peasants. The captains' power also reached into the fiscal and military fields. They supervised the estates' agents collecting the Contribution, as well as the fiscal officials on the manors. They oversaw the furnishing of recruits by the estates in lieu of the Contribution, and the provisioning and quartering of troops.

The Renewed Land Ordinance for Bohemia reaffirmed the king's unfavorable view of the kraj assemblies of the nobility, and after 1648 no such meetings took place. This eliminated with finality the institutional framework for an evolution of the Bohemian kraj, after the model of the Hungarian county, into a unit of noble self-government and autonomy. The precipitous numerical decline of the lower nobility in any case was undermining the social basis for such a development.

The king's authority in royal towns continued to increase as well. In 1621 the appointed royal *rychtář* (judge) reappeared in the Bohemian towns, and was newly introduced into the towns of Moravia. The conditions of Bohemian and Moravian towns were further equalized by the adoption in Moravia of the legal code of Pavel z Koldína, observed by the Bohemian towns since 1579. Instructions issued for the royal *rychtáři* in the 1650s stressed their position of primacy in the town councils, and their oversight of public order, the town finances, and the observance of royal rights and interests. Increases in the subchamberlain's power, mainly after 1688, also diminished the urban self-government. Above all, he was charged with the periodic renewals of the town councils. The subchamberlain himself was losing his status as an estates' representative and turning into an agent of the Bohemian Chamber and the Chancellery. Early in the eighteenth century the towns also lost control over their own financial affairs. In 1706 royal officials—called "economic inspectors"—were appointed in Bohemia to manage town finances. In Moravian towns this function was assigned in 1724 to the Economic Directorates (*Wirtschaftsdirektion*) responsible to the Imperial Economic Commission in Brno. The royal and princely towns of Silesia also received the institution of the royal *rychtář*, but retained their fiscal autonomy.

Manors

The manor remained the basic unit of local government. The apparatus of seigneurial officials grew more elaborate, including on larger estates a specialist for legal and judicial matters, the justiciar. The manor's "economic office" (*hospodářský úřad*, *Wirtschaftsamt*), aside from economic management, performed public functions deriving from the seigneurial authority in local police, judiciary, taxation, and military matters.

In Bohemia and Moravia the Renewed Land Ordinances reconfirmed the system of serfdom; in Silesia a law of the princely diet did the same in 1652. After 1620 a distinction emerged between the "settled" peasants with hereditary right to their homesteads and the "nonsettled" ones, who could be removed from their land at any time. Both categories were equally enserfed. Without the seigneur's permission the peasants could not migrate, marry, have their children educated or apprenticed outside the manor, incur major debts, or dispose of property by sale or testament. Their children had to serve on the demesne for a minimal compensation. It was illegal for the peasants to bear arms or to hunt. The serfs' heaviest economic obligation was the compulsory unpaid labor (*robota*) on the demesne. In addition, they paid the seigneur dues in money and in kind. Typically they were required to purchase certain goods or services only from their seigneur, or sell others exclusively to him.

While the onset of second serfdom in the late sixteenth century had been connected with price revolution favoring agricultural products, its culmination in the 1670s and 1680s, to the contrary, was caused mainly by the agricultural depression following the Thirty Years' War. Seeking to lower production costs by minimizing expenditures on wages, implements, and draft animals, the seigneurs substituted heavier reliance on the serfs' unpaid labor and tools. In order to compensate for the shrinkage in extramanorial markets, they stepped up reliance on compulsory purchases by their own subjects. The intense dependence on compulsory labor opened a vicious cycle of declining labor productivity and consequent application of even heavier exactions.

The peasant situation in the Bohemian Lands contrasted unfavorably not only with Upper and Lower Austria, where serfdom remained virtually nonexistent, but also with Inner Austria, where the mitigative intervention of state authority into the seigneur-serf relations dated to the sixteenth century. On the other hand, it was less oppressive than in Poland, the classical land of neo-serfdom, since the seigneurs, unable to depend on exports, were concerned with sustaining the capacity of their rural and urban subjects to provide internal markets.

Additional relief was forthcoming through an incipient intervention of central political authorities, breaching the monopoly of seigneurial authority over the peasants. Though not very effective in the late seventeenth century, these measures were gaining significance after the turn of the century. Thus in a still largely symbolic gesture, the Moravian and Silesian diets in the 1650s placed the peasants under the protection of the officialdom of the *kraj* and of the Land. After a major peasant uprising in Bohemia, the king for the first time intervened in the seigneur-serf relations by the patent of 1680, which granted the serfs a limited recourse of appeal to the *kraj* captains. More seriously, the royal patents of 1717 for Bohemia and Moravia gave peasants the right to appeal successively to the following authorities: the seigneur himself, the *kraj* captain, the Lieutenancy or the Tribunal, and finally the Bohemian Chancellery. A new patent of 1738 ordered the *kraj* captains to protect peasant petitioners from seigneurial reprisals, and established within the Lieutenancy Council a commission to process peasants' complaints.

In a parallel process, the exercise of criminal justice by manorial courts came gradually under the supervision of king's officials. From 1644, all criminal sentences, based on doubtful evidence, had to be examined by the Prague Council on Appeals. After 1707, subject peasants could appeal any criminal verdict. The patent of 1738 extended protection to the life and health of peasants under arrest. This did not infringe, however, on the patrimonial jurisdiction of the seigneurs in cases of minor civil claims and petty criminal offenses.

The patent of 1680 for Bohemia introduced the first royal regulation of the *robota*. The maximum amount was set at three days per week, except at harvest time when the seigneur could require six days per week and up to sixteen hours per day. The same regulations were applied to Moravia by the patent of 1713, and reconfirmed for both Lands by the patents of 1717 and 1738.

ECONOMIC LIFE[3]

Agriculture

Agricultural production in the Bohemian Lands suffered enormously from the destructiveness of the Thirty Years' War. Because of heavy population losses, a large proportion of peasant lands remained uncultivated. Rough estimates of the population sizes before and after the war indicate a reduction from 1,700,000 to 950,000 for Bohemia, and from 900,000 to 600,000 for Moravia. Aside from direct effects of warfare, the losses resulted from famine, epidemics, and flight. Official surveys determined that 25 percent of peasant lands were still abandoned in Moravia in the 1650s, and 20 percent in Bohemia in the 1680s. Agricultural output did not fully recover until the end of the seventeenth century.

The recovery was slowed down by a severe agricultural depression which followed the Thirty Years' War. The crisis was alleviated only in 1685–1714 when grain prices on the Prague market on the average exceeded the levels of 1655–84 by 50 percent. Subsequently the price rise continued more slowly, amounting to 15 percent between 1715 and 1744.

Techniques of agricultural production failed to improve under the intensified second serfdom, with its reliance on the inefficient peasant forced labor. In fact, some retrogression occurred. Thus incipient movements toward crop rotation, evident late in the sixteenth century, were stifled, and the three-field system prevailed completely from the mid-seventeenth to the mid-eighteenth century. As a result, harvests averaged only 2.5 times the amount of grain planted on the royal es-

---

3. Economic data in this section are derived from *Přehled československých dějin* (Prague: Československá akademie věd, 1958), 1:407–43, 476–508; František Kavka and Josef Válka, *Dějiny Československa. 2. 1437–1781*, 2d ed. (Prague: SPN, [1970]), pp. 170–237; Eduard Maur's candidate dissertation *Český komorní velkostatek v druhé polovině 17. století: Příspěvek k otázce 'druhého nevolnictví' v českých zemích* (Prague: Universita Karlova, 1972–73) 2 vols., also published in an abbreviated form in 1975 (Prague: Universita Karlova); Arnošt Klíma, *Manufakturní období v Čechách* (Prague: Československá akademie věd, 1955), pp. 19–253; *Přehled dějin Československa* (Prague: Academia, 1982), I/2:220–36.

tates, administered by the Bohemian Chamber, and probably not much more on private noble estates. The yields were higher on the more carefully cultivated peasant lands.

In agricultural organization, increases in the size of the demesne estates continued in the second half of the seventeenth century. The latifundia of the great nobles absorbed not only parts of abandoned peasant lands but also the bankrupt estates of the lower nobles, who lacked sufficient subject peasantry to withstand the postwar agricultural crisis. It was this process that led to the virtual disappearance of the small landed nobility by the early eighteenth century. By that time the demesne's share of total arable land on a manor averaged between one-fifth and one-quarter. In addition, the demesne, in most instances, included just about all the forests and pastures on a manor.

The crop production on the enlarged demesne estates was destined more for the domestic than the foreign market. Emphasis remained on the traditional grains, although the assortment changed significantly in the second half of the seventeenth century. Reflecting increased use of barley by seigneurial breweries, the output of barley expanded at the expense of wheat. Cutbacks in draft horses on the demesne estates, typical of the intensified second serfdom, accounted for a decline in oats cultivation. The destruction of vineyards in the Thirty Years' War drastically reduced wine production, which recovered slowly in Moravia but failed to do so in Bohemia. Increased demand for wool by cloth producers stimulated sheep raising, perhaps the most distinctive new departure in seigneurial entrepreneurship during the second half of the seventeenth century. Late in the century income from sheep raising on demesne estates constituted typically 60 percent of the total from animal raising. The rest of this income was made up by sales of butter and milk (24 percent), beef and pork (6 percent each), and poultry (4 percent).

Among other entrepreneurial activities of manorial seigneurs, pisciculture declined, owing to damages to ponds in the Thirty Years' War, and failed to recover its sixteenth-century importance. With intensified exploitation of forests on the demesnes, lumbering emerged as a major source of manorial income by the early eighteenth century. Breweries kept and even increased their importance in the manorial economy, and came close to furnishing half the total income.

Crafts, Industry, and Mining

Despite its destructiveness, the Thirty Years' War stimulated a short-range prosperity in some branches of nonagricultural production, such as iron, armaments, and textiles (for army uniforms). In the long run, however, the towns suffered greater setbacks than the countryside. Most suburbs were destroyed, houses were demolished even within the city walls, and enterprising Protestant burghers were forced to emigrate. The royal free towns were affected most seriously. In disfavor of their Habsburg masters for their part in the 1618 uprising, and stripped of political influence, they failed to reach their pre-1620 population or number of craftsmen even as late as the first half of the eighteenth century. A large proportion of their inhabitants were engaged in agriculture. In Prague, for instance, 1,200 artisans still remained in 1620, but by 1674 their number had diminished to 355. Craft production, rigidly controlled by conservative guilds, showed little capacity for improvement or innovation. The guilds concentrated on restricting the number of craftsmen by prescribing long periods of apprenticeship and journeyman status as well as time-consuming and costly masterpieces. Frequently, definite limits were imposed on the number of masters.

In the seventeenth and early eighteenth centuries the subject towns and even the manors offered more favorable settings for industrial and craft development. Assisted by their seigneurs to evolve into manorial economic centers, the subject towns could provide the meeting ground for the merchants and individual producers. This function was essential to the organizational network of the putting-out system, which by the end of the seventeenth century paved the way for the first manufactories. Not surprisingly, certain subject towns exceeded royal free towns in population and output of goods.

Textiles continued to lead the way in the development of new modes of production. In particular, linen production was largely emancipated from the guilds after the Thirty Years' War, and fell under the sway of the putting-out system, organized mainly by Silesian, Saxon, and English merchant firms. In the countryside the manorial authorities became receptive to the system; they allowed freedom of operation to the merchants' agents, sold them spun flax obtained as dues from the serfs, and occasionally wished to act as intermediaries between the serfs and the commercial firms. Particularly in northern Bohemia, thousands of weavers worked for the merchants, and the putting-out system in linen production occasionally advanced into the form of dispersed manufactory, with certain finishing operations performed in a single plant.

Woolen cloth even after the Thirty Years' War was produced mainly within the traditional guilds. The master craftsmen raised capital and acquired raw materials independently of the cloth merchants. One of their major concerns was to prevent exports of the finer types of wool in order to keep them available for domestic processing. Toward the end of the seventeenth century, however, woolen cloth fabrication witnessed the emergence of the most advanced contemporary form of production, the centralized manufactory, in which not only the finishing work but more basic operations, such as weaving, were performed in a single plant. In part stimulated by military demand for woolen cloth, most of these manufactories sprang up on noble estates, whose seigneurs possessed sufficient capital, sources of energy, and raw materials, as well as serf labor, for unskilled tasks. While in Lower and Upper Austria the first textile manufactories had appeared in the 1660s and 1670s, the four earliest ones in Bohemia were established between 1697 and 1717, and two in Moravia in 1701 and 1704. During the 1720s seven more manufactories sprang up in Bohemia alone, all producing woolen cloth, except for one silk and one cotton manufactory. As a special concession, the government permitted employment of non-Catholic specialists from Holland and England in these enterprises.

Among other important centers of nonguild production were the glassworks. Produced in small enterprises, especially in northern Bohemia proper, Bohemian glass greatly improved in quality during the second half of the seventeenth century and—particularly painted and cut glass—became world famous. After the turn of the century it constituted the second most important article of industrial export from Bohemia, although lagging far behind textiles. For instance, in 1735 its export amounted in value to 97,000 florins compared with 1,300,000 florins' worth of linen and yarn. Paper production continued in small paper mills—often owned by noble seigneurs—in quantities sufficient for export as well as domestic consumption. In Bohemia sixty papermills operated at the end of the seventeenth century, and seventy-three by 1746. In contrast to glass and paper production, mining and metallurgy were in deep decline from the mid-seventeenth to the mid-eighteenth century. Only iron output based on traditional technology maintained its modest level in small enterprises, scattered within areas such as Brdy and the Bohemian-Moravian Highlands.

To foster new modes of production, particularly the manufactories, it was essential to limit the powers of the guilds. Although the Lieutenancy Council in Bohemia urged such measures as early as 1699, Vienna long hesitated to intervene, regarding the artisan organizations as important means of economic and social control, especially in preventing labor disturbances. At last in 1731 a general patent placed the guilds under state supervision through special inspectors. It abrogated their power either to restrict the number of employees for individual masters or to prevent the opening of new enterprises. In 1739 a set of General Articles for guilds revoked their authority to set uniform prices and thus eliminate competition. Nevertheless, during the first half of the eighteenth century, in most areas, guild craftsmen were responsible for greater output than producers outside the guilds.

Trade

In the second half of the seventeenth and early eighteenth centuries, the conditions of external trade of the Bohemian Lands—especially of Bohemia proper and Moravia—provided fertile ground for mercantilist criticism. Exports involved mainly raw materials, such as wool and grain, or semifinished goods, such as unbleached linen and paper. One major exception among finished goods was glass, which found its way to most European countries, the Ottoman Empire, and North America.[4] Imports included highly processed articles, such as woolen cloth, finished linen, iron and steel implements, and chemical dyes.

Appeals to the emperor by two burghers of Brno, Pavel Morgenthaler in 1653 and Fabián Malivský ten years later, voiced, for the first time in the Bohemian Lands, proposals for trade reforms along the mercantilist lines. Independently of each other, they argued that the country was weakened by imports of goods that could be produced domestically. Characteristically they urged development of new industries with the help of foreign specialists, combined with prohibition on imports of corresponding goods. By the 1690s, government agencies in Prague were beginning to voice similar opinions. The Bohemian Chamber asked for high tariffs on foreign textiles in 1690, and in 1693 for a compensatory development of domestic woolen, silk, and linen manufactories. In 1699 the Bohemian Lieutenancy Council put forth a comprehensive plan for customs reform, including high tariffs on imports of finished goods and on exports of raw materials, and low tariffs on imports of raw materials and exports of finished goods. A special commission, established to stimulate trade in Bohemia, urged similar measures in the early eighteenth century.

But some forty years and three quarters of a century, respectively, elapsed from the time the mercantilist concepts were broached by administrative agencies and private individuals before the government began to implement them effectively in trade regulations. An imperial edict of 1728 increased substantially the custom duties on some imported goods. In the case of coarse woolen cloth, the new rate represented 100 percent of value. Another edict, applying to the internal market, abolished in 1735 the excise tax on domestic products, while retaining it for imported goods. The comprehensive tariff of 1737 established high duties on imports and low ones on exports. For instance, woolen cloth exported from Bohemia was to pay only one-sixth of the duty charged for the same commodity imported into Bohemia from

4. Stocks of Czech glass were kept by merchants in Baltimore and New York in the early eighteenth century; see Klíma, *Manufakturní období v Čechách*, p. 156.

abroad. A more powerful stimulus to industrialize Bohemia and Moravia was to be provided by the loss of Silesia to Prussia in 1742. On the whole, during the period 1620–1740 the Bohemian Lands, like the rest of East Central Europe, fell economically even farther behind Western Europe.

The Slovenes

THE ESTABLISHMENT OF ABSOLUTISM

The Counter Reformation and Slovene National Life

The Counter Reformation and absolutism prevailed in the Slovene area in the 1620s, at the same time as in the Bohemian Lands. The victory, however, was not so abrupt, resulting rather from a gradual development from the last quarter of the sixteenth century. The climax came in August 1628, when the prince ordered the nobility of Inner Austria, the only class still free to profess Protestantism, either to return to the Catholic faith or face exile within a year. As a reward for their loyalty during the Hungarian (1604–6) and the Bohemian (1618–20) uprisings, the nobles who sold their estates prior to emigration were exempt from the regular sales tax owed to the prince. There was little resistance. Some chose to convert, but a large number emigrated, mainly to Hungary or southern Germany. According to best estimates, about 754 noble families left; according to incomplete records, 250 were from Styria, 160 from Carinthia, and 104 from Carniola. Virtually all of them had departed by 1631.

The victory of the Counter Reformation also marked the end of the era when the prince shared basic political power with the estates. Subsequently the latter could no longer defy him on matters of taxation, or confront him with effective military forces of their own. All significant political decisions were now in the hands of the prince; yet until the 1740s the new absolutist regime did not dismantle the preexisting administrative and judicial institutions created and maintained by the estates. Instead, the prince used them as instruments of his own will, serving his own objectives. The basic shift of political power was not even expressed in formal documents, comparable to the Renewed Land Ordinances for Bohemia and Moravia. The formal legal order remained unaltered. The estates opposed any change, assuming that reforms would be to their disadvantage, and the princes condoned the existing legal machinery once they achieved in the 1620s an effective de facto control of its operation.

From the standpoint of ethnic demography, as in Silesia, the Counter Reformation resulted in a weakening of the German influence in the Slovene area. The Italians gained considerably, especially in towns where they arrived as artists, doctors, and lawyers. A greater cultural role for Italy was favored by the ban on study at German Protestant universities, a greater economic role by the decline of the South German mercantile companies. The bishop of Ljubljana recorded in 1631 that the common people in the town spoke Slovene, the public authorities used German, and the educated people mostly Italian. While the peasantry remained Slovene speaking, the evidence based on the language of oaths administered in towns indicates that the higher officials were German, the lower ones Slovene, and the burghers a mixture of Germans, Italians, and Slovenes. The nobility remained predominantly German, but the existence of a number of feudal oaths in Slovene indicates that, until the mid-eighteenth century, a segment of the lower nobility did not know German. In this period trials involving Slovene peasants were conducted in Slovene before patrimonial and ecclesiastical courts, and in Carniola also before the captain of the Land and the *vicedom*. The Italian impact was most pronounced and lasting in Gorizia, where by the early seventeenth century Italian permanently displaced German as the language of the upper classes. The peasantry even there, of course, was and remained mostly Slovene speaking.

Printing of Slovene literature ceased entirely after 1615, following a period of lively production, first under Protestant, then—and to a lesser extent—under Catholic auspices. Until 1672 Slovene was used only in manuscript literature, mostly ecclesiastical, and in manuscript translations of a few official regulations, such as a new version of the legal code concerning the vineyards (*Gorske Bukve*) in 1646. Subsequently, printing in Slovene resumed, involving mostly aids to Catholic clergy for their pastoral work. In 1715, however, the Slovene grammar of Adam Bohorič, dating to the Protestant period, was reprinted, still anonymously, and in 1726 the first book for the laity appeared, a sixteen-page calendar in thirty thousand copies printed in Augsburg. It continued as an annual publication.

Of the approximately eighty elementary schools operating in the Slovene territory in 1600–1750, most used German, the rest—in Gorizia—Italian. Slovene was admitted to some extent only in religious instructions. Prior to 1742 the only Slovene textbook was a reader used from 1725 by the Protestants in the Prekmurje region of Hungary. Of the five *gymnasia* in the Slovene area, three (Ljubljana, Ruše near Maribor, Klagenfurt) used German, and two (Trieste and Gorizia) Italian, as an auxiliary language in the first grade. Latin prevailed in the other grades, as well as in the Jesuit University of Graz, composed of the faculties of philosophy and theology.

Compared with its lively manifestation in the Protestant period, the Slovene ethnic consciousness was rarely expressed in an articulate fashion during the Counter Reformation. A conspicuous exception was the writings of the Capuchin monk Hippolytus (1667–1722), who urged the use of Slovene in the educational system. The established cultural and social elite, represented by Johann Ludwig Schoenleben (1618–81) and Johann Weigand Valvasor (1641–93), wrote in Latin or German. Territorial patriotism centered on a particular Land, combined with loyalty to the Habsburg dynasty and pride in the Holy Roman Empire. Both the German and Slovene ("Carniolan") languages were considered native, and the gap between them bridged by a theory, originating in the Humanist period, that the Slovenes were descendants of the Germanic Vandals, and thus the German nobles and the Slovene peasants formed one organic community. Even the Italian nobles of Gorizia requested a rescript which in 1626 affirmed the inclusion of their Land in the Holy Roman Empire.

An incident in the mid-seventeenth century sheds light on the contemporary view of ethnic relations. A priest born in Ljubljana was considered for appointment in the Roman college of Saint Jerome, reserved for the "Illyrian"—that is, South Slav—clergy. To an official inquiry from Rome the estates of Carniola responded in 1651 that Carniola was part of Germany, not of Illyria; hence the candidate did not qualify. The famous Croatian priest, Jurij Križanić, also consulted in the case, initially in 1652 upheld the view. Under pressure from an ecclesiastical superior, however, he reconsidered and declared the Carniolans to be part of the Illyrians, that is South Slavs. He added that it would have been even less proper to consider them Germans than to classify the inhabitants of Dalmatia as Italians.

The Slovenes lived under distinctive conditions in the Prekmurje region of southwestern Hungary. In the seventeenth century the area lay so near the border of the Ottoman Empire that at times the Turks asserted their authority there together with the Hungarian agencies. Protestantism, the dominant religion by 1600, survived the Counter Reformation, though on a diminishing scale. Weakened by the waves of persecution in the 1620s and 1670s, it suffered a crippling setback in 1681 when the diet of Sopron (Ödenburg) did not sanction a single Protestant church in the area.[5] After new repression the Protestants shrank to about one-quarter of the population in the 1730s. The nobles, unlike those of Inner Austria, preserved their earlier rights and privileges, not only in relation to the royal authority but also with respect to their serfs. As a result, the peasants remained in a tighter per-

5. On the religious decrees of the diet of Sopron see pp. 139–40.

sonal bondage and under heavier economic obligations than in other Slovene areas.

The Administrative Organs of Inner Austria

With the election of Ferdinand II as emperor in 1619 and the full establishment and reestablishment of the central administration in Vienna, Inner Austria lost a resident prince, but not its status as a distinct political entity. The central princely agencies for Inner Austria remained in Graz, with the exception of the *Hofkanzlei*, which was transferred to Vienna. In the Viennese Austrian *Hofkanzlei*, newly organized in 1620, a section for Inner Austria functioned as the sole intermediary between the prince (now in Vienna) and the Inner Austrian Lands. As such, it was charged with transmitting instructions from the other central governmental agencies in Vienna. The function of the Inner Austrian section resembled that of the Bohemian Chancellery, and from the administration point of view the Lands of Inner Austria formed an entity akin to the Bohemian Lands, though lacking a comparable historical tradition.

The most important agency in Graz was initially the *Geheime Rat*, which served as the principal channel of communication between the Viennese *Hofkanzlei* and the other agencies in Graz, especially the *Hofkammer* and the *Hofkriegsrat*. Gradually, it was overshadowed by its competitor the *Regierung* (a lineal descendant of the sixteenth-century *Regiment*), which was responsible for public administration and performed an important judicial function as a trial court for certain classes of individuals, especially government officials, and an appellate court from certain courts in the individual Lands. The Graz *Hofkriegsrat* maintained its responsibility, in conjunction with the estates of Carinthia. Carniola, and Styria, for the defense and administration of the Croatian and Slavonian military borders. The Inner Austrian *Hofkammer* enjoyed, at least formally, a greater degree of independence from the Viennese *Hofkammer* than the corresponding agencies in the Bohemian Lands, including the Bohemian Chamber.

Reforms under Joseph I in 1705–9 brought Inner Austria's administrative status more closely in line with the post-1620 situation in Bohemia. The Graz *Hofkammer* was directly subordinated to the Viennese *Hofkammer,* and the Graz *Hofkriegsrat* transformed into a mere branch office (*Kriegsstelle*) for Inner Austria of the Viennese *Hofkriegsrat.*

The territory of Inner Austria did not change substantially in this period. The one exception was the sale of the Gradisca region of Gorizia by Ferdinand III to Prince Eggenberg in 1647. Subsequently this essentially Italian-inhabited area returned to Habsburg rule in 1717 and reunited with Gorizia in 1754.

Fiscal and Military Organization

The system of public finance in the Slovene area continued to be divided into two basic components—the ordinary income, which was controlled directly by the prince, and the Contribution, a new seventeenth-century designation for the former "extraordinary" tax. The Contribution, as well as several lesser taxes, still required in principle the approval of the estates. The estates were also charged with its collection, while the prince's agents gathered the ordinary or cameral income.

Although the contribution was still based on the mid-sixteenth-century registers of income from property (*Gültbücher*), estimating the seigneurs' yield from peasant dues, by the early seventeenth century this tax had reached 400 perent of the original rate. At that time, in addition to this "ordinary" Contribution (the original "extraordinary" tax) a new tax called "extraordinary" Contribution (*extraordinari, Zinsgulden*) was introduced. Based on the *Gültbücher,* its rate also increased, reaching by the first half of the eighteenth century a level between four and six times the original sixteenth-century assessment. The right of the estates to approve the Contribution was in practice limited to negotiations over the amount of the "extraordinary" part. The "ordinary" Contribution had been paid only by the peasants since 1606. The nobles also succeeded in shifting gradually to their serfs the entire burden of the "extraordinary" Contribution. Until 1667 they paid a share—rarely the major part—of the quota; between 1668 and 1728 very little or nothing; and subsequently nothing at all. The seigneurs remained responsible for the delivery of the total amount of the tax from their manors. The towns, which also paid the Contribution, selected their own methods of assessment, such as a tax on houses or on trades, an indirect tax, or payment from other revenues at the town's disposal.

Early in the eighteenth century the estates' fiscal power was further weakened by the requirement that the Contribution be granted for several years in advance. After 1714, grants for ten-year periods (the so-called decennial recessions) became common. The estates continued to retain a portion of direct taxes for special purposes, chiefly the maintenance of the military borders and of their own administrative apparatus.

The cameral income remained in the Slovene area in this period of almost equal significance with the Contribution. Of the older sources, the regalian rights in mining were particularly lucrative, primarily because of the mercury mine in Idrija, jointly administered by the Inner Austrian *Hofkammer* and a special commission in Vienna. After 1670, when the prince's agents directly operated the facility, the annual revenue fluctuated between one and two hundred thousand florins. In 1674–

77 it represented 12.5 percent of the cameral income, and 4 percent of the entire state revenue from the Habsburg Lands. Of the new types of cameral revenue the most burdensome for the common people were the indirect taxes on the production and sale of foodstuffs and other consumer goods. In the seventeenth century the princely authorities found them particularly attractive because they did not require the diets' consent. State monopolies represented another new approach to revenue raising. Private merchants frustrated attempts by the state to take over the salt trade, but the government, after an initial failure in 1670, did secure a monopoly of tobacco processing and sale in 1723, as well as of the sale of gunpowder. Early in the eighteenth century the total cameral income from Inner Austria was 780,000 florins (in 1717), compared with the total Contribution of 911,000 (in 1719).

After the peace with Venice in 1617 the Slovene territory was spared major warfare. The Turkish danger, however, continued until the peace of Karlowitz in 1699, and raids by the Turks into southern Styria, emanating largely from Kanizsa, were common in 1640–81. Subsequently, the same area suffered from penetration of the Hungarian insurgents, the *kurucok,* especially in 1685 under Thököly, and in 1703–10 under Rákóczi.

The old-fashioned military levy was called out twice, during Leopold I's Turkish wars of 1663 and 1683. Even at these times the estates preferred to hire mercenaries rather than mobilize the peasantry, for fear of future insurrections. Until the mid-eighteenth century the nobles of Inner Austria continued to hold most of the officers' posts in the Croatian and Slavonian military borders, as a compensation for the financing of this area by their Lands. The vestiges of the indigenous military organization in Inner Austria became completely overshadowed by the imperial mercenary army. From the beginning of the eighteenth century each Land was assigned an annual quota of recruits, and these were apportioned to the individual manors and towns. Between 500 and 2,500 recruits had to be furnished each year from the Slovene territory. The estates supplied either the recruits themselves or the money to hire the prescribed number of soldiers.

THE POWERS OF THE ESTATES

The Administrative Organs of the Lands

While the governmental organs in Graz for all of Inner Austria were largely agencies derived from direct princely power, the administrative and judicial institutions in the individual Lands were staffed and maintained primarily by the estates. The latter exerted their influence mainly through the diets, which continued to be composed of four colleges (*curiae*). In Carniola, the first *curia* included three bishops (of Ljubljana, Freising, and Brixen), two provosts, three abbots, and seven canons of the Ljubljana cathedral; the second *curia* was made up of nobles with the title of prince, count, or baron; the third, all other nobles (*Landleute*); and the fourth, the urban judges (*Stadtrichter*) as representatives of the towns. The influence of towns declined sharply compared with the pre-1620 situation. In Styria—as in Bohemia and Moravia—all the towns jointly were entitled to just one vote in the diet; in Carniola and Gorizia the burghers were no longer eligible for the Committees of the Land. The character and composition of the noble class had changed, chiefly through emigration of the most dedicated Protestants, the infusion of new members (partly from the townspeople and partly from foreigners, especially the Italians), and grants of higher titles to nobles loyal to the prince. Nevertheless, the nobility was not entirely submissive. The court and the bureaucratic nobles were not representative of the nobility as a whole. The class as such resented the policy of absolutism and centralism, although it did not dare to resist actively. The participation of Counts Hans Erasmus Tattenbach and Kàrl Thurn in the conspiracy of Hungarian and Croatian magnates in 1670 may be considered an exception that confirmed the rule.[6]

Aside from sharing in the control over the administration and the judiciary of the individual Lands, the diets still played a significant role fiscally, and the frequency of their sessions often depended on the length of the term for which taxes were granted. They also had significant rights and functions with respect to defense, especially in the Croatian and Slavonian military borders.

The highest official in each Land was the captain (*Landeshauptmann*). Drawn from the domiciled high nobility, he was appointed by the prince; in some Lands the estates retained the right of nomination. He swore the oath of allegiance to both the prince and the estates, and received pay from both. Other officials, who assisted the captain, were either selected by the prince or the estates. Thus the high officials of the Lands in the Slovene area were not so one-sidedly dependent on the ruler as those in the Bohemian Lands after 1620.

In Carniola, the captain of the Land was assisted by the administrator of the Land (*Landesverwalter*), who acted as his general deputy, and by the magistrate (*Landesverweser, praetor provinciae*), who often took the captain's place specifically in judicial proceedings. In addition, the diet elected a group of delegates (*Verordnete*) as its standing committee, which was specifically in charge of financial affairs. The three officials together with the delegates formed the highest administrative body of the Land.

6. On the conspiracy of 1670 see pp. 137–38 and 168.

The only public official in each Land who was responsible solely to the prince and entirely independent of the estates was the *vicedom*. His jurisdiction was limited to the properties of the prince, in particular the princely towns, mines, princely estates, and customhouses. His power over the towns increased markedly during this period.

The estates continuned to dominate the Courts of the Land, which under the captain of the Land had jurisdiction over cases affecting the nobility. The assessors of these courts were usually elected by the diets. In Carniola this privileged noble court, called *Landschrannengericht*, conducted two types of proceedings, either under the Law of the Court (*Hofrecht*), in cases involving acts of violence and injury to property, or under the Law of the Land (*Landrecht*) in matters affecting noble privileges, grants, and charters, such as inheritance, guardianship, fiefs, and injury to honor. Independently of the *Landschrannengericht,* the captain handled appeals from subject peasants against their seigneurs, as well as from certain town courts.

The territorial division of the Lands into quarters (*Viertel*), carried out for the purposes of defense in the sixteenth century, remained the basis for raising the obsolescent military levy. Of greater importance as administrative subdivisions were the more numerous territorial jurisdictions of the criminal courts entitled to dispense justice involving capital crimes (except for nobles and clergy). Their judges (*Bannrichter*) were appointed and controlled by the *Regierung* in Graz.

Large towns were headed by a mayor (*Bürgermeister*) and all had a judge (*Stadtrichter*), both of whom since the end of sixteenth century had to be confirmed in office by the prince. The *vicedom* heard the appeals from the town courts. By the early seventeenth century the principle of self-perpetuation largely replaced that of genuine elections of the town councils. In Ljubljana for instance, according to the statutes confirmed by Leopold I in 1660, the town council was divided into two parts: "inner" and "external." The "inner" council, composed of twelve members, was elected by the burghers for life from the richest and most prominent inhabitants. This council then elected a mayor from its own ranks. The "external" council of twenty-four members was named annually by the "inner" council. The "people" or the "community" (*Volk Gemeine*), composed of 101 men, selected the town judge from two candidates nominated by the inner council. By the second half of the seventeenth century only merchants were members of the two councils, while the "community" included plain artisans.

The Peasants and the Seigneurs

Most of the peasant population in the Slovene area continued to live under the manorial authority, with the seigneur serving as the judge—

except in serious criminal cases—and as the local administrator who, among other functions, collected taxes and maintained military registers on behalf of the Land. Only in southern Gorizia and northern Istria did the peasants enjoy extensive self-government under their own mayors and councils. The prince's victory over the estates did not immediately ameliorate the peasants' situation. In fact, in 1635 the heavy tax burden and the arbitrary procedures of manorial courts provoked a peasant uprising which spread from lower Styria into parts of Carniola. The insurgents destroyed thirty-four manor houses before troops from the military borders suppressed the rebellion.

In the longer run the prince could use his enhanced authority to intervene on behalf of the peasants. Although in the seventeenth century and into the early eighteenth this intervention remained sporadic and limited in effectiveness, it preceded by almost a century analogous measures in the Bohemian Lands. Since the end of the sixteenth century the serfs had been given princely assurances (in 1579, 1618, and 1622) that they could appeal from the manorial courts not only to the captain of the Land but also to the *Regierung* in Graz. Emperor Ferdinand III (1637–57) stipulated further that the peasants were entitled to speedy trials before the seigneurial justice. The right of appeal to the *Regierung*, however, continued to be of questionable value because of the distance involved, and the peasants' inability to speak or understand German, let alone command the language in writing. Moreover, the petitioning peasants ran the risk of being treated as rebels by their seigneur.

The prince's efforts to regulate the economic obligations of the serfs also remained on a modest scale. The seigneurs were prohibited to require subject labor on Sundays and holidays. Through regulations dating to the mid-sixteenth century, they continued to be barred from forcibly evicting the peasants from their homesteads or from requiring their subjects to sell products to them rather than directly in towns. From 1679 the seigneurs were no longer permitted to appropriate the largest head of cattle from a deceased peasant's estate.

The nobles were eager to maximize the yield of dues and services from their serfs. In the case of peasants settled outside the demesne, the seigneurs were barred from increasing the dues in kind or money above the level registered in the *Gültbücher*. Instead they sought to raise the amount of compulsory labor and also charged high fees for the transfer of peasant homesteads. The latter consideration led them after 1600 to oppose the conversion of lease tenures to hereditary ones, such as had been implemented on the princely estates in the second half of the sixteenth century. In the case of the peasants settled on the demesne, where the protection of fixed fees did not apply, the seigneurs were free to step up their exactions. Often a single parcel of land in the demesne brought the noble landlord more income than an entire homestead outside of it.

The weight of the economic obligations further varied with the geographic area. In general, the peasants' burden was heavier in the plain and rolling country of southern Styria and eastern Carniola than in the more westerly Alpine regions. This was particularly true of the labor obligation, because the seigneurs tended to retain a larger proportion of the demesne under their own cultivation. While in other areas the *robota* was relatively moderate, and by the seventeenth century some seigneurs even permitted its replacement by money payments, in the eastern part of the Slovene territory the labor obligation could mount up to sixteen hours daily, and at harvest time each homestead could be required to furnish two or more workers.

Except for Istria and southern Gorizia, the Slovene peasants were subject to hereditary personal bondage, which, though more benign than in the Bohemian Lands, were still onerous. The peasants could not change their occupation or migrate without the seigneur's permission. In southeastern Carinthia the landlord retained the right to recall a peasant, even if he had left with his permission. In the seventeenth century the freedom to migrate became still more restricted. If he held a hereditary homestead, the migrant owed the seigneur between one-tenth and one-third of the sale price of his property. The serfs also needed the seigneur's permission to marry, although by the sixteenth century this requirement had become in practice reduced to the payment of a fee. In Istria and southern Gorizia not only was the manorial authority limited in the exercise of public functions but the peasants were personally free and their economic obligations involved simply rents with no labor dues. Typically, the peasant signed a lease (*libello*) for an amount of land for a number of years at certain annual payments. He was free to terminate the lease and simply leave.

ECONOMIC LIFE[7]

Agriculture

The agricultural techniques remained relatively stable in the Slovene area from the mid-seventeenth to the mid-eighteenth century. There was some occurrence of the four-field system, under which a piece of land would lie fallow only every fourth year, but the three-field system remained most common, with certain coastal areas following the even

7. Economic data in this section are derived from *Historija naroda Jugoslavije* (Zagreb: Školska knjiga, 1959), 2:676–81, 893–917; and Bogo Grafenauer, *Zgodovina slovenskega naroda* (Ljubljana: Kmečka knjiga, 1961), 4:83–94, 102–21; *Zgodovina Slovencev* (Ljubljana: Cankarjeva založba, 1979), pp. 330–45.

less efficient two-field cycle. There were no marked improvements in the kind of equipment used. The most essential implement was the heavy wooden plow, which required the draft power of two pairs of horses or from three to five pairs of oxen, thus necessitated cooperation among the peasants.

Significant changes, however, did take place in crop production. Among the new crops buckwheat grew in popularity, especially in Carniola by the end of the seventeenth century. Planted after the regular harvest, it made possible more intensive utilization of land. Of major importance outside Carniola was corn, which had penetrated into Gorizia from Venetia in the late sixteenth century, and into Styria somewhat later from Hungary. By 1670 in Styria corn, together with millet, became the principal foodstuff of the peasants, who used the traditional grains to pay their dues to the seigneurs and to raise money for taxes. Since corn was not mentioned in the traditional registers of feudal dues, the seigneurs had difficulties collecting a share of its output from their serfs. Finally an imperial decree for Styria in 1733 granted the landlords one-twentieth of the corn harvest, instead of the conventional tenth due from other peasant crops.

Considerable changes also occurred in the utilization of land. The total area of arable land tended to expand. In the seventeenth century this took place mostly through deforestation. Also, mainly in Gorizia, vineyards and fields grew at the expense of pastures. Later, in another type of change, mulberry trees began to replace vineyards and olive groves in Istria. These shifts created conflicts of interest. In the early eighteenth century further reductions of pastures were prohibited in Gorizia. Elsewhere, wishing to preserve the forests as a source of charcoal for fuel, smelter owners clashed with noble seigneurs bent on clearing more land for peasant homesteads. The princely authorities sought compromise solutions through new forest ordinances (*Waldordnungen*) for Styria in 1695 and for Carniola a year later.

In the overall balances of crop outputs, Gorizia and most of Carniola produced surpluses of grain. Istria and the eastern part of lower Styria exported wine but had to import grain—the former mainly from Gorizia, the latter from Hungary and Croatia. The Alpine areas of the Slovene territory (the Gorenjska region of Carniola, southern Carinthia, and the western part of lower Styria) were more or less self-sufficient in grain output.

In animal production from the mid-seventeenth to the mid-eighteenth century the raising of cattle, sheep, pigs, and poultry continued to predominate. Cattle raising was generally dispersed. The demesnes in Carniola, for instance, averaged no more than 30 to 40 head of beef. The aggregate volume of production, however, was impressive, especially in the Alpine areas, from which cattle were exported in large numbers to Italy. Thus in 1716–22 a single large Italian firm shipped 10,000 oxen from southern Carinthia and Styria alone. Horse raising increased markedly in the early eighteenth century. Its spread among the peasants was stimulated by a growing demand for transportation, especially along the trade routes. The first horse-breeding station was opened in Lipica in 1728, almost half a century before such facilities for other animals.

Crafts, Industry, and Mining

The nonagricultural production in the Slovene area did not suffer so serious a disruption by the Thirty Years' War as was the case, for instance, in the Bohemian Lands, where the devastation due to warfare was catastrophic. Still, severe economic difficulties occurred in the seventeenth century. Currency, its value already diminished by the monetary crisis of the previous century, was becoming scarce because of the emigration of Protestant nobles and burghers. The Inner Austrian *Regiment* finally in 1631 prohibited further export of capital and authorized instead payment of interest to the émigrés. Another source of difficulty was the disruption of commercial and economic relations with Germany, owing partly to war devastation and partly to proscription of contact with Protestant areas. The substitution of trade links with Italy was a slow and gradual process. In general, the Slovene area during the seventeenth century shared in the economic decline characteristic of East Central Europe.

Mining and smelting continued to stand out in the nonagricultural production of the Slovene territory. Iron production actually peaked during the Thirty Years' War. Subsequently, with decline in demand, the output decreased. By the end of the seventeenth century the annual production averaged 1,650 tons per year, a level below the best years of the sixteenth century. Ironworks were still scattered throughout Carniola, with eight major enterprises in the Alpine section of the country. Some were situated in Carinthia and Styria. Stagnation in the rate of iron production went hand in hand with the employment of obsolescent technology. Not until 1704, in the Kanalska Dolina of Carinthia, were conventional furnaces requiring emptying and restarting replaced by the more advanced models enabling continuous operation. Among the enterprises using iron for finished products the most important were the gunsmiths' shops in Borovlje (Ferlach) in Carinthia. In the early eighteenth century some two hundred masters employed there turned out almost 15,000 muskets and twice as many pistols annually.

The mercury mine at Idrija maintained its exceptional importance. The government did not permit production there to decline even during the Thirty Years' War. The output, in fact, reached a record high of 192 tons per year in 1623–30, compared with 50 tons in the second half of the sixteenth century. In the second half of the seventeenth century the production declined to an average of 70 tons per year. The mine proved tremendously profitable. Most of its output was marketed in Amsterdam, where by midcentury a ton of mercury brought 2,000 florins, with only about one quarter of this sum representing the cost of production and transportation. Compared with sixteenth-century production, lead mining declined in Bleiberg, in Carinthia; the mine at Rabelj near Trbiž, with an annual output of 150 tons, was the leading source of lead in the Slovene area.

Outside the area of mining and metallurgy the new mercantilist attitudes stimulated plans for textile manufactories. This industry was particularly relevant to Inner Austria because of the obligation to supply cloth to the military borders in Croatia. The first attempt to establish a woolen manufactory in Klagenfurt failed soon after 1700. Another manufactory, however, started operations in Ljubljana in 1725, working exclusively for the army until 1740.

In craft production, the urban artisans met increasingly stiffer competition from village craftsmen. While in the seventeenth century the princely authority and the town governments had still sought to limit, if not suppress, the peasant artisans, the situation changed significantly after 1700. The state realized that the income derived by the peasants from crafts, as well as from trade, strengthened its principal tax base. In addition, the peasant craftsmen found powerful allies in the urban merchants who began to engage in the putting-out system on a larger scale. Under this system important production developed in Carniola (woolen cloth, linen, and hosiery) and in Gorizia (silk).

Trade

The directions of trade in the seventeenth century reflected the major economic reorientation from Germany to Italy. Italian imports included wine and salt. Iron and lumber (from the Littoral) played an important role in the exports to Italy, as did grain and cattle, partly originating outside the Slovene territory—in Hungary and Croatia. During most of the seventeenth century the conduct of trade was shared in various degrees by the town merchants, the peasants, and the holders of government monopolies. Near the turn of the century a new class of wholesalers gained prominence. Mainly from Italy, these entrepreneurs settled in such commercial centers as Ljubljana, Škofja Loka, Villach, and Trieste.

Early in the eighteenth century the renewal of commercial relations with the East was made possible by the Habsburg reconquest of central Hungary and the Banat, as well as by the government's promotion of free navigation on the Adriatic after 1717. As part of the latter policy, Trieste and Rijeka were declared free ports in 1719 and the Oriental Company was chartered in the same year to further trade and industries on the coast. The Slovene hinterland benefited by the demand for lumber and hemp in the two flourishing free ports, and from the improvement of transportation routes toward the coast. In 1718–29 in Carniola alone, 100,000 florins were spent to rebuild roads from Trieste and Rijeka through Ljubljana to Klagenfurt and Graz. Work to improve the navigability of the Ljubljanica and the Sava began in the 1730s. Early in the same decade the eastern trade, however, suffered a severe setback from the collapse of the Oriental Company. A recovery would occur only later in Maria Theresa's reign.

The Magyars

In the seventeenth century and into the early eighteenth the political evolution of Hungary under Habsburg rule contrasted with that of the Bohemian Lands, or the Slovene territories of Inner Austria. While in the areas to the west absolutism and—except for Silesia—the Counter Reformation triumphed as early as the opening phase of the Thirty Years' War (1618–48), in Hungary the power of the estates and—to a lesser extent—religious toleration survived. Although until the 1680s the Habsburgs governed only the western and northern portion of the Hungarian Kingdom, the pattern of Hungary's distinctive political development was established on this limited territory. It was later adapted on a larger scale to the reunited kingdom after the Turks were forced to leave the country toward the end of the century. This atypical development was facilitated by several factors. The Habsburgs were unable to curb the estates in all their Lands simultaneously. During the Thirty Years' War, the era of the rise of princely absolutism in the Habsburg Lands, the Hungarian nobles could exploit the kings' preoccupation with emasculating the estates of Austria and Bohemia. A persistent domestic factor was the unusual numerical strength of the Hungarian nobility, mostly the gentry, combined with the effectiveness of the county governments as obstacles to royal absolutism. Of the greatest importance was the factor of foreign military and diplomatic aid. The Hungarian estates could enlist successively the support of Transylvania, the Ottoman power, and indirectly France in mounting armed resistance to their imperious kings. After their initial success, owing to the intervention of Gábor Bethlen, prince of Transylvania and for a time Hungarian counter king, in the 1620s, the Hungarian nobles withstood at least three major royal assaults on their position of political power.

This part of the story is more fully discussed in volume V of this series.[8] Merely for the sake of clarifying the situation in the part of Hungary permanently under Habsburg control, some main events, briefly traced here, should be remembered. In the process, three major and one minor rebellion occurred and several major agreements between sovereign and estates were concluded. The agreements or compromises of 1645, 1681, and 1711 are particularly important in our context.

THE CHALLENGE OF ABSOLUTISM 1620–83

From the Treaty of Mikulov (1622) to the Treaty of Linz (1645)

After the treaty of Mikulov (Nikolsburg) in 1622, Bethlen continued to champion the twin cause of Protestantism and the estates' rights in intermittent warfare with Emperor-King Ferdinand II (1619–37). The agreement concluded in Vienna in 1606 between Emperor-King Rudolf II and István Bocskai, prince of Translvania, which had been confirmed by the treaty of Mikulov, was twice reconfirmed: in Vienna (1623) and in Pozsony (1626). Aside from safeguarding the estates' privileges and the Protestants' freedom in Hungary, the document provided that the prince of Transylvania recognize the overlordship of the Habsburg rulers. In view of the Turkish rule in central Hungary, this was a matter of principle rather than one of much current political significance. In fact, several Hungarian counties were ceded to the ruler of Transylvania.

Shortly after signing the treaty of Pozsony, Ferdinand II—in blatant disregard of its provisions—launched a compaign of attrition against Hungarian Protestantism. The Counter Reformation had advanced significantly, largely because of the influence of the learned Cardinal Péter Pázmány, the primate of Hungary since 1616, as well as the power of the Viennese Court. Most magnates gradually embraced the Catholic faith, and as early as 1625 a Catholic was elected *palatin,* the first one since the restoration of the office in 1608. Arbitrary oppression of the Protestants—particularly seizures of their churches—mounted, and from 1638 complaints against violation of religious freedom dominated the Hungarian diet's proceedings. The antagonisms, engendered by the religious conflict, sharpened so much that the diet of 1642 had to be dissolved without any concrete accomplishments.

The threat to the Hungarian constitutional order was averted by an uprising of the nobility in conjunction with renewed Transylvanian intervention. Prince George Rákóczi (1630–48) invaded Hungary as an

---

8. Peter F. Sugar, *Southeastern Europe under Ottoman Rule, 1354–1804* (Seattle and London: University of Washington Press, 1977).

ally of France and Sweden in the concluding stages of the Thirty Years' War. Exploiting the preoccupation of Emperor-King Ferdinand III (1637–57) elsewhere, he succeeded in concluding the advantageous treaty of Linz in 1645, which once again reaffirmed the settlement of 1606. In addition, of the seven counties ceded by Ferdinand II to Bethlen in 1622,[9] Rákóczi secured Szabolcs and Szatmár for Transylvania permanently, and Abaúj, Bereg, Borsod, Ugocsa, and Zemplén for his own lifetime. The Hungarian diet of 1646–47 enacted the provisions of the treaty of Linz into law. Although only ninety out of four hundred churches seized from the Protestants were restored, effective laws for the protection of religious freedom were now adopted. Violation of Protestant churches or other properties became an offense punishable by a fine of six hundred florins. Judgments in such cases were pronounced by special Parity Commissions dispatched by the county authorities. The diet heard appeals from their decisions. The Protestants were encouraged so much that at the diet of 1655 a group of their gentry in a move highly offensive to the dynasty proposed to abolish any restrictions on freely elective kingship.

The Rebellions of Wesselényi (1670) and Thököly (1678)

In 1661 under Leopold I (1657–1705) the Viennese government initiated another major effort to subvert the Hungarian constitution and to extirpate heterodoxy in Hungary. This attack would continue with growing intensity into the following decade. The situation seemed propitious because of the drastic eclipse of Transylvania's power after George Rákóczi II's (1648–57) adventurous war with Poland in 1657, an event that seemed to deprive the Hungarian estates of effective support from abroad. Vienna's tactics called for inciting the Hungarian nobility to revolt, by taking arbitrary measures, and then using the suppression of the rebellion as an occasion for annihilating the estates' political power. The government's pressure became evident at the diet of 1662 when the Protestants' demands were not met. They were simply told to present their grievances to the county authorities. Following the session, Leopold I issued an edict ominously ordering the diet in the future to consider royal propositions as its first order of business. Even more provocative was the behavior of imperial mercenaries, stationed in the border fortresses, who engaged in pillage and other acts of oppression. The final factor in sharpening the nobility's discontent was the Turkish war of 1663, which ended abruptly a year later with the treaty of Vasvár (Eisenburg) on terms surprisingly favorable to the Turks. Hungarian nobles saw in this unusual denouement an implicit bribe to the Otto-

9. See p. 56.

mans to let the Habsburgs deal freely with the Hungarian opposition.

Vienna's tactics of provoking the Hungarian nobility succeeded in their initial objective. The sphere of discontent expanded beyond the traditional Protestant circles to embrace Catholics as well in common detestation of the "German" governmental system and in defense of Hungary's autonomy. Ironically, the success of the Counter Reformation began to interfere with the other chief objective of the Habsburgs, the introduction of absolute rule. It diminished the chances of linking the imposition of absolutism with an ideological crusade against Protestantism. By the mid-1660s no lesser figures than the *palatin*, Ferenc Wesselényi, and the *iudex curiae*, Ferenc Nádasdy, entered a widespread anti-Habsburg conspiracy. The rebellion, named after Wesselényi— though he died in 1667 before its outbreak—could not, however, compare in force and consequences with the subsequent uprisings of Thököly and Rákóczi. Aside from its rather contrived character, due to Vienna's manipulations, the conspiracy failed to secure significant foreign aid, although both the French and the Turks had been approached. It did not pose a real threat to Vienna, which was well informed about the moves of the conspirators, and the final show of force in 1670 was most disappointing. A peculiarity of the rebellion was a notable Croatian involvement, represented by the magnates Petar Zrinski (Zrínyi) and Fran Frankopan.[10]

The Wesselényi rebellion did not lead to another compromise with the king. Instead, it conformed to Vienna's expectations in seeming to offer an opportunity for a drastic repression, such as had occurred in Bohemia fifty years earlier. On the advice of Emperor Leopold I's first minister, Prince Wenzel Lobkowitz, and the Austrian Court chancellor, Johann Paul Hocher, the Hungarian constitution was suspended in 1671 and entirely abrogated two years later. Without a functioning diet, taxes were imposed by royal decrees. In 1671 each county became responsible for maintaining imperial troops stationed on its territory, and the war tax from a peasant homestead was increased ten times (up to sixty florins). In May 1672 excise taxes, applicable to the nobles, as well as the peasants, were introduced on the sale of spirits, meat, and—in some areas—grain. Protestants suffered severe repression under the direction of the archbishop of Esztergom, György Szelepcsényi, and the bishop of Nitra (Nyitra), subsequently archbishop and cardinal, Count Leopold Kollonich (Kollonitsch). In 1672 Jesuits, accompanied by soldiers, traveled through the country forcibly converting the dissidents. Catholic magnates confiscated Protestant churches and schools on their estates, expelling ministers and teachers. In 1673 an authoritarian form of government was established, headed by Johann Kaspar Ambringen, a

10. On Croatian participation see p. 168.

Hungarian-born grandmaster of the German Order. Ambringen, bearing the title of governor, was assisted by a council of four Hungarians and four Austrians. Another wave of persecution struck mainly non-Catholic ministers and teachers, of whom ninety-three received death sentences, subsequently commuted to galley slavery. The Protestants lost eight hundred churches. The religious repression created an international scandal.

The conduct of the new government, and especially that of the imperial army—the main instrument for enforcing authoritarian rule—at last produced a rebellion strong enough to check the political ambition of Vienna. Sporadic resistance began in 1672 by bands of so-called *kurucok,* composed of fugitive peasants, deserters from the border fortresses, and elements of the gentry. It was strengthened by support from Transylvania, and also from France, with which the emperor had been at war since 1674. The rebellion became a major threat in 1678 when the magnate Imre Thököly assumed its leadership and with Turkish aid conquered thirteen counties of northern Hungary by 1680.

The Sopron Compromise (1681)

Under these circumstances and in the face of an approaching war with the Turks, Leopold I was at last ready to retreat on the political front in Hungary. In 1679 the governorship was abolished, and with it the activities of Ambringen and his administration came to an end. The stage was set for a new compromise between the king and the estates, which was consummated at the diet of Sopron in the spring of 1681. The diet was permitted to elect a new *palatin*—the first one since Wesselényi's death in 1667—and the old constitutional order was restored. Hungarian troops were no longer to form an integral part of the imperial army; the non-Hungarian imperial contingents were allowed to stay in the country until the restoration of order, but had to observe local laws strictly. The nobility's traditional rights and privileges were reaffirmed, and a special diet commission was to review the post-1671 confiscations of noble property. The sales taxes, imposed by royal decree, which the nobles found particularly objectionable, were abolished. The Hungarian Chamber, its staff purged of foreign councilors, was to cooperate with, but not be subordinate to, the Viennese *Hofkammer.* Traditional courts resumed their functions, and sentences passed under the special judiciary of 1671–79 were mostly invalidated. In return for these concessions, the diet voted a general levy (*insurrectio*) of nobles for the anticipated Turkish war.

The compromise of Sopron reflected an ascendancy of political over religious issues. While the political rights of the estates were restored at a level in some respects more satisfactory than in the original compromise of 1606, religious rights, which had drawn most attention at the previous settlements (1606, 1622, and 1645), were assuming a secondary importance. The magnates, now mostly Catholics, would have preferred to ignore them altogether, and the Sopron compromise addressed the religious issue in terms significantly less favorable to the Protestants than the previous settlements. Religious freedom was guaranteed to the nobles and to the burghers of royal towns, but no longer to the subject peasants. Protestants could retain the churches they still held, but those confiscated in the 1670s were not restored. If none were left in a county, the non-Catholics were authorized to build two or three new ones. Such churches were called "inarticulated"—that is, permitted under article 26 of the law of 1681.

UNIFICATION AND INSURRECTION, 1683–1711

Hungary Reunited

The settlement of Sopron was soon undermined by a striking reversal in the military fortunes of the Viennese government. The critical situation of the early 1680s, culminating in the Turkish siege of Vienna in 1683, was rapidly followed by the brilliant victories of the imperial armies, which by 1686 conquered most of central Hungary, including the town of Buda, which had been in Turkish possession since 1541. Thus the painful division of Hungary into three parts was essentially terminated, and the entire ancient kingdom came under Habsburg sovereignty.

In the process of expelling the Turks, the forces of Thököly were routed as well, and in 1687 the so-called Slaughterhouse of Prešov (Eperjes) was enacted in eastern Slovakia, where the imperial general Count Antonio Caraffa had several of Thököly's prominent followers sentenced to death and executed. Leopold I was free once again to launch an attempt at reducing the power of the Hungarian estates. This time the tactics were more subtle than those used in the 1670s. Instead of applying royal command and naked military force, the king pressured the Hungarian diet into agreeing to constitutional changes.

Against the background of the impressive imperial victories and the bloody events at Prešov, the new policy was initially successful. The king had now gained the upper hand in his dealings with the recalcitrant estates. The diet at Pozsony in 1687 renounced the right of royal election and recognized a hereditary succession of the Habsburg dynasty in the male line. It also consented to abrogating article 31 of the Golden Bull of Andrew II, conferring on the Hungarian estates the right to resist (ius resistendi) if the king violated their privileges. Almost equally serious as the initiation of the hereditary succession was an article included in the newly drafted Inaugural Diploma, which each new king had to confirm for himself and his successors. It stipulated that while the ruler would preserve all the laws of the land and the lawful rights of the inhabitants, the exact meaning of these laws and rights would be determined by mutual agreement between the king and the estates. The ambiguous phrasing of the Diploma, on which the estates had to yield for the time being, opened the way to questioning the validity of all aspects of the Hungarian constitution.

The diet's concessions of 1687 represented only the opening stage in the renewed contest between the king and the estates, a contest that was to continue for more than twenty years. Principles of absolute rule were applied to the bulk of the territory, which was wrested from the Turks in central Hungary. Under the duress of military management and control accompanying the reconquest of Hungary under a non-Hungarian imperial command, functions previously assigned to the Hungarian administrative agencies were now exercised by the Viennese *Hofkammer* in most of the reconquered territories. Its organ, the *Neoacquisita Commissio*, established in 1688, adjudicated claims to properties in the area, and successful claimants were charged large fees (*ius armorum*), amounting to 10 percent of the value of the retrieved estates. The rest of the formerly Turkish central Hungary was administered by the *Hofkriegsrat*, and these territories were in 1701–2 organized into two new military borders: one between the Danube and the Sava in Slavonia, and another along the rivers Tisza and Mureş farther to the east.[11] Only Transylvania, which came under Habsburg rule in 1691, retained its traditional form of internal self-government.

Preparations for further revisions of the Hungarian political order proceeded immediately after the diet of 1687. In October a special group, including the heads of the Bohemian Court Chancellery, the *Hofkriegsrat*, and the *Hofkammer*, as well as Bishop Kollonich, began to consider how the newly acquired Hungarian territories should be administered on a permanent basis. In 1688 Leopold I also requested suggestions and proposals in this matter from such diverse sources as his personal adviser, the *palatin*, the *personalis*, and even Count Caraffa. This approach ominously resembled the procedure that in the 1620s had led to the reduction of the Bohemian constitution. The elaboration of a definite proposal was entrusted to a subcommission headed by Kollonich and composed of the councilors of several Viennese government agencies. The resulting document, entitled *The Organizational Task* (*Einrichtungswerk des Königreiches Ungarn*), envisaged a reorganization of the Hungarian Court Chancellery and wide-ranging reforms of the administration and judiciary, as well as of fiscal and military management. A

11. On the formation of these military borders see also pp. 169–70, 182.

striking feature of the plan was a partial equalization of all personally free Hungarian inhabitants before the law, including an abrogation of the nobility's immunity from taxation. The proposals inclined toward royal absolutism, but still left more power to the estates than the Renewed Land Ordinance of 1627 in Bohemia. Further changes, including introduction of Austrian laws into Hungary, were, however, envisaged in conjunction with the planned revision of the *Tripartitum*.

Because of serious obstacles, the implementation of the *Einrichtungswerk* was not attempted before the mid-1690s. Kollonich's own premature disclosure of the planned reforms permitted an ardent Hungarian opposition to gather under the *palatin,* which, incensed by the proposal to tax the nobility, scored the impropriety of an intervention in the internal affairs of Hungary by the king's foreign advisers. In addition, certain aspects of Kollonich's project were questioned by a conference of high Viennese dignitaries, including the supreme Bohemian chancellor, who were assigned to review the *Einrichtungswerk.* Most important, by 1690 Leopold I was moved to caution under the shadow of military events. Aside from the unfinished war against the Ottoman Empire, the monarchy had become involved since 1688 in the War of the League of Augsburg against France. This diversion delayed the final confirmation of the conquest of central Hungary and Transylvania for over a decade—until the treaty of Karlovci (Karlowitz) in 1699.

As to religious matters, the diet of Pozsony in 1687 weakened also the guarantees secured by the Protestants in 1681 at the diet of Sopron. It qualified the religious assurances by a proviso that they were valid only "for the time being" and based on special royal favor. Moreover, the guarantees were omitted from the text of the Inaugural Diploma. In practice, however, the Protestants' situation did not change substantially. Answering their renewed remonstrances in 1691, the king amplified in the *Explanatio Leopoldina* the dissidents' status by distinguishing between the public and private exercise of religion. The Protestants could maintain their own ministers, and sever completely the ties with the Catholic Church, only in the "inarticulated" places. Elsewhere, they could practice their faith privately without ministers or common gatherings, and had to share in financing the local Catholic clergy.

The Rákóczi Insurrection

Not until the late 1690s did Leopold I move once more onto a collision course with the Hungarian estates by choosing to implement a highly sensitive aspect of Kollonich's project, the part dealing with taxation. The main objectives were to make the war tax (now called the

Contribution) stable and permanent, increase its yield, and—as in Bohemia or Inner Austria—make the nobility pay a share. In 1697 a high commission (Ministerial Deputation) in Vienna under Cardinal Kollonich, who had in the meantime served as the head of the *Hofkammer*, was charged with reviewing Hungarian taxation from the standpoint of the king's overall fiscal needs. The Deputation recommended that the Hungarian quota be set at four million florins, out of the total Contribution of twelve million from the entire monarchy. The following year the king convened in Vienna a large gathering, including Hungarian magnates, as well as representatives of counties and towns, to negotiate concerning the proposed Hungarian quota. When no agreement was reached, the tax was established by an imperative royal rescript.

This step represented a sharp break with the existing practice and a blatant resort to unconstitutional procedures, closely resembling those employed in the 1670s. Since the local administrative machinery was in the hands of the offended estates, the cumbersome and vexatious method of using the imperial army had to be adopted once again to collect the new tax. To this major grievance another one was added when, with the emperor's involvement in the War of the Spanish Succession, Hungarian peasants in 1702 became subject to forcible induction into the imperial army. Thus the effort to break the power of the estates exasperated the broad strata of the common population as well. The answer to the dynasty's third major attempt (since 1620) to impose absolute rule on Hungary was another major rebellion, which broke out in 1703 under the leadership of the magnate Prince Francis Rákóczi II (1676–1735).

Like Thököly in the 1670s, Rákóczi was able to take advantage of the king's preoccupation with a French war, which virtually denuded Hungary of imperial troops. It was easy for him to gain the support of the urban Protestants with their standing grievances. More remarkable was the ability of this dynamic personality to channel the struggle of the lower class *kurucok*. Inspired by hatred against social oppression, they were now persuaded to acknowledge to a point the political and social privileges of the upper classes.

The rebels seized control of most of the territory recently freed from the Turks, as well as of northern Hungary. The turning point of the uprising was the assembly of Ónod in 1707, which declared the Habsburgs deposed as kings of Hungary. Most nobles preferred a compromise with the dynasty to a complete break, particularly as the conflict of interest between them and the *kurucok* grew more difficult to contain. Negotiations for a compromise between the king and the estates, begun during the brief reign of Joseph I (1705–11), were successfully concluded under his successor Charles VI, as king of Hungary Charles III, (1711–40) at Szatmár (Satu-Mare) on April 30, 1711.

THE SZATMÁR COMPROMISE, 1711–40

The King and the Estates

The settlement at Szatmár was no less than the fifth one between the Hungarian estates and the Habsburg kings since the beginning of the seventeenth century, but it proved to be the most significant one. It established the broad lines of Hungary's distinctive political and social development for over two hundred years. The agreement itself confirmed the rights and liberties of the nobles of Hungary and Transylvania. It offered amnesty to the rebels if they returned to obedience within three weeks. It renewed the existing religious guarantees, and promised to settle other grievances at the next diet. At the diet, which met from 1712 to 1715, the king restated his promise to govern Hungary only according to the existing laws and those that would be passed by the diet. More important, he gave assurances that the ambiguous clause of the Inaugural Diploma, which implied a risky latitude in the interpretation of the actual meaning of Hungarian laws, would not be used to introduce into Hungary the system of government prevailing in other hereditary Lands. A major compromise was achieved on the interrelated issues of the army and taxation. On the one hand, the estates agreed to assume the support of the standing Hungarian army, which had, in fact, been created by a royal fiat in 1702. They acknowledged the need for a continuing tax for that purpose. On the other hand, the diet maintained its right to consent to the necessary taxes and subsidies. It also vindicated the nobles' immunity from taxation, shifting the entire burden to other classes, primarily the peasantry, on the largely obsolete grounds that the nobility had to fulfill its military obligation in person through the general levy (*insurrectio*). Rákóczi, now a political exile, had in the end failed in his efforts to bring about a solution more acceptable to the peasants.

For the record, the diet of 1712–15 requested the establishment of a distinctive Hungarian War Council to control all the troops in the Land, but tacitly it condoned the continued authority of the Viennese *Hofkriegsrat*, recognized since 1569. As another major royal concession, the *Neoacquisita Commissio* was abolished in 1715 and the jurisdiction over the newly acquired territories, except for the military borders, was transferred from the Viennese *Hofkammer* to the regular Hungarian administrative agencies. When, however, a few years later in 1718 the Habsburgs gained the Banat of Timişoara (Temesvár) from the Turks by the treaty of Passarowitz (Požarevac), the territory remained under the jurisdiction of the *Hofkriegsrat*. The ambitious project of settling foreign colonists in the new territories also remained under Vienna's direction.

The series of accommodations of the Hungarian estates to continued Habsburg rule was essentially completed by the diet of 1722–23. It adopted the Pragmatic Sanction with some variations from the version accepted by the estates in the other Habsburg Lands. The hereditary right was limited to male and female descendants of Charles VI, Joseph I, and Leopold I; the right of free royal election was explicitly reserved on the eventual extinction of all these lines; and the affirmation of the Inaugural Diploma by each new ruler was stipulated. The document of accession to the Pragmatic Sanction spoke of the Habsburg monarchy as a union between Hungary and undifferentiated "other Lands." This quasi-constitutional language foreshadowed for the first time the creation of a dualist state as a solution for the Hungarian problem in the Habsburg empire, a process which would come to a full fruition in the Compromise of 1867.

The Hungarian diet emerged after Szatmár with many of its traditional powers, although those given up in 1687 and those qualified by the Pragmatic Sanction were not restored before October 1918. In foreign affairs it retained the right to approve treaties and declarations of war affecting Hungary. It was to possess a plenitude of legislative power, not sharing it with any other organ in Vienna or elsewhere. The diet could exercise a measure of influence on the administrative apparatus as well. It alone could elect the *palatin*, who held his office for life, and by wielding the power to grant the right of domicile, it could assure that no undesirable aliens would be appointed to office in Hungary. Only the diet was authorized to grant taxes, except under circumstances most carefully defined in 1715. If a military emergency did not permit convocation of the diet, the king could assemble within Hungary the highest officials of the Land, as well as deputies from nearby counties. This gathering, called *concursus regnicolarum,* was authorized to deal with the emergency, but no other matters. The Hungarian diet did not have a permanent executive committee comparable to the Committee of the Land in the Bohemian Lands or in Inner Austria. As the need arose, it merely selected temporary commissions (*deputationes regnicolaris*) to carry out specific tasks implementing its directives. Inevitably, Charles VI (Charles III in Hungary) found it difficult to deal with the Hungarian diet and limited the number of its sessions. It was not convoked between 1715 and 1722, and then again from 1729 to 1740.

Central Administration

Partly on the recommendation of commissions appointed by the diet in 1715, a reorganization of Hungary's central administration and judiciary was carried out in 1722–23. The chief administrative body in Hungary, the Lieutenancy Council (*consilium regium locumtenentiale, mag-*

yar királyi hegytartó tanács), which remained in Pozsony, retained a greater degree of independence from the king than its counterpart in Bohemia, mainly because its head, the *palatin,* had to be elected by the diet. However, the twenty-two councilors who now constituted its membership were appointed from domiciled Hungarians and paid by the king. The Council was concerned with all aspects of civil administration except fiscal affairs, for which the Hungarian Chamber remained responsible. In this capacity it was also charged with supervising the truculent county governments. Otherwise it was responsible for furnishing military supplies through a subordinate commissariat. Unlike the Bohemian Lieutenancy Council, it exercised no judicial functions. To safeguard Hungary's autonomy, it was to operate independently of the central agencies in Vienna, and entertain no official relations with corresponding administrative bodies in other Lands. The instructions of 1723 admonished the Council explicitly not to carry out any measures inconsistent with the laws of Hungary, and to execute precisely the diet's decisions.

The reorganization of 1722–23 applied also to the Hungarian Court Chancellery in Vienna, which emerged as an adjunct of the Hungarian Lieutenancy Council rather than a supreme administrative and judicial body of the Land like the Bohemian Chancellery. Provisions were made for rotation of members between the Council and the Chancellery. An instruction of Charles VI (III) of 1727 stipulated along the same lines that the Chancellery should serve primarily as a channel for transmission of royal ordinances rather than as a decision-making body in its own right. The officials of the Hungarian Court Chancellery included the Court chancellor (after 1731 always a layman), the vice-chancellor, and twelve court councilors, selected from Hungarian prelates, magnates, and lesser nobles. The third major Hungarian administrative body, the Hungarian Chamber, remained in a state of ambiguous dependence on the central bureaucratic apparatus in Vienna. In 1715 the diet passed a law that the Chamber should be independent of the Viennese *Hofkammer,* as indeed it should have been according to the agreements of the diet of Sopron in 1681. The king accepted this proposition in principle, but insisted that royal decisions ("resolutions") would still be transmitted to the Hungarian Chamber through the *Hofkammer.*

The upper levels of the judiciary were thoroughly reorganized in 1723. The two high judicial bodies, because of the finality of their decisions, preserved greater independence from royal authority than the administrative agencies operating at a corresponding level. The two courts, the Septemviral Table (*tabula septemviralis*) and the Royal Judicial Table (*tabula regia iudiciaria*), had existed in the seventeenth century, but operated only intermittently, often with interruptions of several years owing to warfare and other disorders. Now both were fully institutionalized and regularized. The former, headed by the *palatin,* or his deputy the *iudex curiae,* and including fifteen assessors appointed by the king, met twice a year in Pest. The highest court of all the Lands of the Hungarian Crown (including Croatia and Transylvania), it heard appeals in the most serious cases, and its decisions were not subject to any further review. The Royal Judicial Table was headed by the *personalis,* and included seventeen judges, most of them appointed by the king, others by the *palatin* and the *iudex curiae.* Sitting permanently in Pest it heard appeals from all courts in Hungary proper in matters not serious enough to be reviewed by the Septemviral Table. There was no further recourse from its appellate decisions. In addition, it had original jurisdiction over certain types of cases (*causae tabulares*), such as political offenses and validity of royal privileges. From its judgments in such cases, appeals to the Septemviral Table were possible. The Royal Judicial Table in Hungary proper was an institution analogous to the *Banus'* Table (*Banaltafel*) in Croatia, or the Transylvanian Royal Judicial Table. Cases of original jurisdiction could also be appealed from the latter two courts to the Septemviral Table in Pest. New institutions of intermediate appellate jurisdiction were created in 1723 in the form of the four District Tables (*Distriktualtafeln*), each of them covering a segment of the Land. They were instances of first appeal from the county courts, which remained unaffected by the reforms of 1723. The District Tables replaced the itinerant protonotorial courts existing since the mid-seventeenth century, under which the protonotary with his scribes traveled through the Land and conducted trials wherever relevant cases were found.

The cause of Protestantism was no longer intimately linked with that of Hungarian constitutionalism. It is true that the limited toleration granted in 1681 and 1687 was reconfirmed "for the time being" by the diet of 1715, but the new Hungarian regime tended to weaken further the Protestants' position. Only Catholics were appointed to offices in the central Hungarian administration, and confiscations of Protestant churches and schools began once more. At the diet of 1728–29, Protestant members of a commission were fined for rejecting an oath of office according to a Catholic formula. At this critical juncture, the Habsburg king found himself in a paradoxical position of upholding, on appeal, the Protestants against the diet. In 1731 a royal pronouncement, *Carolina Resolutio,* reaffirmed the established distinction between the public and the private exercise of religion.

Local Administration

The importance of county governments as guarantors of the constitutional order increased during the long intervals between the diet sessions. Execution of royal ordinances remained in their hands, and they could simply ignore any directives contrary to the existing laws. The central government lacked the means to coerce the elected county officials. Most recently, the counties had proved their capacity to obstruct the exercise of absolute royal power during 1698–1703 prior to the Rákóczi insurrection. New regulations issued by the diet in 1723 stipulated that the *főispán* had to hold elections for new county officials at least once every three years, nominating four candidates for each post. The crucial principle that the *alispán* had to be elected by the local nobility was reaffirmed. It was also decreed that the decisions of the general county assemblies could not be altered by the *főispán*, the *alispán*, or a meeting of the county officials (special or particular assembly).

Royal towns suffered from the mounting assertiveness of the nobility. In 1647 the nobles, resident in towns, had been exempted from the jurisdiction of urban authorities. At the same time, a town had to answer to county authorities for an attack on a nobleman within the city walls. The rural seigneurs' pursuit of their own narrow economic interests also helped to weaken urban crafts and commerce. The county assemblies even assumed in 1625 an exclusive jurisdiction over the setting of price and wage levels. While powerless in the diet and suffering encroachments from an overbearing nobility, the Hungarian royal towns—compared with those of Bohemia or Inner Austria—were relatively free of intervention by royal authorities. Only the heads of town councils needed the king's confirmation. Except for the climax of the absolutist campaign in the 1670s, royal officials were not authorized to intervene in the selection of town councils or in management of town finances.

The exploitation of the peasants mounted chiefly owing to the nobility's unwillingness to share in public financial burdens. The peasantry remained responsible for almost all the state taxes, in addition to the dues to the seigneurs and to the church. From 1715 onward the tax burden increased to cover the cost of the standing army, for which the peasants had to supply recruits as well. The labor obligations also kept increasing in the seventeenth century as the seigneurs undertook to cultivate their demesnes more intensively.

Emigration into the territories reconquered from the Turks appeared as an attractive alternative, offering easier living conditions. In response, county ordinances attempted to restrict the right of free movement, which Hungarian peasantry had enjoyed since 1547 (in contrast with the situation in the Bohemian Lands or in the Slovene territories). In 1715 severe penalties were enacted for failure to return peasant fugitives, including the loss of villages by the seigneurs who provided havens for such migrants. The seigneurs were forbidden to shift their own serfs from one manor to another if the latter lay in a different county. Fortunately for the peasant serfs, these restrictions on migration proved largely unenforceable. In addition, the king began to recognize the need to protect Hungarian peasants as a way of safeguarding the tax base. Under royal prompting the diet passed laws in 1715 and 1723 requiring county authorities to protect the peasants against abuse of power by their seigneurs. The value of these enactments, however, was even more problematic than that of analogous measures in the Bohemian Lands, or in Inner Austria, since the lords' right of tax exemption remained in essence unchanged.

AGRICULTURE, INDUSTRY, AND TRADE[12]

Ascendancy of Agriculture over Industry, 1620–1711

The marked predominance of agricultural production over crafts and mining, which had developed in the Habsburg-controlled part of Hungary in the sixteenth century, continued throughout the next century as well. The main agricultural products also remained the same: grain, cattle, and wine. Grain was destined primarily for the domestic market, especially for consumption by the standing armies stationed in the border areas. Cattle constituted the main part of Hungary's exports, and were mostly sent to Austria, the Bohemian Lands, southern Germany, and Venetia. Wine was both marketed internally and exported, particularly to Silesia and Poland. The large demesne estates focused on raising grain, especially suitable to serf labor. The share of the demesne estate averaged between one-quarter and one-third of the total grain output on a manor. Its share in viticulture, and particularly in cattle raising, was substantially smaller. Peasant homesteads accounted for between six-sevenths and seven-eighths of the wine production on a manor, and the demesne estates often did not keep more cattle than a well-to-do peasant would. Nevertheless the seigneurs—because of their monopolistic rights to trade with the products of their subject peasants—reaped considerable profits also from cattle and, above all, wine trade.

Because of price fluctuations, Hungarian agriculture, however, did not enjoy the relative prosperity after 1620 that it had known in the second half of the sixteenth century and the opening decades of the

12. Economic data in this section are derived from Ervin Pamlényi, ed., *A History of Hungary* (London: Collet's 1975), pp. 148–50, 182–86, 190–91; *Istoriia Vengrii* (Moscow: Nauka, 1971), 1:453–56; L. Makkai, "Die Hauptzüge der wirtschaftlich-sozialen Entwicklung Ungarns im 15.–17. Jahrhundert," in *La Renaissance et la Réformation en Pologne et en Hongrie* (Budapest: Akadémiai Kiadó, 1963), pp. 35–46; J. Szűcs, "Das Städtewesen in Ungarn im 15.–17. Jahrhundert," ibid., pp. 129–64; V. Zimányi, "Mouvement des prix hongrois et l'évolution européenne, XVIe–XVIIIe s.," *Acta Historica* 19 (1973): 305–33; Zsigmond P. Pach, "Le commerce du Levant et la Hongrie au XVIe siècle," in *La Pologne et la Hongrie aux XVIe–XVIIIe siècles* (Budapest: Aкадémiai Kiadó, 1981), pp. 45–55.

seventeenth. Agricultural prices in Hungary, as well as in the rest of East Central Europe, were adversely affected by marked improvements of West European agricultural productivity, especially by the agricultural revolution in Great Britain and the Netherlands. As exemplified mainly by the market of Sopron in western Hungary, the effect was particularly noticeable for grain and cattle. Grain prices leveled off in the period 1620–60, and were actually declining from the 1660s to the 1680s. The price of cattle was subject to periodic declines from 1620 to 1680, and began to rise only in the 1680s and 1690s. As an exception, the price of wine rose steadily throughout the seventeenth century, although at a more moderate rate than during the sixteenth. The effect of the less favorable structure of agricultural prices was cushioned in Hungary—compared with some other parts of East Central Europe—by two circumstances. In the first place, since grain did not play a significant role in Hungary's exports, the drops in price did not have the same disruptive effect as in a heavily grain-exporting country like Poland. In the second place, the rising price of wine to some extent compensated for the instability in the price of cattle.

In contrast to the relative vigor of agricultural production, crafts continued to stagnate at a low level in the royal towns. Artisan production of a more rudimentary type still grew in the countryside, and most rural towns and larger villages acquired representatives of the basic crafts, including cobblers, tailors, blacksmiths, locksmiths, potters, furriers, millers, and weavers. These rural artisans not only excluded urban craftsmen from the peasant market but threatened them on their home ground by seeking to trade in the larger towns as well.

The urban craftsmen, particularly in the royal towns, constantly strove to bolster their shaky position. One way was to band together for mutual defense. Thus the pervasiveness of guild organization reached its climax toward the end of the seventeenth century, when crafts consisting of three or four masters would no longer be considered too small to form a guild. The guilds in turn increased their efforts to suppress competing forms of artisan production. They elicited prohibitions on the sale (in towns) of products, such as shoes or hats, by the rural artisans, and they also, on the whole successfully, fought the emergence of the putting-out system. The latter efforts were particularly damaging to the prospects of Hungary's industrial development. Accordingly the techniques and organization of artisan production in Hungary remained essentially unchanged since the fifteenth century. There was no development of the putting-out system or the manufactories as, for instance, in the contemporary Bohemian Lands.

The pattern of external trade changed little. The almost exclusively agricultural exports focused on cattle, and imports consisted predominantly of artisan products—especially cloth. The ruination of many

Hungarian traders by the ravages of the Thirty Years' War facilitated the assumption of Hungary's external trade by Austrian commercial firms in the second half of the seventeenth century, including the crucial cattle exports and cloth imports. Also by mid-seventeenth century the spice trade from the Ottoman Empire no longer passed directly into Hungary. Instead it had been monopolized by Dutch and English intermediaries.

Economic Reconstruction, 1711–40

The Hungarian territories freed from the Turks after 1683 now rejoined those held by the Habsburg continuously since 1526. Because the quarter of a century before the peace of Szatmár of 1711 was filled with external wars and internal strife, the economic reconstruction of the regained lands and their integration with the rest of Hungary began only in the second decade of the eighteenth century. Repopulating the newly occupied territories was a major challenge. The surveys of 1715–20 showed that although they represented over half of Hungary's total area, these territories contained only one-fifth of the total population. Many peasants living under oppressive conditions in the Hungarian counties, which had been under Habsburg sovereignity since 1526, preferred to migrate into the reconquered regions, where they became exempted from feudal dues and state taxes for one or two years. The lower nobility remained opposed to the peasant exodus, and county ordinances after 1713, seeking to bar migration, expressed primarily its wishes. These measures were not truly effective mainly because the government had little interest in returning the escaped serfs to tax-exempt nobles. The county of Szabolcs alone lost 1,347 peasant families between 1724 and 1735. The government also wished to induce foreign peasants to settle in the areas conquered from the Turks. In 1723 the diet passed a law exempting them from feudal dues and state taxes for six years. Vienna preferred to attract Catholic Germans, who—aside from their economic contribution—would spread the German language and strengthen the Catholic Church.

Hungary's agricultural production steadily expanded as increasing amounts of land were cultivated by the new settlers. Vienna welcomed this trend, since its new mercantilist policy viewed Hungary as a supplier of cheap foodstuffs to other parts of the monarchy. The export of cattle, destined for Vienna, northern Italy, and elsewhere in the monarchy, not only maintained its traditional volume but increased to some extent during the first half of the eighteenth century. For the first time, grain became a major component of Hungary's exports, although considerable amounts were also consumed by the standing army created in Hungary in 1715. Wine exports, disrupted by the previous warfare and insurrection, once more flourished after 1711. Particularly Sopron and Tokay wines were shipped to Poland, Russia, and northern Europe. These directions of trade had the advantage of avoiding transit through Austrian territory, where Hungarian wines were subject to discriminatory tariffs.

Hungary's agriculture also improved qualitatively during the first half of the eighteenth century. New plants were cultivated, including tobacco, corn, potatoes, and feed crops. More intensive methods of cattle raising, such as use of dry fodder, were sought to offset the diminution of pasture land as more of it was put under the plow. Royal towns also strove to increase the yield of wheat and wine on their agricultural lands.

The development of urban crafts started from a low point after the compromise of Szatmár in 1711. The situation was bad enough in the areas originally held by the Habsburgs, where artisan production had stagnated in towns for the last two centuries. It was even worse in the territories wrested from the Turks. In general, only 1 percent of Hungary's inhabitants were employed in crafts or trade, and most of them resided in the older Habsburg territories of Hungary. Overall, not more than 10 to 20 percent of the population in towns were artisans, and even they could not depend for their maintenance only on their craft. As a rule they also held agricultural land, especially vineyards, and periodically closed down their workshops in order to till the soil.

The situation of urban crafts noticeably improved toward the middle of the eighteenth century, as with the increase of agricultural trade the demand for domestic artisan goods also grew. In larger towns, artisans were at last able to concentrate on their crafts to the exclusion of agriculture. In twenty or thirty towns the proportion of artisans reached between a fifth and a quarter of the total population, and the number of different crafts rose to between fifty and sixty.

Aside from certain stillborn ideas about industrial development in Cardinal Kollonich's *Einrichtungswerk,* mercantilist thought first stirred in Hungary in the second decade of the eighteenth century, some sixty or seventy years after its beginning in the Bohemian Lands. The Hungarian diet provided the occasion by appointing a commission in 1715 to propose reforms in public life. A member of the commission, Sándor Károlyi, urged establishment—with the aid of foreign specialists—of manufactories in Hungary to turn local raw materials into finished goods instead of exporting them. He also advocated the abolition of artisan guilds as obstacles to achieving higher forms of production. These appeals had little effect in official circles, since Vienna did not favor Hungary's industrial development, and the diet was too conservative to endorse any new departures. The idea of manufactories (to produce cloth, iron, china, or glass), however, sparked the interest of several Hungarian aristocrats in the 1720s. Károlyi himself established the first manufactory in 1722 to fabricate woolen cloth. Soon afterward similar enterprises were founded by János Pálffy and the Esterházy family. Although these early manufactories were destined to fail by midcentury, they represented the first stirrings of a new spirit of economic entrepreneurship. The older forms of nonguild industrial production—mining and metallurgy—continued in the Slovak area of northern Hungary, as well as in the newly acquired Romanian territories of Transylvania.

The commercial development of Hungary was impeded during the first half of the eighteenth century by poor conditions of roads and other means of communication, lack of credit facilities, and the narrowness of the local market. External trade remained relatively strong. The traditional preponderance of agricultural exports and industrial imports persisted, although significant changes occurred within this basic framework. Among the exports the proportion of cattle diminished from four-fifths to one-half as the weight of wine and grain increased. As a reflection of Vienna's mercantilist policies, imports originated increasingly from other parts of the Habsburg realm rather than from foreign countries. In the organization of Hungary's trade the so-called Greek merchants played a new role. Ethnically not only Greek but also Serbian, Bulgarian, and Armenian, these subjects of the sultan originally traded with imports from the Ottoman Empire. Before long they handled products of Hungarian origin as well.

The Slovaks

EMERGENCE OF NATIONAL CONSCIOUSNESS, 1620–1711

Czech Influence

Several themes continued to characterize the history of the Slovak territory in the seventeenth century: the devastating struggle of Hungarian nobility against the Habsburg kings, the recurring waves of repression against the Protestants culminating in 1671–73, and the threat of the neighboring Turkish power, the detrimental effects of which were only partly offset—from the standpoint of Slovak national interest—by isolating the Slovak territory from an overwhelming Magyar impact. The earlier influence of Czech culture intensified after 1620 with the arrival of Czech Protestant émigrés, estimated at five thousand families, who settled mostly in Nitra and Trenčín counties. They included such important literary figures as Jakub Jakobeus (1591–1660) and Jiří

Třanovský (1592–1637), who contributed significantly to the development of Slovak culture.

Essentially, Czech remained the language of correspondence and administration in the Slovak areas. The Protestants, for whom it was still the language of religious services, used it more often in literature than the Catholics, who were also less concerned with maintaining its literary norms. While the language of the standard Protestant hymnal, *Cithara Sanctorum* (1636), was purely Czech, that of its counterpart, *Cantus Catholici* (1655) of Benedikt Szölösi, contained many traces of Slovak. The Catholic milieu around the Jesuit university of Trnava produced a special kind of Slovakized Czech toward the end of the seventeenth century. This process culminated in the sermons of Alexander Máčaj, published in 1718, so strongly affected by the West Slovak dialect as to be considered the first book in genuine Slovak. With some exceptions, the most notable of which was Daniel Sinapius-Horčička in his catechism of 1683, Slovak Protestant writers advocated the retention of standard Czech. Tobiáš Masník in 1696 stressed the need for interchangeability of literature with the Czechs. Matúš Michalovič around 1700 declared Czech to be the literary form of Slovak, while the highly respected Daniel Krman (1663–1740) at the same time held that Slovak was related to Czech as a primitive mother to a more advanced offspring.

Slovak National Consciousness

The seventeenth century witnessed the birth of a Slovak national consciousness reflected in both Protestant and Catholic publications. The real or potential bearers of this consciousness were segments of the nobility and the burghers, for whom the patriotic authors primarily wrote. Jakobeus dedicated his work *Lacrumae gentis slavonicae* (1642) to three specific nobles, Horčička his *Neoforum* (1678) to the noble youth of five Slovak counties, and Ján Fischer Piscatoris his *De origine, iure ac utilitate linguae slavonicae* (1697) to several burghers of Banská Bystrica. Jakobeus in his *Lacrumae* deplored the condition of the Slovaks and of their homeland among the vicissitudes of the seventeenth century. In a lost history he traced their origin to the time of the Tower of Babel. Szölösi in his introduction to *Cantus Catholici* spoke of the Slovaks as the Pannonian nation, and proudly linked them with the tradition of the ninth-century Great Moravia and the mission of Cyril and Methodius. Horčička exhorted the Slovaks to take pride in their language and national past. The Jesuit author, Martin Szentiványi in his *Dissertatio paralipomenica* (1699), presented the Slovaks as the original inhabitants of ancient Pannonia. He thus argued against the claims of original settlement—hence superior rights—in Hungary by German and Magyar writers on behalf of their own nations.

A salient feature of the emerging national consciousness was the sense of kinship with other Slavs, of belonging to a single *natio slavica*. Although this sentiment occurred in the thought of other Slav nations, the Slovaks probably experienced it most intensely. Among the Catholics, Slav feelings were undoubtedly strengthened by the international ambiance of the university of Trnava, which in its faculty and student body mixed the Slovaks with members of virtually all the other Slav nationalities. The nationally conscious writers, cited above, took special pride in the size of the "Slav nation," spreading from the Adriatic to the Baltic, and all the way to China in the east. The Slav tongue was praised, especially by Piscatoris, for its antiquity, beauty, and usefulness—among other things, as a tool of commercial transactions with the vast Russian Empire. Attention was called to its designation as one of the three liturgical languages by the popes since the ninth century. The Slovak writers felt Slav unity so strongly that it becomes difficult at times to determine whether, when referring to the *Slavi* or *Slováci,* they meant the "Slavs" in general or specifically the "Slovaks," unless they used special modifiers, as in the expressions *Hungaro-Slavi* and *Slavi Pannoniae.*

Slovak-German Conflict in Towns

The towns remained the main arena in which the issue of Slovak nationality played a political role. The struggle of Slovak burghers with the dominant German patriciate continued. In the second quarter of the seventeenth century it focused on Banská Bystrica, although the Hungarian diet in 1635 also had to deal with national conflicts in Košice and Prešov. Agents of the Hungarian Chamber in the crucial Banská Bystrica were hostile to Slovak aspirations, warning the emperor persistently into the 1640s that weakening the German burghers' power there and in other towns would simultaneously undermine the authority of imperial officials. Not until 1650 did the Slovaks receive equal rights in the town government of Banská Bystrica, thanks to the *palatin's* intervention.

In the second half of the seventeenth century, especially during the reign of Leopold I, the Slovaks benefited from the imperial government's loss of interest in supporting the German burghers, whom Vienna now viewed as disloyal heretics, no more reliable than the rebellious Hungarian nobles. Without external support the Germans had to yield power to the Slovaks in the last quarter of the seventeenth century in most of the mining towns of central Slovakia, and early in the following century even in the most important centers of the region, Banská Bystrica and Banská Štiavnica. The Counter Reformation also weakened German elites in the towns of western Slovakia, especially Pozsony, and in such towns of eastern Slovakia as Levoča, Prešov, and Košice. An indication of Slovak gains in the latter part of the seventeenth century was the increasing appearance of guild regulations in Slovak in previously German-dominated towns. The advance in the towns, however, was of limited value for Slovak national life. Having satisfied their local objectives, Slovak burghers, failed to embrace wider national goals. Moreover, the value of towns as a political power base, never very great in Hungary, was further depreciated by their current economic decline.

Seigneurs and Peasants

Slovak peasantry experienced increasing insecurity because the Hungarian county governments, though effective instruments for defense of noble privileges against royal authority, failed to provide for the physical safety of the rural populace. For self-protection the peasants were forced to organize armed groups to fight bandits and Turkish raiders in villages, districts, and finally entire counties. The first such group sprang up in Tekov county in 1607. Known as *sedliacka stolica* (peasant county), this kind of organization received official recognition in the 1630s.[13]

Partly as a result of the nobility's increased powers after 1608, the personal dependence of the peasantry on their seigneurs tightened during the seventeenth century, fully instituting the conditions of the second serfdom. County ordinances virtually abolished the former freedom of migration, and direct rule by seigneurs replaced self-government in the villages. The peasants' economic obligations likewise grew more burdensome. Because of the expansion of the demesnes and the decline in peasant population, the amount of compulsory labor (*robota*) increased often to three or four days a week per household, compared with the previous century's statutory limit of one day. The dues in money (*census*) rose to between four and six florins per household from the rate of one florin established in 1548. The seigneurs also exacted larger payment in kind, above all in grain, which they either marketed or used in brewing beer. Exactions by the state mounted as well. The main tax (*contributio*) rose to twenty florins from one or two at midcentury, and four to six in the late sixteenth century. The length of compulsory labor on military fortifications was doubled in 1657 to twelve days per year.

The enlarged demesne estates directly cultivated by the seigneurs required expansion of the administrative apparatus on the manors.[14] The

13. According to Štefan Janšák, the *sedliacka stolica* of northern Hungary was of purely Slovak origin; see his *Slovensko v dobe uhorského feudalizmu* (Bratislava: Čs. Zemedelské Muzeum, 1932), p. 22.

14. With the increasing importance of agricultural activity and the decline of the military function of the manor, the economic official or *provisor* rose to the top of manorial officialdom, overshadowing the *castellanus*, who turned from a military commander into a police chief (*polkoráb, burggraf*), supervising also animal raising, forestry, and construction activities. As the seventeenth century progressed, the *provisor* enlarged his staff, con-

oppressive system of manorial management and increased exactions led to major uprisings of Slovak peasants. One occurred in the Borsod county, spreading to Zemplín, Šariš, and Spiš in 1631–32; another broke out in Orava county in 1672. The campaigns of Thököly (1674–78) and Francis Rákóczi (1703–11) were also accompanied by peasant insurrections.

End of the Turkish Threat

The Turkish menace to Slovak territory persisted until its abrupt termination in the great Turkish war of 1683–99 (the second Turkish war of Leopold I). Marauding raids by the Turks increased in frequency in the 1620s and 1640s, mainly into western and central Slovakia. In the full-fledged war of 1663–64 (the first Turkish war of Leopold I) the Ottoman troops conquered the key fortress of Nové Zámky and penetrated deeply into western Slovakia, seizing temporarily Nitra (Nyitra), Hlohovec, and Levice. Nové Zámky became the center of a new paşalik that was to include sancaks carved out of the newly conquered territories. Before the end of the war, however, the Turkish conquests were drastically reduced, and after the peace of Vasvár (1664) the Turks administered the remains of the new paşalik centrally from Nové Zámky. The pivotal war of 1683 resulted in a rapid and permanent conquest by the imperial army of Esztergom (1684), Nové Zámky (1685), and Eger (1687), the three centers from which the Turks had ruled strips of Slovak territory, and subjected much wider zones to their extortionary practices.

AFTER SZATMÁR, 1711–40

Demographic and Ethnic Trends

After the peace of Szatmár (1711), following a decade of insurrection by Hungarian nobles, Slovak territory was in a state of devastation akin to that of the Bohemian Lands after the Thirty Years' War. On the whole the open plains of the south suffered more than the mountainous regions of the north. Even the relative stability and tranquility of the period after Szatmár still was marred by political persecution and natural disasters. Of the former, the repression of the Protestants became particularly severe in the 1720s, and subsided only with the *Re-*

---

sisting of the scribe and the controller of alcoholic beverages (*cellarius*), by the addition of an accountant (*perceptor*) and an overseer of crop production (*frumentarius*). Officials with the title of *spanus* (*dvorský*) managed, in the name of the *provisor*, estates located outside the administrative center of the manor.

solutio Carolina of 1731. Of the natural calamities, two waves of plague—probably cholera epidemics—were especially devastating. In 1708–12 the disease hit eastern Slovakia; in 1739–42 the contagion spread in western Slovakia from Poland, and in eastern from Transylvania.

A measure of relief for Slovak counties from overcrowding and seigneurial oppression came with the new opportunities for both licit and clandestine migrations. The largest exodus occurred in the northern counties. Many of the migrants settled in more southerly Slovak counties, for instance in the vicinity of the central mining towns, which had suffered severe population losses during the Rákóczi uprising and in the plague of 1708–12, and which offered employment opportunities as economic activity regained its momentum. Others moved into central Hungary and farther south. Altogether an estimated fifteen thousand Slovak families migrated in the first half of the eighteenth century. As a result, the border of Slovak ethnic settlement, which had retracted north two hundred years earlier, once more moved farther south, especially in the area of Košice and east of Pozsony. The population movements also helped to generate a sense of Slovak ethnic unity, as the arrival of settlers from the north into central and southern Slovak counties tended to blur regional linguistic and psychological idiosyncrasies.

Emerging Conflict with the Magyars

The issue of Slovak nationality continued to play a political role. It was less conspicuous in towns where the struggle of Slovak burghers with German patricians was subsiding, although the Hungarian diet still had to intervene in 1723 and again in 1729 to prohibit limitations on access of Slovaks to guild memberships. A new, more significant national conflict emerged, involving the right of the Slovaks to play a political role in the Hungarian state. In 1722 Michael Bencsik, professor of Hungarian law in Trnava, in a book addressed to the diet, contested the political rights of the burghers and nobles of Trenčín county—and by implication of all Slovak nobles and burghers—on the grounds that they were descendants of the nation of Prince Svatopluk (d. 894), who had sold his land to the Magyars for a white horse, and was subsequently defeated by them. Therefore, the Slovaks were subject to the Magyar nation by the right of conquest. The assembly of Trenčín county commissioned a rebuttal by the learned Jesuit, Ján Balthazár Magin. Magin in his *Murices sive apologia* (1728) claimed that the Magyars had not defeated Svatopluk. Instead, the Slovaks had received them hospitably and agreed voluntarily to unite in a single state. Thus the relationship between the two nations was based not on conquest of one by the other but on a free contract between equals. Bencsik's challenge was also answered, among others, by another Jesuit, Samuel Timon, who in his *Imago Antiquae Hungariae* (1733) added another twist to the quasi-historical argumentation by maintaining that Svatopluk was the ruler of a distinct Moravian nation and not a Slovak. The Slovaks, conquered and oppressed by the Moravians, had turned for help to the Magyars and, after the defeat of Svatopluk, had entered as equals into a political union with the Magyars. The debate precipitated by Bencsik may be considered the opening or preliminary phase of the political contest between the Slovaks and the Magyars.

Seigneurs and Peasants

In the Slovak countryside the process of enlarging the demesnes at the expense of peasant lands occurred in the first half of the eighteenth century on a much larger scale than ever before. The seigneurs usually seized the land that had been abandoned by the peasants. Large tracts thus became available as a result of war devastation, plague, famine, and migration. For instance, between 1715 and 1720 in Šariš county 12,000 Pozsony morgen[15] of land were abandoned, and in Liptov county 8,600 morgen. Many peasants left their homesteads also in the counties of Nitra, Tekov, Turiec, Hont, and Gemer. Where conditions did not favor expansion of the demesnes, this abandoned land was usually leased by the seigneurs to peasants, but for a higher return than the usual one-ninth of the harvest required from regular serfs.

The economic obligations of the serfs remained high. Labor dues averaged three days per week, almost nowhere falling below two days, and in some localities rising to four or five. Moreover, it became common to exact the full quota not only from holders of a whole hide but also from those who held only a fraction of a hide. In general, the required amount of labor tended to be higher in the south of Slovakia, where the demesnes were bigger, than in the north, where the conditions were less suitable for large estates. The required amount of money dues (*census*) varied greatly depending on the locality and tended to be in inverse ratio to the amount of labor due. It ranged from less than a florin to over ten florins per household. The rates were usually higher in the north and the east of Slovakia and lower in the west and south. A definite decline occurred in the required amount of dues in kind, which lost importance for the seigneurs with the expanded cultivation of the demesnes. In particular, the traditional ninth of the grain harvest was often replaced by a sum of money or a fixed amount of grain. The

15. A morgen represented a plot of land that could be plowed during one morning. The precise amount varied between 0.66 and 2 acres. The Pozsony morgen was the basis of the later generally used Hungarian morgen, which amounted to approximately 4,300 square meters.

peasantry was harmed economically by mounting restrictions on the use of the forests, resulting partly from the conservation policy of the state and partly from the seigneurs' new interest in wood trade.

With the introduction of the standing army, the Slovak area was subject to exceptionally heavy taxation. The counties of central and southern Hungary, recently regained from the Turks, failed to provide a proportionate share of revenue because of special exemptions and the still rudimentary and not very effective machinery for tax collection. Thus the Slovak territory had to make up the difference and was assigned a disproportionate number of taxation units or *portae*.[16] For instance, in 1734 Slovakia was allotted 2,260 *portae* out of 5,405 for all of Hungary. Accordingly, the Slovak area had to pay almost half the total taxes while representing only 20 percent of the territory of Hungary proper (without Transylvania and Croatia). In that year, Trenčín county protested that it alone was assigned more *portae* than nine counties of southeastern Hungary altogether. The quartering and provisioning of army units in the villages—in the absence of military barracks—represented an additional levy. Although the cost was deductible from the taxes, the deductions never equaled the market value of these services. In addition, Slovakia had to supply disproportionately large numbers of soldiers for the standing army, because the quotas of recruits corresponded to the number of assigned *portae*.

Because emigration provided a safety valve, no peasant uprisings occurred in Slovakia during the three decades after the peace of Szatmár. Social discontent, however, was reflected by the bands of outlaws infesting the mountains of northeastern Slovakia, especially in the 1710s and 1730s. Recruited primarily from the remnants of the *kurucok* detachments and army deserters, these marauders were at times viewed as fighters against an unjust social order, and one of their leaders, Juraj Jánošík (executed in 1713), turned into a legendary folk hero.

AGRICULTURE, CRAFTS, AND TRADE[17]

Continuing Crisis, 1620–1711

Because of Turkish incursions and noble insurrections, Slovak economy not only stagnated but even regressed in some sectors during the seventeenth century. Its backbone, agriculture, remained at a primitive

16. Having undergone several conceptual transformations since the sixteenth century, the Hungarian *porta* after 1723 represented merely an abstract unit of taxation.
17. Economic data in this section are derived from *Dejiny Slovenska,* ed. Ľudevít Holotík (Bratislava: Slovenská akadémia vied, 1961), 1:297–362; Pavol Horváth, *Poddaný ľud na Slovensku v prvej polovici XVIII. storočia* (Bratislava: Slovenská akadémia vied, 1963), passim; Anton Špiesz, *Manufaktúrne obdobie na Slovensku, 1725–1825* (Bratislava: Slovenská akadémia vied, 1961), pp. 21–36; Otakar Mrázek, *Vývoj průmyslu v českých zemích a na*

level, normally employing the three-field system, and in some areas, such as Orava county, the two-field system. The soil had to lie periodically fallow not only because of lack of fertilizers but because heavy planting of grains was exhausting the soil. The yields exceeded the amounts of seed only three or four times in the south, and two to three times in the mountainous north.

The size and number of estates directly cultivated by the seigneurs were increasing, stimulated in part by the demand for agricultural supplies for the military units stationed in Slovakia. The growth, however, was less rapid in the seventeenth century (particularly in its second half) than it had been in the second half of the sixteenth century. There were also reversals owing mainly to confiscations of noble properties. A noble estate ordinarily did not yet exceed the combined size and grain production of several peasant homesteads. Thus peasant households continued to account for the bulk of agricultural output.

With the exception of a few areas, cereals dominated agricultural production. After rye, which was the most common grain, the second place belonged to barley, wheat declined from its previous position of primacy to a third place and oats remained last. All principal types of grain were grown in most areas with little regional specialization. Grape crops were second in importance to grain in Slovak agriculture. In a few districts, especially in the southwest, grapes became the main product. Wine still surpassed grain as an article of export, and was therefore particularly valued as a source of cash income. In the seventeenth century the area of viticulture reached far to the north, up to the line of Trenčín-Bánovice–Nová Baňa–Krupina in the west and Vranov–Humenné in the east. Cattle raising was important not only for domestic consumption but above all for export. The center of cattle production and trade was in Pozsony and Zvolen counties. In the former, subject peasants held over 30,000 head of cattle toward the end of the seventeenth century. Sheep raising was widespread in northern and central Slovakia. Forestry and lumbering developed strongly in the northern mountains, responding to the needs for charcoal by smelters and for timber in mines and anti-Turkish fortifications.

The towns were declining economically in the seventeenth century, not only because of the direct ravages of warfare and insurrections but also as a result of the crushing tax burden to maintain the military establishment. In 1638 Pozsony had to pay 12,000 florins as a royal tax to the Hungarian Chamber, Košice 10,000 florins, Levoča, Trnava, and the central mining towns 6,000 each. The rate kept increasing, amount-

Slovensku od manufaktury do roku 1918 (Prague: Nakl. politické literatury, 1964), pp. 42–44; Anton Špiesz, *Remeslo na Slovensku v období existencie cechov* (Bratislava: Slovenská akadémia vied, 1972), pp. 41–102; *Přehled dějin Československa* (Prague: Academia, 1982), I/2:289–301.

ing for Pozsony, for example, to 18,000 florins in 1665. At first, the urban population held steady despite economic decline, because the towns afforded greater physical safety, but it began to decrease in the last third of the seventeenth century. For example, in Levoča the number of houses started to diminish after 1667, and the population of Rožňava sank from 3,000 inhabitants to 240 families by the end of the century. The towns were also harmed by the nobility's assumption of power (early in the century) to regulate, through the county governments, the prices of both agricultural and artisan products. Inevitably these regulations discriminated against urban crafts and commerce. Despite the stagnation or decline of crafts, the number of guilds was rising in some towns, but this reflected an increase in specialization not in the total volume of production. In seven large towns the guilds ranged from twenty to forty-five. At the turn of the century, a total of about 1,000 guilds was divided among 160 localities. The decline of urban crafts, and of the power of the guilds, was accompanied by a partial transfer of crafts to the countryside, particularly in the form of cottage production. In seventeenth-century Slovakia, the domestic industries were engaged above all in making linen, and to a lesser extent coarse woolens. The first textile manufactory on Slovak soil, established in 1666 by the archbishop of Esztergom in Hubice on Žitný Ostrov, represented a short-lived experiment to produce better quality woolen cloth.

In the traditionally important sector of mining and metallurgy the production of precious metals suffered from repeated warfare, with the mines alternately plundered by the Hungarian insurgents and the imperial troops. Only in the chief center, Banská Štiavnica, did silver production flourish from the 1670s into the 1690s. The output of copper diminished compared with the sixteenth century, especially in Banská Bystrica, owing to poor maintenance of the mines, lack of investment capital, and competition of cheaper Swedish and overseas metals on the European market. The copper production in Spiš county was not so adversely affected. The output of iron, stimulated by military needs, flourished above all in Gemer county. Iron metallurgy traditionally employed small furnaces, the so-called Slovak ovens, but in 1680 the first high furnace was erected in Dobšina. Annual production of iron in Slovakia reached a capacity of 3,500 tons by the turn of the century. The first known use of gunpowder to extend mineshafts, anywhere in Europe, occurred in Banská Štiavnica in 1627.

The ravages of the seventeenth century interfered with the volume of trade, and this detrimental effect was not completely offset by the rising demand for military supplies. Internal trade in western Slovakia centered in Pozsony (wine and cattle) and Trnava (grain); in the east in Košice, Prešov, and Levoča. Aside from the towns and the nobility, the peasantry also marketed internally such articles as grain, salt, wood, and linen. The competition of rural seigneurs, as well as foreign merchants, caused the trade of royal towns to reach a low point around 1700. External trade was relatively well developed. Exports consisted chiefly of foodstuffs (cattle, wine, grain) and raw materials (copper, iron). Cattle exports, dominated by Austrian merchants favored by the *Hofkammer,* were directed especially to Vienna, Moravia, and Silesia. Reaching a peak in the first half of the seventeenth century, wine exports went mostly to Poland from east Slovakia (more than 63,000 barrels in 1637–41), and to Vienna and Moravia from western Slovakia. Imports included finer kinds of woolens, silk cloth, manufactured products, and overseas goods. An exceptional position was occupied by Prešov, which acted as a commercial hub for Transylvania's exports and imports.

Slow Recovery, 1711–40

Because of the large-scale abandonment of homesteads by the peasantry, the amount of cultivated land seriously diminished in the beginning of the eighteenth century and increased only gradually after the compromise of Szatmár in 1711. Rye, barley, wheat, and oats—in that order of importance—remained the basic crops. Only in the valleys of central Slovakia did the dominant rye yield its primacy to barley, and in the high mountainous areas of the north to oats. Viticulture remained important and relatively widespread. The vineyards, however, had suffered particularly serious damage from warfare at the turn of the century, and the recovery was retarded by growing competition from other parts of Hungary. Among other crops, the cultivation of flax, especially in the north, and of hemp in the south increased in importance with the growing demand for textile fibers, and to a lesser extent for oil (from the seeds). Two new crops had appeared by 1712—corn and tobacco. Tobacco production rose so rapidly that by 1727 it could be exported from western Slovakia to Moravia and Austria. Cattle raising was particularly significant in northern and central Slovakia, above all in the Kysúce region and Zvolen county respectively. In southern Slovakia, where pasture land was relatively scarce, cattle were raised primarily for draft power rather than for milk or meat.

Agricultural implements were primitive, with wood prevailing over metal in the construction of plows and harrows. Rollers remained unknown, and scythes were used only for grass, while cereal grains were cut with sickles. Agricultural techniques also remained at a low level. The most common three-field system involved a sequence of winter cereals, spring cereals, and the fallow. The peasants often violated the system by planting such crops as millet, buckwheat, or hemp on the fallow, evading seigneurial regulations and further exhausting the soil. The scarcity of fertilizers, due to the small number of cattle and their meager diet, permitted manuring a field only about once every six years.

In the beginning of the eighteenth century urban craft production was in deep crisis because of the extreme deterioration of towns. The population of even the royal towns was now only between 1,500 and 3,000, except for Pozsony (10,000), Banská Štiavnica (7,000), Kremnica (5,000), and Košice (4,000). There were only about 5,000 guild craftsmen in Slovakia, but even these did not find sufficient demand for their products, and supplemented their income with agricultural activities. They suffered greatly from the competition of village artisans, whom the guilds were unable to suppress. From the 1710s into the 1730s, however, the situation began to improve with the general slow rise in the level of economic activity. A prime example was the mining towns of central Slovakia, where the miners created a sizable market for artisan products. The craftsmen of this area, in addition, carried their goods south into the Magyar territory as far as Kecskemét and Szeged. Specialization of craft production began to develop not only in individual towns but in entire counties. Production of iron articles was concentrated in Spiš and Gemer counties, and leather tanning in Trenčín county. In certain towns, especially Kežmarok and Levoča, crafts and trade could once more become the dominant occupation of the population.

The relative overpopulation of the countryside in Slovakia (compared with the Magyar territory), as well as the need to raise cash for feudal dues and state taxes, favored further development of domestic production by the peasants. In addition to earlier linen weaving, the making of shingles and wooden implements and vessels spread in the mountainous north. The peasants also produced charcoal for the smelters in central Slovakia, cheese from sheep's milk in Orava and Liptov counties, and famous medicinal oils from herbs in Turiec county, exported as far away as Russia.

The development of trade, like that of the crafts, followed a moderately ascending curve during the three decades after the compromise of Szatmár (1711). Peasants' opportunities for trading were significantly increased in 1723, when the exclusive right of the seigneurs to purchase many peasant products was curtailed. In larger towns, trade was still dominated by merchants associated in guilds who jealously guarded their privileges. Nonresident and foreign merchants could sell only at annual fairs. Slovak merchants, in turn, attended fairs abroad, particularly in Wrocław (Breslau), Leipzig, and Vienna. As elsewhere in Hungary, in Slovakia a special problem was posed by so-called Greek merchants, subjects of the sultan, who were permitted to import goods from the Ottoman Empire. Soon exceeding their authorized functions, they engaged in internal trade, particularly with linen, wool, wine, grain, and cattle. Merchants of Slovakia complained against such activities as early as 1715, but it was only in 1741 that they secured a measure of redress.

Although all of Hungary lagged markedly behind other parts of the monarchy in the development of manufactories, within Hungary in the first half of the eighteenth century the Slovak area afforded the best preconditions for an emergence of this more advanced mode of production. The peasant domestic output could supply the required fibers and semifinished goods, while the presence of a large proportion of Hungary's privileged population (42 percent of all nobility and clergy), as well as town dwellers (24 out of 39 royal towns), offered an attractive potential market. The first manufactory in this period, established by several burghers in Banská Bystrica in 1725 to produce woolen cloth, failed after six years, but in 1736 a more enduring enterprise, a cotton manufactory, was founded in Šaštín by Francis of Lorraine.

The Croats

STRUGGLE AGAINST ABSOLUTISM, 1620–83

The War and Relations with Vienna and Hungary, 1620–48

Unlike the Bohemian and the Slovene Lands, Croatia avoided imposition of royal absolutism during the Thirty Years' War. The main reasons were the following: (1) the enthusiastic Catholicism of the estates removed a religious consideration for the suppression of their rights; (2) their support was needed by the king against insurgent Hungarian nobles; and (3) their power was already restricted to "civil" Croatia—on the whole, it did not pertain to the military borders.

At the outbreak of the Thirty Years' War the Croatian estates wholeheartedly supported Ferdinand II. In August 1620 they even considered a military alliance (confederation) with Inner Austria to fight the king's enemies in Bohemia and Hungary. An internal crisis, however, initially hampered the effectiveness of Croatia's military contribution. At the *Sabor* in Šemovec in October 1620, the lower nobility, offended by the haughtiness of *Banus* Nikola Frankopan (1616–22), demanded to sit in a separate chamber from the magnates. Royal commissioners prevented the division of the *Sabor* and thus preserved its unicameral character, but the tensions between the aristocracy and the gentry did not subside until 1622 with the replacement of Frankopan as *banus* by Juraj Zrinski (Zrínyi, 1622–26).

Shielded by their loyalty to the Habsburg kings, the Croatian estates maintained their autonomy in relation to Hungary. Croatia, it is true, continued to send representatives to both chambers of the Hungarian diet. By 1625 these Croatian deputies had also gained the right to participate in the election of the *palatin*. The laws of the Hungarian diet, however, lacked validity in Croatia, unless specifically reenacted by the *Sabor*. In 1636 Ferdinand II reasserted—despite objections from the Hungarian Chancellery—the equal weight of Croatian laws with those of Hungary by granting a special sanction to twenty-nine measures adopted by the *Sabor* between 1609 and 1635. The *Sabor* also jealously guarded Croatia's independence from Hungary in executive and judicial matters. This in 1642 it protested vigorously against interference by the Hungarian *personalis*, in the decisions of the *Banus'* Table (*tabula banalis*).[18]

Croatia's overall assistance to the Habsburgs during the Thirty Years' War was substantial. On the average between twenty and thirty thousand Croats participated in the campaigns of the imperial armies in Germany. In addition, troops of the *banus* fought Hungarian insurgents during both the rebellions of Bethlen (1620–26) and Prince George Rákóczi (1644–45), settled by the treaty of Linz in 1645. In recognition of the Croatian contribution, Ferdinand III insisted in 1646 on the election of *Banus* Ivan Drašković (1640–46), a staunch Catholic, as *palatin* by the Hungarian diet. Nikola Zrinski, who had distinguished himself in the campaign against Rákóczi, was in turn elected *banus*.

Military Borders, 1620–83

The main grievance of the Croatian estates against the dynasty was the failure—despite the promises of Ferdinand II in 1620—to transfer the military borders to their jurisdiction from that of the imperial commanders responsible partly to the *Hofkriegsrat* in Graz and partly to the estates of Inner Austria. Two successive royal commissions (in 1623 and 1626) examined the situation in the Varaždin Generalate (the so-called Slavonian Border). The attitude of the resident Vlakh (mostly Orthodox Serbian) colonists, abetted by the Styrian estates, convinced the commissioners to advise against transfer of the territory to Croatian authority for fear of a Vlakh rebellion. Although the *Sabor* in 1629 offered to exempt the Vlakhs from feudal services to Croatian seigneurs if they submitted to the *banus,* Ferdinand II resolved the issue a year later by his famous *Statuta Valachorum* in favor of continued government in the Varaždin Generalate by imperial commanders. In return for the standing obligation of military service, the Vlakhs were granted by the *Statuta* autonomy at the village level under an elected headman (*knez*).[19]

18. Two years later the *Sabor* attempted to strengthen the indigenous executive apparatus by providing the *banus* with a body of six assistants, an organ resembling the Committee of the Land (*Landesausschuss*) in other Habsburg realms.
19. Initially, an assembly of village representatives elected judicial officials for each

Although the *Statuta Valachorum* did not formally apply to the Karlovac Generalate (the so-called Croatian Border), this territory also remained outside the jurisdiction of the Croatian government. A major factor favoring the status quo was the changed attitude of the estates of Carniola and Carinthia toward cooperation with Croatian nobility. Having failed in their own struggle against royal absolutism, the Carniolan and Carinthian nobles lost their previous incentive to bolster the power of their Croatian confreres in the military borders. To the contrary, they agreed in 1625 to take over from the *Hofkriegsrat* in Graz the direct financing of the garrisons in the Karlovac Generalate, obtaining in exchange the right to appoint officers there up to the rank of lieutenant. Nevertheless, until the conspiracy of 1671, Croatian nobles continued to wield more influence in this generalate than in the Varaždin Generalate. Customarily they secured imperial appointments to the highest military posts, including the office of the general held from 1626 to 1652 by the Croatian magnate Vuk Frankopan.

Thus in the border territory only the *Banus'* Border—from Karlovac to Ivanić—remained subordinate to the *banus* and the *Sabor*, as well as on the local level to Croatian seigneurs. The war tax (*dica*), collected in Croatia, however, was often insufficient to pay the troops there, and part of the *Banus'* Border (Petrinja Capitanate) in fact had to be garrisoned from the Varaždin Generalate.

Defense of Autonomy in Civil Croatia, 1648–71

Following the Thirty Years' War the Croatian estates continued to guard vigilantly their autonomy from Hungary. The *Sabor* in 1655 challenged the Hungarian diet's reference to Croatia as a realm subject to Hungary (*partes adnexae* or *subiectae*), and in 1660 declared invalid a Hungarian law of the previous year that sought to extend the authority of the *palatin* into Croatia. The main apprehensions, however, focused on the intentions of the Viennese Court, which, no longer in urgent need of the Croats' military aid, felt freer to encroach on the rights of the estates. Vienna, in fact, delayed the confirmation of Zrinski as *banus* for two years until 1649, and attempted to limit his judicial powers. From 1649 on the estates maintained a permanent agent (*agens aulicus*) to defend their rights at the imperial court. In 1651 they resisted royal pressure to forge constitutional links with the Lands of Inner Austria.

---

of the three Capitanates in the Varaždin Generalate, but this right was abrogated after a rebellion in 1665–66, caused by the Vlakhs' resentment over exactions in money and in labor on fortifications. Another source of grievance for the mostly Orthodox colonists, leading to an uprising in 1672, was the efforts of the Catholic bishops of Zagreb to bring the Vlakhs' Orthodox diocese, based on the monastery of Marča, into union with Rome.

The fear of Vienna's absolutist pretentions increased after Leopold I's accession to the throne in 1657.[20]

An additional source of grievance against the dynasty, mounting in the 1650s, was the apparent lack of determination to press the struggle against the Turks to recover the lost Croatian areas. When the war finally came in 1663, as in Hungary, its result merely heightened the dissatisfaction, since the hasty peace of Vasvár in 1664 failed to achieve any territorial gains. This disappointment, combined with the fear of royal absolutism and a resentment over the status of the military borders, led some Croatian magnates to join the Wesselényi conspiracy against the dynasty. In this unique departure from the usual pattern of Croatian enmity to Hungarian rebels, the *banus*, Nikola Zrinski, became the first leader of the conspiracy in Croatia. After his death in November 1664, his brother and successor as *banus*, Petar Zrinski, and another magnate, Fran Frankopan, shared the leadership. The conspirators counted first on the aid of the French, then (from 1669) on the Turks, who had promised to grant Croatia under their suzerainty a status analogous to that of Transylvania.

Despite the personal prestige of the aristocractic conspirators, their position was weak. Their Hungarian allies distrusted them, although some of them, particularly the Zrinski family, were partly Magyarized. The Croatian lower nobility in turn traditionally disliked both the magnates and the Magyars. Croatian prelates were repelled by the alliance with Hungarian Protestants, and even more so by the subsequent prospect of Turkish suzerainty. In additon, the third most important magnate family in Croatia, the Erdődys, opposed the planned uprising. As a result, the Viennese government easily stamped out the conspiracy. Zrinski and Frankopan were arrested in April 1670, and executed a year later.

Aftermath of the Zrinski Conspiracy, 1671–83

The humilation of the powerful Zrinski and Frankopan families weakened the political power of the estates, and in the 1670s Vienna appeared ready to impose on Croatia, as well as Hungary, the absolutist form of government familiar in the Austrian and Bohemian Lands since the 1620s. The office of the *banus* was left vacant, and instead Leopold I appointed, in April 1670, two *banal* lieutenants, Nikola Erdődy and Martin Borković, for military and civil affairs respectively. The chief commander of the Karlovac Generalate, Johann von Herberstein, in 1671 drafted proposals for the reorganization of Croatia. The *Banus'*

---

20. In 1658 the *Sabor* revived the Committee of the Land, consisting of six members (*državni deputati*), to provide greater stability in the estates' administrative system.

Border was to be abolished and its territory split between the Karlovac Generalate and the Varaždin Generalate. Croatia as a whole was to be fully detached from Hungary, and administered on the model of the Inner Austrian Lands under a semibureaucratic *gubernium*. Although a number of lesser Croatian nobles petitioned the king in 1672 to attach Croatia to the Austrian Lands, Herberstein's proposals were not implemented. The *Hofkriegsrat* in Graz was not enthusiastic, and the *Sabor*—which unlike the Hungarian diet continued to meet after 1670—rejected them. Determined resistence by Erdődy prevented the abolition of the *Banus'* Border. Nevertheless the king ignored repeated petitions of the *Sabor* to appoint a regular *banus*, without whom the traditional constitutional order could not function. Above all, without the *banus* the operation of the judiciary was disrupted, and the *Sabor* had to prohibit recourse to alien, especially Hungarian, judges.

The ominous threat of complete absolutism receded only in the late 1670s, when Vienna once more needed Croatian help against Hungarian rebels. In April 1680, Erdődy was installed as a full-fledged *banus* (1680–93). A major success, which marked a solemn recognition of constitutional continuity in Croatia, was the formal sanction by Leopold I in August 1681 of twenty laws passed by the *Sabor* since 1643. One of these measures, moreover, reaffirmed the autonomy of the *banus* in the exercise of his executive and judicial powers. Siding with the king against the Thököly rebellion, the Croats raised a general levy (*insurrectio*) in 1682, and early the following year troops under the *banus* operated in Hungary against the insurgents.

RECONQUEST OF LOST TERRITORIES, 1683–1711

Recovered Regions, 1683–1711

The great Turkish war of 1683, which broke out in conjunction with the Thököly rebellion, at last resulted in the reconquest of large Croatian territories lost to the Turks since the sixteenth century. In 1687 imperial troops seized most of eastern Slavonia between the rivers Drava and Sava. The area of Lika and Krbava near the Adriatic coast was conquered in 1689 by troops from the military borders, and two years later Croatian soldiers under the *banus* occupied a sizable area between Una and Sava in the intermediate sector. These conquests were retained when the treaty of Karlowitz was signed in 1699.

The expectations of the Croatian estates that the newly acquired regions, as well as the older military borders, would be administratively integrated with Croatia were largely doomed to disappointment. Vienna, in fact, assigned eastern Slavonia to the jurisdiction of the *Hof-*

kriegsrat and the *Hofkammer* in the 1690s. The organization of the territory as the Sava-Danube Military Border in 1702 formalized this arrangement. The population was divided into the military colonists (militia) and the ordinary civilians. The former were under the military authorities headed by the general at Osijek, responsible to the Viennese *Hofkriegsrat*. The Viennese *Hofkammer* or the local noble seigneurs exercised jurisdiction over the civilian population.

The area of Lika and Krbava was occupied by troops from the Karlovac Generalate, and civil control was assumed by the Viennese *Hofkammer*. Despite a promise by Leopold I in 1693 to turn the two counties over to the Croatian government, they were transferred a year later by the Viennese *Hofkammer* to the *Hofkammer* in Graz. The local population became subordinated to the officers of the generalate in military matters, while judicial, civil, and economic authority was vested in the officials of the *Hofkammer* in Graz, or in the noble seigneurs who purchased estates in this territory.

The two old military borders, the Karlovac Generalate and the Varaždin Generalate, lost their significance as frontier defense zones by the peace of Karlowitz. This was particularly true of the Varaždin Generalate, and following repeated petitions by the *Sabor* and the *banus*, Leopold I in 1703 promised its reunion with Croatia. After a delay because of the Rákóczi insurrection, the promise was not kept and both generalates remained under the joint jurisdiction of the Graz *Hofkriegsrat* and the estates of Inner Austria. The subordination of the Graz *Hofkriegsrat* to the Viennese one in 1705 had no immediate effect on the administration of the two generalates.

Thus within the Croatian territory under the Habsburg dynasty two separate jurisdictions—the counties of Lika and Krbava, and the Sava-Danube Military Border—were added after the treaty of Karlowitz to the earlier four: Croatia outside the military borders, the *Banus'* Border, the Karlovac Generalate, and the Varaždin Generalate.

Conflict with Hungary, 1683–1711

The pressure of war emergencies, often interfering with regular meetings of the *Sabor,* made the estates anxious to assure continuity in Croatian administration. The Committee of the Land (called the *Banus'* Conference after 1689) was reactivated in 1685 and met regularly. Proposals were advanced for a more structured permanent body, the *Consistorium,* which would execute decisions of the *Sabor* and the *Banus'* Conference, especially with regard to taxation. The plan failed in 1697 after arousing a spirited opposition among the lower nobles, who feared that the proposed body would be dominated by the magnates and might usurp powers from their particular stronghold, the *Sabor*. In 1701 even the *Banus'* Conferene was temporarily abolished, but it soon revived and acquired a permanent secretary in 1714.

While during the three decades after the Thirty Years' War the estates had to defend their rights mainly against the king, after 1680—with the subsiding of royal pretensions—the focus shifted to defense of autonomy from Hungary. The political mobilization of the lower nobles strengthened this trend, since they were more eager to assert the separate political identity of Croatia than the magnates, who valued the support Hungarian estates and institutions could provide for their rights and privileges. Issues disputed with Hungary included matters of ecclesiastical jurisdiction, such as the creation of a separate Croatian province of the Pauline order (after 1684) and raising the see of Zagreb to an archbishopric in 1708.

During the Rákóczi uprising of 1703–11 under Prince Francis Rákóczi II, the Croatian estates loyally supported the dynasty despite appeals from Rákóczi (in 1704–6) reminding them of their grievances, above all in the matter of the military borders. In 1704 *Banus* János Pálffy (1704–32) raised a general levy and prevented a rebel invasion of Croatia by defeating their forces in Medjumurje. Subsequently Croatian troops operated within Hungary.

The Croatian dispute with Hungary revolved mainly around the status of the *Sabor*. The Hungarian diet after the peace of Karlowitz attempted to undermine the legislative independence of Croatia, since the Hungarian estates resented distinctive Croatian laws such as the proscription of Protestantism, solemnly sanctioned by the king in 1636. At first the diet sought to downgrade the enactments of the *Sabor*, claiming that they were not genuine laws and thus should not receive royal sanction. When the king rejected this view, the loyalist Hungarian diet at Pozsony in 1708 proposed the principle that only those enactments of the *Sabor* that were consistent with the laws of Hungary could receive royal sanction. The diet was dissolved before it could formally adopt this measure.

STABILIZATION AND RECOVERY, 1711–40

Continued Conflict with Hungary, 1711–22

The treaty of Szatmár (Satu-Mare), signed in April 1711, left the Hungarian estates still in a powerful position, and thus did not allay the Croatian apprehensions, especially those of the lower nobility about Hungary's encroachments on the rights of Croatia. The *Sabor* demonstrated Croatia's independence by sending a separate delegation to Vienna in December 1711 to pay homage to the new King Charles III (as emperor, Charles VI). The *Sabor* was in turn offended by a letter of the Hungarian Chancellery inviting it to choose two, instead of the customary three, delegates to the Hungarian diet, convoked for April 1712.

The *Sabor* feared particularly that the diet might press the new king to recognize the principle of concordance between Croatian and Hungarian laws. It devised an ingenious tactic to forestall such an attempt. In March 1712 it adopted a law, embodying the idea of the future Pragmatic Sanction, namely the right of the royal Habsburg succession in the female line. It was certain that such a measure would be unacceptable to the Hungarian diet, which cherished its right gained in 1687 to elect a king freely if the dynasty was extinct in the male line. The *Sabor* presupposed that the king just as surely would not repudiate its new law, so favorable to the dynasty. Thus the legislative independence of Croatia from Hungary, including disparate laws, would be clearly vindicated. Within Croatia this strategy sparked another flare-up of the smoldering conflict between the gentry and the aristocracy. Most of the magnates, reluctant to offend the Hungarian estates, opposed the measure and absented themselves from the *Sabor*. The *Sabor*, in turn, decreed heavy penalties—aimed at the magnates—against those who would bypass Croatian authorities and turn to Hungarian officials with petitions or suits.

The anti-Hungarian tactic of the *Sabor* succeeded to the extent that the Hungarian diet, in August 1712, actually recognized the legislative autonomy of Croatia, admitting that the king could sanction enactments of the *Sabor* whether or not they harmonized with the laws of Hungary. This law was approved by the king in 1715, but the Hungarian estates were, in fact, able to block new royal sanctions for the laws of the *Sabor*. When the Croatian estates sought in Vienna confirmation for several measures enacted between 1682 and 1715, the Hungarian Chancellery throughout 1716 repeatedly refused to submit them to the king. Thus the laws remained unconfirmed.

Subsequently the tensions with Hungary subsided and Croatian apprehensions focused once more on the Viennese government's penchant for royal absolutism. The rapprochement with Hungary went so far that the Croatian estates failed to protest against the version of the Pragmatic Sanction, adopted by the Hungarian diet in 1722, which stipulated the indivisibility of the lands of the Hungarian Crown. This provision denied in principle the right of the Croats to seek complete separation from Hungary.

Royal Reforms and Centralization, 1722–40

In the 1720s and 1730s the immediate threat to Croatian autonomy emanated from judicial and administrative reforms proposed from Vienna. The reform of 1723 instituted as the highest court in Croatia the *Banus'* Table (*Banaltafel*), which was the ultimate court of appeal from the county courts. It also possessed original jurisdiction in certain very serious matters (*causae tabulares*), and in such cases appeals were possible to the Hungarian Septemviral Table. At the same time, a District Table (*Districtualtafel*) was established mainly to provide an intermediate level of appeal between county courts and the *Banus'* Table. By 1725 the *Sabor* had to accede to a serious limitation of Croatian autonomy by agreeing to the right of the Viennese government to appoint and pay the assessors of the *Banus'* Table.

The *Sabor* resisted more successfully encroachments in the sphere of executive power. In 1725 it effectively opposed an attempt at intervention in Croatian affairs by the Lieutenancy Council, the chief executive body for Hungary, established in 1723. The estates restated the principle that in Croatia executive and administrative power was vested in the *banus* and the *Sabor,* or the *Banus'* Conference, and was independent of the Hungarian officialdom. In 1730 the *Sabor* again had to resist efforts of the Lieutenancy Council to intervene in Croatia by dealing directly with the *županije* (counties). It remonstrated that the *županije,* less autonomous than the Hungarian counties, were under the exclusive jurisdiction of the *Sabor.*

The Croatian estates were also eager to see the *banus* closely identified with the interests of the Land. *Banus* Pálffy was, in fact, a Hungarian aristocrat, but operated primarily as an imperial army officer. When the *Sabor* complained in 1726 that he had been absent from Croatia for twenty years, the king appointed a Croat, Count Ivan Drašković, as *banal* lieutenant. Upon Pálffy's resignation, another Hungarian, Count József Esterházy, took his place as *banus* (1733–41). As a concession the king enjoined him to reside primarily in Croatia.

Newly Acquired Territories and Military Borders, 1711–40

The Croatian territory under Habsburg rule was expanded by the easternmost section of Slavonia as a result of the treaty of Passarowitz (Požarevac), ending Charles VI's (III) first war with the Turks (1716–18). This acquisition, near the confluence of the Sava and the Danube, was retained after the king's unsuccessful second Turkish war (1737–39). Of the territories gained by the treaty of Karlowitz, the counties of Lika and Krbava had disappeared as special administrative units. The *Hofkammer* in Graz in 1712 turned the area over to the Karlovac Generalate.

In the Sava-Danube Military Border (eastern Slavonia) the condominium of the Viennese *Hofkriegsrat* and *Hofkammer* continued until 1720, when the civil jurisdiction was transferred from the Viennese *Hofkammer* to the Hungarian Chamber in Pozsony, while the *Hofkriegsrat* retained responsibility for defense and the military colonies. By that time, most of the "civilian" peasantry (as distinct from the military colonists) were already under the jurisdiction of the noble seigneurs, who had purchased estates from the *Hofkammer.* The rapacity of the seigneurs and the Chamber officials gradually caused so much peasant unrest that in 1733 the new commander of the border, Count Ferdinand Khevenhüller, was directed to propose reforms. At his suggestion, the king undertook in 1737 to define the mutual rights of seigneurs and serfs in the famous *Carolina Urbarialis Regulatio.* A new agency, *Landesdeputation,* established in Osijek (Eszék), struggled to implement the *Regulatio* against seigneurial opposition. The military colonists in the Sava-Danube Border also had serious grievances, focusing on payments and services demanded by their officers. After 1737 Khevenhüller, on his own authority, sought to mitigate the officers' exactions.

The older military borders suffered increasingly from the obsolescent form of administration permitting unchecked exploitation by the estates of Inner Austria. The colonists in the Karlovac Generalate frequently complained of mistreatment by their noble officers from Carniola and Carinthia, particularly about irregularities of pay and lack of provisions. The situation was still worse in the Varaždin Generalate, where the Styrian noble officers surpassed their Carniolan and Carinthian confreres in greediness. In addition, the sizable Orthodox population was continuously pressured to submit to a Uniat bishop. The conditions were not improved by an inept attempt at reform by Count Kaspar Cordua, who in 1733 abolished the *Statuta Valachorum* (last confirmed by Charles VI in 1717) without replacing them by another charter. Stability was restored in the Varaždin Generalate only in 1737 by Prince Joseph Sachsen-Hildburgshausen, whose tact, above all indulgence toward the Orthodox, appeased the colonists under new statutes, reaffirming their local self-government.

AGRICULTURE, CRAFTS, AND TRADE[21]

Intermittent Economic Recovery, 1620–1711

The decrease in Turkish raids and open warfare after the peace of 1606 created more favorable conditions for economic development

21. Economic data in this section are derived from *Historija naroda Jugoslavije* (Zagreb: Školska knjiga, 1959), 2:684–750, 998–1089; Rudolf Bićanić, *Doba manufakture u Hrvatskoj i Slavoniji, 1750–1860* (Zagreb: Jugoslavenska Akademije Znanosti, 1951), pp. 87, 94, 144, 163–64, 393–97; Miroslava Despot, *Pokušaji manufakture u Gradanskoj Hrvatskoj u 18. stoljeću* (Zagreb: Jugoslavenska Akademije Znanosti, 1962), pp. 21, 36–44, 62–63; Josip Adamček, *Agrarni odnosi u Hrvatskoj od sredine XV do kraja XVII stoljeća* (Zagreb: Sveučilišna Naklada Liber, 1980), pp. 497–769.

during the seventeenth century compared with the sixteenth. Even so, Croatia lagged considerably behind the neighboring lands to the west, particularly in nonagricultural production.

Trends in agricultural production augmented the economic obligations of manorial peasantry during the seventeenth century. Formally the labor obligation on the demesne amounted to six days per week for every hide (*sessio*). The peasants with less than one-sixth of a hide were no longer freed from compulsory labor; they owed one day of work per week. The peasants also suffered from a steady diminution of the amount of land available to them, as the seigneurs attracted by production for the market continued to expand their demesnes. As a result, the size of the hide was decreasing. Thus, during the seventeenth century on the Zagreb Chapter's Sisak manor, the hide became equal to the amount of land that could be plowed in eleven to fourteen days, instead of the traditional seventeen. Though the demesne estates were partly enlarged through clearing and deforestation, the main source of expansion was seizure of peasant lands.

The rising agricultural production on the demesne estates was accounting for an increasing proportion of crops at the disposal of the seigneurs. Conversely, peasant dues in kind, which remained essentially stable, represented a declining share. While in the sixteenth century the seigneurs had typically derived from 50 to 70 percent of their wheat and millet, and more than 90 percent of their wine, from peasant dues, in the seventeenth they normally obtained more than 50 percent of their grain, and often as much of their wine, from the demesne estates. On most manors the income from the demesne estates exceeded the yield from the peasant dues. In terms of value, vineyards occupied the first place, fields and meadows the second and third, and forests the fourth. In contrast to other parts of East Central Europe, particularly the Bohemian Lands, pisciculture did not yield a major component of manorial income. Fresh-water fish were raised mainly for the seigneurs' own consumption rather than for the market.

Artisan production remained underdeveloped during the seventeenth century, as the towns were slow to recover from the earlier damages inflicted by Turkish warfare. This was particularly true of those close to the border, such as Koprivnica, while urban centers deeper in the interior, such as Zagreb and Varaždin, were better protected. Nobles residing in royal free towns also retarded economic recovery, since they refused to bear a fair share of municipal burdens. Towns subject to noble seigneurs were often reduced to the status of serf villages. Certain towns, especially those in Turkish proximity, did not begin to organize craftsmen's guilds until the beginning of the seventeenth century. A new trend in artisan organization was to combine several crafts in a single guild. Thus in the Kaptol section of Zagreb craftsmen of several types joined in 1660 into a grand guild, patterned after one in Varaždin. While the combination of different crafts into a single guild may be considered a sign of economic backwardness, it was also true that new kinds of craftsmen emerged, such as wheelwrights and barrelmakers. On the whole, however, the guilds tended to impede industrial growth, especially by severely restricting the number of new masters. Town governments tried to combat this practice in order to prevent stagnation or even decrease of population.

Outside urban artisan production, a major enterprise was the old copper mine in Rude near Samobor. After a succession of noble owners, it became in 1697 the property of the *Sabor* in partnership with a burgher of Senj. Early in the eighteenth century the mine employed 134 workers and produced 448 tons of copper annually. Petar Zrinski established sizable ironworks in Čabar in 1651 to use the ore mined on his estate in Gorski Kotar. Skilled masters came from Carniola and about 200 serfs supplied ordinary labor. The products, particularly the plows and swords, were marketed all over Croatia.

Although the directions of trade remained stable, there was significant growth in volume. Supplies to the military borders involved an important commercial activity. Merchants increased their profits by smuggling into the borders cloth for civilian consumption along with that destined for the military, which was exempted from customs. Several such entrepreneurs accumulated considerable capital and attained important public offices, especially in fiscal administration. An unorthodox, but lucrative, form of trade consisted of exchanging captives, usually seized in the Turkish territory by the Vlakhs, for ransom. Commercial activities of the nobility, especially magnates such as the Zrinskis and the Frankopans, grew in importance. They not only engaged in export trade but also competed in the domestic market with urban merchants.

Roots of Agricultural Prosperity, 1711–40

After the period of war and rebellion, which had marked the end of the seventeenth century and the opening decade of the eighteenth, the prospects for economic development improved greatly. In agriculture, production of livestock gained new importance. Cattle raising became widespread, especially in eastern Slavonia, which was then thinly populated and permitted extensive grazing. Greek and Armenian merchants often leased large vacant areas to raise cattle in great quantities. Trade in cattle represented the strongest component in Croatian exports. Extensive pig raising prospered in areas of oak and beech forests, particularly around Turopolje and Karlovac, and in Slavonia. The pig trade involved a regional division of labor. Thin young pigs were imported from Bosnia or Serbia, fattened in the forests of Croatia, and taken to market in Sopron for eventual consumption in Vienna and elsewhere in Central Europe. The chief traditional crop was grain (millet, barley, wheat, rye, spelt, oats), yielding poor harvests of between three to five times the amount of seed. The cultivation of corn, introduced in the previous century, spread rapidly. The crop throve in Croatia, with a relatively small proportion of the harvest needed for seed; its use was versatile—it could feed both men and beast; and it was usually exempted from feudal dues, since it was not listed in the old books of obligations. Vineyards, widespread in Croatia, provided the main source of money income for the peasantry, which was permitted after 1715 to engage in wholesale trade with wine.

Agricultural techniques remained primitive. The traditional three-field system prevailed, although in Lika and other mountainous areas fields were allowed to lie fallow for seven to thirty years after having been planted for two or three. Plowing was mostly done with heavy wooden plows, which had to be pulled by three to five pairs of oxen guided by four to six persons. The cooperation of several homesteads was usually required.

Urban crafts experienced a period of revival after the peace of Szatmár, with the number of artisans rising and new types of crafts developing. Artisan techniques had become diversified. To those of Central Europe and the Mediterranean area were added the oriental ones established in the territory recently acquired from the Turks. Mining operations continued, especially extraction of copper in Rude. Iron mining spread in the Gorski Kotar, giving rise to small ironworks. The older mines in Čabar engaged in limited production because of severe flood damage in 1711. Shipbuilding newly emerged on the Adriatic coast, first in Rijeka in 1722, then in 1730 also in Senj. Extensive forests of Gorski Kotar, Istria, and Carniola provided a convenient source of raw materials for this activity.

Attempts were made to introduce manufactories in the 1720s, to produce glass in Gorski Kotar and candles and ships' rigging in Rijeka, but all three enterprises failed. While a continuous tradition of manufactories dated in Bohemia to the late seventeenth century, and even in Hungary to the 1720s, it failed to develop in Croatia before 1750.

The development of trade advanced significantly. The abolition in 1715 of internal custom houses greatly facilitated its flow, benefiting particularly the important transit trade. The main routes leading through Croatia were those from Constantinople to Vienna (via Zemun and Osijek), from Venice through Ptuj and Varaždin to Buda, Pest, or Vienna and from Ljubljana along Sava to Sisak and farther east. The last-named route was substantially improved by the regulation of the Sava in 1722.

The Viennese government attempted to promote a new direction of trade through the Adriatic ports to the east. The declaration of the Adriatic as an open sea by Charles VI in 1717, the commercial treaty with the Turks in 1718, the founding of the Oriental Company, and the establishment of Rijeka and Trieste as free ports in 1719, were all part of this effort. In 1726 a highway, constructed from Karlovac to Rijeka, linked the Danube and the Adriatic. Until the mid-eighteenth century Croatian trade with the Ottoman Empire involved mostly exports of agricultural products and raw materials. Imports from Turkey included manufactured products—cotton cloth, saffian (leather), rugs, silver objects—and colonial goods, coming either directly from the east or through western intermediaries (English or Dutch).

The Ruthenians and the Serbs

THE RUTHENIANS

Extension and Consolidation of Habsburg Rule in Transcarpathia, 1620–1740

The extent of Habsburg power in the three counties of western Transcarpathia fluctuated in the first half of the seventeenth century. In 1621–29 and 1645–48 under the treaties of Mikulov (Nikolsburg) (1622) and Linz (1645) respectively, the counties of Bereg and Ugocsa fell under Transylvania's sovereignty together with several counties of eastern Slovakia, so that Ung county constituted a Habsburg enclave surrounded by Transylvanian territory. Even when Bereg County was formally under Habsburg rule, royal authority was seriously circumscribed there because once again, from 1633 to 1660, members of the Rákóczi family were seigneurs of the crucial Mukacheve castle and proved recalcitrant vassals. The conditions for the exercise of royal power improved in 1660–80 when the manor passed into the hands of the widow of George Rákóczi II, Sophia Báthory, who reverted to Catholicism after her husband's death.

The configuration of power within Transcarpathia affected the Habsburgs' cherished project of spreading the *Unia*—acceptance of papal jurisdiction—among the Orthodox on the high tide of the seventeenth-century Counter Reformation. In contrast to the stubborn rejection of the *Unia* by the Orthodox Serbs in the military borders of Croatia, the concept appealed to the Orthodox Ruthenians under the special circumstances prevailing in Transcarpathia. Thus the Ruthenians resented the Calvinist pressure of some of their seigneurs to simplify the liturgy, while the *Unia* assured full preservation of their cherished ritual. In addition, the *Unia* promised personal freedom to the Orthodox priests, whom their seigneurs usually treated as serfs. It was adopted in Ung county, still the domain of the Catholic Drugeths, by the Uzhhorod Union of 1646, but could be extended to Bereg county only in 1664 under Sophia Báthory, when a Uniat bishop replaced the Orthodox one in Mukacheve.[22]

The split of Transcarpathia between Habsburg and Transylvanian sovereignty ended as a result of the Turkish war of 1683, when the Habsburg empire acquired Máramaros county through the annexation of Transylvania in 1688. Transcarpathia suffered severely from the warfare of the late seventeenth and early eighteenth centuries. The fortress of Mukacheve manor served as a major center of anti-Habsburg resistance during the Thököly uprising in 1678 and under Helena Zrinski (Zrínyi) during the Turkish war in 1685–88, as well as during the rising of Francis Rákóczi II in 1703–11.

After the compromise of Szatmár, Charles VI (III) made fresh efforts in 1711–40 to strengthen royal authority in Transcarpathia. Although the most rebellious nobles, especially the Rákóczis, disappeared from the region, the nobility tended to perpetuate the Hungarian tradition of insubordination. The king therefore sought to lean on the Uniat clergy against the nobles. The *Unia* was extended to Máramaros country, where the separate Orthodox diocese ceased to exist in 1720. The entire Transcarpathia thus fell under the jurisdiction of the Uniat bishop of Mukacheve, who had been recognized by the papacy in 1716 as an apostolic administrator under the Latin bishop of Eger.[23]

Agricultural Decline and Flourishing of Crafts, 1620–1711[24]

The renewal of warfare in the seventeenth century seriously damaged agriculture, which had flourished in the latter part of the previous century. The situation became especially critical after the 1670s, with the size of the peasant population greatly diminished. Thus on the Mukacheve manor from 1682 to 1688, villages declined from 145 with 3,700 serfs to 115 with 955 serfs. On the Uzhhorod manor the number of

22. The establishment of the *Unia* in western Transcarpathia led in turn to the consolidation of an Orthodox diocese in Máramaros county, which was under the jurisdiction of the Transylvanian princes.

23. The exercise of royal power in Transcarpathia was also strengthened by the subordination of the Máramaros salt mines directly to the financial authorities in Vienna. Royal administrators, attached to the mines, as usual exercised functions far beyond economic management, and acted, in fact, by the 1720s as protectors of the Ruthenian population against abuses by local Magyar authorities. Eger was elevated to an archbishopric in 1804.

24. Economic data in this and the following section are derived from Ivan G. Kolomiets, *Ocherki po istorii Zakarpat'ia* (Tomsk: Izd-vo Tomskogo universiteta, 1953–59), 1:38–115; 2:89–90; *Zakarpats'ka oblast'* (Kiev: Ukr. Rad. Entsyklopediia, 1969), pp. 78, 112.

peasant households decreased from 1,195 to 587. Primitive techniques of cultivation further depressed agricultural output. Another indicator of decline was the diminution of livestock. On the Mukacheve manor, for instance, between 1645 and 1711 the number of horses decreased to approximately a quarter, and between 1625 and 1729 the number of cattle to one-sixth, and of goats and sheep to one-seventh.

In contrast to agriculture, urban crafts prospered and several towns developed into commercial centers, not only for local but also for transit trade. This was particularly true of Berehove (Beregszász, Beregovo), where major fairs were held regularly, featuring foodstuffs, cattle, and cloth. Uzhhorod boasted nine artisan guilds toward the end of the century. In addition, noble estates encouraged industrial production, based on artisan methods and serf labor. Thus the Uzhhorod manor maintained sawmills, wood-processing workshops, charcoal production, and— until the 1690s—glassworks. On the Mukacheve manor several villages engaged in small-scale iron production. Francis Rákóczi established the first manufactory in Transcarpathia at the opening of the eighteenth century in Máramaros. It produced colored leather under the direction of Turkish masters.

Agricultural Recovery and Decline of Towns, 1711–40

Following the compromise of Szatmár, agriculture in Transcarpathia began a slow recovery from the era of destructive warfare and rebellions. In 1715–20 uncultivated tracts still encompassed on the average half of the peasant lands, and on the Mukacheve manor even as much as three-quarters—844 out of 1,178 homesteads. The losses in animal holdings were by no means made up as late as 1734. Thus on the Mukacheve manor the level of animal holdings per serf family, compared with the mid-seventeenth century, represented one-half for horses and oxen, one-third to one-fourth for cows, one-fifth for sheep, and one-tenth for pigs. Except for the lowlands of Ugocsa county, Transcarpathia in the first half of the eighteenth century did not yet experience the trend—common elsewhere in East Central Europe—toward enlargment of the demesnes directly cultivated by the seigneurs. Instead, the noble landlords still relied on peasant dues in kind, and the production on the demesnes remained minor. On the Mukacheve manor, for instance, only 4.5 percent of cultivated land belonged to the demesne, which in 1734 held no more than 86 oxen and 132 cows. Methods of cultivation also remained primitive. For example, the vineyards at Berehove had not been fertilized for thirty years prior to 1744. The spread of corn represented the one novelty in agriculture. By 1720 (at least on the Mukacheve manor) it was the third leading crop, after oats and wheat, and ahead of rye and barley.

The seigneurs of Transcarpathian towns, especially the Counts Schoenborn, the new owners of Mukacheve, strove afresh after 1730 to attract immigrant craftsmen, especially from Germany. Thus the artisans in Bereg county increased from 79 in 1720 to several hundred by 1746. Nevertheless, towns declined economically, especially as trading centers, compared with the seventeenth century. The Schoenborns failed in their efforts to increase commerce between Mukacheve and Poland. Likewise, attempts to develop manufactories or large-scale artisan production on the big manors were rarely successful because of scarcity of capital, the limited local market, remoteness of external markets combined with poor communications, and the competition of eastern Slovak towns.[25]

THE SERBS

Settlement in the Bačka and the Banat, 1690–1740

The Habsburgs acquired the Serb[26] territories of southern Hungary as a result of the Turkish war of 1683–99. In the fall of 1689 the imperial armies had set out to conquer Serbia from the Turks. A disappointing attempt was made to enlist the services of Đorđe Branković, a nobleman who claimed descent from Serbia's medieval rulers and proposed to form a state of Orthodox South Slavs under the suzerainty of the Habsburgs. After penetrating as far as Macedonia, the imperial armies were forced to withdraw across the Danube by the fall of 1690. Many Serb refugees, including the patriarch of Peć, Arsenije III Crnojević, shared in the retreat. Their number eventually reached almost 200,000, and they settled mainly in the area between the Danube and the Tisza, conquered from the Turks by the Habsburgs in the 1680s. Based on earlier promises, Leopold I granted them in August 1691 a set of privileges (*Diploma Leopoldinum*) that not only assured religious toleration and internal autonomy, including education, to the Serb Orthodox Church but also endowed its metropolitan (who eventually settled in Sremski Karlovci) with substantial secular powers, particular judgment in civil disputes, collection of feudal dues, and disposal of heirless properties. Inasmuch as these privileges were granted to the Serb Orthodox Church as a body and to the individual church members, but not to the territory inhabited by Serbs, we may consider the

25. Two glass manufactories, however, did start production on the Mukacheve manor. Also the salt mines of Máramaros revived under the royal management from the decay caused by the time of troubles in the latter part of the seventeenth century.

26. The adjectival form "Serb" is applied to Serbs outside the Serbia proper; for those in Serbia the adjectival form "Serbian" is used.

Diploma as one of the earliest examples of personal autonomy in cultural affairs.

For the next decade the Serbs resisted efforts by Hungarian authorities to extend into the reconquered southern Hungary the jurisdiction of manorial seigneurs and the county governments, especially that of Bačka (Bács) county, which was restored in 1696. After the treaty of Karlowitz the imperial government resolved the conflict in favor of the Serbs through the establishment in 1702 of the Tisza-Mureş Military Border, where a large part of the Serbs were concentrated. The border was administered jointly by the Viennese *Hofkriegsrat* and the *Hofkammer*, with Serb self-government at the village level.

The Serbs' subsequent loyalty to the Habsburg emperors was a natural outgrowth of their dislike of the Hungarian nobles, who wished to enserf them, and this loyalty in turn helped to safeguard their ethnic identity. During the Rákóczi insurrection in 1706, Emperor Joseph I reconfirmed their privileges, and two years later the Serbs were able to set an important precedent of holding a National Church Council (*narodno-crkveni sabor*). Meeting in Krušedol, the body consisted—in addition to clergy—of officers of the military border, nobles, burghers, and village chiefs. Aside from its main official task—election of a new metropolitan—the Council voiced distinctly political demands for an administratively autonomous Serb territory, equal rights for Serbs in towns with German and Magyar burghers, and the appointment of two Serb councilors at the Viennese Court. A reconfirmation of the old Serb privileges in 1713 by Charles VI was as much an insurance for the likelihood of a new Turkish war as an oblique expression of royal displeasure about Hungarian hesitation to adopt the Pragmatic Sanction.

Serb territory under Habsburg rule expanded greatly in 1718 with the treaty of Passarowitz, by which the Habsburg power reached the greatest territorial extent of its history. Of these acquisitions, northern Serbia was to be lost again (by the treaty of Belgrade in 1739), but the Banat, with its mixed Serb and Romanian population, represented a permanent gain. As a sign of distrust toward the Hungarian nobles and of favor to the Serbs, the Banat was not incorporated into Hungary or divided into counties, but retained under the jurisdiction of the Viennese *Hofkriegsrat* and the *Hofkammer*. Even private seigneurs were excluded until 1779. The Serbs of the Banat received the protection of the *Diploma Leopoldinum* in 1720, and Count Florimond Mercy, who administered the territory in 1720–34, created twelve districts of which four were designated as special military areas (*Obercapitanate*). Military officers headed the districts, peasant chiefs the villages.

Seeking a higher population density, the *Hofkammer* in the 1720s organized immigration of German colonists into the Banat, and to a lesser extent into Bačka and Baranya counties, where private seigneurs also introduced Slovak, Magyar, and Ruthenian settlers. The Serbs' chief concern, aside from preserving their privileges (somewhat weakened by the imperial *declaratoria* of 1727 and 1729), was to prevent oppression by the landlords outside the military borders. The National Church Councils of 1730, 1731, 1732, and 1734 protested such abuses. Irate peasants in the Bačka demanded abolition of the county government and transfer of political administration to the *Hofkammer*. Continued seigneurial oppression provoked, in May 1735, an insurrection involving mostly Magyar peasants but led by Pero Jovanović Segedinac and several other Serb officers from the military border. The emperor-king hastened to reconfirm the established Serb privileges, but feudal exactions from the manorial peasantry outside the military borders—as elsewhere in Hungary—remained outside royal regulation.

Agriculture, Crafts, and Trade in the Bačka and the Banat, 1690–1740[27]

When the Habsburgs acquired the Bačka and the Banat, local agriculture was in a primitive state. In the second decade of the eighteenth century either hard steppe or, especially in the Banat, swamps still covered most of the territory. The few rural inhabitants engaged mainly in seminomadic cattle raising, resorting to crop cultivation only for their household needs and moving to new lands instead of fertilizing the old ones. In the 1720s and 1730s the *Hofkriegsrat* and the *Hofkammer* launched an ambitious modernization of agriculture, especially in the Banat, where the *Hofkammer* owned large estates. Imitated to some extent by the private seigneurs in the Bačka, this successful effort owed much to the energetic leadership of Count Mercy. Aside from increased immigration to augment the labor force, the process involved draining of marshes, especially in conjunction with the regulation of the Bečej, which also relieved from floods the fertile central Banat. While extensive animal raising still predominated, the government focused on expanding crop production, mainly grain, grapes, rice, and industrial plants such as flax, hemp, indigo, and mulberry bushes. The *Hofkammer* estates, and some private ones as well, pressed on with the "clover revolution," which, by augmenting feed crops, lessened dependence on pasture lands and fallow for cattle raising.

Craft production in the Bačka owed its origin to the Serb artisans who had joined the exodus under Patriarch Arsenije and had found better working conditions under the Habsburgs than in the Ottoman Em-

27. Economic data in this section are derived from *Historija naroda Jugoslavije* (Zagreb: Školska knjiga, 1959), 2:1138–149, 1173; *Istoriia Iugoslavii* (Moscow: Izd-vo Akademii Nauk SSSR, 1963), 1:265; *Enciklopedija Jugoslavije* (Zagreb: Izd. Leksikografskog zavoda, 1971), 8:10–12; J. H. Schwicker, *Geschichte des Temeser Banats* (2d ed.; Budapest: Aigner, 1872), pp. 320, 365; Sonja Jordan, *Die kaiserliche Wirtschaftspolitik im Banat im 18. Jahrhundert* (Munich: Oldenbourg, 1967), pp. 13–74.

pire. There were 298 artisan workshops in the Bačka before the turn of the century, and 37 in Petrovaradin alone by 1720. Other towns with strong Serb crafts by the third and fourth decades of the eighteenth century were Novi Sad (Neusatz, Újvidék) in the Bačka and Veliki Bečkerek (Zrenjanin) and Pančevo in the western Banat. Count Mercy promoted more advanced forms of industrial production in the Romanian section of the Banat, involving several manufactories in Timişoara (Temesvár) as well as copper and iron mining in the region of Oraviţa.

Rising agricultural production favored the development of trade. Exports, encouraged by the *Hofkammer*, still involved mainly cattle. In turn, the Bačka and the western (Serb) part of the Banat were highly dependent on imports, since the area lacked stone, lumber, and metals. The treaty of Passarowitz in 1718 expanded trade opportunities with Serbia, Bosnia, and other Balkan lands.

CHAPTER 4

Royal Absolutism and Bureaucratic Administration, 1740–1847

The Czechs

In the beginning of the reign of Maria Theresa (1740–80) the Bohemian state faced the threat of partition among several foreign countries engaged in the War of the Austrian Succession (1740–48). The queen's opponents concluded in 1741 the agreement of Frankfurt, according to which Bavaria's share was Bohemia proper, Saxony's was Moravia and Upper Silesia, and Prussia's was Lower Silesia.[1] Charles Albert of Bavaria (as Holy Roman emperor, Charles VII), in fact, conquered Bohemia with French aid and controlled the Land from November 1741 to December 1742. He received homage of part of the Bohemian estates and created a new government under a chancellor assisted by a Court Deputation of seven Bohemian nobles. In the end, Maria Theresa lost only the two Silesias, which she yielded to Prussia by the Peace of Berlin in July 1742, except for the duchy of Těšín (Teschen) and the southern parts of Opava (Troppau), Krnov (Jägerndorf), and Nisa (Neisse). The loss was reconfirmed by the treaties of Dresden (1745) and Hubertsburg (1763). By this partition—together with the earlier loss of Upper and Lower Lusatia to Saxony in 1635 by the Peace of Prague—the Bohemian Crown was deprived of almost half of its territory. The Bohemian Lands after the War of the Austrian Succession contained the Czech ethnic core and corresponded approximately to the Bohemian state as it had existed under the Přemyslids in the High Middle Ages.

1. Maria Theresa, prior to the election of her husband Francis of Lorraine as Holy Roman emperor, was generally referred to as queen of Hungary and Bohemia.

In internal affairs the era from the mid-eighteenth to the mid-nine-teenth century witnessed an intensification of royal absolutism. The old division of state power between the king and the estates virtually dis-appeared. The king alone came to represent the state and exercised his authority increasingly through professional bureaucrats instead of the officials of the estates. The integral network of royal officialdom ab-sorbed the government of the individual Lands as well as those of the circuits (*kraje*), and exerted ever-tightening control over the lower ech-elons of public administration: the manors and the towns. The dawning era of bureaucratic absolutism would encompass the phase of "enlight-ened" absolutism marked by dynamic reforms under Maria Theresa and Joseph II (1780–90), and the reactionary phase of "police" abso-lutism characterized by political stagnation and decay under Francis I (1792–1835) and Ferdinand V (as Austrian Emperor Ferdinand I) (1835–48). The brief reign of Leopold II (1790–92), who in his intentions though not his achievements was much closer to the enlightened than the police absolutism, served as a transition between the two.

Bureaucratic absolutism also intensified political centralization. Within the relatively static centralism created by Ferdinand I and embracing foreign, military, and financial affairs of the entire monarchy, a new dynamic "dualist" centralism arose which sought to coordinate the Bo-hemian and the Austrian Lands (though not the Hungarian ones) by creating a common administration and judiciary. This trend aimed at fusing the Bohemian royal power with the Austrian archducal one, and at merging the Bohemian state into a broader polity called the "German hereditary lands." Certain vestiges of separate Bohemian statehood nevertheless remained. Among them perhaps the most conspicuous, though in practice not a very significant one, was the coronation of the Habsburg rulers—except for Joseph II—with the Crown of Saint Wen-ceslas in Prague.

ENLIGHTENED ABSOLUTISM, 1740–92

Reforms of Central Administration, 1740–80

In political affairs the decisive break with the past occurred under Maria Theresa. Several reasons can be given for the zeal with which she pursued the policy of modified centralization and bureaucratiza-tion. She wished to emulate Frederick II of Prussia, and strengthen the financial and military power of the state. She considered the Bohemian nobles to be haughty and arrogant, and these feelings intensified after the temporary defection of many of them to Charles Albert of Bavaria in 1741–42. The disloyalty of the estates provided, though on a more limited scale, an opportunity to reduce their power and the autonomy of the Bohemian state, such as had presented itself to Ferdinand II after the battle of the White Mountain.[2] Maria Theresa was a very conservative personality, anxious to preserve her royal prerogatives. Yet the wish to improve the clumsy administrative apparatus and to raise the standard of living in all her Lands undoubtedly served as a major motivation in the Queen's domestic policies. To what extent she succeeded is, of course, another question.

The most consequential reform took place in 1749 with the abolition of the Bohemian Court Chancellery, the supreme administrative and judicial body for the Bohemian Lands. Its powers were divided between two new agencies, whose jurisdiction covered the Austrian Lands as well. Their creation, therefore, marked a decisive step toward merging the Bohemian state into a new, wider political entity. One of the new governmental agencies of the Bohemian-Austrian conglomerate, the *directorium in publicis et cameralibus*, obtained the former Chancellery's administrative authority, as well as most of the financial powers up to then exercised by the *Hofkammer*. The other agency, the *Oberste Justizstelle* was to perform the functions of a supreme court. The president of the *directorium* now signed measures concerning Bohemia, which had previously required the signature of the Bohemian chancellor. With the disappearance of the Bohemian Court Chancellery the Bohemian state lost not only an effective expression of its political separateness and distinctiveness but also a most significant bond of its internal unity. Accordingly, while the relationship between the Bohemian and the Austrian Lands became closer, the special ties among the Bohemian Lands themselves began to dissolve.

During a second wave of reforms in 1762 the *directorium* was renamed the Bohemian and Austrian Court Chancellery. Aside from political administration, the new body retained control over direct taxation (*contributionale*), while the *Hofkammer* resumed management of indirect taxation (*camerale*). Headed by the "supreme Bohemian and first Austrian chancellor," the Chancellery was internally subdivided into a Bohemian and an Austrian Senate in 1776. When later in the same year Galicia was added to the Bohemian-Austrian conglomerate, it was placed under the Bohemian Senate. In the *Oberste Justizstelle* a third division was created for Galician affairs.

The desire for central bureaucratic administrations within the individual Bohemian Lands, spearheaded by the queen's leading advisor, Count Friedrich Haugwitz, was first realized in the fragment of Silesia that remained under Habsburg rule. In 1742 the Royal Office (*královský*

2. Some Czech historians, above all Joseph Pekař, have maintained that the political and administrative reforms of Maria Theresa, rather than those of Ferdinand II, signified the real destruction of Bohemian statehood. See František Kavka, *Bílá Hora a české dějiny* (Prague: Státní makl. politické literatury, 1962), pp. 12–13, for further reference.

úřad) under a president and two councilors, a genuinely bureaucratic body independent of the estates, assumed administrative and fiscal authority in the crownland. More oblique procedures succeeded in Bohemia and Moravia. In 1748 the deputations, purely bureaucratic agencies, were established in each Land to manage the newly reorganized system of direct taxation (*contributionale*). In 1749 the deputations were renamed "royal representations and chambers" and absorbed the central administrative authority of the traditional institutions, which had been under a vestigial influence of the estates, the Lieutenancy Council in Bohemia and the Tribunal in Moravia. The Lieutenancy Council disappeared and the traditional "highest officials" of the Land were formed into a *concessus*, retaining only the slender judicial agenda previously assigned to the Council. The Tribunal remained, but was also restricted to its former judicial functions. In the financial area, the chambers and representations absorbed—in addition to the management of the Contribution—the functions hitherto performed by the Bohemian Chamber and the Moravian master of rents, the early prototypes of royal bureaucracy.

In a concession to the estates, which was more apparent than real, the representations and chambers, renamed royal *gubernia*, were placed in 1763 under the traditional heads of the estates, the supreme count palatine in Bohemia, and the captain of the Land in Moravia. Their membership remained otherwise bureaucratic. As another concession in Bohemia, the entire *concessus* of the "highest officials" of the Land was added in 1764 to the *gubernium*, but the effect of this provision was neutralized in 1771 by isolating this group in a special judicial section (*gubernium in iudicialibus*), and thus from the truly consequential administrative section (*gubernium in publicis*). Nothing analogous occurred in Moravia, and the *gubernium* in Brno remained devoid of judicial functions.

Maria Theresa likewise did much to emasculate but not destroy the strongholds of the estates, the Bohemian and Moravian diets. The reform was intended in part to increase royal power versus estates' power. In part the objective was undoubtedly to break the reactionary inertia of estate policies dictated by the narcissism of ecclesiastic and secular aristocrats based on landed property. The results of the government's actions were, however, less clear than its objectives. In her campaign the queen focused, first of all, on the crucial fiscal area. In 1748 a system of granting the Contribution for a ten-year period (the "decennial recession") deprived the diets of their power of annual fiscal negotiations. Simultaneously, the diets and the estates lost control over the assessment and collection of the Contribution as well as over the related recruitment of soldiers in lieu of the Contribution. Initially in 1748 the short-lived deputations managed the Contribution, and after 1749 this responsibility shifted to the central bureaucracies of each Land—the "representations and chambers" until 1763, subsequently the *gubernia*. New cadasters regulated the assessment of the Contribution. Prepared for Bohemia in 1749–57 and for Moravia in 1749–60, they covered the lands outside as well as within the demesnes. The traditional exemption of the demesnes from taxes finally ended, but progress was still limited because feudal land was taxed at a rate of less than one-third the rate for peasant land. The executive organs of the diets, the Committees of the Land, also greatly declined in importance with the loss of the estates' power to collect the Contribution. Moreover, by 1770 they became accountable to the *Hofrechenkammer* in Vienna for the management of even the modest revenue (Domestic Fund) which had remained at the disposal of the estates.[3]

In Silesia the diet (*Fürstentag*) was reconstituted after 1742. Maria Theresa reduced its powers to the level of the Bohemian and Moravian diets. Occasionally it met in a less solemn manner as the *conventus publicus* with functions analogous to the Committees of the Land in Bohemia and Moravia.

Under Maria Theresa the use of the Czech language diminished further in public life. One of the implied principles of the later stages of enlightened absolutism was the concept that a single language (German) should correspond to the requirements of a single centralized state, although it was never proclaimed the "state" language. With the abolition of the Bohemian Chancellery (1749), Czech disappeared from the central government organs in Vienna, except for rare uses for a time at the *Oberste Justizstelle*. Inside the Bohemian Lands it vanished from administration and judiciary as these functions were bureaucratized. The rights of Czech were safeguarded only in external contacts of government agencies with private parties, because enlightened absolutism expected from its officials the ability to communicate with the common people.

Reforms of Local Administration, 1740–80

Maria Theresa extended the apparatus of state officialdom to a level just above the manors and the towns through a bureaucratization of the governments of the individual circuits (*kraje*). Silesia served as the testing ground for this process, as it did for the takeover by the state officials of the administration of the individual Lands.[4] In Bohemia and

3. In 1779–80 the government went on to promulgate new by-laws for the Committees, requiring them to submit each month the minutes of their proceedings for approval of the *Hofkanzlei* in Vienna.

4. In 1744 the crownland was divided into three distinct (*obvody*), each managed by an elder of the Land aided by commissioners. These officials were independent of local estates and responsible to the bureaucratic Royal Office in Opava.

Moravia the decisive step in the bureaucratization of the circuit administration occurred in 1749 when the *kraj* captains became subordinated in political, fiscal, and military affairs directly to the "representations and chambers." In 1751 the state assumed the payment of salaries to the chief *kraj* officials, including the captains whose number in Bohemia was reduced to one per *kraj*.

Manorial administration was coming under increasing control of state bureaucracy. To safeguard the solvency of the peasant serfs, Maria Theresa sought to shield them from excessive seigneurial exactions. Special agencies were established in 1748 to conduct trials in such cases. By 1753 they had stabilized under the name of *concessus in causis summi principis et commissorum*. The *kraj* offices investigated peasant complaints, and after 1772 also tried cases arising from them that could be appealed. Manorial officials were increasingly subjected to state regulations. A patent of 1773 required the economic officials to register with the quasi-governmental Agricultural Society, which supervised their conduct and could remove them from office for malfeasance. An edict of 1775 obliged the manorial officials, concerned with the Contribution, to pass a qualifying examination and be registered at the *kraj* office. Most manorial courts lost jurisdiction over capital offenses through judicial reforms, which reduced the number of courts dispensing "higher justice" from 200 to 30 in Moravia between 1752 and 1754, and from 365 to 30 in Bohemia in 1765. The exercise of criminal justice by the manors in lesser cases (patrimonial jurisdiction) became also more closely regulated in 1769–70. The *kraj* offices had to review all verdicts involving confiscation of a homestead, forcible recruitment into the army, or incarceration.

Under Maria Theresa, the state was increasingly concerned as well with the peasants' economic obligations. The emphasis was on strict regulation of the amount of *robota* in each of the Bohemian Lands. In Silesia a state commission, established in 1768, made an official record (*urbarium*) of the traditional peasant obligations on each manor, and a patent of 1771 outlined the manner of their fulfillment. The *robota* patents for Bohemia and Moravia, issued in 1775, reflected in part Vienna's apprehensions over the widespread peasant revolts in Bohemia earlier that year. As a new departure, they disregarded the customary obligations and established general norms for obligatory peasant labor based on the amount paid in Contribution. The patents had to be enforced against adamant opposition of the Bohemian seigneurs. Eleven different rates were stipulated, ranging from thirteen days per year of personal labor (for peasants who paid no tax) to three days a week of labor with one draft animal. At the same time, the government began to experiment with complete abolition of the *robota*. In 1776 Julius Raab, director of the cameral and formerly Jesuit estates in Bohemia, was authorized to divide the demesnes into peasant homesteads and convert obligatory peasant labor into monetary rents. "Raabization," as the reform was later called, was applied to 105 manors in Bohemia, and fewer in Moravia. On the whole, the reform did not appeal to the private seigneurs.

The town governments in the Bohemian Lands also were subjected to an ever mounting state regulation. Bureaucratization was advanced in 1749 by the requirement of formal legal training from candidates for administrative posts in royal towns. Two years later the Contribution, police, and public health in towns were placed under supervision of the *kraj* officials. The internal fiscal autonomy of Silesian towns ended in 1751 when royal agencies (the economic directorates) began to manage town properties. Many towns lost the right to exercise "higher justice" through the judicial reforms of 1752–54 in Moravia and of 1765 in Bohemia.

Culmination of Reforms and Retreat, 1780–92

Joseph II (1780–90) followed his mother's example, advancing even further the tendencies toward centralism and bureaucracy in general, and toward Germanization in particular. At the same time, the efforts not only to increase royal power but to right social injustice were more pronounced. With his penchant for centralization at the top level, Joseph II sought to concentrate administrative, financial, and judicial power in a single agency in Vienna. In the end, the United Bohemian-Austrian Chancellery in 1782 (like the *directorium* in 1749–62) assumed fiscal responsibilities in addition to political administration, but the *Oberste Justizstelle* retained its status as a supreme court.

Joseph II further weakened the ties uniting Bohemia with Moravia and Silesia by refusing to be crowned king of Bohemia, by abolishing in 1783 the common office of the master of coinage, and by transferring its functions to the *gubernia*. Through his judicial reforms of 1782–84 the Prague Court of Appeals lost the last vestige of its status as an institution common to the Bohemian Lands. From 1782, appeals from Silesia went no longer to Prague but to the Tribunal in Brno (renamed Moravian-Silesian Court of Appeals in 1783), which had obtained appellate jurisdiction in Moravia as early as 1753. Silesia was also tied more closely to Moravia in 1782, when it was placed under the authority of the *gubernium* in Brno. The separate Silesian diet, however, remained.

Joseph II reduced even more drastically than his mother the surviving institutions of the estates. The Committees of the Land in both Bohemia and Moravia were abolished in 1783. Instead, the estates in each Land could elect from six candidates, nominated by the government, two deputies (the so-called estate representation), who were attached to the *gubernia*. With the abolition of the Committees of the Land, the state assumed the tax collection for the Domestic Fund, as well as its management. The socially progressive judicial reforms of 1782–84 likewise transformed the Courts of the Land (the trial courts for criminal and civil cases involving the nobles). From domains of the "highest officials" of the Land, still under considerable influence of the estates, these courts turned into realms of state bureaucracy. In Bohemia the Court of the Land also absorbed the judicial powers previously exercised by the "highest officials" of the Land in the *gubernium in iudicialibus*. The traditional "highest officials" thus lost their remaining collective functions. Some of them became heads of bureaucratic institutions, such as the Prague Court of Appeals, or the reformed Moravian Court of the Land, just as earlier (in 1763) the supreme count palatine and the captain of the Land had assumed the presidencies of the *gubernia* respectively in Prague and Brno. In his zeal to downgrade the estates, Joseph II proceeded to nullify even this concession. Breaking with tradition he began to confer the dignities of the "highest officials" on state bureaucrats instead of the leaders of the estates. In such respects he differed from his mother, who like him wanted to reduce if not destroy vested estates' interests in substance, but unlike him had attempted to placate the estates by maintaining their prerogatives at least in outward traditional appearance. Even under Joseph II the diets did not disappear in the Bohemian Lands entirely, but they were restricted to hearing royal propositions and could express their views only at the ruler's request. A patent of 1789, establishing a fixed permanent land tax, deprived them of the opportunity to negotiate over taxes. This decree accompanied the promulgation of a new cadaster, which at last equalized the tax rate in the demesnes and the peasant lands.

In religious affairs a dramatic move by Joseph II, the Toleration Patent of October 13, 1781, ended the century-and-a-half-long ban on Protestantism in Bohemia and Moravia. Restrictions on the status of Jews were considerably modified. As for Protestants, the surviving Bohemian Brethren still lacked the freedom to profess their faith, but had to embrace Lutheranism or Calvinism. In any case, the Counter Reformation had been so effective that only fifty thousand persons dared to join one of the two Protestant denominations, securing their clergy mostly from Slovakia or other parts of Hungary. Even in the late nineteenth century, 95 percent of the population would maintain membership in the Catholic Church.

At the lower echelons of government, Joseph II completed the bureaucratization of the *kraj* administration by making commoners eligible for the position of captain (in 1782), requiring formal legal training from *kraj* officials (1784), and stipulating explicitly (in 1785) that the captains should be chosen from experienced civil servants ("good secretaries"). The subordination of the *kraj* offices to the *gubernia* became more rigorous.

The legal position of the peasantry was fundamentally improved in the Bohemian Lands when Joseph II, by a special patent of November 1, 1781, abolished the condition of personal bondage and substituted a "moderate subjection" (*Unterthanigkeit*) corresponding to the peasants' legal status in Lower and Upper Austria. The peasants were now free to migrate, to marry without permission, to have their children educated or apprenticed in towns, to dispose of or mortgage their land. They still owed economic obligations to their seigneurs, although shortly before his death Joseph II had contemplated a conversion of all *robota* obligations into monetary rent. The judicial and administrative authority of the manor also persisted, though subjected to additional state checks and regulations. Since 1781 the manors had to submit regular reports to the *kraj* offices, which two years later began to keep the service records of higher manorial officials. A major reform introduced in 1788 required the seigneurs to appoint and pay qualified legally trained officials, or justiciars, to take charge of the manorial courts. Thus distinctive judicial offices (*Justizämter*) emerged in the manors, separate from the general "economic" offices, and virtually independent of the seigneur's authority.

Also in the towns Joseph II further reduced self-government in favor of bureaucratization with the intent of improving standards and raising the competency of administrative officials. A decree of 1783 stipulated that town councilors in royal towns could be elected only from a list of candidates prepared jointly by the *gubernium* and the Court of Appeals. Three years later, all royal and large subject towns had to adopt a uniform system of municipal government, the so-called regulated magistracy. The magistracy consisted of several paid councilors, selected as stipulated in 1783, and divided according to their functions into three categories: judicial, political-administrative, and economic. In addition, a burgher committee elected three municipal representatives to assist in the management of town properties. Small towns that were not entitled to a professional magistracy had to delegate their judicial functions to a larger town or to a manorial justiciar.

Leopold II (1790–92), after the premature death of Joseph II, had to face the accumulated resentments of vested interests violated by the reforms of his predecessor. Although a convinced adherent of enlightened absolutism, he was obliged to make concessions to the estates. Diets in each of the Bohemian Lands were convoked in 1790 and asked to prepare their requests of *desideria*. On the whole, the aspirations of the estates were quite modest compared with those of the early eighteenth century when the *elaborata* for a constitutional reform had been put forth. There were no demands for the restoration of a government for the Bohemian Lands, separate from the government for the Austrian Lands. Basically each diet requested restoration of the estates' rights as they had existed under Maria Theresa. The Moravian diet did not go beyond this, and the Silesian diet added requests for administrative separation from Moravia.

The boldest were the *desideria* of the Bohemian diet, above all in the demands that the central administration and judiciary of the Land be staffed using the diet's advice, and that the councilor responsible for Bohemian affairs in the Bohemian-Austrian Court Chancellery be a Bohemian noble. Echoing the ideas of West European enlightenment, the diet asked for replacement of the Renewed Land Ordinance of 1627 by a new constitution based on a free contract between the king and the "nation." Such notions would of course soon be discredited by the radical phases of the incipient French Revolution. The diet could not reflect the views of the broader strata of society. The initiative belonged entirely to the aristocrats, who were divided into a faction favoring historical rights, headed by Baron William Macneven and Count Johann Bouquoi, and a centralist faction supporting strong imperial authority, under Count Rudolf Chotek. The other three *curiae* counted for little: Joseph II's ecclesiastical reforms weakened the prelates; the few knights were mostly empoverished and represented largely by ennobled state officials; and the representatives of the towns were mostly minor bureaucrats from the magistracies.

In response to the estates' desiderata, Leopold II promised to continue presenting to the diets in "propositions" all matters that had been customarily referred to them, and consented to the diets' exercise of legislative initiative in minor matters. The Committees of the Land, consisting of two representatives from each *curia* in the diet, were restored in Bohemia and Moravia, and the management of the Domestic Fund reverted to them from the *gubernia*. In 1791 Leopold II symbolically reaffirmed the unity of the Bohemian Lands through his coronation as the king of Bohemia in Prague. Ironically, this act was opposed by the Moravian estates, among whom the sense of ethnic and political unity with Bohemia had greatly weakened during the seventeenth and eighteenth centuries. The government had to persuade them to send delegates to the coronation.

Origins of Czech National Renaissance

The estates' opposition to Joseph II's policies was accompanied in the Bohemian Lands—first of all in Bohemia proper—by an incipient Czech national awakening, which was to gain political importance in the following century. Although under Leopold II it appeared as an appendage of aristocratic discontent, its ideological orientation was distinctive.

It focused on the interests of the common people, not the privileged classes. It was less interested in the institutions of the past than in a cultural and political mission of the future. Czech ethnicity and language were central, not peripheral, to the concerns of this cultural renaissance.

Although overtly reacting to the Germanizing policies of Joseph II, the Czech national revival owed a heavy philosophical debt to the Josephin enlightenment. From this source its leaders derived their aim of integrating the lower classes into the life of a national society, as well as their commitment to learning and the pursuit of scholarship and science. Their zeal for education and public enlightenment, supported by a few enlightened Bohemian aristocrats, such as Counts Franz Spork (1662–1738), Franz Kinsky (1739–1805), and Kaspar Sternberg (1761–1838) was truly remarkable. By a deliberate assault on the "darkness" of the Counter Reformation, Josephism had also facilitated the rearmament of the Czech national movement by rehabilitated features of the distinctive Protestant (Hussite) past. In the Josephin view of Czech history, documented for instance in an official textbook from 1783,[5] the events following the battle of the White Mountain became deplorable results of the intolerance of the times. John Hus and in a way also the Bohemian Hussite king, George of Poděbrady (1458–71), were seen as victims of excessive, often ruthless, religious zeal.

An ideological trait of the Czech awakening, most remote from the purview of the aristocratic opposition, was the emphasis on Slavdom. Except for contacts with the Slovaks, awareness of a wider Slavic community had not been a conspicuous part of Czech cultural heritage prior to the battle of the White Mountain. Subsequently, a sense of Slav kinship was promoted by the Counter Reformation, with its introduction of Polish priests into the Bohemian Lands, as well as by the multinational setting of the Habsburg monarchy, where the Czechs encountered other Slavs, such as students in Vienna or soldiers stationed in various parts of the empire. The connection between the Slav interests during the Counter Reformation and during the national awakening is most directly attested by the influential *Dissertatio apologetica pro lingua slavonica, praecipue bohemica* of the famous Czech scholar Bohuslav Balbín, originally written around 1672 but not published until 1775. As the title indicates, the defense of the Czech language stresses as its special advantage the kinship with a large family of other Slav tongues. The founder of Slavic linguistics, Josef Dobrovský (1753–1829), also served as one of the main progenitors of Slav consciousness in the Czech national movement, a consciousness of a distinctly Russophile orientation. A prime

5. Johann Heinrich Wolf, *Geschichte des Konigreichs Boheim zum Gebrauche der Studierenden Jugend in den K. K. Staaten* (Vienna: Johann Thomas von Trattner, 1783), pp. 128, 132, 152, 192.

example is his celebrated address before Leopold II in 1791, as the representative of the Bohemian Learned Society, on the significance of the Slavs. In it, he not only eulogized the Austrian Slavs but dwelt on the glory of the Russians and the power of their empire.

The national awakening was still in its infancy during the last quarter of the eighteenth century, and there was some question whether the trend toward Germanization would stop, or whether it would prove irreversible like the process that led to the loss of the Celtic language among the Irish and the Welsh. The leaders of the awakening as yet lacked a substantial following. The largest reservoir of potential strength for a national movement was the Czech-speaking peasants, who, quite naturally, were more concerned with social and economic issues than ethnic ones, as they had demonstrated in the major uprising in Bohemia in 1775. On the other hand, the formation of the modern Czech nation was favored by the reforms of enlightened absolutism, in particular the patent of 1775, which had limited the service obligations of the peasants, and by their subsequent personal emancipation of 1781. The introduction of widespread secular primary education also helped greatly. Furthermore, the increasing integration of the Czech-speaking lower classes with the rest of society was to make the use of Czech in government and in secondary and higher education an increasingly real and even pressing issue. The formation of a modern Czech nation was considerably complicated by the presence—especially in the peripheral areas—of a sizable German population. The most reliable estimates give the ratios of Czechs to Germans toward the turn of the century as 60 to 40 in Bohemia and 70 to 30 in Moravia, while in the small Silesia the 22.5 percent who were Czechs were outweighed by 42.5 percent who were Germans and the 35 percent who spoke Polish.

While general education, from the highest to the lowest levels, had deteriorated drastically after the battle of the White Mountain, when Jesuits and Piarists assumed control of cultural activities, the equality of languages—German and Czech—was preserved at least in principle. Under the influence of the centralistic reforms of Maria Theresa, however, Czech lost ground steadily, and by 1775 the Germanization of the school system in Bohemia was practically completed. On the other hand, general education broadened greatly under the guidance of Prelate Johann Ignaz Felbiger with the assistance of Joseph Sembdera. Ferdinand Kindermann, and others in all Lands of the Bohemian Crown in the 1770s. When the Jesuit order was dissolved in the Habsburg monarchy in 1773, the secondary schools of learning, the *gymnasia*, received a much improved, modernized curriculum, in some ways similar to the one the Jesuits had established almost exclusively for the training of nobles. Under Joseph II, elementary education was expanded further but higher education was more and more restricted, in line with the emperor's strictly utilitarian approach. The Germanization policy, however, gradually began to be reversed under Leopold II and his son Francis I (II) when the estates and the even more influential clergy came out strongly for the promotion of Czech. Obviously in this respect the rising Slavic Renaissance made its weight felt as well.

REACTION AND NATIONAL AWAKENING, 1792–1847

Era of Police Absolutism

In the period of reactionary police absolutism (1792–1847) the government's policy of centralization and Germanization—contrary to that of Maria Theresa and her sons—continued more from the inertia of the bureaucratic apparatus than from conscious direction. Although both Francis I and his feeble minded son, Ferdinand V (I) were crowned as kings of Bohemia, the distinctiveness of the Bohemian state further diminished as a result of Francis I's adoption in 1804 of the title of Austrian emperor and the subsequent derivative concept of an Austrian imperial state (*der Österreichische Kaiserstaat*) which subsumed its component units.

During the first decade of police absolutism, the Bohemian-Austrian Chancellery, which had been limited to political administration under Leopold II, experienced several reorganizations, based on permutations of the relationships between administrative, financial, and judicial powers. In 1792 it was combined with the *Hofkammer* and under the name *directorium in cameralibus germanicis et hungaricis et in publico-politicis germanicis* exercised both administrative and financial powers. As the name suggests, its financial jurisdiction now extended also to Hungary. In 1797 the name of the Bohemian-Austrian Chancellery was restored; while fiscal responsibilities were transferred to the newly established *Finanzhofstelle*, the Chancellery was now entrusted with the judicial agenda of the *Oberste Justizstelle*, which was abolished.[6] In 1802 the status quo was restored.[7]

The United Court Chancellery was henceforth headed by the supreme chancellor with subordinate chancellors, whose number after the Napoleonic wars stabilized at three: Bohemian-Galician, Austro-Illyrian, and Lombardo-Venetian. In the period 1801–8, the United Court Chancellory did not constitute the highest administrative echelon for

6. Between 1797 and 1802 the Bohemian-Austrian Chancellery did not have jurisdiction over Galicia. A separate Galician Court Chancellery functioned in Vienna during that period.
7. The United Court Chancellery was restricted to political administration, and the *Oberste Justizstelle* was reestablished as the supreme court. Financial administration came under the reestablished *Hofkammer*.

the Bohemian Lands. The superior administrative body then operating was the State and Conference Ministry (*Staats- und Konferenzminister-ium*). Having replaced the advisory Council of State (*Straatsrat*) in existence since 1760, it combined under three departments the supreme direction of governmental affairs. The United Court Chancellery as well as the Hungarian and the Transylvanian Chancelleries, and the *Hof-kammer*, were subordinated to the internal department, while the *Hof-kriegsrat* and the State Chancellery (*Staatskanzlei*) were respectively in the military and foreign departments. After the Ministry's abolition in 1808, the restored Council of State was once more a purely advisory body divested of direct administrative responsibility. The same was true of the State and Conference Ministry (or Council) upon its modified reincarnation in 1814. During the reign of the feeble-minded Ferdinand V, or the pre-March (*Vormärz*) period (1835–48), the supreme power in the monarchy was wielded by a triumvirate: Archduke Louis (brother of the late Francis I, as chairman), Prince Clemens Metternich, and Count Franz Anton Kolowrat. This period—in fact the entire Restoration regime since the Napoleonic wars—was usually associated with the name of the notorious Metternich.

The *gubernia* in Prague and Brno remained the central bureaucracies within the Bohemian Lands, serving as administrative arms of the government in Vienna. Their jurisdiction covered education, religious cults, ordinary police, public health, and commerce, as well as direct taxation. After 1815 the *gubernia* were in a way overshadowed by the police directorates in Prague and in Brno. Hallmarks of Metternich's repressive regime, charged with state security and censorship, these agencies communicated directly with the supreme police and censorship office (*Oberste Polizei- und Zensur-Hofstelle*) in Vienna, headed from 1817 to 1848 by Count Josef Sedlnitzky.

The state continued to tighten its control over local administration in the Bohemian Lands, mainly during the first two decades of police absolutism. In the manors, where the exercise of justice by the *Justizamt* had fallen under state control in 1788, the function of public administration was also separated from the general "economic" office (*Wirtschaftsamt*) before the end of the eighteenth century and assigned to a distinct "superior" office. This *Oberamt* or *Direktorialamt* was subordinated to the circuit (*kraj*) office (to the virtual exclusion of the seigneur's authority) in the exercise of its functions, which included police, taxation, public works, social welfare, and military affairs. The *Oberamt*, together with the *Justizamt*, represented a transitional stage toward a complete *étatisation* of public administration and judiciary on the manors. The manors differed greatly in size—from one or two villages with under a hundred inhabitants to several dozen villages with thousands of people. For instance, the population of the manor of Český Krumlov was sixty thousand.[8]

In the early nineteenth century, town self-government was further reduced. After 1803 the judicial councilors of the magistracies were no longer merely nominated but directly appointed by the *gubernia* and the Court of Appeals. Five years later the posts of political and economic councilors also became appointive. Only the municipal representatives, who shared in the management of town properties, were still elected by a committee of the guilds.

Even before the end of the eighteenth century the use of Czech within the Bohemian Lands disappeared from the internal operations of those administrative and judicial agencies that had been converted into state bureaucracies, such as the Courts of the Land (in both Bohemia and Moravia) and the town magistracies. In the first half of the nineteenth century, Czech persisted as an internal official language only in the agencies still left outside the formal framework of state officialdom, particularly in manorial offices and in the councils of towns too small to have a formal magistracy. In addition, the estates used Czech as a ceremonial language, particularly to open and close the diet.

The use of Czech in external contacts by government agencies, especially the courts, however, was still recognized. It was specifically guaranteed by article 13 of Joseph II's ordinance of judicial procedures, which gave the parties and their representatives the right to use languages "customary" in the Land. The Prague Court of Appeals determined in 1803 that Czech, as well as German, was a language "customary" in Bohemia. It further determined in 1836 that even in such largely German areas of Bohemia as Cheb (Eger), a plaintiff was free to file a suit in either Czech or German.

Under police absolutism the élan of Germanization became blunted and some concessions were granted, especially in the education field. Besides the establishment of the chair of Czech language and literature at the University of Prague, Czech lessons were initiated in the *gymnasia* of Bohemia in 1816 in order to ensure a supply of bilingual Czech-German officials. Such concessions were often weakened by the state officialdom, which championed German and had a habit of ignoring instructions. They emanated from Metternich's colleague and rival, the Conference Minister Count Franz Anton Kolowrat in Vienna, and favored the official use of Czech as a strictly limited expression of the concept of historic rights. In the meantime, support for the Czech language emerged from a revived opposition movement within the Bo-

---

8. The smaller manors could not afford to maintain their own *Oberamt* and *Justizamt*, and were authorized to delegate their administrative and judicial authority to a neighboring manor.

hemian aristocracy, and above all from the popular "national awakening" led by Czech intellectuals. By the mid 1840s both movements had formulated demands for equality of Czech with German in public life, which was guaranteed by the Renewed Land Ordinance of 1627 and still formally valid.

Opposition of the Estates

Notwithstanding Kolowrat's personal preferences, the estates' political role, after a slight reprieve under Leopold II, was kept at a minimum by the Viennese government according to Metternich's wishes. The diets dealt with royal propositions, and routinely consented to established taxes. Minor laws of local significance and new taxes, but not major laws, were presented to them for advice. Moreover, the diet sessions were often delayed so that propositions would reach them only after their implementation. The Committees of the Land were tightly supervised in their management of estates' properties, and of the Domestic Fund.

Partly responding to the example of the Hungarian nobility, an aristocratic opposition revived in the Bohemian diet in the late 1830s. The main protagonist was Count Frederick Deym, who, like his more illustrious Hungarian contemporary, Count Stephen Széchenyi, admired the British constitution and its definition of the role of the nobility. The maneuvers of the new Bohemian opposition, in fact, initially resembled modern parliamentary tactics more than the archaic procedures of submitting petitions, still employed by the oppositionist nobles in 1791. Deym's supporters launched an attack on the supreme count palatine, Count Karel Chotek (1825–43), in 1842 for violating the financial rights of the estates in the administration of the Domestic Fund. Among other issues subsequently raised was the diet's competence to raise taxes for the estates' treasury and to subject royal propositions to genuine scrutiny. When the Viennese government rejected in 1845 the complaints of the malcontents, the oppositionists set out to draft a defense of their rights, the so-called deduction. At the same time, in pamphlets published abroad, they voiced their basic demands—in particular, the appointment of a Habsburg archduke as royal lieutenant in Bohemia, the union of Bohemia, Moravia, and Silesia under a single Court Chancellery, and an equality of Czech with German in public life. In May 1847 the diet voted to submit the "deduction" to the king and in August refused to sanction the proposed taxes. Thereupon it was dissolved by the government, which proceeded to collect the taxes without its consent.

The Czech National Movement

Independently of the estates and the diet, the Czech national movement began to mature, especially after 1815. Its supporters paradoxically came from two diverse occupational and social strata, those who felt threatened by the current process of modernization but also those who were beneficiaries of the process. The former included Catholic parish priests in Czech areas, manorial officials who often did not know German and feared displacement by the advancing German bureaucracy, and Czech craftsmen and shopkeepers in towns facing the competition of German-dominated industrial and commercial enterprises. Among the groups favored by modern social development, support for the national movement came from those who were enabled to teach, study, or enrich themselves. They included teachers of elementary schools, of which there were about five thousand in the 1840s. Nationalism appealed also to Czech university students for whom Czechization of public life would improve their competitive position in relation to the Germans for scarce professional posts in the Bohemian Lands. It would reduce the likelihood of less appealing service in other parts of the empire, such as Galicia. A special role was played in the national movement by a stratum of Czech entrepreneurs and wealthy lawyers who were able to purchase noble estates. Such men often patronized Czech cultural and political endeavors, acting to a degree as surrogates for a nationally minded lower nobility. On the other hand, into the 1840s, national publications and cultural activities (by such organizations as the National Museum and *Matice česká*, established respectively in 1820 and 1831) received relatively little support from the particularly numerous Czech-speaking peasantry.

The national revival in Moravia was still channeled mainly into a provincial form of Moravianism (*moravanství*). Although not necessarily anti-Bohemian, it had not yet embraced a Czech national consciousness as it was evolving in Bohemia. Around 1830 forlorn attempts were made to replace standard Czech with codified local speech as a transitional medium to the Slovak dialects.

The government inadvertently provided the first political education for the broader masses of the Bohemian Lands when in the 1790s it mobilized Czech newspapers and clergy to combat the ideas of the French Revolution. Later, Russia's role attracted attention, while the presence of Russian troops in Bohemia in 1805 and 1813 heightened the sense of Slav kinship. After the Napoleonic wars, Russia's success in the Turkish war of 1828–29 was greeted as an advance of Slavdom. The event that most effectively stimulated and refined political thought was the Polish insurrection against Russia's rule in 1830. The older generation tended to condemn the Poles. Thus the famous linguist and, after Dobrovský, the most prominent leader of the Czech cultural revival, Josef Jungmann (1773–1847), was still a firm believer in the virtues of enlightened absolutism and held Tsar Nicholas I in special regard. He welcomed the Polish defeat. The younger generation, however, was inspired by liberal ideas and passionately sided with the Polish cause. Several amateurish attempts were made in Prague by radical youth between 1830 and 1836 to plot an uprising in emulation of the Poles.

After 1840, Czech middle-class leaders sought to define, in pamphlets published abroad, a national political program along the lines of Western liberalism. Most of them turned from anticipating Russia's intervention to a more realistic Austroslav program advanced by Karel Havlíček (1821–56) in agreement with the famous historian František Palacký (1798–1876), and others such as František Čelakovský and František Brauner. Their objective was to safeguard the future of the Czechs, as well as the South Slavs, through political equality and autonomy within the Habsburg empire. Havlíček became, in 1846, editor of the leading Czech newspaper *Pražské Noviny*, and under the risky conditions of police absolutism sought to spread liberal ideas, as far as censorship permitted. Above all, he advocated participation of commoners in the diets, equality of Czech with German in government and education, and peasant emancipation from the vestiges of seigneurial tutelage. Czech liberal leaders met and exchanged ideas in Prague in two organizations tolerated by the government: the Union for the Encouragement of Industry and the patriotic society, *Měšťanská Beseda* (Civic Club), established respectively in 1833 and 1845. A group of radicals under Karel Sabina and Emanuel Arnold, seeking to subvert absolutism through illicit agitation, formed in 1847 a secret society, the Repeal.[9] Arnold was imprisoned in the same year for disseminating an anti-Jesuit leaflet.

AGRICULTURE, CRAFTS, AND INDUSTRY[10]

The Period of Manufactories, 1740–92

Although in the Bohemian Lands the efficiency of agricultural production was generally low owing to the system of compulsory labor,

9. The name was suggested by the contemporary Irish movement for a repeal of the act of union between Ireland and Great Britain.

10. The economic data in this section are derived from František Kavka and Josef Válka, *Dějiny Československa. 2. 1437–1781*, 2d ed. (Prague: SPN, [1970]), pp. 273–95; Jozef Butvin, *Dějiny Československa* (Prague: Státní pedagogické nakl., 1968), 3:19–81; Alois Míka, *Nástin vývoje zemědělské výroby v Českých zemích v epoše feudalismu* (Prague: Státní pedagogické nakl., 1960), passim; Václav Průcha, *Hospodářské dějiny Československa v 19. a 20. století* (Prague: Svoboda, 1974), pp. 15–24; Jan Kapras, *Právní dějiny zemí koruny*

some improvements did occur in the second half of the eighteenth century as agricultural prosperity (contrasting with the long-range depression of the seventeenth century) was gradually mounting. New plants, especially potatoes and sugar beets, were introduced first on the demesnes, then on peasant lands. But even potato growing spread slowly. Initially cultivated mainly in northwestern Bohemia, potatoes attracted attention elsewhere only after the near-famine conditions in the 1770s. Flax and hemp were the most common industrial plants. Eager to improve the linen production in Bohemia after the loss of Silesia, the imperial government encouraged the cultivation of flax and sponsored imports of high-quality seed from Latvia.

A distinct advancement was the modification, in some regions, of the standard three-field system by planting feed crops, such as alfalfa, clover, and beets, instead of fallow. Yet, progress remained limited, with less than 1 percent of cultivated land planted in feed crops in Bohemia in 1787, and the added yields did not suffice to permit substantial increases of livestock. Sheep remained the most abundant agricultural animal. According to available statistics, their number averaged one and a half million in Bohemia between 1776 and 1783. In the last quarter of the century their breed was improved by introducing merino sheep, primarily on the noble estates. Ironically, the transition to crop rotation was retarded by the interests of sheep raising, since the animals customarily grazed on the fallow. The state encouraged horse raising for military use, particularly in the 1760s and 1770s. As a result, the number of horses rose in Bohemia from 81,000 in 1762 to 164,000 in 1780. In the same period the number of oxen (next to horses the main source of draft power) also increased substantially—in Bohemia, for instance, from 142,000 in 1762 to 245,000 in 1786. The herds of beef cattle remained limited, failing to satisfy domestic consumption. The yield in dairy products was also modest. Pigs provided the main source of meat, especially for peasant consumption. In Bohemia in 1770–87 the number of pigs (250,000) amounted to about one-sixth the number of sheep.

Nobles anxious to modernize agriculture established in 1770 agricultural societies in Bohemia, Moravia, and Silesia. After 1790 a chair of agronomy at the University of Prague (later transferred to the Prague School of Technology) provided for scientific study of agriculture. De-

---

české (Prague: Česká Grafická Unie, 1920), 3:55–71; Jaroslav Purš, *Průmyslová revoluce v Českých zemích* (Prague: Státní nakl. technické literatury, 1960), pp. 26–106; William E. Wright, *Serf, Seigneur, and Sovereign: Agrarian Reform in Eighteenth-Century Bohemia* (Minneapolis: University of Minnesota Press, 1966), pp. 151–64; *Přehled dějin Československa* (Prague: Academia, 1982), I/2:340–47, 435–41, 480–91; Josef Křivka, "Průměrná roční produkce obilovin v Čechách v první polovině 19. století," *Československý časopis historický*, 31 (1983): 378–91.

spite these hopeful events, progress in agricultural techniques was sluggish at best. Peasants had little cash and limited amounts of land (in
the 1780s 41 percent of all land was still in the demesnes) to pioneer
major improvements. Abundance of cheap labor diminished the seigneurs' incentive for technological advances.

The noble estates throughout the eighteenth century favored the
production of grain, for which strong demand continued, including export opportunities to Saxony, Bavaria, and Franconia from Bohemia,
and to Silesia and Austria from Moravia. The focus on grain detracted
from other kinds of agricultural production, particularly animal raising
and cultivation of new crops. At the same time virtually no improvement occurred in grain productivity. In both Bohemia and Moravia the
return of three to five times the amount of planted grain had remained
almost constant since the sixteenth century. The relative importance of
individual grains in the total production also held steady. Rye led
the others as the most important foodstuff before the massive spread
of the potato. It was a prevalent custom to plant one of the fields, in
the three-field system, largely in rye. Oats occupied second place because of their use as horse feed. Third place was shared by wheat and
barley, used more in brewing beer than for food.

Regarding guilds as obstacles to industrial progress, the government
continued to curtail their powers, and Maria Theresa even wished to
abolish them entirely in 1750. Instead, a less drastic approach was adopted
of selectively declaring certain crafts as "free" and not subject to guild
organization. Linen came under the free classification in 1755, lacemaking in 1766, and altogether eighty-four crafts by 1776. Under Joseph II the certification of new masters was transferred from the remaining guilds to town and manorial officials. The guilds, however,
were still considered essential in maintaining order and discipline in
certain crafts.

A salient feature of the economy was the development in the Bohemian Lands of manufactories, which the government favored under
enlightened absolutism. Moreover, Bohemia was to replace Silesia as
the focal point for textile production within the monarchy. Under Maria
Theresa special government agencies were charged with the encouragement and regulation of industry and commerce in the individual
Lands until 1772, when this function was entrusted to the *gubernia*. Initially the government granted exclusive production rights to certain entrepreneurs, as well as subsidizing and making advanced payments to
individual enterprises. By the 1770s the system of privileges and sup-
ports was curtailed to encourage competition and avoid monopolies.

During the second half of the eighteenth century, textile manufactories were naturally most numerous, producing linen, woolens, and
some cotton fabric. They relied largely on manual labor, but with a

considerable degree of specialization. The manufactories themselves, often employing over a hundred workers, usually performed the final processing of the cloth, while peasants or guild craftsmen spun and wove in their own homes. Most manufactories operated in regions with plentiful water power: northern Bohemia and northern Moravia with the adjacent parts of the vestigial Silesia. Aside from foreign entrepreneurs, domestic nobles and merchants took part in industry. By 1780 the number of manufactories reached twenty-four in Bohemia alone.

The glass industry continued to expand after midcentury until the 1770s, when a slowdown occurred owing partly to English and Dutch competition and partly to a diminution of export opportunities in Southeastern and Eastern Europe. Compared with the advances, particularly in textile production, ironworks failed to improve technologically. An increased number of traditional plants accounted for an expansion of output. Thus in Bohemia the production of wrought iron rose modestly between 1700 and 1753 from 3,600 to 4,000 tons, and more markedly by 1790 to 7,000 tons.

Despite the prominence of manufactories, until the end of the eighteenth century much more of the textile production came from individual artisans. For instance, in Moravia by 1791 the share of manufactories in the production of woolen cloth was just one-fifth of the total. The field of textiles as a whole, combining the output of manufactories and individual craftsmen, enjoyed an enormous preponderance in the industrial sector. Thus in Bohemia in 1780, compared with 230,000 workers producing textiles, the next two leading industries—glassworks and ironworks—employed only 3,622 and 2,354 workers respectively. In fact, despite the marked development of industry, the Bohemian Lands remained a predominantly agricultural area during the second half of the eighteenth century.

Long-distance commerce of the Bohemian Lands suffered a major disruption with the loss of most of Silesia to Prussia in 1742. In particular, Wrocław previously had served as the principal center of foreign trade. Attempts to channel trade with Russia and Poland through Opava and Těšín proved futile. Although the commercial importance of both Prague and Brno increased, Wrocław's predominant position in the international commerce of the Bohemian Lands was eventually inherited by Vienna. In order to facilitate trade, uniform but separate tariffs were promulgated in 1752 for each of the Bohemian Lands. In 1775 Bohemia and Moravia with Silesia were included in a customs union, which also covered the Alpine Lands and, after 1783, Galicia. Thus the Lands of the Bohemian Crown never formed a single separate customs territory.

In the external trade of the Bohemian Lands the value of exports greatly exceeded that of imports—in the 1760s, for instance, approximately three times. Industrial articles of export included, above all, linen, then woolen cloth, linen yarn, glass, and tin, while wool, grain, and hops ranked highest among the agricultural ones.

Beginning of Industrial Revolution, 1792–1847

From the end of the eighteenth century into the first decades of the nineteenth, improvement of agriculture was still a slow process in the Bohemian Lands. Initially, population growth and the need for military supplies during the Napoleonic wars stimulated agricultural production. Large estates experimented with supplanting the three-field system and the cultivation of potato increased somewhat owing to the shortages of grain, but more advanced equipment was the chief gain. The first sowing machines appeared at the turn of the century. The use of rollers to break up clumps of soil was spreading, and scythes were replacing sickles in the cutting of grains. The most notable advance in the late 1820s was a new type of plow (*ruchadlo*), which improved the mixing and turning of soil, as well as the depth of plowing. A postwar depression caused a temporary setback. With the crucial grain prices declining between 30 and 50 percent during the 1820s, the noble seigneurs intensified sheep raising for wool, the price of which was not affected by the crisis.

Agricultural progress accelerated in the 1830s and 1840s. The incentive stemmed largely from the rise in grain prices, reflecting, in turn, a continued rapid increase of population, which rose in the Bohemian Lands from 4.8 million in 1815 to 6.7 million in 1847. The area of arable land expanded between 1830 and 1847 from 7.7 million morgen to 8.6 million in Bohemia, and from 4.2 to 4.5 million in Moravia and Silesia.[11] The three-field system and fallow finally disappeared, replaced usually by the rotation of crops according to programs often planned for years ahead. Occasionally the system of free planting was used, replacing fixed rotation with the planting of those crops that in a given year would be most profitable. More intensive production required greater use of fertilizers. The Prague Agricultural Society promoted the importation of guano, which led to regular use of artificial fertilizers on large estates from 1843.

Animal raising did not progress as rapidly as crop production, because the beneficial impact of increased output of feed crops (due to the system of crop rotation) could not be felt before midcentury. Traditional sheep raising now reached its final era of prosperity, providing on the average one-quarter of the large estates' income. In the early 1840s there were some 2.5 million sheep in the Bohemian Lands. In the sector

11. Much of the new land was previously covered by ponds, the area of which had decreased from 76,000 hectares in 1786 to 35,000 hectares in the 1840s.

of crop raising, the all-important grain cultivation—after two centuries of stagnation—at last improved in productivity with the introduction of crop rotation and seed selection. Among the new crops, potatoes finally spread to all regions. Often planted in the fallow, potatoes contributed to the demise of the three-field system. This crop became so important that decline in harvests due to plant disease in the late 1840s caused a nutritional crisis among the rural poor. Sugar beet production spread more slowly and almost exclusively on large estates. Cheap cotton had caused stagnation in the output of flax, which averaged, in the early 1840s, 230,000 centners in Bohemia and 60,000 centners in Moravia and Silesia. Hemp remained significant in Moravia and Silesia, with 26,000 centners harvested in 1841. Viticulture continued its two centuries of decline. Foreign competition, and encroachments by grain fields, reduced by the 1830s the once extensive vineyards to mere fragments amounting to 30,000 and 2,000 hectares respectively in Moravia and Bohemia.

The chief driving force of economic progress continued to emanate from industry. Inauspiciously the reactionary Viennese government wished to stem the tide in the early nineteenth century, viewing the rise of large-scale production as socially disruptive and thus politically dangerous. In vain, it tried to curtail industrial development. Napoleon's Continental Blockade in 1806 stimulated production in Bohemia, and after a brief slump, following the blockade and the state bankruptcy of 1811, a fresh economic upsurge marked the beginning of the industrial revolution in the Bohemian Lands. The 1820s witnessed the appearance of genuine factories with mechanized production, often propelled by steam engines. The decisive impetus was the competition of cheap English textiles flooding European markets in the post-Napoleonic period.

Machinery was used primarily in textile production, but its spread was uneven, taking place at different times in different branches of the industry, and also in different operations of the same branch. The spinning of cotton was largely mechanized in the 1820s, and the printing of designs on cotton cloth by 1848. Manual labor, however, persisted in the weaving of cotton cloth. Introduction of spinning machines for flax was delayed until the 1840s, while linen production leveled off, owing to competition from cheaper cotton textiles. Machinery prevailed in the spinning of wool in the 1830s, but weaving and finishing of woolen cloth was still performed in 1848 by individual artisans or the old-fashioned manufactories.

Other industries lagged behind textiles in volume and value of production, as well as in mechanization. Artisan techniques prevailed in glass and porcelain production and in the older types of food processing, especially in breweries and distilleries. Mechanization of sugar refining, however, was just beginning, with 4,000 tons of sugar produced in 1847–48.

Requirements of railroads and machine building stimulated iron production. The first furnace using coke was erected in Vítkovice in 1836, and five puddling refineries and twenty-nine rolling mills were in operation by 1846. Nevertheless, the major share of production still originated on noble estates in the old ironworks relying on charcoal. The output of raw and cast iron rose in the Bohemian Lands from 17,000 tons in 1825 to 47,000 tons in 1845. The use of coke and the spread of steam engines encouraged coal mining, and the production rose between 1819 and 1848 from 33,000 to 184,000 tons of soft coal, and from 61,000 to 429,000 tons of hard coal. Concentrating on textile machinery and steam engines, the machine-tool industry was in its infancy before 1848, with production performed manually in workshops, typically employing less than fifty workers.

Improvements in the system of communications accompanied the onset of the industrial revolution. The first railroad, still horse-drawn, was completed between České Budějovice and Linz in 1832. A steam-powered railroad reached Brno from Vienna in 1839, and Prague from Olomouc in 1845. A telegraph line from Vienna to Brno was constructed in 1846, and extended to Prague a year later.

Concomitant with the industrial revolution, a sizable factory labor force appeared in the 1840s, causing government concern about working conditions. A decree of 1842 prohibited child labor under the age of nine, and limited the working hours for older children and adolescents. In 1844 the first modern labor strife occurred in Prague. Textile workers protested the lowering of wages and, in particular, the introduction of cloth-printing machines, which they sought to destroy. In response, an investigatory commission was established at the *gubernium*, and its recommendations resulted in strict regulation of workers' organizations.

The advance of the industrial revolution in the Bohemian Lands can be measured, to some extent, by the number and distribution of steam engines in individual industries. Of a total of 156 in 1841, 52 percent were in textile industries, 18 percent in mining, 13 percent in ironworks, and 12 percent in sugar refineries and flour mills. Brno appeared more industrialized than Prague; it boasted twice as many steam engines with a population (50,000 in 1834) substantially smaller than Prague's (155,000 in 1846). Excluding Hungary, the Bohemian Lands accounted for 60 percent of industrial steam engines in the rest of the Habsburg monarchy in 1846. The progress of the industrial revolution placed the Bohemian Lands, together with Lower and Upper Austria and Lombardy-Venetia, well ahead of the other Habsburg lands in economic development. While containing only 19 percent of the monarchy's population, the Bohemian Lands accounted in 1841 for 29.2 percent of the total value of industrial production, including 75 percent of woolens, 42 percent of cotton textiles, and 78 percent of glass. Excluding Hungary, they also mined 75 percent of coal in the rest of the monarchy.

The Slovenes

Enlightened Absolutism, 1740–92

Introduction of Bureaucratic Absolutism in the 1740s

In the first decade of Maria Theresa's reign the estates in the Slovene territory lost control over the chief administrative organs of the individual crownlands, which—like those in the Bohemian Lands—became a part of the state bureaucratic apparatus. Under Count Friedrich Haugwitz's guidance in 1748, collegiate bodies of state officials (called representations and chambers after 1749) took charge of political and fiscal administration in each of the crownlands: Carniola (jointly with Gorizia), Carinthia, and Styria. A similar body, the Commercial Intendancy, assumed analogous functions in the area of Trieste and Rijeka (Fiume), now called the Mercantile Province of the Littoral. The entrenchment of direct state power in each Land obviated the need for agencies of state authority at the intermediate level and led to the dismantlement of the governing apparatus for Inner Austria in Graz. The office of *vicedom*, hitherto in charge of princely properties in the individual Lands, was also abolished. In the judiciary as well, the power of the estates diminished greatly with the introduction of new Courts of the Land, likewise staffed by state officials. For administrative purposes, the Lands were subdivided into circuits (*Kreise, okrožja*), each headed by a circuit captain (*Kreishauptmann, okrožni glavar*) who served as a point of contact between state power and individual manors and towns. Carniola was divided into three circuits (with Gorizia attached as a fourth), Carinthia into three, Styria five, and the Littoral two.

Parallel fiscal reforms further reduced the estates' influence. In addition to taxing the land of the demesnes, the state placed the apportionment and collection of taxes under close scrutiny of the circuit officials. The approval of the Contribution, now requested for three to ten years at once, became a mere formality. In Carinthia the tax was to be collected from 1750 to 1770 despite repeated refusals of a sanction by the local diet. In 1748 the Lands of Inner Austria were relieved of responsibility for financing the Croatian military borders,[12] and the pertinent revenue was partly converted into a general military tax.

With the extension of the bureaucratic apparatus, the state now intervened more systematically in the seigneurs' relations with their serfs. Circuit officials were specifically charged with protection of the peasantry. After 1747, manorial courts lost jurisdiction over disputes between seigneurs and serfs, and such cases were assigned to newly created state judicial agencies, which in 1753 assumed a stable form under the name *concessus in causis summi principis, commissorum et subditorum.*

Later Reforms of Maria Theresa, 1763–80

The latter part of Maria Theresa's reign witnessed several administrative adjustments in the Slovene area. In 1763 Gorizia regained its status as a separate Land, and the names of chief administrative organs were charged to *gubernium* in Styria and to Land Captaincy (*Landeshauptmannschaft*) in Carinthia, Carniola, and Gorizia. In 1776 the Province of the Littoral was dissolved, with the Rijeka area added to Croatia, other parts to Gorizia, and only Trieste designated as a separate administrative unit.

A decree of 1774 introduced a new educational system providing for the establishment of elementary ("trivial") schools in every parish, lower secondary schools (*Hauptschule*) in major towns, and teachers' colleges in the capital of each Land. The reform resulted in substantial use of Slovene in the elementary schools and the lower grades of the *Hauptschule* in Carniola and Gorizia. In the elementary schools of Styria and Carinthia, Slovene was confined mainly to religious instructions.

Important measures were adopted to improve conditions of the peasantry. In 1772 the government in Vienna proposed to the estates of the Lands within the Slovene territory a reduction of compulsory peasant labor to two days per week. The Gorizian estates consented, while the others insisted on six days per week. The government then independently by a patent of 1778 fixed the norm for Carinthia and Styria at three days regardless of the size of the peasant holdings. In Carniola, where the seigneurs proved particularly recalcitrant, the settlement was delayed until 1782, when Joseph II was to set the quota at four days (two with draft animals, two without) for a full hide of peasant holdings with decreases in the quota for fractions of a hide. Maria Theresa also took the initiative to ensure land tenure for the peasants on private estates. An imperial decree of 1772 transformed land leases into hereditary possessions in Carinthia. In Styria and Carniola, where the estates had agreed in 1769 to negotiate directly with the peasants, con-

---

12. Concerning the administrative reorganization of the military borders in Croatia see p. 259.

version of leases into ownership was a very slow process. Especially in Carniola, it was not to be fully completed before the peasant emancipation of 1848.

As among other national groups of the Habsburg monarchy, among the Slovenes, the concern of enlightened absolutism for the welfare and education of the common people facilitated the rise of a national movement. During the latter part of the eighteenth century, however, entrenched localisms hampered the formation of a single national consciousness. Thus in 1758–62 a Catholic catechism was printed in three different Slovene versions; Styrian, Carinthian, and Carniolan.[13] Slovenes outside of Carniola described themselves as *Slovenci* and their language as *slovenski*, the same terms they applied to Slavs in general. The Carniolan Slovenes referred to themselves as *Kranjci* and to their language as *kranjski*.

Like other national groups in the Habsburg monarchy, the Slovenes were to find the cultural revival, stimulated by enlightened absolutism, a seedbed for the growth of ideas that would animate the national political programs of the nineteenth century. In the latter part of Maria Theresa's reign the use of Slovene in print began to increase, promoted by the clergy and to a lesser extent by lay writers. Even the government started issuing some of its decrees and circulars in Slovene translation. The most important of the early national "awakeners" was an Augustinian monk, Marko Pohlin (1735–1801), who in his *Kraynska Grammatika* (1768) deplored the preference given to German over Slovene, the usage of which he advocated in education and literature. While Pohlin adopted a narrowly Carniolan viewpoint, rejecting links with Slovenes outside Carniola, his contemporary, the Jesuit linguist Ožbalt Gutsman (1727–90), though recognizing the distinction between the *Slovenci* and *Kranjci*, proposed a single dictionary and literature language for both. Among the lay figures of the nascent Slovene national movement the most prominent one was the merchant and manufacturer Žiga Zois, who in the 1770s supported a circle of Ljubljana intellectuals delving into Slavic languages and affairs.

Culmination of Enlightened Absolutism, 1780–92

Joseph II's (1780–90) chief administrative reforms in the Slovene area aimed at consolidation of administrative units. In 1782 Carniola and Carinthia were placed together with Styria under the *gubernium* in Graz, and Gorizia under a newly created *gubernium* in Trieste. The Lands were no longer administrative entities, and the circuits (*Kreise*) became directly subordinated to the *gubernia*. Wishing to reduce further the

---

13. The Slovene Protestants of Prekmurje also preferred to use the local dialect in their literature.

estates' influence, the emperor rendered the diets entirely powerless, and abolished the Committees of the Land, with only two members of each attached to the *gubernia* as councilors. He severely curtailed the judicial power of the seigneurs by requiring that trained lawyers conduct the manorial courts. In towns the traditional judgeships, as well as the internal and external councils, were abolished. Instead, administration and justice were entrusted to the magistracy, a group of officials whose election by the burghers was little more than a formality.

The Toleration Patent of 1781 affected relatively few communities in the Slovene area.[14] The abolition of manorial restrictions on personal freedom by a patent of 1782—patterned closely on the 1781 patent for the Bohemian Lands—brought substantial relief to the entire peasant class. The patent covered Styria, Carinthia, Carniola, and the Littoral. The peasants obtained further protection through the reform of manorial courts, as well as through an increase in the supervisory powers of circuit captaincies. An additional relief measure—substituting monetary rent for compulsory labor—could be applied only on a few governmental estates in southern Styria.

During the brief reign of Leopold II (1790–92), the estates of the Lands in the Slovene area had an opportunity to complain against the reforms of enlightened absolutism. The Carniolan diet asked for return to the political conditions of the 1760s; the Carinthian diet wished to reverse even Haugwitz's reforms of the 1740s. In their statements— issued, to be sure, before the radical phase of the Revolution in France— the estates (like their confreres in Bohemia) embraced elements of modern constitutional theory, speaking of themselves as the people's representatives, and of the ruler's powers as based on the consent of the governed. In the end, Leopold II granted relatively modest concessions. Each Land again became a separate administrative unit with the Captaincies of the Land restored in Carniola, Carinthia, and Gorizia. The Committees of the Land and certain other agencies of the estates were reestablished. The influence of towns increased somewhat in the agenda of the estates; in particular, Committees of the Land in Styria and Carinthia were to include burgher representatives.

The Slovene national awakening benefited more than it had suffered from Joseph II's reforms. The Germanization policy had little effect in Carniola, Carinthia, or Styria, where German had already dominated not only state agencies but also secondary and higher education; in Gorizia and in Triest, German was introduced largely at the expense of the Italian language. The cause of Slovene national awakening gained from the encouragement of popular religious and didactic literature. An outstanding example was the new Slovene translation of the Bible in 1784–

---

14. The most significant group was the Protestants of Prekmurje.

1804 by Jurij Japelj (1744–1807). Even more significant was the work of Anton Linhart (1756–95), a member of Zois's circle. His history of Carniola and the South Slavs of Austria (1788–91), though written in German, contributed substantially to the development of a national ideology by stressing the historical unity of all Slovenes. Tracing this initial oneness to the early medieval realm of Karantanija, Linhart attributed subsequent divisions of Slovene territory into the existing Lands to the effects of foreign domination, which acording to him persisted.

The nascent Slovene national movement gained relatively little from the reaction against the Germanization plans of Joseph II. The diet of Carniola in its memoranda of 1787 and 1790 did refer to the existence of a distinct language in the Land, but it did not follow up these pronouncements with concrete requests for greater use of Slovene in government or education. Thus, even in this Land with the largest percentage of Slovene inhabitants, the estates failed to link provincial patriotism with Slovene nationalism.

NATIONAL AWAKENING, 1792–1847

Napoleonic Wars and the Illyrian Provinces, 1792–1813

As a result of the Napoleonic wars, by the treaty of Campoformio in 1797, the Habsburg monarchy acquired additional Slovene populations in Venetian Istria (Venetia Euganea) and in so-called Venetian Slovenia (Venetia Julia) located northeast of Gorizia. Venetia Euganea became a separate Land under a president with the capital in Koper (Capodistria), while Venetia Julia remained under the lieutenant (*Statthalter*) in Venice. Subsequent reforms in the old Habsburg territories once again concentrated on the creation of administrative units larger than the traditional Lands. In 1803 Gorizia was subordinated to the Captaincy of the Land (*Landeshauptmannschaft*) in Carniola, and a year later Carinthia was placed under the Styrian *gubernium*.

The cause of Slovene national awakening made slow but steady progress. It was aided by the gradual increase in the number of elementary schools; by 1809 every seventh child in the Slovene territories was able to receive some formal education. The Viennese government encouraged a limited number of publications in Slovene, especially official propaganda to popularize the struggle against Napoleon and the French. Zois's circle continued to play an important role. Its ranking member, Valentin Vodnik (1758–1819), launched the first Slovene newspaper, *Lublanske Novize* (1797–1800). Another major landmark was the appearance in 1809 of a dictionary by the famous linguist Jernej Kopitar (1780–1844) covering jointly the Slovene language in Carniola, Carinthia, and Styria, a work that further advanced the cause of Slovene linguistic, hence national, unity.

By October 1809 almost all Slovenes (except those of Styria and Prekmurje) had fallen under the domination of Napoleon. His newly created Illyrian Provinces included Carniola, western Carinthia, Gorizia, Trieste, and Croatia south of the Sava (ceded by Austria in 1809 by the treaty of Schönbrunn), as well as Istria and Dalmatia, already acquired by Napoleon in 1805 by the treaty of Pozsony, and Dubrovnik. Slovene territory was divided among three of the seven provinces: Carniola, Carinthia, and Istria (including, besides Istria proper, Trieste and Gorizia). Ljubljana was the capital of the Provinces and the seat of the governor-general. Individual provinces were headed by the intendants, and their subdivisions, based largely on the preexisting Austrian *Kreise*, by the subdelegates. French reforms brought an advance of the state judicial and administrative power in the Slovene area at the expense of manorial courts and administrative offices, which were abolished. Economic obligations of the peasants to their seigneurs, however, remained in force. This, together with the rather high rates of taxation and military recruitment, tended to alienate the peasant masses from the French regime despite its progressive features.

In the area of language use, the Illyrian Provinces employed French, German, or Italian in higher education and administration, but local administration and education (including lower secondary) favored the use of the local Slav languages. Although initially the French wished all the Slavs of the Illyrian Provinces to use Croatian, Slovene opposition (articulated above all in a memorandum by Vodnik in July 1811), caused them to recognize the rights of the Slovene language in administration and education within the Slovene area. Reaching the peak of his influence, Vodnik was charged by the French with preparing school textbooks and translating official acts into Slovene. In the *Télegraphe Officiel*, he published the poem "Ilirija oživljena," which applauded Napoleon's Illyrian Provinces for uniting the South Slavs and for freeing them from long alien subjugation. This work expressed in an embryonic form the crucial concept of "United Slovenia" which was to emerge in 1848.

The French benevolence toward the Slovene language elicited a response in the territories still under Habsburg rule. In particular, the government established in 1812 a chair of Slovene language at the Graz *lyceum* to prepare officials and clergy for service in the Slovene territories. Also, for the first time the teaching of Slovene made some headway, albeit modest, in the elementary schools of Styria and Carinthia.

Reaction and the Rise of a National Movement, 1814–47

Austrian troops occupied the Illyrian Provinces in late 1813, and the area was formally restored to Habsburg rule in 1815. A year later the territory, except for Dalmatia, was renamed the Illyrian Kingdom, but divided for actual administrative purposes into two units: one, under a *gubernium* in Ljubljana, included Carniola and before 1825 the western part of Carinthia, and after 1825 all of Carinthia; the other, under a *gubernium* in Trieste, covered Gorizia, Istria, and until 1822 Croatia south of the Sava. Styria, lying outside the ephemeral Illyrian Kingdom, retained its *gubernium* in Graz. While Styria also had retained its traditional *Kreise*, these subdivisions had to be reintroduced into Carniola and Carinthia, once the French occupation had ended. Below the *Kreise* level, traditional manorial administration and judiciary continued in Styria and eastern Carinthia, but they were not restored in Carniola or western Carinthia, where the French had removed them as outmoded vestiges of the feudal system. Instead, in a unique departure from the existing practice in the Habsburg empire, the administration was entrusted to district commissioners and judicial power to state courts. Agencies of the estates—above all, the diet and the Committee of the Land—had continued to exist for Styria and Carinthia, but had disappeared in the territories under the French rule. Gorizia and Istria remained without them, but in Carniola in 1818 a diet was reintroduced together with a committee of four members (the *Verordnete Stelle*) to administer current affairs of the estates.

The use of Slovene in public life was still growing, though at a slow rate. Translations of laws and ordinances, as well as popular literature, particularly on agricultural topics, were increasing. Expanding educational facilities, especially at the lower levels, generated new demands for Slovene textbooks. In the area under the Ljubljana *gubernium* between 1817 and 1847 the number of elementary schools rose from 220 to 350. While in 1810 in the Slovene territory only every seventh child was able to attend school, by 1847 every third could, although the situation varied greatly according to localities, from the enrollment of 77 percent in the Maribor *Kreis* of Styria to 16 percent in the Novo Mesto *Kreis* of Carniola. Still excluded from the seven *gymnasia* within the Slovene territory, Slovene had been offered as a subject in the institutions of more advanced learning, the *lycea*: in Graz since 1812, in Ljubljana since 1817, and in Gorizia since 1847.

The Slovene national movement, which was conspicuous by the 1830s, suffered from a major weakness—the difficulty of enlisting the rising middle class, which seemed to prefer the adoption of German, or (in the Littoral) Italian, or (in Prekmurje) Magyar. Nevertheless, dedicated national leaders, especially intellectuals, did emerge. While the existing police absolutism prevented articulation of a definite political program, the Slovene future was vigorously debated between representatives of conservative and liberal trends. Aside from condoning the existing social system, the conservatives (above all clergymen) tended to restrict their aspirations for the use of the Slovene language, doubting that it could replace German in higher scholarship and culture. The liberals, who gathered around France Prešeren (1800–1849) and published the almanac *Čbelica* (1830–34), championed an unlimited application of their native tongue. Socially progressive, they urged full legal equality for Slovene peasants with other social classes.

In the 1830s Prešeren's group also combated belated schemes for separate literary languages for the Slovenes of Carniola, Styria, and Carinthia. Such efforts had increased since the 1820s and, in some cases, inspired idiosyncratic new alphabets, such as that of Peter Dajnko for the Styrian dialect. While opposed to a splintering of the Slovene language community, Prešeren and his followers equally rejected submergence of the Slovene language into a wider South Slav linguistic community, above all the Illyrian movement, which favored Serbo-Croatian as the literary language for the Slovenes. The Illyrian movement, in fact, found few Slovene converts and mostly in southern Carinthia and Styria. Its main Slovene advocate, Stanko Vraz (1810–51), moved to Zagreb, where he became identified with the Croatian politics and literature.

Prešeren's circle was losing influence in the 1840s and did not participate in the direction of the new Slovene periodical *Novice*, which had appeared in Ljubljana since 1843. Its editor, Janez Bleiweis, a cautious man destined to play a leading role in Slovene politics, then stood closer to the conservative camp.

AGRICULTURE, INDUSTRY, AND TRADE[15]

Period of Manufactories, 1740–92

Influenced by physiocratic doctrines, enlightened absolutism paid special attention to agriculture. The emphasis on individual initiative, partly reflected in efforts to ensure the peasants' hereditary land tenure, led the government in 1768 to decree for the Slovene area a division of common pasture lands among individual peasant owners. The loss of pasture—confining cattle to barns and creating a need for feed crops—stimulated a complex of changes, sometimes called an "agricultural revolution." Feed crops (particularly clover) replenished the soil after grain crops and facilitated elimination of the fallow. Increased availability of manure (accumulating in the barns) for fertilizer also eased the transition to crop rotation.

15. Economic data in this section are derived from *Historija naroda Jugoslavije* (Zagreb: Školska knjiga, 1959), 2:932–85; Ferdo Gestrin and Vasilij Melik, *Slovenska zgodovina od konca osemnajstega stoletja do 1918* (Ljubljana: Državna založba Slovenije, 1966), pp. 16–89; Toussaint Hočevar, *The Structure of the Slovenian Economy, 1848–1963* (New York: Studia Slovenica, 1965), pp. 15–21; *Zgodovina Slovencev* (Ljubljana: Cankarjeva založba, 1979), pp. 358–70, 414–32.

In addition to governmental edicts, new agricultural methods were promoted by agricultural societies, established in quick succession between 1764 and 1767 in Klagenfurt, Graz, Gorizia, and Ljubljana. The societies sponsored experimental farming, publications, prizes for cultivation of new crops or improved animal breeding, and agricultural schools, one of which operated in Ljubljana from 1771 to 1780. The use of German by the agricultural societies, however, limited their impact on Slovene peasants. The first work on agricultural improvements in Slovene did not appear until 1789.

Of the new crops, corn was most common in southern Styria, where its cultivation became a part of the regular system of crop rotation. The growing of potatoes, first known in Carniola in the 1730s and in Styria in 1740, increased very slowly even after the poor harvests of 1767–72, when the government undertook free distribution of seed potatoes. Clover spread rapidly as a result of the agricultural revolution described earlier. Efforts to introduce mulberry trees failed in Carniola and Styria but succeeded in Gorizia, where their number increased in 1764–80 from 53,000 to 185,000. Among older crops, previously flourishing viticulture declined somewhat in the late eighteenth century. As for stubble grains, the cultivation of wheat decreased mainly in favor of the sturdier oats and to some extent rye. Toward the end of the century, for instance, Carniola and Styria produced almost three times more oats than wheat, and Carinthia over five times more.

Although the agricultural revolution, on the whole, improved production, the curtailment of pastures at its onset did cause some decline in the volume of cattle raising. For instance, in Styria the number of cattle diminished in 1778–1807 from 99,000 to 60,000 head. The remaining animals, however, were better fed and larger. The emphasis in animal raising was on cattle, sheep, and horses. Pig production lagged because of easy and plentiful imports from Croatia and Hungary.

In the industrial production of the Slovene area, mining and metallurgy continued to be of major importance. The largest enterprise was still the mercury mine in Idrija, employing some 500 workers in the second half of the eighteenth century. Technological improvements were introduced, and annual production from 1725 to 1785 averaged 148 tons. The traditional output of iron grew moderately. Seven substantial ironworks operated in Carniola, which in 1781 exported an estimated 1,680 tons of iron and iron products. Styria had a major ironworks at Mislinja; in Carinthia iron was produced in small plants, employing artisan methods. The Zois family [16] controlled most of iron exports from Carniola and a substantial part from Carinthia. It acquired major ironworks, particularly at Bohinj and Javornik in Carniola, where high fur-

16. The family was first headed by Michelangelo Zois (1698–1777), then by his son Žiga (1747–1819).

naces were installed before the turn of the century. Under Joseph II the iron industry of the Slovene area was weakened when the government withdrew its special privileges with respect to supplies of raw materials and market protection. Its competitive position, especially on the Italian market, was shaken. Lead was mined and smelted in the Slovene area of Carinthia. The largest enterprise, located at Rabelj, produced 448 tons per year.

Enlightened absolutism placed special emphasis on encouraging manufactories, which sprang up primarily in the production of textiles. A woolen manufactory in Ljubljana, dating to 1725, continued to flourish, and employed 150 workers in the 1750s. New ones were added in Klagenfurt and in Vetrinj in southern Carinthia.[17] A silk manufactory prospered in Fara in Gorizia; another founded in Ljubljana before mid-century failed by 1756. Glassworks, started with foreign workers, represented another important type of manufactory. They were largely concentrated southeast of Maribor (four) and in the Trnovski forest of Gorizia (five). Two more were situated in Styria, and two in Carniola. In the field of paper production, manufactories operated in Ajdovščina and the town of Gorizia; four other plants in the Slovene territory used artisan methods. Several other enterprises, particularly in porcelain and leather production, probably rose above the artisan level to the status of manufactories in the second half of the eighteenth century.

Based on the putting-out system, domestic production flourished and spread into new regions. Linen was a prime example; its exports from Carniola by sea alone reached the value of 360,000 florins in the 1760s. In various Slovene areas lacemaking and the production of straw hats and small iron implements became significant cottage industries.

Beginning of the Industrial Revolution, 1792–1847

In the first half of the nineteenth century the agricultural revolution, launched under enlightened absolutism in the previous century, was essentially completed in the Slovene territories. Crop rotation in three- or four-year cycles (without the fallow) prevailed everywhere. With corn and feed crops firmly established, the potato was at last commonly accepted even among the peasantry following the famine of 1817. By 1848 approximately one-third of the cultivated land was planted in corn, potatoes, and feed crops. The cultivation of stubble grains also increased. Moreover the ratio of wheat to oats improved. In Carniola, in particular, during the first half of the nineteenth century the volume of wheat

---

17. Established respectively in 1762 and 1788.

produced almost doubled, and by midcentury it equaled more than four-fifths of the volume of oats harvested.

Large estates pioneered advances in agricultural techniques as the seigneurs strove to increase their income. Agricultural societies reviving after a lapse at the turn of the century, promoted land improvements (especially draining of swamps), agricultural machinery, new crops, and new branches of agriculture, such as fruit growing and beekeeping. Their activities now had a substantial impact on the peasantry, in part through the mediation of village priests. Forestry became subject to rational management, including planned exploitation and restoration of forests, under intensified state supervision through agencies at the *Kreis* level. The seigneurs began to restrict more severely the peasants' traditional rights of exploiting the forests.

In the second quarter of the nineteenth century the Slovene area experienced the impact of the industrial revolution, though with lesser force than the German-Austrian or Bohemian Lands. Mechanized factories did emerge, but old-fashioned manufactories still outnumbered them. An abundance of water power also tended to retard the application of steam engines. Although the first one was installed in a sugar refinery in Ljubljana in 1835, by 1841 only 4 of the 231 steam engines of Cisleithania operated in the Slovene territory. By 1847, however, over a dozen factories were equipped with them.

According to the classical pattern of the industrial revolution, factory production penetrated relatively early into the textile industry. Mechanized spinneries of cotton sprang up in Ljubljana (1838), Prebold (1839), and Ajdovščina (1843). A woolen factory emerged through an upgrading of the old manufactory in Vetrinj. Silk spinning and weaving failed to reach the factory level; and even the manufactory production, which had prospered in Gorizia, was virtually wiped out during the first half of the nineteenth century by competition from Lombardy and Venetia. In other branches of industry, sugar refining became concentrated in two factories (Gorizia in 1819 and Ljubljana in 1829), belonging among the largest enterprises of their kind within the empire. Since 1842 paper production had boasted a large mechanized mill in Vevče, which exceeded the combined output of the other eight paper mills in the Slovene territory, still of the manufactory type. Also, the mercury mine in Idrija, rising to the challenge of modernization, was equipped with new furnaces in 1842. Its output stabilized in 1805–47 at 157 tons per year, down from the peak of 635 tons per year reached in 1786–98.

In the important iron industry the situation was mixed. Five of the older ironworks[18] were modernized in the 1830s and 1840s, through

---

18. They were located at Prevalje, Ravne, Lipica, Bistrica v Rožu, and Dvor pri Žužemberku.

the installation of puddling furnaces and rolling mills. The other six-teen ironworks remained at the manufactory level. The total output of iron in the Slovene territory rose from 2,240 tons in 1825 to an annual average of 4,648 in 1843–47. About three times as much iron as was locally produced was annually processed in the Slovene area before 1848, especially into railroad rails, wire, and nails. To make up for the deficit of pig iron, caused primarily by the scarcity of iron ore in the Slovene territory, additional pig iron was imported mostly from the German interior of Carinthia. The expansion of iron production stimulated coal mining; the output of coal in the Slovene area increased from 28,000 tons in the early 1830s to 50,400 in the late 1840s, when over half was mined at Leše near Prevalje. By then the railways generated further demand for coal, as the Vienna to Trieste line reached Celje in 1846 and pushed on toward Ljubljana. Glass production maintained its pros-perity originating in the mid-eighteenth century. Generally of the man-ufactory type, numerous glassworks depended mostly on exports to It-aly.

On the whole, the advance of the industrial revolution in the Slovene territories, while significant, did not exceed a modest level by midcen-tury. On a per capita basis, the nonagricultural entrepreneurial income derived from "industry, crafts, and other independent enterprises" was to amount in 1856 to 5 florins (4.70 in Carniola). It was below the most advanced industrial areas of the monarchy—Lombardy-Venetia, and the Austro-German and Bohemian lands—but above the level of all the other regions of the Habsburg empire, including Bukovina, Galicia, Hungary, Croatia, and Dalmatia, but excluding the Vojvodina and the Banat of Timişoara, which virtually equaled the Slovene area.[19] Paral-leling the economic growth, the population of the Slovene territory in-creased by 57 percent in 1771–1857 from some 700,000 to 1,100,000.

19. The following table illustrates conditions compared with other parts of the Habs-burg empire in terms of nonagricultural entrepreneurial income per capita in 1856 (Source: Hočevar, *The Structure of the Slovenian Economy*, pp. 19–20):

AREA	FLORINS
Lower Austria	37.71
Upper Austria	8.15
Bohemia	6.77
Slovene territory	*5.00*
Vojvodina and the Banat of Timişoara	4.88
Hungary	3.79
Bukovina	3.51
Galicia	3.48
Croatia-Slavonia	3.12
Dalmatia	2.56

The Magyars

ENLIGHTENED ABSOLUTISM, 1740–92

Moderate Reforms, 1740–80

During the eras of enlightened absolutism and the subsequent re-action (1792–1847), despite the intentions of its Habsburg rulers, Hungary essentially preserved both the power of the estates and its autonomous status, although absolutism and centralism advanced significantly. In the first instance, Maria Theresa (1740–80) was deterred from imposing centralism and bureaucratization to the degree she did in the Bohemian Lands, far less by gratitude to Hungarian nobles for their very limited aid against Prussia in 1741 than by the fear of habitual Hungarian uprisings in defense of constitutional rights. Altogether her policy was one of rather moderate centralization within the framework of ancient institutions, sanctioned by tradition.

Compared with Maria Theresa's politico-administrative reforms in Bohemia, those affecting Hungary were obviously on the cautious side. In the area of central administration, however, she did in 1746 elevate the Hungarian Court Chancellery in Vienna to a supreme organ of royal administrative and judicial control. While hitherto the Chancellery had been coördinate with the Lieutenancy Council in Pozsony and lacked judicial powers, it was now superior not only to the Council but also to the Septemviral Table and the Royal Judicial Table in Pest. Thus the administrative and especially judicial autonomy of Hungary was compromised. [20] An ascendancy of the *Hofkammer* continued to curtail the independence of the Hungarian Chamber. After the Council of State was established in Vienna in 1760, this chief advisory body on Austrian and Bohemian affairs often included Hungarian matters—especially military ones—in its deliberations. Moreover, in 1765 the queen neutralized the *palatin's* office by conferring its functions on her son-in-law, Albert of Sachsen-Teschen, as the lieutenant.

Relying to some extent on trends initiated late in the seventeenth century with the reconquest of central and eastern Hungary, Maria Theresa sought to attract Hungarian aristocrats to the Viennese Court and to high imperial offices, as a way of attaching Hungary closer to the rest of the monarchy. As early as 1746 she established in Vienna a school for the aristocratic youths of her lands, the *Theresianum*, with emphasis on training for governmental service. A special Hungarian

---

20. The Hungarian Court Chancellery thus came to resemble closely the Bohemian Court Chancellery of the period from 1627 to 1749.

bodyguard was organized in 1764. The overtures were successful in transforming prominent magnates, such as the Pálffys, Balassas, Esterházys, and Apponyis, into more loyal subjects. In association with the imperial court, or the lesser court of Duke Albert in Pozsony, the Hungarian aristocracy changed their manners, dress, and life style, and increasingly adopted French—sometimes German—as their language.

With the alienation of the upper class, another mark of Hungarian distinctiveness, the Magyar language went into decline after flourishing for a time in the seventeenth century. Its use in public life persisted, thanks to the lower nobility, largely in local administration. County officials employed it, along with Latin and local languages; and it, with Latin, remained the medium of official communication among a number of counties, especially in the Tisza region. For certain county assemblies it was the language of proceedings, although official records were kept in Latin. In the diet the official language was Latin, with Magyar restricted to a few ceremonial occasions. Under the influence of central Viennese agencies, German penetrated into the higher levels of Hungary's administration. In particular, the Hungarian Chamber, because of its peculiar dependence on the *Hofkammer*, used it as its official language. After midcentury, German prevailed not only in polite society but also in science and literature. Even the first Hungarian newspaper in a language other than Latin began to appear in German in July 1764—the *Pressburger Zeitung*.

The aristocracy's subservience, however, did not prevent it from joining the lower nobility in resisting tax increases proposed by the queen under the strain of the Prussian wars. After the diet's refusal in 1751 to increase the Contribution, Maria Theresa endorsed a tarriff system, established in 1754 to augment Hungary's fiscal contribution.[21] In the mid-1760s she proposed to increase Hungarian revenues in two ways: by making the nobles subject to taxation (relieving them of the obligation of personal military service), and by enhancing the peasants' tax-paying capacity by specifying and limiting the feudal dues. The nobility resolutely opposed both approaches. It clung stubbornly to the exemption of all nobles from taxation, solemnly enacted by the diet in 1741. It denounced even the existing tax on ecclesiastical estates, dating from 1703, raised in the 1750s, and theoretically justified in 1764 in a treatise by the Slovak Jesuit, Adam František Kollár, whose views were at least unofficially backed by Vienna. The nobles feared that a tax on ecclesiastical estates made the secular ones automatically vulnerable, since Werbőczi's *Tripartitum* equated the privileges of both types of property. Ordering Kollár's book burned, the diet of 1764–65 refused either to trade the military obligation (*insurrectio*) for a permanent tax or to discuss the peasants' feudal obligations.

21. On the new tariff system see p. 237.

Henceforth, Maria Theresa dispensed with the diet for the rest of her reign, and proceeded to enact at least the second aspect of her program by royal rescript. In 1767 she issued the so-called *Urbarium,* regulating peasant feudal dues. Although the impact of peasant revolts of 1765 in the western counties of Vas, Zala, and Somogy helped to lessen noble resistance, the opposition of the seigneurs and county authorities delayed until 1774 the full implementation of the *Urbarium* by royal commissioners. The patent determined maximum peasant obligations on the basis of holding one hide of land. The hide, in turn, was defined as consisting—depending on the quality of soil—of between sixteen and forty holds (one hold equaled 0.57 hectares) of fields, and between four and fifteen holds of meadows. A peasant with one hide of land was obliged to work for his seigneur 52 days per year with his own implements and draft animals, or 104 days without them. In addition, he owed the seigneur each year one florin in cash, one-ninth of his harvest, smaller amounts of poultry and dairy products, and two days of service on long hauls of goods. The *Urbarium* did not affect the peasants' compulsory labor on public works for the county or their payment of tithes to the church or taxes to the government.

The queen's reforms left virtually intact the wide patrimonial jurisdiction over the serfs. In regard to criminal offenses by serfs, the seigneurs still exercised jurisdiction more sweeping than in the Austrian or the Bohemian Lands, since it included frequently the *ius gladii*—the right to pass death sentences in capital cases. Gradually matters of this kind were transferred to the county courts, but even there a very limited right to appeal death sentences was not introduced until 1778. The class character of the judicial system was changed for the better only by the Revolution of 1848.

Maria Theresa's reforming activities left on the whole a positive legacy in the area of education. Secular elementary instruction, though not compulsory, was introduced in Hungary during the last decade of her reign. Her *ratio educationis totiusque rei literariae per regnum Hungariae et provincias eidem adnexas,* which outlined the educational policies of the regime, was issued in 1778.[22] As to secondary education, considerable conflict and competition existed between the Jesuit academies and Piarist and Benedictine *gymnasia* on the one hand, and Lutheran and Calvinist institutions on the other. The Jesuit academies focused on the promotion of faith among clerics and secular nobles and the training of the latter to fight for it in high public office. Benedictine and particularly Piarist *gymnasia* were more bourgeois, and perhaps also more democratic, in character. Here vocational training in regard to agriculture and applied science was not entirely neglected.

22. These provisions were considerably strengthened by a second *ratio educationis* of 1805, extending, in principle, elementary education for a period of two or three years to the villages.

The Protestant and in particular Calvinist schools, foremost among them those in Sárospatak and Debrecen, were more domestic in character than the Jesuit schools, although most of the teachers had studied abroad in Germany and Western Europe. They were especially interested in the instruction of the professional class of commoners and the county squires but, unlike the Jesuits, not in the education of the aristocracy. Teaching in the sciences was superior to that in the Catholic secondary schools. Altogether these Protestant institutions began to emphasize a conscious Hungarian nationalism directed against Rome and empire.

The transfer of the Jesuit-founded university of Trnava to Buda under Maria Theresa, and later to Pest under Joseph II, did much to establish the center of higher learning in the core area of Hungary. In education too, major stimuli for change had to await the Revolution of 1848.

Radical Reforms, 1780–90

Joseph II (1780–90) did not exercise his mother's caution, but set out to establish in Hungary the same kind of centralistic absolutism he desired and partly succeeded in installing in the other Habsburg Lands. To avoid an oath of support for the Hungarian constitution, he refused to submit to a coronation as king of Hungary. To avoid sharing legislative or executive authority with the Hungarian estates, he dispensed during his entire reign with the diet, and left the *palatin's* office vacant. Disregarding traditional usages, he proceeded to enact his reform program autocratically through imperial decrees.

In line with his enlightened philosophy—the chief inspiration of his policies—one of his major initial concerns was religious reform. His Toleration Patent of October 25, 1781, granted free exercise of religion, as well as access to civil and military offices, to Protestants and Greek Orthodox. In the following two years, two-thirds of all monasteries were abolished—those not engaged in charitable, educational, or agricultural work. The state assumed the direction of Catholic seminaries.

The goal of modernization, as seen from a strictly utilitarian standpoint, led the emperor to press for the replacement of Latin by German as the official language in Hungary. According to a decree of March 1784, the Hungarian Chancellery and the Lieutenancy Council were to begin using German in 1784, county and town offices in 1785, and judicial organs in 1787. In the mid-1780s Germanization engulfed the educational system. Lectures at the university, transferred from Buda to Pest, were given in German, which also became officially the language of instruction in the secondary schools and pedagogical institutes by 1787.

The emperor's reformist zeal was inevitably impeded by the lack of royally controlled administrative apparatus at the county level. The traditional system of county government had remained essentially the nobles' tool, despite attempts dating to 1768 to strengthen the sole quasi-royal official, the *főispán*. Joseph II resorted to an unprecedented solution, as far as Hungary was concerned: bureaucratization of the lower levels of public administration. As an intermediate step, in 1785 Hungary was divided into ten circuits (*Kreise*),[23] each headed by a royal commissioner who was charged with supervising the county governments. A year later, royal free towns also fell under the commissioners' authority. Concurrently, county administrations were transformed into full-fledged bureaucracies. Instead of being elected by county assemblies, the county officials were now appointed: the *alispán* by the king, and the lower officials by circuit commissioners. County assemblies virtually disappeared. Their sole remaining function, election of diet deputies, was voided by Joseph II's determination not to convoke the diet. Thirty-eight royal lower courts, staffed by appointed judges, replaced in 1785–86 the county courts, the bulwarks of noble self-government.

The reforms of Hungary's central administration were less drastic. Headed by a royal bureaucrat in the absence of the *palatin*, the Lieutenancy Council absorbed the powers of the Hungarian Chamber in 1782 and was transferred from Pozsony to Buda in 1783. In 1785 the Hungarian Chancellery lost most of its administrative functions to the Lieutenancy Council, and its judicial ones to the Septemviral Table. Although, as a symbol, the Chancellery was preserved, Hungary's distinctive political status was disregarded in practice. Thus the Council of State now routinely considered Hungarian matters with the affairs of the other Habsburg lands. Promulgated in 1787–88, the criminal code and the code of criminal procedure applied equally to Hungary as to the rest of the monarchy.

Having abolished the county autonomy, Joseph II proceeded to challenge the nobility's feudal and fiscal privileges. Preserving the peasants' economic obligations (as defined in the 1767 *Urbarium*), a patent of August 22, 1785, personally emancipated the peasantry by granting the right to migrate and to choose occupation freely, and by voiding the restrictions on marriages. A subsequent judicial reform of 1787 abolished the manorial courts, and instead provided for the appointment of village notaries charged with enforcing the laws, protecting peasants' rights, and serving as links between the state and the people. In 1786 the emperor ordered the preparation of a cadaster of noble land as a

23. Namely, Győr, Pest, Nitra, Banská Bystrica, Košice, Mukacheve, Timişoara, Pécs, Oradea, and Zagreb.

prelude to the momentous step of 1788, the imposition of tax on noble property. This last measure, however, was nullified by a virtual collapse of public authority in the counties, caused by the nobles' determined resistance. A similar fate met the despot's effort of 1789 to convert the peasants' personal services into monetary fees. In a largely barter economy, the peasants themselves feared the burden of cash payments.

Angered by the emperor's administrative and social reforms, Hungary's nobles were mounting the most serious challenge to royal power since 1711, ultimately exploiting once again the monarchy's military difficulties. Initially the nobles' protests focused on the imposition of German as the official language. They demanded either a restoration of Latin or its replacement by Magyar. Paradoxically the campaign in favor of Magyar did not emanate primarily from the Magyar counties of central Hungary and Transdanubia, but from the largely Slovak areas of Upper Hungary, where the anti-Habsburg sentiments were strongly embedded among the Magyarized nobles, and the Magyar language (difficult for outsiders to master) was viewed as a shield against "alien" modes of government. The noble disaffection became a serious menace by 1788 when the emperor engaged in an exacting war with the Ottoman Empire. Now a hostile Prussian government offered the opposition covert support for Hungarian independence. Under the threat of a Prussian war, superimposed on the Turkish one, Joseph II lacked resources to suppress the Hungarian dissidents by force. While he could have anticipated the nobles' resentment, the peasant unrest came as a surprise. Aside from certain aspects of the agrarian reform, especially the introduction of monetary dues, it stemmed from forcible army recruitments required by actual or anticipated wars.

In the end, Joseph II chose to capitulate and yielded to the Hungarian estates. As early as 1789 the traditional county governments were restored, and in January 1790, a month before the emperor's death, all reforms concerning Hungary were revoked except religious toleration and peasant emancipation.

Retreat, 1790–92

Promising to respect the Hungarian constitution, the new emperor, Leopold II (1790–92), convoked the diet for June 1790. Preliminary county assemblies, convened to elect diet deputies, furnished the nobility with platforms from which to voice its grievances and request guarantees against absolutism, centralism, and Germanization. In the eyes of many counties, the Habsburg dynasty's right to hereditary succession had been forfeited by the unconstitutional conduct of Joseph II, and its restoration required a new settlement between the estates and the king. The terms proposed by the counties would emasculate royal authority according to the Polish constitutional model. Wielding virtually unlimited legislative power, the diet would override royal veto simply by readopting a measure. Executive authority would be vested in a Senate, both elected and held accountable by the diet. The Prussian king would guarantee the new constitution.

In addition to voicing radical constitutional demands, the lower nobility, which dominated the county assemblies, assailed the magnates as abettors of Joseph II's designs, and proposed to abolish titles of higher nobility, or to terminate the magnates' right (recognized in 1606) to sit as a separate, Higher Chamber (Table) of the diet. Royal free towns also fell under suspicion as potential allies of the king, and only those recognized in 1687 were to continue enjoying their privileged status.

The language issue remained important. By 1790 the use of Magyar, next to Latin, was spreading not only in the counties' assembly proceedings but in their administrative functions and official correspondence. The case for Magyar was strengthened by its literary revival, largely thanks to a group of writers around György Bessenyei (1742–1811). The first cultural and scholarly journals in Magyar were launched. Unlike their Czech contemporaries, the leaders of the incipient Magyar national movement could enlist the lower nobility's support. Of the forty-nine counties sending deputies to the 1790–91 diet, twenty-two favored Magyar as the official language, nineteen voted to retain Latin, and eight advocated the concurrent use of Latin and Magyar.

The Hungarian estates gained considerably less at the diet of 1790–91 than the county assemblies had initially demanded. The Magyar strength was eroded not only by the conflicts between the lower nobles and the magnates, and between both and the townsmen, but also by the emerging challenge of non-Magyar nationalities, either on the issue of the official language, as in the case of the Croats (willing to accept Latin, but not Magyar), or the issue of self-government, as in the case of the Serbs. The consolidation of the Habsburg monarchy's external position was, however, the decisive factor. In 1790–91, Leopold II reached settlements with both the Ottoman Empire and Prussia, and secured the imperial crown in Germany.

Thus strengthened, the emperor was ready to state his terms, and accepted no other limitations on his power as the king of Hungary than those of the Diploma of 1712. The diet, now in a chastened mood, agreed to his coronation. It also accepted his son Alexander as the *palatin*, thus inaugurating a tradition that neutralized this potentially powerful office by entrusting it to a junior member of the dynasty.

To fortify Hungary's autonomy, the diet of 1790–91, however, legislatively reaffirmed the traditional constitutional principles, above all that the king could not govern through edits, patents, or rescripts, but only according to laws passed jointly by him and the diet, which had to meet at least once every three years. It further stipulated by law that Hungary was a distinct realm that must be ruled separately from the other lands. Finally, the diet accepted two major items of the Josephin legacy, reenacting the substance of the Toleration Patent of 1781 and the Patent of Peasant Emancipation of 1785.

Other decrees of Joseph II concerning the peasantry, as well as the tax on noble lands, remained abrogated. His judicial reforms were annulled and the judiciary reverted basically to the pattern established in 1723. The Lieutenancy Council remained dependent on, and responsible to, the king. The Hungarian Chancellery stayed in Vienna to be used as the imperial government's main instrument for implementing high policy in Hungary.

The desire of many counties for Magyar as the official language was not satisfied. The diet of 1790–91 did prohibit the introduction of German, but restored, at least provisionally, the use of Latin even in formal records and correspondence at the county level. As a minor concession, Magyar became an optional subject of study in all secondary schools. A more significant advance occurred at the diet of 1792, when Magyar became an obligatory subject in the secondary schools of Hungary proper, and its knowledge was eventually to be required of all appointees to public office. Thus the most important effect of the Josephin language legislation, even though it was rescinded before his death, was a powerful impetus given to Magyar nationalism in regard to the language question and in fact in every aspect of cultural activity.

REACTION AND NATIONAL AWAKENING, 1792–1847

Royal Supremacy, 1792–1825

The settlement at the diet of 1790–91 restored a political dualism of royal and estates' power approximately as it had existed under Maria Theresa—that is, with the royal side enjoying a significant advantage. Soon after the diet, Leopold II himself strove to strengthen further the royal authority through restrictions on county governments and tighter controls over the central administration of the Land. A truly reactionary phase set in with the reign of Francis I (1792–1835; as Holy Roman emperor until 1806, Francis II), which at its outset focused on combating the French Revolution and its influences. Sharing the court's fear of revolutionary radicalism, which threatened their own privileges, most Hungarian nobles for the rest of the 1790s tolerated a measure of repression and supported the French wars with money and men. An additional reason for the estates' docility was the discovery and bloody suppression of the so-called Jacobin Conspiracy.

Small groups of Hungarian intellectuals had, in fact, become intrigued by the radical French ideas, partly influenced by the constitutional debates and revolutionary tensions in neighboring Poland. By 1793 they had formed several reading clubs, with József Hajnóczy, Ferenc Szentmarjai, and János Laczkovics playing notable roles. Before long the leadership was assumed by the ex-Franciscan of Serb descent, and former police informer, Abbé Ignatius Martinovics (1755–95), who proposed to replace the archaic monarchy with a modern democracy. Moreover, the new Hungary was to become a federation in which three non-Magyar national districts, "Slavonica" (the northwest counties), "Illyrica" (southern Hungary and Croatia-Slavonia), and "Valachica" (part of Transylvania and the Banat) would enjoy autonomy. In the spring of 1794 Martinovics, in Machiavellian fashion, organized two secret societies with disparate objectives. The first, the moderate Society of Reformers, was to enlist the discontented nobles with its advocacy of a constitutional monarchy. The other, the Society of Liberty and Equality, was to appeal to the radical intellectuals through its aim of an egalitarian republic. Within three months, before the police intervened, the two societies enrolled about three hundred members. Arrests began in the summer of 1794, and the following spring Martinovics and five colleagues were executed in Pest. While the direct impact of the Jacobin Conspiracy was hardly significant, the fact that it was supported by government officials, a priest, and intellectuals impressed Francis I and sharpened the reversal of the government's course in a conservative antienlightened direction.

With the threat of French revolutionary radicalism waning, an opposition reemerged at the Hungarian diet of 1802 to combat the king's fiscal proposals encroaching on the traditional immunities from taxation. In particular, the diet rejected payment of the Contribution by peasants settled on the demesnes, and taxation of the nobles for the purposes of the Domestic Fund (*fundus domesticus*), a treasury mainly for internal public works. With his propositions rebuffed, the king dissolved the diet before it presented its own requests (*gravamina*).

Another source of friction with the Hungarian estates was Francis I's practice, inherited from his predecessors, of entrusting Hungarian affairs to central imperial agencies in violation of Hungary's constitutional laws, most recently enacted by the diet of 1790–91. Thus the supreme body of imperial administration, the State and Conference Ministry, functioned in 1801–8 as the directing organ of the Hungarian court Chancellery. Its replacement, the advisory Council of State, from 1808 also covered Hungarian affairs, and a Hungarian member was to serve in each of its four sections (legal and judicial, administrative, financial, and military). In addition, financial matters at the highest level were administered jointly for Hungary and the other Lands, successively by the *directorium in cameralibus germanicis et hungaricis* (1792–97), the *Finanzhofstelle* (1797–1802), and the restored *Hofkammer* (from 1802). Needless to say, the *Hofkriegsrat* continued to merge Hungarian military affairs with those of the rest of the monarchy.

Tensions between the king and the Hungarian diet subsided at the height of the Napoleonic challenge. Suspicious of Napoleon's policies, the Hungarian estates ignored French appeals to revolt against Vienna in 1805 and 1809. Instead, the diet loyally supported Francis I's struggle against the heir of the French Revolution. In turn, in 1805 it won a significant language concession—permission for Hungarian government agencies to correspond with the Lieutenancy Council in Magyar. With the recession of the Napoleonic threat by 1812, the relations between the king and the estates rapidly deteriorated into the most severe constitutional crisis since the Josephin reforms of the 1780s. The diet now rejected the imperial decree of 1811 devaluating the currency (actually the declaration of state bankruptcy) and refused to assume one-half of the monarchy's public debt.

Vienna once more took the risk of governing Hungary without the diet, although a more flexible approach was tried than the traditional naked autocracy. The government requested recruits and taxes directly from the counties, and sought compliance through a manipulation of county elections and assembly proceedings. The main objective was to weaken the middle layer of the nobility, which excelled in political activity as well as hostility to Vienna. Initially the government relied on the magnates, who could dominate county proceedings thanks to the vague voting procedures of not counting but "weighing" the votes. After 1819, in a diametrically opposite approach, Vienna courted the lowest stratum of the nobility. Against the existing usages, the government insisted on the poor nobles' right to vote, and attracted their favor at election time through lavish entertainment and other forms of bribery. Comprising almost three-quarters of the estimated 136,000 noble families, the poor nobles could outvote the middle nobility even in the counties where the latter were strongly entrenched.[24] They now dominated the restoration assemblies, choosing county officials favorable to Vienna. The system for a time yielded money and recruits helping to cover the costs of Austria's intervention in Naples in 1821.

The following year, however, the government overplayed its hand, demanding tax payments in silver coins instead of the depreciated paper money, thus in effect raising the tax rate 150 percent. A number of counties refused to obey, and Vienna adopted the ill-advised and counterproductive method of direct coercion. Royal commissioners, mostly Hungarian generals, were sent into the recalcitrant counties to

---

24. Such as Borsod, Komárom, Sopron, Vas, Zala, and Nógrád.

enforce compliance with the aid of soldiers, if necessary. Clashes occurred in several counties, especially Komárom, Nitra, Nógrád, and Zemplén, while most counties resorted to passive resistance. In an extreme case, all local officials resigned in Bars county, leaving nobody with whom the royal commissioner could deal. The impasse forced Francis I in 1825 to retreat from the unconstitutional position. The king once again promised regular convocations of the diet, as the only competent authority in fiscal and military matters. A single diet seemed preferable to dealing with fifty-two counties.

Moderate Opposition, 1825–40

The convocation of the Hungarian diet of 1825–27 was the first significant setback for absolutism in the reign of Francis I. The mood at the diet resembled that of 1790–91, except that the allegiance to the king was not in question. A heatedly debated but unresolved issue was whether the royal commissioners were punishable for following unlawful royal commands. As yet, the basic objective of the diet was restoration, not reform. Even expansion of the official use of Magyar—corresponding with the growth of national consciousness—was rejected by the Table of Magnates, many of whom still lacked fluency in that language.

Nevertheless, the diet witnessed the emergence of a new patriotic generation, desiring cultural, social, and economic progress. The leading protagonist was a wealthy aristocrat, Count Stephen Széchenyi (1791–1860), later called "the greatest Magyar," who after travels in Western Europe resented his homeland's underdevelopment. In his writings, particularly in three books written between 1830 and 1833, he proposed comprehensive reforms, including legal equality of peasants with nobles, abolition of peasant labor dues (*robot*) and noble immunity from taxation, and political franchise for all inhabitants. He also advocated economic development to be sustained by adequate credit facilities.

The social reformism, championed by Széchenyi and other young men, did not yet affect the brief diet of 1830. On the contrary, the French July Revolution revived fears of social upheavals, and the Hungarian estates readily assented to Vienna's demands for recruits. As compensation, the diet exacted additional language concessions. The Lieutenancy Council and the higher courts were to process and answer Magyar petitions in Magyar, the knowledge of which was henceforth a prerequisite for appointment to public office, and—after 1833—for admission to the bar.

Following the diet of 1830, two events highlighted the need of social reform for the Hungarian gentry. One was the failure of the 1830–31 Polish uprising against Tsarist Russia, which was widely attributed to the deep social cleavage between Polish peasantry and gentry. More important, the most serious peasant uprising since the Dózsa rebellion of 1514 erupted in 1831 in Hungary's own northeast. Against this background the counties tended to choose for the next diet, opening in 1832, not only inspired nationalists but liberal reformers, notably Ferenc Kölcsey, István Bezerédi, and especially Francis Deák (1803–76). Still, the diet, which lasted from 1832 to 1836, was more productive in language rights than social reform. Magyar became the authorized language of Hungarian laws, and the language of all proceedings before the Royal Judicial Table, as well as of church registers in those communities where it was used in preaching. Opposed by the magnates and the Viennese court, peasant emancipation failed to advance significantly. The noble immunity from taxation was breached only in token ways by subjecting nobles to bridge tolls between Buda and Pest and to taxes on peasant lands if cultivated as parts of the demesne estates. Perhaps the most significant result of the diet of 1832–36 was the rise to prominence of the great Lajos Kossuth (1802–94), who helped to popularize the liberal cause through skillful summaries of diet proceedings, issued as newssheets. After the diet, he thus publicized the subsequent debates of county assemblies.

The surge of liberal reformism at the diet of 1832–36 alarmed the Viennese government as well as the Hungarian noble conservatives who feared for their privileges. In addition, Austria's ally, the Russian government, indicated its displeasure with the Hungarian diet's criticism of tsarist policy in Poland. Seeking to stifle the liberal movement, Vienna in 1836 appointed an old-fashioned conservative, Count Fidelis Pálffy, as Hungarian chancellor, and filled other top posts in the Hungarian administration with men of the same ilk. Repression followed in 1837 when Kossuth and other young liberals were arrested. Kossuth was sentenced to four years in prison for criticizing the government in print, and a magnate, Baron Miklós Wesselényi, was confined for the same offense.

The interlude of repression ended in 1839 under the impact of external affairs, notably the growing tensions in the Near East. Vienna replaced Pálffy as chancellor with a more moderate conservative, Count Antal Majláth, and the diet convened within the appointed term. While the number of liberals increased in the Lower Table, a liberal faction emerged even in the Table of Magnates, including the famous future leaders, Count Lajos Batthyány (1806–49) and Baron Joseph Eötvös (1813–72). In addition, a group under Count Aurel Dessewffy formed a "prudently progressive" or neoconservative faction, receptive to social reforms, though only in agreement with the imperial government. Following Deák's lead in the diet, the liberals debated royal propositions, but refused to pass any legislation. In need of recruits, Vienna had to yield further and release both Kossuth and Wesselényi, as well as sanction a minor reform act permitting peasants to buy their way out of the *robot*. It was clear that the impecunious peasantry could not be emancipated in this way. The device had failed a generation before under Joseph II.

Radical Opposition, 1841–47

The diet of 1839–40 left the Hungarian liberals deeply dissatisfied. The 1840s were marked by the liberals' intensifying struggle against the imperial government and its domestic allies, with the focus shifting from the socioeconomic to the more sensitive political issues. In its political maneuvering, Vienna used first language concessions then promises of economic reform to deflect the most unpalatable political demands prior to 1848.

Kossuth's journalistic activity sharpened the opposition's mood. After his release from prison he became, in 1841, editor of the leading Hungarian newspaper, *Pesti Hírlap*, and his editorials were highly critical and inflammatory, though not always consistent. At times he glorified the system of noble self-government as an essential guarantee of the constitution; at other times he urged abolition of the estates' priviliges and an extension of political rights to the townsmen and peasants. He wished to end the peasants' juridical and economic dependence on the seigneurs, yet feared that an outright emancipation might give advantage to the non-Magyars. Against the primacy of economic development, championed by Széchenyi (by now his determined opponent), Kossuth stressed the political struggle against Vienna aimed at loosening the ties of Hungary's dependence. In this dispute the liberal opposition, including Deák, inclined toward Kossuth's viewpoint over Széchenyi's.

After the diet of 1839–40 the political turmoil spilled over into the counties, where the assemblies indulged in unusually long sessions. Some passed the legislation blocked at the diet, and the government in turn proceeded to annul such measures as beyond the counties' competence. Fierce contests between conservatives and liberals for control of county assemblies and courts prompted electoral illegalities ranging from bribery to terror.

In the elections for the diet of 1843–44 the imperial government revived the alliance with the lower and predominantly poor nobility, whose acts of intimidation and outright terror helped to elect conservative candidates. Because of this intervention, the progovernment and the opposition deputies were almost evenly balanced at the diet. The liberal opposition focused on an objective combining economics with politics. It proposed to vest control over Hungarian tariffs in the diet so that the tariff would be used—in full reversal of the current intent—to protect Hungarian industries from external competition. Inevitably, Vienna refused to yield. Instead, as usual, it compensated for its socioeconomic rigidity by granting further language concessions. The sway of Magyar, at least in theory, now reached its apogee. The diet of 1839–40 had already prescribed it for its own proceedings, the internal service of government agencies, and all church records. Henceforth it became not only the official language of all courts and religious consistories but also—as a particularly sweeping measure—the language of instruction in all schools. Even the deputies from Croatia were required to speak Magyar in the diet.

After the diet of 1843–44 the imperial government attempted to stabilize the Hungarian situation in a novel way, masterminded by Metternich himself. To weaken the liberals, moderate economic reforms would be sponsored selectively. At the same time, liberals would be restricted through more rigorous administration in the counties. The chosen instrument of the new policy was the neoconservatives, whose leader, Count György Apponyi (Dessewffy had died in 1842), was appointed vice-chancellor in 1844, and two years later on Majláth's death, chancellor. Enticed by the government's economic projects, even Széchenyi agreed to serve the new regime as a member of the Lieutenancy Council. On the positive side, Vienna's economic program mainly envisioned a lifting of the tariff barrier between Hungary and the rest of the monarchy. As a compensation for the loss of customs revenue, indirect taxation, including the tobacco monopoly, would be extended to Hungary. Apponyi undertook to implement the other—the repressive—aspect of Vienna's new approach. He focused on ensuring that the county chiefs would function, not just in theory but in fact, as agents of the government. In part he employed a valid, though hitherto unenforced law, permitting the government to appoint administrators in those counties in which the *főispán* was incapacitated or, in the case of a hereditary office, a minor. He was able to install in thirty counties either temporary administrators or reliable new *főispánok,* all of whom connived to weaken the opposition and produce majorities for the government.

The liberals were slow in responding to the government's new challenge, mainly because of a sharp division in their own ranks over the value of the county governments. Most leaders, including Kossuth and Deák, the so-called municipalists, still viewed them with traditional awe as bulwarks of constitutional liberty. A smaller but exceptionally gifted group of "centralists," led by Eötvös, became repelled by the corruption of county proceedings and their evident susceptibility to Vienna's manipulation. They argued for centralizing the struggle for national emancipation in the diet, and for replacing the archaic county institutions with more efficient local governments.

Pressures for the liberals to reunite, however, were formidable. The neoconservatives gained strength by organizing a regular progovernment party in 1846, and it seemed possible that their regime might in fact erode support for the liberals. The relative success of Apponyi's administrators cast significant doubt on the reliability of county nobles as guarantors of Hungary's autonomy and independence. Moreover, the outcome of the Galician uprising of 1846, in which Polish peasants helped the imperial government destroy Polish noble insurgents, highlighted the need to emancipate the Hungarian peasantry if it was not to serve as Vienna's Trojan horse. Mainly under the impact of the Galician events, the opposition at last coalesced in June 1847 around a new program, written mostly by Kossuth, though for tactical reasons attributed to Deák. This Opposition Declaration called for a diet based on popular representation, a Hungarian ministry responsible to the diet, and complete legal equality for all inhabitants, including an end of the peasants' service obligations (with compensation for the seigneurs) and abrogation of the nobility's immunity from taxation.

This program served as the liberals' platform in the ensuing diet elections. Marked on both sides by unprecedented bribery and corruption, the elections left both parties once more evenly balanced. In the first three months of the diet, convened in November 1847, the liberals gained nothing of significance from the government and its neoconservative allies. Substituting for the absent Deák, Kossuth faltered in his leadership. He even failed to unite the liberals behind a censure motion against Apponyi's use of county administrators. Fearing the loss of the gentry's support, he did not dare to broach peasant emancipation. Unexpectedly the opposition's cause was salvaged in March 1848 by the news of the revolution in Paris and its subsequent repercussions within the Habsburg empire.

AGRICULTURE, CRAFTS, AND INDUSTRY[25]

Agricultural Expansion and Industrial Retardation, 1740–92

The second half of the eighteenth century was, on the whole, a period of major expansion in Hungary's agricultural production. This occurred despite the tariff system, instituted early in Maria Theresa's reign,

---

25. Economic data in this section are derived from Ervin Pamlényi, ed., *A History of Hungary* (London: Collet's, 1975), pp. 195–254; *Istoriia Vengrii* (Moscow: Nauka, 1971–72), 1:453–69; 2:9–91; Gyula Mérei, *Über einige Fragen der Anfänge der kapitalistischen Gewerbeentwicklung in Ungarn* (Budapest: Akadémiai Kiadó, 1960), passim; Ján Novotný, *Vývoj priemyselnej výroby na Slovensku v prvej polovici 19. storočia* (Bratislava: Slovenská akadémia vied, 1961), pp. 76–87, 197–214, 252–55; I. T. Berend and G. Ranki, *Hungary: A Century of Economic Development* (Newton Abbot: David and Charles, 1974; New York: Barnes and Noble), pp. 28–38.

which initially harmed Hungarian agriculture by cutting off exports, particularly those of cattle to Italy and wine to Poland. The response of the noble landlords, however, was to compensate for the decline in agricultural prices by increasing production. To augment the output they continued to raise the serfs' labor obligations, and greatly accelerated the expansion of the demesnes at the expense of peasant lands. The Counts (later Princes) Festetics, for instance, on one of their large manors in the Vas county, enlarged the area cultivated in the demesne ten times between 1738 and 1783.

A larger proportion of demesne cultivation did not yet lead to modernization of production. In fact, portions of such land were often leased to landless peasants on advantageous terms because such tenants, in consequence of occupying demesne land, were exempt from taxation. The improvements that did occur were due largely to the expanding cultivation of new and more intensive crops—tobacco, corn, potatoes, and feed crops. One effect of the enlargement of the demesnes and cultivating more land was the constant diminution of pastures available to market towns in the great plains. This trend continued to promote the transition from extensive to intensive cattle raising.

The increased exploitation of serf labor was the major cause of peasant unrest in western Hungary, which in turn supplied the impetus for issuing the *Urbarium* of 1767. The prohibition of further incorporation of peasant lands into the demesnes by the *Urbarium* clashed with the rising demand for agricultural products, generated since the 1760s by the enlarged imperial military establishment and by the growing industrialization of other Habsburg lands. In order to circumvent the prohibition, the seigneurs placed meadows under cultivation, evicted peasant tenants from the demesnes, and seized freshly cleared peasant lands (unprotected by the *Urbarium*). The increased production on the demesne estates accounted for the fivefold rise in Hungarian grain exports from 1748 to 1782, reaching the annual volume of 100,000 tons, as well as for the growth of wool exports from an annual average of 1,000 tons in 1748–64 to 5,600 tons by 1782. The typical products of peasant homesteads, cattle and wine, became relatively less important components of Hungary's exports.

Not until the 1780s did some of the large estates in the Magyar areas begin to adopt production improvements: replacement of the three-field system by crop rotation, more thorough preparation of the soil, selection of grain seeds, and import of foreign livestock, especially merino sheep. The modernized latifundia achieved significant results as early as the 1780s. For instance, the grain harvest became from seven to eight times larger than the amount of seed, while elsewhere, especially on peasant land, it was at most five times larger. The Viennese government promoted technical advances through agronomic literature as well as through specialized schools and research. And a chair of agronomy was established at the University of Pest.

In contrast to the agricultural sector, industry on the whole presented a depressing spectacle in the second half of the eighteenth century. Maria Theresa's tariff policy, destined to last almost a hundred years, was not designed to stimulate Hungarian industries. The initial intent was to redirect Hungarian trade from Silesia (after its loss in 1742–48) to the other Habsburg Lands. After the Hungarian nobility definitely refused to relinquish its immunity from taxation, the intent of the new tariff of 1754 shifted to favoring the industry of Austria and Bohemia in order to compensate these Lands for a heavier fiscal burden. Establishing high customs barriers between the monarchy and the rest of Europe, the tariff also imposed high duties on products exported from Hungary into other parts of the monarchy, except for industrial raw materials and agricultural goods needed by the Austrian and Bohemian Lands. Low preferential tariffs, on the contrary, favored imports of Austrian and Bohemian manufactured goods into Hungary. As a result, in 1770 Hungary's external trade—87 percent of exports and 85 percent of imports—was mostly with the rest of the monarchy. As measured in 1767, the exports remained almost entirely agricultural (52 percent cattle, 26 percent other foodstuffs, 16 percent raw skins and wool, 5 percent tobacco). Among the imports, 80 percent consisted of industrial goods (more than half textiles), and 20 percent such overseas goods as coffee, tea, and spices.

Stabilized in the 1780s, the tariff rates amounted to 2 percent of value on exports of Hungarian raw materials needed by Austria and Bohemia, and 3 to 5 percent of value on Hungarian exports potentially competitive with industries in the western Habsburg Lands. Customs on imports into Hungary from outside the monarchy amounted to a virtually prohibitive 20 percent. Post-1945 research[26] has emphasized two points about the imperial tariff policy. In the first place, it is claimed that under it Hungary—in relation to its population size—actually contributed more than its share of common expenses. In the second place, it is recognized that the tariff did not prohibit industrialization outright, and that the industrial retardation of Hungary was due only in part to the restrictive tariff policy, and at least as much to the social, economic, and cultural underdevelopment of the Land.

Yet, stimulated by the rise in agricultural production, towns began to emerge from their stagnation by the mid-eighteenth century. Crafts revived and new guilds sprang up in towns, marketplaces, and villages. Much of the internal trade still remained in the hands of the Greek,

---

26. Mérei, *Über einige Fragen der Anfänge der kapitalistischen Gewerbeentwicklung in Ungarn,* p. 12; Pamlényi, ed., *A History of Hungary,* pp. 193, 200; Novotný, *Vývoj priemyselnej výroby na Slovensku v prvej polovici 19. storočia,* pp. 7–24.

Serbian, and Armenian merchants who had settled in colonies in the towns along the Danube.

During the second half of the eighteenth century, the growth of towns resulted primarily from trade with the Austrian and Bohemian Lands. The towns of the Magyar interior benefited in contrast to those of the Slovak northern fringe. They served as assembly points of such agricultural products as grain, wine, leather, cattle, and wool for further shipment, usually along the Danube. Crafts flourished, serving in part the internal consumption of the towns and in part the need of the external traffic and its carriers. The census of 1785–87 registered an urban population of 400,000, which, however, constituted less than 5 percent of the total in the Land. The larger towns were concentrated near the Danube in the former Turkish territory. In the Magyar area, Buda, Szeged, and Debrecen led with over 20,000 inhabitants, while a dozen others followed with between 10,000 and 20,000.

Aside from artisan production, the manufactories originating in the 1720s had mostly collapsed before midcentury. The rise in agricultural production, however, stimulated another wave of entrepreneurship in the 1760s. Usually established by landed aristocrats, most manufactories produced textiles. While several of the largest operated in the Slovak area of northern Hungary, a major woolen manufactory was founded in Hatvan in central Hungary in 1768. By the late 1770s several enterprises had sprung up in Buda and Pest, including a dispersed manufactory turning out stockings, another producing silk, and a large tannery employing scores of workers. Aside from a core of technically skilled workers, usually recruited abroad, the offspring of peasant tenants performed most of the labor in the manufactories. In addition, these enterprises drew upon peasant spinners and weavers working in their own cottages. Aside from textiles, larger enterprises appeared also in the iron industry—especially, in the Magyar area, the state-owned ironworks of Diósgyőr.

Nevertheless, the progress of crafts and industries remained very limited. All the guild artisans and manufactory workers constituted under 1 percent of the nine and a quarter million people of Hungary in 1785. A census of 1777 had registered in the larger towns a total of 30,921 artisans, including masters, journeymen, and apprentices. Large-scale industrial production encountered particularly severe obstacles. In contrast to her treatment of the Bohemian Lands, Maria Theresa did little to weaken the power of the guilds in Hungary, and Joseph II's efforts in that regard (dating to 1785) proved ineffectual. Fearing capitalist industry, the guilds were determined to prevent the emergence of manufactories in towns. Other impediments included a lack of skilled workers, reliable credit, an organized market, and an adequate transportation network. The nobility's immunity from taxation played a peculiarly ambiguous role in relation to industrial development. In one respect it was a retarding factor, providing the major cause for Vienna's imposition of the restrictive tariff policy. In another respect, it favored industrial development, since it represented an actual subsidy for the aristocratic manufactories in the form of exemptions from taxes and tolls. Viewed in this light, the nobility's fiscal privileges functioned in Hungary as a partial substitute for the protection provided elsewhere by mercantilist government policies.

Fluctuation in Agricultural Prosperity, 1792–1847

The French and Napoleonic wars for almost a quarter of a century (1792–1815) heightened the prosperity of Hungary's agriculture. The needs of large imperial armies generated rising demand for agricultural products. The wholesale grain trade now drew into its network previously isolated areas. Not only the latifundia but also the estates of the middle and lower nobility benefited. Even the peasants expanded their production. Hungarian exports in 1800 were 63.8 percent above the level of 1787, and Hungary served as the principal source of grain, cattle, and wool for the imperial army, and Austrian and Bohemian industry. In the year 1801–2, for instance, Hungary exported 12,400 tons of wool, 536,000 sheep, and 170,000 lambs.

Only, as an exception, the large estates responded to this surge of prosperity with modernization of production, introducing equipment such as threshing machines, horse-drawn harrows, and seeding machines. In most cases the noble landlords still relied on the traditional methods of increasing compulsory peasant labor (often by 50 to 100 percent) and of adding peasant lands to the demesnes through various methods of resurveying or seizure of newly cleared lands.

The peasants intensified their production mainly in the vicinity of larger towns in order to meet the demand of townsmen for fruit and vegetables. Elsewhere their techniques tended to remain primitive, characterized by the two-field system, by the use of wooden plows that penetrated the soil only 6 to 12 centimeters, and by harvesting with sickles rather than scythes. The poor quality of seed and inadequate fertilization kept the grain harvests at levels of three to four times the amount of seed planted.

The end of the Napoleonic wars in 1815 precipitated a major crisis in Hungary's agriculture that was not fully overcome for fifteen years. The demand to supply large armies ceased. Penetration of external markets was impeded by the competition of Russian grain, the relatively poor quality of Hungarian wheat, and the high cost of transport due to the underdevelopment of the Hungarian transportation network. Moreover, the Austrian market had to be increasingly shared with Galician landlords, whose production, it is true, was low in quality, but also exceptionally low in price. Hungary's shrinking share of the Austrian market could be largely satisfied by the estates located in the western Hungarian counties.

Confronted with this crisis, a number of large landowners abandoned production for the market, preferring to rent their demesnes to merchants or—in small parcels—to landless peasants. The more enterprising seigneurs, who wished to remain competitive on external markets, had trouble raising capital needed for the modernization of production. Sources of credit were severely limited, partly by the capital scarcity following two currency depreciations and partly by the legal inalienability of noble estates (*avicitas*), in consequence of which noble lands in Hungary could not be pledged as security for loans. As an exception, wool continued to command a good price in the 1820s and, with the production increasing on some large estates, the total Hungarian wool exports rose from somewhat over 10,000 tons in 1818 to 19,000 tons in 1827.

Genuine recovery occurred in conjunction with the growing food deficits in the Austrian and Bohemian Lands, and with the revival of industrial production, beginning in the 1830s and accelerated in the next decade. The rising demand for agricultural products presented the large landowners with new incentives to cultivate their demesnes directly and to improve efficiency, particularly by supplementing obligatory peasant labor with free wage labor, found to be three times as productive. Many latifundia stressed cattle raising, employment of agronomists, and—above all in western Hungary—the use of agricultural machinery. The modernized latifundia proceeded to establish food-processing plants: flour mills, distilleries, and sugar refineries. Their harvests exceeded the average yield by 100 percent, while the quality of their products—grain, cattle, and wool—improved markedly. Hungarian wheat exports, which had sunk below 100,000 tons in 1827, reached almost 250,000 tons in 1845.

Even peasant producers shared (within limits) in the prosperity, finding opportunities in the 1830s, and still more in the 1840s, to sell crops at the newly emerging fairs and marketplaces, as well as to the distilleries and sugar refineries springing up on noble estates. Influenced by the changed market conditions, they tended to cultivate more plants for industrial processing (potatoes, sugar beets, tobacco, flax) instead of the traditional wheat, rye, and corn. There was also an incentive to intensify production by shifting from the two-field system to the less primitive three-field one.

Only a segment of the peasantry, however, could benefit significantly. Those peasants were particularly advantaged who held larger parcels of land and were at least partly exempt from feudal services, such as certain village officials and rural town residents. Owing to the expansion of the demesnes, which had continued into the first quarter of the century, peasant lands constituted little more than one-quarter of the total (11.6 million holds compared with 32.6 million of noble lands). Of the entire subject peasant population, not more than 40 percent held land, and of these 85 percent disposed of less than half of a hide.

Obstacles to Industrial Revolution, 1792–1847

The period of the French and Napoleonic wars further stimulated Hungarian trade and industries. Crafts alone were unable to meet the increased demand for uniforms, armaments, and other military equipment. With the ensuing territorial losses in the western Habsburg Lands (1805–13), Vienna was less reluctant to shift some of the production to Hungary. Closing the trade routes from the Baltic and the North Sea, Napoleon's Continental Blockade (1806–13) enabled Hungarian merchants to share in the trade with overseas goods through the Mediterranean and the Balkans. Ensuing capital accumulation made it possible for merchant families to join wealthy aristocrats in establishing new manufactories. Occasionally, sizable enterprises evolved from workshops of artisan masters, who succeeded in breaking the restraints of the guilds in order to enlarge their output.

New manufactories emerged in the period 1792–1815, especially in textile production. A woolen manufactory, founded by Archduchess Maria Christina in Mosonmagyaróvár, employed over 3,000 workers, of whom all but 160 worked at home. Another manufactory in Pest-Rákospalota and Majk employed 300 workers. Also, new ironworks were established by the state and by wealthy noblemen, most of them in the Slovak area of northern Hungary except for two in Borsod county. An armaments manufactory came into being at Diósgyőr. During 1792–1815, textiles and iron were far ahead of other industries, such as production of glass, paper, leather, and ceramics, or wagon building.

Despite this limitation, the manufactory in the period 1792–1815 was no longer an isolated phenomenon, but a spreading form of industrial production in Hungary. The number of capitalist enterprises functioning outside the guild system increased from 66 in 1785 to 175 in 1815. The proportion of persons employed in crafts and trade was also rising. While the total population increased between 1785 and 1828 from 9.25 million to 11.5 million, the number of artisans rose from over 30,000 to 95,000 and shopkeepers from 4,000 to 9,000.

The end of the Napoleonic wars brought about an industrial depression, as the impact of declining demand for military supplies was magnified by the simultaneous decline of purchasing power on the internal market, due in turn to unsalable surpluses in the agricultural sector.

Moreover, with the competition of English and other advanced West European industries creating export problems, Vienna wished to aid producers in the western Habsburg Lands by facilitating sales in Hungary and by preventing competition from Hungarian industries. A striking example of this policy was the new tariff of 1817. Under it, the customs fee for one centner of cloth was 120 florins if exported from Hungary into the western parts of the monarchy and only 20 florins if imported into Hungary from the latter. As the industrial revolution began to spread in the Austrian and Bohemian Lands, in particular during the 1820s, the unfavorable impact of their competitive advantage on Hungarian production became even more pronouned.

The influx of cheaper industrial goods not only depressed the inefficient Hungarian crafts, it undermined a number of capitalist enterprises of the manufactory type, established in the preceding era of prosperity. Official statistics registered fewer such enterprises in 1818 than in 1814–15, and a further decline occurred by 1825. Several textile plants went bankrupt, and Hungary's textile industry fell into an eclipse destined to last into the late nineteenth century.

In the longer run, however, the industrial revolution in the Austrian and Bohemian Lands had a stimulating effect on certain aspects of Hungary's economy through an increased demand for agricultural and industrial—mostly semifinished—goods. A revival of Hungarian industrial activity began in the 1830s and, after an interruption in 1837–39, accelerated in the 1840s. In contrast to the previous period of industrial prosperity (1792–1815), with textiles no longer playing a major role, the food-processing industry initially took the lead. An important stimulus was the persistent competition of Galician grain, further facilitated by a new railroad through Moravia to Vienna, completed in 1845. This challenge motivated Hungarian producers increasingly to export flour instead of wheat. The first large flour mill, powered by steam, opened in Sopron in 1836 on Széchenyi's initiative, followed in the 1840s by similar mills in Pest and Debrecen. About the same time there were instances of applying steam power and modern machinery to sugar refining and distilling. The expansion of sugar refining, beginning in the 1830s, was especially significant, although many enterprises were small and transient. By 1848, nineteen sizable refineries were in operation. Under the impact of Austrian competition the few surviving manufactories were converted into genuine factories in the mid-1830s.

In the 1840s, ironworks led in the expansion of industrial output. Their growth responded to the demand for iron in other parts of the monarchy, mainly generated by railroad construction and implement manufacture. From 1841 to 1848 the output of pig iron doubled in Hungary, rising from 11,158 to 22,524 tons. Among the other Habsburg Lands only Carinthia and Styria, although far smaller than Hungary, produced more pig iron, and only Bohemia and Moravia (with Silesia) more cast iron. The increase in production was due mainly to a larger number of enterprises rather than to technological improvements, which lagged behind the western parts of the monarchy.

Most of the iron output was exported because local facilities for its processing were meager. The tool and machinery industry, still in its infancy, consisted of small foundries and machine workshops, mainly in Pest. A major exception was the shipyard in Óbuda, which in 1847 employed about 1,000 workers with an average production capacity of one ship a week, including ten steamships a year. In the mining of hard coal, Hungary in 1841 with 44,380 tons stood within the monarchy in the fourth place after Bohemia, Silesia, and Lower Austria.

The proportion of persons employed in crafts and industry rose significantly between 1828 and 1846. While the total population of Hungary increased from 11.5 million to 12 million, the number of craftsmen and artisans rose from 95,000 to 233,000, not including 78,000 journeymen and apprentices. In addition, 23,400 workers were employed in 1846 in capitalist enterprises, and around 50,000 in the mines. The number of capitalist enterprises rose from 175 in 1815 to 251 in 1840 and 547 in 1845, but a large number of them were just small manufactories, and relatively few employed more than one hundred workers. The population of towns reached the total figure of 710,000 in the early 1840s. The fastest growing city, Pest, rose from 62,000 inhabitants in 1829 to 110,000 in 1848. The number of capitalist enterprises within its precincts increased from 16 in 1815 to 32 in 1840 and 49 in 1846.

Legislation enacted by the diet of 1839–40 undermined the guilds and helped to foster industrial development. Ownership of enterprises and employment of masters, artisans, and workers became independent of such extrinsic criteria as the noble status, guild membership, or religious preference. Foundation of joint stock companies was facilitated. A credit law, passed by the same diet, stimulated the development of a modern banking system, beginning in 1836 with a savings bank in Pest. The first commercial bank was founded, also in Pest, in 1841. By 1848 Hungary had thirty-six financial institutions, virtually all savings banks, with total capital of 9 million florins, and able to cover at least part of the credit needs of the Land.

The transportation network also began to improve. In the 1830s, river traffic advanced greatly with the regulation of the Danube, Tisza, and Drava. Regular steamship service developed, beginning with the Danube route from Pest to Vienna in 1831. In 1837 the Hungarian river fleet consisted of 1,409 ships. The first steam-powered railroad was opened between Pest and Vác in 1846, and between Pest and Szolnok a year later.

The Hungarian achievements in the field of crafts and industry, however, remained modest when measured against the progress of most of the other Lands of the monarchy. In 1840 there was one artisan, tradesman, or worker for every 89 inhabitants in Hungary, compared with 9 in Lombardy and Venetia, 13 to 15 in Lower and Upper Austria, and 80 in Galicia; in 1843 the proportion of those employed in agriculture to those in crafts, trade, and industry was 78:1 in Hungary, compared with 8:1 in Lombardy, 15:1 in Lower Austria, and 80:1 in Galicia. Measured by the value of industrial production per capita, Hungary in 1845 with 5 florins was in the lowest place, except for Dalmatia with 3 florins. The value for Lower Austria was 77 florins, 29 for Moravia-Silesia, 27 for Bohemia, and 8 for Galicia.[27] The 547 capitalist enterprises existing outside the guild system in Hungary in 1846 represented probably no more than 5 percent of such establishments in the entire monarchy. The level of mechanization was also low. For instance, of the 242 steam engines (with 3,069 horsepower) in operation in the monarchy in 1841, only 10 (with 116 horsepower) were in Hungary.

The pattern of modern industrialization differed in Hungary from that characteristic of Western Europe, as well as the Austrian and Bohemian Lands. During the first intimations of an industrial revolution in the 1830s and 1840s, significant advances occurred not in textile industry[28] but in the mechanization of food processing and the expansion of ironworks. This peculiarity stemmed from Hungary's dependence on the more advanced Lands of the monarchy, which inhibited the manufacture of textiles while stimulating the production of foodstuffs as well as of pig iron required by the industries of those other Lands. Thus in Hungary the onset of industrialization was not only delayed but also deflected in a special direction.

The Slovaks

ENLIGHTENED DESPOTISM, 1740–92

Spread of National Consciousness

The component ideas of Slovak or Hungaro-Slavic national consciousness which had developed in the seventeenth century continued

---

27.   For the other Lands it was: Lombardy and Upper Austria, 25; Venetia and Tyrol, 22; Carinthia, Carniola, and the Littoral 21; Styria, 16; and Transylvania, 7. See Mérei, *Über einige Fragen der Anfänge der kapitalistischen Gewerbeentwicklung in Ungarn*, p. 21; *Istoriia Vengrii*, 2:55.

28.   In contrast to the relative strength of the textiles industry during the manufactory period of 1792–1815.

to diffuse in the reign of Maria Theresa, especially among lower nobles and among burghers, whose ranks were augmented through a lively growth of small towns and marketplaces. Notable instruments in the strengthening of national consciousness were Pavel Doležal's *Grammatica Slavo-Behemica* (1746) and M. Markovič's *Historie Církevní* (1765). Both of these widely read texts contained prefaces, respectively by Matej Bel and Adam Škultéty, which dwelt on the earlier views about the greatness of the "Slav nation," the importance of its language, and the antiquity of its settlements in Hungary. Daniel Krman's writings had foreshadowed a new idea, which was explicitly developed by the Moravian historian, Krištof Jordan, in 1746, namely that the Slovak area was the original Slav homeland, and local speech (*dialectus Hungaro-Slavicus*) the purest of the Slavic tongues and dialects. Among Slovak intellectuals upholding this view was the famous Adam František Kollár (1718–83).

The division with respect to literary language persisted. Perpetuating Máčaj's tradition in the intellectual ambiance of Trnava University, Catholic literati developed a form of Czech so permeated by elements of the west Slovak dialect that the medium was called "Hungarian Slovak." This trend found expression in the dictionary by Romuald Hedbavný, *Syllabus Dictionarii Latino-Slavonicus* (1763). On the other hand, the Protestants treasured standard Czech, as codified in the grammatical works of Doležal.

At the end of Maria Theresa's reign many elements of the national self-definition were synthesized in the first history of the Slovaks, Juraj Papánek's *Historiae Gentis Slavae* (1780). Following in the footsteps of Szölösi, this work highlighted the Slovaks' historical tie with the Great Moravian Empire and its famous ruler Svatopluk. As a petty noble, however, Papánek minimized the disruptive effect of the empire's demise. Instead, he emphasized the successful integration of Slovak nobility into the ruling elite of the new Hungarian state. Subsequently, Juraj Sklenár in his *Vetustissimus Magnae Moraviae Situs* (1784), echoing Timon's arguments, sought to disassociate the Slovaks historically from Great Moravia and hence from the Cyrillo-Methodian mission, but this effort failed to leave a lasting impression.

The policies of Joseph II (1780–90) contributed significantly to the development of Slovak nationalism. The moves toward social equalization, which marked the enlightened despot's rule, favored cultivation of the vernacular tongue and broadening of the national community beyond the nobles and burghers. The Toleration Patent of 1781 not only stimulated an intellectual renaissance among Slovak Protestants but paved the way to an eventual national unity transcending religious differences, although in the short run the linguistic and literary cleavages widened. Joseph II's reforms, as a temporary measure, also reduced the administrative fragmentation of Slovakia—an obstacle to national unification—by combining the fourteen existing counties into three administrative circuits in 1785.[29]

In retrospect, the evolution of "Hungarian Slovak" as a literary language consummated by the literary endeavors of Jozef Bajza in 1783 and the grammatical works of Anton Bernolák (1762–1813), published in 1787 and 1790, was the foremost achievement of Catholic intellectual life in the Josephin era. Thus a trend of literary development spanning one and a half centuries reached a culmination at the General Seminary of Pozsony, which had replaced Trnava University as the main intellectual center for Catholic Slovaks. Therewith the felling of distinct Slovak identity increased markedly. According to Bernolák, the Slovaks formed an independent stock within the Slavic nation, with their own literary tongue, the purest among the Slav languages. He modified Papánek's outline of Slovak history in one fundamental respect. He viewed the demise of Great Moravia and the emergence of the Hungarian state as a national catastrophe which caused disintegration of the Slovak polity and interference of Latin, Magyar, and Czech with the development of the Slovak language.

Reacting to the views and activities of Bernolák and his colleagues, Protestant writers propounded the concept of a single Czechoslovak stock, based largely on the three-hundred-year-old tradition of the common Czech literary language. Such authors as Jur Ribay, Bohuslav Tablic, and Ladislav Bartholomeides researched Slovak cultural relations with the Czechs. The impact of Czech Hussites on fifteenth-century Slovakia received a special emphasis. Ján Hrdlička published a stirring eulogy of the Czech language in 1785–86. The grant of religious toleration facilitated contacts of Slovak Protestant intellectuals with scholars and writers of the Bohemian Lands and led to common efforts at justifying the concept of Czecho-Slovak ethnic unity. Thus Ribay developed close relations with Josef Dobrovský. A periodical, *Prešpurské noviny,* edited in Pozsony by Slovak Protestants in 1783–87, was published in Czech.

Seigneurs and Peasants

The humanitarian aspect of enlightened absolutism was reflected in Slovakia primarily in the attempts to lessen peasant exploitation. Slovak peasants also found some relief in the possibility of resettling in the economically less oppressive southern Hungary. In any case, Slovakia was spared the peasant disturbances such as occurred in the Magyar-inhabited western Hungary in the 1760s. The safety valve was so much

29.   These circuits were centered in Nitra, Banská Bystrica, and Košice. In the same vein, under Maria Theresa the First Partition of Poland in 1772 had ended the Polish administration of sixteen towns in Spiš county.

more important as the population of Slovakia was increasing very rapidly during the eighteenth century: from some 700,000 in 1715–20 to about 2,000,000 in 1780.

Maria Theresa's *Urbarium* of 1767 was implemented in Slovakia mainly between 1768 and 1774. Although the nobility generally objected to these royally inspired proceedings, the reform in Slovakia was largely carried out to the serfs' disadvantage. With the quality of the soil arbitrarily adjudged higher than the actual conditions warranted, the number of hides—the basic units of taxation—doubled or tripled in most Slovak counties.[30] The average hide in 70 percent of the villages (between 16 and 20 Pozsony morgen) amounted to only three-quarters of the average hide in the more fertile Magyar lowlands. In Orava county, where the hide was reduced to one-sixth of the pre-*Urbarium* size, peasant resistance delayed implementation of the reform until 1780. Violent opposition occurred also in rural subject towns when—in conjunction with the *Urbarium*—their seigneurs reduced them to the status of common villages.

The most important and lasting reforms of Joseph II, promulgated in 1785, granted the peasants freedom of movement and occupation, and recognized their claim to the land. Therewith clear title to the land and abolition of serfdom—though not abolition of personal services—were accomplished. With the opportunities for urban employment and advanced education more limited, the grant of personal freedom, however, did not have the same effect on social mobility as, for instance, in the Bohemian Lands.

A consequence of Maria Theresa's and her oldest son's reforms was a more elaborate manorial administration. Increased legal functions mandated by the 1767 *Urbarium* necessitated the addition of a trained lawyer to the manorial officialdom. This *fiscalis dominalis* presided in the seigneur's name over the manorial court (*sedes dominales*), and later also chaired a new commission (*sedes officiosae*), which was to replace litigation of civil cases by arbitration. Flowing from the status of the manor (until 1848) as the lowest echelon of public administration, other functions of the *fiscalis* included supervising village governments (above all, their accounts) and representing the seigneur in county assemblies in such matters as assessment of military and county taxes and the quartering of troops. The rise of the *fiscalis* left the previously dominant official, the *provisor*, with only the functions of economic management. The *provisor* was reduced to the status of equality not only with the *fiscalis* but also with the newly emerging chief financial official, the *rationum exactor*. Maria Theresa's forest ordinance of 1769 brought yet another manorial official: the forest master (*sylvarum magister*).

---

30. On the *Urbarium* of 1767 and its principles see also p. 223.

National Awakening, 1792–1847

Weakness of the National Movement, 1792–1815

The development of modern nationalism encountered peculiar difficulties among the Slovaks. Aside from economic underdevelopment, Slovak territory suffered from serious fragmentation as a result of its mountainous geography and numerous administrative (county) boundaries. Discounting the controversial Great Moravia, it lacked a tradition of distinctive statehood, or even a town with the prestige of a recognized national and cultural center. The Catholic-Protestant division hindered agreement not only on a single literary language but on a single difinition of national identity.

A serious impediment to the national movement was the commitment of the middle nobility and the upper urban strata to the idea of a unitary Hungarian statehood and, from the 1790s on, to the policy of Magyarization. The Hungarian Jacobins, some of whom were from Slovakia, provided an isolated instance of the privileged classes' interest in the Slovak national cause. Their 1794 draft of a Hungarian constitution broached for the first time in modern history the idea of Slovak political autonomy. Otherwise the task of inspiring and organizing a national movement fell to nonnoble intellectuals drawn largely from the Catholic and Protestant clergy, who appealed primarily to the lower middle class and the politically weak petty nobility.[31]

The policy of Magyarization, initiated by the laws of 1791–92 and 1805, played a major role in stimulating the Slovak national movement. Juraj Fándly in his *Compendiata Historia Gentis Slavae* (1793) urged expanded teaching of Slovak to counter the laws of 1791–92 favoring Magyar in education. Juraj Feješ (in *De Lingua* in 1807) argued, against the even more severe law of 1805, that constitutionally all languages of Hungary should enjoy equal status. Some Slovak counties applied the 1805 law far beyond its intent, making Magyar the official language of county courts and administration in both internal and external contacts. Most counties, however, while approving Magyarization in principle, wished to postpone the adoption of Magyar until it became sufficiently known in their area. These objections helped to reverse the essentially illegal Magyarization measures by a royal decree of 1812. With the subsequent suspension of the diet, further pressure in favor of Magyar ceased until 1825.

Slovak national activity, after the linguistic achievements scored in the 1780s in Pozsony, was led until 1815 by adherents of the humanitarian

31. For instance, in the 1790s Bernolák's nationally activist *Slovenské Učené Tovaryšstvo* included some four hundred priests in its membership of five hundred. The rest consisted of burghers, craftsmen, merchants, and petty nobles.

ideals of the Enlightenment. On the Catholic side, the Bernolákist *Slovenské Učené Tovaryšstvo*, originating in 1792 in Trnava, established branches throughout the Slovak territory from Pozsony to Prešov and Košice. Although the society was in decline after the turn of the century, it had achieved lasting gains for the new Slovak literary language, securing its wide use among Slovak intellectuals, its introduction as an auxiliary language in secondary schools and seminaries, and its diffusion through a sizable popular literature. After the deaths of Fándly (1811) and Bernolák (1813), the moving spirit behind Bernolákist activities was Juraj Palkovič, a canon in Esztergom. The movement also enjoyed the support of Alexander Rudnay, another prelate of Slovak background, destined for the primatial see of Esztergom by 1819.

In competition with the Catholic initiatives, the Protestants planned their own institutions for cultivating Slovak literature and culture in the Czech language. Ambitious projects proposed by Ribay were realized on a modest scale in 1803 through the founding of a chair of Czechoslovak language and literature in the Lyceum of Pozsony. Its first occupant, Juraj Palkovič, also engaged in publishing activities, including a weekly newspaper (1812–18).[32] A leading figure among the Protestants of central Slovakia, Bohuslav Tablic, established in 1810 a learned society, *Societas Litteraria Slavica Montana*, which in turn sponsored a chair of Czech in the Lyceum of Banská Štiavnica. Several Czech cultural leaders from Bohemia, indluding Dobrovský, became members of Tablic's society.

Strengthening National Ideology, 1815–30

The post-Napoleonic period witnessed the rise of a new romantic generation of leaders in both camps of Slovak national activity, and a fuller development of a national ideology. Magyar national demands again supplied an important stimulus. Starting in 1817 the Magyar press (for example, *Tudományos Gyűjtemény*) assailed Slovak claims of a distinct nationhood, asserting that a single state in Hungary presupposed a single political nation, the language of which could be no other than Magyar.[33]

The leading opponent of Magyar views, Ján Kollár (1793–1852), elaborated on the Protestant side in the 1820s a new basis for the national assertion of the Slovaks. Utilizing German romantic ideas stemming from Herder and Hegel, he made the language the primary criterion of nationhood, and the nation so defined was for him, as a natural

32. This Juraj Palkovič (1769–1850) must be distinguished from his Catholic contemporary of the same name (1763–1835), the canon of Esztergom, mentioned earlier.
33. The Slovaks made use of the foreign press to justify their national cause. Thus Ján Čaplovič published an article in defense of Slovak rights in a Prague German periodical in 1818, and Ján Kollár did the same in a Swiss journal in 1821.

entity, inherently superior to the state, an artificial construct. Thus he directly contradicted the official Hungarian view that the state and its historical evolution generated the nation. The Slovaks now acquired a conceptual justification for their national claims despite their lack of an incontestable historical statehood.

Kollár and other Protestant leaders, above all Pavel Šafárik, continued to write in Czech and to regard the Slovaks as part of a single Czechoslovak stock. In fact, their cooperation with the Czechs was so close and substantial that both Kollár and Šafárik became key figures in the Czech (as well as the Slovak) national revival. The Catholic leaders, centered in Buda, decisively rejected the concept of Czechoslovak ethnic unity. The use of Slovak (in Bernolák's version) as a literary language received in the 1820s the continuing patronage of Rudnay and Palkovič, who sponsored a translation of the Bible and publication of school textbooks. The Bernolákists had their most active organizer in Martin Hamuljak, an official of the Hungarian Lieutenancy Council, and their leading artist in the poet Ján Hollý, a priest in Madunice.

Both wings of the national movement shared the traditional Slovak enthusiasm for the idea of Slav cultural, if not political, unity, and an admiration for Russia, enhanced by the tsarist victories over Napoleon and over the Turks in 1828–29. Kollár, in part echoing Herder, ascribed outstanding, indeed sublime virtues to the Slavs, and expected them to play a dominant role in the further development of mankind. Among the Bernolákists, some, like Hamuljak, anticipated that the Russian language would become a bond of unity among the Slavs; others, in particular Ján Herkel, looked forward to the emergence of a common Slavic tongue.

Restored in 1825, the Hungarian diet generated new Magyarization pressures. Although the king-emperor blocked the original enactments of 1825–27, illegal Magyarization recurred. In a drastic example in 1827, the authorities resorted to whipping to make Lutheran Slovak peasants accept Magyar liturgy and sermons in the region of Lajoskomárom. Fear of Russian power was an additional reason cited in the late 1820s for the imposition of Magyar on the Slovaks, thereby breaking the bond of Slavic kinship. In fact, the peasant insurgents of eastern Slovakia in 1831 hoped that the Russian army would intervene in their behalf and free them from the burden of manorial exactions.

Origins of the Political Program and National Organization in the 1830s

The foundations for the political stage of Slovak nationalism were laid in the 1830s. Intensified pressure toward Magyarization supplied a negative incentive, based on new diet legislation and amplified by county ordinances. Special commissions were established after 1830 in Pozsony, Orava, Gemer, and Spiš counties in order to spread the use of Magyar, particularly through education. By 1840 most Slovak counties had adopted Magyar as their official language with exceptions normally made for the general assemblies, the judiciary, and external administrative contacts. Lacking access to the decision-making institutions (the diet and the county assemblies), Slovak national spokesmen, in particular Samuel Hoič, L'udovít Šuhajda, and Michal Kuniš, resorted in 1833–34 to the press, assailing Magyarization in pamphlets written in German. They scored the new language legislation as violating both the natural rights of the Slovak nation and the alleged respect for language equality in Hungary, embedded above all in the laws of 1608–9. Questioning the character of Hungarian statehood, Šuhajda said quite frankly that it was a more natural condition for the boundaries of a state to coincide with those of an ethnic group. He drew a political conclusion from Kollár's theory of nationhood.

On the positive side, the social base of the Slovak movement was broadened with a diffusion of national consciousness in the 1830s, especially in the towns of northwest and central Slovakia. As a novel social element, Slovak entrepreneurs emerged from the ranks of linen wholesalers and owners of medium and small enterprises, such as iron mills, glassworks, paper mills, and sawmills. Many of them showed interest in national publications and other undertakings. A growing maturity in the national movement was also marked by cooperation across the religious barriers. Although the basic division between the Catholic Bernolákists and the Protestant Czechoslovakists persisted, the two camps were able to collaborate in a cultural society, *Spolok Milovníkov Reči i Literatúry,* established on Hamuljak's initiative and under Kollár's chairmanship in Buda in 1834. The society's annual, *Zora,* published contributions in both Czech and Bernolákist Slovak.

The first signs of transition to political activity were evident among student societies in both Catholic seminaries and Protestant lyceums. Including a particularly active group led by L'udevít Štúr (1815–56) at the Pozsony Lyceum, these associations moved from literary to political subjects, influenced by the Hungarian political ferment and by the revolutionary events elsewhere in Europe, especially in neighboring Poland. Ideas were exchanged with Czech and Polish student groups in Vienna. After the suppression of the existing Slovak student societies in the spring of 1837, substitute organizations quickly sprang up. They were coordinated to a degree by several intellectuals, who formed in Pozsony a group called *Vzájemnost* (Solidarity, 1837–40). Led by a lawyer, Alexander Vrchovský, and including among others Michal Hodža (1811–70), Jozef Hurban (1817–88), and Samo Chalúpka, Solidarity espoused as its main objective the enhancement of national sentiments, especially through contacts between students and the common people.

Vrchovský expected that strong national consciousness would necessarily lead to the emergence of a distinct Slovak territory with economic and administrative autonomy.

Formation of the Political Program and National Organization, 1840–47

Under the challenging circumstances of the 1840s, the Slovak national movement entered the political arena. As early as 1840 a Slovak petition was drafted protesting the law that instituted Magyar record keeping in the Lutheran Church. After the petition's confiscation even before reaching the diet, the preparation of new petitions provided a momentous occasion for discussing Slovak political goals. Štúr advocated a plea that the Slovak territory be transformed into a separate crownland with its own diet on the pattern of Croatia, if Magyarization could not be stopped. The more moderate proposal of Kollár asked for the use of Slovak in education and by county authorities, as well as a separate Slovak representation in the Hungarian diet. The final version of the petition (*prestolný prosbopis*), actually submitted to the Viennese government in 1842, was for tactical reasons again limited to the grievances of Slovak Lutherans.

The failure of even this modest petition was followed by a crucial turning point in the development of Slovak national ideology. The initiative was taken by Štúr, who after the disintegration of Solidarity in 1840 had rapidly become the key person in the national movement. His own efforts convinced him of the implacability of the Bernolákists' opposition to the Czechoslovakist viewpoint. Doubting the efficacy of Czech support for the Slovak objectives in Hungary, Štúr concluded by 1843 that the interest of the national movement required a general adoption of the Bernolákist view of the Slovaks as a separate nation with its own literary language. This step would deprive the Magyar opponents of the main reason for charging the Slovak movement with foreign roots and connections. Above all, wishing to rally the common people behind the national ideals, Štúr now believed that the peasant masses would respond more readily to a language and style closest to the national idiom. For that reason he and his collaborators, Hodža and Hurban, urged instead of the Bernolákist language, based on western Slovakia (and thus closer to Czech), the standardization of the central Slovak dialect, approaching a common Slovak norm.

For Štúr and his followers the promotion of a Slovak literary language and a distinct national identity was only a part of a broader program of organizational and political mobilization. A new organizational structure was promoted, including reading clubs, self-help peasant circles, and above all a network of rural temperance societies that had formed in cooperation with Catholic priests since 1843. A central cultural organization, *Tatrín,* emerged under Hodža's leadership in 1844; a year later, Ján Francisci formed a national student association. At a momentous meeting of *Tatrín* in 1847, a majority of some seventy Catholic and Protestant leaders agreed to adopt the literary language advocated by Štúr. The most important dissident was Kollár, who retained the Czechoslovakist commitment for the rest of his life.

The main organ for uniting and guiding national opinion was a newspaper, *Slovenskje Národňje Novini,* which Štúr launched in 1845. Because of the Viennese government's dislike for Magyar liberals, he enjoyed considerable latitude in criticizing the latter's Magyar nationalism. After Kossuth rejected in 1846 his plea for a Magyar-Slovak reconciliation, Štúr definitely sided with Vienna, despite the qualms of Francisci's group, which still hoped for rapprochement with Magyar liberals. In October 1847 the town of Zvolen honored Štúr by electing him its representative in the Hungarian diet. In the winter of 1847–48 *Tatrín* sponsored a national petition for submission to the diet, but the onset of the revolutionary events of 1848 interrupted this campaign.

AGRICULTURE, IINDUSTRY, AND TRADE[34]

Slow Agricultural and Industrial Growth, 1740–92

Agriculture, which remained the basic occupation of the Slovak population, made slow progress during the second half of the eighteenth century despite the policy of enlightened absolutism to foster improvements. The main obstacle to increased productivity was the persistence of the two- and three-field system. The two-field system still occurred even in the fertile southern lowlands. Before midcentury, although the fallow was occasionally planted with various crops, regular crop rotation was virtually unknown in Slovakia. The perpetuation of traditional methods not only prevented an increase in grain production but also hindered the spread of new crops like potatoes and clover, on which in turn the expansion of cattle raising depended. The imperial government under Maria Theresa following the 1767 *Urbarium,* and even

34. Economic data in this section are derived from *Dejiny Slovenska,* ed. L'udevít Holotík (Bratislava: Slovenská akadémia vied, 1961), 1:362–80, 404–39, 479–96; *Přehled československých dějin* (Prague: Československá akademie věd, 1958), 1:722–34, 750–61; Ján Novotný, *Vývoj priemyselnej výroby na Slovensku v prvej polovici 19. storočia* (Bratislava: Slovenská akadémia vied, 1961), passim; Otakar Mrázek, *Vývoj průmyslu v českých zemích a na Slovensku od manufaktury do roku 1918* (Prague: Nakl. politické literatury, 1964), pp. 42–54, 78–84, 140–48; Karol Rebro, *Urbárska regulácia Márie Terezie a poddanské reformy Jozefa II. na Slovensku* (Bratislava: Slovenská akadémia vied, 1959), pp. 119–204; Anton Špiesz, *Remeslo na Slovensku v období existencie cechov* (Bratislava: Slovenská akadémia vied, 1972), pp. 103–6; *Přehled dějin Československa* (Prague: Academia, 1982), I/2:383–93, 554–58, 573–81.

more actively under Joseph II, sought to encourage crop rotation by prohibiting—despite opposition of the Slovak nobility—the collection of feudal dues from the crops grown in place of the fallow. Still, crop rotation made little advance on peasant lands, and not much more on noble estates. The demesne estates continued to grow from midcentury, mainly through the cancellation of land leases to peasants on the demesnes.

Among other notable trends in agriculture was a continuous expansion of viticulture, particularly in the southwest. The raising of sheep also flourished; according to estimates, their number exceeded 3,000,000 in Slovakia in the 1770s. The use of horses as the principal draft animals, instead of oxen, was spreading, especially in the lowlands.

Industrial production in Slovakia expanded moderately in the period of enlightened absolutism, particularly in textiles and metallurgy. There was a marked fluctuation in the emergence of new manufactories. Only a single one (a porcelain manufactory in Holíč in 1743) was added before 1765. By the end of the decade ten manufactories had sprung up, mostly in textiles. The two largest, one for cotton cloth in Čeklís and another for woolens in Halič near Lučenec, each employed over a hundred workers. After restrictions on Hungarian industrial enterprises by Maria Theresa's government in 1771, the cotton manufactories in Šaštín and Čeklís closed down, others limited their production. Under Joseph II this regressive trend was reversed and five new manufactories were added. Two of them (in Devín and Pozsony) were the first in Slovakia to introduce modern machinery (spinning jenny machines).

Mining operations had been facilitated since the 1760s by new techniques of water removal. Copper output rose to an annual average of 1,293 tons in 1775–9, representing up to 12 percent of the world total. Having reached a maximum level of 2,429 marks of gold and 92,261 of silver in 1744, the production of precious metals stabilized at an average annual rate of 1,250 marks of gold and 58,500 of silver for the rest of the century. Iron production suffered from Austrian, especially Styrian, competition. In 1776, with 129 "Slovak ovens" and six high furnaces in operation, the annual output of iron was 6,700 tons.[35]

With the number of manufactories limited, most industrial production in Slovakia originated in the domestic industries of the villages, or in the guild crafts of the towns. Linen production was particularly important in the villages, especially in Spiš county. According to a census, the number of urban craftsmen in Slovakia amounted in 1777 to over 12,000, about 40 percent of Hungary's total. An estimate, taking into

35. The iron production was divided among the counties of Gemer (72.5 percent), Zvolen (10.8), Spiš (9.1), Abov (6.3), and Liptov (1.3).

account also small towns and marketplaces, gives the total number of artisans for Slovakia in 1770 as over 40,000, including 22,500 masters (compared with 7,500 in 1720), and 18,000 journeymen and apprentices. In comparison, toward the end of the century about 2,000 permanent employees worked in the manufactories, supported by some 30,000 domestic spinners and weavers. Around 1770 the largest number of artisan workshops was in Pozsony (1,000), followed by Banská Bystrica and Komárno (450 each). The artisan production grew most rapidly in Slovakia between 1725 and 1765. After this zenith, it began to suffer from competitive imports from the Austrian and Bohemian Lands, as well as from the underdevelopment of the domestic market.

In the commercial area, the guild merchants of Slovak towns, numbering only 778 in 1777, faced the competition of both domestic and Austrian manufactories, which sold directly on the market. The Hungarian tariff system restricted Slovakia mostly to trade with the Austrian and Bohemian Lands. Imports included fine textiles and luxury articles; exports consisted mainly of agricultural products (grain, wine, cattle, rawhides, wool) and industrial raw materials, primarily metals. The customs regulations particularly hampered the traditional wine exports from western Slovakia to Silesia and Germany, threatening the future of viticulture. As an exception to the imperial commercial policy, large amounts of copper were exported outside the monarchy, especially to Germany, France, and Italy, and some iron to France.

Prosperity, Crisis, and Recovery, 1792–1847

The Slovak economy followed a cycle from prosperity during the French and Napoleonic wars to decline after 1815 and resurgence beginning in the 1830s. The progress remained painfully slow in agriculture. Among the large estates a few introduced planting of clover instead of the third-year fallow, making possible increases in cattle raising, and thus also in the volume of manure for soil improvement. The peasantry, in particular, remained attached to the fallow as pasture, and its cultivation was further discouraged by a feudal rent on the "third planting" imposed in 1806. New crops, such as potatoes, corn, and paprika, spread on large estates at the turn of the century, while the conservative and suspicious peasants were reluctant to raise them, especially when urged to do so by the seigneurs. During the postwar depression the peasants were particularly affected by the decline in grain prices, which plummeted between 1818 and 1824 to 30 percent of their previous level. The impact was somewhat cushioned on the large estates by the continuous demand for wool, the prices of which even increased by 70 percent in 1820–26.

With the return of relative prosperity in the 1830s, the demand by distilleries helped to stimulate the cultivation of potatoes by the peasants. In Spiš county, for instance, by the 1840s potato raising was beginning to supersede that of flax. The estates of the south initiated the growing of corn for animal feed. Otherwise the traditional predominance of rye and barley over wheat persisted. Although the iron plow made its first appearance on peasant homesteads in the 1830s, agricultural techniques in general remained at low levels. Even on the large estates the harvest lasted two months, and threshing—though flails replaced horses' hoofbeats—the entire winter.

As for industrial development, at the turn of the century Slovakia still enjoyed more favorable preconditions than the rest of Hungary. It possessed old traditions of crafts and urban life, and was endowed with substantial natural resources. As the century progressed, however, the industrial ascendancy of the western parts of the monarchy was stifling—with some exceptions—the realization of this potential. This retardation was reflected in the fact that during the first half of the nineteenth century, rural population growth (17 percent) outstripped urban growth (12 percent).

In mining and metallurgy, iron was gaining in importance over precious metals. Its production received strong impetus during the Napoleonic wars. With the price of iron rising 175 percent from 1795 to 1805, the demand led to the formation of large enterprises, especially in Gemer county. Technology still kept pace with the western parts of the monarchy. For instance, between 1776 and 1825 the number of high furnaces increased from 6 to 30, while the primitive "Slovak ovens" declined from 129 to 27. After a slump in the 1820s, production recovered by 1830 and then rose sharply. In 1831 the Slovak output of pig iron (8,377 tons) represented 78.2 percent of the Hungarian total, and 9.9 percent of the entire output of the Habsburg monarchy. The percentages for cast iron (918.5 tons) were respectively 64.2 and 8.9. By the mid-1840s the annual production of all iron in Slovakia averaged 27,826 tons or 81 percent of the Hungarian total. After 1830, however, the Slovak iron industry was slow in applying the new techniques, which by the 1830s were initiating the industrial revolution in the Bohemian and Austrian Lands. Nevertheless certain innovations did take place and Slovakia excelled in that regard over the rest of Hungary.[36]

In the opening years of the century the annual copper output of 1,568 tons still represented 10 percent of the world total. After a decline in the 1820s, it recovered its previous level in the following decade but not its significance on the world market. The output of precious

---

36. For instance, in 1841 there were two puddling refineries and six rolling mills in Slovakia, and none of either type elsewhere in Hungary.

metals averaged annually in the first decade of the century 1,600 marks of gold and 72,000 of silver. By 1842–46 the annual average for gold had risen to 2,148 marks, while for silver it had declined to 46,445 marks, representing respectively 31.1 and 43.8 percent of the monarchy's total. By this time, however, the production costs had begun to exceed the income of the generally government-owned gold and silver mines.

The textile industry experienced most drastically the stifling effect of Austrian and Bohemian competition. After 1815 the textile manufactories generally failed to develop into factories, and their network was, in fact, disintegrating. The decline was particularly striking in cotton: by the 1840s virtually all manufactories were wiped out. The woolen manufactories fared slightly better, with five surviving into the 1830s and another added in the early 1840s. Linen production maintained its strength, but merely as a domestic industry.

On the other hand, advancing industrial sectors were papermaking and sugar refining. Small paper mills increased from forty in the 1820s to seventy twenty years later (or 85 percent of Hungary's total). More important, in the 1840s four large enterprises emerged as mechanized factories, transcending the manufactory stage. Similar progress occurred in sugar refineries, which began to spring up after 1830. In 1847–48 eleven mechanized refineries, out of the Hungarian total of nineteen, operated in Slovakia. Usually organized by joint-stock companies, they accounted for 60 percent of the modernized Hungarian sugar production.

Contrary to the situation in the Magyar part of Hungary, flour milling did not advance conspicuously in Slovakia, since grain production did not play as important a role. The first two modern flour mills did not begin operating until after 1846. Breweries and distilleries also remained small and based on artisan methods of production. Among other light industries, glass and ceramics, while retaining their importance, did not advance beyond the stage of manufactories. Glassworks increased in number from fourteen at the turn of the century to twenty-six in the 1840s, and at least eight ceramics manufactories existed in Slovakia in the first half of the nineteenth century.

Thus the first intimations of an industrial revolution in Slovakia occurred neither in textile production, despite the ephemeral appearance of textile machinery as early as the 1780s, nor in metallurgy, although iron production was relatively high. Moreover, flour milling did not play an important role, as it did in the Magyar part of Hungary. Instead, genuine factories first appeared in the 1840s in the sectors of papermaking and sugar refining, thanks to the investment of Austrian and foreign capital. Compared, for instance, with the Bohemian Lands, first signs of the industrial revolution in Slovakia were delayed by at least twenty years and its onset even longer. In the 1840s the level of mechanization was still very low. Thus in 1841 there were only three steam engines in Slovakia (out of a total of ten in Hungary), compared with 156 in the Bohemian Lands and 242 in the entire monarchy. Only three more were added by 1848.

Lacking a central hub, the Slovak territory remained seriously fragmented commercially. While contacts between the western and central parts were substantial, the underdeveloped east was largely isolated from the rest of Slovakia. Pozsony and Trnava in the southwest and Košice in the east maintained their leadership in the structure of trade, and Banská Bystrica emerged as an important new market for central Slovakia. The problems of commercial and economic integration of the Slovak territory continued to mirror the difficulties of Slovak national unification.

The Croats

ENLIGHTENED ABSOLUTISM, 1740–92

Reorganization of the Military Borders, 1740–55

While Maria Theresa's reign in Croatia, as elsewhere, aimed at centralizing governmental power in Vienna, she was willing to make an exception in the 1740s. In order to retain the Croatian estates' support in the War of the Austrian Succession, she transferred in 1745 most of the Sava-Danube Military Border from a condominium of the Viennese *Hofkriegsrat* and the Hungarian Chamber to Croatian civil administration. Three new *županije* (Virovitica, Požega, Srijem) were organized there on the model of the Hungarian counties; only the area along the Sava was reserved for the new Slavonian-Syrmian Military Border. Politically, however, the new Slavonian *županije* were not fully integrated with the three preexisting Croatian *županije* (Zagreb, Varaždin, Križevci) of the traditional "civil" Croatia. They were under the general administration of the *banus* and represented in the *Sabor*, but their finances were controlled by the Hungarian Lieutenancy Council, and after 1751, unlike the Croatian *županije*, each one was entitled to direct participation in the Hungarian diet. The Croatian estates naturally resented the anomalous ascendancy of Hungarian authorities over part of their territory.

The queen's interest in centralization and administrative uniformity affected first of all the military borders. In the mid-1740s only the new Slavonian-Syrmian Border was under the jurisdiction of the Viennese *Hofkriegsrat*. The *banus* and the *Sabor* administered the *Banus'* Border;

and the Graz *Hofkriegsrat* jointly with the estates of Inner Austria controlled the old Karlovac Generalate and Varaždin Generalate.[37] In 1743 the Graz *Hofkriegsrat* was renamed *Militär-Direktorium* as a prelude to its complete abolition in 1749, and the financial responsibility of Inner Austrian estates for the two old generalates terminated in 1748. Thus by 1749 both generalates were financed and administered directly from Vienna. In 1750 Vienna assumed fiscal jurisdiction over the *Banus'* Border; officers there were henceforth commissioned by the *Hofkriegsrat*, and the regiments swore allegiance not to the Croatian Kingdom but to the king. The last vestiges of local self-government were wiped out in the generalates of Varaždin and Karlovac by 1754. In 1765 a common inspectorate for the four military borders would crown the work of centralization.

Royal Regulation of Peasants' Obligations

Serious peasant discontent, which prevailed in the areas outside the military borders (in the domains of private seigneurs), erupted into uprisings in 1755. In Slavonia the basic cause was the increase in the nobility's power with the organization of the *županije*, while in Croatia the even more intense violence was sparked mainly by the recent imposition of a military tax for the maintenance of the *Banus'* Border by Vienna. Maria Theresa's government now intervened to regulate the serf's economic obligations. A royal commission, assembled at Virovitica, recommended a set of rules, based on the *Carolina Regulatio* of 1737, which were promulgated as the Slavonian *Urbarium* in 1756. Another commission under Michael Althan, sitting in Zagreb, proposed regulations for the Croatian *županije* in 1755, although the resultant Croatian *Urbarium* was not completed until 1780.

The two *Urbaria* reflected major differences between the Croatian and Slavonian *županije*. The hide—the basic measure of the serf's obligations—was larger in Slavonia (24–40 morgen) than in Croatia (14–22 morgen). Dues in both kind and money applied in Croatia; in money alone in the better developed Slavonia. With the ratio of nobles to peasants 1:240 in Slavonia and only 1:30 in Croatia, the basic labor obligation was more than twice as onerous in Croatia (104 days per year) than in Slavonia (48 days).

---

37. As he had done in the Varaždin Generalate in 1737, Prince Sachsen-Hildburgshausen replaced in the Karlovac Generalate in 1743 the obsolete captaincies with regimental districts, elective lower officers with appointive ones, and introduced German as the language of command. In the new Slavonian-Syrmian Border the standard regimental organization was instituted by Baron Engelshofen in 1747, and the military rules of the Varaždin and Karlovac generalates were applied even more closely by Johann Serbelloni in 1753.

Centralist Reforms, 1755–79

Beginning in the mid-1750s Maria Theresa's government set out to restrict the autonomy of the Croatian estates. Althan's commission first broached in 1755 the idea of a semibureaucratic *gubernium* for Croatia, resembling the later *gubernia* of the Bohemian and Austrian Lands. For the time being, a lesser reform was adopted, enabling the Viennese government to bypass the *Sabor* and transmit instructions directly to the *županije* through the *banus*.

After the hiatus of the Seven Years' War (1756–63), the absolutist trend gathered new momentum, and the idea of a new executive organ for Croatia was embodied in 1767 in the *consilium regium*, headed by the *banus* and modeled on the Hungarian Lieutenancy Council. In effect it replaced the archaic but nonbureaucratic *Banus' Conference*. The *Sabor's* fiscal power was also severely curtailed. The imperial government independently decreed a basic reform in 1770, replacing the traditional chimney (*dim*) by the Hungarian *porta* as a unit of taxation, and equalizing the *dica* in Croatia with the Hungarian one. A tax assessment according to the new formula in 1772 was likewise carried out without the *Sabor's* participation. Equally serious was the loss of control by the *Sabor* over the collection and disbursement of the *dica* (called now the Contribution). By 1772 the *županije* had to deliver the tax proceeds directly to the imperial authorities, and a year later the Hungarian Chamber assumed entirely the financing of the administrative organs of the Croatian Kingdom.

Croatia's autonomy further suffered in a series of dramatic events before the end of Maria Theresa's reign. Seeking to further perfect the administrative uniformity in the military borders, the empress wished to eliminate the anomaly of private manors in the *Banus* Border. She failed to placate the estates by a transfer of the Rijeka region (an autonmous entity since 1670) to a joint Croatian-Hungarian jurisdiction in 1776. Despite her gesture, the *Sabor* in late 1777 refused to approve an expropriation of noble estates in the *Banus'* Border. After the *Sabor* was dissolved (early in 1778) and dissatisfaction mounted, the empress abolished the *consilium regium* in August 1779, and transferred its powers to the Hungarian Lieutenancy Council. Thus, in addition to the financial domination by the Hungarian Chamber since 1773, Croatia found itself for the first time explicitly subordinated to Hungarian political administration.

Culmination of Absolutism, 1780–90

As elsewhere in the Habsburg monarchy, also in Croatia, enlightened absolutism culminated in the reign of Joseph II (1780–90). Of the two cardinal liberalizing measures, religious toleration was decreed in 1781, and the abolition of peasants' personal bondage in 1785. The effort to elimate the estates' political power focused on bureaucratizing the *županije* administrations. German personnel were introduced, and in 1784 German was decreed to become the official language of the *županije* within two years. In addition, to overcome local opposition to the reforms, a system of administrative circuits was superimposed on the *županije* in 1785, disregarding the Croatian-Hungarian boundary. [38] The *Sabor*, until its suspension in 1785, gathered solely for ceremonial installations of officials appointed from Vienna. The *banus* entirely ceased to represent local estates.

The breakdown of the new administrative system under the impact of Joseph II's unsuccessful Turkish war (1788–91) led to the abolition of the circuits in late 1789. Allowed to gather for the first time in two years, the *županije* assemblies called for a meeting of the *Sabor* and proceeded to expel German officials as well as to eliminate the German official language. Before his death in early 1790, the emperor promised to convoke the *Sabor* and to recognize the Croatian constitution as of 1780.

Partial Submission to Hungary, 1790–92

During the conciliatory era of Leopold II's reign (1790–92) the memory of his predecessor's onslaught on their privileges caused the Croatian nobles to sway in the direction of close alliance with the Hungarian estates. Although this trend was not unique, it surpassed its precedents. In a striking decision of May 1790, the *Sabor* endorsed Croatia's subordination to the Hungarian Lieutenancy Council, thus in fact sanctioning the autocratic act of 1779 flowing out of Maria Theresa's centralistic policy. The *Sabor* also surrendered its basic financial power by requesting that the size of Croatia's Contribution be negotiated only at the Hungarian diet. Both wishes of the *Sabor* were approved by the Hungarian diet and the emperor.

As early as 1790, however, the outlines of future Croatian conflicts with Hungary began to emerge. In a move bearing on the old issue of "concordance" between Croatian and Hungarian laws, the Croatian delegates vigorously opposed the proposals at the Hungarian diet that civil rights be granted to Protestants in Croatia. Likewise, they refused to accept Magyar as the official language, insisting on the traditional Latin. In the end, confronted with the Croatian challenge to its competence,

---

38. The three Croatian *županije* and a Slavonian one (Požega) were combined with a Hungarian county (Zala) to form the Zagreb circuit. The Slavonian *županije* of Virovitica and Srijem, together with three Hungarian counties, composed the circuit of Pécs. The royal commissioners heading the circuits controlled appointments of the *županije* officials.

the diet relented and restricted both measures to Hungary proper. The *Sabor*, still in a spirit of accommodation, made a minor concession on the language issue, and decreed in June 1791 that Magyar should be offered as an optional subject in Croatian schools.

REACTION AND NATIONAL AWAKENING, 1792–1847

Acquisition of Dalmatia and Istria, 1792–1815

The struggle against revolutionary France, which erupted shortly before the accession of Francis I (II) in 1792, tended to establish a common interest between king and estates and to submerge their conflicts. The war itself resulted in 1797 in a major expansion of ethnic Croatian territory under Habsburg rule. Dalmatia and Istria were included in the Austrian acquisition of the Venetian Republic and a large part of her possessions. Of these, Dalmatia was placed under a *gubernium* in Zadar and subordinated directly to Vienna. Boka Kotorska, separated from the rest of Dalmatia by the independent Dubrovnik Republic, obtained its own administration. Thus the imperial government showed no inclination to unite Dalmatia with Croatia despite a formal petition by the Croatian estates in 1802. Further north, Venetian Istria retained its separate status from the smaller (ethnically Croatian) Austrian Istria, which still formed a part of Carniola.

By the treaty of Pozsony in December 1805, Dalmatia and Istria, together with the other former Venetian territories, were ceded to France. Napoleon made them a part of his Kingdom of Italy with the capital in Milan. Dalmatia was organized as a *provenditura generale* headed by Vinzenzo Dandolo as *provenditore*. Dubrovnik, seized by the French in 1806, was administered together with Boka Kotorska by a separate *provenditore* from 1808. Reforms by Dandolo created a system of bureaucracy and judiciary more modern than anywhere in the Habsburg monarchy. The formerly Venetian Istria became a department of the Italian Kingdom and was administratively reorganized in 1807 according to the French pattern under a prefect in Koper.

During the Napoleonic wars the relationship between the Croatian and the Hungarian estates began to deteriorate, as the Hungarian diet in exchange for supporting the war effort tried to elicit from the king-emperor concessions in the area of language. The Croatian delegates had to oppose in 1805, 1807, and 1811 the introduction of Magyar into administration, education, and the army, and to insist on the retention of Latin. A conflict erupted also over the joint possession of Rijeka. In 1808 the king reconfirmed the Croatian-Hungarian condominium.

By the treaty of Schöbrunn in October 1809, the Kingdom of Croatia suffered a painful loss of its territory south of the Sava to the French.

This area included a segment of civil Croatia and six regimental districts of the Karlovac Generalate and of the *Banus'* Border. It became part of the seven so-called Illyrian Provinces newly created by Napoleon, which included also (1) Carniola, western Carinthia, Gorizia, and Trieste likewise ceded to France by the treaty of Schönbrunn, and (2) Dalmatia, Dubrovnik, and Istria now detached from the Kingdom of Italy. Thus constituted, the Illyrian Provinces formed a part of the French Empire with an administrative center in Ljubljana, headed by a governor-general. An intendant was in charge in each of the six "civil" provinces. The military border south of the Sava constituted a special "military" province, and the existing internal organization was preserved under a French military intendant. "Civil Croatia" formed a separate province with the capital in Karlovac; attached to it were the Rijeka area and initially the old Austrian Istria. Venetian Istria formed a department within the province of Istria, which further comprised Trieste and Gorizia. In 1811 the old Austrian Istria was detached from the province of "Civil Croatia" and merged with Venetian Istria into a single department within the province of Istria. Thus all of Istria was administratively united for the first time in four centuries. Dalmatia and Dubrovnik each constituted a separate province.[39]

The French authorities encouraged to some extent the use of the Croatian or "Illyrian" language, especially in the lower administration, elementary schools, and lower sections of the *gymnasia*. Also, the university-level Central School in Dubrovnik provided for the study of the Croatian language. Otherwise, French, Italian, and Latin dominated higher education. In contrast to the Slovene areas of the Illyrian Provinces, the French measures did not stimulate a genuine national movement in the Croatian territory, where the native majority was socially less advanced. The French rule, though far more progressive than the Austrian, remained, on the whole, unpopular among the Croats, who widely resented its ecclesiastical reforms, taxation policies, curtailment of maritime commerce, and recruitment for foreign armies.

Struggle Against Absolutism, 1815–30

With the collapse of Napoleon's power, the territory of the Illyrian Provinces was reoccupied by the Austrian army in late 1813, and the area was definitely reassigned to the Habsburg monarchy by the Congress of Vienna two years later. The change of sovereignty, however, did not result in an administrative unification of ethnic Croatian territories. The military border south of the Sava reverted to its status

39. Of the seven provinces, stabilized by Napoleon's *Décret sur l'organisation de l'Illyrie* of April 15, 1811, four were inhabited by Croats (Civil Croatia, Military Croatia, Dalmatia, Dubrovnik), two by Slovenes (Carniola, Carinthia), and one by both (Istria).

before 1809. Dalmatia together with Dubrovnik and Boka Kotorska became a separate crownland with a *gubernium* in Zadar, headed by a lieutenant (*Statthalter*). The provincial government was purely bureaucratic without a representative diet, and Austrian laws replaced the French ones. With most officials recruited from Italian territories under Austrian control, Italian and German became the official languages.

To the bitter chagrin of the Croatian estates, Napoleon's former "Civil Croatia" was not initially reunited with the Croatian Kingdom. Instead, shorn of the Rijeka area, it was first attached to Carniola, and in 1815 subjected to Austrian laws and German official language. Then in 1816 its territory was incorporated into the newly proclaimed Illyrian Kingdom, and administratively subordinated to the *gubernium* in Trieste as the *Kreis* Karlovac. Thus it was joined with the so-called Austrian Littoral (*Küstenland*) consisting of three other *Kreise* (Trieste, Rijeka, and Gorizia).[40] Not until 1822, after persistent petitioning by the Croatian estates, did the king-emperor relent and agree to reunite "Civil Croatia" south of the Sava with the Croatian Kingdom, and to restore Rijeka to joint Croatian-Hungarian rule.

Istria was divided in 1814, with the former Venetian part included in the Trieste *Kreis* and the old Austrian one in the Rijeka *Kreis*. By 1825 the two parts of Istria were reunited and assumed the stable form as a separate crownland with administrative center in Pazin, but without a diet.

Late in the Napoleonic wars the Croatian estates entered a new phase of struggle against royal absolutism. Since 1812 the king had not convoked the *Sabor* (or the Hungarian diet), and had sought to obtain revenue and military recruits directly from the *županije*. Both the conduct of the Viennese government toward the *županije* and the ensuing resistance of the latter resembled the contemporary situation between the government and counties in Hungary. Working through the *veliki župani*, Vienna used such expedients as restricting the *županije* assemblies to officials or alternately flooding them with compliant poor nobles. By 1821 the *županije* had grown recalcitrant, so that in 1822 royal commissioners had to be appointed in Zagreb and several other *županije* to enforce compliance in a purely dictatorial manner.[41]

The restoration of constitutional government in 1825 revived among Croatian nobles a desire for alliance with the Hungarian estates against recurrence of royal absolutism. As a friendly gesture, the *Sabor*, in 1827, surprisingly endorsed the teaching of Magyar as a compulsory subject

40. Although officially the designation persisted until 1849, the Illyrian Kingdom remained an ephemeral entity, since its other part continued to function under a separate *gubernium* in Ljubljana. See also pp. 214–15.

41. The estates of Zagreb still refused to comply. For corresponding events in Hungary see pp. 230–31.

in Croatian secondary schools. The rapprochement soon faltered, inasmuch as the Hungarian diet of 1825–27, not satisfied with minor concessions, insisted on Magyar as the official language for Croatia, and moreover revived the perennial issue of Croatia's legislative conformity with Hungary. The diet of 1830 pressed the Hungarian demands more insistently.

National Awakening, 1830–47

At this point Croatia was developing new intellectual premises for the approaching clash with Hungary. A Croatian national movement was at last emerging, spearheaded by Ljudevit Gaj's group of young intellectuals. Influenced by Kollár and Šafárik during his studies in Pest, Gaj (1809–72) settled in Zagreb in 1831 as a champion of unity among Slavs in general, South Slavs in particular. To promote this specific objective he initiated the so-called Illyrian movement, and propagated the adoption of the Štokavian dialect (spoken by a majority of Croats and by virtually all Serbs everywhere) as a literary language in place of the Kajkavian dialect of Zagreb, hitherto prevalent in Croatian literature. The political program of the new national movement was articulated by the aging Count Janko Drašković (1770–1856). In a treatise published in 1832 in the Štokavian dialect, he envisioned a "Great Illyria," which would include not only Croatia-Slavonia, Rijeka, the military borders, and Dalmatia, but also the Slovene areas of Inner Austria. Drašković also urged Croatia's administrative independence from Hungary with the *banus* responsible directly to the king, as well as adoption of the Štokavian dialect as the official language.

Offended by the Hungarian intentions to abolish feudal services and to equalize the Protestants' civil status, pressed by the diets of 1832–36 and 1839–40, Croatian nobles and clergy began to rally behind the national movement. Autonomy from Hungary acquired an added appeal and led the Croatian estates to request a separate administrative body for Croatia which would supersede the authority of the Hungarian Lieutenancy Council. In need of allies against the assertive Hungarian estates, the Viennese government also gave qualified support to the Croatian national movement. Thus the King refused sanction to Hungarian laws, passed by the diets of 1832–36 and 1839–40, which sought to institute Magyar as the official language in Croatia within ten years.

The Illyrian movement did not remain unchallenged. A pro-Hungarian faction, known as the Magyarones, organized in February 1841, under the leadership of Antun Josipović and the Barons Juraj and Levin Rauch. Mobilizing the poorer nobility, the Magyarones sought to gain control of the *županije* assemblies and then the *Sabor*. This scheme failed in 1842, but the Magyarones' charges of Russophilism against the national faction, compounded by Turkish complaints against Illyrian agitation among Bosnia's Catholics, led the Viennese government to restrain the Croatian national program. The new *banus*, Franz Haller, a Transylvanian appointed in June 1842, proscribed the use of the term "Illyrianism" and its derivatives, and tightened the censorship. His measures were, in fact, followed by a reorientation of the national movement from broad cultural goals to narrower political issues contested with the Hungarian estates and the local Magyarones. A specifically Croatian focus was also gradually prevailing over the comprehensive South Slav (Yugoslav) vision of Illyrianism.

On the whole, Vienna, for reasons of its own, continued to back the national faction in its political struggles. Thus in April 1843, when the Magyarones assembled large numbers of dependent poor nobles in Zagreb, *Banus* Haller frustrated their attempt to dominate the *Sabor* by postponing the opening session. After the impecunious nobles departed, the *Sabor* met, safely controlled by the national faction. When the Hungarian diet of 1843–44 passed Magyarization measures affecting Croatia, the king again refused to sanction them, except for the least onerous law requiring Croatian deputies to speak Magyar in the Hungarian diet within six years. In January 1845 the ban against the term "Illyrianism" was lifted if the word was used in a cultural or linguistic (not a political) sense. In September 1845 the king's intervention permanently undercut the Magyarones' electoral tactics by formally excluding the poor nobles from direct participation in the *Sabor*. A royal decree restricted *Sabor* membership to the customary group—persons invited by the *banus*, and the designated representatives of the *županije*, towns, and religious chapters. The national faction celebrated its victory by renewing the *Sabor*'s petition for Croatia's administrative separation from Hungary, such as existed under the *consilium regium* in Maria Theresa's time (1767–79).

The last Croatian *Sabor*, based on feudal representation, met in October 1847, and finally moved to implement a cardinal point of the national program—the replacement of Latin by Croatian in the *Sabor* itself, in other government agencies, and in education. The Hungarian diet now shifted its tactics from imposing Magyar in Croatia to forestalling Croatian as the official language. Before the onset of revolutionary events, it passed a law in January 1848 requiring continued official use of Latin in Croatia and Slavonia.

In ethnic Croatian areas outside the Croatian Kingdom, the national movement developed more slowly. A strong Italian ascendancy became apparent in Dalmatia, although most inhabitants—except for relatively few nobles, burghers, and higher clergy—were not Italian. Since 1844 the first local Croatian journal, the Zadar *Zora Dalmatinska*, had sought to stimulate national sentiments and the use of Croatian language in public life. The prospects were less favorable in Istria, where the largely Italian townsmen supported the dominant flourishing culture. The Croatian as well as the less numerous Slovene peasantry was not yet nationally conscious. The only educated Croatian group was the rural clergy, still slow in the 1840s to assimilate national impulses emanating from Zagreb.

AGRICULTURE, INDUSTRY, AND TRADE[42]

Rise of Crop Production and Beginnings of Manufactories, 1740–92.

The cardinal change in agriculture during the second half of the eighteenth century was the gradual shift from extensive cattle raising to crop production. Reflecting growing population density, and facilitated by improved transportation and public security, the process was most advanced in western Croatia and began to engulf Slavonia as well. The one notable increase in animal raising by the end of the century was in the breeding of horses as draft animals, especially in Gorski Kotar, Lika, and the region of Karlovac. Cattle and pig raising remained strong in Slavonia and certain parts of Croatia. On the other hand, efforts to stimulate sheep raising failed during the reign of Maria Theresa.

Among the crops, the popularity of corn spread fastest, its high yield and labor intensity complementing the population increase. Wheat production also grew rapidly, especially on the demesnes, destined—unlike corn—primarily for export. Of other grains, the production of barley and rye remained stable, while millet and spelt declined except in Lika and the mountainous areas. A fast-growing new crop was tobacco, widely exported, particularly from the Požega region, into Italy, Spain, and other Mediterranean countries. Viticulture maintained its importance, mostly on peasant lands. In the late eighteenth century, civil Croatia alone produced annually over 1 million barrels (each 56.6 liters) of wine. The trend toward crop expansion increased tensions, as the seigneurs sought to extend the demesnes while blocking the enlargement of peasant fields at the expense of the forests.

---

42. Economic data in this section are derived from *Historija naroda Jugoslavije* (Zagreb: Školska knjiga, 1959), 2:1052–1104; Rudolf Bićanić, *Doba manufakture u Hrvatskoj i Slavoniji, 1750–1860* (Zagreb: Jugoslavenska Akademije Znanosti, 1951), pp. 85–181, 209–29; Miroslava Despot, *Pokušaji manufakture u Građanskoj Hrvatskoj u 18. stoljeću* (Zagreb: Jugoslavenska Akademije Znanosti, 1962), pp. 7–89; Igor Karaman, *Privreda i društvo Hrvatske u 19. stoljeću* (Zagreb: Školska knjiga, 1972), pp. 9–22; I. I. Leshchilovskaia, "K voprosu o razlozhenii feodal'no-krepostnicheskoi sistemy i razvitii kapitalisticheskikh otnoshenii v pomeshchich'em khoziaistve Khorvatii i Slavonii v kontse XVIII–pervoi polovine XIX v.," *Uchenye Zapiski Instituta Slavianovedeniia Akademii Nauk SSSR* 18 (1959): 114–56.

Artisan production grew in volume and diversity during the eighteenth century, eventually encompassing some seventy kinds of crafts. While a few crafts became obsolete and extinct, many new craftsmen emerged, such as watchmakers, gunsmiths, cabinetmakers, and fanciers of metal objects such as needles, nails, horseshoes, and locks. Public regulations tightened for craftsmen supplying basic necessities in towns, such as butchers, bakers, and masons; others, the so-called commercial crafts, were released from many of the traditional guild restrictions under enlightened absolutism. In the 1770s, efforts to stimulate underdeveloped artisan production in the military borders included the establishment of artisan guilds covering entire generalates.

In the second half of the eighteenth century manufactories finally appeared in civil Croatia, established mainly by lay and ecclesiatical seigneurs. Encouraged by the Viennese government's mercantilism, seven such enterprises were founded in the 1760s, and paradoxically thirteen more in the 1770s when the government began to frown on industrialization in the eastern parts of the monarchy. At least six were added by 1792. The discouraging record of the manufactories, above all in the crucial textiles and metallurgy, illustrates the artificiality of this industrialization process. The first woolen manufactory, established in 1750 in Zagreb, closed down in 1781, but it outlasted four others, founded in the 1760s and 1770s. None could withstand the competition of Bohemian cloth. Similarly short lived were two linen manufactories, established in Ozalj (1768) and Vidovec (1772). Only silk production succeeded. With the silkworm introduced in 1761, two manufactories for spinning and two for weaving silk prospered in Slavonia. In the field of metallurgy, two iron manufactories operated precariously in Bregana and Brod na Kupi from the late eighteenth century. A copper wire manufactory functioned in Ozalj in the early 1770s.

A relatively successful area was glass production. Of four manufactories, two (established in 1766 and 1781) continued into the nineteenth century, generating significant exports to Spain, France, Italy, Egypt, and Turkey. Another area of success was potash production, also destined for export, with seven manufactories springing up after 1764 in Virovitica *županija*. The record of paper production was mixed. A manufactory at Zagreb flourished from 1771, another established at Vidovec in 1772 soon failed. Efforts to start large-scale production of leather (in 1767) and china (in 1775) did not succeed.

The twenty-eight manufactories that emerged in 1750–92 were evenly divided between civil Croatia and civil Slavonia. In Slavonia almost all were in textiles and potash; in Croatia they represented textiles, metals, glass, paper, and leather. Over half the manufactories were located in the *županije* of Zagreb and Virovitica. Of the twenty-eight only eleven survived the turn of the century.

In the military borders the industrial development was weaker than in civil Croatia-Slavonia. Two woolen manufactories, founded in the 1780s near Karlovac, failed in the next decade. The borders surpassed the civil territory only in silk production. At the other end of the spectrum, the area of Rijeka had several manufactories: two tanneries, a sugar refinery, and a candle manufactory. In addition, two shipyards perpetuated the traditional shipbuilding, launching in 1785–95 alone twenty-two vessels, fifteen of them large.

The growth of trade was particularly significant in 1740–92. The number of major fairs increased from 48 in 12 towns to 187 in 48 towns between 1755 and 1804. The flow of trade was facilitated by a new highway (*Josephina*) from Karlovac to Senj, regulation of the Kupa and the Sava from Karlovac to Zemun by 1756, and a new combined river and land route from Karlovac to Trieste. Except for glass and potash, export trade concentrated on agricultural commodities. Reflecting the structural change in agricultural production outlined earlier, cattle yielded primacy to grain among agricultural exports by 1770. Wine maintained its importance in exports, and lumber—from the coastal area and Gorski Kotar—became a prominent export article destined for shipbuilding in the Mediterranean region. Flourishing imports of textiles from the Bohemian Lands, and of iron products from Carniola and Styria, helped to undermine domestic textile manufactories and ironworks. The trade with the Ottoman Empire tended to shift after 1755, prompted by mercantilist policies, to imports of raw materials and exports of finished products.

Agricultural Crisis and Age of Manufactories, 1792–1847

During the first half of the nineteenth century the respective importance of cattle raising and crop production stabilized. Crops clearly prevailed in Croatia and reached an equality with cattle raising in Slavonia. Only in Požega *županija* did cattle raising still predominate, encouraged by uncultivated tracts in the swampy riverine regions, and the proximity of major markets (Sopron and Kanizsa). Large-scale pig raising also continued in the beech and oak forests of Požega and Virovitica *županije*. In the overall agricultural economy on the Croatian territory, however, crops were most important. Grains, mainly wheat, dominated the export trade. More land was planted in wheat than in rye. Vineyards were still widespread in Croatia, while tobacco fields were concentrated in Požega *županija*. Flax and hemp production served almost exclusively the needs of clothmaking by peasant households. The cultivation of hops for beer and of plums for *slivovica* brandy (particularly in Slavonia) gained in importance.

As a major weakness, Croatia's agricultural techniques increasingly lagged behind the improving standards of its western and northern neighbors. The three-field system prevailed. The peasants used primitive implements both on their own land and on the demesne. Cultivation was carried on with wooden plows, hoes, and harrows; harvesting with sickles, scythes, and rakes; and threshing by stomping of oxen or horses. These primitive techniques caused also a qualitative decline in Croatian viticulture below the standards of Carniola and Styria by the 1830s.

After 1829 Croatian agriculture was more centrally challenged by the competition of Russian grain, which—benefiting from the low cost of sea transportation—could undersell Croatian grain even in the coastal areas of Dalmatia and Istria. The tightening of the export market brought on the additional competition of Hungarian grain, which was of superior quality and penetrated internal Croatian markets in the areas of grain deficiency, especially the western military borders. The slackening of demand further lessened incentives to improve agricultural techniques. After 1841, modernization was propagated by the Croatian-Slavonian Agricultural Society, but the results were modest.

In industrial development, Croatia made some advances in the first half of the nineteenth century, but poor in capital, lacking in credit facilities, and exposed to the competition of Bohemian and Austrian goods, it remained among the least developed areas of the Habsburg monarchy, lagging behind even the Magyar and particularly the Slovak territories of Hungary.

Sectors of industrial strength included shipbuilding after its recovery from a turn-of-the-century crisis. The number of shipyards rose from two in 1819 to eight in 1823, located in Rijeka, Bakar, and Kraljevica. Ship construction increased from 13 averaging 300 tons in 1839 to 23 averaging 380 tons in 1847. In 1845–49 Croatia accounted for 41 percent of newly constructed shipping in the Habsburg monarchy, and Dalmatia for an additional 9 percent. Glass production also remained an area of relative strength. The two older manufactories were replaced by four new enterprises by midcentury, exporting five-eighths of their output to Italy, Spain, the Ottoman Empire, North Africa, and America. The related production of china and bricks was represented at midcentury respectively by three manufactories and sixty-three brickyards, the latter engaged largely in exports to the Balkans. Potash production flourished initially, spreading after 1810 from civil Croatia to the military borders. A decline occurred in the 1840s as the value of lumber increased. Wood processing was, in turn, gaining strength. The demand for wood for shipbuilding was supplemented and soon surpassed by the demand for barrel staves, first from France (after 1824), then from Germany (after 1830). Improved transportation enabled exploitation of forests increasingly remote from the coast. Of the twenty-four water-powered sawmills in Croatia in the 1840s, the three largest could process 14,000 cubic meters of wood annually.

Metallurgy and textiles, ordinarily basic to industrialization, continued to languish. Iron production revived on a small scale in the military borders at Kosna in 1794, with added facilities in neighboring Trgovi by 1806. This sole significant ironworks in Croatia did not produce more than 85 tons of iron per year until 1838. Subsequently the rate rose to 140 tons in 1839 and 252 in 1847. Even then the Croatian output remained modest, equaling no more than 1 percent of the contemporary production of pig iron on the Slovak territory, the main center of Hungary's metallurgy. Peasant production of linen, and to a lesser extent imported woolen cloth, satisfied the need for textiles. The peasant production remained strictly individualized.[43] Only silk production continued to thrive, receiving added impetus during the Napoleonic wars. Civil Croatia produced 121,000 pounds of raw silk per year by 1840 and the military borders 215,000 pounds. Ninety percent of this output, however, was spun outside Croatia, mainly in Lombardy.

Although domestic and artisan methods usually prevailed in food processing, more advanced forms of production did emerge in flour milling and sugar refining for export. Five large flour mills came into existence, three in Rijeka and one each in Karlovac and Ivanec. Although the old sugar refinery in Rijeka, utilizing sugar cane, declined and closed down in 1828, two modern refineries were established after 1830 to process sugar beets (in Čepin and Virovitica).

On the whole, the manufactory still represented the most advanced form of industrial production in Croatia. It was most significant in flour milling, wood processing, shipbuilding, and sugar refining, which by midcentury together accounted for about two-thirds of the total value of the output of Croatian manufactories. Manufactories producing potash, silk, iron, glass, and bricks were responsible for most of the remaining third. The distribution of manufactories followed the pattern established in the late eighteenth century. The highest concentration was in Rijeka, with sixty-five enterprises in the 1840s. Second place belonged to the towns of civil Croatia, particularly Osijek, Zagreb, Karlovac, and Varaždin. The military borders had the fewest manufactories—no more than seventeen in 1842.

By 1848 Croatia had felt no significant impact of the industrial revolution, lagging in that respect some thirty years behind the Bohemian Lands, and ten years behind Hungary, especially the Slovak territory. There was no notable machinery production before 1848, and very few enterprises were sufficiently mechanized and equipped with steam en-

---

43. Textile production did not even reach the organizational level of the putting-out system or the dispersed manufactory. After the demise of the older textile manufactories in the 1790s, the first new one did not emerge until 1847 in Varaždin.

gines to qualify as genuine factories: one paper mill, two sugar refineries, and one flour mill. Thus at midcentury Croatia still remained essentially in the age of manufactories.

The Ruthenians, the Serbs, and the Romanians

THE RUTHENIANS OF TRANSCARPATHIA AND BUKOVINA

Enlightened Absolutism, 1740–92

Transcarpathia. The history of the Ruthenians, who are frequently referred to as the most forgotten national group under the Habsburg scepter, is closely interwoven with their church organization. This is a sociopolitical phenomenon typical of an oppressed peasant people in early modern history. Maria Theresa continued her predecessors' policy of seeking to protect the Uniat Church in Transcarpathia against discrimination by the largely Magyar and German nobles. In 1741 she reconfirmed the diplomas of Leopold I and Charles VI granting full equality to the Uniat with the Latin clergy. Inevitably the county assemblies hesitated to promulgate the new decree. Bereg complied in two years, Ung in four, and Máramaros procrastinated until 1761. Subsequently the queen sought to shield the Uniats from excessive interference by the Latin rite hierarchy, especially the bishops of Eger, to whom the Mukacheve Uniat diocese was subordinated as a vicariate. Concerned since the early 1760s about the emerging pro-Orthdox and Russophile moods among the Transcarpathian Ruthenians, Maria Theresa finally prevailed on the Vatican to grant full autonomy in 1771 to the Mukacheve diocese,[44] ending its dependence on Eger. In addition, Vienna encouraged the dynamic bishop of Mukacheve, Andrii Bachyns'kyi (1773–1809), to improve the training of the clergy, and develop a program of publication in Church Slavonic to terminate the Uniats' dependence on liturgical books from the Russian Empire.

The remarkable bishop also cared for the development of village elementary schools, meeting with considerable success by the turn of the century. In addition to a *gymnasium*, a teachers' college was established in Uzhhorod in 1794. These institutions used mostly Latin, while the primary schools instructed in the local Ruthenian language.

After increasing exactions by the Transcarpathian seigneurs, the Ruthenian peasantry benefited from Maria Theresa's protective mea-

---

44. In 1780 the seat of the diocese was transferred to Uzhhorod.

sures, in particular the well-known *Urbarium* of 1767, as well as those of Joseph II, whose emancipation decree of 1785 was promulgated in the Ruthenian language. The resulting gratitude and loyalty to the Viennese government were to last among Ruthenian peasants well into the nineteenth century.

Bukovina. The number of Ruthenians in the Habsburg empire increased substantially with the acquisition of Galicia in 1772,[45] which later led to the annexation of the partly Ruthenian Bukovina. The Viennese government exacted the Bukovina from the Ottoman Empire, and its vassal state Moldavia, in 1774–75 largely to obtain a land zone connecting Galicia with Transylvania. From 1775 to 1786 the Bukovina remained under military administration, headed by a military governor, with local affairs managed largely by the established landed nobility, the boyars, almost entirely Romanian by nationality. To augment the local predominantly Ruthenian population amounting to only 75,000 in 1775, the military government encouraged immigration, which came mostly from Transylvania, Moldavia, and Bessarabia and resulted in a Romanian majority before the end of the century.

After 1780 Joseph II applied a wide range of reforms to the new territory of his empire. The peasants were personally emancipated in 1781, and obtained hereditary right to their lands in 1788. Modest development took place in elementary and secondary education, mainly in German. The local Orthodox diocese of Rădăuți (Radautz), the religious organization of most of the Ruthenian and Romanian population, was released in 1781 from the jurisdiction of the metropolitan of Jassy in Moldavia and its seat transferred to Chernivtsi (Czernowitz, Cernăuți). The diocese was subordinated to the metropolitan of Karlovci (Karlowitz, Karlócza) in 1783. In 1786 the Orthodox Religious Fund, managed by the government, was created to assume the administration of ecclesiastical estates.

The military administration approached its end in 1786 when an incorporation of Bukovina into Galicia was decreed. In 1787 Bukovina was constituted as a circuit (*Kreis*) of Galicia, headed by a circuit captain (*Kreishauptmann*), who resided in Chernivtsi and was responsible to the *gubernium* in Lviv (Lemberg, Lwów). Several deputies and district commissars, almost all of them Germans or Poles, assisted him. Also, in the spring of 1787, the noble estate in Bukovina was regularized, with most of the traditional nobles confirmed in their dignities and entitled to seats in the consultative Galician diet (*Sejm*) in Lviv.

---

45. The history of the Ruthenians of eastern Galicia, 1772–1918, is discussed in volume VII of this series: Piotr S. Wandycz, *The Lands of Partitioned Poland, 1795–1918* (Seattle and London: University of Washington Press, 1974).

Reaction and the Approach of Revolution, 1792–1847

Transcarpathia. The chief Ruthenian ethnic organization in Transcarpathia, the Uniat Church, had been isolated from Russian religious influences by Maria Theresa's reform of the 1770s. Unintentionally, however, the improvement in the education standards of the Ruthenian clergy led to forging new intellectual links between Transcarpathia and the Russian Empire. By the early nineteenth century an oversupply of Transcarpathian scholars, trained in Vienna and Lviv, could not find employment locally, and many sought appointments within the expanding Russian university system.[46] Thus the prospects of Russophilism in Transcarpathia and of Russia's interest in the area were strengthened. At the same time, intellectuals from Transcarpathia had opportunities in Vienna and Lviv to meet other Slavs from the Habsburg monarchy, in particular fellow Ruthenians from Galicia.

Within Transcarpathia, the passage of Russian troops during the Napoleonic wars in 1799 and 1813–14 promoted awareness of mutual kinship, as did a visit by Tsar Alexander I in the area of 1821. The Russian victories during the Turkish war of 1828–29 were celebrated in the poems by Aleksander Dukhnovych (1803–65), after Bachyns'kyi the most notable cultural leader of Transcarpathian Ruthenians. There were also contacts with the more immediate Slav neighbors. The prominent leader of the national revival among Galician Ruthenians, Iakiv Holovats'kyi, traveled repeatedly to Transcarpathia in the 1830s and publicized local conditions. Starting in the 1830s the Slovak national movement, led by Štúr, directly stimulated cultural and educational interests among Ruthenian intellectuals.

This interaction inevitably elicited charges of disloyal Panslavism against Ruthenian leaders from the Magyar side, including Kossuth's own *Pesti Hírlap.* As elsewhere in Hungary, the increasing sway of Magyarization affected public administration and education of Transcarpathia during the second quarter of the nineteenth century.

The bulk of the Ruthenian population of Transcarpathia—the peasantry—had experienced unusual hardships since the beginning of the century. After 1811 periods of poor harvests had been followed by outbreaks of epidemics, the most serious of which, a cholera epidemic, flared up intermittently from 1827 to 1841. Major peasant disturbances in Transcarpathia, as well as in adjacent parts of Slovakia, in 1831 helped to induce the Hungarian diet to seek improvements in peasant conditions during the 1830s.

In the absence of royal free cities, the small urban population of

46. The most notable case, but by no means an isolated one, was that of Mykhailo Baludianskyi (1769–1847), who became the first rector of St. Petersburg University in 1819.

Transcarpathia was concentrated in towns subject either to private seigneurs or the Hungarian Chamber. The mayors were appointed by the seigneurs or by the *prefectus cameralis*, while the privileged burghers elected town councilors. A complicating factor in towns was the presence of nobles, who averaged, early in the nineteenth century, about 5 percent of the urban population. Initially the nobles often clashed with the burghers over the conduct of municipal affairs and the observance of local ordinances. By the 1830s and 1840s, however, with developing interest in crafts and trade, they tended to ally with the burghers against the greedy and imperious seigneurs. Data available for the 1840s indicate that the largest towns were Uzhhorod and Mukacheve, with over 6,000 inhabitants, followed by Berehove, Khust (Huszt), and Sevliush (Nagyszöllős) with over 3,000 each. Ruthenians constituted no more than 25 percent of Transcarpathia's urban population. Somewhat later, in 1850, in Uzhhorod, Ruthenians represented 27 percent of the inhabitants, Jews 32 percent, and Germans and Magyars together 41 percent. The total Ruthenian population in northeastern Hungary amounted to some 400,000 in the 1840s.

Bukovina. Bukovina remained administratively a part of Galicia during the entire first half of the nineteenth century. Many Ruthenian peasants from Galicia settled in Bukovina during this period, attracted not only by availability of land but also—until 1830—by the exemption from the obligation of military service. This immigration was the chief factor in raising Bukovina's population from 190,000 in 1801 to 337,000 in 1848.

Prevailing conditions, however, did not favor Ruthenian national development. The office of the *Kreishauptmann* in Chernivtsi was held by either a German or occasionally a Romanian, while German served as the official language with a subsidiary use of Romanian. Polish influences from Galicia also interfered with Ruthenian ethnic consolidation. With central control over lower education in Bukovina assumed by the Catholic consistory in Lviv in 1815, Polish was introduced into elementary schools of the Ruthenian areas. Exceptions were made only for religious instructions, which could be conducted in Ruthenian for the Uniats (after 1816), and were given according to a Serb catechism to the more numerous Orthodox. Segments of the Ruthenian population in northern Bukovinian towns became Polonized in the early nineteenth century.

Concomitant with the rise of Ruthenian ethnic awareness in Galicia, the Polonizing trend subsided in Bukovina in the 1840s. The imperial government as well began to take note of Ruthenian ethnic interests. Thus the Court Educational Commission (*Studienhofkommission*) in Vienna ruled in 1844 that Ruthenian, rather than Polish, should be the language of instruction in Orthodox schools north of the Prut. This decision, however, was not implemented before 1848.

The administrative and judicial subordination to Galicia also tended to exacerbate social conflicts in Bukovina, inasmuch as the now applicable Galician laws favored an ultrarigorous interpretation of peasants' feudal obligations. The most serious frictions developed in the northwestern highlands of Bukovina inhabited by the Hutsul branch of the Ruthenians. The Hutsuls repeatedly (in 1803, 1814, 1815, and 1825) showed their resentment over increases in compulsory labor, demanded by their seigneurs mostly for lumbering. By the 1830s, conflicts had also arisen between local bureaucrats in Bukovina, wishing to protect the peasants, and their superiors in Lviv, more eager to serve the seigneurs' interests.[47] A major outbreak of peasant disorders occurred in the Hutsul area in 1842–43. Another wave of unrest developed in the fall of 1846, fomented by Lukian Kobylytsia. His arrest in the summer of 1847 did not still the rebelliousness of Bukovina's Ruthenian peasantry.

Economic Life, 1740–92[48]

Transcarpathia. In the second half of the eighteenth century, agricultural modernization remained confined to large estates in the fertile and easily accessible lowlands of southern Transcarpathia, with the introduction of plows, better use of fertilizers, seed selection, crop rotation, large-scale sheep raising, and selective breeding of cattle. In most of Transcarpathia, however, including the Mukacheve manor, agricultural methods employed on the demesnes did not differ substantially from those used by the peasants on their own lands. Increases in production depended on heavier exploitation of peasant labor. Demesne estates expanded the raising of pigs and sheep, but remained weak in cattle. A major new trend was the increasing concern with viticulture in the three western counties of Transcarpathia. On the Uzhhorod manor, for instance, vineyards represented one-quarter of all income-producing property. Government efforts to encourage potato growing had little success.

Crafts and industry grew in the second half of the eighteenth cen-

47. These tensions were climaxed in the removal from office of the Bukovinian *Kreishauptmann*, Kasimir von Millbacher, in 1840 after his ordinance for a reflief of peasantry was countermanded from Lviv.

48. Economic data in this and the following two sections are derived from Ivan G. Kolomiets, *Ocherki po istorii Zakarpat'ia* (Tomsk: Izd-vo Tomskogo universiteta, 1953–59), 1:170–90; 2:8–32, 63–103; Denys Kvitkovs'kyi, ed., *Bukovyna: ïi mynule i suchasne* (Paris and Philadelphia: Zelena Bukovyna, 1956), p. 209; *Pivnichna Bukovyna: ïi mynule i suchasne* (Uzhhorod: Karpaty, 1969), p. 48; *Hauptbericht und Statistik über das Herzogthum Bukowina* (Lemberg: Selbstverlag der Handelskammer, 1872), pp. 157–73, 203–8, 230.

tury, but slowly and in a limited way. The number of craftsmen kept increasing in such towns as Mukacheve and Berehove. Industrial enterprises on large manors (flour mills, distilleries, brickyards, sawmills, and tanneries) were also rising in numbers, although their relative significance in the total manorial economy remained relatively small. They were usually based on artisan methods, rarely rising to the level of a manufactory. Of notable importance was the iron manufactory on the Mukacheve manor, which in 1771 acquired the first high furnace in Transcarpathia. The government-owned salt mines in Máramaros remained the largest mining enterprise.

Bukovina. When Bukovina was formally annexed in 1775, agricultural land in the area was extremely limited, with villages surrounded by dense forests. The peasants grew small amounts of corn, millet, flax, and hemp. In addition, silkworms were cultivated in the valleys of the Prut and the Suceava (Suczawa). Animal raising was the dominant agricultural occupation, especially in the Romanian parts. German and Magyar colonists in the 1780s helped to introduce new crops—rye, wheat, and barley. The state-managed Orthodox Religious Fund, which from 1786 held one-quarter of the agricultural land and half of the forests in Bukovina, became the chief driving force for agricultural progress, introducing on its estates new techniques to be emulated by the rest of agricultural producers.

The first significant industrial enterprises in Bukovina in the 1780s included ironworks and saltworks, all located in the southern Romanian section.

Economic Stagnation in Transcarpathia, 1792–1847

Large estates in Transcarpathia increased their income fairly rapidly in 1800–1812 (in response to demands generated by the Napoleonic wars), and more slowly in 1812–47. The rising income was due primarily to expansion of the demesnes, which increased in size by 20 percent during the first half of the nineteenth century. Improvement of productivity through modernization, hampered by scarcity of capital and dependence on compulsory labor, did not play a significant role. The archaic two-field system still prevailed in the north, and remained mixed with the three-field system in the south. Some manors, however, substantially expanded animal raising.[49] Among the crops grown in Transcarpathia, corn maintained its importance, though it was challenged by potatoes, which at last (since the 1790s) were spreading rap-

49. For instance, by the 1840s on the Mukacheve manor the demesne held 15 percent of all cattle and 70 percent of all sheep and pigs, compared with 6.5 and 50 percent respectively in the mid-eighteenth century.

idly. The chief crop, accounting for up to 50 percent of sown areas, however, was oats until the 1830s, subsequently—reflecting the demands of the market—wheat and rye began to take the lead among the stubble grains at its expense. Wine production had stagnated by the 1820s and 1830s because of declining demand and failure to adopt new techniques.

Artisan guilds in Transcarpathian towns suffered from restrictions imposed by the seigneurs, and the development of crafts lagged behind that of the neighboring royal free towns of eastern Slovakia. Most of the artisans in Transcarpathia were still German or Magyar; the estimated number of Ruthenian craftsmen in the beginning of the nineteenth century was between 1,000 and 1,200. Toward midcentury the total number of artisans amounted to 6,000 to 7,000, constituting under 2 percent of the population of Transcarpathia. Among other types of production, the salt mines in Máramaros expanded their output by 60 percent in 1819–46. The most important manufactory was still the ironworks on the Mukacheve manor, which operated ten high furnaces by the beginning of the nineteenth century, and exported iron implements to other parts of Hungary as well as to Galicia and Bukovina. Those were, however, the only two bright spots in the generally gloomy picture of industrial decline. Elsewhere, the old-fashioned manufactories on noble estates were suffering severely from competition from the more advanced industrial enterprises outside Transcarpathia. The proportion of manorial income derived from industrial enterprises (never particularly high) now dropped sharply.[50] Transcarpathia was being reduced to the least industrially developed region of Hungary.

Agricultural Advance in Bukovina, 1792–1847

The agricultural population of Bukovina continued to expand rapidly in the early nineteenth century, with most immigrants arriving from Galicia. Simultaneously, impressive advances in agricultural techniques and production were taking place. Aside from governmental initiatives, a powerful incentive for the peasants to improve their land was the greater security of tenure assured by the land surveys of 1818–20. In the 1820s, crop rotation (instead of the three-field system) was promoted by government estates and widely adopted first by the private latifundia, then by the peasantry. As for the new crops, growing of potatoes spread rapidly after the poor grain harvests of 1812–14. Managers of the government estates also successfully encouraged the extension of flax and grain production into the mountainous areas in the

---

50. Even on the Mukacheve manor it decreased from 15.7 to 6.3 percent in 1800–1847.

1830s, and promoted cultivation of feed crops to expand animal raising in the 1840s.

Outside the dominant agricultural sector, the main economic activity in Bukovina was mining and metallurgy (iron, silver, and copper), concentrated in the Romanian districts except for the ironworks at Lopushna on the Siret (Seret), established in 1840. Based on the abundance of forests, lumbering began to flourish by 1812 in the Ruthenian area of the northwest, where the Cheremosh River provided a convenient export route. With the improved navigability of the rivers in central and southern Bukovina by the 1840s, Romanian districts, however, were gaining predominance in the lumber trade. Artisan production also developed substantially in Bukovina during the first half of the nineteenth century. The number of craftsmen rose between 1804 and 1851 from 1,399 to 5,306, most of whom were German with relatively few Ruthenians among the rest.

THE SERBS OF VOJVODINA

Enlightened Absolutism in the Bačka and the Banat, 1740–92

In the first part of Maria Theresa's reign, her policy toward the Serbs of the Bačka[51] and the Banat was molded by the contradictory objectives of placating the Hungarian nobility while maintaining the allegiance of the Serb military manpower. To please the Hungarian nobles, the queen promised in 1741 the abolition of the Tisza-Mureş Military Border and its incorporation into Hungary. Sharp Serb protests, led by the metropolitan, delayed the implementation of this pledge, and yielded new concessions to the Serbs. Thus their traditional privileges were confirmed by the queen in 1743. Also at the request of the National Church Council of 1744 for special officials at the court, the Illyrian Court Commission was established in 1745. This supervisory body for Serb ecclesiastical and cultural affairs (renamed Illyrian Court Deputation in 1747) tended to clash with the Hungarian Court Chancellery, which regarded Serb matters as part of its own jurisdiction.

When the actual demilitarization of the Tisza-Mureş Border began in 1749, the Serbs bitterly resented the approaching transfer under the jurisdiction of Hungarian counties and seigneurs. Around three thousand of them preferred to emigrate to Russia in 1751–52. An intervention of the *Hofkriegsrat* and the Illyrian Court Deputation led once again to mitigative measures. A small Šajkaš Battalion area in southeast

---

51. The term "Bačka" is used to designate the Serb-inhabited territory to the west of the Tisza (Theiss) River in southern Hungary. The more specific area of the Hungarian county of that name (Bács) is referred to as "Bačka county."

Bačka was exempted from demilitarization and finally in 1764 was organized as a new military border with Titel as its center. A much larger territory along the Tisza obtained a special status in 1751 as the Tisza Crown District. Subordinated directly to Vienna, the district enjoyed considerable autonomy under a Serb *magistrat* in the capital of Bečej. As for the rest of the former Tisza-Mureş Border, which was in fact incorporated into Hungarian counties, individual Serb families desiring to emigrate were resettled, mostly in the southern Banat. The Banat remained for the time being directly under the Crown. The one major administrative change in 1751 involved clearer demarcation between the civil and the military areas.[52]

In the latter part of Maria Theresa's reign, following the Seven Year's War, jurisdictional reforms in the Banat deeply affected the Serbs. In 1764 the transformation of the southern Banat into a regular military border was initiated. The border assumed a stable form ten years later as two regimental areas, the German and the Illyrian-Wallachian. In ethnic composition, the former was mostly Serb, the latter Romanian. With the rest of the Banat slated for incorporation into Hungarian counties, the Serbs obtained another significant concession. A sizable area along the eastern side of the Tisza was transformed in 1774 into the Kikinda Crown District, similar to its autonomous status to the Tisza district on the other side of the river. Elsewhere the introduction of the Hungarian county system began in 1779.[53]

Another source of friction in the last decade of Maria Theresa's reign was Vienna's intervention in Serb religious affairs and concomitant restrictions on their national autonomy. Two decrees (*Regulamente*), issued respectively in 1770 and 1777, abolished the metropolitan's secular powers, and revised ecclesiastical rituals, while a new school constitution of 1776 placed Orthodox schools under governmental supervision. The reforms, especially those of 1777, provoked Serb anger and led to threats of violence against their own Orthodox hierarchy, willing to condone the changes. Above all, the elimination of Russian and Serb saints from the calendar was regarded as a preparatory step to imposing a Uniat status on the Serb Orthodox Church. Upset by what she considered inept implementation of her policy, Maria Theresa abolished the Illyrian Court Deputation in 1777 and assigned its functions to the Hungarian Court Cancellery. Thus the Serbs lost a valued symbol of their autonomy, and a *declaratorium* of 1779 essentially reaffirmed the curtailment of Orthodox Church power.

52. Three districts along the Turkish border were assigned primarily to the *Hofkriegsrat*, while the remaining eight districts came primarily under the *Hofkammer*, which administered them through the *Landesadministration* in Timişoara. Between 1759 and 1769 the Wiener Stadtbank held the Banat as security for state loans, and was entitled to all revenues from the province.

53. The counties in question were Torontal, Temes, and Krasso-Szereny.

Throughout Maria Theresa's reign a systematic colonization of the Bačka and the Banat was carried on with most of the immigrants— German at first, and from the 1760s also Magyar, Slovak, and Ruthenian. Many took the places vacated by the Serbs who had left to escape serfdom under county and seigneurial jurisdiction. Peasant conditions in Bačka and Baranya counties were regulated in 1772 by an application of the Hungarian *Urbarium* of 1767. The *Urbarium* was extended to the Banat in 1780, but with some alleviations for the serfs, designed to lessen the peasants' resentment against the imposition of the seigneurial system.

Compared with the discontents of Maria Theresa's reign, the policies of Joseph II were almost uniformly popular among the Serbs. The odious transfer of the Banat to Hungarian jurisdiction was blocked in 1781 by its restoration to the authority of the central Viennese agencies. All Serbs benefited from the Toleration Patent of 1781, and there were few Serb nobles to resent the personal emancipation of peasants in 1785. Even the reorganization of Orthodox ecclesiastical courts and the introduction of consistories into the dioceses by an imperial edict in 1782 did not arouse significant opposition. Joseph II's popularity among the Serbs reached its zenith in the final phase of his reign, while it was at its lowest point almost everywhere else in the monarchy. At the outbreak of the Turkish war of 1788, Serb clergy and laity alike hoped for a reunion, under Habsburg rule, with their liberated conationals from the Ottoman Empire.

After the accession of Leopold II in 1790, the Serb objective of genuine territorial autonomy at last seemed close to realization. In need of allies against the truculent Hungarian estates, the new king authorized the meeting of a national council in Timişoara in August 1790. The membership included Orthodox bishops from the Bačka and the Banat as well as from Transylvania and Bukovina, three imperial generals, twenty-five nobles, and twenty-five representatives of burghers and of the *zadruge* (agricultural communes) from the military borders. Although the council also formally represented the Romanians, the Serbs dominated its proceedings. Their chief request was the creation—out of the Banat, the Hungarian county of Bačka, and the Croatian *županija* of Srijem—of a unified self-governing Serb territory, separated from Hungary and subordinated directly to Vienna. Leopold II's initial response, the establishment of an Illyrian Court Chancellery, appeared as the harbinger of territorial autonomy under Vienna. Instead, a reconciliation between the king and the Magyar nobles dashed the Serbs' hopes. In 1791 the Hungarian county system was introduced into the Banat outside the two regimental areas, while the Serbs remained exempt from Hungarian jurisdiction only in the Tisza and Kikinda districts and in the military borders. The Hungarian diet, however, did promise those Serbs who had settled in the Hungarian counties equal rights of citizenship, religious freedom, and maintenance of their traditional privileges, as far as consistent with the laws of Hungary. The token of prospective Serb autonomy in a self-governing province, the Illyrian Court Chancellery, was abolished in 1792.

The National Awakening of the Serbs in Southern Hungary, 1792–1847

The demise of the Illyrian Court Chancellery in 1792 left the Serbs of southern Hungary without any central administrative institution of their own. The promise, made in 1792, of regular representation in the central Hungarian bureaucracy was not honored either. No Serb was appointed to the Lieutenancy Council, and the single Serbian councilor in the Hungarian Court Chancellery left by 1805. Even the National Church Councils were suspended from 1790 to 1837. From 1792, however, the Serb metropolitan and bishops had the right to participate in the Hungarian diet. Administratively the Serb territory remained fragmented into six units: three between the Danube and the western bank of the Tisza (Bačka county, the Tisza Crown District, and the military border of the Šajkaš Batallion), and three in the western Banat (Torontal county, Kikinda Crown District, and the German regimental area). The Serb population in southern Hungary, as well as in Croatia-Slavonia, rose from 667,200 in 1797 to 896,900 in 1847.

The strength of Serb ethnicity had to compensate for the lack of administrative cohesion. In the early vigor of their national consciousness, the Serbs surpassed the other Slavs in the monarchy in general and their fellow South Slavs—the Croats and Slovenes—in particular. Reinforced by the National Council of Timișoara in 1790, their national awareness was rooted in a long literary tradition, a pride of military prowess, and a tenacious resistance to religious and social oppression. It found institutional expression in the Orthodox Church, in such educational establishments as the *gymnasia* in Sremski Karlovci and Novi Sad (founded respectively in 1791 and 1810) and the teachers' college (started in Szentendre in 1812 and transferred to Sombor in 1816), and especially in the *Matica Srpska,* created in 1826 as a counterpart of the Hungarian Academy of Sciences. The *Matica* provided a model for similar institutions among the other Slavic nations of the Habsburg monarchy.

The Serbs looked alternately to the Russian tsar and the Austrian emperor for the realization of their national desiderata. A wave of Russophilism rose during the 1804 uprising in Serbia. The metropolitan of Karlovci, Stefan Stratimirović (1790–1836), asked Tsar Alexander I in a secret memorandum to establish a Russian protectorate that would include the Serb area of southern Hungary together with Serbia and

Bosnia. The bishop of the Bačka, Jovan Jovanović, dispatched a similar plea to the metropolitan of St. Petersburg. On the other hand, Serb troops demonstrated their loyalty to the Austrian emperor by their bravery during the Napoleonic wars, as well as during the later Habsburg interventions abroad under the aegis of the Holy Alliance. A number of Serbs rose to high ranks in the imperial army, including major general and lieutenant field marshal.

Although unable to participate in the central government agencies in either Vienna or Pest, the Serbs still enjoyed their traditional self-government in the Tisza and Kikinda Crown Districts, reconfirmed in 1800 and 1817. Elsewhere, their representatives played varied roles at local government levels. They were particularly influential in the towns of Novi Sad, Sombor (Zombor), Veliki Bečkerek, and Vršac (Werschetz). In the royal free towns, as well as in the free "communes" of the military border, positions in municipal governments were distributed according to a nationality key. For instance, in Novi Sad the Serbs were entitled to half the members in the *magistrat,* and every other year to the mayoralty. In the royal towns, the privileged burghers usually exercised their electoral rights with minimal interference from either the Lieutenancy Council or the Hungarian Court Chancellery. In the "communes" of the military borders, the military authorities appointed the three principal officials, while the burghers chose only two additional officers, the senators. Represented mostly among the poor nobles, the Serbs carried little weight in the Hungarian county governments. With no Serbs among the magnates, only the relatively few middle nobles could participate in the assemblies of Bačka and Torontal counties. County offices were held almost exclusively by Magyars or Germans.

The Serb national movement continued to gain strength after the foundation of the *Matica Srpska.* By the 1830s two Serb newspapers were launched, and the number of other publications increased steadily. The center of cultural life was shifting from Vienna and Pest to Novi Sad, where the Serb Reading Club (*Čitaonica*), founded in 1844, became another major focus of both cultural and social activity. The town also sheltered two publishing houses and an amateur theater. The prominent role of the Orthodox hierarchy tended to impart a certain intellectual as well as social conservatism to the Serb national movement in southern Hungary. Thus the national leadership tenaciously favored the archaic (Russian-flavored) Church Slavonic as a literary medium over the current form of the Serb language, the so-called Štokavian dialect, which had been promoted by the famous writer Vuk Karadžić (1787–1864) since the 1810s. The ascendancy of the Orthodox bishops stemmed in large part from the Serb intelligentsia's dependence on the ecclesiastical establishment. In 1846–47, for example, its largest contingent consisted of 700 priests, as well as 400 teachers employed mostly in Orthodox schools. Serb representation was relatively weak in the distinctly secular professions. Thus between 1773 and 1827 only 227 Serbs obtained licenses as lawyers, and no more than 30 were physicians in 1848. Nevertheless, by the 1830s some Serb students seeking education in the Lutheran *gymnasia* of the north were influenced by modern secular and liberal ideas, above all in the circles of Štúr and Kollár, respectively in Pozsony and Pest.

After 1830 the Hungarian diet's measures of Magyarization helped to intensify Serb national ardor. The governments of royal towns, such as Novi Sad, had to replace Latin with Magyar as their official language. By 1840 ecclesiastical records had to be maintained in Magyar, which in 1843 also became by law the language of instruction in all schools. The Serb teachers' college in Sombor, for instance, had to change its registers from Latin to Magyar in the academic year 1844–45. Mounting Serb resentment against these measures of denationalization would become evident in 1848.

While seeking to fend off Magyarization, the Serbs were, in turn, in conflict with the emerging Romanian intelligentsia which wished to lessen the Serb ascendancy—exercised through the metropolitanate of Karlovci—in the Orthodox establishment of the Banat and the Crişana area of Hungary. After the issue was raised in 1812, Metropolitan Stratimirović decreed in the 1820s that the bishops of Arad, Timişoara, and Vršac should be either Romanians or able to speak Romanian. Pressure, however, continued for expanded use of Romanian in religious services, records, schools, and monasteries.

Outside cultural and educational institutions, the Serbs remained severely restricted in the pursuit of their national goals during the 1830s and early 1840s. A National Church Council met at last in 1837, but its agenda was limited to the election of a new metropolitan. Thus it failed to meet the Serbs' wish for a "debating" (*raspravni*) council that would deal with issues of Serb national interest, which could not be effectively done either through the Hungarian counties or the regimental administrations in the military borders. Nevertheless the same restriction applied in 1842 to the next council, which elected Metropolitan Josif Rajačić. On that occasion, however, forty-two delegates formally petitioned the king-emperor to permit a genuine *raspravni* council. Delayed until August 1847, the authorization could not be implemented before the Revolution of 1848. In the meantime, Metropolitan Rajačić, under the pressure of Serb public opinion, was taking a more active part in the Hungarian diet than his predecessors. His protest at the session of 1843–44 concerning the lack of Serb representatives in the central organs of Hungary resulted in the appointment of a Serb to the Lieutenancy Council, and of an Orthodox Greek to the Hungarian Court Chancellery.

Government-Sponsored Economic Development, 1740–92[54]

Under enlightened absolutism the Viennese government, particularly the *Hofkammer* and the *Hofkrriegsrat,* continued to promote agriculture vigorously in the Bačka and the Banat. In the 1740s a Dutch expert was engaged to direct canal construction in the southern Banat. The acquisition of new lands for cultivation through draining, as well as a systematic agricultural colonization, favored reduction of extensive animal raising and expansion of crop production. Crops were to predominate in the total agricultural output before the end of the eighteenth century, although animal raising—shifting to an intensive basis—was also increasing in absolute terms. Within the sector of animal production, cattle received continuing emphasis and the stock was improved through crossbreeding of diverse types imported by the colonists. With established tradition in the area, sheep raising, concentrated on large estates, was oriented to wool export. In the late eighteenth century the government encouraged horse breeding, and pig raising expanded partly under the influence of the transit trade in pigs from Serbia.

In crop production, grain continued to predominate, with wheat in the lead. Otherwise rice, tobacco, and indigo retained their importance. Cultivation of potatoes—introduced by the German colonists—and of corn, both for local consumption, was initially on a modest scale. Silkworm raising persisted despite the termination of state subsidies in the late eighteenth century.

Craft production continued to expand in both the Bačka and the Banat. In 1760 Novi Sad, for instance, had 173 artisan workshops, representing 31 different crafts—with tailors, furriers, and shoemakers most prominent. The first guild in the area is known to have existed in 1761 also in Novi Sad. Subsequently, guild organizations spread to other royal towns, free "communes" of the military border, and smaller towns. Because of relative scarcity of artisans in the region, guild rules eschewed restrictions, customary in other parts of the monarchy, on the number of masters, journeymen, and apprentices.

In contrast to its modernizing efforts in agriculture, the government in Vienna was much less concerned with introducing advanced technology in the industrial sector. Selective encouragement of iron and copper mining, as well as wood processing, persisted, but only in the Romanian part of the Banat where Timişoara remained a center of

---

54. The economic data in this and the following section are derived from *Historija naroda Jugoslavije* (Zagreb: Školska knjiga, 1959), 2:1144, 1170–183; *Istoriia Iugoslavii* (Moscow: Izd-vo Akademii Nauk SSSR, 1963), 1:411; Dušan Popović, *Srbi u Vojvodini* (Novi Sad: Matica srpska, 1963), 3:105–6, 133–35; *Enciklopedija Jugoslavije* (Zagreb: Izd. Leksikografskog zavoda, 1968–1971), 7:532–33; 8:10–15; Sonja Jordan, *Die kaiserliche Wirtschaftspolitik im Banat im 18. Jahrhundert* (Munich: Oldenbourg, 1967), pp. 75–204.

manufactories. In the Serb portion of the Banat several manufactories were located in Pančevo, Vršac, and Veliki Bečkerek, including silk fila-tures, a brewery, a distillery, and a woolen manufactory. As for the Bačka, two breweries (established in 1748) and, since 1770, processing plants for silk and tobacco operated in Novi Sad.[55]

Trade, especially export of agricultural products, was strongly en-couraged by the *Hofkammer* in both the Banat and the Bačka. Corre-sponding with the basic trend in agricultural production of the region, the share of cattle in exports of the second half of the eighteenth cen-tury was diminishing in relation to grain, wine, wool, indigo, and to-bacco. The main trade routes, above all for grain, followed combina-tions of rivers and roads through Croatia to the Adriatic coast, particularly to Trieste, Rijeka, or Senj.

Agricultural Expansion and Industrial Underdevelopment, 1792–1847

Agricultural production continued to expand in the first half of the nineteenth century as additional areas were placed under cultivation. In particular, in the Banat military borders the amount of arable land tripled between 1786 and 1817. Production of stubble grains flour-ished, with the river ports of Novi Sad, Bečej, and Zemun (Zimony, Semlin) serving as principal export centers. While the raising of pota-toes, promoted by officers in the military borders, increased signifi-cantly, corn as yet was grown on a limited scale and in a primitive man-ner with seeds scattered over unplowed land. Viticulture prospered around Subotica (Szabadka, Maria-Theresiopel) and Vršac, as well as in the Serb part of the Banat military borders. Silkworms were culti-vated in the Bačka and to a lesser extent in the southern Banat.

Contrary to the prevailing trend in the area, the Serbs showed a marked preference for raising animals rather than crops. More than the Ger-mans or the Magyars, they engaged in sheep raising, and the wool from the Bačka was especially valued on the Pest market. They were well-known producers of pigs, supplying the great regional market in Baja. The Serbs also exceeded the Germans, though not the Magyars, in cat-tle raising. Nevertheless, contemporary observers considered the over-all standards of Serb agriculture in its equipment and methods inferior to the other nationalities in the area, except possibly the Romanians.

In the situation of flourishing agriculture and industrial underde-velopment, artisan production remained essential in both the Bačka and the Banat. In fact, the first half of the nineteenth century became known

---

55. Otherwise manufactories, such as the large flour mill in Futog, were rare and isolated phenomena. A putting-out system of cloth production, however, became well developed in the area of Odžaci by the 1760s.

as the "golden age" of crafts. Guilds persisted as the typical craft organizations, although their authority had diminished. They were often divided along religious or ethnic lines. Thus in Novi Sad in the mid-nineteenth century ten guilds were specifically Serb, with the furriers' guild the most prosperous.

Manufactories were still relatively few and largely restricted to silk filatures, large breweries, and distilleries. In the Bačka probably only Novi Sad, and in the Serb part of the Banat only Pančevo and Bela Crkva contained more than a single manufactory. As for genuine factories (mechanized and steam-powered enterprises), there is evidence for only five in the entire area before 1848: two flour mills, a textile mill, a candlemaking enterprise, and an oil press.

Improvements in transportation facilitated external trade. The Francis Canal, constructed in 1793–1802, connected the Tisza with the Danube through the Bačka and shortened the passage to Western Europe by as much as twenty days. Steamships were introduced on the Danube in 1834, on the Tisza in 1844. Newly emerging commercial hubs included Beliki Bečkerek (cattle), Vršac (wine), and Apatin (hemp), in addition to several centers for grain exports. Voluminous trade, especially in cotton, wool, and leather, passed through the Banat and the Bačka in transit from Wallachia or Turkey westward.[56]

THE ROMANIANS OF BUKOVINA

Enlightenment Era in Bukovina, 1775–92

While sizable Romanian territories became part of Hungary in the late seventeenth and early eighteenth centuries (in Transylvania, the Crişana-Maramureş area, and the eastern Banat),[57] the one significant group of Romanians outside of Hungary was introduced into the Habsburg monarchy with the annexation of Bukovina in 1775. The initial Austrian military administration in Bukovina (1775–86) sought to enlist local—mostly Romanian—nobility into the service of the state. As early as 1777 Bukovinian nobles became state functionaries in Chernivtsi, Suceava, and Rădăuţi. Nevertheless, some preferred to emigrate to Moldavia, especially to avoid an oath of allegiance to the emperor required in 1779. The ranks of Romanian émigrés were later augmented by priests

56. Credit facilities were not so scarce as, for instance, in neighboring Croatia. Prior to 1848, they included two savings banks in Veliki Bečkerek, and another in Apatin.

57. The history of the Romanians living in Hungary is discussed in volume VIII of this series: Charles and Barbara Jelavich, *The Establishment of the Balkan National States, 1804–1920* (Seattle and London: University of Washington Press, 1977).

and monks antagonized by the ecclesiastical reforms of Joseph II, including the creation of a consistory for the Orthodox bishopric of Chernivtsi in 1781, the dissolution of all but three Orthodox monasteries a year later, and the placing of ecclesiastical landed properties under the management of the state-controlled Orthodox Religious Fund in 1786.

The Romanian emigration from Bukovina was greatly exceeded by the Romanian immigration, encouraged by the Austrian military government, mainly from Transylvania, Moldavia, and Bessarabia. This immigration policy was to increase the population of Bukovina from 117,000 in 1778 to 190,000 by 1801. An unofficial estimate of 1804 fixed the number of Romanians as high as 141,000. Aside from Ruthenians, the rest consisted of Jews, Germans, Poles, and Magyars.

In addition to its administrative, ecclesiastical, and demographic reforms, the military government paid at least limited attention to education. By 1786, thirty-two schools with mostly German-speaking teachers were in operation, including junior high schools (*Hauptschule*) in Chernivtsi and Suceava. Local populations distrusted these institutions and in Chernivtsi only five out of sixty-eight pupils were Romanian. A seminary for Orthodox clergy was established in 1786 in Suceava and transferred to Chernivtsi three years later.

The outstanding personality among the Romanians of Bukovina in the late eighteenth century was the aristocrat Basilius von Balsch. A supporter of Habsburg rule, he was appointed to the *Hofkriegsrat* in 1783 as chief adviser on Bukovinian affairs. When the military rule ended in 1786 and Bukovina became a circuit (*Kreis*) of Galicia under the *gubernium* in Lviv, Balsch joined the United Court Chancellery. He was among the first to propose a comprehensive Austrian solution to the overall Romanian problem, suggesting to Leopold II (1790–92) that he annex Wallachia and Moldavia to the empire.

The Sway of Austrian Bureaucracy and Polish Catholicism, 1792–1847

The decision to subordinate Bukovina to Galicia remained unpopular with Romanian nobles, some of whom refused to participate in the Galician diet at Lviv. The resentment against the introduction of the Austrian bureaucracy was not diminished even by the appointment of Balsch as circuit captain (*Kreishauptmann*) in Chernivtsi in 1792. In fact, he was eventually driven from office by the hostility of his peers.

Nevertheless, the Romanian nobles showed a basic loyalty to the Habsburg empire by organizing a militia against the invading Polish revolutionaries who wished to launch an anti-Habsburg uprising in Galicia in 1797. The same fidelity was displayed by the nobles, as well as the peasants, during the Napoleonic wars of 1809 and 1813. With German as its official internal language, the imperial administration made limited provisions for the use of Romanian in external contacts, while neglecting the linguistic rights of the increasingly numerous but socially disadvantaged Ruthenians. Accordingly the state bureaucrats in Bukovina were expected to learn some Romanian, although the United Court Chancellery in 1804 noted deficiencies in that regard. In any case, altogether ninety-eight official announcements came out in Romanian between 1778 and 1848, and the Circuit Office (*Kreisamt*) in Chernivtsi employed a Romanian translator.

While receiving limited recognition in public administration, Romanian ethnic interests were slighted in the educational and religious spheres in the early nineteenth century. Assuming control of the school system in Bukovina in 1815, the Catholic consistory of Lviv restricted teaching positions to Catholics. Besides having the problem of a language barrier, the new teachers, mostly Poles, were shunned by the Orthodox Romanians on religious grounds. Thus the educational system languished with only twenty-seven elementary schools in 1815–22. The highest educational institution in the Land was the German *gymnasium* in Chernivtsi, established in 1808. The head of the Bukovinian Orthodox Church from 1789 to 1822, Bishop Daniel Wlachowicz of Chernivtsi, was of Serb origin. Regarded as a partisan of Slav interests, he instituted the Slavicization of Romanian names in church registers and fostered Ruthenian immigration from Galicia.

In the second quarter of the nineteenth century, Vienna showed an increasing concern over the national interests of the Romanians. In the area of state administration, the Council of State specified in 1833 that a candidate for the post of Bukovinian circuit captain (*Kreishauptmann*) should know Latin, French, and Italian so that he might easily learn Romanian. In 1837 a Romanian, Georg Isecescul, was appointed deputy circuit captain (*Vice-Kreishauptmann*). In 1844 he became the first Romanian circuit captain in Bukovina since Balsch. In ecclesiastical affairs, the bishop of Chernivtsi, Isaia Balaşescul (1822–35), restored the Romanian ascendancy within the Orthodox Church. His successor, Evhen Hakman (1835–73), essentially condoned this state of affairs, although he made some concessions to the Ruthenian language in ecclesiastical administration in 1838. In the educational field, the Court Educational Commission in Vienna proposed in 1844 to restrict the jurisdiction of the Lviv consistory to schools in Catholic communities, and place those in Orthodox areas under the Orthodox consistory of Chernivtsi. The Commission further stipulated that Romanian be used in all Orthodox elementary schools, except in a small area north of the Prut reserved for Ruthenian. These measures—overgenerous to the Romanians—were under implementation at the outbreak of the 1848 revolution.

Economic Life, 1775–1847[58]

After the annexation of Bukovina to the Habsburg monarchy, animal raising predominated over crop production in the Romanian regions. Agricultural modernization through the estates of the Orthodox Religious Fund (under full state control in 1786) was concentrated in the Romanian areas, where four out of the six Chamber Economic Offices (*Kameral Wirtschaftsämter*), established in 1786, were located (St. Illie, Solka, Gura Humorului, and Cîmpulung), while only two were in the Ruthenian areas (Kitsman' and Zhuchka). In the first half of the nineteenth century the chief impetus to improvements emanated from the estate at Rădăuţi and its economic director (1818–38), Gottfried von Asboth. Inspiring emulation by private landowners, Asboth pioneered the replacement of the three-field system by crop rotation, reclamation of swamplands, and clearing of forests for agriculture. His accomplishments included regulation of the Suceava River and the construction of a major road through its valley. Asboth's successor at the Rădăuţi estate, Karl Wilhelm Ambrosius, was primarily concerned in the 1840s with self-sufficiency in animal fodder. He introduced the cultivation of clover and alfalfa, as well as planting of meadows with nourishing and fast-growing grasses. Imitated not only by private estates but also by the peasants, these improvements was particularly germane to the Romanian areas where animal raising continued to dominate agriculture.

The number of artisans and the range of crafts had been extremely limited in Bukovina during Turkish rule. The Austrian authorities began to remedy the situation as early as the 1780s by encouraging immigration of foreign, mainly German, craftsmen into towns—within the Romanian area, especially into Suceava. The formation of artisan guilds started in 1804.

Mining and metallurgical activities, begun in Bukovina in the late eighteenth and early nineteenth centuries, were concentrated in the Romanian regions of Cîmpulung and Gura Humorului. The first major ironworks, using essentially artisan methods, were established by several boyars at Iacobeni in 1784. Two saltworks (in Solka and Cacica), managed by the Orthodox Religious Fund, were in operation by 1790. The ironworks at Iacobeni, under new management since 1796, erected a high furnace in 1800, and expanded operations to include the mining of silver in Cârlibaba (in 1797–1820) and copper in Pojorita (from 1821). By the 1840s the iron industry in Bukovina, consisting then of three

58. The economic data in this section are derived from Erich Prokopowitsch, *Die rumänische Nationalbewegung in der Bukowina und der Dako-Romanismus* (Graz and Cologne: Böhlaus Nachf., 1965), pp. 93–96; *Hauptbericht und Statistik über das Herzogthum Bukowina* (Lemberg: Selbstverlag der Handelskammer, 1872), pp. 159–71, 203; Kvitkovs'kyi, ed., *Bukovyna*, p. 209.

ironworks, entered a period of crisis because of technological obsolescence.

Industries exploiting the forests were also particularly strong in the Romanian regions where wood was abundant. Glassworks were established in 1803 in Krasna Putna and Krasna Il'ski between the Siret and Suceava rivers, and somewhat later at Karlsberg and Fürstenthal west of Rădăuţi. With the depletion of surrounding forests the first two moved to Chudyn, and glass production at Karlsberg ceased in 1827. Potash production was pursued intensively in both state and private forests in the early nineteenth century, until rendered uneconomical by the rising timber prices. Except for the valley of the Cheremosh, lumbering was also concentrated in the Romanian regions. Starting in southeastern Bukovina in the 1810s, it was long hampered by poor navigability of rivers and insecurity of passage through Moldavia. With both obstacles overcome by the 1840s, lumber exports moved freely into the Black Sea region, giving rise to numerous sawmills along the Bistriţa-Aurie and its tributaries.[59]

59. The second most important area of lumbering in the Romanian area evolved in the Suceava river valley after Asboth's initiative assured its navigability.

CHAPTER 5

Constitutional Era, 1848–1918

The Czechs

REVOLUTION AND REACTION, 1848–59

Political Rebirth, 1848–49

The political debut of the Czechs as a modern nation in 1848 amid the general revolutionary situation in the Habsburg empire rested largely on the program developed in the—often veiled—discussions earlier in the 1840s. It began at the historic meeting at the Saint Wenceslas Baths in Prague on March 11. Although convoked by the radicals of the Repeal society, the assembly was dominated by moderate Czech liberals led by Palacký, František Rieger (1818–1903), and Havlíček; and several German liberals also participated. A standing group selected by this gathering, the Saint Wenceslas Committee, adopted two petitions, drafted by František Brauner, which, besides civil and language rights, requested self-government as well as some form of confederation for the Bohemian Lands. Vienna's response, in the imperial Rescript (*kabinetní list*) of April 8, promised equality of Czech with German in public life and creation of a representative diet and a responsible executive body for Bohemia, but reserved the question of a constitutional link with Moravia and Silesia for decision by the forthcoming imperial *Reichstag*. The supreme count palatine, Count Leo Thun, was to prepare for self-government in Bohemia in cooperation with the National Committee, a successor to the Saint Wenceslas Committee.

The aristocrats in Bohemia remained virtually passive during the events of 1848. The diet did not meet, and they found the national and liberal character of the Czech movement uncongenial. In Moravia and Silesia the aristocracy, however, continued to dominate local politics through diets, reorganized to admit town and village representatives. The degree of Czech national consciousness was still much lower in Moravia than in Bohemia, and the Czech representatives in the Moravian diet, led by Alois Pražák (1820–1901), acquiesced in the provincial separatism of the nobility, opposing closer ties with other Bohemian Lands.

The Bohemian Germans soon turned from benevolence concerning Czech national aspirations to decisive opposition, when the Czechs rejected the idea of a unified Germany including Bohemia. This rejection was proclaimed in Palacký's famous letter of April 11, 1848, to Frankfurt denouncing Czech participation in the provisional Frankfurt assembly (*Vorparlament*), and then confirmed by Czech boycott of the elections to the Constituent Assembly in Frankfurt. The differences sharpened, and by August a German congress in Teplice (Teplitz) raised for the first time the ill-fated demand to partition Bohemia into Czech and German sections.

Opposed to the inclusion of the Bohemian Lands in a general German confederation, the Czech leaders adhered to the idea of Austroslavism, pledged to preserve a fully independent Habsburg empire, which would be reformed to assure free development of its diverse, especially Slavic, nationalities. A Slav Congress was convened in Prague on June 2 to support the Austroslav program, but it was disrupted on June 12 by the Pentecostal Uprising, led by Czech radicals under Josef V. Frič and abetted by Mikhail Bakunin, a Russian émigré participant in the Congress.

Although opposed by the principal Czech leaders and easily suppressed after five days by the imperial garrison, the riots prompted Vienna to scrap the plans for a legislative diet and responsible government in Bohemia, which the National Committee had prepared. With the main concession of the Rescript of April 8 abrogated, language rights represented the chief gain from this document. Czech was now used widely in Bohemia by governmental agencies not only in contacts with external parties but to some extent in internal operations as well. Czech as the official language advanced somewhat even in Moravia. After bilateral arrangements with Vienna had failed to secure autonomy and self-government, Czech politicians had to shift their efforts to the multilateral framework of the forthcoming *Reichstag*.

Despite promises in the Rescript of April 8, the Viennese government continued to treat the Bohemian Lands as an integral part of the administrative structure composed of the non-Hungarian Lands. The traditional agencies of centralism, exclusive of Hungarian autonomous rights, remained, although their names were changed in March: the United Court Chancellery became the Ministry of the Interior, and the *Oberste Justizstelle* formed the basis of the Ministry of Justice. New ministries of education and commerce were added later in the year. After the recognition of a separate constitution for Hungary on April 10, 1848, a provisional centralist constitution was promulgated by Vienna for the other Lands, including the Bohemian ones, on April 25. It was, in turn, abrogated in late May, and the drafting of a constitution for the non-Hungarian Lands was assigned to the imperial parliament, the *Reichstag*.

Elected on the basis of virtually universal manhood suffrage, the *Reichstag* met in Vienna from July to October 1848, and reconvened in the Moravian Kroměříž (Kremsier) in November. The Bohemian Lands held 138 seats out of the total of 283. In addition to 22 Czechs from Moravia and one from Silesia, only a few as yet nationally committed, the *Reichstag* included 55 Czechs from Bohemia, who spearheaded the national cause. Most of the latter, accepting the lead of Palacký and his future son-in-law Rieger, were either moderate conservatives or moderate liberals. Few embraced the radical democratic orientation represented by Frič and Karel Sladkovský, who sympathized with the revolutionary sentiments of the Viennese radicals.

Palacký expressed the Czech aims on restructuring the empire in two consecutive proposals, neither of which adhered fully to the framework of Bohemia's historical rights, asserted in earlier programmatic statements. The first proposal, of September 1848, applied only to the non-Hungarian part of the empire, and envisaged broad autonomy for each of the Bohemian Lands, without, however, associating them constitutionally. The second proposal, advanced in January 1849, applied to the entire monarchy, and based its component units strictly on the ethnic principle. The Czech unit would exclude the German areas of the Bohemian Lands but receive as compensation the Slovak area of Hungary. The *Reichstag* majority, however, did not favor ethnicity as the basis for restructuring the empire beyond the circuit (*Kreis*) level. In any case, this assembly did not complete its work, although the draft of the constitution, which represented a genuine compromise with the national group outside of Hungary, was an outstanding achievement on the path to evolution of genuine representative government in the Habsburg empire.

After a premature dissolution of the *Reichstag* on March 7, 1849, by the arbitrary action of prime minister, Prince Felix Schwarzenberg, condoned by the new youthful emperor Francis Joseph (1848–1916), the Viennese government decreed the so-called Stadion Constitution, named after its author, the minister of the interior, Count Franz Stadion. Unlike the Kroměříž draft, it applied to the entire monarchy including Hungary and provided for an empire-wide *Reichstag* elected on the basis of restricted suffrage. Even this "decreed" constitution was never put into effect. Instead, a new era of absolutism began.

Neo-Absolutism, 1849–59

Czech conservatives, liberals, and radicals opposed the new absolutist regime. The radicals participated in an unsuccessful wide-ranging conspiracy, directed from Saxony in April and May 1849 by Bakunin, with the grandiose aim of ridding all of central Europe of reactionary regimes. Expression of opinion was gradually curtailed, with the last independent Czech newspaper suppressed in June 1851. By that time the liberal politicians had either retired from public life or left the country, and the radicals ended up in jail. The Bohemian Lands were once more governed bureaucratically. The central body of administration in each Land—even in Silesia, since 1849 administratively separated from Moravia—was the Lieutenancy (*Statthalterei, místodržitelství*), headed by a lieutenant (*Statthalter*). Administrative significance of the Lands greatly diminished, as most of the powers of the former *gubernia* were assigned to the newly created circuits or *kraje* (seven in Bohemia and two in Moravia), much larger than the pre-1848 *kraje*. The *kraj* governments were immediately subordinated to the Ministry of the Interior in Vienna.

Absolutism not only in fact but in name was also reinstituted by the New Year's Eve Patent of 1851, which formally invalidated the Stadion Constitution. After the death of Schwarzenberg in April 1852, Alexander Bach, minister of the interior, and a renegade from revolutionary radicalism, became the leader of the new absolutist regime. The sole nonbureaucratic elements within the governmental structures of the Bohemian Lands were the old Committees of the Land, which under the lieutenant's chairmanship perpetuated their earlier meager functions. Since the diets no longer met, the Committees until 1861 maintained their composition as of 1847 in Bohemia and Moravia, and as of 1848 in Silesia. The process of Germanization also resumed. In Bohemia an ordinance of 1852 excluded Czech as a language of internal transactions from government agencies. The same happened in Moravia without a formal decree. In Silesia in 1851 Czech, as well as Polish, was excluded even from official contact with outside parties, and government agencies became purely German. The realm of state bureaucracy advanced another basic step from the level of the *kraj* to encompass administrative and judicial functions previously performed by manors and towns.

This extension of the civil service network responded to the peasant emancipation from economic services to their landlords, and to the concomitant abolition of the seigneurial exercise of public functions. The basic law of emancipation passed the *Reichstag* on September 7, 1848, and was implemented in the Bohemian Lands by the imperial decree of March 4, 1849. The landlords received, over a twenty-year period, a compensation for two-thirds of the estimated value of the lost peasant services and dues, with the payments equally divided between the peasants and the governments of the Lands. The remaining third was deemed an equivalent of state taxes hitherto paid by the landlords on the value of peasant dues and services, and thus requiring no compensation. By March 1849 the seigneur's authority had been replaced in the villages by municipal self-government, functioning through the elder (*starosta*), a Municipal Committee (*obecní výbor*), and a narrower Municipal Council (*obecní rada*). Subsequently, Bach absolutism seriously limited the municipal self-government without entirely destroying it.

The replacement of seigneurial jurisdiction at the manorial level was more complicated. In 1848 in Bohemia alone there were 1,421 administrative patrimonial jurisdictions, as well as 868 patrimonial courts. The new administrative agencies began to operate in January 1850. They were called Captaincies (*hejtmanství*) and their territorial jurisdictions *okresy*. Headed by a captain (*hejtman*), they represented the lowest echelon of state bureaucracy in public administration. In Bohemia, 79 *okres* captaincies were created, in Moravia 25, and in Silesia 7. In Bohemia and Moravia, their supervisory agencies were the governments of the newly enlarged *kraje,* headed by presidents. In Silesia they were responsible to the Lieutenancy.

The replacement of patrimonial courts with state courts occurred in July 1851. Less serious civil and criminal offenses were tried by a single judge in the *okres* courts. The judicial *okresy* were smaller than the administrative ones: on the average the latter contained three to four of the former. In Bohemia, 220 judicial *okresy* were organized, in Moravia 80, and in Silesia 25. The *kraj* courts tried the more serious cases, and decisions were made by colleges of judges ("senates"). The judicial *kraje* largely coincided with the smaller pre-1850 administrative *kraje*. In Bohemia 13 were established, in Moravia 6, and in Silesia 2. Appeals from the *kraj* courts went to the Superior Courts of the Land (*vrchní zemský soud*). One for Bohemia was located in Prague, another for both Moravia and Silesia in Brno. The final appellate jurisdiction belonged to the Supreme Judicial and Cassation Court (*Oberster Gerichts- und Kassationshof*) in Vienna.

A major reorganization of governmental agencies took place in May 1855. The lowest echelons of public administration and judiciary were combined through the establishment in every judicial *okres* of Mixed District Offices (*smíšené okresní úřady*), which assumed the functions of both the *okres* captaincies and the *okres* courts. At the next higher level the number of administrative *kraje* increased and more or less corresponded to the old (pre-1850) administrative *kraje* and the new (post-1850) judicial ones.[1] The higher density of administrative agencies fa-

---

1. In Bohemia their number was raised from seven to thirteen, and in Moravia from two to six. Silesia still had none.

cilitated tighter controls and surveillance over the population. At the same time, the importance of the Lands increased in relation to the *kraje*. The Lieutenancies became the main administrative echelon between the *okresy* and the Ministry of the Interior in Vienna. Henceforth the *kraje* served mainly as channels for transmission of official business between the Lieutenancies and the *okresy*. In Silesia the Lieutenancy was renamed Government of the Land, and its chief was president of the Land (*Landespräsident*).

QUEST FOR AUTONOMY, 1860–78

The reintroduction of parliamentarianism in the Habsburg empire in the early 1860s enabled Czech political leaders—after a twelve-year hiatus—to press for national autonomy and self-government. Imitating the Magyars' tactics in neighboring Hungary, they focused for almost twenty years on a restoration of the ancient rights of the Bohemian Crown, securing a limited support of the Bohemian aristocracy. The tactics, which succeeded in Hungary, failed in Bohemia. In Hungary, not the aristocracy but the lower nobility (which the Czechs lacked) provided the main sociopolitical driving force for national autonomy. Unlike Hungary, the Bohemian Lands had the imperial bureaucracy, entrenched since Maria Theresa and perfected under the neo-absolutism of the 1850s, which could—in combination with the politically and socially advantaged German minority—neutralize efforts to paralyze the government's operations through passive opposition. As for external support, the Germans proved more interested and effective allies for the Magyars than the Russians or the French for the Czechs.

Nevertheless, in a less dramatic but more fundamental way the process of modern Czech nation building was advancing, greatly indebted to the liberal social and political reforms sponsored by the Viennese government at the onset of the constitutional era.

Constitutional Experimentation, 1860–65: From Federalism to Centralism

After the collapse of Bach absolutism in the summer of 1859, largely due to the Austrian defeat by France and Piedmont, Czech political leaders did not directly participate in the initial moves to restore a constitutional order. At the first stage, in the Enlarged (*Verstärkte*) *Reichsrat* of March-September 1860, the Bohemian Lands were represented by several nobles, led by Count Jindřich Clam-Martinic, who urged autonomy for the individual Lands based on their historical rights. The subsequent constitutional charter, the October Diploma of 1860, seemingly adopted this federalistic approach. While instituting a general legislature for the entire monarchy, the broader *Reichsrat*, as well as a special legislature for the combined non-Hungarian Lands, the narrower *Reichsrat*, the Diploma implied that most legislative power would be reserved for the diets of the individual Lands.

With the revival of political life in the Bohemian Lands, facilitated by the reemergence of a vigorous press, particularly the *Národní Listy*, the Czech leaders, headed once more by Palacký and Rieger, gravitated under the impact of the Diploma toward the program of historical rights partly abandoned in 1848–49 in favor of the ethnic criterion. Since it became clear that—unlike in 1848–49—the aristocracy would play a major role in the new representative organs, they also sought in January 1861 a rapprochement with the aristocratic autonomists around Clam-Martinic, even though the nobles' reservations toward Czech ethnic nationalism limited the area of consensus. Despite its plausibility, this alliance, destined to last off and on for thirty years, had serious disadvantages for the Czechs. It further alienated the German liberals, while it did not really please the emperor, Francis Joseph, who disapproved of the conservatives' claims for historical rights. Moreover, the "autonomists" constituted only one faction within the Bohemian and Moravian aristocracy; the other faction, the centralists or "constitutionalists," like the German minorities in Bohemia and Moravia, wished to perpetuate a unitary state merging the Bohemian with the Austrian Lands.

The actual implementation of the constitutional order by the February Patent of 1861 under Anton von Schmerling's ministry (December 1860 to June 1865) represented—from the Czech viewpoint—a disappointing shift from federalism to centralism. The Patent restricted the diets to such secondary areas as agriculture, public works, and social welfare, and, within the framework of imperial legislation, to municipal, educational, and religious affairs. It divided other matters between the broader and narrower *Reichsrat*, in both cases consisting of two chambers, the upper largely appointed by the emperor, the lower elected by the diets. Out of the total membership of 223 in the lower chamber of the narrower *Reichsrat*, and 343 in that of the broader *Reichsrat*, Bohemia was assigned 54, Moravia 22, and Silesia 6 deputies.

The diets in the Bohemian Lands were elected in March 1861. The Bohemian diet had 241 members, the Moravian 100, and the Silesian 31. Most deputies represented four electoral colleges or *curiae*: the nobles, the towns, the chambers of commerce, and the villages.[2] The franchise in towns and villages followed complicated rules, but in general those who paid at least ten florins of direct tax per year could vote. To administer the affairs within their jurisdiction, the diets elected Com-

---

2. In Bohemia the ratio of deputies representing the individual *curiae* was (nobles, towns, chambers of commerce, villages) 71:72:15:70; in Moravia 30:31:6:37; and in Silesia 9:10:2:9.

mittees of the Land, headed by the supreme marshal of the Land in Bohemia, and by a captain of the Land each in Moravia and Silesia.

Owing to the property-based franchise, the economically advantaged Germans, though a minority in both Bohemia and Moravia, equaled or outnumbered the Czechs among the diet deputies elected from the three lower *curiae*. The balance of power in the Bohemian and Moravian diets was held by the deputies of the nobles. The autonomists ordinarily allied with the Czechs, and the centralists with the Germans, and thus the prevalence of one of the noble factions determined the orientation of the entire diet. Lacking any aristocratic autonomists or—until the late 1860s—any Czechs, the Silesian diet was entirely dominated by the centralists.

A crucial development within the Czech political camp was the rapprochement between the Bohemian and Moravian Czechs. The Moravians' abandonment of separatism and endorsement of association with Bohemia at the 1861 diet were due largely to the leadership of Alois Pražák, who had come to admire both Palacký and Rieger in 1848 at the *Reichstag* in Kroměřiiž. In general, the fusion of Czech nationalism in Bohemia and Moravia was fully consummated in the 1860s. Among the Bohemian Czechs, tensions developed between the more conservative leaders and the more liberal group, stemming partly from the radicals of 1848 and including Karel Sladkovský and the brothers Julius and Eduard Grégr. A persistent issue between the two factions, called the Old Czechs and Young Czechs, was the degree of political cooperation with the Bohemian aristocracy. Moreover, an open conflict broke out over the Polish uprising of 1863 in tsarist Russia. While the Young Czechs favored the Polish insurgents, Palacký and Rieger deplored the struggle as detrimental to Slav interests.

In both the Bohemian and Moravian diets the Czechs with the noble autonomists constituted minorities until 1865. Their one significant success was in Bohemia, where, with the support of both noble factions (the centralists as well as the autonomists), they gained an increase in the number of Czech academic high schools (*gymnasia*). Efforts to ensure a more equitable Czech representation in the diet, by lowering the tax requirement for voting, were not supported even by the autonomist nobility.

After initial hesitation, the Bohemian Czechs, urged on by the noble autonomists, decided to focus their struggle for national autonomy on the Viennese *Reichsrat* and, following the example of the Moravian Czechs, participated in the election of *Reichsrat* deputies by the diet in April 1861. Twenty Czech deputies were elected in Bohemia and only four in Moravia. Within the *Reichsrat* the Czechs wished to forge a coalition of federalists, mainly the Austrian Slavs, for a drive to revise the February Patent in the spirit of the October Diploma. Failing to rally an effective opposition to Schmerling's centralist government, the Bohemian Czechs decided in 1863 to imitate the Magyars and boycott the *Reichsrat.* The Moravian Czechs left the Viennese legislature a year later. After the setback for national decentralization at the *Reichsrat,* Palacký restated in 1865, in his *Idea of the Austrian State,* the Austroslav position of 1848, but with much less optimism. He predicted that the empire would lose its reason for existence if it either perpetuated the current unitary centralism or instituted a dualist one accommodating the Magyars, while neglecting the national aspirations of the Slavs.

Constitutional Experimentation, 1865–67: From Federalism to Dualism

Count Richard Belcredi's ministry (July 1865 to February 1867), accompanied by a suspension of the February Patent in September 1865, initially appeared as a turn toward an empire-wide federalism. There were other signs favorable to the Czech position. Through by-elections in the *curia* of the nobility, the Bohemian diet acquired for the first time an autonomist majority in late 1865, and in the Moravian diet the autonomists fell only three votes short of a majority. During 1866 Belcredi's government, moreover, enforced the use of Czech by courts and administrative agencies in external contacts with private parties in both Bohemia and Moravia.

The impact of foreign affairs terminated the federalist interlude. The Austrian defeat by Prussia in the summer of 1866 and the ensuing Compromise of May 1867 with Hungary introduced the dualist centralism against which Palacký had warned so sternly. As a result, the non-Hungarian Lands in 1867 acquired separate constitutional laws (*Staatsgrundgesetze*), the so-called December Constitution, which in essence retained the narrower *Reichsrat* and the diets of the February Patent. The Bohemian Lands thus remained part of a centralized political entity henceforth called officially "Kingdoms and Lands represented in the *Reichsrat,*" and unofficially Cisleithania, or simply Austria. Retaining their quotas of deputies in the *Reichsrat,* Bohemia also received ten seats, Moravia four, and Silesia one, in the Cisleithanian Delegation of sixty, which was to meet annually with its Hungarian counterpart to pass on the entire monarchy's foreign policy, military affairs, and related financial matters. One positive aspect of the laws forming the December Constitution was—in the eyes of the Czechs—a comprehensive bill of rights, above all a guarantee of equal rights of languages "customary" in a given Land in schools and government agencies.

The adoption of the new constitution also approximately marked the time by which the public administration and judiciary, inherited from the period of Bach absolutism, were reformed to correspond with the spirit of the new era of mild liberalism. The reorganization signified a decisive victory of the Lands as units of public administration. The administrative *kraje* were abolished in Moravia in 1860 and in Bohemia in 1862, and their functions reassigned to the Lieutenancies and the Mixed District Offices. In a final separation of administration from the judiciary at the lowest echelon in 1868, the Mixed District Offices were abolished, and the *okres* courts and *okres* captaincies restored in approximately the same form in which they had existed in 1850–55. Thus each administrative *okres* contained more than one judicial *okres*. The *kraj* courts and the judicial *kraje* remained, as an intermediate echelon between the *okres* courts and the Superior Courts in Prague and Brno. The right to trial by jury in serious criminal cases was granted in 1867.

Local self-government also expanded under the official liberalism of the 1860s. Towns and villages regained their municipal autonomy in 1863–64. Mayors and councils were elected by municipal committees, which in turn were chosen by voters divided into three classes according to the size of their tax payments. The Committees of the Land, the executive arms of the diets, directly supervised the municipal governments in Moravia and in Silesia. In Bohemia another stratum of institutions, the *okres* representations (*zastupitelství*), was interposed between the municipalities and the Committee of the Land. Created in 1864, the representations were elected by four classes of voters, analogous to those choosing the four *curiae* in the diet, and in turn selected an executive organ, a six-member committee headed by the elder (*starosta*). Their territorial jurisdictions coincided with the judicial *okresy*. Aside from supervising municipal governments, the *okres* representation dealt chiefly with public works and the institutions of public health and social welfare. The organs of self-government (municipalities, *okres* representations, and Committees of the Land) operated independently of the agencies of state administration (*okres* captaincies, and Lieutenancies) in a peculiar system of administrative dualism, comparable to that between the *zemstva* and the *gubernii* in the contemporary Russian Empire.

Failure of Trialism, 1867–71: The Fundamental Articles

Despite undeniably liberal features of the December Constitution and the concomitant reforms, Czech political leaders reacted bitterly to the Compromise of 1867. They saw their quest for national autonomy persistently ignored despite their loyalty to the dynasty, demonstrated both in 1848 and, more recently, in 1866 during the Prussian occupation of Prague, when they rejected Prussia's overtures transmitted by the radical émigré Josef V. Frič. Abhorring the dualist centralism, they intensified the campaign for national self-government. Following the earlier example of the Magyars, they had embarked as early as April 1867 on a boycott of the diets and the *Reichsrat,* and, in alliance with the autonomist aristocracy, based their claims for autonomy strictly on the historical rights (*státní právo*) of the Bohemian Crown. In substance the goal was a constitutional status equal to that of Hungary, which would transform the Habsburg monarchy from a dualist into a "trialist" state. The Czech desiderata reached the strongest expression in the Bohemian Declaration, adopted in August 1868 by Czech deputies from both the Bohemian and the Moravian diets. It demanded negotiations between the emperor-king and the nation to restore the traditional rights of the Bohemian Crown.

The Declaration evoked a vigorous response from the Czech population, expressed especially in widespread outdoor mass rallies (*tábory*), reminiscent of O'Connell's "monster meetings" in Ireland in the 1840s. Mobilization of the masses behind the national program strikingly revealed the effect of the recent liberal reforms. The degree of national consciousness was clearly heightened by the proliferation of newspapers and journals, by the spread of patriotic societies such as the *Sokol* gymnastic organizations, and by the expansion of educational facilities. The Czech national movement had clearly reached a mature stage by the late 1860s.

Again following the earlier example of the Magyars, Czech leaders sought foreign support for their cause. As early as the spring of 1867 they journeyed demonstratively to St. Petersburg and Moscow on the occasion of an ethnographic exhibit. The visit reflected the growing Russophilism among the Old Czechs, especially Palacký himself, as well as a disillusionment with the Poles on the part of the Young Czechs, who resented the Galician deputies' support for the Compromise of 1867 in the *Reichsrat*.[3] In another initiative in 1869, Rieger submitted a memorandum to Napoleon III, arguing that France would benefit from a more influential position of the Slavs in the Habsburg empire, which under German and Magyar domination inevitably gravitated toward Prussia. In the same vein, in December 1870, Czech diet deputies expressed sympathy for both France and Russia in the *promemoria,* presented to Chancellor Count Friedrich Beust, which condemned Germany's annexation of Alsace-Lorraine and defended Russia's right to remilitarize her Black Sea coast. Since the Cisleithanian and Hungarian delegations in January 1871 voted for rapprochement with Imperial Germany, Czech views clashed with the official foreign policy of the Habsburg monarchy.

After the Czechs had rejected as inadequate offers of minor concessions within the framework of the December Constitution by Prime Minister Count Alfred Potocki in late 1870, the Czech aspirations for autonomy of the Bohemian Crown came close to fulfillment in the fol-

3. Despite their disappointment with the politics of the Poles of Galicia, the Czech delegates did raise in Moscow the highly sensitive issue of national rights for the Russian Poles, risking the displeasure of their Russian hosts.

lowing year. An attempt to reconcile the Czechs was made in the summer and fall of 1871 by the cabinet of Count Karl Hohenwart, which, as a good-will gesture, included two imperial bureaucrats of Czech background, Karel Hrabietinek and Josef Jireček. Conducted by a progressive cabinet member from South Germany, Minister of Commerce Albert Schäffle on behalf of the government, and by Rieger, Pražák, and Clam-Martinic for the Czechs and Bohemian autonomist aristocrats, the principal negotiations resulted in the draft of eighteen Fundamental Articles.

Although they recognized certain common affairs of the non-Hungarian Lands, thus retreating partially from the Bohemian Declaration of 1868, the Articles on the whole would have greatly strengthened Czech historic rights in proposing a special bond joining the three Bohemian Lands through a general diet. They were to entrust to each Land the conduct of public administration, judiciary, and education, as well as direct taxation. A Congress of Delegates was to replace the *Reichsrat* and legislate concerning the reduced agenda of common Cisleithanian affairs (commerce, industry, and communications), as well as apportion common expenses among the individual Lands. The Austrian cabinet was to include, in addition to the heads of functional ministries, the chief executives of the Lands. Among the latter the Bohemian Court chancellor (presumably Rieger) would head the governments in the three Bohemian Lands.

The proposed settlement with the Czechs inevitably aroused formidable opposition. The leading Hungarian statesmen, Francis Deák, and the prime minister, Gyula Andrássy, considered it a violation of the Compromise of 1867. Chancellor Beust in a lengthy attack reminded the emperor, among other things, of the unorthodox Czech views on foreign policy. Even the German Emperor William I warned Francis Joseph that the Bohemian Germans might turn to Berlin for support if the Bohemian settlement was implemented. Finally, determined opposition in the Crown Council meeting of October 20, 1871, definitely persuaded Francis Joseph to abandon the project. The main significance of the "trialist" episode of 1871 was a reminder to the Germans and the Magyars that loyalty to the dynasty was the price for the dualist system that assured a Magyar and (more limited) German hegemony within the monarchy. Thus the net result was to strengthen the status quo.[4]

Passive Opposition, 1872–78

The failure of the Fundamental Articles to secure adoption led the Czech political leaders in 1872 to renew their boycott of the Bohemian

---

4. See also pp. 353–54.

and Moravian diets. The stanchest support for the policy of abstention came from the Bohemian Old Czechs and their allies in the autonomist nobility. Palacký, in his last political testament of 1872, saw in the failure of Hohenwart's federalist reform a definite confirmation of the nonviability of the Habsburg empire. For the long run he put his faith into the rising power of Russia. Even for the present, he felt that the Russian government had a moral obligation to sustain the Czechs, since the antipathy of the Germans and the Magyars to them ultimately stemmed from their ethnic kinship with the Russians.

Rieger, by now the undisputed leader of the Old Czechs, was in fact confirmed in the stance of uncompromising opposition by the rising turmoil in the Balkans and Russia's involvement there after 1875. He hoped that the impact of external events might lead to yet another restructuring of the Austrian empire, which Russia might influence—inspired by Slavic solidarity—in favor of the Czechs. To attract Russia's benevolence, the Old Czechs sponsored and otherwise supported expressions of enthusiasm for Russian victories in the Turkish war of 1877–78, including religious services of thanksgiving and congratulatory messages to the Panslav journalist Ivan Aksakov and the chancellor, Prince Alexander Gorchakov. In March 1878 Rieger requested the Russian ambassador in Vienna, Count Nikolai Ignat'ev, to intercede with the Austrian government for Czech autonomy. Ignat'ev's apparent indifference, combined with Russia's containment in the Balkans, at last convinced Rieger to abandon hopes for Czech autonomy through Russian intervention.

In the meantime, the policy of abstention had suffered major attritions in any case. The Moravian Czechs had reentered the diet in November 1873, and the *Reichsrat* the following January. The Bohemian Young Czechs broke with the Old Czechs over the parliamentary boycott in September 1874, and in December organized an independent party, the National Liberal Party, leaving to the Old Czechs the previous common designation, the National Party. In the fall of 1878, even the Old Czechs abandoned the boycott and entered the Bohemian diet, forming there a joint club with the Young Czechs under an agreement between Rieger and Sladkovský.

QUEST FOR LANGUAGE RIGHTS, 1879–1914

Beginning in 1879 Czech leaders shifted the focus of national policy from immediate restoration of national autonomy and self-government. In addition to the failure of passive resistance and boycotting the organs of state authority, the chances of a drastic reorganization of the empire had greatly diminished owing to other stabilizing developments.

The Compromise of 1867 with the Magyars, and the quasi compromise with the Galician Poles in 1871, stabilized the monarchy internally, as the alliance with the new German Empire, consummated in 1879, consolidated its position externally.

Until World War I, the immediate goal of Czech policy, persisting despite changes in party leadership and structure, was to strengthen social solidarity through economic and cultural development, as well as to advance national integration through expanding public use of the Czech language. Instead of uncompromising opposition to governments of the unitary Cisleithania, the new approach called for trading parliamentary support for piecemeal concessions, especially in the language area.

National self-government, however, remained the ultimate objective, and the historical claims of the Bohemian Crown to an autonomous statehood were restated by Czech deputies at the opening of every *Reichsrat*.

Old Czech Leadership, 1879–90

The government of Count Eduard Taaffe (1879–93) facilitated the new departure. The premier sought a *Reichsrat* coalition independent of the German liberals, the mainstays of Cisleithanian centralism, who had dominated the Austrian cabinets for most of the 1870s, mainly under the prime minister, Count Adolf Auersperg (1871–79). In September 1879 the Old and Young Czechs of Bohemia entered the *Reichsrat*, as part of the basically pro-Slav conservative government coalition, and formed a Czech club jointly with the Moravian Czechs and the autonomist nobles from Bohemia and Moravia. Pražák served in the cabinet, first without portfolio, and from 1881 as administrator of the Ministry of Justice.

The Czechs won safeguards in the area of language use. The Stremayr Ordinance of 1880 (by the then minister of justice, Karl von Stremayr) restated the traditional principle of external use of Czech by the judiciary and public administration in Bohemia and Moravia. Moreover, the Pražák Ordinance of 1886 for the first time sanctioned Czech as an internal official language, though only in the processing of Czech cases at the superior courts in Prague and Brno. A more limited measure, the Pražák Ordinance of 1882, applicable to Silesia, had admitted Czech and Polish as external languages in courts of certain *okresy*. Concessions in the area of education were crowned by the emergence of a purely Czech university in 1881–82, when the University of Prague, the oldest in Central Europe (established in 1348), was divided into Czech and German institutions. Czech *gymnasia* increased in number in Bohemia and Moravia, and the first one was founded in 1883 in Silesia.

Among the major gains early in the Taaffe era was an increase in Czech political influence with the substantial lowering of franchise requirements. In 1882 the electoral rules for the *Reichsrat* became distinct from those for the diets,[5] and the right to vote in the *curiae* of towns and villages was given to the five-florin taxpayers. A similar reform applied to the Bohemian diet in 1885 assured a permanent Czech and autonomist majority, and led to a German boycott of the diet from 1887.

Nevertheless, as the 1880s progressed, the Czech club coalition was disintegrating. The Young Czechs felt that their dominant partners, the Old Czechs, paid a price to the government and the rest of the imperial establishment not commensurate with the concessions obtained. A prime example was Rieger's deference to the Magyar statesmen, inspired by the memory of their role in the demise of the Fundamental Articles. To guard against their interference with Vienna's newly benevolent attitude toward the Czechs, Rieger hastened in 1880 to assure Premier Kálmán Tisza and his entourage that the Czechs would not publically criticize the treatment of Slav minorities in Hungary. When in 1884 the Young Czechs feted in Prague the prominent Slovak, Samo Tomášik, Rieger apologized to Budapest. Similarly, in deference to the emperor, the Magyars, and even the Poles, the Old Czechs felt it was prudent not to criticize the Austro-German alliance, or to express pro-Russian or pro-French sentiments.

The Young Czechs' dissatisfaction mounted after 1886, when further expansion of Czech in the state apparatus and in secondary education was halted. In relative terms, however, progress was substantial. The preliminary and provisional separation of Czech and German boards of education was made permanent by 1890. Separate agricultural advisory boards were likewise established, and the appearance of a Czech university in 1882 could be considered a major breakthrough. Spurred on by success, seven Young Czech deputies, led by Eduard Grégr and Josef Herold, formally broke with the Old Czechs at a party congress in 1887, and accordingly seceded from the Czech club in the *Reichsrat*. Unrestrained by coalition loyalties, they felt free to criticize the government. Not excluding the sensitive foreign policy, they attacked the German alliance and advocated rapprochement with France and Russia to counteract German power. The Young Czechs' fighting stance appealed to voters, particularly those newly enfranchised, and launched them on the road to national leadership. In five *Reichsrat* by-elections they won four seats, and in the summer of 1889 almost quadrupled their representation in the Bohemian diet, winning 39 to the Old Czechs' 58 seats.

The decline of the Old Czechs turned into a debacle over an agree-

5. The election of the *Reichsrat* deputies already has been transferred from the diets directly to the voters in 1873.

ment (*punktace*) with the Bohemian Germans, negotiated by them in Vienna in January 1890 under pressure from Taaffe, who wished to end the German boycott of the Bohemian diet. *Punktace* appeared as a move to split Bohemia into a German zone, from which official use of Czech would be virtually excluded, and a Czech zone in which Czech would be admissible in external use but German would remain the internal language of state bureaucracy. In the spring of 1890 the Young Czechs fought vigorously at the Bohemian diet against the adoption of the agreement. Their campaign had an electrifying effect on Czech public opinion. Sensing disaster, Rieger implored Vienna to help the Old Czechs by sanctioning Czech as an internal official language in the Czech zone. Taaffe, however, remained passive, considering the situation of Rieger's party beyond repair.

Young Czech Leadership, 1890–1906

The consistently liberal and nationalist Young Czechs assumed political leadership as a result of the *Reichsrat* elections in March 1891, when they won in Bohemia thirty-seven seats compared with the Old Czechs' two mandates. Only in Moravia, where the Young Czechs' anticlericalism cost them popularity, did the Old Czechs for the time being retain their ten seats. In their moment of triumph the Young Czechs benefited from an accession of the dynamic Realist group, led by the influential university professor Thomas G. Masaryk (1850–1937). Although the independent-minded Masaryk was to leave the party soon, two of his colleagues, Josef Kaizl (1854–1901) and Karel Kramář (1860–1937), provided new leadership for the Young Czechs within a decade, superseding the aging Eduard and Julius Grégr.

After their victory, the Young Czechs initially persisted in their opposition to the government in the *Reichsrat*. In the Delegations in 1892 and 1893 their attacks on the German alliance caused particular consternation. In the Bohemian diet they concentrated on preventing an adoption of the *punktace* agreement. Political excitement in Bohemia characterized the period of Young Czech opposition. Arrival of foreign delegations to the Jubilee Industrial Exposition of 1891 created occasions for expression of pro-French and pro-Russian sentiments. Subsequently, youthful radicals of the *Omladina* group organized political demonstrations accompanied by defacement of symbols of imperial authority and circulation of leaflets insulting Francis Joseph. The government responded in 1892 by imposing martial law in Prague, and by jailing the *Omladina* leaders, including Alois Rašín.

After six years in opposition the Young Czechs resumed the policy of trading parliamentary support for national concessions. In 1897 Premier Count Kazimir Badeni (1895–97), formerly lieutenant in Galicia, promised them what Taaffe had denied the Old Czechs: the internal use of Czech by state bureaucracy. In April the Badeni Ordinances for Bohemia and Moravia stipulated that government agencies, under the jurisdiction of the Interior, Justice, Finance, Commerce, and Agriculture ministries, would process entirely in Czech the cases initiated in that language. Hence officials in such agencies would have to be proficient in Czech as well as German within four years. Inasmuch as practically all educated Czechs knew German but relatively few Germans knew Czech and perhaps even fewer wanted to learn it, this measure obviously would have worked to the Germans' disadvantage.

When violent German opposition and disorders spilled from the *Reichsrat* into the streets of Vienna, the emperor dismissed Badeni. An interim prime minister, Baron Paul Gautsch, attempted appeasement by new ordinances, in February 1898, which eliminated the requirement of bilingualism for officials. Otherwise the provisions of Badeni's ordinances were followed in Moravia and in the nationally mixed zone in Bohemia. In the Czech and German zones in Bohemia, however, the internal processing of cases was to be respectively in Czech or German regardless of the language in which a case was initiated. The first phase of the Young Czechs' opportunistic policy reached its peak of success under the cabinet of Count Francis Thun (March 1898 to September 1899), in which Kaizl served as finance minister. Within the limits of the Gautsch Ordinances, Czech in fact began to be introduced as the internal official language—that is, the language used by government agencies in administrative matters not to be communicated to the parties involved.

In response to renewed German protests and obstruction in the *Reichsrat,* another interim government was appointed under Count Manfred Clary-Aldringen, which repealed the Gautsch Ordinances in October 1899. It proceeded to reintroduce German despite the Young Czechs' pleas that Czech could be retained as the official internal language, without any legislation or administrative decrees, simply on the basis of the 1867 constitution and its guarantees of language rights. In the end, however, Czech was tolerated as the internal language of bureaucracy in some localities, including the town of Plzeň.

Electoral reforms and the ensuing democratization of political life foreshadowed a decline of the Young Czechs' hegemony. Just as the reforms of the mid-1880s enfranchising the lower middle classes favored the Young Czech ascendancy, so the spread of franchise among the urban and rural lower classes, starting in the mid-1890s, would diminish their political power. The electoral reform of 1896 lowered the tax requirement to four florins for voting for the *Reichsrat* in the *curiae* of towns and villages. Moreover, a newly created fifth *curia* (represented by twenty-seven deputies in the Bohemian Lands) extended the suffrage to those not entitled to vote in the other *curiae.* In 1901 the tax requirement for voting for the Bohemian diet was likewise lowered to four florins in the *curiae* of towns and villages.

New political parties could appeal to the social interests of the lower classes. Above all, the Social Democrats now acquired political weight. The Czech faction within the Austrian Social Democratic Party gained an autonomous status in 1896, and its executive committee moved from Vienna to Prague in 1900. Factions representing workers and peasants within the Young Czech party established their independence respectively in 1898 as the National Socialists under Václav Klofáč (1868–1942) and in 1899 as the Agrarians under the youthful Antonín Švehla (1873– 1933).

Other parties responded to more particular interests. Catholic party organizations sprang up by the mid-1890s, especially in Moravia, providing a haven for clerical elements from the crippled Old Czechs. The socially progressive and liberal Realists maintained their independence from 1900 under the leadership of Masaryk, whose extraordinary political mission lay in the future. Stemming from the *Omladina,* the Radicals revived the claims for immediate national self-government, which had dominated Czech politics in the 1860s and 1870s.

Despite their divergencies on social and other issues, the Czech political parties formed, in June 1900, a standing consultative National Council in Prague to coordinate policies on common national interests. Moreover, the Young Czechs maintained their preponderance into the opening years of the twentieth century. While in the 1897 *Reichsrat* elections they won 63 seats (the Catholics 1, and the Social Democrats 5), in 1901 they still captured 53 mandates compared with 13 for the other Czech parties (Agrarians 5, National Socialists 4, Catholics 2, and Social Democrats 2).

During the last phase of their dominance, the Young Czechs maintained a highly ambiguous relationship with the ministry of Ernst von Koerber (January 1900 to December 1904). The cabinet included successively two Young Czechs, first Antonín Rezek, then in 1904 Antonín Randa, who as Czech ministers-countrymen (*Landsmannschaftsminister, ministr krajan*) served as intermediaries between the premier and Czech politicians. The Young Czech party itself was committed to nonviolent obstruction in the *Reichsrat* in protest against the revocation of the Gautsch Ordinances.

A minority of Young Czechs, including Eduard Grégr and Josef Fořt, urged the use of obstruction in an uncompromising way in order to force constitutional change to federalism in Cisleithania. Led by Kaizl, and after his death in 1901 by Kramář, the majority favored the established policy of extracting specific concessions from the government and was willing, in exchange, to suspend obstruction periodically. On this basis, it gained appropriations for regulation of Bohemian rivers and for urban renewal in Prague in line with Koerber's policy of empire-wide economic development. Cultural gains included an art gallery in Prague and the first Czech pedagogical institute in Silesia. The issue of a second Czech university (for Brno) was raised, but not resolved. Koerber made the satisfaction of the main desideratum—Czech as the internal language of government agencies—dependent on a prior reconciliation of Czechs and Germans in Bohemia and Moravia. Negotiations for that purpose failed in 1900, and again in 1903, over the issue of ethnically delimited administrative *kraje*. Koerber's endeavors to achieve a comprehensive Czech-German compromise in the language question and in regard to dietal representation were, of course, not successful either.

During the ministry of Gautsch (January 1905 to April 1906), which retained Randa as the minister-countryman, the Young Czechs changed from obstruction to simple opposition in the *Reichsrat* in return for a commitment that Czech, as internal language of state bureaucracy, would be introduced into Czech areas *via facti* (that is in circumvention of the politically sensitive formal legislation or ministerial ordinances). In addition, individual Czechs received senior posts in the imperial ministries and courts in Vienna. Although the issues of administrative jurisdictions and language use in provincial organs remained unsettled in Bohemia, Czech and German politicians concluded a limited agreement in Moravia, where the nationality conflict was less intense. The Moravian Compromise of 1905 reformed the diet on the basis of national *curiae*, assuring a Czech majority while granting the Germans veto power in certain areas. It also regulated the official language of municipalities.

Multiparty Representation, 1907–14

The Young Czech dominance in Czech politics ended with the full enfranchisement of the workers and peasantry. Under the ministry of Baron Max Beck (June 1906 to November 1908), the laws governing the *Reichsrat* elections, adopted in January 1907, replaced the system of *curiae* by general and equal manhood suffrage. Out of 513 deputies, Bohemia was assigned 130, Moravia 49, and Silesia 15. The Czech districts in the three Lands were allotted 108 seats. The elections of May 1907 reflected the new social distribution of electoral strength. Twenty-six Young Czechs were chosen, compared with 28 Agrarians, 24 Social Democrats, 17 Catholics, 9 National Socialists, 2 Realists, and 2 Independents. The redistribution of electoral power was further refined in the next *Reichsrat* election of 1911. Young Czechs won only 19 seats, while the Agrarians obtained 36 mandates, Social Democrats 26, National Socialists 16, Catholics 7, Realists 1, and Radicals 1.

Despite the proliferation of parties, Czech politics exhibited an essential continuity with the period of Young Czech dominance. At the openings of the *Reichsrat,* the Czech deputies, except the Social Democrats, repeated the traditional protest against Cisleithanian centralism as a denial of the historic rights of Bohemian statehood. But even the Social Democrats joined the other parties in the assertion of Czech language rights. The issue of Czech national interests produced a split in the party into the "autonomist" majority and the "centralist" minority. The majority entirely separated in 1911 from the central Austrian party in Vienna, which in its opinion toed the German line. The centralists received minor support in Moravia and Silesia, and elected one *Reichsrat* deputy in 1911.

The Czech parties, in particular the Agrarians, the Young Czechs, and the Catholics, tended to coordinate their policies in the *Reichsrat* and continued the tactics of trading political support for national concessions, including equalization of Czech with German in parliamentary proceedings in 1907. Within the *Reichsrat* the Czechs also sought cooperation with other Slavs. Thus in 1909–10 the nonsocialist Czech and South Slav parties formed a parliamentary coalition, the Slav Union, but the Polish and Ruthenian deputies did not participate. The main desideratum of Czech national policy, a full-fledged Czechization of state bureaucracy in Czech areas, as well as the demand for a Czech university in Moravia, remained unfulfilled. The lack of progress on national issues led to a general parliamentary opposition of Czech parties by 1913, with the Agrarians and the National Socialists reviving the tactics of obstruction. The customary two Czech ministers in the Cisleithanian cabinets between 1907 and 1914 were either nonpolitical bureaucrats or, if political figures, did not officially represent their parties.

Concerned with the national conflict in Bohemia (unresolved since the *punktace* of 1890), Prime Minister Count Richard Bienerth (appointed in November 1908) and his successor Count Karl Stürgkh (since June 1911) pressed for a settlement by an agreement between the Czechs and Germans. Negotiations failed repeatedly in 1909–10 and 1913. The basic German demand for strictly delineated German circuits (*kraje*) was viewed as a step toward the denationalization of Czech minorities. Czech apprehensions in that regard were strengthened in 1909 when the diet of Lower Austria voted to exclude Czech from schools and municipal governments. After the failure of negotiations, German obstruction in the Bohemian diet led to a suspension of the provincial organs. The diet was dissolved in July 1913, and the Committee of the Land was replaced by a bureaucratic commission.

In the increasingly critical area of foreign policy the Czech parties overtly perpetuated the position established in the period of Young Czech dominance. Abandoning the radical opposition for an opportunistic policy in 1896, the Young Czechs tempered their demands for an outright abrogation of the Austro-German alliance. Instead, they pleaded against exclusive dependence on Germany and for improved relations with Russia and France. After 1907 the Young Czechs shared with other parties representation in the Delegations dealing with the imperial foreign policy. Masaryk and Klofáč, next to Kramář, emerged as prominent Czech spokesmen in this forum.

The Russian Revolution of 1905 intensified the traditional Czech pro-Slav sympathies. Russia appeared more attractive as it seemingly shed its anachronistic autocracy, and Czech politicians proceeded to foster closer relations between Austrian and outside Slavs. This ideological and political trend of neo-Slavism led to Slav congresses in Prague in 1908 and in Sofia two years later. As the official Austrian policy moved in an opposite direction to the neo-Slav aspirations, toward sharpened hostility with Russia, especially by 1913, Kramář and Klofáč discreetly approached Russian officials, including Foreign Minister Sergei Sazonov, with assurances of Czech sympathies and inquiries about Russia's attitude toward the Czechs in case of a major European war.

AGRICULTURE, INDUSTRY, AND FINANCE[6]

Agricultural Prosperity, Depression, and Recovery

The agricultural prosperity in the Bohemian Lands, originating in the 1840s, continued into the 1870s in response to the needs of a growing industrial population, which before the full development of railroad networks was satisfied mostly from domestic production. Increases in production, especially of the marketable portion, came through technological improvements such as the introduction of machinery, fertilizers, and grain feeds. These were usually pioneered on the large estates, which still comprised one-third of the land and benefited considerably from the capital obtained in compensation for the loss of peasant services in 1848. A measure of these improvements was the increase in labor productivity. Between 1848 and 1900 the production of grain per agricultural inhabitant doubled, and that of meat and milk almost quadrupled. Market demands determined shifts in production.

6. Economic data in this section are derived from Václav Průcha, *Hospodářské dějiny Československa v 19. a 20. století* (Prague: Svoboda, 1974), pp. 38–57, Otakar Mrázek, *Vývoj průmyslu v českých zemích a na Slovensku od manufaktury do roku 1918* (Prague: Nakl. politické literatury, 1964), pp. 224–67, 314–410; *Přehled československých dějin* (Prague: Československá akademie věd, 1960), 2:318–23, 496, 827; Richard L. Rudolph, *Banking and Industrialization in Austria-Hungary: The Role of Banks in the Industrialization of the Czech Crownlands, 1873–1914* (Cambridge: Cambridge University Press, 1976), pp. 122–55; *Die Habsburgermonarchie, 1848–1918* (Vienna: Österreichische Akademie der Wissenschaften, 1973), 1:415–7.

For example, flax was increasingly replaced by sugar beets in the lowlands and by potatoes elsewhere.

The fragmentation of peasant holdings increased after 1868, when division of homesteads was permitted. Surveys taken in 1896 and 1902 showed that almost 80 percent of peasant homesteads in the Bohemian Lands contained less than 5 hectares of land, and altogether held only 13 percent of the total amount of agricultural land. A marked differentiation developed between the richer peasants, whose income permitted use of advanced implements and techniques, and the poorer ones, who had to rely on intensification of their own labor, or had to supplement their income by outside employment. Unlike marginal crafts, the marginal homesteads tended to survive. At the other end of the spectrum, except for some magnates in Hungary, the aristocracy in Bohemia and Moravia such as the Schwarzenbergs, Lobkowitzes, and Liechtensteins, enjoyed the largest land holdings in the empire.

An extended agricultural depression began in the 1870s, triggered by the industrial crisis of 1873, and greatly worsened after 1878 by large-scale importation of Russian and overseas grain. In the mid-1880s the crisis affected sugar beet production, and the low point was reached in 1894–95. The prices of wheat and of rye declined respectively to 66 and 75 percent of the predepression level (1871–75), while the price of barley—retaining its high reputation in beer brewing—fell only to 82 percent. The slump led to further shifts in production, above all to increased cultivation of potatoes, barley, and hops, and to an emphasis on livestock raising, which was less severely affected by the crisis.

A rise in agricultural prices terminated the depression in the late 1890s and prosperity followed in 1904–11, assisted by the establishment of soaring protective tariffs in 1906. An incentive was provided for further intensification of agricultural production through use of machinery and mechanical propulsion, expanded use of artificial fertilizers, and the introduction of selective breeding. Besides the large estates, the richer peasants and to some extent the smallholders shared these advances.

The spread of cooperatives of various types significantly facilitated increases in agricultural production among the peasants toward the end of the century. Some were devoted to purchasing, sales, and warehousing, others to processing of agricultural products—giving rise to such local enterprises as dairies, bakeries, distilleries, and flour mills. Credit cooperatives started even earlier, and expanded rapidly from granting loans to individuals to financing commercial activities of other cooperatives. The network of cooperatives, combined with other agricultural organizations, provided a major base for the Agrarian Party, which represented largely the interests of the richer and middle peasantry.

Before World War I the Bohemian Lands were, in fact, the most highly developed agricultural area of Cisleithania, accounting for 60 to 70 percent of its total crop production. Nevertheless, agriculture lagged behind the rapid development of industry, and its share of the gross national income was declining.

From Industrial to Technical Revolution

The industrial revolution continued in the Bohemian Lands until the economic crisis of 1873. Its most pronounced impact was still in the area of textiles. By the 1870s the production of woolen and cotton cloth was almost entirely mechanized; only linen production was to some extent performed manually. The great process of technological transformation, however, began to affect other branches of industry as well. In food processing, stimulated by the era of agricultural prosperity, the leading position belonged to sugar refining, which had converted to factory production by the 1860s. While textiles had been the main source for an accumulation of German capital, sugar refining would serve the same function for Czech capital. Other kinds of light industry undergoing mechanization after 1848 were those producing glass, porcelain, paper, and leather.

The advances in light industry, the construction of railroads, and demand for agricultural implements stimulated the development of heavy industry. Iron production slowly discarded the old-fashioned methods prevailing in the ironworks on noble estates. By 1871, 38 percent of iron production came from blast furnaces fueled by coke, especially in Vítkovice, Kladno, and Třinec. Although the output of pig iron rose to 128,900 tons in 1873, it was still insufficient to satisfy domestic demand and constituted a mere 35 percent of Cisleithania's iron production. Coal by now was the basic fuel, and mining of it greatly expanded, reaching, in 1873, 4,120,000 and 4,720,000 tons of hard and soft coal respectively.

The development of machine-tool industries was a characteristic result of the industrial revolution. The most prominent factories were located in Prague and its suburbs (Ringhoffer, Daněk, *První Českomoravská Strojírna*) and in Plzeň (Wallenstein machine works, acquired by Emil Škoda in 1869). The domestic market consumed most of their production, which included steam engines, railroad equipment, agricultural machinery and implements, and equipment for the food processing industries, mines, and ironworks. Despite its diversity, the machine-tool industry failed to meet the requirements of domestic consumers. Equipment for textiles industries, metalworking machines, and more complicated agricultural machinery all had to be imported.

Unquestionably after the loss of Lombardy in 1859, if not before, the

Bohemian Lands became the most important area of industrial development in the empire. While in 1880 their share of Cisleithania's territory was 25 percent, and of its population 37 percent, they accounted for 64 percent of its industrial production. Almost one-third of their population was employed in industry, and industrial entrepreneurs began to supersede noble landowners in economic importance.

The depression, which began in 1873, caused a substantial decline in production, above all in iron and machinery, but the crisis was substantially shorter in industry than in agriculture. The industrial advance resumed after 1880, and continued with minor interruptions—such as the depression of 1901–03—until 1914. It was marked by new techniques in iron and steel production, and, after 1900, by the more general technical revolution with the emergence of new sources of energy (electricity, gaseous and liquid fuels) and methods of propulsion (electric, and internal combustion motors). The growth rate of heavy industries in this period exceeded that of light industries.

Iron and steel production received a major stimulus from the introduction of the Thomas process in the 1880s, enabling use of local ores high in phosphorus content. The Bohemian Lands then became a leading center of iron production, and maintained their strength in the related branches of heavy industry. Their share of Cisleithania's iron production rose from 35 to 61 percent between 1876 and 1896. They produced 89,500 tons of pig iron in 1880, 485,000 in 1900, and 797,000 in 1913. In the same time spans the production of hard coal rose from 5,528,000 to 9,766,000 to 14,271,000 tons, and that of soft coal from 6,281,000 to 17,551,000 to 23,017,000 tons.

The production of alkalis and artificial fertilizers occupied the most important place in the growing chemical industry. Competition of the more advanced German industry, however, hindered development of new types of chemical manufacturing, such as production of organic dyes. The beginnings of an electrical industry in the 1880s were connected with the names of two inventor-entrepreneurs, František Křižík and Emil Kolben. Initially electricity served to illuminate public places and factories, later to provide a source of energy for industry, transportation, and agriculture. Construction of large electric power stations began in the first decade of the twentieth century.

Multiplication of industrial branches rapidly expanded and diversified the machine-tool industry. New types of production included motors, automobiles, and equipment for electrical industries. In the beginning of the twentieth century the demand for armaments offered another stimulus for expansion. The Škoda Works, with 10,000 employees, was by 1914 one of the largest munitions producers in the world. Yet the machine-tool industries of the Bohemian Lands still did not satisfy the highly diversified domestic demand for producers' goods, and imports of machinery and instruments were rising. The problem was that though the demand existed its volume was not sufficient to warrant the domestic development of the full range of machine-tool industries. Likewise the relative weakness of the domestic demand for consumers' goods hindered the introduction of the assembly line and other techniques of mass production.

In the total production of the Bohemian Lands in the early twentieth century light industries still predominated over heavy ones, though their rate of expansion was slower. The Bohemian Lands maintained their leading role in Cisleithania's industrial production, accounting for almost all the sugar, glass, and porcelain output, more than half of the iron, mining, and textile industries, and approximately half of the machine-tool, chemical, and construction industries. They contained 53.3 percent of persons active in industry in Cisleithania.

The Bohemian Lands depended heavily for industrial investment on external capital, especially Austrian and German. This was particularly true of iron production, coal mining, and related enterprises. Investment of Czech capital, accumulated in agriculture and craft production, began by the mid-nineteenth century with food processing and the production of fertilizers and agricultural machinery. Later it expanded to construction materials and machine-tool, electrical, chemical, and linen production. Early in the twentieth century Czech banks also made substantial investments in cotton textile industries. Originally concentrated in Bohemia, Czech capital gradually penetrated into Moravia and Silesia; but as late as 1914 only about one-third of investments in the industries of the Bohemian Lands were of Czech origin.

Despite the growth of factory production, artisan crafts survived, though their share in the total industrial output was declining. Virtually extinct in some areas, especially cloth weaving, they persisted in others in which the penetration of large-scale production was retarded (clothing, furniture making) or in which they performed subsidiary functions (plumbing, locksmithing, construction). Still, in the last twenty years of the nineteenth century the number of independent craftsmen declined by 20 percent.

The growth of the factory labor force is impossible to determine because of inadequate census data. Estimates indicate that in Bohemia alone the labor force more than doubled between 1846 and 1880. In all the Bohemian Lands it increased by 90 percent from 1880 to 1902, and again by 20 percent between 1902 and 1910. In 1910 there were 1,935,827 persons employed in both factory industry and artisan crafts. At that time 35.3 percent of the population was active in industry (including mining and crafts), compared with 38.9 percent in agriculture.

By the 1860s the immediate aspirations of industrial workers were centered on a shorter workday. Through strikes they succeeded in bringing it down to eleven or twelve hours in the textile industries of northern Bohemia, and by 1872 to ten hours in the machine-tool factories in Prague. In the 1870s industrial labor became better organized to press its demands. In response, Taaffe's government inaugurated a new era of social legislation, including establishing factory inspectors in 1883, shortening the workday to ten hours in mining in 1884 and to eleven hours in the large industries a year later, and instituting accident and sickness insurance in 1887–88. Subsequently, only a few concessions were gained through legislation, mainly the right to a twenty-four hour rest period once a week in 1895, and a further limitation of the workday in mining to nine hours in 1901. Additional demands for a shorter workday and a paid annual vacation were not successful. In practice the workday in industry varied between nine and eleven hours in 1906. In contrast, agricultural workers, not covered by the social legislation, had to work between twelve and fourteen hours.

Nominal wages had been rising since the 1880s, especially in mining and the metallurgical and machine-tool industries, but the rising cost of living, particularly after 1900, tended to nullify the increases. The first decade of the new century witnessed an upsurge of labor discontent, resulting in an increase in strikes and demonstrations for both economic and political objectives, such as universal suffrage, or lower prices, taxes, and tariffs. Workers' membership in the Social Democratic Party and the labor unions also rose steadily.

Czech and German Capital

A network of credit facilities developed during the industrial prosperity from 1848 to 1873. Viennese commercial banks had established branches in the Bohemian Lands since the 1850s, and local German capital financed the Mährische Escompte-Bank in Brno and the Böhmische Escompte-Bank in Prague, both in the 1860s. In 1864 the Bohemian diet established the Hypoteční Banka, guaranteed by the Land, mainly to provide mortgage loans. The diets of Moravia and Silesia founded similar banks. By the late 1860s the accumulation of loan capital in Czech hands, especially in local savings banks and associations, made possible the organization of Czech commercial banks. Thus Živnostenská Banka in Prague and Záložní Úvěrní Ústav in Hradec Králové were both founded in 1868. Before the crash of 1873 the number of commercial banks in the Bohemian Lands had reached thirty-three.

The original local credit institutions were the municipal *spořitelny* (savings banks), guaranteed by the municipalities, and specializing in mortgage and municipal loans. The *občanské záložny* (citizens' savings and loan associations), based on the ideas of Hermann Schulze-Delitzsch, penetrated into the Bohemian Lands in the 1850s. They appealed particularly to shopkeepers and craftsmen, providing cheap short-term credit for their members. The *okresní hospodářské záložny* (agricultural savings and loan associations) performed similar services for the better-off peasantry. They sprang up mainly from the 1860s to the 1880s as outgrowths of the earlier grain reserves dating to the feudal period.

The depression of the 1870s caused reduction or consolidation of the major credit institutions, leaving in 1890 only seven commercial banks—three Czech and four German. In the same year, the Zemská Banka was established by the Bohemian Diet to serve as a central institution of the municipal and *okres* savings banks, and provide credit for public works, railroads, and municipalities. Besides accepting deposits, it issued its own bonds. Analogous institutions were founded by the Moravian and Silesian diets.

The 1880s and 1890s were the time of the major development of the self-help credit cooperatives in the villages. Based on the ideas of the Prussian Friedrich Raiffeisen, they were often called *kampeličky* after their Czech propagator Cyril Kampelík. Each limited to one or a few villages, they were managed by volunteer elected functionaries. In the 1890s the various types of local savings and loan institutions formed central associations, and even proceeded to establish new commercial banks; such as the Ústřední Banka Českých Spořitelen (1903) and Agrární Banka (1911).

Aside from the local savings and loan banks, the main source of the rapid growth of Czech commercial banks from the mid-1890s was credit and investment in industrial enterprises. The largest among these banks, Živnostenská, Pražská Úvěrní, and Česká Průmyslová, came to control substantial segments of industry in the Bohemian Lands. Some capital was exported, mainly to the developing regions of the empire, as well as to the Balkans and the Ukraine. Often Slavic areas were preferred in the expectation of a more hospitable reception.

The expansion of Czech commercial banks was particularly rapid from 1907 to 1913, at which time their capital grew at a faster rate than that of local German banks. By 1913 twelve Czech banks had a joint-stock capital of 225 million crowns, and reserve funds of 46 million crowns, compared with respectively 109 million and 41 million crowns held by the twelve local German banks. Their share of the total bank capital in Cisleithania rose between 1900 and 1913 from 5.3 percent to 16.7 percent. Nevertheless, the dominant position still belonged to the Viennese banks, which in 1914 maintained over ninety branches in the Bohemian Lands. Despite their rapid growth, the holdings of the Czech commercial banks in 1913 did not significantly exceed one quarter of the stock capital of the Viennese commercial banks.

QUEST FOR INDEPENDENCE, 1914–18

Hopes and Uncertainty, 1914–16

The Czech political tradition diametrically opposed supporting the empire in a war involving an alliance with Germany against Russia and France. The outbreak of the conflict in the summer of 1914 inevitably produced serious alienation from the Habsburg monarchy and led several important political personalities to consider the idea of complete separation of the Bohemian state, preferably in union with the adjacent Slovak territories of Hungary. Aside from Masaryk, who left the empire in December 1914 to work for Czech and Slovak independence abroad, the early partisans of independence included the Young Czechs Kramář and Rašín, the Realists Eduard Beneš (1884–1948) and Přemysl Šámal, and virtually all the Radicals, who in March 1915 formed a secret group, later called *Mafie*, mainly for the purpose of communicating with the independence movement abroad. The organization was headed by Beneš, and after his departure into exile the following September, by Šámal.

The successful Russian advance in Galicia, begun in August 1914, engendered hopes of Russia's aid in line with the Russophile orientation of much of Czech public opinion. These feelings found their most dramatic expression in the desertions of Czech soldiers to the Russian side, including two entire regiments in the spring of 1915. The rout of the Russian army in May 1915, however, ended such expectations. At the same time, the Austrian government initiated a repression which culminated in the arrest of several leading proponents of independence, most notably Kramář and Rašín.[7] Although they did not lead to violent protests as the Austrian military authorities had anticipated, the arrests did produce further alienation from the dynasty and its councilors, who were perceived as imposing repression while demanding sacrifices of blood and property in a most unpopular war.

After the arrests, the political leadership tended to pass to the "activists" who counted on the continued existence of the empire after the war, and sought to protect national interests under such circumstances. The prominent members of this group were the Agrarian Švehla, the Social Democrat Bohumír Šmeral, and the Young Czech Zdeněk Tobolka. Since normal political life had been disrupted after the outbreak of the war by the indefinite suspension of the *Reichsrat*, the "activists" sought to form a common organ of the Czech political parties which could represent the nation in relations with the government. Negotiations carried on from September 1915 until April 1916 failed to reach

---

7. Klofáč had been arrested earlier, in September 1914. Released from prison in July 1917, before his case came to trial, he resumed his activities as *Reichsrat* deputy.

this objective. At last in November 1916, shortly before the death of
Emperor Francis Joseph, most political parties agreed to form two common organs, a joint club of *Reichsrat* deputies, *Český Svaz*, and a representative body in Prague, *Národní Výbor*. The dominant figure in the
former was the Social Democrat Vlastimil Tusar, in the latter Švehla.
Only the small Realist and Radical parties, unalterably opposed to pro-
Habsburg "activism," refused to participate in either organ.

Of particular concern for the activists were the demands of the Austro-German parties, which considered war a favorable time to realize
their national aspirations. Their Easter Program of 1916 called once
more for a German Cisleithania, excluding Galicia, Bukovina, and Dalmatia and restricting the national rights of the Czechs and the Slovenes
to a minimum. Noting that the Germans in the *Reich*, including the
famous Friedrich Naumann in his treatise *Mittel-Europa*, often advocated a more tolerant treatment of the smaller nations of Central Europe, some of the "activists" tried to enlist the aid of intellectuals in the
German Empire to restrain the Austro-Germans. The most notable of
these unsuccessful efforts was an approach to Naumann himself, initiated by Šmeral in March 1916. In the opening months of Charles I's
reign the government was, in fact, ready to satisfy by decree the German claim for an ethnic partition of Bohemia. This intent was blocked
less by the exertions of the *Český Svaz* than by the new concern for the
rights of small nations.

In the meantime, the idea of an independent state joining the Czechs
with the Slovaks had received the support of most Czech and Slovak
immigrant settlers in the Entente countries soon after the outbreak of
the war. In January 1915 the Czech and Slovak immigrant groups of
France, Russia, and England established in Paris a joint National Council of Czechoslovak Communities, but personal conflicts rendered this
body ineffectual. The true leadership for the independence movement
came from the most distinguished émigré, Masaryk, who shortly after
the outbreak of the war concluded that the Western powers, above all
Great Britain, would determine the fate of postwar Europe. As early
as April 1915, in a memorandum to the British and French governments, he advocated the creation of an independent Czechoslovakia.
Russia's military reversals in the spring and summer of that year increased the authority of his pro-Western attitude. After the arrival of
Beneš in September, he established the Czech Foreign Committee in
Paris, which gained speedy recognition by most of the Czech settlers in
the Entente countries. In November the Committee issued a solemn
declaration of its objectives, ranging the Czechs on the side of the Entente. In February 1916 it was reorganized as the Czechoslovak National Council, and included in its leadership, besides Masaryk and Beneš,
a recently escaped Agrarian *Reichsrat* deputy from Bohemia, Josef Dürich,

and a Slovak émigré with influential connections in the French government, Milan Štefánik (1880–1919). The authority of the Council was challenged by the organizations of Czech and Slovak settlers in Russia at the instigation of the tsarist government, which distrusted Masaryk's Western orientation. Dürich, sent to Russia to represent the Council, ended up by joining the schism. The tsarist intrigue ended with the February Revolution of 1917, and the liberal Provisional Government favored Masaryk's leadership of the Czechoslovak cause. In the meantime, Masaryk's movement had gained some support from the Western governments. In February 1916 he was received by the French prime minister, Aristide Briand, who expressed his private sympathies for Czechoslovak independence. The greatest triumph, however, was achieved in December; largely thanks to Beneš's exertions at the French Foreign Ministry, the Entente powers explicitly referred to the Czechoslovak case in their reply to President Woodrow Wilson's request to state their war aims. Issued on January 10, 1917, the document listed the "Czechoslovaks" among those to be liberated from foreign domination.

The brief period of elation in Masaryk's camp was replaced by an extended phase of uncertainty. Ironically it was the influence of President Wilson, rising steadily with the increasing involvement of the United States in the war, that sustained the still existing willingness of the British and French governments to preserve the Habsburg empire and conclude a separate peace with it. The American statesman, too, felt that the empire could be detached from the German alliance, if merely autonomy, not full independence, were requested for most of the constituent nationalities, including the Czechs. A period of complex and protracted approaches to the Austrian government for a separate peace ensued.

Toward Independence, 1917–18

In the meantime, however, the year 1917 opened up a more eventful phase in the Bohemian Lands themselves. It began, it is true, inauspiciously with a denunciation of the Entente's reply to Wilson by the *Český Svaz* in late January 1917. The Czech deputies in a letter to the Austro-Hungarian foreign minister, Count Ottokar Czernin, stated that the note misinterpreted the desire of the Czechs, who wished to remain under the scepter of the Habsburgs. The abject declaration aimed primarily at checking the government's implementation of the Austro-German program, such as the partitioning of Bohemia. As it happened, it proved unnecessary, because in the meantime Vienna had become highly sensitive to the issue of self-determination for the smaller nationalities, which had been raised to a level of basic importance by Wilson, and to a lesser extent by the pronouncements of the new revolutionary Kerensky government installed in Russia. Nevertheless, the Czech deputies needed encouragement to take advantage of the more permissive atmosphere in Austria under the new Emperor Charles. The impetus came from 222 Czech writers and scholars, who signed a declaration on May 17, 1917, urging the politicians at this critical juncture in history to proclaim a clear program of national liberation. The *Český Svaz*, in fact, announced as its goal, at the opening of the *Reichsrat* on May 30, the creation of a free democratic Czech state, including the Slovaks, though still under the Habsburg dynasty.

Czech public opinion now turned sharply against the leaders of the "activist" trend. Kramář, Rašín, and Klofáč, all released from prison in early July,[8] enjoyed rising moral authority. Within the Social Democratic Party the chief "activist" Šmeral lost influence by September to the less compromised František Soukup and Gustav Habrman. Nevertheless, the leaders of the major parties still counted on the continued existence of the dynasty. In particular, the *Národní Výbor* in Prague persisted in developing projects for federalization of the empire with an autonomous Czech-Slovak component.

Another phase in the loosening of the political and psychological ties with the empire began in the winter of 1917–18, after the Russian November Revolution. On December 25 Czernin answered the Bolshevik call, at the peace negotiations of Brest-Litovsk, for national self-determination by maintaining that the subject was not a matter for international negotiations. A joint meeting of Czech *Reichsrat* and diet deputies in Prague on January 6 dissociated itself from Czernin's view. Its Epiphany Declaration, written mainly by Rašín, asked for a free, independent, and sovereign state, including the Bohemian Lands and the settlements of the Slovaks, and made no reference to the dynasty. The impact of this omission was somewhat softened at the insistence of the Moravian Catholics, the most pro-Habsburg group, by a statement of adherence to previous declarations in the *Reichsrat*, which had pledged allegiance to the reigning house. While the politicians moved closer to open espousal of independence, popular discontent with the war and economic privations mounted and was increasingly reflected in strikes and protests by industrial workers. The Social Democrats and the National Socialists assumed leadership of the initially spontaneous movements, and organized mass demonstrations on January 22. After the Epiphany Declaration the remaining advocates of an "activist" policy gradually lost influence. The *Národní Výbor* stopped meeting at the end of March 1918.

The uncertainty about the ultimate attitude of the Entente toward the preservation of the Habsburg empire was a basic concern for the

8. Kramář and Rašín received death sentences in 1916, which were commuted to long prison terms. In July 1917 they were released from prison but did not obtain full pardon.

advocates of Czechoslovak independence both at home and abroad. The movement abroad had concentrated during 1917 on bolstering the claim to independence through the formation of military units to fight alongside the Entente armies. These so-called legions were recruited primarily from Czech and Slovak prisoners of war. Beneš received permission from the French government for the formation of a legion in August 1917, and in December the National Council was recognized by the French as the supreme political authority over this armed force. Masaryk, who had gone to Russia in May 1917, made similar arrangements with the sympathetic Provisional Government, and the legion there became 30,000 strong by October. Italy permitted the creation of labor battalions from prisoners of war in December 1917, but a genuine fighting force was not formed until April 1918.

The Entente's efforts to separate Austria from Germany persisted into the spring of 1918. In January, Prime Minister Lloyd George explicitly, and Woodrow Wilson implicitly, gave assurances that the breakup of the empire was not among the war aims of the Entente. The idea of a dissolution was, however, publicly revived in Italy by March, largely as an effort by the hard-pressed government to weaken the Habsburg empire before its feared spring offensive on the Italian front. Accordingly at a Congress of Oppressed Peoples in Rome, April 8–11, 1918, the Czechs and Slovaks together with the other nationalities of the empire could voice demands for full independence. Within a month, in the wake of the so-called Sixtus letter, and the agreement of Spa between the Central Powers, the Entente at last was losing interest in a separate peace with Austria. In the aforementioned secret letter addressed to his brother-in-law, Prince Sixtus de Bourbon, Emperor Charles had approved of the "just" French claims to Alsace-Lorraine. When the French prime minister, Georges Clemenceau, provoked by an indiscretion of the Austro-Hungarian foreign minister, Count Czernin, revealed this clause, the emperor declared it to be a forgery. In the subsequent meeting with Emperor William II at German headquarters in Spa he was forced to submit totally to German leadership. The United States now assumed the lead in sanctioning the complete self-determination of all the repressed nationalities of the empire. On May 29, 1918, Secretary of State Robert Lansing openly endorsed the claims of the "Czechoslovaks" and the other nationalities voiced at the Rome Congress, and the other major Entente powers concurred with his statement on June 3. The Czechoslovak cause was promoted in the United States by Masaryk, who had arrived there from Russia in late April 1918. However, he did not meet Wilson until June 19, much after the crucial declaration by Lansing. The struggle of the Czechoslovak legion in Siberia against the Bolsheviks also inspired sympathy for Czechoslovak independence during the summer of 1918. At last, on September

2, the U.S. government recognized the Czechoslovak National Council as a de facto government. This act was preceded by lesser degrees of recognition by France on June 29 and Britain on August 9. Both powers matched the U.S. measure on October 15 and 23 respectively.

By the spring of 1918 the activities of Czech political leaders at home were becoming coordinated the those of the Czechoslovak National Council abroad. On May 16–17 a major celebration was held in Prague, ostensibly to commemorate a jubilee of the National Theater. Its real purpose, prompted by a message from Beneš in February, and supported by all major parties except the Catholics, was to provide a counterpart to the Rome Congress. Representatives of almost all nationalities of the Habsburg empire met in Prague and adopted a solemn resolution asking for self-determination in their own independent states. A Slovak delegation also participated in the Prague celebrations, and earlier, on May 1, 1918, a gathering in Liptovský Sv. Mikuláš had called for self-determination of the Slovaks as the "Hungarian branch of the Czechoslovak stock." It was followed by the Pittsburgh Agreement of Slovak representatives with Masaryk on May 30, 1918, which assured, with some reservations, the Slovaks of full autonomy in the Czechoslovak republic of the near future.[9]

An important event, marking the rally to independence in Bohemia and Moravia, was a message from Beneš of May 10, 1918, announcing the ultimate failure of the Entente's separate negotiations with the Habsburg empire. Another was the news of the French official recognition of Masaryk's National Council as the representative of the Czechoslovak nation on June 29. The following month a new *Národní Výbor* was created, in place of the defunct "activist" one, with Kramář as chairman, Švehla and Klofáč as deputy chairmen, and Soukup as secretary. Its aim was in fact to prepare the groundwork for an independent Czechoslovak state. In September the National Socialists and Social Democrats formed a joint organ, the Socialist Council, which pressed for a declaration of independence in connection with the one-day general strike planned for October 14. The move was vetoed by the *Národní Výbor*. Three days later the *Výbor*, concurring with the *Český Svaz* in the *Reichsrat*, rejected as inadequate the last-minute imperial manifesto of October 16 offering to transform Cisleithania into a federation along ethnic lines.

On October 19, 1918, a delegation of the *Národní Výbor*, led by Kramář and Klofáč, obtained permission to go to Switzerland for consultations with the Czechoslovak National Council, represented by Beneš. Meetings held in Geneva from October 28 to 31 approved the actions of the resistance movement abroad, as well as its obligations toward the En-

9. Concerning the circumstances of the subsequent accession of Transcarpathian Ruthenians to the Czechoslovak state, see p. 424.

tente. In the meantime, the news of the unconditional surrender of the Habsburg empire prompted the declaration of Czechoslovak independence by the *Národní Výbor* in Prague on October 28, 1918. On October 30, Slovak political representatives meeting in Turčiansky Sv. Martin declared the adherence of Slovakia to the new state. The death throes of the Habsburg empire were also the birth pangs of the new state.

Czech history under Habsburg rule can in retrospect be divided into four periods. The first is from the Habsburg accession in 1526 to the loss of most existing liberties in the Lands of the Bohemian Crown at the Battle of the White Mountain in 1620. The second period of nearly complete political and cultural submission to Habsburg centralism lasted roughly to the 1740s. The third phase is characterized by the cultural revolution under the auspices of the Slavic Renaissance and the simultaneous gradual betterment of the lot of the peasants and improved administrative and educational procedures as promoted by the reforms of Maria Theresa and Joseph II in the 1770s and 1780s. The final period covers the era from the Revolution of 1848 to the emergence of the Czechoslovak republic in 1918 as a consequence of the dissolution of the Habsburg empire in World War I.

Of these four periods, the years considered the darkest in Czech history before 1939 were not quite so hopeless as it might seem at first glance, those of evolution conversely not so bright as they may appear. The Bohemian Lands under Habsburg rule until 1620 managed to preserve their political identity; yet the German language advanced further into Czech language territory, the religious conflict among the Protestant factions themselves and between Protestantism as a whole and the Catholic Church grew in intensity. The outcome of the struggle in a predominantly Catholic empire could hardly be in doubt. This, however, is a hindsight view. It was not recognized in the early seventeenth century that the unresolved religious conflicts and the estates' struggles between ecclesiastic and temporal dignitaries, nobles, and towns foreshadowed future defeat.

The catastrophe of the White Mountain and its uncontested, far-reaching consequences for the slowdown—but by no means the complete destruction—of Czech political and cultural institutions and chances of further development must be acknowledged. But at least the shell of the political institutions of the Bohemian Crown could be preserved; and while this shell was until the end of the seventeenth century an empty one, it made it possible to be filled with new life at the beginning of the new century when the question of imperial succession came up. Foreign nobility that had taken over the estates of the expelled or executed Czech Protestant nobles assimilated gradually to Bohemian conditions in the course of a century. Thus they became advocates, however conservative, of historical state rights of the Bohemian Crown. The cultural situation, it is true, was in a state of hibernation but the religious conflict, which had been so harmful to Czech national life, was now muted without destroying the chance for a revival of Czech Protestantism. The decline of urban life was an indirect consequence of the victory of the Counter Reformation in all Habsburg Lands, but under the influence of mercantilist theories and practices, and of the favorable conditions for industralization and especially mining in Bohemia, it was less comprehensive than in the Alpine Hereditary Lands and in those of the Hungarian Crown.

The gradual evolution of the Czech position at the time of the late Enlightenment was determined foremost by the impact of the Slavic Renaissance; but although the Maria Theresan and Josephin reforms had little influence on the new rise of Czech national life, they helped greatly to uplift the miserable position of the unfree peasants and strengthened the towns. The losers, though still losers in a very comfortable situation, were the lords. Yet the stupendous progress of the Czech bourgeoisie and of Czech national life in all its ramifications between 1848 and 1918 would have been unthinkable without the prior strengthening of lower- and middle-class standards. True, this development was mainly an unintended side effect of the enlightened reform period in the Habsburg empire, but this does not change the fact itself.

Cultural, economic, and political progress between 1848 and 1918 is uncontested, some temporary setbacks notwithstanding. The Czechs, though still not in full possession of their political rights, had sufficient possibilities to participate in the public life of the Habsburg empire to enter the republican era fully prepared for their new task. It was, however, an illusion to believe that the nationality and minority problems that had haunted the Czechs in particular during the last seventy years of the Habsburg empire would go away as soon as they became masters of their own destiny. These problems were to stay with them and, in fact, worsen. The debatable impossibility of solving them within the Habsburg empire became an uncontested certainty in the tragic history of the Czechoslovak republic, with its new problems in international relations. In fact, this problem showed itself now where it previously was believed not to exist, in the relationship between the two master national groups of the new state, the Czechs and the Slovaks. Here also, conditions, as compared with the last half-century of the Habsburg era, became even more complex, not less. Social conflict too, between agricultural and commercial-industrial interests on one side and industrial management and labor on the other, while certainly not irreconcilable, became more difficult to solve because some problems that had been camouflaged by the nearly united front against Habsburg rule came now increasingly to the fore. This applied in particular to foreign relations, where the Czechs, who previously had been partly suppressed but also partly protected by Habsburg rule, finally found themselves isolated in the face of the threat of a huge aggressive military power. None of these factors invalidated in any way the Czech claim to national independence. Yet is is undeniable that the Czechs, when they entered their new state, carried with them an inheritance of the old empire that was neither as bad as it appeared to many nor as good as it seemed to some.

The Slovenes

THE REVOLUTION OF 1848 AND ITS AFTERMATH

Beginning of National Politics, 1848–49

The news of the March Revolution in Vienna led among the Slovene peasants to expressions of social discontent rather than national or political demands. Among the nationally conscious intellectuals, however, the onset of revolutionary events stimulated the evolution of modern political thought. From this ferment of ideas, much of it originating outside of Carniola, above all in Vienna, there emerged the first Slovene political program, adopted on April 20, 1848, by the newly established *Slovenija* society in Vienna. Its essence was the creation of a United Slovenia, which would combine all the ethnically Slovene territories into a separate kingdom as part of the Habsburg empire, but with its own diet and Slovene as the language of administration and education. The program, implying an abolition of the traditional crownlands, was endorsed by *Slovenija* societies established in Graz and Ljubljana. The Slovene national movement, however, failed to acquire central direction. Throughout the stormy events of 1848–49, it was hindered by the lack of a single national political organization, such as the Croats had in their *Sabor,* or the Serbs in their *Skupština* based on the traditional National Church Council, and other nationalities obtained in their unofficial national committees.

Clerical and other conservative figures, initially also Janez Bleiweis, regarded with distrust the program of United Slovenia and preferred to seek limited concessions from the established diets and administrative authorities. The Carniolan diet had in fact on April 6, 1848, adopted a fairly strong resolution in favor of the use of Slovene in public life, and its demand was to some extent met by the government in Vienna, especially in the area of education. Slovene became a subject offered in the *gymnasia,* and in 1849 Slovene lecture courses in criminal and civil law were initiated.

Slovene national leaders remained essentially Austroslav in political orientation and opposed to the cause of all-German unification, represented by the Frankfurt Assembly, for reasons similar to those articulated by Palacký on behalf of the Czechs. Their sympathies were directed toward other Slavs, primarily the Croats, and the Serbs of Vojvodina. They also participated in early June in the Prague Slav Congress, which approved the program of United Slovenia presented by five Slovene delegates. Shortly thereafter this program was strengthened through its endorsement by Bleiweis, who assumed the chairmanship of the *Slovenija* society in Ljubljana on June 6.

The elections for the Viennese *Reichstag* in June 1848 resulted in the selection of sixteen Slovene deputies. Most of them, however, were peasants who failed to share the national aspirations of their colleagues from the intelligentsia. This became especially evident after the transfer of the *Reichstag* from Vienna to Kroměříž in November 1848, when the Slovene peasant deputies did not join the Slav Club, but rather voted with the Germans. In the crucial Constitutional Committee of the *Reichstag,* one of the five Slovene members, Matija Kavčič, introduced a proposal for the restructuring of the Austrian empire which called for the creation of an autonomous Slovenia, including Carniola and the Slovene parts of Styria and the Littoral. When this proposal was ignored by the Committee, most of the Slovene deputies voted for one of Palacký's unsuccessful projects, the federalization of the empire along ethnic lines. In any case, first credit for a proposal to reorganize the empire along ethnic lines belonged to a Slovene as representative of demands raised by his people. It was, of course, no accident that these demands evolved within the ranks of a nation that lacked a tradition of political autonomy, even within strictly historical lines.

Neo-Absolutism, 1849–59

The new absolutist era, following the dissolution of the *Reichstag* in March 1849, brought on major administrative reforms. The *gubernia* were replaced by Lieutenancies in Styria and Carniola, Carinthia was again separated from Carniola under its own Lieutenancy. The Littoral remained a separate administrative unit, with Gorizia and Istria organized as circuits (*Kreise, okrožja*). The circuits were abolished in Carniola and Carinthia but retained in Styria, where the Maribor circuit coincided essentially with the Slovene area. At a lower level, new organs of political administration, the district captaincies (*Bezirkshauptmannschaften, okrajna glavarstva*), were introduced in all the Lands. They also replaced the manorial jurisdictions persisting in the Littoral, eastern Carinthia, and Styria. New judicial districts (numbering usually two or more in each captaincy) assumed the former functions of the residual manorial judiciary, where it had persisted. In 1853–54 the district captaincies were temporarily abolished. As a retrogressive step, a "mixed district office" was created in each judicial district, combining administrative with judicial functions.

The consistent abolition of manorial jurisdictions was part of the peasant emancipation from traditional feudal services. Ordinances issued in September 1849 implemented this reform in the Slovene Lands in consequence of the legislation enacted by the *Reichstag* of Vienna in September 1848 and by the imperial government in March 1849. As in the Bohemian Lands, the seigneurs were entitled to compensation for two-thirds of the value of lost services and dues, with the cost borne equally by the peasants and the Lands. The lords still retained a large proportion of the land. For instance, in Carniola 334 estates contained over 1,000 hectares each, while peasant holdings rarely exceeded 10 hectares.

The Slovene national movement suffered temporary reversals in the new absolutist era. As for language use, the official gazette was no longer published in Slovene, and by 1852 the Slovene text of laws was no longer considered authentic. Slovene gains in elementary education persisted, but the *gymnasia* again became thoroughly German. Political activity to advance national objectives was suspended. The *Slovenija* society in Ljubljana under Bleiweis as early as spring of 1849 renounced political concerns for purely cultural ones, and was entirely abolished in 1853. Most of the Slovene periodicals, launched in 1848, also disappeared by 1850. The tolerated cultural activities were usually performed under ecclesiastical auspices. Since 1851 Društvo Sv. Mohorja had rendered important service to the national cause, above all in book publishing. Although established in Klagenfurt, it was to serve the entire Slovene territory, and its membership reached a peak of 1,000 in the mid-1850s. The leading role of ecclesiastics, such as Anton Slomšek and Luka Jeran, in Slovene national life in the 1850s helped forge the strong bond subsequently evident between Slovene nationalism and Catholic clericalism. The absolutist regime totally silenced the liberal minority, and proscribed the ideal of United Slovenia as subversive of the established order of the traditional crownlands.

CONFLICT BETWEEN CENTRALISM AND AUTONOMISM, 1860–93

Constitutional Experimentation, 1860–67

With the opening of the new constitutional era, under the February Patent of 1861, the Lands of the Slovene area (including Gorizia and

Istria) were provided with diets, elected by the four *curiae* standard in Cisleithania (big estates owners, chambers of commerce and trade, towns, and rural communities).[10] Administrative reforms of the 1860s restored the district captaincies, placing them directly under the Lieutenancies. The intermediate administrative circuits (*Kreise*) were eliminated entirely. The Lieutenancies were headed by lieutenants (*Statthalter*) in Styria and the Littoral (including Trieste, Gorizia, and Istria), and by presidents of the Land in Carniola and Carinthia.

The Slovene national leaders as yet lacked adequate political organization in 1861. Only thirteen Slovenes out of a total membership of thirty-six were elected to the diet in Carniola, seven out of twenty-one in Gorizia, and none at all in Styria, Carinthia, or Istria. Because of their weakness in the diets, the Slovenes' representation in the *Reichsrat* amounted to no more than three deputies. A deputy from Carniola, Lovro Toman, joined the Czech opposition against Schmerling's centralism. The other two, both from Gorizia—abandoning the goal of United Slovenia as an immediate possibility—supported the government for minor concessions. The most significant gain was the introduction, within the jurisdiction of two Superior Courts of the Land (in Graz and in Trieste), of Slovene as an external language in judicial proceedings, whenever possible, if a party knew no other language. Over the issue of political objectives, a dichotomy emerged within the Slovene national camp between the more cautious, conservative wing or the Old Slovenes, guided by Bleiweis and his journal *Novice,* and the more radical Young Slovenes seeking to revive the idea of United Slovenia, whose spokesman was France Levstik and whose platform was first the journal *Naprej (Forward)* (1863), then *Slovenec* (1865–67).

During the 1860s the Slovene national movement gained genuine strength from the widespread awakening of national consciousness among both peasants and townsmen, particularly in Carniola, Styria, and Gorizia, and to a lesser extent in Carinthia and Istria. New cultural and social organizations, such as the popular reading clubs, played a leading role in this process. They could proliferate under the newly granted freedom of association. Ljubljana led the way as a center of national activity with the establishment of the *Sokol* gymnastic organization in 1863, *Slovenska Matica* in 1864, and the dramatic society two years later.

Thus the era of Count Richard Belcredi as Austrian prime minister, with its renewed federalist overtones, beginning in mid-1865, found the Slovene movement a more potent force than hitherto. In order to accommodate the premier's emphasis on historical rights of the tradi-

---

10. Also conforming to the standard Cisleithanian pattern, the diets in turn elected Committees of the Land to administer the limited affairs within the diets' jurisdiction. Captains of the Land (*Landeshauptmänner*), appointed by the emperor, chaired these committees.

tional crownlands, the leading Slovene politicians put forth in September 1865 the so-called Maribor Program. In it they proposed (without success) to approach the goal of a United Slovenia through the dubious expedient of linking the Lands of Styria, Carinthia, Carniola, and the Littoral through a common diet, evoking their historical association as "Inner Austria." The Slovenes, however, secured real gains in the existing diets. In June 1866, shortly before the war with Italy, the Italian majority in the Gorizian diet was reduced from 14:7 to 11:10 through a reform of the *curia* of big estate owners. In elections to other diets in January 1867, the Slovenes improved their position, including the gain of a majority of 25 (out of 36) in Carniola. In all the diets, the number of Slovene deputies rose from 22 in 1861 to 44 in 1867.

Within a month of these diet elections a reversion to centralism took place in Cisleithania with the accession of Baron (Count) Ferdinand Beust to power. New elections to the Carniolan diet were held, which reduced but did not eliminate the Slovene majority. The Slovene parliamentarians, however, were able to extract concessions from Beust by adopting an opportunistic policy in the *Reichsrat* and voting for the Compromise of 1867. In this, they broke solidarity with the Czechs and followed the example of the Galician Poles. They went even further than the Poles by voting for the December Constitution as well. Their major reward was the establishment of Slovene, in September 1867, as an obligatory—rather than merely recommended—external language in judicial proceedings in Carniola, if a party knew no other language. At the same time Slovene began to be used in the transactions of the Carniolan diet. Beust also promised to appoint Slovenes to the Supreme Judicial and Cassation Court in Vienna, and as officials in the Ministries of the Interior and Education.

Liberalism and Centralism, 1868–78

The introduction of dualism, despite its opportunistic support by the Slovene deputies in the *Reichsrat*, caused great resentment among the Slovene public. The campaign was led by the Young Slovenes, especially through their new organ, *Slovenski Narod (The Slovene Nation)*, launched in April 1868, and edited by Anton Tomšič until 1871, then by Josip Jurčič. Against dualism, they championed federalism, and revived the idea of United Slovenia and of Slav cooperation, particularly with the Croats and Serbs. This program was endorsed by student congresses held in Ljubljana in 1868 and 1869, and by mass outdoor meetings, organized on the model of the Czech *tábory* in 1868–71. The latter contributed to political mobilization of the wider strata of the Slovene population. Moreover, Slovene deputies raised the issue of United Slovenia in 1868–70 in the diets of Styria, Gorizia, and Carniola. The strongest manifestation of the Slovenes' affinity for the other South Slavs occurred at the so-called Yugoslav Congress in Ljubljana in early December 1870, at a time when the aggressive ascendancy of Prussia was raising doubts about the preservation of the Habsburg monarchy. The Congress signified the Slovenes' wish for a union with the Croats and the Serbs, if a fundamental rearrangement of political boundaries became a necessity in East Central Europe.

The era of subsequent German liberal dominance in the empire, extending from 1871 to 1879, at its start sharpened the conflict between the Old Slovenes, who joined the conservative Hohenwart Club in the *Reichsrat*, and the Young Slovenes, who occasionally voted with the German majority on issues of liberal reform. The struggle culminated in the *Reichsrat* elections of 1873, with each faction presenting its own slate of candidates. Four Young and three Old Slovenes won seats. By the end of 1874 a reconciliation took place, and the Young Slovenes also joined the Hohenwart Club, both factions however preserving their own organizations and press organs. In order to conform to the emphasis on the historical rights of the traditional crownlands upheld by Czech and Polish political leaders, the joint program of the two Slovene factions deemphasized the ahistorical concept of United Slovenia and stressed limited administrative concessions within the existing Lands. It was hoped that these could be achieved gradually through supporting, rather than opposing, the government.

Slovene national life advanced only within narrow limits during the 1870s. Slovene strength in the diets actually regressed. In Styria, Slovene representation was reduced to four by 1875, and by 1877 the Germans had regained control of the diet in Carniola. The usage of Slovene in government agencies had progressed no further since Beust's concessions. Elementary schools instructing in Slovene did expand under the compulsory education act of 1869, again mainly in Carniola, Styria, and Gorizia, and newly—against Italian opposition—in Istria. The situation in Carinthia remained unsatisfactory. The one bilingual German-Slovene *gymnasium*, established under Hohenwart in 1871, became completely German in 1874.

Concessions of the Taaffe Era, 1879–93

After the assumption of office in August 1879 by the cabinet of Count Eduard Taaffe, who promised concessions to the non-German nationalities of Cisleithania, Slovene deputies in the *Reichsrat* shifted with the Hohenwart Club from opposition to the support of the government. The Slovenes in fact significantly benefited through administrative measures of the Taaffe cabinet. Except for Carinthia, the number of Slovene officials noticeably increased in the Slovene area. In Carniola a Slovene, Andrej Winkler, was even appointed to the office of *Lan-*

despräsident (1880–92). The administrative organs no longer exerted pressure in favor of German representation in the diets, so the German party sank into virtual impotence in Carniola; and in Styria the Slovenes recovered the strength in the rural *curia*, which had been lost in the 1870s. The Slovene representation remained extremely restricted only in Carinthia. An ordinance of the Justice Ministry in 1882, applicable to Carniola, southern Styria, and the Slovene districts of Carinthia, made the use of Slovene as the external language in judicial proceedings obligatory if specified by a party. In the same year, Slovene became the official internal language of the municipality of Ljubljana. Although still limited, a notable advance was scored in secondary education. A mixed Slovene-German program—in addition to a purely German one, which had existed in Ljubljana since 1875—was introduced into the lower *gymnasia* in Kranj (Krainburg) and Novo Mesto in 1882, Maribor (Marburg) in 1889, and Celje (Cilli) in 1895. On the model of similar German and Italian organizations, the Society of Saints Cyril and Methodius was established in 1885 by Ivan Vrhovnik to organize and maintain private Slovene schools in nationally mixed areas.

Early in the Taaffe era the Slovene political leadership changed. Both Bleiweis and Jurčič died in 1881, and Fran Šunklje (1849–1935) and Karel Klun (1841–96) became the leaders of the liberals and the conservatives respectively. In the spirit of the limited aspirations of the Taaffe era, the joint program of Slovene politicians, masterminded by Šunklje, shelved the ideal of a United Slovenia for the modest goals of greater autonomy of the traditional crownlands and the introduction of national *curiae* into the diets of the latter. Šunklje and his colleagues— derisively labeled "elastics"—came under fire for their minimalist program from young radicals, led by Ivan Tavčar (1851–1923) and Ivan Hribar (1851–1941), who in their review *Slovan* (1884–87), in irreverent disregard for historical boundaries, highlighted the concept of a United Slovenia. In addition, they advocated Slav cooperation both within and beyond the frontiers of the Habsburg empire. The conflict between the radicals and the "elastics," however, had begun to subside by 1886 because of the challenge to both groups from the rising clericalism. The clerical involvement in politics, promoted by Pope Leo XIII, mounted steadily during the 1880s. In 1883 the clerical newspaper *Slovenec* became a daily, and the even more influential *Rimski Katolik* was launched in Gorizia in 1888 by the zealous prelate, Anton Mahnič.

DEMOCRATIZATION AND POLITICAL DIFFERENTIATION, 1893–1914

Liberal-Clerical Conflict, 1893–97

Even before the end of the Taaffe era, a sharp conflict between the liberals and the clericals sundered the unity within the Slovene political

camp. In Carniola the two factions had evolved into separately organized parties by 1892. The clericals, or the Catholic National Party, tended
to emphasize issues of social reform, while the liberals, or the National
Party, stressed more the cause of national autonomy. The antagonism
intensified so much that in the Carniolan diet the nine liberals formed
against the sixteen clericals in 1896 an unlikely coalition with the eleven
Germans, an alliance which was to last for twelve years.

A Christian Social movement represented a dynamic wing within the
clerical party. Transcending the narrowly political framework, it was
stimulated by the papal encyclical *Rerum Novarum* of 1892. Skillfully
guided by a priest, Janez Krek (1865–1917), its activities focused on
the countryside. In 1894 Krek launched a successful cooperative movement first in the field of credit, then in various forms of agricultural
activity. The Christian Social movement did not entirely ignore the urban workers either. One of Krek's chief aids, Jože Gostinčar, organized
a number of workers' societies with both educational and political objectives. The mounting tension between the Christian Social and the
conservative wings threatened at the time of the 1897 *Reichsrat* elections
to split the clerical party openly. The schism was only averted thanks
to Krek's conciliatory skills.

In addition, prior to the 1897 elections, a Yugoslav Social Democratic
Party appeared on the political scene as an independent factor. Organized in Ljubljana in August 1896, its activities were to encompass in
addition to the Slovene areas all of Dalmatia and Istria. Because of the
scarcity of industrial workers in the latter two areas, the members and
leaders of the party under Etbin Kristan (1864–1953) were mostly Slovene. Even the Slovene cadres, however, were not sufficiently numerous. Thus the German-Austrian Social Democrats actually organized
the Slovene areas of Carinthia and the Maribor district of Styria.[11]

Political Diversification, 1897–1907

The polarization between the liberals and the clericals persisted in
the Slovene political camp after 1897. A formal split into two political
parties—after the pattern of Carniola—occurred in 1899 in Gorizia and
in 1906–7 in southern Styria. The Slovenes remained united in a clerical organization only in Carinthia, and within a joint Slovene-Croatian
party in Istria. In Carniola, the clericals, known by 1905 as the People's
Party, under the leadership of the priest Ivan Šušteršič (1863–1925),
avoided further splits despite the persistence of the conservative and
Christian Social wings. Liberals (renamed the National Progressive Party
in Carniola in 1905) attempted to weaken the clericals by sponsoring a

11. The Celje district of Styria was controlled by the Yugoslav Social Democrats, as
far as Social Democratic Party activities were concerned.

peasant party. Independently of these efforts a small peasant party appeared only in Gorizia by 1907. The liberals also sought to weaken the Social Democrats through the establishment of a national workers' organization in Trieste in 1907 and later in Gorizia and Istria, unsuccessfully attempting to emulate the Young Czechs' launching of the National Socialist Party in the Bohemian Lands.

A revolt against the liberal party was represented by the National Radical movement that emerged after 1900 and was fostered by young intellectuals, especially those educated at the Vienna University, who scored the liberals for ignoring social and economic issues. Under the leadership of Gregor Žerjav (1882–1929), the National Radicals held their first congress in 1905, which resulted in a party organization and in the launching of a cooperative movement. The party, however, was not destined for long independent existence. In 1908 it was to fuse with the liberals, with Žerjav as the secretary general of the rejuvenated liberal party. Another numerically small but influential political group (the Realists) consisted of former students of Thomas Masaryk at the Prague University. Their journal *Naši Zapiski* (*Our Notes*) appeared first in Ljubljana (1902–7), then in Gorizia (1909–14). Led by Anton Dermota and Dragotin Lončar, and critical of both liberalism and clericalism, the Realists advocated concrete work to uplift the common people economically, politically, and culturally.

The Yugoslav Social Democrats failed to elect a single candidate of their own into the *Reichsrat* or the individual diets, but they could affect the electoral process. Although in 1907 the party finally endorsed Slovene national autonomy on the basis of a United Slovenia, the Social Democrats in ethnically mixed areas frequently detracted from the Slovene national movement. This tendency was particularly evident in Carinthia and Istria, where—because of the clericalism of the local Slovene parties—the socialists preferred to support, in close elections, German or Italian liberals against their own Slovene conationals.

After the electoral reform of 1897, the Slovenes were assigned 15 of the total 425 seats in the *Reichsrat*, with 9 from Carniola, 4 from Styria, and 2 from the Littoral. After forming a single club in the *Reichsrat* in 1897–1900, the liberals and the clericals established their own clubs, but still cooperated on matters of national Slovene interest. They oscillated between opposition and support of the government on the basis of piecemeal concessions, especially in language rights.

The Era of Universal Suffrage, 1907–14

The electoral reform of 1907 raised the number of Slovene representatives in the *Reichsrat* to 24 (out of 516); Carniola sent 11, Styria 7, Gorizia 3, and Carinthia, Istria, and Trieste one each. The electoral reforms of the individual diets usually consisted of the addition of a fifth or general *curia* of voters, but on the whole the diets remained unreflective of the actual numerical strength of the Slovenes. The Slovenes failed to reach a majority in either the Gorizian or (with the Croats) the Istrian diet; in the former (according to the reform of 1907) the Italian-Slovene ratio was 15 to 14, in the latter (reform of 1908) 26 Italians to 16 Croats and 2 Slovenes. They remained flagrantly underrepresented in the Carinthian diet, with two seats out of 41 (reform of 1902), and in the Styrian diet, with 13 out of 84 (reform of 1908). In Carniola the reform of 1908 raised the number of Slovenes in the diet to 39 out of 50. At the same time it gave an absolute majority of 26 to the clericals and ended the dominance of the coalition of the Slovene liberals and the Germans, who were reduced to 12 and 11 seats respectively. In 1909 the clericals of Carniola merged with those of Styria and Gorizia to create an All-Slovene People's Party. The dominance of the clericals was even greater in the *Reichsrat* delegation with 17 elected in 1907 and 19 in 1911, compared with 4 and 2 liberals respectively. By 1911 the Slovene deputies, with one exception, formed a joint Croat-Slovene parliamentary group with 7 Dalmatian and Istrian Croats.

The Slovenes' national life had grown in strength early in the twentieth century, but their ethnic territory had not yet fully stabilized. The heaviest losses occurred in Carinthia, where, as noted below, Slovene national rights continued to be slighted. In the southern regions of Carinthia, where the Slovenes had constituted 91 percent of the population in 1880, their proportion declined to 45.5 percent by 1910. In southern Styria the ethnic boundary receded somewhat, partly because of the German nationalist Südmark organization, established in 1889; one of its tasks was to purchase Slovene homesteads for sale to German peasants. Slovene language rights in elementary education were reasonably secure except in Carinthia, where only three purely Slovene schools existed before World War I. In secondary education another advance was achieved in 1908 in Carniola, where some Slovene was introduced into four higher *gymnasia*; in Styria, Slovene remained restricted to two lower *gymnasia*. The only purely Slovene *gymnasium* was in Gorizia. While German, or in some instances Italian, remained the internal official language of government agencies and courts, Slovene was widely used as the external official language in all Slovene territories with the exception of Carinthia. A parallel growth of the number of Slovene officials occurred in all the Slovene Lands except once again in Carinthia, where by 1914 only fifteen administrative officials and four judges were Slovenes.[12]

12. The Slovenes had to wait for a representative in the Viennese cabinet until World War I, when Ivan Žolger would hold a ministry without portfolio from August 1917 to May 1918.

Between the annexation of Bosnia-Herzegovina in 1908 and the outbreak of World War I, all the Slovene parties favored closer ties with the other South Slavs in the empire. The clericals looked to Vienna, above all to the Archduke Franz Ferdinand and the influential army circles, to achieve an association between the Slovenes and the Croats. Having cultivated intimate contacts with kindred Croatian groups since 1911, they made a serious attempt at a conference in Ljubljana in October 1912 to unite with the Croatian Starčević Party of the Right, as well as with the Croatian *Frankovci*. The liberals issued declarations in 1909 and 1913 in favor of a union with the Croats and Serbs through a federalistic or trialistic reorganization of the empire. The Social Democrats, in their Tivoli Resolution of November 1909, went so far as to advocate a complete fusion of all South Slavs into a single Yugoslav nation. While the three major parties sought a solution within the monarchy, from 1912 the radical *Preporodovci* (the Renaissance group), in touch with other South Slav revolutionaries such as the Young Bosnia, felt that Yugoslav unity required a secession from the empire, because German and Magyar opposition would inevitably block all attempts at federalism or trialism in the Habsburg monarchy.

AGRICULTURE, INDUSTRY, AND FINANCE[13]

Agricultural and Industrial Progress, 1848–90

As a new departure in Slovene agriculture, the removal of the feudal obligations in the 1850s encouraged the peasants to diversify crop production. Nevertheless, there was still a heavy reliance on grains that facilitated efficient use of land. In particular wheat, barley, and rye could be planted in the fall, and their early harvest enabled replanting in the summer. Viticulture suffered further losses with the spread of phylloxera, and the recovery was slow. Cultivation of hops began to spread in the 1870s. The agrarian crisis of the 1880s, caused by imports of overseas grains to Europe, had only a minor impact in Slovenia, for local grain was consumed mostly by the producers.

The prevalent use of crop rotation, even among the peasants, accounted by midcentury for an increased production of feed crops and potatoes. Abundant fodder facilitated the expansion of animal stocks, except for sheep raising, which was declining in the Kars and Alpine

13. Economic data in this section are derived from Ferdo Gestrin and Vasilij Melik, *Slovenska zgodovina od konca osemnajstega stoletja do 1918* (Ljubljana: Državna založba Slovenije, 1966), pp. 91–337; Toussaint Hočevar, *The Structure of the Slovenian Economy, 1848–1963* (New York: Studia Slovenica, 1965), pp. 7–117; *Zgodovina Slovencev* (Ljubljana: Cankarjeva založba, 1979), pp. 479–92, 527–41.

areas. The production of cattle and pigs benefited most. Horse raising prospered only in Carinthia.

Advances in agricultural production and industrial development were reflected in the use of more modern implements. By the 1850s iron generally began to replace wood in plows and in the teeth of harrows. By the 1870s and 1880s more advanced machinery—such as straw cutters and threshing, mowing, and sifting machines—was introduced on the large estates, though not yet on peasant farms. The estates also started employing more advanced techniques, in particular the use of artificial fertilizers and the coordination of production with the demands of the market.

As for industrial development, in the mid-nineteenth century the industrialization of the Slovene territory, though on a modest scale, had the appearance of a well-balanced process as in no other South Slav area of the Habsburg monarchy. Iron and textile industries played the classical leading role, and many other industrial activities were represented, including light industries such as food processing. Nevertheless, in the second half of the century the vigor of industrial growth was weakened by a shift of technology from wood to coal as fuel, and from water to coal as propellent. By the 1880s it became evident that the focus of industrial activity had moved to the more northerly coal-rich regions of the empire.

Within the iron industries the old smelters based on the manufactory type of production were yielding by the 1860s to modern plants. The newly created Carniolan Industrial Society in 1869 took over the ironworks in Jesenice, which became a major production center in the 1880s. The ironworks at Prevalje was similarly modernized in the 1870s, and operated by the Alpine Mountain Company from 1881. While, on the whole, extraction of iron ore declined, coal mining expanded significantly, particularly in the Trbovlje area with the establishment of the Trbovlje Coal Mining Company in 1873. The annual production grew from 236,000 tons in 1874 to 500,000 tons in the 1880s, though mainly to meet the demands of the railroads rather than of industries. Lead mining also expanded in southern Carinthia.

The textile industry experienced modest growth. To the four existing factories, a woolen factory was added in Ljubljana in 1862, and two cotton mills in Tržič and Litija in the 1880s. Among other branches of light industry, factory production developed in food processing. The first steam-powered flour mill was founded in Celje in 1850, others later in Ljubljana (1859) and Kranj (1870). Before the end of the century eight steam-powered mills were in operation, processing grain from as far away as Bessarabia, Bulgaria, and Turkey.[14] Modern breweries,

14.   Factories producing coffee substitutes sprang up in Ljubljana and Maribor.

such as those established in Ljubljana and Maribor in the 1860s, began to overshadow the older ones based on artisan methods of production. In addition to food processing, modern industry emerged in paper production. The factory in Vevče expanded its output from 900,000 tons in 1855 to 1,500,000 tons in 1870. Three other mechanized paper mills sprang up during the 1880s.[15] In glass production, the mechanized glassworks, established in Zagorje and Hrastnik in 1860–61, were replacing the vanishing plants of the manufactory type.

Of particular significance for the future was the growth of wood processing reflected in the emergence of steam-powered sawmills. With improvements in transportation, the value of lumber for export made the use of wood as industrial fuel uneconomical. This development in turn contributed to the decline of manufactory style iron- and glassworks in the Slovene territory.

Agricultural Prosperity and Industrial Retardation, 1890–1914

After the end of the agricultural depression in the 1890s, a long era of relative prosperity began in Slovene agriculture. Use of machinery started to spread among the peasants, thanks to the cooperative movement launched in the 1890s particularly by the clericals under the leadership of Janez Krek. The machinery cooperatives made available to the peasant smallholders straw cutters and threshers, and later on cultivating and harvesting machines. Although the use of artificial fertilizers was restricted to big estate owners and richer peasants, the yield per acre generally improved. Agriculture did not advance equally in all areas. Carinthia, Styria, and in Carniola the regions of Ljubljana and the north were the most developed, while Gorizia and the regions of southern and eastern Carniola lagged behind.

With the growth of industry and population the demand for grain outstripped production, and imports had to cover the deficit. Viticulture (recovering from the pest), and fruit growing, especially in Gorizia and southern Styria, gained importance. Hops production, mainly in the Savinjska Dolina, amounted to 1,000 tons per year, mostly for export. In animal raising, the number of cattle in Carniola alone rose in the period 1869–1900 from 190,000 to 254,000, and of pigs from 63,000 to 108,000. Horses registered a smaller increase, from 20,000 to 25,000, while the number of sheep declined from 85,000 to 39,000. After 1900 an emphasis was placed on improved breeds and efficient feeding of animals.

The overall production of Slovene agriculture assured a favorable balance of agricultural exports amounting in 1913 to 36 million crowns

15. In Sladka Gora, Podgora near Gorizia, and Radeče.

compared with 22 million in imports. The favorable balance was due to the excess of livestock exports over imports (20 million crowns), which offset the excess of crop imports over exports (6 million crowns). As a crucial indicator of the degree of advancement of Slovenian agriculture, livestock constituted 47.8 percent (207 million of 433 million crowns) of the total value of agricultural production in 1913. This was somewhat better than the 46 percent in the neighboring Croatia, but still a low proportion compared with the agriculturally advanced parts of Europe.

The mounting crisis in industrial development of the Slovene area became fully evident in the period 1890 to 1914. While a modest overall growth occurred, the advance became more uneven and the volume of production fell further behind the Austro-German and Bohemian Lands of the empire. The crisis was reflected in the condition of the industries basic to the nineteenth-century process of industrialization: textiles and iron. While the production of textiles stagnated, some of the existing ironworks were actually curtailed, usually because of scarcity of iron ore combined with poor railroad connections. In 1898 the Carniolan Industrial Society established new ironworks near Trieste, and only vestigial operations remained in Jesenice. The Alpine Mountain Company closed down the ironworks at Prevalje, and iron production also ceased in Dvor pri Žužemberku in the 1890s.

Established industrial branches that continued to grow modestly included metal processing. Machinery production, especially the manufacture of turbines and wood-processing equipment, was established in Ljubljana in the 1890s. A large factory in Celje produced metal utensils. Mining also continued to expand for coal (especially in Trbovlje), lead (Litija and Mežica), and zinc (in Litija). Altogether in the Slovene territory the coal production grew from 650,000 tons per year in the 1880s to 1,450,000 tons per year before World War I. In 1913 the annual output of lead and zinc amounted respectively to 15,000 and 4,300 tons. The traditional mercury production at Idrija stabilized at a level of 800 tons per year.

Among the established light industries, the one exceptional sector to undergo rapid expansion was wood processing. It became the leading industry of the Slovene area. Before World War I, from 40,000 to 50,000 carloads, or one million cubic meters, of lumber were exported annually. In addition, seven local plants produced finished wooden goods. As to other light industries, tanneries and shoe manufacture expanded substantially, while food processing grew more slowly, adding to the older flour mills new factories manufacturing dough products.[16]

As to new industries, several developed slowly in the late nineteenth

---

16. In Ljubljana, Maribor, and Ilirska Bistrica.

and early twentieth centuries, including chemicals, building materials, and electric industries. The most important chemical plants (in Hrastnik and Celje) began producing fertilizers in the 1890s. Construction of another large chemical factory in Ruše began just before World War I. In addition to numerous brickyards, large cement factories operated in Trbovlje, Zidani Most, and Mojstrana by 1914. Although steam propulsion still prevailed, individual enterprises began to turn to electricity after 1897. The Committee of the Land drafted in 1909 a comprehensive plan for the electrification of Carniola.

A growth of credit institutions accompanied the industrial expansion at the end of the nineteenth century and the beginning of the twentieth. Loan cooperatives began to multiply in the 1880s and became linked in the so-called Celje federation. In the 1890s the clericals launched a movement of smaller credit cooperatives of the Raiffeisen type, which penetrated into villages, particularly in Carniola. In 1907 the liberals started a third series of cooperatives. All of these institutions, amounting to 512 in 1910, operated throughout the Slovene territory and contributed to its economic integration. The growth of savings banks was much less rapid, with 15 in 1890 and 28 by World War I. As for commercial banks, no special Slovene ones existed before 1900, and reliance had to be placed on outside institutions, especially in Graz or Vienna. Not until the twentieth century did matters begin to change slowly.[17]

In assessing the industrialization of the Slovene territory in the second half of the nineteenth century and the opening decade of the twentieth, it can be pointed out that the number of industrial enterprises increased in 1852–1912 (in Carniola and southern Styria) from 116 to 441 and the number of workers from 6,633 to 36,230. Still, the number of enterprises per 100,000 inhabitants amounted only to 29.0 in Carniola, which was below the average of 59.8 for Cisleithania.[18] Turning to another measure of industrialization, agricultural population declined significantly on the Slovene territory after 1880, when the percentage was 81; it fell to 73 in 1900 and 67 in 1910. Even by 1910, however, the percentage was comparatively high; the corresponding figures, for example, were 61.8 for the territory of present-day Slovakia and 34.2 for the Lands of the Bohemian Crown.

Of the total gross national product in the Slovene territory, 35.2 percent originated in 1913 from nonagricultural production, which was

17. In 1900 Ljubljanska Kreditna Banka was organized with half a million crowns in stock capital, of which 47.6 percent was contributed by the Živnostenská Banka in Prague and the rest by Slovene businessmen and cooperatives. Numerous branches were established in the Slovene territory, and beyond it in Split (1903) and Sarajevo (1910). The stock capital grew to 3 million in 1909 and 8 million in 1912. The Committee of the Land sponsored the establishment in 1910 of the Kranjska Deželna Banka, designed primarily to hold land mortgages and underwrite municipal bonds.

18. In Bohemia it was 93.6.

about the same proportion as in contemporary Hungary. Of the total value of industrial production a disproportionately high share of 44.2 percent belonged to wood processing. Mining, metallurgy, and metal-working accounted for 26.8 percent, despite the recession in iron production. The stagnation of textiles was offset by the growth of leather and shoe production, to keep the share of apparel industry at a respectable 15.7 percent. Because of its very modest growth, food processing accounted for only 4.9 percent. All other industrial branches together amounted to less than 10 percent of the total value of industrial production.

Despite limitations of its industrialization, the Slovene area was the most heavily industrialized among the various South Slav territories within—and for that matter also outside—the Habsburg empire. The capital invested in industry per capita by 1918 was to be 192 dinars there, while only 124 dinars were invested in the Vojvodina, 113 in Croatia, 107 in Serbia, 73 in Bosnia-Herzegovina, and 13 in Montenegro.

WORLD WAR I AND SELF-DETERMINATION

Although all Slovene political parties had before World War I endorsed the idea of association with other South Slavs, in almost all cases they had envisioned such a grouping within the Habsburg empire. Not surprisingly, the clericals, the staunchest advocates of a trialistic reorganization of the monarchy, pledged their loyalty to the Habsburgs at the outbreak of the war, and the liberals echoed these pledges, though with less enthusiasm. But a wave of governmental repression, especially in Styria and Carinthia, helped to engender popular discontent. During the first fourteen months of the war, 469 persons suffered the death penalty in the Slovene territories for political crimes. German nationalist pressure to strengthen the position of German as the official language also mounted from 1915. As a gesture of resistance, individuals escaped to Serbia to volunteer for the local army, and voluntary surrenders of Slovene units occurred, especially on the Russian front.

Several public figures had emigrated in order to work abroad for the separation of the Slovene territories from the Habsburg empire. The Yugoslav Committee, organized in London in April 1915, included three Slovene representatives. A Slovene periodical, edited by F. L. Tuma, also had begun to appear in St. Petersburg by October 1916, advocating the inclusion of the Slovenes in an independent federated Yugoslav state. A Slovene delegate, Bogumil Vošnjak, participated on behalf of the Yugoslav Committee in the negotiation of the Corfu Declaration of July 1917, expressing greater concern for Yugoslav unity than for guarantees of the component nations' internal autonomy.

Within the Habsburg monarchy the movement toward self-determination among the Slovenes, as among other nations, was gaining momentum by the spring of 1917. In particular, the reconvening of the *Reichsrat* provided an opportunity for the Slovene deputies, associated with their South Slav (Croatian and Serb) colleagues from Istria and Dalmatia, to restate more emphatically in the May Declaration of 1917 the demand for an autonomous political body, embracing all the South Slavs within the monarchy. The principles of the Declaration were reiterated in September 1917 in the Ljubljana Statement, signed by Bishop Anton Jeglič, numerous members of the clergy, and other representatives of both the clericals and the liberals. The Statement evoked widespread popular support. The intensification of the movement toward self-determination precipitated schisms among the Yugoslav (i.e., Slovene) Social Democrats and among the clericals. In September 1917 the so-called Socialist *Omladina* (Youth Movement) denounced the majority of the Social Democrats for clinging to the Tivoli Declaration of 1909, which was less explicit on the issue of South Slav statehood than the May Declaration of 1917. A loyalist wing under Šušteršič seceded from the clericals to form in November 1917 a Slovene Peasant Party, pledged to preserve the Habsburg monarchy as a shield against Serbian ascendancy and Italian encroachments. Clinging to the pro-Habsburg orientation, this faction was to denounce in the Carniolan diet the Yugoslav Committee of London for high treason as late as June 1918.

By the late spring of 1918, however, both of the main parties, the clericals and the liberals, had begun to move from an autonomist to a separatist position. In June 1918 the liberals of Carniola and Styria united under Tavčar's leadership, characteristically adopting the name Yugoslav Democratic Party. Independently the Social Democrats were also abandoning their traditional loyalism to the Habsburg empire. In July 1918 they organized a large demonstration in Ljubljana in favor of an independent Yugoslav state. In mid-August the major Slovene parties created a National Council under the presidency of the clerical, Anton Korošec, later a Yugoslav prime minister, to work toward the same goal.

In early October the Slovene parties, still excluding Šušteršič's faction, but including the Social Democrats, agreed to join the National Council in Zagreb, organized to coordinate the preparation for an independent statehood of the South Slavs of the Habsburg monarchy. Subsequently the Slovene leaders associated themselves with the actions of this Council up to the declaration of an independent state of the Slovenes, Croats, and Serbs on October 29, 1918. The declaration was promulgated in Ljubljana on the same day, and on October 31 the Slovene National Council replaced the authority of Vienna with a national government for the Slovene area, headed by Josip Pogačnik and including seven clericals, five liberals, and one Social Democrat. Fears of internal disorders and of Italian encroachments during November led the Slovene authorities to associate themselves with the wish of the Croat leaders to accept on December 1, 1918, a union with the Serbian Kingdom without prior guarantees of internal autonomy for either the Croats or the Slovenes.

The Magyars

FROM REVOLUTION TO DUALISM, 1848–67

Revolution and War of Independence, 1848–49

The impact of the French February Revolution completely transformed the relationship of forces in the Hungarian diet in favor of the liberals and Kossuth's leadership. On March 3, 1848, Kossuth presented proposals, based on the opposition program, for liberalization of the constitution and far-reaching autonomy of Hungary under a separate ministry. Disturbances in Vienna and popular demonstrations in Pest itself helped to secure the consent of the diet, as well as of the imperial government. The emperor on April 7 sanctioned a Hungarian Ministry headed by Lajos Batthyány and including, among others, such outstanding men as Lajos Kossuth, Count Stephen Széchenyi, Baron Joseph Eötvös, and Francis Deák.

The set of provisions, defining the new constitutional order, and adopted by the diet, was to a large extent confirmed by the emperor on April 11. According to these April Laws, the Ministry, responsible to the diet, replaced the earlier organs of central administration: the Hungarian Court Chancellery, the Lieutenancy Council, and the Hungarian Chamber. The reformed diet was to meet annually in Pest, with the lower chamber elected every three years, no longer solely by the nobles but by all citizens meeting certain educational and tax requirements. Magyar became the official language of the state, and its knowledge a precondition for service in the diet. Civil liberties, including freedom of the press, assembly, and religion, were granted; the nobility's immunity from taxation was abolished; and the emancipation of the peasants from patrimonial jurisdiction, as well as seigneurial obligations, was enacted. The counties retained self-government, but all voters, not just nobles, were represented by the county assemblies, which were authorized to choose standing county committees for the supervision of other county agencies. All of historic Hungary was to form a unitary state, with even Croatia reduced to the status of mere province.

The new constitution could not unilaterally determine the relation of

Hungary to the bulk of the monarchy, but it assumed a Hungarian status similar to that of an ally of the empire under a Habsburg king rather than as part of the empire. Despite warnings of his more moderate colleagues, Kossuth exacerbated the problem by seeking an independent financial and military system. As the finance minister, he insisted on an entirely separate Hungarian budget, and, chiefly at his urging, the constitution provided also that Hungarian troops could not serve outside the country without the approval of the cabinet and diet. The emperor-king refused to sanction these financial and military provisions, which were inconsistent with the structure of an even moderately centralized empire. Nevertheless, mainly on Kossuth's initiative, the diet, meeting according to the new constitution, appropriated funds on July 11 to create a Hungarian army of 200,000 men.

Vienna could rely on the non-Magyar nationalities to curb the actions of the Magyar-dominated Hungary. Although they made up about half of Hungary's population, the new constitution ignored their particular interests. Their leaning toward Vienna for protection had been foreshadowed as early as 1790, and was to reemerge periodically in the future. With the revolution restrained in Italy, the imperial government in September 1848 used the threat of a Croatian invasion of Hungary by *Banus* Joseph Jelačić as a means of inducing the more moderate elements in Pest to compromise. Although supported by Batthyány and Deák, the attempts at peaceful settlement broke down when Jelačić's troops entered Hungary from the south and the royal commissioner, Count Francis Lamberg, was killed in Pest on September 28 by an unruly mob.

While the Magyars were united in their will to defend the complete autonomy, if not sovereignty, of Hungary against Habsburg power, they were no less resolved to suppress the risings of the non-Magyar nationalities in the country. The demands of the Transylvanian Romanians for preservation of their autonomy directly under the jurisdiction of Vienna were rejected, as was the more limited Slovak request for autonomy within Hungary. Serb risings in pursuit of their claims for expanded autonomy were fought in bloody clashes. Therewith the Magyar revolution, which in many ways stood for the cause of liberalism, was compromised by the narrow nationalism of its charismatic, brilliant leader Kossuth.

Through a manifesto of October 3, the crown declared a substantial part of the revolutionary legislation in Hungary void, dissolved the diet, and introduced a state of siege. In defiance of these royal decrees the diet declared itself in permanent session. After the resignation of Batthyány, semidictatorial powers were transferred to Kossuth. His intransigence, and the harshness and indirectly the military incompetence of the new imperial commander in Hungary, Prince Alfred Windischgrätz, aggravated the conflict further. Trusting in their superior military leadership under Generals Artur Görgey and György Klapka, the Magyars were now as little inclined to compromise as the crown. They refused to recognize the new emperor-king, Francis Joseph (1848–1916), who succeeded the feeble-minded Ferdinand V (1835–48) after his abdication on December 2, 1848. Obviously a coronation of Francis Joseph in Hungary had by now become impossible.

Undaunted by the loss of Buda and Pest to imperial troops, the revolutionary Hungarian government moved to Debrecen in early January 1849. In April the national assembly declared the Habsburg dynasty deposed. An independent Hungarian state under Kossuth as governor (kormányzó elnök) was proclaimed. Beginning in January 1849, the Hungarian revolution was transformed into a war of independence. Notwithstanding armed conflict with the Serbs in the Banat, and the Saxons (Germans) and Romanians in Transylvania, the Magyar military forces gradually gained the upper hand against imperial troops. Weakened by the crisis in Germany and the spring campaign against Piedmont in Italy, Francis Joseph in May 1849 was forced to ask Tsar Nicholas I for help in Hungary. It was readily granted in the spirit of counterrevolutionary solidarity.

With the support of Russian troops the victory of the imperial cause under a particularly brutal commander, Julius Haynau, was a foregone conclusion. Kossuth finally managed to escape to Turkey, and on August 13, 1849, Görgey was forced to capitulate at Világos (Şiria). The Hungarian generals who had surrendered to the Russians were hanged, the others shot. This shameful action ordered by the government of Prince Felix Schwarzenberg, and executed by its foul henchman Haynau, was never forgotten, and although it was patched over in the 1860s, it was never really forgiven by the Magyars. The future relationship with Austria was to become a marriage of convenience but never evidence of genuine friendship. There can be little doubt also that the brutal suppression the Magyars had to suffer in the following decade made them even less inclined to comprehend the viewpoint of the nationalities with whom they were at odds in 1848–49. No good could result from the errors and follies committed on either side.

Neo-Absolutism, 1849–59

The defeat of the Hungarian revolution by means of military occupation and administration led to a short phase of almost complete unitary centralism in the empire. With the abrogation of the April constitution, Hungary had lost its character as a distinct state and its former self-government. In possession of exclusive legislative power, the emperor issued laws in the form of patents, ordinances, and other autocratic decrees. Executive power also belonged to the emperor, and was exercised through a series of agencies hierarchically subordinated to the ministry in Vienna. Transylvania and Croatia reverted to the status of separate Lands, albeit under absolutist government, and Hungary proper was reduced further by the formation of its southeastern, partly Serbian, territory, the Serbian Vojvodina and the Banat of Timişoara, as a new and separate crownland.

The new civil administration emerged in Hungary provisionally in the fall of 1850, after the end of a military dictatorship, and assumed a definite form by a law promulgated in 1853. The Lieutenancy was formally restored, and was headed until 1856 by the civil and military lieutenant, subsequently by the governor-general. The Land was newly divided into five districts of civil administration, delimited to some extent according to national lines. The prevalent national groups in these districts were respectively the Magyars (in the district of Pest-Buda), the Slovaks (Pozsony), the Slovaks and Ruthenians (Košice), the Romanians (Oradea, Nagyvárad), and the Germans (Sopron). Each district was governed by a section of the Lieutenancy, located in its chief town and headed by a deputy chairman of the Lieutenancy. Each section was, in fact, if not in theory, directly subordinated to Vienna, rather than to the Lieutenancy in Pest, which in practice functioned only through its sections. Under the new districts were the traditional counties and their subdivisions, the *járások*. Both, however, had been transformed from units of self-government into those of bureaucratic administration, staffed by professional civil servants who were often recruited in the Austrian and Bohemian Lands.[19]

The new judicial system, introduced in 1853, also functioned as part of a centralized structure, charged with enforcing the same legal codes in Hungary as in the rest of the monarchy. At the lowest level, the offices of the *járások* combined administrative with judicial functions. The county courts tried more serious cases and accepted appeals from the *járások*. The district chief courts represented the next level of appellate authority. It was another reflection of the tendency to emphasize the importance of the five districts over that of the Land that there was no supreme court for Hungary as a whole, and appeals from the district courts went directly to the Supreme Judicial and Cassation Court in Vienna. A customs union accompanied the introduction of uniform codes of law. The tariff between Hungary and the rest of the monarchy was suspended in October 1850 and permanently abolished in July of the next year. The government compensated for the loss of customs

19. The counties in their administrative functions became very much like the Bohemian *kraje* (*Kreise*), the *járások* like the Bohemian *okresy* (*Bezirke*). The "districts" were peculiar creations which in their operations resembled more the *Länder* than the *Kreise* of Cisleithania.

revenue by introducing into Hungary indirect Austrian taxes and the tobacco monopoly, as well as a land tax paid by both peasants and nobles at the rate of 16 percent of net income from land.

Of the major reform measures adopted by the Hungarian diet in the revolutionary period 1848–49, the only one that the absolutist regime did implement was the emancipation of the peasantry. The law of March 1853 assigned directly to the peasants the land outside the demesnes, basically as recorded in the Urbarium of 1767. The noble seigneurs were compensated for the loss of peasant services by a sum equal to seventeen times the estimated annual value of such services. The state paid the entire compensation so that Hungarian peasants, unlike those in the Bohemian and Austrian Lands, were absolved from redemption payments.

The old Hungarian political groups in varying degrees opposed the absolutist centralist regime. The neoconservatives, represented by magnates such as Count György Apponyi and Baron Sámuel Josika, were relieved that the revolution had failed, and hoped for restoration of the pre-1848 constitutional order. In 1857 they made an unsuccessful attempt to present their wishes in a memorandum to the emperor. At the other extreme, Kossuth with his fellow émigrés clung to the idea of Hungary's complete separation from the Habsburg monarchy through another revolution, supported by Romania and Serbia, and possibly resulting in a Danubian confederation centered in Hungary. The middle ground was occupied by moderate liberals, both magnates and middle nobility, among whom Deák gained increasingly in authority. Insisting on the validity of the April constitution, he awaited propitious circumstances to campaign for its restoration.

Toward Dualism, 1860–67

The absolutist regime having collapsed in the wake of the empire's defeat by France and Piedmont in the Sardinian War of 1859, the conservatives briefly enjoyed political dominance in Hungary. Led by the Counts Anthony Szécsen and Emil Dessewffy, they played a prominent role in 1860 in the Enlarged *Reichsrat* and in the adoption of the October Diploma. Their influence led to a restoration of many of the basic aspects of the pre-1848 constitutional order in Hungary. In April 1860 the five administrative districts were abolished, and in December the Serbian Vojvodina was reincorporated into Hungary proper. In October the government announced the reestablishment of the Hungarian Court Chancellery, the Lieutenancy Council, and the diet and the traditional institutions of county self-government. After the restoration of the Septemviral Table and the Royal Judicial Table in January 1861, a two-month-long Iudex-Curial Conference was held to decide a provisional replacement of the Austrian law codes introduced in the period of Neo-Absolutism. In May 1861 the traditional county courts began to function as part of the restored county self-government.

The ascendancy of the conservatives ended with a crushing victory of the liberals in the diet election of April 1861. The liberals themselves were divided in the diet into the Anti-Address Party, led by the returned émigrés Kálmán Tisza (1830–1902) and Count László Teleki, and the slightly larger Address Party, led by Deák and Count Gyula Andrássy (1823–90), another former political exile. The followers of Tisza and Teleki refused to deal with Francis Joseph until he was formally crowned in accordance with the April constitution of 1848. The supporters of Deák and Andrássy were ready to start negotiations with the king, although they also insisted on the validity of the April Laws, above all the provision for a separate Hungarian Ministry. Both factions challenged the legality of the October Diploma (1860) and the February Patent (1861), and they especially rejected as unconstitutional a common legislative body with the other Lands of the monarchy—the *Reichsrat*. When the diet refused to elect deputies into the *Reichsrat*, it was dissolved in August 1861 by the government of Anton Schmerling (1861–65), which held that the Hungarian uprising of 1848–49 nullified the April Laws.

The restored administrative and judicial organs of county self-government also fell under the control of champions of the April Laws. The conservative magnates, who dominated the central organs of Hungarian administration, were powerless to deal with the counties' opposition to the empire-wide semicentralist system, instituted by the February Patent. The counties wielded the traditional weapon of passive resistance, centered on the refusal to collect state taxes or to supply army recruits. To undermine central authority further, the counties demanded abolition of the state gendarmerie, created in the 1850s, and proceeded to recruit their own police units, largely from the veterans of the revolutionary army of 1848.

The Viennese government reacted to the collapse of state authority in Hungary by reintroducing absolute rule, known as the Schmerling *Provisorium*. In October 1861 the county assemblies were proscribed, royal commissioners appointed in the counties, and offenses by public officials made punishable by military courts. A bureaucratic system of local government reemerged. The royal commissioners absorbed the functions of county assemblies, committees, and elective officials. Civil servants of the Neo-Absolutist era regained their posts. The counties also lost their traditional fiscal autonomy. Officials of the central administration undertook to collect not only state taxes but also taxes required for the maintenance of the county administration.

The pressure of international events, notably the approach of a military conflict with Prussia, however, once more induced Francis Joseph to end the policy of repression in Hungary. To bolster the empire's external position, he charged, in July 1865, the new government of Count Richard Belcredi to seek settlement with Deák's party. The new Hungarian chancellor, Count Antal Majláth, proceeded to regularize the county governments. The bureaucrats appointed during the Schmerling *Provisorium* were dismissed and replaced, particularly in the posts of *főispán* and *alispán,* as county executives by adherents of Deák, who in turn were trusted to ensure election of Deák's supporters to the diet. To prevent a more radical current of opinion from prevailing in the counties and hence in the diet, the county self-government was not restored. Deák's followers, in fact, dominated the Hungarian legislature, which met in December 1865. Francis Joseph then signified his willingness to accept the April Laws if the diet supplemented them— in the spirit of the October Diploma—by recognizing a legislative body common to the entire monarchy to deal particularly with matters of military and foreign policy. In February 1866 the diet appointed a committee under Count Gyula Andrássy to draft proposals for a settlement, which provided for Hungary's participation in the common affairs of the monarchy but avoided the creation of a common parliament.

These proposals, with certain modifications, formed the basis of the famous Austro-Hungarian Compromise in 1867 following the defeat of Austria by Prussia in the summer of 1866. After the monarchy's external position was seriously and permanently weakened, the emperor finally felt compelled to make the necessary concessions in the domestic crisis. Baron (Count) Ferdinand Beust, former Saxon prime minister, now Austrian prime and foreign minister with the title of chancellor, conducted the negotiations with Hungary. They had a better chance of succeeding if taken up by a foreigner. A chief obstacle was finally removed: the idea of an overall imperial parliament. In February 1867 a Hungarian Ministry headed by Andrássy was appointed, and in June Francis Joseph was crowned king of Hungary. The Compromise itself had been enacted as a series of amendments to the April Laws by the Hungarian diet in May, and approved by the *Reichsrat* the following December. Executive authority over common affairs of the monarchy—foreign, military, and joint financial expenditures, chiefly for the armed forces—was assigned to three common ministers. Legislative authority over the common affairs was entrusted to the Delegations of the Hungarian diet and of the Cisleithanian *Reichsrat,* each consisting of sixty members and meeting in Vienna and Budapest in alternate years. The Compromise retained common currency and a joint Austro-Hungarian bank of issue was established in 1878. Economic and financial agreements between Hungary and the rest of the monarchy were to be renegotiated every ten years. Above all, they covered the customs union and the quotas of contribution to the common expenses. The Hungarian quota was initially set at 30 percent, but was later raised slightly.

The dualistic Compromise, in particular its interpretation by Magyar constitutional law, made an empire-wide reform of the nationality problem impossible. Yet even if one takes the short-range view, the necessity of ten-year economic compromises within the overall Compromise led to a state of chronic crisis in relations between Vienna and Budapest. These differences, like the more emotional and potentially more serious ones about the issues of unified armed forces and common interests in foreign policy, could to a point be adjusted but never really solved. And yet, the Compromise made possible the Austro-German alliance of 1879, which for half a century protected the Magyars from the dangers of despotic tsarist absolutism. Under a right-wing Panslav flag it might otherwise have enslaved Hungary, possibly as early as the 1870s. If the Magyars enjoyed constitutional government under the Compromise, it must not be forgotten that the non-Magyar national groups had to pay the price for the privileged Magyar position. Yet, would they have fared better under tsarist tutelege? Furthermore, it could not be predicted that the Austro-German Alliance of 1879, anchored in the premise of the Compromise of 1867, would lead to a world war. In any case, the Compromise represented not an unmixed blessing but certainly not an outright disaster.

DUALISM IN ASCENDANCY, 1868–1905

The Deákists in Power, 1868–75

The Compromise of 1867, which signified a victory for Deák's policy, brought Hungary a degree of autonomy unprecedented since 1526. Moreover, internal power was almost entirely retained by the Magyars. Aside from the common affairs, the organization of legislative and executive authority followed the pattern established in 1848. The diet turned into a parliament with the Table of Magnates (renamed the Upper House), remaining partly hereditary and partly appointive, and the Lower Table (now called the House of Deputies) of 453 members being elected on the basis of a highly restricted franchise. The electoral rules originating in 1848, and essentially reaffirmed in 1874, entitled only 6 percent of the population to vote. The Council of Ministers once again replaced the Hungarian Court Chancellery and the Lieutenancy Council. The office of the *palatin* also disappeared. The king had the right to appoint and dismiss the prime minister. The latter formed the cabinet, which to govern effectively needed the confidence of the parliament.

The ministry of Andrássy, which continued in power until 1871, consisted entirely of members of Deák's party, formally organized in 1866. While Kossuth himself remained abroad and unreconciled, a number of other political exiles, such as the generals Mór Perczel and György Klapka, and the historian Mihály Horváth, returned and joined the Deákists. The government under Andrássy adopted major constitutional measures and administrative reforms. Transylvania, in violation of previous pledges given by the crown to the four-nation state, was incorporated into Hungary proper in December 1868; Croatia, through an agreement (*nagodba*) as a kind of subdualistic compromise between political unequals, Hungary and the so-called Triune Kingdom, became an autonomous unit within the lands of the Hungarian Crown.[20] The Nationality Law of 1868, drafted by Eötvös in his capacity as education minister, failed to satisfy the wish of the non-Magyar nationalities for territorial autonomy. Moreover, Magyar became the official and state language to be used in the parliament, the courts, and higher education. Other languages were admissible in churches, county and municipal governments, and primary and secondary schools. Nevertheless, the law was a document drafted by a high-minded and enlightened statesman. Although it would not give national groups legal standing as corporate bodies in public law, the national rights of the individuals were fairly wide. At fault was not the intent of the lawgiver but the will to enforce it by the executive and judicial branches of government. In this respect the situation in Hungary was inferior to that in Austria, which was far from ideal.

The reform of county governments was carried out in 1870 and, with amendments adopted in 1886, represented a compromise between the "centralists," who wished to reduce county autonomy to a minimum, and the "municipalists," who cherished the county liberties of the pre-1848 era, briefly reinstituted in 1860–61. Aside from functioning as agents of state administration and local self-government, the counties retained the right to scrutinize national issues and appeal against governmental laws and ordinances viewed as unconstitutional. Reaffirmation of the statute by the appropriate ministry, however, sufficed to override such protests. In addition, the counties had lost their power to instruct parliamentary deputies. The *főispán*, though appointed by the king, was in fact an agent of the Ministry of the Interior. His main concern was the enforcement of governmental statutes, while local self-government was managed chiefly by the elected *alispán*. County assemblies were replaced by municipal committees consisting partly of the

---

20. For discussion of the *nagodba* see pp. 397–98. The Triune Kingdom consisted of Croatia, Slavonia, and Dalmatia. The last mentioned, however, was a crownland under Austrian administration.

highest taxpayers and partly of representatives elected for six years by the other substantial taxpayers.

The Andrássy government also enacted a basic reform of the judiciary. An enactment in 1869 severed the link between local organs of self-government and the courts in the counties and in the *járások*. All judges were to be appointed by the king on the advice of the justice minister, instead of being elected locally. A restructuring of the court system, the most significant one since 1723, was promulgated in 1871. District courts in the *járások* were to try minor cases before a single judge. In the new county courts (Royal Judicial Chairs), replacing the old noble courts or *sedriae*, senates of three judges were to try major cases and hear appeals from the district courts. There were 102 of them until 1875, then 66. Royal Judicial Tables were to serve as courts of appeal from the county courts.[21] The former Septemviral Table, now renamed Royal Judicial Curia, served as the supreme court for the whole country.

After the constructive accomplishments of the Andrássy Ministry, the fortunes of the Deákist party declined rapidly. Much of its distinguished leadership was lost in 1871 with the transfer of Andrássy as foreign minister to Vienna, the death of Eötvös, and the increasing withdrawal of Deák himself from active politics. The ministries of Count Menyhért Lónyay, József Szlávy, and István Bittó, succeeding each other rapidly in the brief span of 1871–75, suffered from financial difficulties and embarrassments, which stemmed partly from the economic crisis of 1873.

The main political challenge to the Deákists emanated not from the Independence Party (later renamed the Party of 1848), which followed the exiled Kossuth, but from the Left Center, originating from the Anti-Address Party of 1861, and led by Kálmán Ghyczy and Kálmán Tisza. The Left Center's Bihar Program of 1868 had accepted Hungary's link with the Cisleithanian half of the monarchy through the dynasty (on the basis of the Pragmatic Sanction), but demanded a separate Hungarian army and diplomatic representation, as well as abolition of the Delegations and of the common Ministry of Finance. While the magnates still played a substantial role among the Deákists, the leadership of the Left Center stemmed almost entirely from the middle nobility. In the parliamentary elections of 1872 the Left Center won 116 seats compared with 38 for the Independence Party. The Deákists still maintained a comfortable majority with 245 seats, but internal dissensions and recurrent malfeasance foreshadowed their political demise.

As the Left Center moved toward its hour of triumph, its immediate aims underwent a striking revision, largely owing to Tisza, who had

21. Their number increased from the initial two to eleven in 1890.

assumed its top leadership. He gradually became convinced that, under existing circumstances, pressure for basic changes in the Compromise of 1867 had little chance of success because Vienna could respond, as in 1848, by turning for support against the Magyars to the non-Magyar nationalities of Hungary. The apprehension that Francis Joseph might not find it unthinkable to place a traditionally dominant nationality under the rule of a disadvantaged one was reinforced by a recent, though abortive, plan to allow the Czechs an ascendancy in the Bohemian Lands under the Fundamental Articles of 1871. Tisza felt that a confrontation with the emperor over the Compromise had to be postponed, while the first priority was to decrease the size of non-Magyar nationalities through intensive Magyarization. Accordingly from 1872 to 1874 Tisza gradually downgraded the main points of the Bihar Program, declaring finally the Compromise not to be the most urgent immediate issue. In March 1875 he joined the cabinet as minister of the interior, and led the Left Center into a fusion with the Deákists to form the Liberal Party. In the ensuing elections the Liberals won 333 seats, the Independence Party 33. In October Tisza became prime minister.

Ministry of Kálmán Tisza, 1875–90

In line with Tisza's conviction that a numerical reduction of the nationalities was the key to future independence from Vienna, the program of Magyarization became a major theme of his long ministry (1875–90). In education, all secondary academic schools (the *gymnasia*) under state jurisdiction were to teach exclusively in Magyar after 1883. For those operated by the churches, Magyar became an obligatory subject and the language of final examinations. Moreover, the number of such schools had been reduced. In the most drastic move, all Slovak *gymnasia* were abolished as early as 1874–75. Municipal and parochial elementary schools were ordered in 1879 to teach Magyar as a compulsory subject for seventeen hours per week. Later the number of hours was raised to twenty-six. In state elementary schools, which began to emerge in significant numbers during the 1870s, all teaching was done in Magyar. Attempts were made to introduce Magyar into the churches in the nationalities' areas. Even those of the Byzantine rite were to be affected through the device of a Magyar sponsored Uniat church. Magyar was increasingly employed by state agencies not only for internal purposes but also for external contacts. It was used exclusively in all official announcements and documents. The courts did not accept petitions in non-Magyar languages; administrative agencies did accept them, but responded in Magyar. The national minorities were unable to seek effective redress through political action. Besides the artificial manipulation of the electoral process by the government, the chances of minorities electing parliamentary deputies were minimized by the franchise, which favored the propertied and well-educated groups. Minorities were grossly underrepresented in these groups.

To cope with the opposition within the enfranchised Magyar public, Tisza developed a powerful political machine and mastery of election management, which kept the so-called Liberal Party in power not only during his ministry but for an additional fifteen years. The procedure of open voting facilitated the tactics of bribery, intimidation, and outright terror. The technique of gerrymandering was also effectively employed. Electoral districts with large numbers of voters (up to 7,000 or 8,000) were created in the purely Magyar areas, which tended to favor Hungary's independence. Districts with a small number of voters (100 to 200) were formed in the non-Magyar areas, where most of the enfranchised population was either employed by or otherwise dependent on the government, and therefore voted for the party in power. A peculiar political trend of this period was for the magnates to abandon the traditional Habsburg loyalty, once this attitude was preempted by the middle nobility under Tisza, and to shift to the opposite extreme of revisionism with respect to the Compromise of 1867.

Tisza's opposition included the traditional Independence Party, led by Gábor Ugron and Gyula Justh, which obtained 88 seats in the elections of 1881, 75 in 1884, and 80 in 1887. A new opposition party, which reproduced the old Left Center position, had begun to emerge after 1877 when the decennial economic agreement with Austria failed to grant a separate national bank to Hungary. Recruited in part from dissident Liberals, in part from former magnate conservatives, the new party, under the leadership of Count Albert Apponyi (1846–1933), adopted the name of Moderate Opposition before the 1881 elections. It elected 84 deputies in 1881, 60 in 1884, and 48 in 1887. Its claim was that, accepting the Compromise in principle, it merely sought certain modifications. Initially the Moderate Opposition, in fact, took issue only with the less sensitive economic and financial effects of the Compromise. Ironically, Tisza's government was notably successful exactly in the fiscal field; it contained the growth of state deficits, and eventually balanced the budget.

The political debate turned more explosive when the Moderate Opposition focused on military affairs. The precipitating cause was the offense to the Magyar public opinion in 1886 by the unveiling of a monument in honor of the imperial General Heinrich Hentzi, who had been killed in the struggle against the Hungarian revolution in 1849. The Moderate Opposition started agitating for more Magyar spirit within the imperial army, and moved closer to the Independence Party's insistence on a separate army for Hungary. Both parties jointly opposed the army bill of 1889, which—contrary to their wishes—lessened the control of the Hungarian parliament over the number of recruits from Hungary and reemphasized the obligation of army officers to know German. Tisza had the bill enacted despite intense opposition, bolstered by boisterous street demonstrations and threats to his personal safety. His political position, however, was shaken by the massive outpouring of hostility, and he chose to resign in March 1890, although his party commanded a solid majority of 77 deputies in the parliament.

End of the Liberal Party Era, 1890–1905

A succession of prime ministers perpetuated the essential lines of Tisza's policy. The rule of the Liberal Party lasted another fifteen years. In the early 1890s the issue of religious reform captured political attention, temporarily eclipsing the issue of the Compromise. The aim was a fuller equalization of churches and a partial secularization of the state. Proposed during the ministry of Count Gyula Szapáry (1890–92) and enacted in 1894–95 under his successor, Alexander Wekerle (1892–95), the reform made civil marriage obligatory, and also civil register of births, marriages, and deaths. It granted full equality to the Jewish religion, and regulated religious upbringing of children in mixed marriages. Catholic objections to the legislation provoked a mild *Kulturkampf*, and brought into being in 1895 the new People's Party (*Néppárt*) under Count Ferdinánd Zichy. It combined a Roman Catholic program with—largely spurious—claims of concern for the interests of the petty bourgeoisie, and even the non-Magyar nationalities. In practice, the People's Party started collaborating closely with the other opposition groups, the Independence Party, which in 1895 gained a new leader in Ferenc Kossuth (1841–1914), the famous hero's repatriated son, and Apponyi's Moderate Opposition, renamed the National Party in 1892. The Liberals continued to contain the opposition, and under Prime Minister Baron Desző Bánffy (1895–99) even surpassed the unscrupulous techniques of election manipulation developed by Tisza. The elections of 1896 yielded the Liberals 287 seats, and only 32 to the National Party, 60 to the Independence Party, and 19 to the new People's Party.

In practice both the Liberals and the opposition agreed on the goal of Magyarization and on the exclusion of lower social classes of whatever nationality from active political life. An expansion of the Magyar language into the nationality areas was further promoted in 1891 through the introduction of compulsory Magyar nursery schools, and by requiring more teaching of Magyar in private schools in exchange for a state subsidy in 1893. The religious reform legislation of 1894–95 also favored Magyarization, since it transferred a large area of official record keeping from churches to the state. To facilitate ethnic repression of the nationalities, the government in Budapest created a special section in 1894 to scrutinize their associations, press, financial institutions, and mutual contacts. The grand celebration of the Millennium of the entry of the Magyar nation into Hungary in 1896 provided an impetus for a required Magyarization of names, both geographic and personal, the latter especially among civil servants.

Among the lower classes, which remained disenfranchised, the peasantry posed the most serious social problem. Consisting largely of cottagers and landless proletarians, it suffered from poverty and unemployment, and created a chronic state of tensions and discontent in the countryside. The government responded to rural protests in 1898 by severely curtailing the freedom of assembly and association among the peasants. Although, in the late 1890s, the Social Democratic Party's influence affected certain rural regions, the main concern of the party, founded in 1890, was to organize the urban workers through trade unions. There was no chance of direct political activity under the existing franchise. By 1900 the trade unions had enrolled between 10,000 and 20,000 urban workers. In 1900 Vilmos Mezőfi's Reorganized Social Democratic Party set out to agitate specifically among the peasants for manhood suffrage and land reform, but opportunism and repression soon dampened the movement's radical fervor.

After the millennial celebrations of 1896, the Liberals and the opposition resumed the struggle over the Compromise of 1867. The decennial negotiations of economic issues with Austria in 1897 provided a point of departure. Even the People's Party, now led by István Rakovszky, ignored its proclaimed social concerns and focused instead on the consitutional conflict in an alliance with the Independence and the National parties. Despite opposition that escalated into parliamentary obstruction, Prime Minister Kálmán Széll (1899–1903) secured in 1900 the approval of a provisional agreement. Although the agreement increased the Hungarian quota for common expenses from 30 to 34.4 percent, it granted significant concessions, particularly more Hungarian influence in the joint Austro-Hungarian Bank and a provision that if a regular agreement was not reached by 1903, Hungary would be free to dissolve the customs and commercial union in 1907.

The opposition once more advanced its campaign, from the issues of a separate tariff and a Hungarian national bank to the most sensitive issue of a separate army with Magyar the language of command. The struggle intensified in September 1903 when Francis Joseph explicitly reaffirmed the unity of the army and his own unilateral right to determine the language of command, which should remain German. Violent obstruction in parliament caused the fall of the short-lived ministry of Count Károly Khuen-Héderváry and the appointment in November 1903 as prime minister of Count István Tisza (1861–1918), son of the famous Kálmán. Although Tisza obtained some concessions from the emperor, especially the use of Magyar in military academies and courts and in correspondence between Hungarian troops and Hungarian civil agencies, the excitement over the military question threw the country into a state of virtual anarchy, and the Liberal Party suffered formidable defections. Opposition groups multiplied. In 1904 Apponyi reestablished the National Party, which he had fused with the Liberals in 1901, and Bánffy formed the New Party, pledged to an immediate tariff autonomy. In November 1904, Gyula Andrássy, Jr. (1860–1929), son of the earlier prime minister and joint minister of foreign affairs, created the Constitutional Party in protest against Tisza's attempts to curb obstruction through modifications of parliamentary rules.

István Tisza sought to resolve the crisis through new elections in January 1905. Whether he deliberately abstained from interference with the electoral process or—as is more likely—the accumulated hostility defied manipulation, the result was a decisive defeat for the Liberals, who secured a mere 159 seats. The Independence Party, combined with Apponyi's National Party, won 166 mandates, Andrássy's Consitutional Party 27, the People's Party 24, and Bánffy's New Party 17. The victors formed a Coalition of National Parties. Thus ended the long reign of the Liberal Party, the mainstay of the Compromise for thirty years. A full-fledged substitute for it would not be found for another five years. The parliamentary majority now shifted to a coalition that envisaged a full restoration of the conditions of April 1848, amounting by intent to little more than a personal union with the rest of the monarchy.

DUALISM IN CRISIS, 1905–18

Crisis, Coalition, Restoration, 1905–14

Victory of the National Coalition plunged Hungary into a deep consititutional crisis. When the Coalition leaders refused to yield on the army issue, Francis Joseph ignored their parliamentary majority, and appointed in June 1905 a cabinet of government officials under a Habsburg loyalist, General Géza Fejérváry. Against truculent opposition, directed by Bánffy, Apponyi, and Andrássy, the prime minister attempted to govern without parliament, and turned directly to the counties for taxes and recruits. When the counties rejected government orders, the minister of the interior, József Kristóffy, appointed new főispánok. In many localities the county officials refused to accept the new chiefs; elsewhere—following the precedent of 1823—they resigned, leaving the főispánok without a governing apparatus.

To overcome the opposition, Fejérváry's government unveiled its most powerful weapon: social and ethnic equalization in politics. It announced its intention to move toward universal manhood suffrage, at the same time easing the restrictions on organizing politically the urban and rural poor. The reform threatened not only to give a political voice to Magyar workers and poor peasants but to make non-Magyars the dominant element in the Hungarian parliament. Rather than face the prospect of this cataclysmic turnover, the Coalition surrendered. First Kossuth, then the other leaders, yielded, and promised the emperor in secret to accept the joint diplomatic service and the unitary army with German as the language of command, and not to alter the economic arrangements unilaterally. In return, they were free to decide the issue of electoral reform. Following this bargain, the emperor in April 1906 appointed the former Liberal, Wekerle, to head a cabinet that included all principal leaders of the Coalition—Kossuth, Apponyi, Andrássy, and Zichy. In parliamentary elections a month later—in the absence of the Liberal Party dissolved by Tisza—almost all seats went to the Coalition.[22]

The election results were meaningless, since the Coalition cabinet did not dare pursue any of the opposition's major original objectives. In the 1907 negotiations with Austria it even acquiesced in a 2 percent rise in the quota of Hungary's contribution to common expenses. In return, however, the new government could simply procrastinate on the promised liberalization of franchise. Moreover, it was free to intensify the Magyarization drive aimed at reducing the liability the non-Magyars represented in the struggle with Vienna. A law, drafted by Apponyi in 1907, required all teachers in non-Magyar elementary schools to be fully proficient in Magyar, and all pupils to demonstrate complete knowledge of the language at the end of fourth grade. Two years later, religious instruction in these schools was to be given only in Magyar.

The Coalition rapidly lost ground among the voters, who—unaware of the secret accommodation with the emperor—were dismayed by its failure to implement its program. The government itself was weakened by internal strife. The largest component, the Independence Party, was split by a revolt against the leadership of the feeble young Kossuth and the intellectually far superior Apponyi, by a faction under the leadership of Gyula Justh. Justh's party campaigned for a moderate franchise reform and for an immediate establishment of a separate national bank for Hungary. Wekerle's resignation in April 1909 prepared the way for a decisive defeat of the Coalition. After protracted negotiations with the emperor, a new cabinet was appointed in January 1910, consisting of former Liberals headed by Count Khuen-Héderváry. Ultimate power, however, belonged to Tisza, who set out to reconstitute the Liberals

22. The Independence Party won 253, the Constitutional Party 89, the People's Party 23, and the New Party 3.

under the name of the Party of National Work in time for elections in early June 1910. The disillusionment with the Coalition, combined with the traditional methods of election management, brought an impressive majority of 258 seats to the new party, and reduced the former Coalition to a minority of contending parties.[23]

After the elections, the situation in the parliament essentially reproduced the state before 1905, with the government party committed to defending the Compromise and the opposition seeking its abrogation. In March 1911, Khuen-Héderváry gained approval for an extension of the common National Bank until 1917. Yet two months later the usual conflict erupted over a new army bill increasing the annual number of recruits. Violent obstruction, led in parliament by Justh's party, caused the resignation of Khuen in April 1912. The impasse was broken only during the following ministry of László Lukács, when Tisza, assuming the position of speaker of the House of Deputies in May 1912, ended the obstruction by having protesting deputies physically removed from the chamber. Finally, the army bill passed, and as *quid pro quo* Francis Joseph withdrew the demand of 1905 for meaningful reform of the suffrage. Instead a token bill, passed in March 1913, continued to exclude Magyar workers and peasants, as well as national minorities, from parliamentary representation.

Despite formidable impediments, workers' and peasants' organizations achieved some advances, notably in the permissive Fejérváry era. The trade unions, sponsored by the Social Democrats, expanded from 70,000 members in 1905 to 130,000 in 1907. After a decline the membership rose again by 1911, and the following May a mass demonstration in Budapest showed the strength of the Social Democrats. Rural laborers became more assertive in 1905, and strikes at harvest time occurred the following year. In March 1906, András Achim organized the Independent Socialist Peasant Party, which agitated for land reform and universal suffrage. The government, highly sensitive to social protests in the countryside, responded with further restrictions on the peasants' right of association in 1907, and gradual suppression of Achim's movement. After 1905 the cause of universal suffrage however gained new champions in a circle of middle-class intellectuals, the Radicals, led by Oscar Jászi (1875–1957). Among the parties actually represented in the parliament only Justh's wing of the Independence Party seriously advocated suffrage reform. In 1913 its leadership passed to Count Mihály Károlyi (1875–1955), who, in addition, favored limited concessions to non-Magyar nationalities in order to strengthen Hungary in relation to Vienna.

In July 1913 the restoration of pre-1905 conditions was underscored

23. Kossuth's Independence Party won 55 seats, Justh's Independence Party 41, Andrássy's Constitutional Party 21, and the People's Party 13.

by Tisza's appointment as prime minister. He now became more eager to mitigate the conflict with the traditional opposition, especially Apponyi's majority wing of the Independence Party and Zichy's People's Party. He also wished to limit the conflict with the nationalities through selective concessions to the Croats. His other initiative in this field, renewed negotiations with the leaders of Transylvanian Romanians, from October, 1913 to February 1914, produced no results, and was pursued mainly to appease the German government, eager to win Romania over to the Austro-German alliance.

World War I

In early July 1914 Tisza prudently tried to prevent the outbreak of war with Serbia, which in its consequences was to be disastrous for the cause to which both his party and the parliamentary opposition—despite their other differences—were equally dedicated. It took an appeal from Francis Joseph to make the Hungarian premier agree on July 18 to the fateful ultimatum to Serbia. Even then he insisted on a proviso that except for relatively minor strategic frontier rectifications, Serbian territory would not be annexed by the monarchy as a result of the war. Nevertheless, once the war did break out, it received full support not only from Tisza and his party but also from the parliamentary opposition (Coalition), headed by Andrássy. The opposition, in fact, offered to join the Party of National Work in the cabinet but demanded the price of Tisza's replacement as prime minister. Even the Social Democrats, who had no parliamentary representation, initially endorsed the war against "tsarist barbarism."

The Tisza government efficiently organized Hungarian war production and mobilization. Magyar troops partook actively in the war, especially on the Italian front from 1915, and against Romania in 1916. Consistent with his prewar policy, Tisza remained firmly loyal to Vienna, as well as to the German war alliance, rejecting all suggestions for a separate peace. In return he expected to avoid any importunity from Vienna for concessions to non-Magyar nationalities, or on the issue of the electoral franchise. To assure perpetuation of the status quo after Francis Joseph's death in November 1916, he pressed for speedy coronation of the new Emperor Charles as the king of Hungary so as to bind him with an oath to preserve Hungary's existing constitutional order and territorial integrity. Using the lever of Cisleithania's dependence on Hungarian foodstuffs, Tisza arranged the coronation for December 30. In return he agreed to a twenty-year extension of the economic agreement with the Cisleithanian half of the monarchy.

Nevertheless, by early 1917 Charles began to press for a democratization of Hungarian politics in order to strengthen the monarchy internally, as well as to improve its image for possible negotiations with the Entente. Rather than alter Hungary's political regime, Tisza resigned in May. After an interlude of a ministry headed by Count Móric Esterházy, the cabinet of Wekerle came to power in September, consisting largely of members of the old Coalition parties. The new minister of justice, Vilmos Vázsonyi, actually prepared a moderately liberal reform of the franchise in December 1917, but the project was defeated in the parliament, where Tisza's Party of National Work still had a majority. A substitute measure, modified according to Tisza's wishes largely to exclude the poor peasantry and the non-Magyar population from voting, was finally passed in July 1918. Even for this relatively small concession the emperor had to pay the high price of agreeing to an independent Hungarian army after the war.

Among leaders of the parliamentary parties, only Károlyi, who had opposed the German war alliance from the very start, espoused the idea of a separate peace by 1917. Outside the parliament he sought a rapprochement with the Social Democrats, who had turned against the war as early as 1915. Their influence among Hungarian workers grew with the increasing wartime privations and the repercussions of revolutionary events in Russia. In the spring of 1917 the trade union membership exceeded 200,000. In part under the influence of Jászi, in the fall of 1917 Károlyi also realized the urgency of major concessions to the non-Magyar nationalities. He wished to answer the insistence of the Western powers on autonomous development of all the nations of the Habsburg monarchy, and thus preserve the territorial integrity of Hungary. Until October 1918, however, he could do nothing specific except urge some concessions to the Transylvanian Romanians.

The government of Wekerle continued to oppose adamantly any suggestions of significant autonomy for the non-Magyars of Hungary, even after the Central Powers came to the brink of defeat. On its insistence, Charles' famous Manifesto of October 16, 1918, had to include a proviso that exempted Hungary from the federalization proposed for the Cisleithanian part of the monarchy. Even so, Wekerle declared in parliament that through the Manifesto the Compromise of 1867 had been abrogated. Therewith Hungary's link to Austria had been reduced to a mere personal union. At the same time, Károlyi called for a complete break with Austria and Germany, granting of autonomy to the nationalities, and immediate peace with the Entente.

Following Wekerle's resignation on October 23, Károlyi formed a National Council including representatives of his own faction of the Independence Party, Jászi's Radicals, and the Social Democrats. Emperor Charles and his representative for Hungarian affairs, Archduke Joseph, favored another cabinet of traditional parliamentary parties; but mounting popular discontent in Budapest convinced them to recognize on October 30 Károlyi's National Council as the new government, which was sworn in the next day. On November 1 this cabinet was released from its oath by Charles, and began to regard Hungary as a fully independent country. Károlyi's attention then focused on safeguarding the traditional unitary character of the Hungarian state, but this effort was doomed to failure, both by the attitude of the Entente and more especially by the non-Magyar nationalities themselves, most of whom had already declared through their leaders their adherence to one of the neighboring states. The dissolution of the tie with Austria thus merely accelerated the inevitable disintegration of the multinational Hungarian kingdom.

AGRICULTURE, INDUSTRY, AND FINANCE[24]

Agricultural Prosperity, Depression, and Recovery

In the period from the Revolution of 1848 to the Compromise of 1867, Hungarian agriculture continued to enjoy the prosperity that originated in the mid-1830s and was fostered in part by improvements in the transportation network. Above all, railroads now joined Vienna through Pest with the grain-growing region of Szeged and the cattle-raising area of Debrecen. The loss of unpaid labor, due to peasant emancipation, further stimulated the large landowners to initiate mechanization. They acquired seeding and reaping machines, and in particular steam threshers, the number of which rose in Hungary between 1864 and 1871 from 163 to 2,420. Most peasants and even the partly noble owners of middle-size estates, however, lacked the capital, or access to credit facilities, to modernize production methods on their land. Peasant farming, in particular, had remained primitive, with the prevalence of the three-field system and obsolete tools. The inefficiency of peasant homesteads was increased by a scattering of the land into small—on the average ten to sixteen—parcels. Still, some improvements came to pass. In the 1850s a gradual transition began from sickles to scythes, and from wooden to iron plows. By 1870 the proportion of iron plows reached 52 percent. Traditional extensive cattle raising continued to diminish with the encroachment of grain fields on pastures.

24. Economic data in this section are derived from Ervin Pamlényi, ed., *A History of Hungary* (London: Collet's, 1975), pp. 291–96, 345–59; I. T. Berend and G. Ranki, *Hungary: A Century of Economic Development* (Newton Abbot: David and Charles, 1974; New York: Barnes and Noble), pp. 13–90; Iván T. Berend and György Ranki, *Economic Development in East-Central Europe in the 19th and 20th Centuries* (New York: Columbia University Press, 1974), pp. 63–65, 123–30; *Istoriia Vengrii* (Moscow: Nauka, 1972), 2:186; Brian R. Mitchell, *European Historical Statistics, 1750–1970* (New York: Columbia University Press, 1975), pp. 363, 393; *Die Habsburgermonarchie, 1848–1918* (Vienna: Österreichische Akademie der Wissenschaften, 1973), 1:462–527.

In the years immediately following the Compromise until the mid-1870s, agricultural exports, mostly grain and flour, were still increasing and prices rising. Large estate owners found it even easier to raise capital for modernization, partly from newly founded credit institutions and partly from rents collected on lands leased to peasants. The effect of the agricultural depression, which began in 1873 and deepened later in the decade with the mounting imports of inexpensive overseas grain, was compounded in Hungary by an uncontrollable blight affecting the vineyards. Before the end of the century, the pest destroyed 50 percent of the vines, and wine production declined to one-fifth. The agricultural crisis caused the loss of land by a large number of peasants and also owners of middle-size estates. About 100,000 independent homesteads disappeared during the last two decades of the nineteenth century. Nevertheless, the effects of the depression were mitigated by governmental intervention, mainly through protective tariffs, which limited the decline of agricultural prices to 17 percent between the 1870s and the 1880s.

The long-range trends of Hungarian agriculture at the turn of the century were shaped to a high degree by the impact of the slump of the 1870s and 1880s. One tendency was to increase production but at the same time lower costs in order to improve the competitive position of Hungarian products. The area of agricultural land increased from 10.4 million hectares in 1871–75 to 11.9 million in 1896–1900, and to 12.9 million in 1911–15. Most of the growth was due to the reclamation of swamplands, which from 1879 to 1918 made possible a gain of 1.4 million hectares. Moreover, an increasing proportion of agricultural land was cultivated, causing the fallow to decline from 22 percent of agricultural land in 1871–75 to 9 percent in 1911–15. The productivity per hectare improved even more dramatically. Between 1871–75 and 1911–15 it almost doubled for rye, barley, and sugar beets; more than doubled for wheat, oats, and corn; and more than tripled for potatoes and fodder beets. The increased yield was due to improved implements and equipment, more intensive crop rotation, and better soil preparation. Between 1871 and 1895 the number of steam threshers more than quadrupled, that of horse-drawn reapers and harvesters tripled, and of horse-drawn seeding machines increased sevenfold. Steam threshers tripled again in number, rising to 30,000 from 1895 to 1914. In addition to more manuring, the use of artificial fertilizers rose from about 5.5 pounds per hold (0.57 hectare) of arable land in 1898 to 26.5 pounds in 1913.

Another trend, setting in toward the end of the nineteenth century, was a significant shift from the traditional grains, most adversely affected by the depression, to other crops, as well as to cattle raising for both meat and dairy products. While the production of wheat, rye, barley, and oats increased only between two to three times from 1871–75 to 1911–15, that of corn rose almost four times, of potatoes more than six times, of sugar beets sixteen times, and of fodder beets seventeen times. The proportion of wheat, rye, barley, and oats decreased from 63.2 percent of total harvest in 1881–85 to 57.1 percent in 1911–15. Among the animal stocks, the largest increase from 1870–75 to 1910–14 was 70 percent for pigs, followed by 38 and 31 percent respectively for cattle and horses. A major decline (43 percent) occurred only in the number of sheep. A qualitative improvement also took place. While in 1884 more than 80 percent of cattle were of a local variety, low in yield of meat and milk, by 1911 less than one-third were of this inferior type.

The agricultural crisis was overcome after the turn of the century, and higher protective tariffs of 1906 ushered in a new wave of prosperity. Thus shielded, Hungarian agriculture acquired virtual monopoly in the expanding market of the Habsburg monarchy. This market offered an added benefit in that the level of agricultural prices, in relation to industrial ones, kept rising until 1914—that is, as long as free market conditions existed.

During the entire period from the Compromise to World War I, Hungarian agriculture established a record of solid growth, although it did not match the rate of industrial expansion. Based on the prices of 1900, gross agricultural production expanded at an annual average rate of 2.2 percent in 1867–1913. Another calculation, using the prices of 1913, has arrived at an average yearly rate of 1.8 percent, with the rate for crops of 2.0 percent, and for animal production of 1.7 percent.[25] Despite this record of growth, the condition of Hungarian agriculture was marked by a number of negative aspects. Technological improvements were delayed in certain parts of the country, particularly eastern Hungary, and resulted in average yields significantly below those of Western Europe. Most of the rural population owned little land or none at all. According to the census of 1895, peasant homesteads under 20 holds or 11.4 hectares (constituting 88.9 percent of all farms) occupied only 29.4 percent of all agricultural land, while estates over 100 holds or 57 hectares (accounting for a mere 1 percent of all farms) took up 48 percent of all agricultural land. According to one estimate,[26] 39 percent of the agricultural work force consisted of landless farm laborers by 1900. One-quarter of them lived on large estates as permanent employees; the rest faced the harsh prospect of day work at harvest time or other occasional employment. The agricultural laborers worked up to 16 or 18 hours in the summer, and were paid only 50 to 60 percent of the average industrial wage. Work opportunities diminished with increasing mechanization on large estates, especially of the

25. Berend and Ranki, *Hungary*, p. 48.
26. Ibid., pp. 77–78.

threshing process. Emigration provided some relief. In 1880–1900 about 500,000 emigrated from Hungary, followed by 1,400,000 between 1900 and 1914. A large majority of the emigrants were non-Magyars.

Toward the Industrial Revolution

Industrial development of Hungary in the period between the Revolution of 1848 and the Compromise of 1867 remained sluggish, and mechanization was not yet sufficiently widespread to speak of a sustained industrial revolution. By 1867 only 480 steam engines with a capacity of 8,100 horsepower operated in Hungarian industry. Traditionally the retardation was blamed on Hungary's lack of political and economic independence, which permitted the western parts of the monarchy to hinder progress of many industrial branches in the east, especially the light industries. In general the tariff policy of the empire then represented a compromise between the economic interests of Austrian industry and banking and those of the large Hungarian landowners.

It can be argued, however, that because of Hungary's relative economic backwardness, and under the prevailing free market economy, a successful industrialization drive could not have been launched then, even if the country had been fully independent.[27] Moreover, it has been pointed out that the common market with Austria, after the abolition of the internal tariff in 1850, had undeniably beneficial effects. It helped to modernize agriculture as a precondition for the industrial revolution. It also stimulated mining and iron industries, as well as construction of railroads, which increased from 178 kilometers to 2,200 kilometers in 1850–67.

Food processing remained the dominant industrial branch, and since the 1850s had attracted investment from grain wholesalers, who in turn accounted for a large share of capital accumulation in Hungary. In food processing, the first place belonged to flour milling. In Pest and Buda alone, there were fourteen large mills by 1867, and the amount of horsepower used in Hungary's flour mills increased almost thirteen times from 1852 to 1863. Important advances occurred also in distilling, and—with the aid of Austrian capital—in sugar refining. Coal mines and ironworks continued to flourish largely thanks to outside financing. Demands of railroads and steamship lines led to the opening of new coal mines, especially near Pécs and in the eastern Banat around Reşiţa and Anina. By 1860 Hungarian coal production reached 480,000 tons, equally divided between hard and soft coal. The increasing demand for iron derived partly from the construction of local railroads and partly from

27. Pamlényi, *A History of Hungary*, pp. 294–95.

advancing industrialization of the Austrian and Bohemian Lands, where until the mid-1850s iron production had leveled off. The Austrian state railroads took the lead in establishing large ironworks in Reşiţa. Another major enterprise, the Rimamurány Company, was formed through the merger of three smaller plants. By 1865 the production of pig iron in Hungary reached 100,000 tons.

Manufacturing of machinery still lagged far behind the output of pig iron, most of which was sent to Austria for further processing. The Austrian-owned railroads and steamship lines (on the Danube) operated plants to produce their own equipment. In addition, certain small enterprises developed into medium-size factories. Specifically, wheels for railroad cars, machinery for flour mills, and agricultural tools and machines were manufactured. Chemical, leather, and woodworking industries were modest in scale. Textile production—elsewhere so important to early industrial development—remained stunted by the heavy competition from the Austrian and Bohemian Lands.

In the period immediately following the Compromise, from 1867 to 1873, industrial development was stimulated by accelerated railroad construction, improved credit facilities, and an influx of outside capital attracted by the new conditions of political stability. While earlier enterprises were mainly individually owned, ownership by joint-stock companies was not spreading. The depression of 1873–79 caused a relatively brief hiatus in the industrial growth. In the 1880s the advance resumed and reached its peak in the period 1890–1913. The 1880s also marked the maturing of the industrial revolution, and the beginning of a systematic promotion of industralization by the government. State support of industry in 1881 assumed the form of fifteen-year tax exemptions for new factories, and after 1890 the government made available interest-free loan and direct subsidies, as well as preferential rates on railroads. After 1900, state subsidies, which represented about 2 percent of the total investment in private industry, focused on selected targets. Thus in 1907 the lagging textile industry was singled out for preferential treatment, and assigned 57 percent of the total subsidies. The state also aided industry in general, and certain branches such as machine building in particular, by purchasing on the average 13 percent of all industrial products. Finally, toward the end of the nineteenth century the Hungarian government became particularly successful in promoting foreign investment in domestic enterprises, especially mining.

The leading branch of Hungarian industry, food processing, continued to prosper in the era of dualism. Hungary became one of the leading European centers of flour milling. A major technological improvement between 1867 and 1873 was the replacement of the traditional millstone by a new roller-milling method. Increases in the production of food-processing industries highlighted the acceleration of industrial advance. The output of flour rose from 150,000 tons in 1867 to 1,600,000 in 1900 and to 2,400,000 in 1913. Of these amounts, 600,000 tons were exported in 1900 and 800,000 in 1913. Sugar production grew from 32,000 tons in 1880 to 198,000 in 1898–99 and to 591,000 in 1912–13.

In the other area of traditional strength, the interrelated fields of coal mining and iron production made great strides. Coal production more than doubled between 1866 and 1873 from 700,000 tons to 1,630,000, mainly because of the opening of new mines, since mechanization of mining operations remained slow. The output was relatively stagnant during the depression of 1874–79, but growth resumed in the 1880s, with the production more than tripling between 1880 and 1900 from 1,810,000 tons to 6,580,000. In 1913 it reached 10,270,000 tons, including 8,950,000 tons of soft coal and 1,320,000 of hard. From the 1880s the largest centers of coal mining, financed chiefly by Austrian, German, and French capital, were in the northern fringes of Magyar ethnic territory in Tabánya and Salgótarján. Production of iron ore almost doubled between 1869 and 1873, from 294,000 tons to 550,000. About 100,000 tons annually, however, were exported directly to Austria, and as a result Hungarian pig iron production in the same period rose less than 50 percent—from 110,000 tons to 160,000. Nevertheless, it was at this time that the Hungarian iron industry started to undergo a fundamental process of technological improvements. Coke was replacing charcoal in smelting, the first Bessemer converter went into operation in 1868, and the first Martin open hearth in 1873. This modernization of iron metallurgy, in turn, provided the main basis for the sustained industrial revolution in Hungary from the 1880s. At the end of the nineteenth and early in the twentieth century Hungary's iron production was concentrated in three large companies, which—benefiting from both state support and the infusion of foreign capital—came to account for 90 percent of pig iron output and 96 percent of steel production. Iron ore output increased from the base of 586,000 tons in 1880 by 224 percent to 1,656,000 in 1900, and by 351 percent to 2,059,000 in 1913. During the depression of 1874–79, the production of pig iron declined from the high of 160,000 tons in 1873 to a low of 118,000 tons in 1879. It began to rise again in 1880, reaching 144,000 tons. Subsequently the rate of increase in output of pig iron exceeded that of iron ore. The production rose from the base of 140,000 tons in 1880 by 325 percent to 456,000 tons in 1900, and by 445 percent to 623,000 in 1913. The steel output, which became significant only in the 1880s, rose from 427,000 tons in 1900 to 800,000 in 1913. Despite major advances, Hungary's iron and steel industry still lagged behind the more developed areas. Measured in per capita output of pig iron, Hungarian production of 64.6 pounds in 1913 was exceeded almost twice by Austria, eight and a half times by Germany, and eleven times by the United States.

Machinery production in Hungary continued to focus on transportation equipment, which generated about two-thirds of the total output of machines. In particular, manufacture of steam locomotives and railroad cars rose sharply in the two closing decades of the nineteenth century. In the same period, the number of shipyards increased from one to four. The manufacture of farm machinery and equipment for food processing industries also expanded. Production of steam turbines, automobiles, and tractors started early in the twentieth century. Just before World War I, ten of the largest enterprises producing machinery employed more than one thousand workers each. Among them was the firm of Manfréd and Weiss on the island of Csepel, the most important armaments manufacturer in Hungary. The need to import machinery, of course, persisted even in such relatively well-developed areas as agricultural machines, in which domestic production could cover only half the demand. In the area of machine tools, in which the output remained particularly weak, the dependence on imports amounted to three-quarters of the total demand.

Two branches of heavy industry were newly developing late in the nineteenth century—chemical and electric. The former concentrated on oil refining and the production of artificial fertilizers. The production of electrical energy began in the 1890s, with the number of power stations reaching 43 in 1900. Subsequently, the output of electical energy rose from 36.4 million kilowatt hours to 220 million in 1913. Important inventions, especially the alternating current transformer, the watt meter, and the three-phase electrical locomotive, originated in the world famous Ganz Electrical Works in Budapest.

Light industries, traditionally overshadowed by heavy industry, showed signs of limited progress from the 1880s on. Greater mechanization, increased output, and larger enterprises became characteristic of the wood-processing, paper, and leather industries. The more crucial textile manufacture, however, remained weak even at the turn of the century. It then covered on the average barely 14 percent of the domestic need, and in the case of wool and cotton cloth only 10 and 3.5 percent respectively. As noted, this industry became, after 1900, an object of special concern to the government, which by 1913 through direct subsidies and guarantees of foreign investments succeeded in raising production by 350 percent. Still, the output covered less than one-third of the domestic need. In comparison, the leather industry satisfied 40 percent of domestic consumption.

The overall growth of Hungarian industrial production has been computed,[28] in the prices of 1900, as amounting to 800 percent in 1900, and 1,450 percent in 1913, over the base year of 1860. Between 1867 and 1913 growth averaged 5 percent per year for all industrial enterprises and 6 percent for factories alone. The share of factory production in the total industrial production—an index of the advancing industrial revolution—kept increasing, as was indicated by several measures. The number of factories rose from several dozen in 1867 to 2,700 in 1898 and 5,500 in 1913; the amount of horsepower used in the factories from 10,000–15,000 (1867) to 307,000 (1898) and 886,000 (1913). The proportion of factory workers in the total industrial work force increased from 21 percent (110,000) in 1880 to 40 percent (305,000) in 1900 and more than 50 percent (563,000) in 1910. By 1910 factory production accounted for almost 75 percent of the total industrial output.

Comparison of the censuses of 1898 and 1913 showed a tendency for the disproportionate dominance of the food-processing industry to diminish. The value of its production declined from 44.1 percent to 38.9 percent of the total value of industrial production. The position of heavy industries remained fairly steady, rising only from 39.9 percent to 41.2. Within this sector, the share of iron and steel rose from 12.6 percent to 15.2 of the total value of industrial production; the share of mining declined from 6.7 percent to 5.4; and that of the other branches (machinery, chemical, electrical, and building materials) remained unchanged at 20.6 percent. The underdeveloped light industries advanced more rapidly than either food processing or heavy industries. Their share of the total value of industrial output increased from 16.0 to 19.9 percent. The most important factor was the rise for textile and clothing industries from 5.0 to 7.3 percent. The share of the other light industries (woodworking, leather, paper, printing) rose more modestly, from 11.0 to 12.6 percent.

The modern industrial working class expanded at a slow rate, even in relation to the growth of industrial output, mainly because food processing, the largest industry, required comparatively few workers. For instance, in 1898, while producing 44.1 percent of the value of manufactured goods, this industrial branch employed only 15.3 percent of factory labor. The working class also contained a large component of non-Hungarians, because most of the specialized labor force, particularly in mining, ironworks, and machinery production, was recruited outside the country, most often in the Austrian or Bohemian Lands. In 1875, foreigners accounted for 35 percent of the labor force in iron and machinery production. Nevertheless, the number of factory workers grew from 23,000 in 1846 to 110,000 in 1880; it almost tripled in

28. Berend and Ranki, *Hungary*, pp. 60–61.

the next twenty years, and virtually doubled between 1900 and 1913, reaching 620,000.

Working conditions in factories improved very slowly. In 1867 a workday of twelve to fourteen hours was common. According to statistics of 1901, a workday of twelve hours or more prevailed in 10 percent of the factories, of ten to twelve hours in 60 percent, and under ten hours in 30 percent. By World War I, labor had won only the most basic elements of social security, such as sickness and disability insurance, a weekly day of rest, protection against accidents, and prohibition of child labor. Yet the working conditions in industry were better than in agriculture. Skilled workers were too scarce for there to be serious unemployment. Only unskilled workers feared competition of migrants from the countryside. Above all, urban workers could unionize for self-protection, and strikes were fairly common early in the twentieth century. Compared with Western Europe, in Hungary the compensation of industrial labor remained lower on the average by 40 or 50 percent. Between 1905 and 1909, according to one estimate, the average Hungarian industrial wage was only 30 percent of the English level, 44 percent of the German, and 60 percent of the French. An unusual wage differential between skilled and unskilled labor was due to the scarcity of skilled labor. Early in the twentieth century, the highest paid 5 percent of the workers earned four to five times more than the lowest paid 20 percent, and three times more than the average wage.

Dominance and Decline of Foreign Capital

The development of credit institutions virtually ceased in Hungary under Neo-Absolutism from 1850 to 1859. The scarcity of liquid capital was not relieved by the Viennese government's restrictions on savings banks. Above all, the law of 1852 prohibited their formation on the basis of joint-stock companies, and limited the interest rate on mortgages to 5 percent. The number of credit institutions between 1848 and 1860 remained virtually unchanged (36 compared to 38), although their capital assets (share capital, reserve fund, and deposits) rose from 22 million crowns to 81 million. Slow improvement occurred from 1860 to 1867; the number of credit institutions, mostly savings banks, increased by 1867 to 107 with capital assets of 175 million crowns.

From the Compromise of 1867 until the crash of 1873 the lifting of restrictive legislation and the general prosperity favored banking activity. Five large banks, mainly based on outside capital, were established, in addition to numerous smaller banks and savings banks, utilizing mostly domestic capital. The number of credit institutions rose to 637, with capital assets of 548 million crowns. The banks concentrated on land mortgages on large estates, financing of trade and transport, and spec-

ulative financial transactions. Banking, however, suffered exceptionally
from the depression of 1873–79 with the collapse of 74 credit institutions. Of the five large foreign-owned banks, only the General Credit
Bank, backed by the Austrian Rothschilds, survived.

Following the depression, foreign capital again flowed into Hungary
in the 1880s, creating new banks and strengthening the established ones.
Although land mortgages still represented 50 to 60 percent of the banks'
assets toward the end of the century, the banks also became interested
in industrial and commercial shares. By 1900 there were 2,696 credit
institutions, and their capital assets reached 2,607 million crowns. Four
large banks, including two pre-1848 institutions, the Commercial Bank
and the First Savings Bank of Pest, as well as the General Credit Bank
and the Discount and Exchange Bank, directly or indirectly controlled
47 percent of the capital resources of Hungary's credit system. Each of
the banks had a special focus—for instance, the Commercial Bank on
financing railroads, the General Credit Bank on floating state loans.

Early in the twentieth century the Hungarian banking system more
than doubled in size, consisting by 1913 of 5,993 credit institutions with
6,691 million crowns in capital assets. The four largest banks, joined by
a fifth one—the Hungarian Bank and Trading Company—grew more
powerful. By establishing branches and gaining ascendency through
consortia over local banks, they controlled 58 percent of all capital assets of the Hungarian banking structure by 1913. The banks also increasingly focused on industrial investments. In 1913, consortia of the
five large banks controlled 47 percent of all industrial corporations in
Hungary. As noted, the dependence of industry on bank financing was
a major cause of the heavy concentration of production. Monopolistic
tendencies were also promoted, leading to restrictive market practices.
Around eighty cartels had sprung up by 1913.

Capital from the Austrian and Bohemian Lands and from abroad
played a crucial role in the economic development of Hungary in the
era of dualism. Its importation, supported by the government, took several forms, especially mortgage loans, subscription to state loans and
municipal bonds, and investment in railroads, banks, and industry.
Nevertheless, the share of foreign capital in the Hungarian economy
declined steadily. Between 1867 and 1873 it represented 60 percent of
all newly invested capital. Its share fell to 45 percent between 1873 and
1900, and to 25 percent by 1913.

Achievements of Hungary's Economy

The overall modernization of the Hungarian economy scored considerable advances in the period from 1850 to 1914, especially after the
Compromise of 1867. Yet the rise of industrial activity did not over-

come the predominance of agricultural production. Agriculture accounted for 80 percent of the national income in 1850, 76 in 1870, 63 in 1900, and 64 in 1911–13, while the share of industry and mining increased in the same years from 12.0 to 16.5, 25.3, and 25.9 percent. The share of commerce fluctuated in the same years from 8.0 to 7.5, 11.7, and 10.1 percent. The proportion of population employed in agriculture changed from 80.0 percent in 1870 to 64.5 in 1910, and the proportion employed in industry, commerce, and transportation from 11.5 percent to 23.6. The pattern of external trade with both Cisleithania and foreign countries reflected the dominance of agriculture, raw materials, and semifinished goods in Hungarian production. The composition of exports, which remained fairly constant in 1900–1913, averaged 50 percent of raw materials, especially agricultural ones, and only 37.5 percent of finished goods, of which in turn some 65 percent consisted characteristically of processed foodstuffs. The composition of imports changed from 70 percent of finished goods and 30 of raw materials and semifinished products in 1900, to somewhat over 60 percent and not quite 40 respectively in 1913.

The real national income in constant prices increased fourfold from 1850 to 1913. The average growth per year amounted to 2.8 percent. In the era of dualism the national income, in terms of the 1900 prices, almost tripled between 1867 and 1900, and rose by another 50 percent by 1913. According to this computation, the average annual rate of growth was 3.2 percent in the period from 1867 to 1913. Hungary continued to lag economically behind Cisleithania, although the gap was narrowing. Between 1850 and 1911–13 Hungary's share of the national income of the entire monarchy rose from 30.0 percent to 36.4. It went from 16.0 percent to 24.1 in industry and mining, 17.0 to 22.8 in commerce and 40.0 to 51.1 in agriculture. Most tellingly, Hungary's national income per capita rose in contemporary prices from 58 percent of the Cisleithanian one (62 to 107 crowns) in 1850 to 77 percent (319 to 426 crowns) in 1913. A comparison with foreign countries showed that Hungary's per capita gross output by 1913 amounted to only 40 to 50 percent of the output of West European nations, and 70 to 80 percent of that of Italy, while it surpassed that of Russia and the Balkan states by some 25 to 30 percent.

The inclusion of Hungary in the common market of the monarchy produced mixed results. Certain branches of the economy, enjoying cost advantages and benefiting from the availability of outside capital and a large market, could experience remarkable advances. This was particularly true of agriculture, transportation, and credit facilities. Other sectors of the economy, however, tended to stagnate at a primitive level, in large part because of their inability to compete in an open market with the more advanced production of the Austrian and Bohemian Lands.

Thus a relatively limited number of highly modernized agricultural estates and industrial enterprises existed side by side with widespread backward peasant farming and artisan production.

In a study that discusses the history of ethnic entities within the Habsburg empire, it is obviously impossible to arrive at clearcut conclusions concerning their economic interrelations, since they developed primarily within the framework of political-administrative boundaries. In the first decades after the conclusion of the Compromise of 1867 the economic association between Cisleithania and Hungary worked fairly smoothly, since it corresponded to the interests of highly influential industrialists in Austria and even more influential big estate owners in Hungary. This understanding was based on the premise that Hungary was an agricultural country and Austria supposedly an industrialized one. Whether true or not—and in this simplified form the assumption was never fully correct—it served the proponents of this postulate well. Actually, however, in spite of considerable industrial progress, Austria until 1918 remained a predominantly rural political entity that included a significant and expanding industrial sector. As to rural holdings, middle-size and small farms played an important role; in industry, heavy industry exercised a decisive influence. Hungary was and remained an even more pronounced agricultural country and one in which big estates were more numerous and larger than in Austria, although the Austrian ones were by no means negligible either. In any case, big aristocratic latifundia owners carried greater weight than in Austria. On the other hand, in the last thirty years before the outbreak of the World War, Hungarian industry developed on a scale that came gradually close to the Austrian level. Aristocratic big estate owners were no longer the only important partners in trade negotiations with Austria. The increasingly mixed economies of the western and eastern parts of the Habsburg monarchy made reaching an understanding more difficult when representatives of either half of the empire were at economic cross-purposes.

Here a relationship to the ethnic factor can be traced. In Austria, in the period under discussion, over 60 percent of the population were Slavs and Romanians, the national groups surveyed here; in Hungary, including Croatia-Slavonia, only about 45 percent were—the rest consisted of Magyars and Germans. Economic tensions, which in the cumbersome economic compromise negotiations every ten years were usually resolved with more concessions to the eastern than to the western part of the monarchy, affected more Slavs and Romanians in the Cisleithanian than in the Transleithanian part of the empire. This is true in percentages as well as in absolute numbers. On the other hand, the distribution of wealth—in Hungary there was far more agricultural wealth than in Austria—was even more uneven in the east than in the west. It was more grossly uneven for the non-Magyar national groups, even though economic discrimination on ethnic grounds was only thinly camouflaged in the west as well. Both lines of development could not fail to exercise an influence on the political history of the peoples surveyed in this study.

The Slovaks

FROM REVOLUTION TO DUALISM, 1848–67

Revolution and Quest for Autonomy, 1848–49

The revolutionary events, opening in Hungary in March 1848, brought the Slovak national leadership into collision with the Pest government, dominated by the nationally intolerant Magyar gentry. Štúr and Hurban led a campaign in April for a petition movement in favor of Slovak autonomy within individual counties and towns. These efforts failed largely because of administrative repression and, as yet, insufficient rapport between the masses and the national activists. About thirty Slovak leaders then assembled in Liptovský Mikuláš and themselves drafted on May 11 in the name of the nation a single petition for submission to the king and to the Hungarian authorities. The Mikuláš Petition formulated publicly for the first time a comprehensive national program of the Slovaks. It envisaged an autonomous Slovakia (within a federalized Hungary) with its own diet, official language, educational system, and also a distinct flag. The Hungarian government responded by imposing martial law and issuing warrants for the arrest of Štúr, Hurban, and Hodža.

In the unequal contest, the Slovak leaders first sought support from their fellow Slavs. In June 1848, about twenty of them, headed by Štúr, took part in the Slav Congress in Prague. In opposition to the Czech liberals, above all Palacký, they tended to cooperate with the Czech and Polish radicals. Seeking (like the latter) to transcend the Austroslav framework, Štúr and Hurban urged cooperation with Slavs outside the Habsburg monarchy, and warned against a close identification of the Slavs with the interests of the dynasty. Most of them, like Hurban, still favored Slovak autonomy within Hungary, though some considered creation of a separate crownland either just Slovak or jointly with the Czechs.

The course of events forced the Slovaks—like the other non-Magyar nationalities of Hungary—to turn, despite initial reluctance, to Vienna for support. In the summer of 1848, Štúr and Hurban hoped that the

Croats, who were authorized by Vienna to negotiate with the Pest government, would also secure national concessions for the Slovaks. When negotiations failed in September, a Slovak National Council was organized by Štúr, Hurban, and Hodža, and launched a military expedition of almost five hundred volunteers under Czech commanders, who in late September briefly penetrated into western Slovakia. After the final break between Vienna and Pest, the Slovak National Council mounted in November a second military expedition in close conjunction with the imperial army. One group, led by Štúr and Hurban, advanced through northern Slovakia to Košice; another, under Hodža, reached Nové Zámky in southern Slovakia. Slovak representatives played some role in the appointment of new county and local officials, but their activities remained circumscribed by the distrust of the conservative commanders and the still powerful loyalist Hungarian magnates on Slovak territory.

The proclamation of the Stadion Constitution in March 1849, offered some encouragement to the Slovaks by its promise of national and language equality in Hungary. Despite warnings of the radicals, such as Janko Král, against reliance on Vienna, a Slovak deputation in late March appealed to the emperor for the creation of a separate Slovak grand duchy. Although the Austrian statesmen wished to weaken the Magyar gentry, only a few (like Bach and Stadion) favored the actual dismemberment of Hungary. Moreover, in the increasingly reactionary atmosphere the truly effective Slovak leaders around Štúr became suspect as subversive liberals. When in March the Viennese government appointed an advisory commission on Slovak affairs, the members were nonpolitical conservatives headed by Ján Kollár. Nevertheless the use of Slovak volunteer detachments continued, particularly in the summer of 1849 (the so-called third expedition). After sharing in the mopping-up operations in central and eastern Slovakia, the detachments were dissolved in November.

Neo-Absolutism, 1849–59

The new absolutist government in Vienna, consolidated by 1850, refused either to separate the Slovak territory or at least to provide for its administrative unification within Hungary. Concessions were more limited and furthermore vitiated by a profound distrust of all autonomous movements. The Slovak territory was split into two parts—though at the same time shielded from the Magyar area—by the organization of the administrative districts of Pozsony and Košice. Language rights were granted in government agencies and in education. Kollár influenced the most important ministers, Alexander Bach and Count Leo Thun, to choose Czech (with minor modifications) as the official language of the Slovaks, which had been used in the official newspaper, *Slovenské Noviny*, since mid-1849. By 1850 the introduction of Czech into lower and secondary education had begun. In 1851–52, for instance, eight gymnasia were conducted entirely, and three partly, in Czech out of a total of twenty-seven in Slovakia; the rest used German or Magyar as languages of instruction. To implement the new language policy Czech officials and teachers were appointed in Slovak areas to supplement available Slovak candidates. Despite their vagaries, the educational and cultural policies of the Bach government helped to increase the number of nationally conscious Slovak intellectuals.

Vienna's support of Czech, however, did not settle the language issue. Štúr and his followers continued to cling to the literary Slovak developed in the mid-1840s. They scored a major success by converting to their point of view the leading group of Catholic intellectuals under Andrej Radlinský and Ján Palárik, who agreed at a meeting in Pozsony in October 1851 to shift from the official Czech to a modified form of Štúrovite Slovak. This version, codified in 1852 in a grammar by Martin Hattala, was destined to prevail within a decade as the final form of literary language of the Slovaks.

Slovak national leaders developed divergent orientations under the Neo-Absolutists regime. While the conservatives around Kollár relied on Vienna and Radlinský's group hoped for cooperation with Magyar liberals, Štúr and Hurban, deeply disillusioned with both Pest and Vienna by the experiences of 1848–49, placed their trust in eventual succor from Slavic Russia. Štúr in the last years before his death (in 1856) even abandoned his earlier liberalism and his belief in the equality of all the Slav nations. In his *Slavdom and the World of the Future* he foresaw a dominant position in Europe for Russia, the political and social system of which he contrasted favorably with Western liberalism and capitalism. Other Slavs could share in Russia's leading role by adopting Tsarism, Orthodoxy, and the Russian language.

Radlinský's group provided the focus of Slovak national activity in the late 1850s. In 1856 they launched under the auspices of the bishop of Banská Bystrica, Štefan Moyses, a campaign for the establishment of a central Slovak cultural institution (*Matica*). In 1857 Palárik started a journal, *Cyrill a Method*, in Slovak (as reformed in 1851–52) and rallied a substantial proportion of Slovak teachers, writers, and officials, both Catholic and Protestant, behind the demand to replace Czech with Slovak in schools and government agencies. This agitation helped to create a measure of cohesion in the Slovak national movement when the Neo-Absolutist system collapsed in the monarchy in 1859.

Between Pest and Vienna, 1860–67

The revival of constitutional life in 1860 deepened the divisions among Slovak leaders. The group around Palárik, called the New School, advocated—especially in view of the current administrative recentralization of Hungary—a rapprochement with Magyar liberals. These people also tried to obtain concessions from the Hungarian diet. Hurban and his followers remained skeptical about the Magyars' attitude, which, in fact, showed little regard for Slovak national interests. As the Magyar gentry regained control, Slovaks were dismissed from county offices, and not a single Slovak candidate could win a seat in the diet in early 1861. In opposition to the New School, a group around Hurban, or the Old School, sought aid from Vienna. In February Hurban himself had petitioned the imperial Interior Ministry to separate administratively the Slovak territory from the rest of Hungary. Nevertheless, the two factions did cooperate in publishing, beginning in March 1861, the newspaper *Peštbudínské Vědomosti* (*Pest-Buda News*), edited by Francisci. They also succeeded in bringing about the final acceptance of Slovak over Czech as the literary language. Largely owing to Štefan Daxner's efforts, the two camps further agreed on a joint program in June 1861, at a meeting in Turčiansky Svatý Martin. This program, the Martin Memorandum, was the most significant Slovak political act before the Compromise of 1867. Hurban consented to consider a solution of the Slovak question within the Hungarian county system. On the other hand, Palárik (despite fear of offending the strictly centralist sentiments of the Magyars) agreed to a demand that Slovak counties achieve at least a nominal unity through the offical designation as the Slovak *Okolie* (territory). The Hungarian diet treated the Memorandum with hostility, but it was itself dissolved by the king in August 1861, in a renewed suspension of constitutional rights in Hungary.

The reintroduction of absolutism under Schmerling's *Provisorium* strengthened those among the Slovaks who trusted in the aid of Vienna. Hurban, Francisci, and Viliam Paulíny-Tóth participated in a delegation led by Bishop Moyses, which in December 1861 presented to Francis Joseph a new memorandum. It went beyond the Martin Memorandum in that the Slovak *Okolie* was to be not a mere descriptive designation for a group of counties but a genuine single administrative entity with a capital in Banská Bystrica. The imperial government offered more limited concessions. The establishment of several Slovak *gymnasia* was promised, although only three (one Catholic and two Protestant) eventually came into existence. Several Slovaks were appointed to important public offices; in particular, Francisci became the *főispán* of Liptov county and Daxner the *alispán* of Gemer county. In February 1863 an imperial resolution established Slovak as the official language of municipalities and lower education in the Slovak area. Perhaps the most significant gain was the permission to establish the Slovak *Matica* in Martin in the summer of 1863. Although intended as a cultural and research institution, in the absence of a central Slovak politicoadministrative organization, the *Matica* could also give political direction to the national movement.

By mid-1865 the restoration of constitutionalism in Hungary, and the Magyar liberals' return to power, endangered most of the imperial concessions. With the Magyar resumption of control over county governments, Slovak officials, including Daxner and Francisci, were once more dismissed. None of the twenty-five Slovak candidates, representing Hurban's pro-Vienna faction, the New School, and an intermediate group of centrists (under Daxner), secured election to the restored Hungarian diet in the fall of 1865. Hurban's group and the centrists continued to hope for yet another reversal in Vienna's attitude, but the outcome of the Austro-Prussian War of 1866 forced Francis Joseph instead to placate the Magyar liberals through the Compromise of 1867 and condone their desire for a centralized Magyar-dominated Hungary.

UNDER DUALISM, 1867–1914

Struggle for National Rights, 1868–74

Affirming in Hungary a centralized statehood dominated by the Magyar gentry, the dualist system put the Slovak national movement in an increasingly difficult position. The former pro-Vienna faction, or the Old School, upheld the principles of the Martin Memorandum. Next to Hurban, Paulíny-Tóth (1826–77) emerged as the most important leader. In 1870 its organ *Peštbudínské Vědomosti* was transferred to Martin and renamed *Národnie Noviny*. The former centrists under Daxner and Francisci fused with the Old School, which became known as the Slovak National Party (*Slovenská Národná Strana*). As the likelihood of Vienna's aid faded, the party increasingly placed its hope—following in Štúr's footsteps—in expectations of Russia's help, a remote contingency at best. The main competing faction, the New School, was strengthened after 1867 by fresh leadership from the ranks of Slovak entrepreneurs under Ján Bobula. Launching a newspaper of its own, *Slovenské Noviny* (1868–75), it espoused what under the conditions of dualism seemed a more realistic policy of renouncing the Martin Memorandum, above all the demand for a Slovak *Okolie*, and rejecting both pro-Vienna sentiments and Panslav aspirations as impediments to national concessions from the Magyar gentry.

During the ascendancy of the Deákist party, both Slovak factions concentrated on efforts first to liberalize the proposed Hungarian nationality law and then, after its adoption in December 1868, to replace it by legislation more favorable to the national aspirations of the non-Magyars.[29] Though Hurban was jailed for his critique of the law, three Slovaks—Paulíny-Tóth for the National Party and two candidates of the

29. On the Nationality Law of 1868 see p. 352.

New School—were elected into the Hungarian parliament in 1869. Paulíny-Tóth, the most dynamic of the Slovak deputies, sought to co-operate with the Left Center, led by Kálmán Tisza. In view of subsequent events this policy appears highly ironic, but at the time the Left Center appealed to the nationally minded Slovaks by its championship of county autonomy, which under altered circumstances could become the basis for asserting Slovak national rights. Neither the government nor the opposition, however, had any intention of amending the nationality law. The Slovaks failed in 1870 even in their more modest objective, a state subsidy for the *Matica*.

In the early 1870s the Hungarian government began to display a less tolerant attitude toward the nationalities, especially the Slovaks. By now it had become obvious that the nationality legislation of 1868, limited as it was from the start, would not be enforced according to the spirit of its sponsor Eötvös. In the 1872 elections not a single Slovak captured a seat in the parliament, and in the same year publication of the Slovak edition of the Hungarian official gazette was discontinued. The assault against Slovak cultural institutions intensified in 1873, led by the *alispán* of Zvolen county, Béla Grünwald, a zealous Magyarizer. This drive resulted in the closing of three Slovak *gymnasia* in 1874, a step entirely eliminating secondary education in the Slovak language. The repression of the Slovak national movement culminated and was consolidated during the Liberal Party rule under Kálmán Tisza beginning in 1875. In that year the crucial cultural institution *Matica* was dissolved, in an act accompanied by Tisza's famous dictum that no such entity as the "Slovak nation" existed in the eyes of Hungarian law. One effect of these events was the disintegration and demise of the New School, whose assumptions of at least limited good will on the part of the Magyar gentry appeared erroneous. The government's attitude toward Slovak national rights was more fundamentally negative than a simple defensive reaction against autonomist claims and Panslav ideas of certain Slovak leaders. Nothing less ambitious than the objective to Magyarize all Hungarian national groups seemed to be the policy of Tisza's government.

Political Passivity and National Decline, 1875–95

The period from 1875 to 1895 represented accordingly the low point in the history of the Slovak national movement under dualism. With the nobility already alienated, the Magyarizing pressure combined with the political impotence of the Slovak national leadership arrested the spread of national sentiments among the middle class. Thereby also the possibilities of mobilizing the lower classes behind the national cause were severely restricted. The one remaining Slovak political organization, the National Party, was still centered in the small provincial town of Martin, where its organ, *Národnie Noviny*, was published. At the critical juncture it suffered the loss of its outstanding leader, Paulíny-Tóth, who died in 1877, and his place was taken by the dedicated but less talented Pavol Mudroň (1835–1914).[30]

The onset of the repressive period witnessed an intensification of the party's traditional pro-Russian sympathies. The success of tsarist armies in the Turko-Russian war of 1877–78 engendered hopes that Russia after destroying the Turkish empire would deal similarly with the Habsburg monarchy. This faith in Russia's future role—partly nurtured by the tsarist government's subsidy to the *Národnie Noviny*—appeared unfounded in the aftermath of the Congress of Berlin of June–July 1878. It had also a detrimental effect on short-range Slovak policies, diverting attention from the more immediate concrete tasks. Moreover, the pro-Russian stance provided a pretext for the Hungarian government's campaign to fight the Slovaks as a distinct ethnic group. The manipulation of the electoral process by the Hungarian government prevented the election of Slovak deputies to parliament. Still, in 1881 the Slovak National Party nominated four candidates, who campaigned for scrupulous observance of the Nationality Law of 1868 as a minimal objective. The desiderata of the Martin Memorandum were overtly upheld as the party's ultimate goal. Subsequently, the party boycotted the elections of 1884, 1887, and 1892, and justified its abstention by solemn denunciations of the government's electoral malpractices above all the bribing and intimidating of voters.

The campaign of Magyarization continued relentlessly. From the late 1870s to the mid-1880s, Magyar was established as the external as well as the internal language of state agencies and courts in the Slovak counties. Henceforth, Slovak applications and petitions were admissible only when an attorney was not involved, and even then responses were issued in Magyar. Simultaneously, measures were launched to insulate further the masses from the influences of the Slovak national movement. In 1878 the peasant temperance societies were dissolved. A year later the introduction of Magyar into elementary schools began. By 1891, the process was extended to the kindergartens. In the early 1890s municipalities were pressured to adopt Magyar as their official language.

With direct participation in politics foreclosed, the Slovak National Party's functions were confined into narrow limits. Its newspaper continued to appear, despite frequent confiscations and other penalties. Unsuccessful petitions were presented in Vienna, one in 1878 to restore the *Matica*, another in 1885 to prevent the use of *Matica's* confiscated

30. The party also acquired the services of Matúš Dula (1846–1926), a former member of the defunct New School, and especially of Hurban's son, Svetozár Hurban-Vajanský (1847–1916), the most articulate spokesman for the party's Russophilism.

property by a new society (*Felvidéki Magyar Közművelődési Egyesület*), dedicated tauntingly to the spread of the Magyar tongue among the Slovaks. But according to the terms of the Compromise of 1867, these
matters were not within the jurisdiction of the government in Vienna.
Of importance to the sustenance of national feelings were the patriotic
assemblies that had been held annually since 1879 in Martin under the
patronage of the women's society *Živena*, and gatherings held, despite
police harassment, to commemorate the twenty-fifth anniversary of the
Martin Memorandum (1886) and the centenary of Kollár's birth (1893),
as well as to dedicate a monument to Hurban (1892).

The Slovak national movement received some support from other
national groups. Non-Magyar deputies in the Budapest parliament, especially the Serb Mihajlo Polit-Desančić, occasionally protested repressive measures applied in Slovakia. Contacts with the Czechs revived in
the late 1870s. Hurban even had proposed in 1875 a return by the
Slovaks to the Czech literary language. Funds were raised to enable
Slovak students to attend Czech *gymnasia* and the University of Prague,
where a Slovak student society, *Detvan*, was established in 1882. Several
Czech writers and artists turned to Slovak themes. On the other hand,
following the fiasco of the Fundamental Articles in 1871 and during
the ascendancy of the Old Czechs, Czech leaders were reluctant to side
with the Slovaks openly, fearing political reprisals by the Hungarian
government via Vienna. The situation changed gradually in this respect
with the ascent of the less timid Young Czechs in the 1880s.[31]

Political Revival, 1895–1914

During the last two decades before World War I, Slovak political activity revived considerably, despite the unrelenting pressure of Magyarization. At the start of this revival the Slovak leaders drew closer to the
other non-Magyar nationalities of Hungary. This cooperation, reflecting mostly Serb initiative, resulted in a joint congress of Slovak, Serb,
and Romanian representatives in Budapest in August 1895. Even more
fundamental was the broadening political participation and improvement in organization by political movements both within and outside
the Slovak National Party (SNP), which had hitherto appealed largely
to the intellectuals and certain established strata of the middle class. A
Slovak Catholic clerical movement developed within the Hungarian
People's Party (*Néppárt*) by 1896 and functioned after 1898 increasingly
as a Catholic wing of the SNP. Not until 1913 did its leader, the priest

31. On the attitude of Czech politicians in the 1880s see p. 306. Although hesitant to
challenge the Hungarian government publically, the Old Czechs, including Rieger, privately favored the Slovak national cause.

Andrej Hlinka (1864–1938), form a fully independent Slovak People's Party. Another new current, emerging in 1897, was deeply concerned with Slovak peasant problems. Inspired mainly by the Czech Agrarian Party, this group sought, under the leadership of Milan Hodža (1878–1944), to create a network of peasant cooperatives and societies. The agrarian movement enjoyed a considerable appeal. By the middle of the following decade its press reached a higher circulation (14,000) than that of Hlinka's clerical (12,000) or the official organ of the SNP (1,000). A more explicitly pro-Czech political group, reviving the idea of Czechoslovak national unity, formed around the journal *Hlas*, launched in 1898. It reflected the views of younger intellectuals, led by Vavro Šrobár (1867–1950), who had studied abroad, especially in Prague. Influenced by Thomas Masaryk, the Hlasists advocated a widespread civic education to arouse political consciousness among the lower social classes. Neither the Agrarians nor the Hlasists sought to establish political parties, preferring to work within the SNP or the clerical organization. The Slovak socialist movement was gaining in significance. Originating in the 1890s as a part of the Hungarian Social Democracy, the Slovak Social Democrats grew increasingly independent with the support of their Czech comrades, particularly after 1905.

The SNP terminated its boycott of Hungarian parliamentary elections in 1896 when it urged its followers to vote for the candidates of Zichy's *Néppárt*, promising to champion the national rights of non-Magyar minorities. Subsequently, in 1901 and 1905 the SNP ran its own candidates on a platform much more modest than the Martin Memorandum, asking merely for a genuine observance of the Nationality Law of 1868. Under the prevailing regime the results could be meager at best. In 1901 three Slovaks, and in 1905 only two, were elected. The latter two, Hodža and a Catholic clerical, joined in parliament with the Romanian and Serb deputies to form the Nationality Party of ten members.

June 1905, with the extraconstitutional cabinet of Fejérváry, ushered in a brief revival of hopes that Vienna might after all free the Slovaks and other non-Magyars from their political impotence through the announced expansion of the electoral franchise. These hopes were shattered, when the old regime—based on the suppression of both Magyar and non-Magyar lower classes—was reestablished de facto under the ministry of Wekerle in April 1906. This in fact launched a new phase of escalated Magyarization. It is true that in the parliamentary elections of May 1906 the repressive mechanism was not yet fully operational, and an unprecedented but still extremely modest number of Slovaks—seven—were elected. However, the following year was marked by the massacre of Černová, in which fifteen of Hlinka's demonstrating followers were killed by Magyar gendarmes (on October 27). In the same year the so-called Apponyi Laws further restricted the use of Slovak in elementary schools. As a result of these curtailments, by 1914 of the 214,000 school-age children in Slovakia only 42,000 were taught at least in part in the Slovak language.

The steady pressure of Magyarization was weakening the Slovaks as an ethnic group both numerically and socially. Between 1880 and 1910 the proportion of Slovaks in Slovakia decreased from 63 percent to 57.6 percent. The Slovaks were grossly underrepresented in the middle as well as the upper classes. Of the 230,000 civil servants, officials, and members of free professions in all of Hungary in 1910, only 2,911 were Slovaks, who constituted more than 10 percent of the population of Hungary (exclusive of Croatia-Slavonia). Of the 6,185 civil servants in Slovakia only 154 were Slovaks. In addition to Magyarization, the Slovak ethnic group (numbering 1,946,000 in 1910) was weakened by mass emigration, the per capita rate of which exceeded that of any other European nation except the Irish. Between 1871 and 1914 some 500,000 Slovaks settled permanently in the United States.

Although by 1910 the Hungarian government was making friendly verbal overtures to the non-Magyar nationalities, including the Slovaks, in that same year official repression prevented the election of all but three Slovak candidates to the parliament, and delegations of the SNP under Mudroň in vain sought redress of cultural and educational grievances from Prime Minister Count Károly Khuen-Héderváry in June 1911, and from his powerful successor, Count István Tisza, in the spring of 1913. Hodža and other Slovak leaders now placed their hopes for national equality in an eventual intervention in Hungarian affairs by the heir apparent, Archduke Franz Ferdinand, who was thought eager to change the political balance in favor of the non-Magyars. Also, contacts with the Czechs had been growing since 1907, cultivated not only by the agrarians, Hlasists, and Social Democrats, but by the leaders of the SNP and the People's Party, who had been traditionally apprehensive about Czech cultural hegemony. In April 1914 representatives of all Czech parties expressed in Prague their support for the Slovaks and urged the conversion of Hungary into a federation of equal nationalities. A month later the SNP under a new chairman, Matúš Dula (Mudroň having died in March 1914) and a new secretary, Jozef Gregor-Tajovský, adopted amendments to its program, stressing close cooperation with the Czechs, repudiating political Panslavism, and endorsing conversion of the entire monarchy into a federation of self-governing nations. At the same time, Dula sought to establish a Slovak National Council that would provide a framework for cooperation of all political movements, including the People's Party and the Social Democrats. This plan could not be implemented before the outbreak of World War I.

AGRICULTURE, INDUSTRY, AND FINANCE[32]

Toward Industrial Revolution, 1848–67

The reforms initiated in 1848 and implemented in the 1850s provided favorable conditions for the modernization of production on large estates, while peasant agriculture remained little affected. Compensation for the loss of feudal dues and improved credit facilities made more capital available to large landowners. Free access to the Austrian market served as incentive to increased outputs, especially in western and southern Slovakia. The more advanced estates, under scientifically trained managers, replaced the three-field system by crop rotation. The demand of agricultural industries stimulated expanded cultivation of sugar beets, tobacco, and potatoes. In southern Slovakia increasing corn production made possible a marked expansion in pig raising. Sheep were still plentiful in the 1860s, amounting to 500,000 in Pozsony and Nitra counties alone. The use of modern agricultural machinery also began to spread, especially on estates in the western and southern counties. Steam-powered threshing machines appeared for the first time in the 1850s.[33] The northern counties lagged behind the rest of Slovakia in agricultural modernization.

After 1848, tentative steps toward an industrial revolution affected additional branches of production in the Slovak area, but progress remained relatively slow and limited. One of the retarding factors was a lag in the development of the transportation network; by 1867, of the 2,342 kilometers of railroads in Hungary only 156 kilometers were in Slovakia. Another important factor, peculiar to the Slovak situation, was the widespread ownership of industrial enterprises by the nobility, not so readily receptive to technological innovation as the middle-class entrepreneurs.

Mechanization at last embraced the most important industrial branch in Slovakia, iron metallurgy. The old "Slovak ovens" were entirely replaced with blast furnaces. By 1856, 54 of the 60 in all of Hungary were in Slovakia. Other advances included preroasting of lower grade ores, preheating of air in blast furnaces, the spread of puddling fur-

32. Economic data in this section are derived from *Dejiny Slovenska*, ed. Ľudevít Holotík (Bratislava: Slovenská akadémia vied, 1968), 2:123–52, 320–402; Ákoš Paulinyi, "Otázky hospodárskeho vývinu na Slovensku v 50. a 60. rokoch 19. stor.," *Historický Časopis*, 11 (1963) 31–54; Otakar Mrázek, *Vývoj průmyslu v českých zemích a na Slovensku od manufaktury do roku 1918* (Prague: Nakl. politické literatury, 1964), pp. 258–61, 362–66, 458–64; Ľubomír Lipták, *Slovensko v 20. storočí* (Bratislava: VPL, 1968), pp. 11–13; *Přehled československých dějin* (Prague: Československá akademie věd, 1960), 2:846; Jozef Butvin, *Dějiny Československa* (Prague: Státní pedagogické nakl., 1968), 3:439.
33. By the late 1860s, 429 of them were used in Slovakia, as well as over 800 horse-powered ones, 420 mowing machines, and 1,500 seeders.

naces, and the transition from hammers to rolling mills. Pig iron production rose rapidly from 22,400 tons in 1848 to 56,000 in 1857, stagnated during the depression of the late 1850s, and then resumed growing at a slower pace, reaching 76,048 tons in 1865. It accounted for about three-quarters of the Hungarian total. Over half of the pig iron output was directly exported from Slovakia. Of the rest most was processed into semifinished products (such as forged iron, rails, and sheet metal), and thus the basis for a machinery industry remained narrow. Only two significant machine-building enterprises evolved from repair shops attached to ironworks.

Food processing was the second most important industrial branch in the Slovak area. Sugar refining became completely converted to factory production. The five refineries in Slovakia (out of the Hungarian total of nineteen) included the largest such enterprise in Hungary. Mechanization was penetrating to flour milling, but—unlike in the rest of Hungary—in Slovakia this industry continued to occupy second place in food processing. In 1863, of the Hungarian total of 146 steam-powered mills, only 7 were in Slovakia. Four were added by 1867. Distilling and brewing remained largely confined to small enterprises with artisan type production.

Among other branches of light industry, papermaking, earlier affected by mechanization, slowed down its growth significantly after 1848. Only one new factory had been added by 1863 to the older four. Mechanization, however, was newly spreading into wood processing, stimulated by the demands of construction and furniture making. The first steam-powered sawmill appeared in 1862; by 1867 there were eight in southwestern Slovakia alone. The textile industry continued to decay, damaged more than any other by the 1851 customs union with Austria.[34] Glassmaking and leather tanning remained at the level of either artisan or manufactory production, although their output reached considerable volume. For instance, in 1856 sixteen glassworks in Slovakia represented half of all such enterprises in Hungary.

Despite the diffusion of mechanization from the older fields (sugar refining and papermaking) into new ones (ironworks, flour milling, and wood processing), the major part of industrial production in Slovakia, especially output of textiles and other consumer goods, remained the domain of guild artisans and cottage industries. The rate of mechanization, moreover, began to lag even behind the rest of Hungary. While in 1851 Slovakia contained 19 percent of Hungary's steam engines with 24 percent of the total horsepower, by 1863 its share declined to 15 and 10 percent respectively.

---

34. Only three significant enterprises producing woolen cloth survived in Slovakia. All of them depended on orders from the army, shielding them from free competition.

Industrial Retardation and Agricultural Adjustment, 1867–1914

The last third of the nineteenth century witnessed significant advances in agriculture. A major stimulus to greater efficiency, born out of necessity, came from the depression of the 1880s and 1890s, although its impact in Slovakia was milder than in the rest of Hungary. The advance of modernization remained uneven. It heightened the advantage of the south over the north of Slovakia, and of the large estates over peasant homesteads.

The amount of arable land increased in Slovakia between 1867 and 1896 by 450,000 morgen, of which almost half was due to plowing up of pastures.[35] The proportion of cultivated land planted in grains decreased somewhat—from 74 percent to 67. Market demands caused substantial shifts in the assortment of production. The growing of wheat and barley increased (by 40 and 30 percent respectively); oats remained stable; and rye declined (by 37 percent). Barley advanced from second to first place, wheat from fourth to second, oats remained in third, and rye declined from first to fourth place. The dominance of barley over wheat—in contrast to the situation in the rest of Hungary—helped Slovakia weather the agricultural crisis, because the price of barley remained relatively stable, reflecting the rise in demand of breweries both domestic and foreign (above all in Germany).

The cultivation of certain industrial crops, especially sugar beets and potatoes, increased further between 1870 and 1900, stimulated by the demands of refineries and distilleries. The cultivation of potatoes rose by 30 percent, and the Slovak output accounted for two-fifth of the Hungarian total. The diminution of pastures and fallow was linked with a dramatic expansion of feed crops. Acreage planted in these crops more than tripled and provided a solid basis for an increase in livestock. A sharp decline in the domestic production of linen helped to account for the halving of the output of flax and hemp.

In animal raising, the increase of cattle from 885,000 to 1,057,000 head between 1870 and 1895 was exceeded by the 50 percent rise in the number of pigs, from 425,000 to 640,000. Yet by 1895 Slovakia accounted for only 10 percent of total Hungarian pig production, and thus did not match the overall rate of increase for Hungary. The number of cattle represented 20 percent of the Hungarian total. The combined effect of the competition of Australian wool and the shrinkage of pasture lands and fallow caused the number of sheep to plummet from 2.7 million to 1.3 million. Fewer horses were needed for carting, owing to the development of railroads, but they were used more in field

35. The amount of land under actual cultivation rose also with the diminution of the fallow from 745,000 morgen in 1870 to 483,000 in 1900.

work with the intensified cultivation of land. On balance, their number declined slightly to 249,000 in 1895 from 255,000 in 1870. The pressure for more efficient production, most notably in the southern counties, promoted a greater reliance on agricultural machinery, which became more readily available with the advance of the industrial revolution.[36]

The development of Slovak industry in the era of dualism was affected by the cycle of prosperity up to 1873, the subsequent depression, and the revival after 1880. While still suffering from Cisleithanian competition, Slovak industry also benefited somewhat from the Hungarian government's industrial subsidies, especially in textiles, after 1880. Yet even within Hungary, Slovakia continued to lag behind the general advance, particularly after 1900, when in fact it suffered sharp reversals in the key area of ferrous metallurgy. Between 1900 and 1910 the industrial labor force increased by only 45 percent compared with 67 percent for the rest of Hungary. By 1914 there was a major erosion of the industrial predominance which Slovakia had enjoyed within Hungary a century earlier.

The one aspect of the iron industry that escaped the long-range decline was the output of iron ore. It rose from 956,000 tons in 1899 to 1,187,000 in 1913. The production of pig iron between 1868 and 1899 increased from 77,000 to 270,000 tons, but its share of Hungary's total sank from 69 to 60 percent. Subsequently in 1900–1913 there was a sharp drop not only relative (to 30 percent of Hungarian total) but also absolute (to 186,891 tons). One factor in this decline was the tendency to shift iron production closer to centers of machinery manufacture, which remained notably underdeveloped in Slovakia. Another factor was the weakness of Slovak coal mining, which in 1900 amounted to a mere 10,000 tons, or less than 0.2 percent of Hungary's total. Only after 1911 did a significant expansion occur, with the output reaching 119,700 tons in 1913.

With the value of iron production declining, food processing became the leading sector of Slovak industry by 1910. The fully mechanized sugar refining industry, after a period of stagnation, resumed its growth in the 1890s. In 1910 eight large refineries employed 4,545 workers. Mechanization advanced steadily in flour milling, and the number of steam-powered mills rose from 47 to 132 between 1871 and 1895. In the new area of tobacco processing the factories increased from one in 1867 to five (with 3,928 workers) in 1910.

The textile industry, the chief beneficiary of the new policy of state subsidies, began to expand by the 1880s and especially grew in the 1890s.

36. By 1895, 41 steam-powered plows were being used in Slovakia. Steam-powered threshing machines rose to 1,346, horse-drawn ones to 13,192, mowing machines to 1,417, and seeders to 7,938.

In 1910 the ten largest manufacturers of cotton cloth employed 5,376 workers. Altogether there were thirty-five textile factories with more than twenty employees, each totaling 10,275 workers. Among other industries, wood processing progressed steadily, accounting for seventy enterprises with more than twenty employees each in 1900, and for 116 (with a total of 8,667 workers) in 1910. Paper production grew more slowly because of keener Austrian competition. In the 1880s and 1890s leather and glass production at last was affected by the industrial revolution. By 1900 twenty-one large tanneries were mechanized. Among the glassworks by 1900 nine used steam for propulsion and eleven used gas to heat furnaces. A significant chemical industry began to develop in the 1870s, with the production of matches, explosives, and starch. In the mid-1890s a major oil refinery was established in Pozsony.

By 1910 food processing accounted for 33.4 percent of the value of industrial production in Slovakia, iron and metallurgy for 23.2 percent, textiles for 12 percent, followed by wood products (7.7), chemical industries (7.4), paper (4.8), and leather (4.3). Within the structure of Hungarian industry, Slovakia shared heavily in the output of unfinished and semifinished products, especially paper (53.7 percent of the Hungarian total), textiles (33.7), leather (27.4), iron (26.9), wood (20.2), and chemicals (17.7). It had only a minor share in the more advanced and profitable production of finished goods, particularly clothing (5.8 percent), machinery (4.1), and printing (1.9). The number of persons employed in industry in Slovakia rose to 227,800 in 1910 from 159,000 in 1890. The growing importance of larger enterprises over artisan workshops was indicated by a further breakdown of these figures. The number of wage workers rose from 85,200 to 150,200, while that of self-employed persons remained virtually constant (somewhat over 70,000). Of the industrial workers 37.5 percent (85,300) in 1910 were employed in 623 enterprises with more than twenty employees each.

Yet on the eve of World War I, Slovakia still remained largely an agricultural area. In 1910, 20.3 percent of the population was employed in industry and trade and 61.8 percent in agriculture, compared with 40.0 and 34.2 percent respectively in the Bohemian Lands. Within a broader framework, Slovak per capita industrial production, and percentage of population employed in industry, represented respectively about one-half and one-third of the European average. While ranking below the lands of Western and Central Europe, Slovakia did exceed in degree of industrialization not only Russia and the Balkan lands, such as Romania and Bulgaria, but also (discounting Budapest) the Magyar territory of Hungary.

Financially the industrial development in Slovakia depended on outside capital—mainly Magyar, Austrian, and German. Most of the larger credit institutions, which began to spring up after 1867, were either branches of Budapest banks or dominated by non-Slovak interests. The Slovak national leaders sought to stimulate the growth of credit facilities controlled by nationally conscious Slovaks. Their achievements were modest. By 1900, discounting credit unions, there were about 130 banks and savings banks in Slovakia with share capital of 17 million florins and total assets of 570 million. Of these, Slovaks controlled twenty-two banks with share capital of 2.3 million (14 percent of the total), and assets of 68 million (12 percent of the total).[37]

WORLD WAR I AND SELF-DETERMINATION

The outbreak of the war found Slovak political leaders unprepared for the new vistas that the historic conflict might open for the realization of national objectives. Slovak representation in the Hungarian parliament had diminished to a single deputy, the clerical Ferdinand Juriga. With tighter controls by the Budapest government over the press and other forms of public expression, the Slovak National Party announced, in August 1914, a suspension of political activity for the duration of the war. Similar official passivity was adopted by the agrarians, the People's Party, and the socialists. A small group of Slovaks in Vienna, under Hodža, sought to promote a comprehensive federalization of the monarchy as a way to assure the autonomy of Slovakia. The Russian Army's advance to the Carpathians in the winter of 1914–15 engendered short-lived hopes of liberation not only among the traditionally Russophile leaders of the SNP but also among the pro-Western Hlasists, such as Šrobár.

In the initial stages of the war the eventual solution of the Slovak question became adumbrated primarily abroad in the resistance movement on the Entente side, which joined the Slovak with the Czech cause under Thomas G. Masaryk. Even before his departure for exile, Masaryk as early as October 1914, in a secret memorandum to England, envisioned, in case of German defeat, the rise of an independent Czech state that could include the Slovak territories as a bridge to Russia. The concept of a joint Czech-Slovak state received widespread endorsement from the large and articulate Slovak community in the United States. In view of the Slovaks' weakness, a link with the Czechs offered a feasible arrangement for separation from Hungary. Apprehensions about Czech cultural and political hegemony were largely stilled by foreseeing

37. The participation of Slovak capital in industrial ownership was even weaker. In 1900 of the approximately fifty joint-stock companies centered in Slovakia, with share capital of 74 million florins, only one was fully, and two or three were partly, owned by Slovak capital, the investment of which did not exceed one million (about 1.5 percent of the total).

the rise of an assertive and distinctly Slovak intelligentsia within a generation of free development. In October 1915 the ranking Slovak organization in the United States, the Slovak League, signed the so-called Cleveland Agreement proposing a federal union of the Slovak and Czech nations in an independent state. The backing of Masaryk's committee, which included a Slovak, Milan Štefánik, by the Slovak League and other emigrant Slovak associations, together with the later participation of Slovaks in the Czechoslovak legions in France (70 percent of the total) and in Russia (10 percent), became known in Slovakia and eventually helped to sway the views of political leaders there. It is important to note that many, if not most, of the influential Slovaks abroad continued to think in terms of a union between two distinct nations. This was the substance, for instance, of a resolution in October 1916 by an important Slovak group in Kiev, headed by Gregor-Tajovský, the exiled secretary of the SNP. The eventual acceptance of the theory of a single Czechoslovak nation by almost all Slovak leaders before the end of the war was due largely to the overwhelming authority of Masaryk. He had made his position clear as early as May 1915 in a memorandum to the British Foreign Secretary, in which he wrote: "Slovaks are Czechs despite the fact that they use their dialect as a literary language."[38] The Pittsburgh Agreement signed on May 30, 1918, by Masaryk and American Slovak leaders already represented a major concession to the Czechoslovakist orientation; while asking for an autonomy for "Slovakia" it avoided any reference to the "Slovak nation."

Within the Habsburg monarchy the first open demand for the inclusion of Slovaks with Czechs in a common state—on the initiative of Šrobár—appeared in the declaration of Czech *Reichsrat* deputies in May 1917. In Slovakia the hope of gaining concessions within Hungary was not yet entirely abandoned. In August 1917 the SNP in fact considered seriously a statement of loyalty to the Hungarian state, provided Budapest would promise restoration of the *Matica*, one Slovak *gymnasium*, and the appointment of Slovaks to county and judicial offices. A joint state with the Czechs was favored most strongly by the former Hlasists, especially Šrobár, the agrarians under Hodža, and the socialists led by Emanuel Lehocký. In the summer of 1917 the leaders of the People's Party, Hlinka and Juriga, expressed a wish to cooperate with the Czechs.

By the spring of 1918 the orientation toward a Czechoslovak state clearly prevailed in Slovak politics. The first public declaration within Slovakia in favor of union with the Czechs was adopted (on the initiative of Šrobár) by a socialist meeting in Liptovský Mikuláš on May 1, 1918. A similar resolution was endorsed by major Slovak leaders assembled under the auspices of the SNP in Martin on May 24. Although not

38. *Slováci i ich národný vývin* (Bratislava: Slovenská akadémia vied, 1969), p. 300.

made public, its contents were confidentially communicated to Czech politicians in Prague.

As the time for decisive action approached, all Slovak political parties and groups formed in September 1918 a joint Slovak National Council. With the pressure to assert Slovak claims to self-determination mounting, Juriga declared in the Budapest parliament on October 19 that the Slovaks no longer recognized the authority of the Hungarian government and that their future could be determined only by their own central political organ, the Slovak National Council. On October 30, 1918, the Council assembled in Martin under Dula's chairmanship to adopt the famous declaration in which it not only claimed the inclusion of Slovaks with the Czechs in a fully independent state but also endorsed the concept of a single Czechoslovak nation. While the joint Slovak and Czech statehood proved an enduring phenomenon, the "Czechoslovakist" orientation was to be just a passing phase in the continuing process of the Slovak nation-building.

The Croats

BETWEEN PEST AND VIENNA, 1848–67

The Revolution of 1848–49

Under the laws adopted by the Hungarian diet in March 1848, and approved by the emperor on April 11, Croatia was to be virtually integrated with Hungary, but the onset of the revolutionary events severed almost all ties between the two countries. A large public meeting, organized by Ivan Kukuljević in Zagreb on March 25, 1848, demanded complete independence from Hungary under a responsible Croatian executive body, and a union of all Croatian territories including Croatia-Slavonia, the military borders, Dalmatia, and Rijeka. The newly appointed *banus*, Josip Jelačić (1801–59), holding also the chief command in the Croatian military borders, prohibited on April 19 local Croatian authorities from accepting any directives from the Hungarian government. In late April, he created a central executive authority in Zagreb, the *Banus' Council (Banalrat)*, including departments for inner and military affairs, justice, religion and education, and finance. Croatia thus gained an administrative independence from Hungary for the first time since Maria Theresa's abolition of the *concilium regium* in 1779.

The *Sabor* elected in late May, on the basis of broadened suffrage, represented the military borders as well as civil Croatia. Assembling on June 5, this body refused to promulgate any laws of the Hungarian diet. It favored a conversion of the entire monarchy into a federation of autonomous Lands with certain common affairs entrusted to a central government and parliament in Vienna. The *Sabor* also reaffirmed the request for unification of all ethnically Croatian territories within the monarchy under the *banus'* jurisdiction. Moreover, it proclaimed emancipation of the peasantry, including the abolition of feudal dues.

Relations with the Hungarian government worsened steadily, and in mid-July 1848 Jelačić intervened in order to prevent annexation of the three Slavonian *županije* by Hungary. Futile negotiations between Croatian and Hungarian representatives took place in Vienna in late July. While previously Vienna had viewed some of Jelačić's anti-Hungarian acts with disapproval, the situation changed drastically by the end of August and the *banus* was encouraged to prepare an invasion of Hungary. Jelačić sought to strengthen Croatia for the approaching conflict through the occupation of Rijeka on August 31. The opening act of his military campaign, which began on September 11, was the seizure of the Medjumurje area in Hungary proper and its annexation to Croatia. Subsequently, Jelačić's troops loyally fought alongside the imperial armies against Hungarian revolutionaries and other opponents.

The accession of Francis Joseph to the throne on December 2, 1848, brought new concessions to the Croats. Above all, on that day, Jelačić received additional appointments as governor of both Rijeka and Dalmatia. Thus he combined the administrative authority over all Croatian territories within the monarchy except for Istria. Disillusionment with the Viennese government, however, set in with the "decreed" imperial constitution of March 4, 1849. In vain did the *Banus'* Council protest in May against its centralistic character—encroaching on Croatia's traditional autonomy—as well as against the establishment of the military borders as a separate crownland.

Neo-Absolutism, 1849–59

At last, in September 1849, the *Banus'* Council acknowledged the new constitution, which, however, was never implemented. The measures of the initial phase of the Neo-Absolutist regime followed. In November two districts (Ilok and Ruma) of Srijem *županija* were entirely separated from civil Croatia and were transferred to the administration of the newly created crownland of Serbian Vojvodina.[39] As a minor compensation, the Medjumurje area was provisionally incorporated into civil Croatia. Upon the introduction of Austrian law codes in March 1850, the courts of the *županije* and the *kotari* were reformed to correspond to the circuit and district courts of the Austrian and Bohemian

39. On the formation of Serbian Vojvodina as a crownland see pp. 426–27.

Lands. Similarly, the *Banus'* Table was transformed into the Superior Court of the Land, with final appellate jurisdiction vested in the Supreme Judicial and Cassation Court in Vienna. The assemblies and elected committees in the *županije* were abolished, and from the administrative point of view the *županije* and the *kotari* became purely bureaucratic institutions, headed by *veliki župani* and *podžupani* respectively. At the top of Croatia's administrative hierarchy stood the *Banus'* Government (*Banalregierung*), which had replaced the independent-minded *Banus'* Council in June 1850, and was responsible to the imperial Cabinet in Vienna. At least temporarily, however, Croatian replaced Latin in government agencies and in secondary education. The proclamation of overt absolutism on December 31, 1851, when the "decreed" constitution of March 1849 was formally abrogated, was followed by a second phase of reforms, largely aimed at an empire-wide administrative uniformity and Germanization. By 1854 the *Banus'* Government was transformed into a Lieutenancy (*Statthalterei*) subordinated to the Interior Ministry in Vienna. The *županije* and the *kotari* were reorganized to correspond respectively to the *Kreise* (*kraje*) and *Bezirke* (*okresy*) of the Austrian and Bohemian Lands. Also in 1854, German became the official language of government agencies, as well as in substance the language of instruction in secondary education. To a large extent the officials of the absolutist system were recruited outside Croatia, particularly among the Austro-Germans, Slovenes, and Czechs. On the more positive side from the viewpoint of Croatia's social and national development, one should cite enactment of the peasant emancipation implemented by a decree of March 2, 1853, and the consistent tendency of the Neo-Absolutist regime to sever administrative, legislative, and judicial links between Croatia and Hungary. The raising of the see of Zagreb to an archbishopric in December 1852 emancipated Croatia from Hungary in the ecclesiastical sphere.

Political life virtually ceased under the new absolutist regime. The suppression of self-government reaching a degree unprecedented since Joseph II's reign, affected not only the *Sabor* (as in 1812–25) but also the *županije* assemblies. The press, not excluding literary and religious periodicals, was subject to rigid censorship. *Banus* Jelačić, reduced now to a figurehead, was failing physically in the late 1850s and died in May 1859.

The Provisorium, *1860–67*

With the trend toward restoration of constitutionalism in the Habsburg monarchy following defeat in the war against France and Piedmont in 1859, Bishop Josip Strossmayer (1815–1905) rose to prominence as a Croatian spokesman within the Enlarged *Reichsrat* in the summer of 1860. In Croatia, German was now replaced by Croatian as the official language. At royal request, an assembly of 55 leading Croat politicians, or an ad hoc "*banus'* conference," met from November 1860 to January 1861 to propose political and administrative changes. In response to their wishes, the king sanctioned the creation in Vienna of a provisional Croatian Court Chancellery (*dikasterij*), headed by Ivan Mažuranić, and the reestablishment of the traditional self-government within the *županije*. The restoration of easternmost Slavonia to Croatia (with the abolition of the Serbian Vojvodina) was counterbalanced by the reincorporation of Medjumurje into Hungary in January 1861. The latter loss, together with reviving conflict over Rijeka, dissipated much of the pro-Hungarian feeling generated among the Croats by the recent common experience of oppression from Vienna. The emperor ignored the request of the *banus'* conference of 1860–61, subsequently echoed by the *Sabor,* for the annexation to Croatia of eastern Istria, including the districts of Labin (Albena), Podgrad (Castelnuovo), and Volosko (Volosca), as well as the islands of Krk, Cres, and Lošinj. Concerning its call for a reunion of Croatia with Dalmatia, the *banus'* conference was told by the imperial government to negotiate with a Dalmatian delegation, which, however, never arrived.

The *Sabor,* elected according to the rules of 1848, met in April 1861. With the military borders represented, the Serbs became now a significant factor within the Zagreb legislature. On the principal issue of relations with Hungary, the majority in the *Sabor* led by Bishop Strossmayer (later called the National Party) adopted a law (article 42) stipulating that the union was one between equal partners based on complete internal self-government. More substantive union was advocated by the minority (the Unionists), composed partly of former Magyarones and partly of Nationalists counting on Hungary's aid against Viennese centralism. A third position rejecting any a priori ties to either Hungary or Austria was upheld by a small radical group (later known as the Party of the Right), including the lawyers Eugen Kvaternik and Antun Starčević.

Vienna's reversion to rigid centralism under Schmerling led to a dissolution of the *Sabor* in November 1861, following its refusal to elect deputies to the *Reichsrat.* Nevertheless, the government continued to favor Croatia's separate identity. Having created in Zagreb an executive authority, independent of Hungary, the Lieutenancy Council (on the basis of the Neo-Absolutist Lieutenancy), and confirmed article 42, the king sanctioned the establishment of a regular Croatian Court Chancellery in Vienna in November 1861 and a supreme court in Zagreb (*stol sedmorice*) in January 1862. Under the direction of the Croatian Chancellery, the Lieutenancy Council controlled political administration, justice, and education in Croatia. A pro-Austrian group, the Independent Party, including Mažuranić andKukuljević, gradually emerged favoring a settlement with Vienna independent of Hungary. But an electoral reform in February 1865, sponsored by Vienna, failed—in the *Sabor* elections in May—to produce a majority for the Independents over the combined strength of Strossmayer's National Party and the Unionists.

With the recurrence of a pro-Hungarian orientation in Vienna under Belcredi, the new *Sabor* was encouraged to negotiate with the Hungarian diet the conclusion of a new union. The negotiations, carried on from April to June 1866, broke down over the Hungarians' refusal to accept the principle of equal partnership embodied in article 42, or to recognize Rijeka and Medjumurje as integral parts of Croatia. The following December, the *Sabor* voted to pursue a settlement with Vienna independent of Hungary. This position became untenable with Vienna's decisive turn toward a Compromise with the Magyar gentry. After the replacement of Austrian Prime Minister Count Richard Belcredi by Count Friedrich Ferdinand Beust as chancellor in February 1867, the *Sabor* was invited to send representatives to the Hungarian diet for the coronation of Francis Joseph. The *Sabor*'s refusal led to its dissolution in May, and the ceremony took place a month later in Buda without Croatian representatives.

Dalmatia and Istria, 1848–67

The second largest segment of Croatian population in the Habsburg monarchy lived in Dalmatia, the union of which with Croatia was a standing desideratum of Croatia's leaders. In 1848, except in the southern region of Dubrovnik, the Italian or Italianized officials and intellectuals of Dalmatia ignored the unification appeals from Zagreb. Limited attempts to introduce Croatian into education and government agencies were interrupted during the Neo-Absolutism of the 1850s, when public administration and judiciary were cast into the standard Austrian mold. Renewed calls from Croatia for a reunion in late 1860 were again rejected by most Dalmatian leaders. Created in 1861 and based on the standard four *curiae*, the Dalmatian diet was initially dominated by 31 autonomists, upholding the status quo, against 13 members of the National Party, favoring annexation by Croatia. Strengthened in 1864 by defections from the autonomists, the National Party in the following year won majorities in most municipalities, except the large towns. Under Belcredi in 1865–66, Vienna briefly favored the Croats. Under the lieutenant (*Statthalter*), Baron Filipović, knowledge of Croatian (in addition to Italian) became obligatory for civil servants. Croatian also secured equality with Italian in the diet, and it was introduced widely into elementary schools, as well as into parallel sections of *gymnasia* classes.

With the approach of the Compromise with Hungary, Vienna's benevolence swayed to the Italians, who supported the dualist system.

In Istria the Italians (60,000 in 1846) were even more powerful politically than in Dalmatia, although they were heavily outnumbered by the combined Croats (134,000) and Slovenes (32,000). In the 1848 *Reichstag* elections four Italians and only one Croat won mandates. Attempts to establish Italian as the sole official language in the Land, however, led to Croatian protest meetings in the winter of 1848–49, requesting a union of the predominantly Croatian eastern part of Istria with Croatia. After the reestablishment of constitutionalism,[40] the Italians dominated all four *curiae* of the newly created diet of 1861, which met in the new capital of Poreč (Parenzo). Outnumbered twenty-five to five, the Croats and Slovenes had to accept Italian as the sole language of the diet and were excluded from the Committee of the Land. Three of the five Slav deputies in the diet were bishops, including the well-known Juraj Dobrila. Neither the Croats nor the Slovenes developed any formal political organizations of their own in the 1860s.

UNDER DUALISM, 1867–1914

Era of Conciliation, 1867–83

After the Compromise with Hungary, Levin Rauch was appointed provisional *banus* in June 1867 to ensure conclusion of a union agreement between Croatia and Hungary. In October a royal rescript increased the number of appointed members of the *Sabor*. Under government pressure, in late 1867 the Unionists won 52 seats against 14 for the National Party. The new Sabor approved in November 1868 an agreement (*nagodba*) with the Hungarian parliament which stipulated complete Croatian autonomy in the area of justice, the interior, and education and religion. Finance, agriculture, trade, and defense were, however, subordinated to the ministries in Budapest. The *nagodba* provided for Croatian representation in the Hungarian parliament and for the appointment of the *banus* by the king on the advice of the Hungarian prime minister. During the implementation of the *nagodba* in early 1869 the Croatian Chancellery in Vienna was replaced by the Croatian Ministry in Budapest, and a Croatian government was established in Zagreb, consisting of three departments—for justice, the interior, and religious and educational affairs.[41] The *banus* alone wielded independent executive power with the heads of government carrying

40. Concerning administrative and judicial reforms in Istria during the 1850s and 1860s see pp. 328, 329–30.
41. A fourth department, for national economy, was not established until 1914.

out his directives. While subject to impeachment by the *Sabor*, he was not responsible to the legislature for the ordinary conduct of government business. As a final act of the initial settlement with Hungary, in the summer of 1870 the *Sabor* provisionally accepted Hungarian administration of Rijeka.

In the meantime, resentment over the *nagodba* and political repression grew intense. In the elections of May 1871 the National Party won 51 seats against 13 for the Unionists. After the government had repeatedly postponed convoking the *Sabor*, the National Party issued a declaration in September 1871 openly repudiating the *nagodba*. In early October, Kvaternik incited an uprising in the military borders aimed at Croatia's independence from both Hungary and the Habsburg empire. After this climax, the radical mood began to subside. The *Sabor* was dissolved before it had a chance to meet, and although the new elections in the spring of 1872 returned a majority of National Party members, the Unionists combined with appointed members gained an overall majority. In July 1872 the chastened National Party agreed to renegotiate the *nagodba* jointly with the Unionists. The Croats sought control of their own finances and independence of the *banus* from the Hungarian prime minister, but the adamant Hungarian parliament conceded only minor points, enacted finally in September 1873.

A relatively peaceful era followed, with Mažuranić appointed *banus* also in September 1873, and the Unionists merged with the National Party to form a new government party under the joint name of the National Party. Constructive legislation was passed in 1874–75, particularly in the area of civil liberties, including a definite separation of the judiciary also at the lower levels from the administration. A university was established in Zagreb in October 1874. A reorganization of the administrative system affected the *županije*, which had already in 1870 turned from agencies of local autonomy into primarily organs of the Croatian government with officials appointed by the *banus* or the *veliki župan* rather than elected by the *županija* assembly. In November 1874 the eight existing *županije* lost most of their administrative functions to the twenty new districts (*podžupanije*) reporting directly to the government in Zagreb. A discordant note was the Hungarian government's efforts to introduce Magyar into railroad administration, even though the *nagodba* obliged agencies of the common ministries in Croatia to use Croatian. A more serious conflict pitted the Croats against the Serb minority over the issue of Bosnia-Herzegovnia, leaving a long-lasting legacy of bitterness and alienation. In the summer of 1876 the *banus* applied repression against the Serbian community (arresting leaders and closing Orthodox schools) for its financial and military aid to the insurgents in Bosnia-Herzegovina. The Serbs, in turn, resented Croatian demands for the annexation of Bosnia-Herzegovina to Croatia after 1878.

The situation further destabilized by Mažuranić's resignation in February 1880 over his failure to obtain financial concessions from the Hungarian government.

Under the new *banus,* Count Ladislav Pejačević (a Unionist), relations with Hungary were soon disturbed by a new measure of Magyarization, when a Zagreb agency of the Hungarian Finance Ministry opened a school to teach Magyar to Croatian officials. In protest, twenty-two deputies left the government party in September 1880, and formed an Independent National Party, called *Obzoraši.*[42] Also the Party of the Right, or *Pravaši,* which had revived in 1878 and rejected the *nagodba* entirely, grew in strength. A peaceful interlude followed during the incorporation of the Croatian military borders (demilitarized since September 1873) into civil Croatia, which was initiated in July 1881. Subsequently, a new crisis erupted over the display of Magyar inscriptions on emblems of the government revenue bureaus in Zagreb in August 1883. Rioting in the capital was followed by violent disturbances in the countryside. The king-emperor suspended the constitution in September and entrusted a royal commissioner with restoration of order. The subsequent appointment of Count Károly Khuen-Héderváry as *banus* in December 1883 opened a new era for Croatia.

Soon after the Compromise of 1867 the situation in Dalmatia changed in favor of the Croats. In 1870 the National Party, uniting Croats with Serbs (16 percent of Dalmatia's population), won 25 seats in the diet against 16 for the mostly Italian autonomists. The National Party survived a temporary split in 1873, when it expelled all of its *Reichsrat* deputies for subservience to the imperial government, as well as permanent defection of the Serbs over the issue of Bosnia-Herzegovina. Although the Serbs formed their own (National) party in 1879, which leaned toward the autonomists, the (Croatian) National Party still won eight out of nine seats in the *Reichsrat* election that year. Early in the Taaffe era (1879–93), the Croats gained concessions, including in 1880 the establishment of two *gymnasia* and a recognition of Croatian as the external official language of government agencies. The latter measure, however, was accompanied by belated and ill-advised steps to introduce German as the internal official language. In 1883 the use of Croatian in judicial proceedings was reaffirmed, and Croatian gained dominance in the diet and in the Committee of the Land, with Italian relegated to a secondary status.

In Istria, the Croats—in cooperation with the Slovenes—were acquiring the rudiments of a political organization. A political journal, issued in Trieste, emerged in 1870, and political meetings were organized as early as 1871. In 1873 one of the two *Reichsrat* deputies elected

---

42. The name was derived from the title of the party's organ, *Obzor.*

in the rural *curia* was a Croat. In 1878 a Croatian-Slovene party was formally organized. The Taaffe era brought limited concessions, in particular the use of Croatian and Slovene in judicial proceedings by 1883. Basically, however, the position of the Croats remained weak. In 1880, Italian still predominated in elementary education, and except for a teachers' institute in Koper, Croatian was not used in secondary schools. From 1857 to 1880 the Croatian population decreased from 132,000 to 121,000, while the Italian population grew from 72,000 to 114,000. The Slovenes increased from 28,000 to 43,000.

Pseudo-Constitutionalism, 1883–1903

Khuen-Héderváry skillfully applied in Croatia the typical Hungarian methods of political and election manipulation, essentially in order to perpetuate the status quo under the *nagodba*. Threatening to rule without the *Sabor,* he gained cooperation of a majority of the old progovernment National Party. In the ensuing elections of September 1884, through imprisonment, intimidation, and invalidation of votes, the *Pravaši* were reduced to 25 seats, and the *Obzoraši* to 13, compared with 69 for the National Party. Afterward Khuen imposed restrictions on the opposition in the *Sabor,* increased the powers of the *veliki župani* in the counties, and abolished the use of jury in trials for press offenses. In February 1886 the *županije* became an intermediate administrative layer between the government in Zagreb and the districts (*podžupanije*). To foster a division between Croats and Serbs, and therewith to weaken the opposition, he made educational and cultural concessions to the Serbs, whose importance in Croatia had increased with the incorporation of the military borders in 1881. In the same vein, the *banus* even attempted to promote a Slavonian separatism.

In the elections of 1887 the opposition was further weakened, and the ensuing period to the mid-1890s represented the zenith of Khuen's pseudo-constitutional regime. An electoral reform in June 1888 reduced the number of voters to a mere 2 percent of the population, probably the lowest level among the contemporary parliamentary systems of Europe.[43] Within the beleaguered and powerless opposition, the *Pravaši* moderated their earlier anti-Austrian and anti-Hungarian radicalism. Losing hope in a disruption of the Habsburg monarchy through Russia's intervention, and witnessing the conflicts between Budapest and Vienna, they acquiesced in a possible solution of the Croatian question within the monarchy, and drew closer to the *Obzoraši*. In 1892 the former archenemies, Starčević and Strossmayer, met to stimulate an advance toward the common program, which was in fact adopted

43. By way of comparison, even in Hungary at least 6 percent of the population could vote.

in 1894, while the two party organizations remained separate. The new program called for the union of all Croatian territories, probably within Hungary, but leaving open the possibility of a trialist solution. Within a year sharp schism rent the *Pravaši*. While the core of the party, now called *Domovinaši*,[44] moved even closer to the *Obzoraši*, a radically pro-Austrian and anti-Serbian wing formed a distinct party of the Pure Right, also known as *Frankovci* after their leader Josip Frank.

In 1895 Khuen's regime entered an unstable phase. In October the stagnant political atmosphere was stirred up by a spirited student demonstration in Zagreb. More important, new political trends were emerging. One of them was clericalism as an anticipatory reaction to the liberal religious legislation in Hungary. Thanks largely to the influence of the clergy in rural areas, the opposition won a third of the seats in the *Sabor* elections of 1897, compared with one-tenth in 1892. After 1901 a progressive current was represented by the group *Omladina*, inspired by young intellectuals who had studied abroad, particularly under Masaryk in Prague. They displayed an avid interest in modern social and cultural ideas, friendship for the Serbs and other Slavs, and concern with educational uplifting of the masses. The *Omladina* also nurtured as its offshoot an agrarian movement, later developed by the brothers Stjepan and Antun Radić. Moreover, the antagonism between the Croats and the Serbs was abating. This was owing partly to an alienation of Serb leaders from Khuen's regime in the late 1890s and to the subsequent rise of younger leaders, above all Svetozar Pribičević, sharing common interests with the Croatian *Omladina*. By 1903 the situation in Croatia was ripe for more vigorous political life.

In Dalmatia the Croatian national movement continued to advance during the last two decades of the nineteenth century. By 1900 the Croatian (or Serbian) language prevailed not only in elementary but also in secondary education (except in Zadar) and in all municipal governments except two. It still was excluded as the internal official language of state government agencies. In the 1880s the National Party came under increasing criticism for subservience to Vienna, and for halfheartedness about a reunion with Croatia. By 1894 the critics had organized the Party of the Right (*Pravaši*), led by Frano Supilo and Ante Trumbić. The more clerical elements split off in 1898 as the Party of Pure Right, and subsequently the *Pravaši* drew closer to the National Party. Under a new leader, Pero Čingrija, the National Party also sought rapprochement with the Serbian Party, which after 1901 was ready to cooperate with the Croats rather than as hitherto with the Italian autonomists. In the diet elected in 1901, the Croats gained 29 seats (the National Party 18, *Pravaši* 9, Pure Right 2), the Serbs and the Italians each 6.

44. The name was derived from the title of the party's organ, *Hrvatska Domovina*.

In Istria, the national advances of the Croats and the Slovenes were less conspicuous. The South Slavs did succeed, however, in winning majorities in most municipalities in the northeast and the center of the Land during the 1880s. By 1889 they had reached the maximum number of diet seats possible under the existing electoral system, 9 out of 30. Only the king-emperor's veto prevented the establishment of Italian as the exclusive language of the diet in the 1890s. Vienna offered merely half-hearted support in the field of education. The first Croatian *gymnasium* (in Pazin) was established as late as 1899. Weak politically, Croatian leaders resorted to private organizations to promote the vigor of national life. A successful cooperative movement was launched in the 1880s, and from 1893 on the Society of Cyril and Methodius focused on establishing schools in Croatian and Slovene villages. The ethnic balance remained precarious. While the ratio between the Croats and the Italians stabilized in the 1880s, the proportion of the Italians was increasing again in the 1890s.

The population of Bosnia-Herzegovina, placed under Austro-Hungarian administration in 1878,[45] was 18 percent Croatian. These Croats represented 10 percent of the entire Croatian population of the monarchy, in which they constituted the third largest Croatian group. In comparison, 62 percent of the monarchy's Croats were in Croatia, 18 percent in Dalmatia, 6 percent in Istria, and 4 percent in Vojvodina. The leadership of the Croatian community in Bosnia-Herzegovina rested initially with the local Franciscan monks, who also controlled the first political journal launched in 1884. Starting with a broadly Yugoslav viewpoint in the spirit of Stossmayer, by the end of the decade the journal shifted toward the more narrowly Croatian orientation typical of Starčević *Pravaši*. Since the 1880s the Franciscans had competed with the local Serb leaders for the national allegiance of the Moslems (38.7 percent percent of the population), maintaining that despite their adherence to Islam the latter were ethnically Croats. The Moslems were, however, repelled by the Croats' pronounced Habsburg loyalism, which mounted in the 1890s particularly under the influence of the *Frankovci*. At last, by 1902, they allied with the Serbs, with whom they shared a religiously inspired dislike of the Austro-Hungarian monarchy.

Political Revival, 1903–14

The year 1903 ushered in a decade of turbulence in Croatia which was to last almost until the outbreak of World War I, and—combined with the parallel crisis of the dualist system—made the maintenance of the status quo under the *nagodba* a most precarious undertaking. In January 1903 the opposition coalition of the *Obzoraši* and *Domovinaši*

---

45. On the administrative system in Bosnia-Herzegovina see p. 431.

was strengthened by the addition of the dynamic *Omladina*. The *Omladina* proceeded to organize protest meetings, demanding broader suffrage and a larger share of the common Hungaro-Croatian finances. Khuen's attempts to suppress the movement incited the first serious riots in the cities and violence in the countryside since 1883. While the new *banus,* Count Teodor Pejačević, after Khuen's appointment as Hungarian premier in June 1903, struggled to perpetuate his predecessor's pseudo-constitutional system, new political groups emerged to channel the aspirations of the hitherto disenfranchised masses, in particular the clerical organization *Hrvatstvo* in May 1904, and Radić's Peasant Party in December. Even the Social Democrats, organized in 1894, now played a noticeable role.

The year 1905, which also climaxed the crisis of dualism, brought about two major shifts in the policy of the principal opposition parties in Croatia. All of them, except the inherently pro-Austrian *Frankovci*, adopted the Rijeka Resolution in October 1905, which called for an alliance with the Hungarian opposition against Vienna in the misguided hope that the opposition would be more generous toward Croatian national aspirations than the pre-1905 ruling party in Budapest, Tisza's Liberals, and would, moreover, support the annexation of Dalmatia to Croatia. In a more durable new departure, the Serbs of Croatia, who with the rising tensions between the Habsburg monarchy and Serbia could no longer count on favors from either Vienna or Budapest, made their peace with the Croats. In December 1905, the major Serbian parties (National Independent and Radical) combined with the Party of the Right (resulting from a fusion in 1903 of the *Obzoraši* and the *Domovinaši*) and the *Omladina* (called the Progressive Party since 1904) into the Croat-Serb Coalition, destined to remain the most important factor in Croatia's politics until 1918. Of the major opposition parties only the *Frankovci* (Pure Right), the Peasant Party, and the clerical *Hrvatstvo* stayed outside the Coalition.

Following the guidelines of the Rijeka Resolution, the Croat-Serb Coalition in fact struck a bargain with the Hungarian opposition, which came to power in Budapest in April 1906 as the National Coalition. The latter withdrew support from the old Croatian government party (National Party), which Khuen had created as a tool for ruling Croatia and managed by underhanded interference. As a result, the Croat-Serb Coalition emerged as the victor in the *Sabor* elections of May 1906. The cooperation between Croatia and Hungary, or the policy of the "New Course," however, was short-lived, since the Hungarian National Coalition proved to be even more zealous about Magyarization than Tisza's Liberal Party. The irreparable break came over a measure sponsored in Budapest by Ferenc Kossuth in May 1907, explicitly legalizing Magyar as the official language of railroad service in Croatia.

A new *banus,* Pavol Rauch, appointed in January 1908, was given the task of calming the ensuing political turmoil in Croatia. More an agent of Vienna than of Budapest, he tried first to bolster the *Frankovci* against the Croat-Serb Coalition. Failing in this, he dissolved the newly elected *Sabor* (containing 22 *Frankovci* against 57 Coalition members) in March 1908, and ruled autocratically. Further efforts to discredit the Croat-Serb Coalition figured conspicuously in the notorius treason trial of fifty-three Serbian politicians, intellectuals, and others in Zagreb in October 1909, in which conviction were secured by the use of forged documents.

By 1910, a sufficiently reconsolidated Hungarian government could reassert its power over Croatia, and in January, Khuen, once again the Hungarian premier, appointed as *banus* his old confidant Nikola Tomašić, who hoped to recreate Khuen's pseudo-constitutional regime. The Croat-Serb Coalition initially responded to Tomašić's overtures when in May 1910 he agreed to expand the franchise from 2 to 6 percent of the population. Subsequently, it refused, however, to play the role of a government party, unwilling to undergo the process of emasculation, such as Khuen had performed on the National Party in 1883. Tomašić's efforts to create a totally new government party also failed. The situation was further complicated by the pro-Austrian *Frankovci,* mobilized under Rauch, who tried to involve Vienna more closely in Croatian affairs. To shed the remnants of their liberal image, and thus become even more attractive to the conservative elements at the Court, the *Frankovci* fused with the clerical *Hrvatstvo* (under the name of Christian Social Party) in September 1910. The search for ideological purity, however, was also a source of weakness for the *Frankovci.* It had caused in 1908 the secession of a faction that opposed a rigidly clerical and anti-Serb orientation. The new group established itself as the Starčević Party of the Right.[46] In the elections of October 1910, reflecting the expanded franchise, Tomašić's government party (Party of Progress) won merely 18 seats, while the Croat-Serb Coalition gained 36, the Starčević Party of the Right 9, *Frankovci* (Christian Social Party) 14, and the Peasant Party 9. After prolonged suspension of the *Sabor,* Tomašić tried new elections in December 1911, but the government party remained in a minority.

46. Nevertheless in 1911 the Starčević Party of the Right and the *Frankovci* resumed cooperation, and in January 1912 they presented to both Francis Joseph and to the heir apparent Franz Ferdinand a joint manifesto calling for an immediate solution of the Croatian question on the basis of trialism under which Croatia, Dalmatia, Istria, and Bosnia-Herzegovina would be placed under Zagreb. Subsequently, the two groups sought to coordinate their policies with the Slovene clericals at the Ljubljana Conference of October 1912 (see also p. 337). The staunch anti-Serbian and anti-Orthodox view of the *Frankovci,* however, caused a permanent rift between them and the Starčević Party of the Right in March 1913.

Tomašić's failure to reproduce Khuen's old system in Croatia forced the Hungarian premier to apply naked authoritarianism. The new *banus,* Slavko Cuvaj, appointed in January 1912, was proclaimed a royal commissioner in April in the first overt suspension of constitutional government in Croatia since 1883. The task of resolving the impasse was inherited in May 1912 by the new Hungarian premier, László Lukács, who, however, was hampered by rising violence in Croatia, as well as by uncertainties about the impact of the Balkan Wars. It was left to the political acumen of Count István Tisza, appointed prime minister in the summer of 1913, to end the decade of political turmoil in Croatia. For the amazingly low price of formally repealing the railroad language regulation of 1907, while retaining its substance in fact, he secured a pledge from the Croat-Serb Coalition to maintain the *nagodba.* In November 1913, Ivan Skerlecz became *banus* and the Coalition won a majority in the elections in the following month. Without surrendering its identity, it became the ruling party in the *Sabor* against the opposition of the *Frankovci,* the Starčević Party of the Right, and the Peasant Party. Without Tisza's support, the pro-Magyar Party of Progress, organized by Tomašić as a potential government party, disintegrated and vanished prior to the elections of 1913.

As for Dalmatia, the opening years of the twentieth century witnessed a mounting tension between the Croatian politicians and the Viennese government. A major source of friction was the attempt, initiated in 1903 by the Lieutenant Erasmus von Handel, to impose German as the internal official language of government agencies. Estrangement from Vienna was increased by the refusal of Francis Joseph in 1903 to receive a delegation of Dalmatian (and Istrian) diet deputies protesting the political suppression in Croatia on the technical grounds that the delegation was unauthorized to intervene in Transleithanian (Hungarian) affairs. Against this background, the Croatian Party of Dalmatia (resulting from a union of the National Party and the *Pravaši* in the spring of 1905) inclined to cooperation with the newly victorious Hungarian opposition against Vienna. This policy of a "New Course," it was hoped, would advance Croatian national interests, above all a union of Dalmatia with Croatia. Thus the Dalmatian Croats, in particular Trumbić and Supilo (having cleared its principles with both Budapest and Belgrade), were the chief architects of the Rijeka Resolution of October 4, 1905.

A major significance of the Rijeka Resolution was its endorsement by the Serbs of both Dalmatia and Croatia, resulting in a program of Serb-Croat reconciliation within the territories settled by Croats in the western and eastern parts of the Habsburg monarchy. The Serb support for the Resolution was signified at a meeting of Serb delegates in Zadar in mid-October 1905, and by the subsequent accession of the Serbs to the Croat-Serb Coalition in Croatia. The Rijeka and the Zadar mani-festoes, supplemented by the call for a Yugoslav union in the socialist-sponsored Tivoli Resolution of Ljubljana of 1909, and by the joint Croatian-Slovene clerical action program, likewise of Ljubljana, of 1912, were of far-reaching importance in the evolution of the South Slav union movement within the empire.

The idea of cooperation with Budapest, or the policy of the "New Course," had even shorter duration in Dalmatia than in Croatia. By 1906 the Croatian Party responded favorably to economic concessions from Vienna, and a new high point of reconciliation was reached in April 1909, when Serbo-Croatian was established as the internal official language in Dalmatia. Nevertheless, Vienna was soon disappointed by the sympathies for Serbia of all Dalmatian factions, except the *Fran-kovci*, during the Balkan Wars of 1912–13. The relative strength of in-dividual political parties, based on the *Reichsrat* elections of 1911, was as follows: Croatian Party four deputies, *Frankovci* four, Serbs two, Pro-gressives one. In the *Reichsrat* the *Frankovci* joined the Croat-Slovene club, while the others remained independent as a Dalmatian club.

In Istria the Croat-Slovene Party demanded more aggressively by 1903 an equitable representation in both the diet and the *Reichsrat.* Under a sympathetic lieutenant of the Littoral, Prince Conrad Hohenlohe, ap-pointed in late 1904, certain national concessions were obtained. Sub-sequently the *Reichsrat* electoral reform of 1907 at least assigned an equal number of seats to the South Slavs (two to the Croats, one to the Slov-enes) as to the Italians (three). But in 1908 a reform of the diet still gave the Italians twenty-six representatives, compared with eighteen for the Slavs (sixteen Croats and two Slovenes), although the South Slavs also obtained the right of veto in certain important areas of legislation. After 1910, continuous conflicts troubled the diet. The Croat-Slovene Party demanded a proportional share of public offices, as well as of cultural and educational expenditures, while the Italians pressed for redrawing town boundaries to preserve their Italian character by ex-cluding Slav-inhabited peripheries.

A secular Croatian intelligentsia was emerging in Bosnia-Herzego-vina in the early twentieth century and tended to perpetuate the po-litical tradition launched by the Franciscans. A Croatian political meet-ing in Doc near Travnik in the summer of 1906 petitioned Francis Joseph in vain for union of Bosnia-Herzegovina with Croatia. In December 1907 Nikola Mandić established a Croatian society, *Hrvatska Narodna Zajednica,* soon to become a political party. In October 1908 the occu-pation of Bosnia-Herzegovina (in 1878) was tranformed into formal an-nexation against vehement opposition from Serbia from the outside, backed to a degree by Russia. Thereupon a limited constitution was granted to Bosnia-Herzegovina in 1910.[47]

In the first diet elections in May 1910 the *Hrvatska Narodna Zajednica* was opposed by the staunchly Catholic and anti-Serb *Hrvatska Katolicka Zadruga*, organized by Archbishop Josip Stadler. The dichotomy between Stadler's and Mandić's groups (both favoring an ultimate union of Bosnia-Herzegovina with Croatia) reproduced the conflict between the *Frankovci* and the Starčević Party of the Right in Croatia. The *Zajednica* won eleven of the sixteen seats assigned to the Croats. By 1912 the *Zadruga* and the *Zajednica* formally merged, but the dichotomy between the two factions persisted. The Croats in the diet then cooperated closely with Vienna, resuming a policy of rapprochement with the Moslem leaders. Relations remained strained with the Serbs, who (unlike their kinsmen in Croatia and Dalmatia) envisaged their ultimate destiny not with Croatia but with Serbia.

AGRICULTURE, INDUSTRY, AND FINANCE[48]

Obstacles to Industrial Revolution, 1848–67

The emancipation of the peasantry, implemented by a decree of March 2, 1853, deeply affected Croatia's agriculture. The loss of unpaid labor caused severe financial problems for the former seigneurs. The larger noble landowners raised money through sales of forest lands, while the smaller ones often ended up in bankruptcy. Scarcity of credit facilities—until 1868 Croatia had only one credit institution—aggravated the situation. Among the peasants the emancipation stimulated replacement of the extended family homesteads (*zadruge*) with single family farms, first in civil Croatia, and from the 1860s also in the military borders. The disintegration of the *zadruga* lessened the area of pasture lands and depressed animal raising. Thus on the Croatian territory between 1857 and 1869 cattle declined from 884,000 to 786,000 head, and the number of pigs from 904,000 to 733,000. Peasant income also diminished because a high tax discouraged the distilling of brandy, and

47. On the constitutional arrangements of 1910 for Bosnia-Herzegovina see also p. 432.

48. The economic data in this section are derived from Jaroslav Šidak et al., *Povijest hrvatskog naroda g. 1860–1914* (Zagreb: Školska knjiga, 1968); Igor Karaman, *Privreda i društvo Hrvatske u 19. stoljeću* (Zagreb: Školska knjiga, 1972), pp. 266–89, 302–48; Rudolf Bićanić, *Doba manufakture u Hrvatskoj i Slavoniji, 1750–1860* (Zagreb: Jugoslavenska Akademije Znanosti, 1951), pp. 85–163, 209–29; Vladimir Stipetić, *Kretanje i tendencije u razvitku poljoprivredne proizvodnje na području NR Hrvatske* (Zagreb, 1959); *Enciklopedija Jugoslavije* (Zagreb: Izd. Leksikografskog zavoda, 1960), 4:192–97; *Hrvatska enciklopedija* (Zagreb: Konzorcija Hrvatske enciklopedije, 1942), 4:478–80; Miroslava Despot, *Industrija Građanske Hrvatske, 1860–1873* (Zagreb: Institut za Historiju radničkog pokreta Hrvatske, 1970), pp. 137–75.

the introduction of a state tobacco monopoly affected tobacco growing unfavorably, above all in the Požega area.

Agricultural marketing depended largely on exports, as low consumption limited the domestic market. Underdevelopment of the transportation network, however, hampered the export trade. A major railroad line did not reach Croatia until 1862. Grain remained the chief export article, followed by cattle, particularly from Slavonia. During the 1850s on the average 20,000 head of cattle and 70,000 pigs were sold abroad annually.

Dalmatia and Istria belonged among the areas of the monarchy with an exceptionally low proportion of arable land within the total of agricultural land. In Dalmatia 57.4 percent of the entire territory at midcentury was covered by pasture, while Istria imported one-third of its grain consumption. Animal raising was well developed. Sheep in 1857 numbered 800,000 in Dalmatia and 300,000 in Istria. Nevertheless, the chief traditional exports of both lands were wine and olive oil.

Industrial development in Croatia during the period 1848–67 started naturally from a lower level than that of the Austrian and Bohemian Lands. Yet it was inferior to that of Hungary as well. Altogether the halting and uneven economic progress made it questionable whether the industrial revolution would take root on Croatian territory. Wood processing remained the main area of strength, satisfying the ever-growing demand for barrel staves in France and Germany as well as for lumber in shipbuilding. Thirteen large sawmills were established in 1849–60. Shipbuilding in Rijeka, Bakar, and Kraljevica reached a peak in 1855 with forty-one ships of 14,400 tons constructed. After a slump in the late 1850s, production stabilized in the mid-1860s; twenty ships of 10,800 tons were built in 1867. Within the sector of food processing, flour milling continued to advance, with seven steam-powered mills added by 1864. In contrast, sugar refining began to stagnate owing to the low sugar content of local beets—6 percent compared with 9 to 13 percent in Bohemia—and increased competition from Austrian and Bohemian producers. After 1853 production was limited to two refineries.

Of the previously flourishing industries the production of potash suffered the sharpest decline, partly because of the rising value of wood for lumber in the 1850s and mostly because of the invention of the Solvay method of soda production in 1863. The output sank from 840 tons in 1829 to 84 in 1869. A more ominous sign concerning the industrial vigor of the Land was the failure of the textile industry to develop. Even the formerly prosperous silk production declined after 1848 and a disease of the silkworm, combined with Italian and French competition, caused its virtual collapse by 1859.

Another crucial indicator of industrial development, iron metallurgy, followed an unsteady course. The old copper mine at Rude shifted to iron extraction in 1852. Its ironworks, as well as those at Trgovi, were modernized in the mid-1850s. Three new iron mines opened in the late 1850s.[49] Further expansion, however, under the conditions of restricted local demand, was impeded by the high cost of transport to the iron-processing plants of Carinthia and Styria. Of the lesser industries, glass production remained confined to four centers, and paper to one large mill in Rijeka. Chemical and machinery industries emerged in the 1850s on a very limited scale, represented by four and two plants respectively.

The mechanization of production, measured by new application of steam power, which had been confined to four plants in 1848, spread to only twenty-two more by 1864, including eight flour mills, five sawmills, three sugar refineries, three chemical plants, two ironworks, and one each of the following: shipbuilding, tobacco processing, and the production of glass, paper, and machinery. The slow, erratic course of industrialization reflected not only the weakness of domestic capital but also the interest of foreign (English, French, Belgian, and German) investors in highly profitable export commodities. Except for sugar, most of the existing factory production was designed for export rather than internal consumption. On the whole, the failure of a modern textile and iron industry to emerge was not offset in Croatia—as happened in the Magyar and Slovak areas of Hungary—by a significant development of a mechanized food-processing industry.

Dalmatia in 1848–67 remained untouched by even the modest beginnings of mechanization discernible in Croatia's industries. With only 2.3 percent of the population engaged in crafts and manufacturing in 1867, it was the least industrialized of all the Lands of the Habsburg monarchy.[50] The first manufactories, based on artisan methods, appeared in the 1850s. Concentrated mainly in the region of Split, they engaged in cloth dyeing and the production of cherry brandy, candles, soap, and leather. Seaborne trade was of considerable importance, with Split again in first place and Zadar tied with Dubrovnik for second. Even so, the volume of trade in Split did not equal more than one-third of Rijeka's.

In Istria in the 1850s and 1860s, crafts were better developed than in Croatia or Dalmatia, but more advanced industrial production was likewise limited. The ranking industrial enterprise was the imperial navy yard in Pula (Pola), established in 1856. Coal was mined near Raša, but of exceptional importance was shipping. In 1853–55 the island of Mali Lošinj concentrated one-fifth of the entire merchant marine of the Habsburg monarchy.

---

49. The output of pig iron increased at Trgovi from 196 tons in 1849 to 333.5 in 1857–8, and at Rude from 472 in 1852 to 823 in 1858.

50. The corresponding percentages, also in 1867, were 8.2 for the entire monarchy, 11.2 for Cisleithania, and 4.2 for Hungary.

Agricultural Imbalance and Industrial Underdevelopment, 1867–1914

The development of Croatian agriculture after 1867 was dominated by a cycle initiated by the depression of 1873. Recovery began in animal raising in the late 1880s, and for crops by 1895. A period of prosperity followed in the early twentieth century.

In crop production, the predominance of grains was further accentuated during the period of recovery and prosperity. In 1885–89, grains occupied 67 percent of arable land; in 1910–14, 70 percent. The production of wheat rose steeply (from 22.5 to 34.4 percent of land devoted to grains), corn more modestly (39.2 to 42.3 percent), barley remained stable, and rye declined sharply. Among other crops, the output of potatoes rose impressively from 263,000 tons in 1885–89 to 681,000 in 1910–14.

As for animal production, the depression did not affect cattle raising adversely—in fact, between 1869 and 1880 there was an increase from 786,000 head to 838,000, but the number of pigs decreased drastically from 733,000 to 472,000. The onset of the recovery reversed the long-term regression of animal production in relation to crops, which had marked Croatia's agricultural development since the mid-eighteenth century. Between 1895 and 1911 the size of herds rose from 1,043,000 to 1,268,000 for cattle, and from 856,000 to 1,117,000 for pigs. In the same period, however, milk production advanced most rapidly (from 183 to 361 million hectoliters), with its value rising by 80 percent (compared to 34 percent for meat). Most important, animal raising as a whole advanced more rapidly than crop production. From 1885–89 to 1910–14 its volume rose by 31.2 percent, compared with 19.8 percent for crops. Despite this improvement, however, animal production still failed to reach even half the total value of agricultural output. Between 1885–89 and 1910–14 its share increased from 41 to 46 percent, falling far short of the 60 to 80 percent prevalent in the developed regions of Central and Western Europe.

Viticulture had its greatest era during the agricultural depression in 1875–92 thanks to the fortuitous circumstance that the onset of the phylloxera pest, which then ravaged the vineyards of Central and Western Europe, was late in reaching Croatian territory. Subsequently, with the spread of the pest to Croatia, as well as the recovery of foreign vineyards, wine production declined from 23.3 percent of the total value of Croatia's agricultural production in 1885–89 to 14.8 percent in 1910–14.

As elsewhere in East Central Europe, in Croatia the proportion of fallow in total arable land declined. In 1910–14 it was down to 6.3 percent from 17.3 percent in 1885–89. It was a deviation from the norm reflecting an imbalance in Croatia's agriculture, that the abandonment of the fallow did not usually lead to the sound pattern of triennial crop rotation, but more often to simple alternation between corn and another grain (mostly wheat), a practice particularly exhaustive of the soil. The basic reason was that animal raising, though increasing, still was not adequate in Croatia's total agricultural production to sustain a massive expansion of feed crops, which would have been required to introduce triennial crop rotation. Between 1885–89 and 1910–14 the proportion of arable land planted with feed crops increased only from 4.1 to 8.4 percent. Thus Croatian agriculture suffered from a peculiar deformation that could not fail to hold down productivity.

The depression of 1873 had a profoundly damaging effect on Croatian industries and dashed the chances for the onset of an industrial revolution based on the development in 1848–67. The crisis struck when the infant industries were particularly vulnerable, and in the absence of strong local authority neither Vienna nor Budapest was interested in their protection. The effects were evident by 1883. Iron production and sugar refining were wiped out and shipbuilding reduced to two shipyards. Flourmilling lost its previous vigor and stagnated, with only five commercially significant mills in operation. Glass production managed to survive, with three medium-size and four small plants. Of the major industries only wood processing had continued to grow substantially, laying the basis for a peculiar imbalance of Croatia's industrial structure. It was represented by thirty-two sizable enterprises.[51]

By 1890 modest advances toward modern industrialization were resuming, this time within a healthier context of a higher share of domestic investment, which tended to diversify production and pay greater attention to domestic consumption. The number of enterprises employing more than twenty workers rose from 110 with 9,800 workers in 1890 to 213 with 18,800 workers in 1900, and to 271 with 23,600 workers in 1910. Of these enterprises, those employing more than 100 workers amounted to twenty-five in 1890, fifty-one in 1900, and sixty-four in 1910. Taking the enterprises with more than twenty workers as indicators of Croatia's modern industrial development, in 1910 wood processing still bore a disproportionately heavy weight, encompassing 101 enterprises, or 37.3 percent of the total. This preponderance, however, was diminishing; in 1890 the proportion had been 54.5 percent. In 1910 food processing was in second place, with 12.9 percent of all enterprises; construction and construction materials came next with respectively 11.8 and 9.6 percent. A particularly encouraging sign was the reappearance of a textile industry (together with clothing and leather production, 5.9 percent of all enterprises) and the existence of machinery production and paper and chemical industry (with respectively

51. Twenty-two sawmills and ten others, mostly engaged in furniture making.

5.2 and 5.5 percent of all enterprises). On the negative side, one must note the continued absence of an iron and steel industry. In the area of mining, a modest development occurred in the production of soft coal (250,000 tons in 1910).

Rijeka and its district still represented an area of relative industrial strength in the Croatian geographical orbit. Enterprises with more than a hundred workers amounted in 1910 to eleven with a total of 6,100 workers. Dalmatia, on the contrary, continued as the weakest Land industrially in the Habsburg monarchy except for Bosnia-Herzegovina. Isolated from the railroad network of the empire, it showed no signs of modern industrialization before 1900. Subsequently, several enterprises deserving the name of factories sprang up, especially distilleries, fish canneries, and cement and chemical plants. After the collapse of sailboat shipping in the 1880s, steam shipping slowly grew, with the largest firm "Dalmatia," incorporated in 1908, owning twenty-four ships. Istria suffered even more from the obsolescence of the sailboat. The shipping tonnage in the former center of merchant marine, the island of Mali Lošinj, plummeted from 84,000 in 1870 to 4,500 in the 1890s. The major industrial enterprise, the naval yard at Pula, increased its work force from 2,400 in 1880 to 8,000 by 1910. The second industrial center was Rovinj, with factories processing tobacco, alcohol, and sardines. The mine near Raša produced, after 1900, about 100,000 tons of coal annually.

The increase in the number of sizable industrial enterprises in Croatia was accompanied by a growth in the number of joint-stock companies from six in 1890 to forty-three by 1905 and fifty-eight in 1910. Their capital increased from 23.6 million crowns in 1905 to 51 million in 1910. An indication of the rising role of domestic (compared with Magyar) investors was the fact that in 1910 only five companies had headquarters in Hungary, with slightly over one-quarter of the total capital; in 1905 the respective figures had been nine companies and half of the total capital. The strength of local capital was also reflected in the increase of credit institutions in Croatia from 123 in 1895 to 933 in 1910 and of their combined capital and savings deposits from 91.7 million to 372.2 million crowns. Czech investors played a significant role in establishing banks in Croatia and thus in strengthening local financial resources in relation to Hungarian and Austro-German capital.

Nevertheless, on the whole, Croatian territories still suffered deeply from industrial underdevelopment in the late nineteenth and early twentieth centuries. In 1890 the percentage of population engaged in agriculture was 86.1 for Dalmatia and 84.6 for Croatia, the highest figures among the individual Lands of the monarchy.[52] Comparable fig-

52. The proportion of agricultural population was higher only in Bosnia-Herzegovina, then administered by the Habsburg monarchy but not yet annexed. For economic developments in that province see pp. 435–37.

ures were 82.8 for Transylvania, 77.3 for Galicia, and 75.7 for Bukovina. Istria came off somewhat better, with 72.8 percent, close to the 71.9 percent for Carniola. In contrast, the percentage of agricultural population in Lower Austria was 24.7 and in Bohemia 40.6. Even in 1910 in its degree of industrial development Croatia stood closer to the Balkans than to Central Europe. Measured against such industrial-fringe areas of Central Europe as the Slovak territory, it had less than half as many enterprises with more than twenty workers (271 to 623); moreover, the average number of workers per enterprise was significantly lower (87 to 137).

WORLD WAR I AND SELF-DETERMINATION

After the outbreak of the war, while the ruling Croat-Serb Coalition adopted in Croatia a noncommittal attitude, the *Frankovci* hailed the conflict with Serbia as offering—in reward for a loyalist stance—new opportunities for a trialist solution of the Croatian question within the Habsburg monarchy. Radić's Peasant Party largely shared these expectations. Nevertheless, Vienna, suspecting the South Slavs of disloyalty, applied harsh repressive measures in Dalmatia against both the Croats and the Serbs. Croatia itself was protected in a way by Tisza's desire not to upset the recent settlement with the Croat-Serb Coalition. Repression there accordingly affected mainly Serbs hostile to the empire. The war caused a substantial deterioration of economic conditions, above all in Dalmatia, where the essential maritime commerce was hampered by the Allied blockade. Subsequently, Italy's entry into the war in May 1915, severely disrupted the economy of Istria. The ensuing hardships led to spontaneous demonstrations and other expressions of popular discontent. By the end of 1915, however, the economic and military conditions of the monarchy improved somewhat, and a period of relative internal tranquility followed in 1916.

Two prominent Dalmatian politicians, Trumbić and Supilo, left the monarchy just before the war and subsequently led a group of South Slav exiles in promoting within the Entente countries the concept of an independent and federated South Slav (Yugoslav) state. In the fall of 1914 and early spring of 1915, Supilo received sympathetic but noncommittal hearing from leading French, British, Russian, and Serbian statesmen. In April 1915 the South Slav exiles were deeply troubled by the Treaty of London, which promised Italy, as a reward for joining the Entente, the Croatian territories of Istria and northern Dalmatia. In early May they formed the Yugoslav Committee, headed by Trumbić, and located in London; one of its prime objectives was to block the Italian claims. On two subsequent occasions between 1915 and 1917, before the United States entered the war, the Entente came close to pledging the separation of Croatia from the Habsburg monarchy.[53]

Within the monarchy the first overt statement by Croatian political leaders concerning the solution of the South Slav question came on May 30, 1917, the day of the reconvening of the Austrian *Reichsrat*. The Croatian deputies from Dalmatia and Istria joined their other South Slav colleagues in issuing the May Declaration, which called for the union of all Croats with the Slovenes and Serbs in the monarchy into a single autonomous political unit. In the Croatian *Sabor* only the Starčević Party of the Right and several Serbian deputies endorsed the Declaration. The Croat-Serb Coalition maintained tactical silence over a proposal that would have destroyed the *nagodba*. The *Frankovci* found the document repugnant, as it represented a "Yugoslav" rather than a purely Croatian approach.

In the summer of 1917, Serbian Prime Minister Nikola Pašić, having lost in tsarist Russia his staunchest ally, sought to bolster his position with the Entente by reaching an agreement with Trumbić's Yugoslav Committee. The resulting Corfu Declaration of July 20, 1917, pledged Croatian, Slovene, and Serbian representatives to the union of all South Slavs, exclusive of the Bulgarians, under the Serbian dynasty in a form decided by a constituent assembly. Since the Entente did not wish as yet to foreclose the possibility of a separate peace with Austria-Hungary, it remained wary of the idea of separating the Croatian and Slovene territories from the Habsburg monarchy. In March 1918 a decisive turn occurred when Italy endorsed the establishment of a Yugoslav state, the boundaries of which would be agreed upon amicably on the basis of national self-determination. Subsequent acceptance of the idea of a Yugoslav kingdom by other Entente powers, however, did not entail recognition of the Yugoslav Committee as the representative body of the South Slavs under Habsburg rule, owing partly to remaining Italian reservations and partly to Serbia's claim for leadership in the union movement.

In Croatia the signs of military and political weakness of the existing regime (especially sailors' insurrections and guerrilla activities by the so-called green cadres composed mainly of military deserters) encouraged the leaders of the Starčević Party and the Social Democrats in late March 1918 to pass beyond the May Declaration of 1917 and embrace the goal of full independence. Soon they were joined by the Peasant Party, terminating its previous cooperation with the *Frankovci*. The Croat-Serb Coalition remained officially aloof, although it had communicated abroad

---

53. For the first time, in the summer of 1915, as a compensation to Serbia for the proposed partial cession of Macedonia to Bulgaria; for the second time, in January 1917, when the liberation of the South Slavs (referred to simply as "Slavs" to spare Italian sensitivities) from foreign domination was included in a formal statement of the Entente's war aims.

its secret agreement with the Corfu Declaration as early as September 1917. The Croats in Dalmatia (together with the Serbs) and in Istria (together with the Slovenes) inclined toward an independent South Slav state by July 1918. Under strong influence of the *Frankovci*, the Croats of Bosnia-Herzegovina delayed a final decision until September 1918.

In early October 1918, with the Habsburg monarchy suing for peace, the political groups in Croatia, which had carried on the March 1918 discussions, were at last joined by the Croat-Serb Coalition. In Zagreb, a National Council of Slovens, Croats, and Serbs, including also representatives from Dalmatia, Istria, the Slovene Lands, Vojvodina, and Bosnia-Herzegovina, was set up as a shadow government for the South Slav territories within the Habsburg monarchy. On October 29, 1918, the *Sabor* officially dissolved Croatia's union with Hungary and proclaimed the Land's entry into the emerging "State of the Slovenes, Croats, and Serbs" (SHS). Under the aegis of the National Council, provisional governments were formed for Croatia and Dalmatia. On October 31 the National Council announced to the Entente the creation of the new state, and entrusted the Yugoslav Committee with the conduct of its foreign relations. After attempting to negotiate a federal union between the new state and Serbia in early November, the National Council in Zagreb, anxious for Serbian military aid against Italy's encroachments on Croatian territory, finally opted for a unitary state, the internal order of which would be decided by a constituent assembly. Accordingly, on December 1, 1918, the Serbian Prince-Regent Alexander proclaimed in Belgrade the union of Serbia with the independent State of the Slovenes, Croats, and Serbs into the Kingdom of Serbs, Croats, and Slovenes. The stormy, yet durable, political association of the Croats with the Serbs was launched.

The Ruthenians, the Serbs, and the Romanians

THE RUTHENIANS OF TRANSCARPATHIA AND BUKOVINA

From Revolution to Dualism, 1848–67

Transcarpathia. During the revolutionary year of 1848, Adolf Dobrianskii (1817–1901) emerged as the first modern political spokesman for the Transcarpathian Ruthenians. Under his influence the Slav Congress in Prague in June 1848 passed a resolution favoring a union of the Hungarian Ruthenians with the Slovaks into an autonomous province. Unable to stay in Hungary, Dobrianskii subsequently associated with the Ruthenian Council in Lviv and supported its program of union of the Ruthenians of Galicia, Transcarpathia, and Bukovina into a single new crownland of the Habsburg monarchy. He returned to Transcarpathia in the summer of 1849, acting as a liaison officer with the Russian army. The presence of Russian troops from July to September 1849 engendered a sense of linguistic and religious kinship and helped to stimulate Russophile feelings among Transcarpathian Ruthenians.

In October 1849, when it was clear that a united Ruthenian crownland was not acceptable to the imperial government, Dobrianskii led a Ruthenian delegation to Vienna to ask for an autonomous province of Transcarpathia within Hungary alone. While genuine autonomy was impossible during the ensuing era of Bach absolutism (1849–59), the Ruthenians received limited national concessions. The four Transcarpathian counties were in fact united into a single civil district of Uzhhorod, which in turn was subordinated to the military district of Košice (Kaschau, Kassa). Dobrianskii himself served briefly as the deputy *főispán* of the Uzhhorod district. The Ruthenian language was introduced into education, including, at the secondary level, the *gymnasium* in Uzhhorod in 1850; and despite strong Magyar opposition, it was used as an external official language in administrative and judicial agencies. Altogether thirty-six Ruthenians were appointed to official positions in the Uzhhorod district.

With the return to a constitutional regime and restoration of the traditional Hungarian county governments in 1860, Magyar became once more the official language in Transcarpathia. Dobrianskii, elected to the Hungarian diet but prevented from taking his seat in 1861, resorted to journalism to advocate a federalistic Hungary in which Ruthenian Transcarpathia would constitute one of several autonomous national districts. Rebuffed by the Hungarian diet, his hopes turned to Vienna and he promoted petitions to the emperor by Ruthenian priests and mayors for Transcarpathian autonomy. With the political situation favoring the restoration of Magyar gentry's political power in Hungary by 1865, he scaled down the national demands to an ethnic delimitation of existing counties and to granting Ruthenian equal status with Magyar as the official languages in Transcarpathia. Such modest goals were endorsed by a gathering of Ruthenian priests, teachers, and peasants in 1867 in Zemplén county in eastern Slovakia. It was to be the last publicly formulated political program of Transcarpathian Ruthenians before 1918.[54]

Bukovina. The excitement of early 1848 caused peasant unrest to flare

---

54. Dobrianskii, himself by this time disappointed with both Pest and Vienna, turned his hopes to Russia's intervention in the affairs of the Habsburg monarchy. The Russophile stance barred him from practical politics in Hungary.

up again in Bukovina, especially since the abolition of peasants' feudal obligations was promulgated in August 1848 rather than May as in Galicia, to which Bukovina was then attached. During the following winter, renewed peasant disorders led to a military repression in January 1849. The *Reichstag* elections in June 1848 in the meantime had resulted, in Bukovina, in the choice of four Ruthenians, three Romanians, and one German. The Ruthenian deputies, all of them of peasant background, opposed in the *Reichstag* in February 1849 the Romanian spokesmen's demands for separation of Bukovina from Galicia, a step viewed as preparatory for joining Bukovina with Transylvania and the Banat into a large Romanian-dominated crownland. Similarly the bishop of Chernivtsi, Evhen Hakman, in February 1849 resisted proposals of the Transylvanian Orthodox bishop, Andreiu Şaguna, for the formation of an autonomous Romanian ecclesiastical organization including the diocese of Chernivtsi, which would become independent of the Slav (Serbian) Orthodox patriarchate of Karlovci. Thus the outlines of the future Ruthenian-Romanian antagonism began to emerge.

Under the "decreed" constitution of March 1849, Bukovina was in fact separated from Galicia as an independent crownland. During the Neo-Absolutist regime (1849–59), it was divided in 1850 into six, then in 1854 into fifteen districts (*Bezirke*), each headed by a district captain (*Bezirkshauptmann*). Since 1853 the president of the Land (*Landespräsident*), assisted by a bureaucratic body, the government of the Land (*Landesregierung*), had headed the administrative apparatus. The teaching of Ruthenian, as well as Romanian, was introduced into the *gymnasium* of Chernivtsi by 1851. In the field of elementary education, however, the Ruthenians had substantially fewer schools than the Romanians; although according to unofficial counts, they were approaching numerical equality with the Romanians.

After the fall of Bach absolutism, Bukovina reverted in April 1860 to the status of a circuit (*Kreis*) of Galicia, but was restored as a separate crownland in March 1861. Its new diet of thirty members was chosen mainly by electors of the four *curiae*, typical of the diets of Cisleithania. The diet, in turn, elected the Committee of the Land, headed by the captain of the Land (*Landeshauptmann*). Vienna continued to direct the administrative system, headed by the *Landespräsident* and his deputy, the *Landeschef*. They supervised the district captains. During the 1860s the Romanians with the Germans dominated the diet and its official apparatus. Even the rural voters in Ruthenian areas tended to elect Romanian and German candidates backed by the district captains, and hardly any Ruthenians were chosen.[55]

55. Although Bishop Hakman was appointed captain of the Land, he did little for Ruthenian national advancement in Bukovina.

Retardation of the National Awakening, 1867–1914

Transcarpathia. After the establishment of the dualist regime in 1867, the scope of Ruthenian national life narrowed considerably in Transcarpathia. The dominance of Magyar expanded from organs of state power to the realm of secondary education, and the teaching of Ruthenian in the Uzhhorod *gymnasium* stopped accordingly in 1868. From 1867 until 1918 not a single Ruthenian was to win election to the Hungarian parliament, and all positions in county and town governments were henceforth held by the Magyars. Initially (until 1875), the Hungarian government did tolerate Ruthenian as the language of instruction in elementary schools, as well as a fair amount of ethnic cultural activity. Of particular significance in the fields of publication and adult education was the Basilius Society (established in 1866), which was modeled on the *Matice* of other Slav nations in the Habsburg monarchy. The consolidation of a national culture, however, encountered an additional hindrance in the unsettled issue of a standard literary language (which would still be unresolved by 1918)—with Russian, a version of Church Slavonic, and the local folk speech vying for recognition.

Beginning with Kálmán Tisza's ministry in 1875, Ruthenian national aspirations in Hungary were subjected to a lengthy period of severe repression. The new departure was signaled by an investigation, launched by the *főispánok* of the main Ruthenian counties, which sought to link Ruthenian national activities with Panslavism, and hence—in the eyes of the Hungarian government—with treason. The Basilius Society was virtually silenced. The Uniat priests, traditionally the principal bearers of Ruthenian national consciousness, were cajoled or coerced—with notable exceptions—to serve as agents of Magyarization. The level of national activity became so low that even the Congress of Nationalities, held in Budapest in 1895, did not evoke any response from the Ruthenians of Transcarpathia.

In addition to the cultural repression, Transcarpathia under the rule of Magyar gentry suffered increasingly from rural poverty, caused by serious economic underdevelopment. The Hungarian government launched minor economic and social reforms in 1898–1902, under the name of the Highlands Action, but these measures failed to improve the living conditions. The per capita rate of emigration from the Transcarpathian region (especially from its western part and mostly to the United States) was probably higher than from any other Slavic area in the Habsburg monarchy.

The Magyarization pressure intensified in the opening decade of the twentieth century. Striking evidence of this was the decrease of elementary schools with Ruthenian as the language of instruction from 353 in 1870 to 64 in 1903 and 18 in 1910. Church Slavonic was replaced by

Greek in 1912 as the liturgical language of a segment of the Uniat Church.[56] Owing to emigration and Magyarization, the number of Ruthenians in northeast Hungary remained virtually unchanged from 1840 (442,903) to 1910 (447,566). A limited but conspicuous form of social and national protest among the peasantry was a responsiveness to the Russian-inspired propaganda for conversion to Orthodoxy. Reacting harshly against this trend, the Hungarian government in the winter of 1913–14 put ninety-four Ruthenian peasant converts on trial in Máramaros Sziget as political offenders. As an alternative to Russophilism, some nationally aware Ruthenian intellectuals, notably the Uniat priest and author Avhustyn Voloshyn (1874–1945), sought association with the Ukrainophile movement among the Ruthenians of Galicia and Bukovina.

Bukovina. The Ruthenians of Bukovina remained politically powerless in the period after 1867 and throughout the 1870s. Although Ruthenian, since 1860, had been held to be one of the three external official languages used by imperial administrative and judicial agencies in Bukovina, only German and Romanian were recognized in October 1869 as the languages of the diet, in which Ruthenian representation was confined to four apolitical peasant deputies. The main political contest in Bukovina in the 1870s as well as in the 1860s, was between the Autonomists, led by conservative Romanian boyars, and the Centralists, a coalition of Romanian and German liberals. The first Ruthenian journal, *Russka Beseda*, and the first political organization, *Russka Rada*, established respectively in 1869 and 1870, pursued a Russophile orientation uncongenial to the Ruthenian masses. The foundation of a new, in essence German university in Chernivtsi in 1875, as a centenary gift by the government in commemoration of the incorporation of the Bukovina into the Habsburg empire in 1775, was of benefit to Ruthenian national aspirations only in regard to the Greek-Orthodox faculty of theology.

During the 1880s and 1890s, the Ruthenian political position improved substantially as Vienna, under Taaffe's ministry, embarked on a more evenhanded ethnic policy. To offset the potentially dangerous Russophilism, Vienna encouraged the Ukrainian movement, or Ukrainophile orientation, which, prevailing in both the *Russka Beseda* and *Russka Rada* in the mid-1880s, at last launched an effective political mobilization of the Ruthenian masses. Fearing Romanian separatism after the emergence of the unified Romanian Kingdom in 1878, Vienna also terminated the preferential treatment of the Romanians. Thus in 1890 the *Landespräsident* of Bukovina instructed the district captains to treat

56. The Vatican vetoed the Hungarian government's wish to use Magyar.

the national candidates with impartiality. In that year the Ukrainophiles elected three deputies to the diet and one to the *Reichsrat*. Their number increased to four in the diet by 1894 and to two in the *Reichsrat* by 1898.

The Romanian political dominance in Bukovina was shaken in the first decade of the twentieth century. By 1903 the Ukrainophiles, or *Narodovtsi*, whose numbers rose to six in the diet, were able to form a coalition with the Germans, Jews, and dissident Romanians to outvote the dominant Romanian National Party. The *Narodovtsi*, competently led by Stepan Smal'-Stots'kyi in the diet, and by Mykola Vasyl'ko in the *Reichsrat*, saw the future of the Ruthenians best safeguarded in a unified Ukranian crownland within a federalized Habsburg empire. By 1906 the close cooperation with Vienna by the *Narodovtsi* (renamed National Democrats a year later) was questioned by young intellectuals, led by Teodot Halip. Halip's group formed a separate Radical Party, based on the militant *Sich* societies.

A reform of the Bukovinian diet in 1910, according to which the voters, mostly Ruthenians, Romanians, and Germans (Jews) were organized into national *curiae* in this most multinational crownland of the Habsburg empire, changed the legal situation somewhat. It gave a fairer share of seats to the Ruthenians (17) in relation to the Romanians (22), though not yet proportionate to their actual numbers (305,000 compared with 273,000 Romanians).[57] The five Ruthenian National Democrats, elected in 1911 to the *Reichsrat* from Bukovina, like their predecessors, cooperated with the Ukrainian deputies (the National Democrats and the Radicals) from Galicia. They also continued to support the Viennese government, a loyalty rewarded by Vienna with favors in Bukovina, especially in the field of education. By 1910–11, of the 531 elementary schools in the crownland, 216 were Ruthenian and only 179 Romanian. In 1912 the National Democrats were shaken by interparty rivalries. Friction also developed between the Bukovinian and the Galician deputies in the *Reichsrat*; and Smal'-Stots'kyi, in opposition to Vasylko's National Democrats, established a separate Ukrainian National Party, dedicated to a more energetic pursuit of a union between the Ruthenians (Ukrainians) of Bukovina and Galicia. Before the outbreak of World War I, and increasingly during the war, the Austrian government became suspicious of separatist tendencies among the Ruthenian Radicals in Bukovina and persecuted their organizations, above all the *Sich* societies.

57. In the diet elections of 1911, the National Democrats won fifteen seats, the Radicals and the Social Democrats one each. The internationally oriented Ruthenian Social Democrats in Bukovina, led by Osyp Bezpalko, had established a party organization in 1906.

Economic Underdevelopment in Transcarpathia, 1848–1914[58]

By the end of the nineteenth century, crops constituted approximately two-thirds of the entire value of Transcarpathian agricultural production. The area of arable land increased in Transcarpathia between 1870 and 1905 from 267,809 to 360,206 hectares, mostly at the expense of the forests, which declined from 54.75 to 47.5 percent of the total surface. The composition of the crop output changed substantially in this period. The share in the total gross yield of crops went up for potatoes and wheat, declined for corn and rye, and remained relatively stable for oats. In 1905, potatoes, as the chief peasant foodstuff, and wheat, attractive to the large estate owners for its market value, represented 48.3 and 17.2 percent of the gross yield. Owing to declining profitability, the area of vineyards decreased by almost two-thirds between 1885 and 1905.

As for animal raising, the number of cattle, horses, and pigs increased modestly between 1870 and 1900, and declined precipitously for goats and sheep. The most notable subsequent trend was the decline in the number of pigs from 1895 to 1912 (from 149,000 to 119,000) below the level of 1870 (123,000). Accompanied by an increase in the number of goats (from 20,300 to 29,800 between 1895 and 1912), this trend reflected a degradation of animal raising on peasant homesteads.

Agricultural productivity in Transcarpathia lagged seriously behind the Hungarian averages. In the 1870s it was 42 percent lower in average yield from one hold of cultivated land; and in the second half of the nineteenth century, 10 to 20 percent lower in the output per cow (milk and meat), and 30 to 40 percent in output in sheep (meat and wool) or pig (meat and fat). Transcarpathian agriculture also fell below the Hungarian averages in quality of implements and in mechanization.[59]

The conditions were even less favorable in industry. During the second half of the nineteenth century, the traditional industrial and mining activities, based largely on manufactory or even artisan methods, continued to decline due to obsolescence of equipment, lack of capital, and severity of outside competition. Production of the salt mines in Máramaros decreased in 1868–1900 from 81.3 to 47.6 tons per year. The thirteen small ironworks still in existence barely managed to sur-

58. Economic data in this section are derived from Ivan G. Kolomiets, *Sotsial'no-ekonomicheskie otnosheniia i obshchestvennoe dvizhenie v Zakarpat'e vo vtoroi polovine XIX stoletiia* (Tomsk: Izd-vo Tomskogo universiteta, 1961), 1:43–162; 2:3–72.

59. In the 1870s only 34 percent of the plows were metal, compared with 60 percent for all of Hungary. In 1895 the 176 steam engines employed in agriculture represented less than 1.5 percent of the Hungarian total of 12,000.

vive. The share of the Transcarpathian flour mills in the amount of grain ground in Hungary, a mere 1.5 percent in 1885, kept declining. A modest advance occurred only in wood processing. Aside from rising exports of lumber, two large furniture-making plants and four chemical enterprises (utilizing woods) were established between 1868 and 1914.

On the whole, industrial activity in Transcarpathia remained at an extremely low level. In 1900, Transcarpathian industry accounted for only 1.25 percent of the total horsepower of steam engines in Hungarian industries, and for only 48 out of 2,261 enterprises employing more than twenty workers.[60] Within the entire Habsburg monarchy, Transcarpathia—with nearly 90 percent of its population in agriculture in 1890 and close to 85 percent in 1910—was probably the least developed area industrially except for Bosnia-Herzegovina.

Industrial Retardation in Bukovina, 1848–1914[61]

In the second half of the nineteenth century, agriculture in Bukovina continued to advance substantially. The large estates in the 1850s and 1860s pioneered a major expansion of animal raising as a supplement and complement to grain production. This was partly stimulated by a rising need for fertilizers and facilitated by the growth of distilleries, the wastes of which—derived from potatoes or corn—were eminently suited for cattle feed. Ruthenian peasants initially lagged behind the large estates in the quality of animal raising, but the situation improved by the early twentieth century. Between 1869 and 1907 the Ruthenian districts registered considerable advances in animal stocks: from 92,968 to 115,312 for cattle, from 21,499 to 32,131 for horses, and from 64,245 to 100,000 for pigs. The Ruthenian areas also maintained their predominance in crop production. The most important crops raised in Bukovina by 1912 were corn (63,000 hectares), oats (42,000), and potatoes (37,000), followed by barley (33,000 hectares), rye (31,000), and wheat (22,000). The growing of sugar beets was not far advanced (2,800 hectares).

The structures of industrial production changed substantially in Bukovina, while remaining on a modest scale during the second half of

60. By 1910 the number of such enterprises in Transcarpathia rose to 65, which still compared unfavorably not only with Slovakia (623 enterprises) but also the Serb area of southern Hungary (157).

61. Economic data in this section are derived from *Hauptbericht und Statistik über das Herzogthum Bukowina* (Lemberg: Selbstverlag der Handelskammer, 1872), pp. 132–33, 165–76, 206–15, 238–39, 256–60; *Bukovina* (London: The Foreign Office, 1920), pp. 27–30; *Pivnichna Bukovyna: ii mynule i suchasne* (Uzhhorod: Karpaty, 1969), p. 58; Denys Kvitkovs'kyi, ed., *Bukovyna: ii mynule i suchasne* (Paris and Philadelphia: Zelena Bukovyna, 1956), p. 252; *Statistisches Jahrbuch des Herzogthums Bukowina für das Jahr 1907* (Czernowitz, 1910), p. 117.

the nineteenth century. Wood processing continued to develop after 1848, although scarcity of capital interfered with its progress. While salt mining prospered, the old metallurgical iron and copper plants languished because of obsolescence. Of other types of industry, food processing took root in Bukovina. By 1871 a large brewery, nine flour mills, and forty-four distilleries met the standards of modern industrial enterprises. Traditionally weak in mining and surpassed by the Romanian districts in wood processing, the Ruthenian areas contained most of the food industry.

With the failure of textile, machinery, or chemical production to develop, the range of industrial activity in Bukovina was still restricted in the late nineteenth and early twentieth centuries. Food processing (flour mills and distilleries) remained significant. Wood processing expanded, with 31 steam-powered sawmills in operation by 1896, and 18,000 railroad cars of lumber exported annually to Russia, Western Europe, and Asia. Except for the persistent flourishing of the Cacica salt mines, mining altered its character entirely. The old iron and copper production vanished, and the extraction of manganese and sulphur attained major importance, not so much for its volume (10,900 and 8,000 tons respectively in 1912), but because of its rarity in the Habsburg empire.

In its degree of industrialization, Bukovina clearly belonged to the underdeveloped areas in the Habsburg monarchy. Yet measured by the percentage of nonagricultural population in 1890, it came—with 24.29 percent—close to the top in this category. It was ahead not only of the neighboring Ruthenian and Romanian areas (Transcarpathia with somewhat over 10 percent, Transylvania with 17.12, and Galicia with 22.62) but also of most South Slav regions (Dalmatia with 13.86 percent, Croatia-Slavonia with 15.36 and Serb southern Hungary with 24).

World War I, 1914–18

Even in the absence of an organized political movement, the population of Transcarpathia manifested spontaneous Russophile feelings during the brief penetration of the area's northern fringes by the Russian army in September and October 1914. About eight hundred Ruthenians were subsequently prosecuted by Magyar authorities for collaborating with the enemy, and many Ruthenians, in turn, deserted to the Russian army. On the cultural front, the Hungarian government sought to take advantage of war conditions to campaign against the Ruthenians' ethnic identity. As a replacement for the Cyrillic script, hitherto used in Ruthenian textbooks and liturgical books, a new Romanized alphabet was devised in mid-1915, based on Magyar phonetic transcription. The use of this alphabet became obligatory in 1916.

In Bukovina at the outbreak of the war, young radical Ukrainophiles formed volunteer detachments, the *Sichovi Stril'tsi*, which fought against the Russian army from September 1914 in Galicia and the Ukraine for the cause of Ukrainian freedom and unity. When the Russian army occupied Bukovina for the first time from October 1914 to June 1915, the Russian authorities persecuted the Ukrainophiles and favored the Russophile elements, whose center was the Orthodox consistory in Chernivtsi. On returning to Bukovina, the Austrian administration, in turn, prosecuted the Russophiles. The principal leaders of the Bukovinian Ruthenians, including the *Reichsrat* deputies, resided mostly in Vienna. In May 1915 seven of them formed with twenty-four Ruthenian leaders from Galicia a General Ukrainian Council with Vasyl'ko as vice-chairman, to coordinate questions of national policy for the Ruthenians of Cisleithania.

During the second Russian occupation from June 1916 to July 1917, Bukovina together with eastern Galicia was formed into a single *guberniia*. A gubernial commissar was in charge of administration in Bukovina. Following the March Revolution of 1917, the Russian Provisional Government permitted a Ukrainization of the administrative apparatus in Bukovina. After the *Reichsrat* reconvened in Vienna in the spring of 1917, both the Ruthenian and the Romanian deputies claimed Bukovina for their wider national communities. In a secret clause of the Brest-Litovsk treaty in February 1918, the Viennese government committed itself to the "Ukrainian" solution—that is, to the inclusion of Bukovina with eastern Galicia into a single Ruthenian crownland.

The postwar destiny of Transcarpathia was adumbrated within the sizable emigrant community of Transcarpathian Ruthenians in the United States. A meeting of their representatives in Homestead, Pennsylvania, in July 1918, voted for a separation of the area from Hungary with the following options, in order of preference: (1) complete independence; (2) union with eastern Galicia and Bukovina in an independent Ruthenian state; and (3) autonomy within another state. The National Council subsequently formed by Transcarpathian Ruthenians in the United States under Gregory Zhatkovich, approached President Woodrow Wilson on October 21, 1918, for advice concerning the three options. The president's suggestion was to discuss a solution according to the third option with the leader of the Czechoslovak National Council, Thomas Masaryk, then visiting the United States. As a result of discussions between Zhatkovich and Masaryk, the Philadelphia Agreement was signed on October 26, 1918, proposing the inclusion of Transcarpathia as an autonomous unit within Czechoslovakia. In Transcarpathia a Ruthenian National Council, which came into being near the Slovak area in Stará L'ubovňa, declared a separation of Transcarpathia from Hungary on November 8, 1918. The actual incorporation of the territory into Czechoslovakia, however, was delayed for several months.

Anticipating the downfall of the Habsburg monarchy, the representatives of the Ruthenians of Bukovina, including the *Reichsrat* and the diet deputies, participated in a meeting in Lviv on October 18, 1918, which approved the establishment of a Ukrainian state and formed the Ukrainian National Council as its provisional government. On October 25 a Ukrainian Committee was established in Chernivtsi, headed by Omelian Popovych, to serve as a branch, for Bukovina, of the Lviv Ukrainian National Council. A competing Romanian National Council was formed for Bukovina on October 27. Bukovina's last Austrian *Landespräsident* transferred political power to the two councils on November 6. Two days later the armed forces of the Kingdom of Romania advanced from the southern into the northern (Ruthenian) parts of the Land, seizing Chernivtsi on November 11. Ruthenian volunteers resisted the Romanian troops for two more weeks in northernmost Bukovina before retreating into Galicia. Romania's control over all of Bukovina thus became an accomplished fact.

The aspirations of the Ruthenians (Ukrainians) of Bukovina for a union with their conationals in Galicia were not attainable as a result of World War I. Instead of a united homeland, the Ruthenians of Bukovina, Galicia, and Transcarpathia would be divided among three neighboring countries, respectively Romania, Poland, and Czechoslovakia.

THE SERBS OF VOJVODINA AND BOSNIA-HERZEGOVINA

Vojvodina from Revolution to Dualism, 1848–67

The news of revolutionary events in Pest and Vienna in March 1848 elicited demands for liberal reforms from major Serb towns in both the Bačka and the military borders (Novi Sad, Pančevo, Zemun). In the countryside, Serb peasants were refusing to render feudal dues and services to their seigneurs. With the Hungarian government unwilling to discuss the Serbs' national rights, a National Assembly (*Skupština*) based on the traditional National Church Council formulated in Sremski Karlovci, in mid-May 1848, the first modern political program of the Hungarian Serbs. It asked for creation of a new crownland, the Serbian Vojvodina, composed of Bačka and Baranya counties, the Banat, the (Croatian) *županija* of Srijem, and all the adjacent military borders. The Vojvodina was to form a federal union with Croatia. The *Skupština* raised Metropolitan Rajačić to the rank of patriarch and chose as *Vojvoda* Stefan Šupljikac, an imperial army colonel. It also created a Chief Committee (*Glavni odbor*) which, located in Sremski Karlovci, was to implement the decisions of the May *Skupština* and conduct governmental business until the election of a national diet (*Narodni sabor*).

For the approaching conflict with Hungary, the *Glavni odbor* gathered a sizable military force, commanded by Đorđe Stratimirović and composed of troops from the military borders, as well as of volunteers from Serbia under Stefan Kničanin. In the summer of 1848 the Serbs' situation appeared critical, since even Vienna considered the *Glavni odbor* illegitimate and authorized military action against its forces. By the fall, however, the imperial government welcomed Serb help against Hungary, and in November 1848 the *Glavni odbor* was recognized as a legitimate administrative organ, operating through three sections—political, judicial, and financial. By October, the Serb movement had assumed a conservative direction under the influence of Orthodox hierarchy. The liberal Stratimirović was replaced as military commander by *Vojvoda* Šupljikac. After the latter's death in late December, Patriarch Rajačić, as chairman of the *Glavni odbor*, secured unquestioned political dominance.

Although Francis Joseph sanctioned the program of the May *Skupština* in December 1848, its realization in the postrevolutionary period suffered from a peculiar distortion characteristic of the Neo-Absolutism of the 1850s. Already the "decreed" Stadion Constitution of March 1849 had proclaimed the establishment of the new crownland of the "Serbian Vojvodina and the Banat of Timişoara," which was to include Bačka county, the Banat, and two districts of the Srijem *županija*, but not the strongly Serb military borders (whether in the Banat or in Srijem, or even the area of the Šajkaš Battalion). As a result, within the prospective crownland, the Serbs were a minority of 321,000 against 390,000 Romanians, 335,000 Germans, and 221,000 Magyars. The creation of this curious entity was designed less to reward the Serbs for their loyalty in 1848 than to punish the Magyars by detaching a sizable territory from the Crown of Saint Stephen, and to please the currently helpful Russian government with its traditional interest in the Orthodox "brethren" abroad.

Rajačić's *Glavni odbor* stopped functioning in November 1849. The subsequently established government in the crownland of Vojvodina, excluding self-rule, was purely bureaucratic with German as its internal official language. A military and civil governor (Count Johann Coronini-Cronberg assumed that post in August 1851) resided in Timişoara and headed the government of the Land (*Landesregierung*), directly responsible to the Ministry of the Interior in Vienna. The Hungarian counties and manorial jurisdictions were replaced by five administrative circuits (*Kreise, okružja*), further subdivided into districts (*Bezirke, srezovi*), each headed by a captain (*Bezirkshauptmann, srezki načalnik*). Equality of all citizens before the law according to the Austrian civil and criminal codes replaced the sway of Werbőczi's *Tripartitum*. The judicial system under the Superior Court in Timişoara operated through the circuit courts in Sombor, Lugoj, and Timişoara, and the lower courts in each of the districts.

Reversal of the Magyarization of the 1830s and 1840s represented a positive side of the Neo-Absolutist regime from the Serb national viewpoint. Thus the Serb language could be used in relations with the agencies of the state and in local government and educational institutions, such as the teachers' college in Sombor. The Viennese government also let the Serbs dominate the Orthodox Church through the patriarchate of Karlovci not only in the Bačka but in the entire Banat (including the military borders), although the number of believers in the three predominantly Romanian dioceses was 1,300,000, and in the four mostly Serb ones only 580,000.

The moves to reintroduce constitutional government in 1860, marked by Vienna's efforts to conciliate the Magyar nobility, spelled an end to the crownland of Vojvodina. In December 1860, the bulk of its territory was reincorporated into Hungary, while the two districts of Srijem *županija* returned to Croatia. A Serb National Council (the so-called *Blagoveštenski Sabor*), however, was permitted to gather in Karlovci in April 1861, to voice its wishes in the light of the altered political situation. Three different viewpoints emerged at the council. A faction under Svetozar Miletić, disappointed by Vienna's ingratitude for Serb aid in 1848, proposed reconciliation and cooperation with the Magyars. A group, led by Jovan Subotić, advanced a "Yugoslav" solution according to which Vojvodina would form with Croatia and Dalmatia a federation, which in turn would confederate with Hungary. The pro-Viennese majority, backed by the influential Orthodox prelates, adopted a program asking for an autonomous but smaller Vojvodina, which—excluding the northern Bačka and eastern Banat—would be more Serb in its ethnic character. Vienna, however, did not help, and the pro-Magyar viewpoint suffered a serious setback in 1861 in a confrontation of views between the Serb leader Mihajlo Polit-Desančić and the Magyar spokesman, Baron Joseph Eötvös, on the prospective Hungarian constitution. Polit envisioned Hungary as an "eastern Switzerland" in which all nationalities would have their own self-governing areas and enjoy the use of their own languages in all spheres of public life, including the parliament. Eötvös, in spite of his generally liberal leanings, opposed the concept of territorial autonomy and insisted on Magyar as the sole language of the central governmental organs in Hungary.

In the mid-1860s Miletić emerged as the leading secular Serb politician. In his newspaper *Zastava*, established in 1866, he championed liberal reforms against the conservative clerical leadership. Also in 1866, a radical political organization, the United Serbian *Omladina*, came into existence in Novi Sad. Ranging in their views from liberalism to socialism, its youthful members sought association with Serbia and envisioned the recreation of a unified Serbian state, which would match in its dimensions the late medieval realm of King Stefan Dušan. Inevitably their views were regarded as seditious by the Hungarian authorities.

The Serbs of Southern Hungary under Dualism, 1867–1914

After the Compromise of 1867 the Serb deputies, cooperating with their Romanian colleagues, pressed in the Hungarian parliament for grants of territorial autonomy to the individual nationalities. They were deeply disillusioned by the Nationality Law of 1868, sponsored by Eötvös. The Serb Liberal Party, organized in 1869 under Miletić's leadership in Veliki Bečkerek, reaffirmed the goal of a federalized Hungary, based on autonomous national areas, as well as cooperation with the other non-Magyar nationalities of Hungary toward that objective. In the parliament, the party continued to urge revision of the Nationality Law.

Other measures of the Hungarian government in the 1870s exacerbated the Serbs' discontent. A source of grievance was the disposition of the military borders, abolished in 1872–73. Budapest rejected Serb pleas for the formation of a predominantly Serb county in the area. Instead, the former borders were divided among the existing nationally mixed counties, with Šajkaš attached to Bács-Bodrog, and the German regimental area of the western Banat split between Torontal and Temes counties. The promotion of Magyarization through the educational system also caused bitterness. This tactic became evident with the establishment of the Magyar *gymnasia* in Sombor (1872) and Novi Sad (1873), and the introduction of the compulsory study of Magyar in Serb elementary schools in 1879.

In 1876, Serb representation in the Hungarian parliament was reduced to a single deputy, Polit-Desančić. The only other representative, Miletić, was arrested for urging young Hungarian Serbs, in his newspaper *Zastava*, to join as volunteers the anti-Turkish struggle in Bosnia-Herzegovina. In the parliament Polit continued to voice the Serbs' concern for Bosnia-Herzegovina, sharply criticizing the Austro-Hungarian occupation and its subsequent policy. Between 1880 and 1883, he particularly exasperated Kálmán Tisza's cabinet by promoting Serb-Croatian friendship in his parliamentary speeches, which denounced attempts to introduce Magyar into Croatia, urged the return of Rijeka (Fiume) to the Croats, and warned his compatriots in Croatia not to antagonize the Croats by accepting favors from the Hungarian government.

After 1884, the electoral manipulation, managed by Kálmán Tisza, precluded the election of any Serb to the Hungarian parliament. The Serb Liberal Party at the same time was rent by a major internal conflict. A radical and socially minded faction under Jaša Tomić was alienated by a new party program, softening the opposition to a unitary Hungarian state, which was adopted in Kikinda in 1884. Assuming control in 1885 of the party newspaper *Zastava*—against which Polit's majority established a new organ, *Branik*—Tomić's faction in 1887 reaffirmed the older, more radically autonomist Bečkerek program of 1869, supplemented by socially progressive planks such as demands for more equitable taxation and support for peasant cooperatives. In 1891 the faction constituted itself as a separate Radical Party.

Unable to voice their grievances in the Hungarian parliament, the Serbs together with the Romanians and the Slovaks agreed on a platform in the joint Congress, held in Budapest in August 1895, which was attended by 150 Serbian delegates, including both the Liberals and the Radicals. A minimalist program, drafted by Polit and adopted by the Congress, no longer called for unified autonomous territories for individual nationalities, but merely for ethnic delimitation and language autonomy of the existing counties. The Congress elected a permanent committee, which acted on two subsequent occasions: in 1896 to protest the Magyar-centered millennial celebrations of the Hungarian state, and in 1898 to condemn the government's pressure for the Magyarization of personal and place names. Throughout the 1890s, no Serb could win a seat in the parliament unless he ran as a candidate of one of the Magyar parties. In 1901 a Serb Liberal, Ljube Pavlović, at last won mandate. Although soon expelled from the parliament, he was able to deliver a plea for national autonomy of the non-Magyars.

Early in the twentieth century, the crisis of the dualist system, combined with the spread of political awareness to wider social strata, revitalized political activity also among the Hungarian Serbs. The political climate favored the Serb Radicals who in 1902 for the first time prevailed over the Liberals in the National Church Council. The Radicals' new program of 1903 further accentuated social and economic reforms, including social insurance, progressive taxation, abolition of excise taxes, and even a major land reform in favor of the peasantry. Like the leading politicians of Croatia, the Radicals implemented the Rijeka Resolution and allied in 1905 with the Magyar Independence Party. Ferenc Kossuth (son of the celebrated Lajos Kossuth) fascinated them by his protestations of sympathy for the South Slavs.

With the government's pressure relaxed in the elections of 1906, the Serbs were able to win a more significant representation in the Hungarian parliament for the first time since the mid-1880s. Although Tomić was defeated, three other Radicals won mandates, as did Polit, the sole Liberal. The four Serbs formed a parliamentary club with the Romanian and Slovak deputies. The three Radicals simultaneously joined the ruling National Coalition of the Magyar parties, following the initial example of the deputies from Croatia.

While the Radicals were henceforth restrained from criticizing the government, Polit was free to resume his pleas for a federalized Hungary ("eastern Switzerland"). Once more adopting a broad South Slav viewpoint, he scored the Austro-Hungarian customs war with Serbia in 1906, Kossuth's railroad language regulations for Croatia a year later, and the annexation of Bosnia-Herzegovina in 1908.

In the meantime, the Radicals' docility toward the Hungarian government was clearly eroding their popularity. They were slow to react even to the notorious educational Magyarization laws of Count Albert Apponyi in 1907. A year later they withdrew their own candidate for the Serbian Orthodox patriarchate to support the government protégé. The party was further weakened in 1907 by the secession of a faction, the Kikinda Democrats, who, against the narrowly Serb orientation of Tomić's leadership, advocated South Slav cooperation. At last in 1909 the Radicals also felt entirely free to criticize the governing Hungarian National Coalition.

With the restoration of István Tisza's ascendancy in Hungarian politics, the government's pressure against the Serbs intensified. In the parliamentary elections of 1910 the Serb Radicals and Liberals could not win a single mandate. The venerable National Church Councils were suspended indefinitely in 1912, and by 1913 Serb leaders were excluded from participation even in such local governing bodies as the city council of Novi Sad and the county assembly of Bačka. Application of the Apponyi laws led to further Magyarization of the educational system. As early as 1909 in Bačka and Torontal counties, with approximately equal numbers of Serbs and Magyars, there were 560 Magyar elementary schools and only 159 Serb ones. Seven *gymnasia* in the area were Magyar, and just one was Serb.[62] Disillusionment with both Tisza and the Magyar opposition was bringing the Liberals and the Radicals closer together. The Serbs' clandestine aid to their compatriots abroad during the Balkan Wars of 1912–13 led to more punitive anti-Serb government measures, and the Serbs' discontent increased accordingly. It was in this atmosphere that World War I was to break out.

The Serbs of Bosnia-Herzegovina, 1878–1914

With the occupation of Bosnia-Hezegovina in July 1878, the Habsburg empire acquired the single largest body of Serbs within its frontiers. By 1910 they were to constitute 42 percent of the total population

---

62. The Croats of southern Hungary were even more disadvantaged culturally. Divided into two subgroups, the Bunjevci and the Šokci, they numbered at least 70,000, but had only one elementary school in the Bačka. Traditionally lacking in national and political consciousness, they formed in 1913 a political organization in Subotica and opted openly for Croatian nationality, as well as for close cooperation with the Serbs.

of the two provinces, or 850,000 inhabitants, compared with 650,000 Serbs in Croatia, 500,000 in southern Hungary, and 100,000 in Dalmatia. After a brief period under the Foreign Ministry, Bosnia-Herzegovina was transferred to the jurisdiction of the joint Austro-Hungarian Ministry of Finance in Vienna. In 1882 the military commander, who served as the chief administrator (*Landeschef*) in Sarajevo, was provided with a deputy (*Adlatus*) for civil matters, responsible to Finance Minister Benjámin Kállay (1882–1903). The central governing body (*zemaljska vlada, Landesregierung*) operated through sections for administration, finance, justice, and public works. The Land was divided for administrative and judicial purposes into circuits (*okružja, Kreise*), and further into districts (*srezovi, Bezirke*).

At the time of the Habsburg occupation of Bosnia-Herzegovina, the Serbs, compared with the local Croats, had developed a clear sense of national identity.[63] The Serbian revolts against the Turks in 1804–15 aroused their national consciousness. Since the mid-1840s the Serbian Principality had supported national propaganda in Bosnia-Herzegovina through paid and voluntary agents (teachers, priests, and merchants). The anti-Turkish uprisings of the 1860s and 1870s augmented and strengthened the ties of the Serbs of Bosnia-Herzegovina with the Serbs of southern Hungary and with Serbia.

During the period of Austro-Hungarian occupation, the Serb community focused on regaining its ecclesiastical and educational autonomy. Under restrictions imposed in 1880, the Austrian government had assumed the right to appoint Orthodox bishops as well as to certify priests and Orthodox school teachers. In the early 1890s the Serbs mounted a powerful broadly based campaign demanding free selection of priests and teachers by their communities, popular voice in choosing the Orthodox metropolitan, and cultural rights, such as the free use of the Cyrillic alphabet. After repeated petitions to the emperor and the government's inability to suppress the movement, complex negotiations ensued between the Austrian government and the patriarch of Constantinople, with occasional Russian mediation. A compromise solution was not reached until August 1905, by which time Baron István Burián (joint Minister of Finance, 1903–12) had replaced the more rigid Kállay.

As the struggle for religious and cultural rights approached its climax in 1902, the Serb leaders concluded an agreement with the Moslem autonomists to oppose an annexation of the Land by Austria-Hungary, and to favor instead autonomy within the Ottoman Empire. Shortly af-

---

63. In contrast, the Croats' sense of national identification was redirected from a specifically Croatian focus to a broader "Yugoslav" one by the Illyrian agitation of the 1830s and 1840s. Subsequently, this was affirmed by their Catholic priests trained from 1853 to 1876, in the same spirit at the seminary of Djakovo, ideologically dominated by Bishop Strossmayer.

terward, however, a new generation of Serb lay intelligentsia began to emerge, which had little liking for either the Habsburgs or the Turks, preferring close ties with the Serbian Kingdom and Montenegro. The first Serb political newspaper, *Srpska Riječ*, in 1904 and *Narod* three years later owed their establishment to this new leadership, which also served as a nucleus for the first Serb political movement in Bosnia-Herzegovina, the Serb National Organization, founded in 1907.

To soften internal opposition against the annexation of 1908, in February 1910 the Austro-Hungarian government granted Bosnia-Herzegovina a constitution, including the provision of a diet. Patterned after the diets of Cisleithania, it had very limited powers, and was based mainly on the system of electoral *curiae*. Moreover, its legislation was subject to control by the *Reichsrat* and the Hungarian parliament, in addition to the joint Ministry of Finance. The fact that the president of the diet was Moslem, and only five of the appointed members of the diet were Orthodox compared with seven Catholics, increased the Serbs' feeling of the government's distrust, already evident in the composition of the civil service of the Land.[64] The first major issue facing the diet was that of peasant emancipation, dramatized in the summer of 1910 by strikes led among Serb peasants by Peter Kočić. A law passed in 1911 enabled unfree peasants (*kmets*) to purchase economic freedom from their—mostly Moslem—seigneurs, but not before the agrarian issue had caused a split of the Serb liberal National Organization into conservative and progressive factions, formed respectively around the newspapers *Srpska Riječ* and *Narod*. The contest over peasant emancipation also destroyed the cooperation between Serb and Moslem leaders, already strained by the anti-Turkish attitude of the new generation of Serb politicians. Aside from Kočić's peasant movement, Serb social radicalism found expression in the organization of the Social Democratic Party of Bosnia-Herzegovina in 1909, following worker unrest centered in Sarajevo.

Serb resentment against Vienna's rule assumed the sharpest form in the conspiratorial group of youthful radicals, Young Bosnia, which attempted to assassinate the *Landeschef*, Baron Marian Varešanin in 1910. The excitement of the Balkan Wars of 1912–13 intensified the radicals' contacts with secret Pan-Serbian organizations in Serbia. The government's countermeasures increased the potential for violence, which the new joint Finance Minister (1912–15), Leon Biliński, belatedly attempted to defuse through economic concessions to the Serb middle

64. According to statistics, there were about twice as many Serbs as Croats in Bosnia-Herzegovina, while native Croats outnumbered native Serbs six to one in the provincial civil service. (In 1906 judiciary had been fully separated from administration. Resembling the Cisleithanian model, 48 district courts and 6 circuit courts functioned under the Superior Court of the Land in Sarajevo. In 1912 the *Landesregierung* added sections for religion and education, and the economy.)

class in the fall of 1913. The fateful climax of these tensions was the assassination of Archduke Franz Ferdinand in Sarajevo on June 28, 1914, by a group of young Bosnian Serbs.

Agricultural Imbalance and Industrial Underdevelopment in Vojvodina, 1848–1914[65]

Crop raising continued to dominate agriculture in both the Bačka and the western Banat into the second half of the nineteenth century. The consequence was an impressive expansion of arable land, which in the Bačka increased from 574,000 morgen[66] in 1826 to 1,113,000 in 1895, while pastures and marshes declined from 839,000 morgen to 207,000. At the same time the fallow diminished. In the Banat, for instance, it declined from 6 percent of arable land in 1875 to 1.1 percent in 1912. The overwhelming dominance of wheat within the total crop production yielded during the second half of the nineteenth century to a virtual parity of wheat with corn, as the pattern of alternate planting of the two prevailed. Early in the twentieth century the only other significant grain, accounting together with wheat and corn for 80 percent of the cultivated area, was oats, needed for horsefeed. The remaining land was planted with hemp, flax, tobacco, and to a lesser extent with sugar beets, feed crops, and potatoes.

The diminution of pasture, combined with a failure to raise feed crops on a large scale, imposed serious restrictions on animal production, affecting particularly cattle and sheep raising. Horses (for draft) and pigs (for the market) were most common. With 307 horses per thousand inhabitants in the Banat and 159 in the Bačka by the end of the nineteenth century, the area was among the most advanced of Central Europe in the replacement of cattle by horses as draft animals. The number of pigs more than doubled in the Banat, and more than tripled in the Bačka, between 1870 and 1911. The amount of cattle stagnated in 1884–95, then began to rise in the Bačka but declined in the Banat.

Modernization of production made slow progress initially even on large estates. Despite the sporadic appearance of machinery in the 1860s, there is little subsequent evidence of its use until after 1890. Then its diffusion was fairly rapid, including steam-powered plows and threshing machines, mechanical reapers, and mowers. Mechanization was favored by a relative scarcity of manpower, caused by an exceptionally low birthrate in the area. Modern agricultural methods were also in-

---

65. Economic data in this section are derived from Stevan Mezei, "Privreda Vojvodine početkom XX veka," *Jugoslovenski narodi pred prvi svetski rat* (Belgrade: Naučno delo, 1967), pp. 521–47; *Istoriia Iugoslavii* (Moscow: Izd-vo Akademii Nauk SSSR, 1963), 1:592–93; *Enciklopedija Jugoslavije* (Zagreb: Izd. Leksikografskog zavoda, 1968–1971), 7:532–39, 8:10–15.
66. One morgen amounted to approximately 4,300 square meters.

troduced. The use of artificial fertilizers became important, helping to offset the effects of imperfect crop rotation, as well as the scarcity of manure, owing to the low level of animal raising.

Industrial development continued to lag behind agriculture in the second half of the nineteenth century for several reasons: the government in Budapest did not favor industrial growth in the peripheral areas of Hungary; labor power was relatively scarce because of the comparative underpopulation of the area; and there was a lack of water power and of such important raw materials as coal, iron and other ores, stone, and wood. Although factories made a sporadic appearance before 1848, a genuine industrial revolution did not take place even by 1914. Instead, the manufactory type of production continued to grow side by side with limited factory production.

Manufactories of the dispersed type dominated the fabrication of textiles, based largely on the putting-out system. Of special importance was the spinning and weaving of hemp, encouraged by the Hungarian government as noncompetitive with the economy of central Hungary. Toward the end of the nineteenth century, in Bačka alone the putting-out system employed some 200,000 domestic workers. Manufactory methods also prevailed in brickmaking, wood processing, and the fabrication of simple metal implements.

The prime area for the penetration of factory production was food processing, for which a solid base of raw materials existed, although advances in this sector were hampered from Budapest in order to protect the food-processing industry of central Hungary from competition. Nevertheless, twenty-six steam-powered flour mills survived in the Bačka by the end of the nineteenth century. Greater development was checked by the Hungarian government's manipulation of railroad rates, which discriminated against the imports of wheat into—and exports of flour from—the Bačka and the Banat. Similarly the Hungarian sugar cartel stifled introduction of sugar refining until 1906. Subsequently three refineries were established by 1913. Aside from food processing factories, mechanized plants appeared in selected areas of the textile industry, especially hemp and silk. Otherwise factory production included several medium-size brickyards, sawmills, and chemical plants.

Despite major impediments, industrial progress did occur in the Bačka and the western Banat. The number of enterprises employing more than twenty workers increased from 58 with 2,571 workers in 1900 to 157 with 9,237 workers in 1910. Nevertheless, the degree of industrialization remained relatively low. In 1890, 76 percent of the population was still engaged in agriculture, which was less than in Croatia (84.6) or Dalmatia (86.1), but more than in Carniola (71.9) or Istria (72.8). The proportion declined to 70 percent by 1910. Although industrialization was limited, the Bačka and the western Banat by 1918 exceeded in capital invested in industry per capita not only Serbia but also Croatia, but they fell below the level of industrial investment in the Slovene territories.

Government-Sponsored Economic Development in Bosnia-Herzegovina, 1848–1914[67]

The Viennese government made special efforts to raise the level of economic life in the retarded provinces acquired from the Ottoman Empire in 1878. The agricultural sector posed a formidable challenge, since in 1910 it still employed 87.9 percent of the total population, the largest percentage of any part of the Habsburg empire. Grain-growing river valleys along the Sava and elsewhere particularly benefited. The government established model estates, settled skilled colonists, and encouraged cultivation of new crops, especially sugar beets. Another area of special attention was the cultivation of southern fruit and tobacco in Herzegovina. Little, if any, progress was made in regions where animal raising prevailed.

Crop production scored impressive gains. Annual yields increased dramatically from 1882–86 to 1911 for corn (from 116,000 tons to 214,000), wheat (44,000 to 77,000), potatoes (17,000 to 58,000), and tobacco (1,388 to 3,256); the increases were less significant for barley (56,000 to 62,000) and grapes (3,723 to 4,748). Despite attempts to improve methods and breeds, animal raising remained largely primitive. In fact, an absolute decline in the number of animals, occurring between 1895 and 1910, was especially marked for sheep (almost one-third) and pigs (over one-fifth), less so for cattle and goats.

Industrial production was promoted even more energetically by the Viennese government. Favorable preconditions existed in Bosnia-Herzegovina's solid raw material base (coal, iron, and lumber), as well as in its abundant water power and cheap labor. The administration of joint Finance Minister Kállay guided the major advances between 1882 and 1903, while interest slackened under his successors. The government was particularly active in selective development of heavy industry. It achieved favorable results in mining and iron metallurgy. State-owned coal mines increased their output from 23,000 tons in 1885 to 394,000 in 1900, and to 847,000 in 1913. Production of iron ore in the state-owned mines at Vareš rose from 2,305 tons in 1890 to 219,000 tons in

67. Economic data in this section are derived from *Enciklopedija Jugoslavije* (Zagreb: Izd-vo Leksikografskog zavoda, 1956), 2:87–90; Peter F. Sugar, *Industrialization of Bosnia-Hercegovina, 1878–1918* (Seattle: University of Washington Press, 1963), pp. 101–67; *Dějiny Jugoslávie,* ed. Václav Žáček (Prague: Svoboda, 1970), pp. 292–93; Vladimir Dedijer et al., *History of Yugoslavia* (New York: McGraw-Hill, 1974), p. 526–28. *Die Habsburgermonarchie, 1848–1918* (Vienna: Österreichische Akademie der Wissenschaften, 1973), 1:537–66.

1913. Also at Vareš, the government erected modern ironworks in 1891, and the output of pig iron amounted to 25,000 tons in 1895 and 53,000 tons in 1913.[68] Through grants of concessions and privileges to private entrepreneurs, the government also successfully promoted the chemical industry. Six major factories came into existence after 1893: an oil refinery, an electrochemical plant, and plants producing soda, wood distillates, cellulose, and turpentine.

The largest industry in Bosnia-Herzegovina, however, was lumbering and wood processing. As late as 1913 approximately half of the territory was covered with forests, about three-quarters of them state owned. The number of sawmills rose from two in 1875 to 174 (31 steam-powered) by 1913. Most of the lumber was destined for export, which amounted in 1913 to 53,000 wagon loads, valued at 28 to 30 million crowns, or one-quarter of total exports.

The successful industries produced semifinished goods and depended heavily on exports. Conditions did not favor industries fabricating finished products with more limited export opportunities. The government ignored some of them, especially textiles and machinery manufacture, traditionally viewed as hallmarks of mature industrialization. Others were encouraged, but with meager results. A paper mill at Zenica and a large tannery at Jelez, established respectively in 1886 and 1890, failed to survive. In food processing, the government discouraged flour milling in order to avoid competing with Hungarian mills.[69]

Despite setbacks, the joint Austro-Hungarian administration did stimulate important advances in the industrial sector. By 1907 there were 145 enterprises with more than twenty workers, employing together 22,913 workers. Among them were ten enterprises with more than 500 workers each. Yet, with an extremely low starting point, industrialization of Bosnia-Herzegovina remained below the level of any other South Slav area in the Habsburg monarchy. Measured in capital invested in industry per capita, it stood in 1918, with 73 dinars, below not only Slovenia (192), Vojvodina (124), and Croatia (113), but—outside of the monarchy—also Serbia (107).[70]

The whole industrial and indeed general economic development of Bosnia-Herzegovina suffered from the transportation problem. Its dif-

---

68. In addition, the state was the principal supplier and customer of the private ironworks at Zenica, built in 1892 to produce steel and a variety of semifinished iron products. The volume of production rose from 3,721 tons in 1895 to 27,000 tons in 1913.

69. Where the state did engage in food-related industries, as in alcohol distillation at Tuzla in 1888, or in sugar refining at Ušora around 1900, these initiatives proved unprofitable. The one area of food processing, conspicuously successful as private enterprise, was prune production. The first plant, established in Brčka in 1888, was followed by two others.

70. Yet a comparison with Montenegro (13 dinars) showed a fair degree of development by the Balkan standards.

ficulties were to a large measure due to political and economic competitive opposition of the Hungarian government against the development of Bosnia. It blocked the establishment of railway links between Dalmatia and Bosnia, in part to maintain that Dalmatia belonged in principle to the Triune Kingdom, a *corpus adnexum* of the Hungarian Crown, but more importantly to protect the interests of the only Hungarian seaport of Rijeka. Likewise Hungary prevented the construction of railway connections between Austria and the Balkans through western Croatian territories.

World War I

The outbreak of the war against Serbia in 1914 exposed the Serbs in the Habsburg monarchy to severe repressions. The government in Budapest suppresed their publications, as well as their political, cultural, and social organizations in southern Hungary. Serbs were subject to arrest on suspicion of contacts with illegal anti-Habsburg societies. Stern reprisals occurred particularly in the Srijem area, which the Serbian army had briefly penetrated in September 1914. Executions, mass arrests, and destruction of entire villages followed.

Persecution of the Serbs was even more severe in Bosnia-Herzegovina, where members of Young Bosnia were mercilessly hunted down, and acknowledged death sentences reached 460. Entire regions in the vicinity of Serbia and Montenegro were ordered evacuated. Appalling conditions prevailed in the internment camps. Thus 60 percent of the inmates perished in a camp for Bosnian Serbs in Arad. With the suspension of the constitution of Bosnia-Herzegovina facilitating repressions, anti-Serb measures included bans on the celebration of Orthodox holidays and on the use of the Cyrillic alphabet in schools and by government agencies.

Early in the war Serbs of southern Hungary were joining in Serbia's defense against the Habsburg monarchy. Some left for Serbia following the outbreak of the war. Others withdrew with the Serbian army from Srijem, most of them perishing in the defense of Belgrade in 1915. Serb draftees into the Austrian army were soon found in large numbers in Russia as deserters or prisoners of war. Until the end of 1915, those wishing to fight for Serbia were permitted to reach the front through Bulgaria. After Bulgaria's entry into the war as an ally of the Central Powers, Serbs from southern Hungary were included in a South Slav division assembled by the Russian government in Odessa in 1916. The division fought against the Bulgarians in the Dobrudzha, and similar formations were later dispatched to the Salonika front. Within the Yugoslav independence movement in the West, the Serbs of the Habsburg monarchy were represented by a member of the Bosnian diet, Nikola Stojanović.

Within the Habsburg monarchy, the persecution of the Serbs had diminished by 1916 under the pressure of world opinion, combined with the wish to project a more liberal nationality policy. Thus the government spared the lives of sixteen Bosnian Serb intellectuals who had been sentenced to death in Banja Luka in April 1916. With the lessening of terror, manifestations of popular discontent began to spread, including strikes and demonstrations as well as acts of sabotage and the formation of underground organizations. As the antiwar sentiments intensified in 1917, desertions from the Austrian army multiplied and many of the deserters entered the "green cadres" waging guerrilla warfare, especially in Srijem. In the spring of 1918 the "green cadres" spread into Bosnia-Herzegovina, often concentrating on a vendetta against the Moslem landowners.

Soon after its establishment in Zagreb in early October 1918, the as yet illegal National Council of the Slovenes, Croats, and Serbs included, in addition to Slovene and Croatian members, ten Serb delegates from southern Hungary and eighteen representatives from Bosnia-Herzegovina. On October 26 a National Council, formed under the aegis of the Zagreb council specifically for Bosnia-Herzegovina, proclaimed the political unification of all Slovenes, Croats, and Serbs. On November 1, 1918 it took over governmental power in the Land. In a parallel development, a meeting convened from November 12 to 25 in Novi Sad, at which 757 Serb delegates from 211 communities of southern Hungary declared the separation of Vojvodina from Hungary and its unification with Serbia within a Yugoslav state.

THE ROMANIANS OF BUKOVINA

Revolution and Reaction, 1848–59

The Romanians of Bukovina were less affected by violent upheavals than most other peoples of the Habsburg empire in 1848, but the revolutionary year did mark their initiation into modern politics. In the spring a committee, comprising several landlords, as well as professors of the Orthodox theological institute, gathered in Chernivtsi to express the Romanian wishes to the emperor and the Viennese government. Led by the brothers Eudoxius, Georg, and Alexander Hormuzaki, this group prepared a twelve-point memorandum urging the separation of Bukovina from Galicia and its establishment as an autonomous self-governing crownland with Romanian as the official language. In early summer of 1848 a meeting of Transylvanian and Bukovinian leaders in Chernivtsi revived the vision—dating at least to 1792—of a united Romania (including Wallachia and Moldavia) under Habsburg rule. On the initiative of the Hormuzaki brothers, the first Romanian newspaper in Bukovina began to appear weekly in October 1848, propagating Romanian national self-determination within a federalized Austrian empire. Printing articles by authors not only from Bukovina and Transylvania but also from Wallachia and Moldavia, the newspaper, entitled *Bucovina,* sought to promote cultural unification of all Romanians.

The constitutional committee of the *Reichstag* in Kroměříž (Kremsier) considered the future of Bukovina in the winter of 1848–49. The German Left proposed continued attachment of the province to Galicia, which was unacceptable to the Romanian leaders. The Czech spokesman, Palacký, favored the division of Bukovina, with the northern (Ruthenian) part remaining with Galicia and the southern part attached to the other Romanian territories (Transylvania and the Banat) within the empire. A delegation of Bukovinian Romanians on January 20, 1849, presented to the emperor the twelve-point memorandum, drafted the previous spring. Another Romanian delegation under the Orthodox Bishop Andreiu Şaguna of Transylvania, received by Francis Joseph on February 25, asked for the administrative unification of all Habsburg-ruled Romanian territories. During a discussion of Bukovina's status in the *Reichstag* three days later, the Bukovinian delegation split: the three Romanians joined by the one German persisted in demanding a separate crownland; the four Ruthenian deputies favored continuing association with Galicia. The Romanians' view was supported by German and Polish speakers and opposed by the Czechs.

The Neo-Absolutist regime of 1849–59 met the Romanians' wish for Bukovina's detachment from Galicia, but without autonomy or self-government. German remained the official language, although the Romanians received limited national concessions, especially in education. Romanian replaced Latin as the language of instruction in the Orthodox theological institute in Chernivtsi; a chair of Romanian language and literature was established in the Chernivtsi *gymnasium;* and the Orthodox consistory by 1851 asumed full control over the Orthodox elementary schools, in most of which Romanian was taught alongside German. In May 1851 several Romanian nobles and *gymnasium* professors took the initiative to found a public library in Chernivtsi. It was destined to serve as a major national institution.

On the whole, Bukovina's Romanians remained politically tranquil in the 1850s. The newspaper *Bucovina* ceased publication in October 1851. There was no sign of opposition movements, nor any need for political arrests and trials. During the Crimean War (1853–56) the Romanians in Bukovina failed to share the excitement of their Transylvanian compatriots over a possible Austrian annexation of the Danubian Principalities. The leading political activist of 1848, Eudoxius Hormuzaki, assumed in the 1850s the role of adviser to the absolutist government on legal and educational matters.

Romanian Ascendancy, 1860–90

With the gradual establishment of the constitutional regime in the Habsburg monarchy, in essence after 1860, the Romanians—mostly because of their preponderance within the nobility—dominated the Bukovinian diet, the Committee of the Land, and the *Reichsrat* delegations. In the 1860s two Romanian parties emerged in Bukovina. The stronger Centralists, led by the Hormuzaki brothers, cooperated with the German liberals. The Autonomists occasionally gained influence with Vienna's support, as in 1870 when their leader Alexander Petrino served as agriculture minister in Potocki's proautonomist cabinet.

The era of cultural and educational growth, launched in the 1860s, helped to strengthen Romanian national consciousness. The network of Romanian elementary schools began to expand. A new *gymnasium*, established in Suceava in 1860, rapidly acquired a Romanian character, and technical secondary education in Romanian was available in Chernivtsi by 1862. In 1863 the *Societatea Pentru Cultura și Literatura* was founded in Chernivtsi to perform cultural and publicistic functions analogous to those of the *Matica* organizations of the Slavic nations. A major disappointment for the Romanian nationalists was the failure of the Orthodox Church to identify fully with their aspirations. Above all, Bishop Hakman opposed an integration of the diocese of Chernivtsi with the Romanian Orthodox ecclesiastical organization in Transylvania, a measure under consideration by the government in 1861–66. In 1869 Ruthenian was officially adopted as the second language of the Chernivtsi Orthodox consistory. In 1873 the raising of the Chernivtsi see to an archbishopric affirmed Bukovina's ecclesiastical independence from Transylvania.

During the 1870s, the era of German Liberal dominance in Vienna, the Centralist Party enjoyed complete control of the Bukovinian diet and of the organs of the Land. After the death of Eudoxius Hormuzaki in 1874, Konstantin Tomaszczuk assumed the party's leadership. Though a Romanian by birth, this firm believer in the civilizing mission of the German language and culture belonged among the principal proponents of the German university, established in Chernivtsi in 1875. Nevertheless, Romanian nationalism continued to grow. A gathering of cultural leaders and students from all Romanian territories, organized in 1871 by the poet Mihai Eminescu at the historic monastery of Putna, served as a powerful reminder to the Romanians of Bukovina that they belonged to wider ethnic community. An early intimation of irredentist sentiments within the Chernivtsi student society *Arboroasă* led to its dissolution by the government in 1877.

Despite the shift of the Viennese government in the 1880s toward a quasi-autonomist position under Taaffe's ministry, the Centralist Party

in Bukovina continued to dominate the diet and the *Reichsrat* delegation. By 1885 its conservatism and artistocratic leadership drew the criticism of a new Romanian political group, *Concordia*, organized in Chernivtsi by professors Ion Bumbacu and Grigori Halip. More important,
the entire Romanian political community was challenged afresh by the
rising Ruthenian nationalism under a new dynamic Ukrainophile leadership. The portent of this challenge was underscored by the 1880 census, which for the first time officially registered a larger number of
Ruthenians (239,000) than Romanians (190,000) in Bukovina. The initial Romanian response focused on systematizing private support for
Romanian schools through the society *Şcoala Română*, established in Suceava in 1883 with branches springing up in other towns of Bukovina.

Romanian Ascendancy Challenged, 1890–1914

In 1892 the Romanians closed their political ranks to form the National Party through a merger of the Centralists, the *Concordia* society,
and the remnants of the Autonomists. Although claiming to represent
all social classes, the new party–like the Centralists before it—was still
dominated by the landed nobility led by Ion Wolczynski. While the
Ruthenians under the Ukrainophile program looked for ethnic support
to Galicia, the Romanians largely barred by the adamant Hungarian
government from contacts with their kinsmen in Transylvania, had little choice but to seek cultural ties in the new Kingdom of Romania.
Inevitably those who entertained such contacts risked suspicions of disloyalty to the Habsburg empire, above all when they involved the essentially irredentist *Liga Culturală*, established in 1891 in Bucharest by
Nicolai Iorga.
    Romanian control of the diet and of the associated organs in Bu-
kovina did not end until 1903 and then only because of a split in the
Romanian ranks. Aurel Onciul, in opposition to the social conservatism
of the National Party, formed a new Democratic Party, which cooperated with the Ruthenian National Democrats as well as smaller Jewish
and Polish political groups. The Romanian National Party, led by Iancu
Flondor, was outvoted by the new coalition, called the Liberal Union
by 1907. It was also challenged from the right by the Group of the
Young, clamoring for more radical nationalist orientation. This radical
faction was represented in the *Reichsrat* from 1900 to 1905 by Georg
Popovici. By 1907 the Romanian Social Democratic Party of Bukovina
had become another serious competitor for Romanian votes. Its leader,
George Grigorovici, won a seat in the *Reichsrat* in 1907 and 1911 from
Chernivtsi with the help of Jewish votes. Nevertheless, the Romanian
National Party retained a solid majority of four out of six Romanian
seats in the *Reichsrat*. In 1909, it experienced a serious crisis when the

majority opinion in the party questioned the *Reichsrat* deputies' invariable support of the Viennese cabinets, but the dispute was soon settled and the traditional policy resumed. In 1911 the Romanian representatives in the *Reichsrat* (except for the one Social Democrat) joined a loose parliamentary alliance, *Unio Latina*, with Italian nonsocialist deputies, permitting each group to define its own attitude toward the government. With the increase in anti-Semitic propaganda before World War I, an unsuccessful attempt was made to launch a Romanian Christian Social Party, appealing primarily to the peasantry and modeled on Karl Lueger's Austro-German party of the same name.

Despite the numerical superiority of the Ruthenians and their steady political advance, the Romanian position remained on the whole stronger in the public life of Bukovina up to the outbreak of World War I. Only in the field of lower education did the Ruthenians attain a position reflecting their larger numbers: 251 elementary schools were purely or partly Ruthenian, compared with 218 purely or partly Romanian ones, in January 1914. A major reform of Bukovina's constitution of the Land (*Landesordnung*) in May 1910 established a *curia* system on an ethnic basis in the diet. The Romanians were now allotted 22 seats, the Ruthenians only 17. As for the higher ranks of civil service in 1914 the ratio of Romanians to Ruthenians stood at 17 to 4 in the political administration, 72 to 32 in the judiciary, and 13 to 8 in fiscal affairs. This privileged position was anchored in the strength of social and cultural tradition and influence rather than in law. Within the Orthodox ecclesiastical organization, while the archbishop was a Romanian and the vicar general a Ruthenian, three out of four members of the diocesan consistory were Romanians, as well as nine out of twelve archpriests, and all four heads of monasteries.

Nevertheless, irredentist propaganda was gaining ground among Romanian students and intellectuals. It continued to emanate particularly from Iorga's *Liga Culturală*. Iorga himself was specifically banned from visiting Bukovina by the Austrian authorities from 1909. Students from Bukovina attended indoctrination courses organized by the *Liga* in Vălenii de Munte in Romania each summer from 1910. The *Liga* also disseminated writings by Romanian authors attacking Habsburg rule in Bukovina.

Economic Life, 1848–1914[71]

A notable trend in Bukovina's agriculture in the second half of the nineteenth century was the decrease in the proportion of large Ro-

71. Economic data in this section are derived from Erich Prokopowitsch, *Die rumänische nationalbewegung in der Bukowina und der Dako-Romanismus* (Graz and Cologne: Böhlaus Nachf., 1965), pp. 93–99; *Hauptbericht und Statistik über das Herzogthum Bukowina* (Lem-

manian landowners. Mainly because of poor management by original proprietors, large estates were passing into the ownership of Armenians, Poles from Galicia, and later Jews. By the end of the century Romanian nationalists blamed the Austrian government for not helping Romanian nobles to retain their lands, and charged that the official passivity reflected a wish to weaken Romanian influence in the crownland. The Romanian peasantry, on the other hand, took full advantage of the unencumbered landownership and independence after the emanicipation of 1848. Prospering and advancing in education, the peasants became aware that, compared with their kinsmen in Moldavia or Wallachia, their own living conditions were better. Developing a Habsburg loyalism, they were relatively immune to irredentist appeals.

In agricultural production the Romanian areas[72] continued to stress animal raising, although their strength in this sector suffered an erosion in relative—and in some instances absolute—terms. Between 1869 and 1907 the number of cattle dropped slightly; that of pigs rose correspondingly, and of horses substantially. More important, of the total number of animals for Bukovina, the Romanian share (in comparison with the Ruthenian areas) declined in 1869—1907 from 58.5 percent to 52.6 for cattle, from 51.8 to 42.7 percent for pigs, and from 48.8 to 46.4 percent for horses. Of the increasingly obsolescent sheep, the Romanian share rose slightly (from 56.8 to 58.6 percent), although the absolute number declined sharply.

While still averaging 50 percent of the total for Bukovina in animal raising in the early twentieth century, the Romanian areas remained weak in crop production. Compared with the Ruthenian areas in 1907, they accounted for half of the total Bukovinian production of major grains only in the case of oats (27,700 tons). As for the other major grains, the Romanian share was two-fifth for corn and substantially less for the rest.[73]

In craft production, the number of artisan workshops in the Romanian area in 1907 (2,211) was considerably exceeded by that in the Ruthenian districts (3,858). The number becomes more nearly equal if the unusually high concentration of artisan workshops in the city of Chernivtsi (1,574) is discounted. Applying the criterion of nationality to individual craftsmen, Romanians were in 1910 in a striking minority of

berg: Selbstverlag der Handelskammer, 1872), pp. 132–33, 148–53, 178, 192–212, 288; *Statistisches Jahrbuch des Herzogthums Bukowina für das Jahr 1907* (Czernowitz, 1910), pp. 117, 119, 180, 206–11; *Bukovina* (London: Foreign Office, 1920), p. 30. This section focuses on economic trends in the Romanian districts. For an assessment of the overall economic developments in Bukovina see pp. 422–23.

72. The Romanian area of Bukovina included the following administrative districts: Cîmpulung, Gura Humorului, Rădăuţi, Storozhynets', Suceava; the Ruthenian area included the districts of Chernivtsi, Kitsman', Siret, Vyzhnytsia, and Zastavna.

73. It was 33.3 percent for rye, 28.9 percent for barley, and 22.1 percent for wheat.

737, compared with 5,091 Jewish craftsmen and 3,494 of other nationalities. Concerned by the Romanian weakness in this economic sector, the National Party in 1907 sponsored in Chernivtsi the Society of Romanian Artisans, which facilitated training of Romanian apprentices. A newly established special state school for woodworkers in Cîmpulung, with Romanian as its language of instruction, promised to increase the number of Romanian craftsmen in the period before World War I.

In the food-processing industry, the Romanian districts lagged considerably behind the Ruthenian ones. In 1871 they accounted for only two out of nine steam-powered flour mills in Bukovina. In alcohol production in 1870 their output represented 30 percent of the Bukovinian total. In the fiscal year 1906–7, 19 out of 59 Bukovinian distilleries were located in Romanian districts and accounted for 33.5 percent of the total alcohol output in Bukovina. In the same year, of the seven large breweries in the crownland three were located in Romanian districts and four in Ruthenian ones, but the former accounted for only 27 percent of the total output of the seven breweries. Sugar refining was also concentrated in the Ruthenian area.[74]

The Romanian districts, however, excelled in wood processing. In 1871 they contained 75.8 percent of the entire forest area in Bukovina. Their average annual production of lumber for the ten years prior to 1871 was 63.8 percent of Bukovina's total. Also, mining and metallurgical enterprises in Bukovina, though by and large declining in importance, were mostly found in Romanian districts. In 1871 the major ironworks and saltworks were located in the districts of Cîmpulung and Gura Humorului respectively. In 1885–90 experiments with oil extraction were conducted in Ruşii-Muldoviţei near Cîmpulung. Of the principal mineral production in the early twentieth century, salt mining was centered in Cacica near Gura Humorolui, and that of manganese between Cârlibaba and Vatra Dornei in the Cîmpulung district.

World War I

When World War I broke out, the broad strata of Romanian society in Bukovina remained loyal to the Habsburg empire, a stance facilitated by the neutrality of the Romanian Kingdom. Unlike the Romanians of Transylvania, those of Bukovina obeyed mobilization orders promptly, fought well, and few deserted. Aurel Onciul, leader of the Democratic Party and a *Reichsrat* deputy, in the fall of 1914 helped to organize a volunteer Romanian Legion, which participated in the defense of Bukovina against the Russian army. A loyalist meeting of ten thousand

74. In 1906–7 the two major sugar refineries of Bukovina were both sited in the Ruthenian area (in Luzhany and Zhuchka).

Romanians in Suceava in November 1914 issued an appeal to the king of Romania to honor his country's alliance with the Central Powers. Several deputies from the Bukovinian diet volunteered to make anti-Russian speeches in Romania in order to discourage sympathies for the Entente there. To improve Romania's attitude toward the Central Powers, Onciul even attempted in February 1915 to persuade the recalcitrant Hungarian government to show more respect for the national rights of the Romanian population in Transylvania.

Overreacting to the danger of treason or espionage within certain segments of Romanian society (especially intellectuals and professionals) in Bukovina, the Austrian government in the fall of 1914 summarily executed a number of suspects (at least forty-two by November), arrested others, and confined many more in the concentration camp at Thalerhof near Graz. These excesses provided some substance to the charges of Habsburg misrule in Bukovina, voiced in Romania by genuinely disaffected escapees. Gathered around two professors from Chernivtsi, Ioan Grămadă and Lazar Gherman, and a lawyer from Storozhynets', Emilian Sluşanschi, these refugees formed in Bucharest, in July 1915, the Bukovina Association with the aim of popularizing the cause of the Entente within Romania. According to Austrian estimates, the number of escapees from Bukovina to Romania rose to 250 by mid-1916; of those definitely identified, 80 were students, 56 teachers, 40 officials and lawyers, and 10 peasants.

Romania finally entered the war on the Entente's side in August 1916, provided with promises of large territorial gains at the expense of the Habsburg empire. The Romanian part of Bukovina had in fact been promised for mere neutrality by a secret treaty with Russia as early as October 1914. In 1916 Romania's share of Bukovina was defined as the area south of the Prut, which would have included, in addition to all of the five Romanian districts, almost the entire area of three Ruthenian ones along with the city of Chernivtsi. After Romania's entry into the war, Romanian war prisoners from Bukovina and other parts of the Habsburg empire both in Russia and in Italy were encouraged to join special Romanian legions and fight against the Central Powers. Having held much of northern Bukovina (including Chernivtsi) since June 1916, Russia, however, showed little consideration of Romania's interests. The tsarist government declared the whole area, occupied until July 1917, part of a new *guberniia* centered in East Galicia. It included territories promised to Romania in August 1916. Romania had occupied two districts (Suceava and Siret) in southern Bukovina, but had to relinquish them early in 1918 when suing for a separate peace with the Central Powers (concluded in May).

Romania's entry into the war posed a difficult problem for the Bukovinian leaders. All five members of the Romanian Club in the *Reichs-*

rat signed a declaration in August 1916 condemning Romania's alliance with Russia as a dire threat to Romanian national existence. After the *Reichsrat* reconvened, Onciul declared in June 1917 that the ultimate goal of the Romanians of Bukovina was the unification, under Habsburg rule, of all Romanian territories, both inside and outside the empire. As late as October 4, 1918, the chairman of the Romanian Club, Konstantin Isopescul-Grecul, asked only for the unification and autonomy of all Romanian areas within the Habsburg empire. He hoped that this self-governing province would serve as a magnet for the Kingdom of Romania to join later. By October 22, his tone had stiffened when he urged Vienna to force Budapest to release Transylvania and other Romanian territories from Hungarian control, and let them join Bukovina in a separate crownland. Otherwise, he warned, the Romanian subjects of the Habsburg empire would have to look for outside help.

During the final stages in the disintegration of the Habsburg empire, the Bukovinian Romanians established their own National Council under the chairmanship of Flondor on October 27, 1918, in Chernivtsi. This Council subsequently repudiated an agreement that Onciul concluded on November 4 with the Ukrainian National Committee for Bukovina (formed on October 25). It had provided for division of the Land along ethnic lines and joint Romanian-Ukrainian jurisdiction over Chernivtsi. Instead, Flondor's Council appealed to the Romanian government on November 7 to occupy the entire Land. Redeclaring war against the Central Powers on November 9, Romania, in fact, seized Chernivtsi on November 11, and soon afterward the rest of Bukovina. The Romanian National Council for Bukovina on November 12 established a new government of the Land under Flondor's presidency. This government convoked a congress, consisting essentially of the National Council augmented by Polish and German representatives, as well as several pliant Ruthenian peasants. In response to a resolution of this congress of November 28, requesting union of the Bukovina with Romania, the Romanian government issued a decree formalizing Bukovina's annexation on December 19, 1918.

With the subsequent acquisition of Transylvania, the Crișana-Maramureș area, and the eastern Banat, as well as Bessarabia, by the Romanian Kingdom, the Romanians of Bukovina as a result of World War I were to be reunited with all their conationals both inside and outside the former Habsburg empire.

CHAPTER 6

Cultural Life

Humanism, Renaissance, and Reformation, 1526–1620

THE MAGYARS

Cultural interrelations stop at neither political nor ethnic borders, and the Magyar cultural evolution is no exception. Nevertheless, the various features that distinguish the Magyars from other nations in East Central Europe have left marks on their cultural history.

One of these features is the splendor and vitality of the Renaissance era under János Hunyadi (ca. 1407/9–1456) and above all his son King Matthias I Corvinus (1458–90). The Turkish invasions, the beginnings of which roughly coincided with the end of Corvinus's reign, destroyed most of the literary treasures and works of fine art of this great era of Hungarian history. But we know from the historian Nicolas Istuanffy (1538–1615) about the splendor of the Corvinian Renaissance; and Ferenc Forgách (1535–1577), a truly distinguished humanist, has transmitted in his *Historia* the tragic events of the first decade after the battle of Mohács. Throughout the dark period of Hungarian history—the era of Turkish occupation during the best part of the sixteenth and seventeenth centuries—Magyar humanists, theologians, linguists, and poets were still active in the small, sparsely occupied eastern and northeastern part of the country.

The expanding Reformation was not as impeded by continuous warfare as late Renaissance culture was. One of its centers was Transylvania, whose princes were protected from the inroads of the Counter Reformation under cover of the Turkish occupation to the east. Of great

importance are the complete translations of the Bible accomplished in
the 1560s by Gáspár Heltai (d. 1574) and by the pastor Gáspár Károli
(1529–91) in eastern Hungary (still in use). The significance of these
translations for the Magyar literary language may well be compared to
Luther's bible translation and High German literature. Péter Bórnemisza
(1535–85), a Lutheran preacher in northwestern Hungary, a territory
free of Turkish occupation, was, like Heltai and Károli, concerned with
theological literature, in his case a collection of sermons; but at the same
time his work vividly describes Magyar daily life, and in his translations
he also deals with secular literature, such as Sophocles' *Electra*. Bálint
Balassi (1554–94), a Protestant nobleman from northwestern Hungary
who later converted to Catholicism, was a genuine secular lyrical poet
equally concerned with love songs and patriotic themes.

THE CZECHS

Czech Renaissance literature in the sixteenth century was confined
largely to Latin poetry by aristocratic writers, led by Jan Starší z Hodějova
(1496–1566). Vernacular literature combined elements of the Renaissance with those of the Reformation. Because of the marked religious
tendency, stemming ultimately from the Hussite movement, fictional
literature favored didactic writings, satirizing alleged vices of contemporary society, by authors such as Mikuláš Konáč z Hodiškova (d. 1546)
and Vavřinec Leander Rvačovský (1525–90). Otherwise belles-lettres in
Czech consisted mainly of translations from Italian, French, and German. Original accounts of travels, especially to the Near East, enjoyed
considerable popularity, as did historical writings. In particular, the *Czech
Chronicle* by Václav Hájek z Libočan, published in 1541, was widely read
for its attractive style, despite its Catholic slant and its failure to meet
the Renaissance standards of scholarship.

Important contributions to the development of Czech literature were
made after 1567 by the Bohemian Brethren, when their initial anti-
intellectualism receded under the impetus of Jan Blahoslav (1523–71),
a distinguished grammarian. The outstanding accomplishment of the
sect was the new translation of the Bible, published at Kralice in 1579–
88, which established the norms of the Czech literary language.

While the Gothic style lingered on in ecclesiastical structures in the
sixteenth century, Renaissance architecture flourished in the numerous
castles and palaces of the nobility that had been appearing in Moravia
as early as the end of the fifteenth century. Moravia still led the way
in the following century with castles erected, for instance, in Telč,
Bučovice, Račice, and Velké Losiny, but Bohemia did not lag far behind
with remarkable Renaissance edifices in Pardubice, Nelahozeves, Opočno,
Litomyšl, and Jindřichův Hradec. The Habsburgs early concentrated

on the renovation of Prague castle, adorning it with the Belvedere Palace (1536–63). By the second half of the sixteenth century a distinct Czech Renaissance style had emerged in smaller towns, combining the Italian influences with local traditions.[1] On the other hand, the court artists of Rudolf II (1576–1612) in Prague were detached from the surrounding Czech culture and worked mostly in the style of Italian mannerism.

Renaissance musical influences reached Bohemia from both central Italy and the Netherlands, leading to the cultivation of complex polyphonic singing. At first, choirs at the court and on aristocratic estates, later special brotherhoods in towns, practiced the new art. The most accomplished composer of polyphonies, particularly motets in the style of the Netherlands, was Kryštof Harant z Polžic (1564–1621). The singing of church hymns remained widespread. During the sixteenth century the Utraquists, the Lutherans, the Bohemian Brethren, and also the Catholics published hymnals. Those of the Bohemian Brethren excelled both on inspirational and aesthetic grounds, above all the Šamotul Hymnal of 1561.

THE SLOVAKS

The Slovak humanist culture that emerged in the sixteenth century had close links with the Bohemian Lands. The outstanding Slovak humanist writer, Martin Rakovský (ca. 1535–79), graduated from the Prague University and for several years taught school in Bohemia before his official appointment to the Hungarian Chamber in Pozsony. In his Latin treatises, written in verse, he was primarily concerned with political theory. He explored the causes of political instability in *Libellus de partibus reipublicae et causis mutationum*, 1560, and advocated strong central authority to curb powerful individuals and ensure equal justice in *De magistratu politico*, 1547. Pavol Kyrmezer (d. 1589), a native of Banská Štiavnica, who was well known for his religious dramas, worked in Moravia, where he sought a rapprochement between the Bohemian Brethren and other Protestants. The University of Prague included prominent Slovaks on its faculty early in the seventeenth century. One of them, Jan Jessenius, a distinguished pioneer in experimental anatomy, served as rector in 1618–21. He paid with his life for participating in the Bohemian uprising. Another Slovak professor, Vavrinec Benedicti z Nedožier, wrote the first systematic grammar of Czech, published in Prague in 1603.

1. Characteristic sgraffito decorations on the outside walls of edifices, together with tombstone sculptures and illustrations in Protestant books, had replaced by then the interior church decorations as the chief expressions of the Renaissance in painting and sculpture.

The Renaissance completely dominated Slovak architecture during the sixteenth century. Several outstanding Renaissance buildings were erected in towns (Banská Štiavnica, Banská Bystrica, Levoča) by the powerful Thurzo family, in addition to a castle in Betlanovce (1564). In connection with anti-Turkish defense many castles were rebuilt in the new style. A striking example of Renaissance urban planning was the locality of Nové Zámky, entirely reconstructed as a fortress town. The new mode penetrated to the villages, where belfries were erected for military purposes. Sculpture, though less important than architecture, found frequent application in the Renaissance fountains, sepulchers, and reliefs on the portals of castles and palaces. A typical decoration was the sgraffito on the parapets of Renaissance houses. In painting, religious themes receded in favor of mythology and secular portraiture in natural settings.

The Reformation loosened both the form and the content of musical compositions. In addition, the more active participation of the congregation in the liturgy encouraged a proliferation of religious songs. Composers of this musical genre in the sixteenth century included Ján Pruno, Šebastián Ambrózy, and Eliáš Láni. Cultivated both in towns and the castles, secular music absorbed elements of Slovak folk culture. In particular the love song attracted attention, and the nobility was to some extent receptive to the patterns of local folk dancing. The historical songs emerged in this period as a distinct musical form. Evoked partly by the anti-Turkish struggle, they celebrated the heroism of Slovak, Croat, and Magyar warriors. Others, anti-Habsburg in orientation, denounced acts of imperial troops and their commanders.

THE CROATS

In Habsburg-ruled Croatia, literary production was meager in the sixteenth century. Two Croatian prose works were published, a translation of the previously noted codification of Hungarian common law, the so-called *Tripartitum Werbőczi,* by Ivan Pergošić in 1574, and a world chronicle by Antun Vramac in 1578. In addition, the first songbook in the Kajkavian dialect appeared in 1593 containing, besides religious hymns, also love and didactic songs as well as an epos about the fall of the fortress of Sighet. Relatively more plentiful were the émigré publications by Croatian Protestants under the direction of Stjepan Konzul Istranin (1521–68) and Antun Dalmatin (d. 1579). In 1561–64 twenty-five Croatian items (twelve in Glagolitic, seven in Cyrillic, and six in the Latin alphabet), mostly catechisms, sermons, and apologies, issued from a press maintained in Urach near Tübingen. Significantly, the Protestant publicists searched for a single Croatian idiom, thus raising an issue not resolved until the Illyrian movement of the 1830s.

Affected by Venice a Dalmatian Renaissance literature flourished during the first half of the sixteenth century in a second generation of Humanist writers. Among them, and indeed within the entire Croatian Renaissance literature, the outstanding figure was Marin Držić (ca. 1508–67) of Dubrovnik. Starting as a poet, he won the greatest renown for his comedies set in his native city and reminiscent of Plautus. The Humanist tradition continued into the later sixteenth century when Dinko Ranjina (1536–1607) enriched the Croatian poetical language by introducing new rhythms and expressions, and Dominko Zlatarić (ca. 1555–after 1609) not only wrote original works but also skillfully translated Sophocles, Ovid, and Tasso.

Even more than in the Slovak territory, in Croatia the architecture in the sixteenth century was affected by considerations of anti-Turkish defense. Adjusted to the use of artillery, the new art of fortification was exemplified by the fortresses of Sisak (1544), Karlovac (1579), and Petrinja (1592). The Renaissance influence, however, was most clearly evident in arcades (sometimes multistoried) adorning castle courtyards, particularly in Veliki Tabor, Varaždin, and Novi Dvori. In sculpture, characteristic examples of the Renaissance style were sepulchers bearing the likenesses of the deceased, most notably Nikola Zrinski's near Čakovec created by the Flemish master Adriaen van Conflans in 1566–74. In pictorial arts, the treasured relics of the Croatian Renaissance include two masterpieces on the altar of the Zagreb cathedral from the first half of the sixteenth century and the illustrations in Protestant books from the latter part of the century.

In Dalmatia, Renaissance art declined after flourishing into the first two decades of the sixteenth century. Subsequently paintings were imported mostly from Venetia, while Dalmatian artists, especially Stjepan Crnota (d. 1548) and Andrija Medulić (d. 1563), worked abroad. Architecture was also at a low ebb on the Dalmatian coast except for Dubrovnik (Ragusa), where by the mid-sixteenth century the Renaissance style prevailed, exemplified particularly by the palace of Skočibuha-Bizzaro, constructed in 1550–53. Subsequently the noted sculptor Nikola Lazanić worked in Dubrovnik in the 1580s in the style of Roman mannerism. Otherwise, two cathedrals were completed in the 1550s, one in Šibenik (Sebenico), the other in Korčula, both combining Venetian Gothic with early Renaissance. The Venetian government also erected administrative and military structures in the Dalmatian towns.[2] An outstanding example of the late Renaissance style was the topmost section of the cathedral belfry in Trogir, built by Trifun Bokanić in 1597–1603.

The tangible evidence of musical activity in Croatia in the sixteenth century is limited to several hymnals and song collections. From the early seventeenth century stems the remarkable *Molitvena Knjižica* of

---

2. Such as arsenals, town gates, and public loggia.

Nikola Krajačević, with religious texts sung to folk tunes. From the Dalmatian coast the names of relatively numerous sixteenth-century composers of Renaissance music are preserved, but few of their works.[3]

THE SLOVENES

The Humanist movement initially had only a tangential relevance to the specifically Slovene culture. A number of important Humanists were from the Slovene area, in particular Tomaž Prelokar, Brikcij Preprost, Bernard Perger, and Matija Hvale—all of whom, gathered around the university of Vienna, participated in the development of Austrian (not Slovene) Humanism. The Reformation, to the contrary, contributed fundamentally to the rise of Slovene literature by pioneering a Slovene literary language and by initiating book printing in Slovene. The key figure in this literary movement, Primož Trubar (1508–86), is credited with the publication of twenty-six Slovene books, starting with a primer and a short catechism both issued in Tübingen in 1550, and followed, among others, by the New Testament, the psalter, and a collection of sermons. As advocate of a distinctive Slovene tongue, he rejected the concept of a common literary South Slav language. Nevertheless, he responded to the needs of other South Slavs, and helped to produce Croatian Protestant books at Urach in 1561–64. Among his followers, Jurij Dalmatin (ca. 1547–89) translated the entire Bible into Slovene, published in 1584 in Wittenberg, and Adam Bohorič (ca. 1520–after 1598) prepared the first Slovene grammar, printed simultaneously with Dalmatin's Bible. During forty-five years the Protestants published fifty Slovene books, the last one (a postil of Luther) in 1595.

The Catholic response to Protestant literary activities remained notably weak, initially consisting of a short Slovene catechism published in Graz in 1574 and an Italian-Slovene dictionary by Gregorius Alasius, printed in Udine in 1607. Subsequently the bishop of Ljubljana, Tomaž Hren, envisaged a broader program of publications, but for lack of collaborators only two more Slovene books were issued: a collection of liturgical texts (1613) and another short catechism (1615), both translated by a Jesuit, Janez Čandek (ca. 1581–1624).

By the mid-sixteenth century the Gothic sway in the formative arts was yielding to the Renaissance on the Slovene territory. Within the Protestant milieu, Renaissance art occasionally bore a Germanic or Dutch imprint, especially in sepulchral sculpture and in book illustrations (for instance, in Dalmatin's Bible). On the whole, however, the Italian Renaissance style predominated in the architecture of fortifications, as well as of castles and palaces with arcaded courtyards. While the Italian Re-

---

3. The oldest surviving compositions are by Andrija Patricij from 1550, followed by several madrigals and motets by Julije Schiavetto from 1563–64.

naissance penetrated to western and central Slovenia directly, in the eastern or Styrian region Venetian and other northern Italian influences were mediated through Graz. In the latter part of the sixteenth century, the Graz variant of the Italian Renaissance came to characterize two notable Lutheran churches, built in Govče and Sevnica.

The Renaissance style in music prevailed in the Slovene region from the late fifteenth century. Its eminent representative was Jacobus Gallus Carniolus (1550–91), a composer of masses, motets, madrigals, and early monodic songs, who popularized in Central Europe, especially in Bohemia, his own elaboration of Venetian musical techniques. Within Slovenia the rise of the Reformation at midcentury interrupted the dominance of the Renaissance mode. The first Protestant hymnal, which appeared in 1567, preserved many medieval Slovene religious songs. Besides Trubar, Sebastijan Semmzer and Wolfgang Striccius stood out as authors of Protestant hymns. By the late sixteenth and early seventeenth centuries the sway of the Renaissance, mixed with elements of early Baroque, was reestablished thanks to the musical activities of Catholic institutions in general and the Ljubljana Jesuit theater in particular. A large number of late Renaissance composers emerged, including Daniel Lagkhner (d. ca. 1607) and Gabriel Plavec (Plautzius, d. 1642). Outstanding among them was Izak Poš (Poschius), composer of Latin motets and monodic songs, as well as a master of the variational suite.

Baroque and Counter Reformation, 1620–1740

THE MAGYARS

Probably the most representative cultural leader of the transition period to Baroque culture was Péter Pázmány (1570–1637), the converted Calvinist who became a cardinal and primate of Hungary. This truly enlightened prince of the church, an outstanding prose writer and translator of theological literature, was also the founder of the Jesuit University of Trnava (Nagyszombat), which under Empress Maria Theresa was transfered to Buda.

The truly outstanding epic and lyric poet Count Nikola Zrinski (Miklós Zrínyi) (1620–64), the scion of a Croatian family linked to the heroic traditions of Hungarian history, and János Czere of Apácza (1625–59), a scholar of Calvinist stock and compiler of an encyclopedia of decidedly West European leaning, both definitely belonged to the Baroque era. István Gyöngyösi (1629–1704), likewise a noble and a Protestant convert to Catholicism, wrote elegant allegorical love epics in which the destiny of princes and mythological gods so typical of the Western Baroque style is freely interwoven. More interesting today are probably the songs of the *kurucok*, the freedom fighters among the peasants against Habsburg rule in the late seventeenth and early eighteenth centuries.

The Turkish occupation impeded if not blocked the development of fine arts; but after the reconquest of Buda by the Habsburg armies in 1686, Hungarian architecture evolved in line with developments in the Bohemian and Austrian Lands to the northwest and west of Hungary. Numerous town palaces in Buda and castles of the aristocracy in particular in western Hungary illustrate this development. In Hungary, as well as in western parts of the monarchy, both fine arts and music advanced under ecclesiastic and princely-aristocratic sponsorship.

THE CZECHS

After the battle of the White Mountain, Czech literature, rooted in Humanism and the Reformation, continued only in exile. Its outstanding representative, not entirely untouched by the Baroque exuberance, was Jan Amos Komenský (1592–1670), whose advanced educational theories made him world famous. In the Bohemian Lands, the Counter Reformation style of Baroque was abruptly introduced and cultivated mainly by the Jesuits. A few Jesuit poets in the seventeenth century achieved artistic distinction, especially Bedřich Bridel (1619–80) in his mystical lyrics, such as *Co Bůh? Člověk?*, and Felix Kadlický (1613–75) in his bucolic verses inspired by the German poet Friedrich Spee von Langenfeld. The preeminent figure in the literature of the Czech Counter Reformation, however, was the Jesuit Bohuslav Balbín (1621–88). Although writing his historical and geographic works in Latin, he deplored the decline of Czech language and culture after 1620. From the end of the seventeenth to the mid-eighteenth century, the demise of an educated reading public, in fact, caused a descent of Czech-language literature to the level of simplistic sermons, legends, and religious songs.

The Baroque style was introduced in architecture with the same abruptness as in literature. By the mid-seventeenth century the north Italian influence was reflected in imposing structures including the Clementinum College and the Czernin Palace, both in Prague. After mid-century the Roman style of Baroque prevailed, represented chiefly by the work of Giovanni Batista Mathey, architect in Prague of the Troja Palace and Saint Francis Church. Finally, the radical Baroque with its exuberant ornateness penetrated Bohemia by the end of the seventeenth century through Austria and southern Germany. It climaxed in the works of Christoph Dientzenhofer (ca. 1655–1722) and his son Kilian Ignaz (1689–1751), particularly in their joint masterpiece, Saint Nicholas Church in the Lesser Town of Prague. Simultaneously, Baroque sculpture attained its high point in two contrasting interpretations: the earthly realistic, of Ferdinand Maximilian Brokoff (1688–1731), and the otherworldly ecstatic, of Matthias Bernard Braun (1684–1738).

In painting, the break with past tradition was less abrupt. The leading painter in the mid-seventeenth century, Karel Škréta (1610–74), was of Czech origin, and although trained in the Italian Baroque style, he avoided the theatrical tendency and his work resembled the sobriety of Rembrandt. His tradition was continued by Petr Brandl (1668–1735), an outstanding portraitist, and Václav Reiner (1689–1743), the painter of monumental ceiling frescoes in the new Baroque churches and palaces. Subsequently, Norbert Grund (1717–67) excelled in the secularized Rococo painting.

The main expression of Baroque music in Bohemia in the seventeenth century was the ecclesiastical song with polyphony replaced by homophony and stress placed on the intelligibility of the lyrics. A notable composer of Czech religious songs was Adam Michna z Otradovic (1600–1674). The end of the century saw a revival of musical activity on noble estates, disrupted by the Thirty Years' War. Instrumental music predominated, and Czech composers contributed to its evolution. The development of counterpoint culminated in the work of Matěj Černohorský (1684–1742), whose influence reached abroad to touch Christoph Willibald Gluck and Guiseppe Tartini. Elements of the sonata were perfected by František V. Míča (1694–1744). The sonata form was further developed by another Czech composer, Jan Václav Stamic (1717–57), a member of the Mannheim school, to become in turn the foundation of classical symphony.

THE SLOVAKS

The transition to the Baroque style in literature was less sudden in Slovakia than in the Bohemian Lands. The Humanist approach endured well into the seventeenth century in the Protestant schools, particularly the *lyceum* in Prešov; but even so, the excited emotionalism and religiosity typical of the Baroque gradually prevailed in literature. Among the poets, Andrej Lucae (1596–ca. 1673) used his chiliastic prophecies as vehicles for criticizing social conditions, Ján Milochovský (ca. 1630–84) applied mostly religious criteria to depict the virtues of the ideal sovereign, and Štefan Pilárik (1615–93) expatiated on his sufferings in Turkish captivity.[4] Of the two most distinguished prose writers of the Slovak Baroque, Daniel Krman (1663–1740), a Lutheran leader, pro-

---

4. The tribulations of the Protestants' religious exile are described by Tobiáš Masník (1640–97) and Ján Simonides (1648–1708).

duced a travel memoir of Poland and western Russia as his major work, while the Jesuit Samuel Timon (1675–1736) has been compared to Balbín for his historically rooted defense of Slovak rights in Hungary.

The Renaissance influence persisted in the secular architecture of Slovakia in the seventeenth century. It was evident in the burghers' houses in towns such as Kremnica and Banská Štiavnica, as well as in the noble mansions of the countryside. A distinct Renaissance style evolved in eastern Slovakia.[5] The Baroque did appear early in ecclesiastical architecture, especially in the university church of Trnava built by Italian masters in 1629–37, as well as in the reconstruction of the Pozsony castle in 1635. It prevailed entirely in the first half of the eighteenth century, without, however, reaching the same vigor as in the Austrian or Bohemian Lands. Except for the churches and palaces of Pozsony, the architectural imprint of the Baroque was relatively weak in towns typically in economic decline during this period. On the other hand, a number of notable Baroque castles and monastic churches appeared in the countryside.[6] Painting and sculpture languished during the seventeenth century, although two artists from Slovakia did achieve fame abroad as portrait painters, Ján Kupecký (1667–1740) in Germany and Jakub Bohdan (b. 1660) in England.[7]

The Baroque period further inspired the cultivation of religious songs. A Protestant hymnal, *Cithara Sanctorum*, compiled by a Czech émigré, Jiří Třanovský, and a Catholic one, *Cantus Catholici*, prepared by Benedikt Szölösi, were published respectively in 1636 in Levoča and in 1655 in Trnava. The continuing tradition of historical songs drew its themes from the Thirty Years' War, the Turkish wars (for instance, the fall of Nové Zámky in 1663), and the Rákóczi rebellion. While the art music had declined in the economically depressed towns by the early eighteenth century, it flourished on noble estates. The enduring impact of folk music resulted in a new musical form, the folk pastorale, produced by composers such as Juraj Paulín Bajan (1721–90).[8]

THE CROATS

The Counter Reformation stimulated literary activity in Habsburg-ruled Croatia. The initially mediocre results were embodied in the publication of legends, sermons, and didactic pieces by early Baroque writ-

---

5. The castles of Kežmarok and Fričovce exhibited this style most clearly.
6. Especially the castles of Továrniki, Bernolákovo, Biela, and Holíč.
7. At the height of the Baroque in 1728–39 the renowned Viennese artist Rafael Donner produced several masterpieces in Pozsony, especially the statue of Saint Martin in the cathedral.
8. The interest in folk music was also reflected in the appearance of the first manuscript collections of folk songs in the late seventeenth and early eighteenth centuries.

ers.[9] Contributions of a higher order were made to Croatian secular lyrical and epical poetry by the famous aristocrats Petar Zrinski (1621–71) and Fran Krsto Frankopan (1643–71). The former produced a translation of his brother Nikola's Magyar work *Adriai tengernek Syrenaia*; Frankopan wrote a collection of love poems in the Italian style mediated through Vienna. The first professional writer in Croatia, Pavao Ritter Vitezović (ca. 1650–1713), was a weak poet, but notable as a historian and a linguist. The Baroque literary tradition in Habsburg Croatia culminated in the poetical depictions of nature by Antun Kanižlić (1699–1777) of Požega, whose works echoed the Dubrovnik school, particularly Djurdjević.

The Dubrovnik school continued the poetical tradition of Dalmatia in the Baroque period. It was represented first and foremost by Ivan Gundulić (ca. 1589–1639), famous for his religious and mythological poems and dramas, then by the Anacreontic poet Ivan Bunić (1591–1658), and by Junije Palmotić (1607–57), author of melodramas reminiscent of Ovid, Vergil, Ariosto, and Tasso. Ignjat Djurdjević (1675–1737) gained fame for his eclogues and erotic lyrics of the late Baroque.

Unlike the Renaissance, the Baroque left a strong imprint on the art and architecture of Habsburg Croatia. The new style became manifest in the Jesuit churches of Zagreb and Varaždin as early as the first half of the seventeenth century, and in the Franciscan churches of Samobor, Zagreb, and Varaždin soon thereafter. Other older churches, including the Zagreb cathedral, acquired Baroque decorations. While early artists usually came from Slovenia, a native, Bernard Bobić, produced impressive altar paintings in the 1690s. By the early eighteenth century, with the recession of the Turkish threat, Croatian nobles were erecting Baroque castles and palaces (for instance, the Oršić-Rauchs in Zagreb, the Patačićs and the Draškovićs in Varaždin). Churches in the flamboyant style of the radical Baroque were built in Zagreb (Saint Francis Xavier), Daruvar, and Rijeka. The preeminent artists of the late Baroque were Ivan Ranger (1700–1753), painter of illusionist frescoes, and Francesco Robba (1698–1757), famous for his marble altars in the churches of Zagreb and Križevci. In Dalmatia, architecture also flourished in the Baroque era after a decline in the sixteenth century. While original palaces, cathedrals, and churches were built, older ones were redecorated in the new style. Above all, Dubrovnik, during the half century after a destructive earthquake in 1667, acquired a new appearance drawing on the radical Baroque of the Roman and Venetian type.[10]

---

9. In particular, Juraj Habdelić (1609–78) and Ivan Belostenec (ca. 1594–1675), as well as Juraj Ratkaj (1612–66), who translated from Magyar.

10. Of the two outstanding Dalmatian painters, Trifun Kokolja (1661–1713) decorated local churches with frescoes and Frederik Benković (1677–1753) was active abroad in Venice, Vienna, Gorizia, and Würzburg.

In Habsburg Croatia the musical production of the Baroque period was limited mostly to church songs. The authoritative Croatian hymnal, *Cithara octochorda*, appeared in 1701. It contained Latin and Croatian hymns of unknown composers, influenced by both Gregorian chant and Croatian folk melodies. In contrast, a tradition of art music persisted in Dalmatia, thriving in the first half of the seventeenth century with Ivan Lukić (ca. 1587–1648) of Split, author of *Sacrae cantiones* (1620) with twenty-seven motets, and Vinko Jelić (born 1596), composer (in the 1620s) of three collections including sacred songs, motets, and *ricercari*. In the eighteenth century, Stjepan Spadina won fame for his violin compositions.

THE SLOVENES

While a few Slovene books had appeared under Catholic auspices, the full victory of the Counter Reformation in the 1620s, obviating the need for responses to Protestant initiatives, halted this modest program of publication for over fifty years. Only manuscripts are available in Slovene from this period—some fifty of them, including legal documents. Not until 1672 was a new Slovene book (an edition of Čandek's compilation of 1613) published by Johann Ludwig Schönleben (1618–81). Genuine Baroque literature in Slovene began belatedly with Matija Kastelec (1620–88), a canon in Novo Mesto, who in 1678–88 issued several religious books (prayers, poems, and meditations). At the turn of the century a number of sermon collections appeared, among whose authors a Capuchin monk, Janez Svetokriški (Tobija Lionelli, 1647–1714), was the most gifted literary stylist of the Slovene Baroque. Another monk, Hippolytus (Janez Gaiger, 1667–1722), was concerned with philological and pedagogical themes. By the mid-eighteenth century religious literature in Slovene (including Protestant contributions from Prekmurje) became more plentiful.

The victorious Counter Reformation intensified Italian influences on the art and architecture of the Slovene area, as revealed most markedly by the spread of stucco decorations and illusionist paintings. The Italian stimuli penetrated Slovenia with some delay, so that in the seventeenth century Slovene architecture and art were still heavily indebted to the essentially pre-Baroque mannerism. Its most striking expressions were the so-called golden altars in the churches of communities such as Crngrob, Muljava, and Suha near Škofja Loka. In certain towns, however, Jesuit presence ensured, as early as the seventeenth century, the appearance of truly Baroque structures, such as the Saint Francis Xavier Chapel in Ljubljana's Saint Jacob Church. By the early eighteenth century the Baroque style gained general acceptance, and Slovenia, moreover, gave birth to a distinct variant, the Ljubljana Baroque, synthesizing Venetian and Central European components. Its influence spread to neighboring Croatia. The principal monument of this style was the Ljubljana cathedral, designed by an Italian, Andrea Pozzo. Gregor Maček was the leading domestic architect of the Ljubljana Baroque.[11]

The Baroque style also dominated the musical life in the Slovene area from the mid-seventeenth century, promoted by the Jesuit theater, the Italian opera (first performed in Ljubljana in 1660), and subsequently by the Ljubljana musical society, Academia Philharmonicorum (1701–69). In the second half of the seventeenth century, Janez Krstnik Dolar, the Slovene composer of ballets, sonatas, and masses, became a major representative of high Baroque in European music. At the turn of the century the leading Slovene composer was Janez Jurij Hočevar (1656–1714), followed by a remarkable number of gifted artists creating oratorios, concertos, trios, cantatas, and masses.[12] The chief representative of a belated Baroque phase in Slovene music was Jakob Zupan (Suppan, 1734–1810), who composed the first Slovene opera, *Belin* (1780 or 1782).

Enlightenment, Classicism, and Romanticism, 1740–1847

THE MAGYARS

Enlightenment in Magyar Hungary reflects perhaps less the national spirit than did Renaissance and Baroque, after the ordeal and challenge of the Turkish invasions had been overcome by the early eighteenth century. The Jesuit priest, lyric poet, and playwright Ferenc Faludi (1704–79) represents well the transition period from Baroque to Enlightenment. György Bessenyei (1742–1811) was already a distinct disciple of the French Enlightenment in his prose writings and in his plays in the style of the *tragédie classique*. Sándor Kisfaludy (1772–1844), an imperial officer moved further into the spirit of classicism, which he linked to national Hungarian history, the main theme of his dramatic work. The outstanding lyrical poet of the Magyar Enlightenment was Mihály Cso-

11. Sculpture in this style was best represented by the famous Francesco Robba (1698–1757). In painting, the outstanding figure was Giulio Quaglio, decorator of the Ljubljana cathedral, who in turn influenced the native Slovene painter, France Jelovšek (1700–64). A distinctive (the so-called Styrian) style of Baroque developed in eastern Slovenia with a center in Maribor and under the influence of Graz.

12. They included Mihael Omerza (1679–1742) and Janez Krstnik Polec (Polz, 1685–1750).

konai Vitéz (1773–1805), who came from a petty burgeois milieu. His lyrics represent the political and social aspects of the Enlightenment at their best.

Romanticism was even more strongly associated with the memories evoked by Hungarian history, above all the tragic experience of the Hungarian revolution and War of Independence of 1848–49. Three men whose work is still largely alive today are the outstanding representatives of this era. The first, Mihály Vörösmarty (1800–1855), was the creator of the Hungarian national epos *Zalán's Flight* and of lyrics that gripped the hearts of Magyar patriots. In this respect he was the equal of Sándor Petőfi (1823–49), the great song writer who fell in battle during the War of Independence. János Arany (1817–82), an epic and lyric poet, was the third in this romantic trio.

Mór Jókai (1825–1904), though also closely associated with the revolutionary experience of 1848–49, spanned a much wider range of time and themes. He became quite a realistic novelist of the revolutionary era and the following period that restored the power of Magyar aristocracy and established that of an increasingly wealthy bourgeoisie.

Hungarian fine arts during that period were largely dominated by the pseudo-historic eclectic styles of the West; but in music we find Ferenc Erkel (1810–93), an original composer of national operas, and the famous Franz Liszt (1811–86), who as composer belongs as much to the Hungarian as to the German orbit.

THE CZECHS

The Enlightenment spirit was first manifest in Czech literature by attacks on the Counter Reformation view of national history. Above all, Gelasius Dobner (1719–90) embarked in the 1760s on his monumental critique of Hájek z Libočan's *Chronicle*. The next phase focused on justifying the use of the Czech language in public life. Starting with Count Franz Kinsky in 1773, these "defenses" stressed the practical utility of Czech. Rococo playfulness and Anacreontic classicism characterized the first collection of modern Czech poetry, published in 1785 by Václav Thám and his collaborators. A series of almanacs, issued by Antonín Puchmajer (1769–1820) and his literary circle between 1795 and 1814, reflected a more advanced stage of classicist poetry, containing all forms from odes to epigrams.

The first Czech romanticist works of lasting literary value were the poems of the Královédvorský and Zelenohorský manuscripts "discovered" in 1817–18 and alleged to stem from the early Middle Ages, but actually forged by Václav Hanka (1791–1861) and Josef Linda (1789–1834). The outstanding poet of Czech romanticism, František L.

Čelakovský (1799–1852), echoed in his major poetical collections Russian (1829) and Czech folk songs (1839). Prose works, both stories and dramas, of enduring interest by Josef K. Tyl (1808–56) often drew their patriotic themes from Czech history, especially the Hussite period. An exceptional literary phenomenon was the disciple of Byron and the Polish romanticists, Karel Hynek Mácha (1810–36). Despite his youth, he created—particularly in his brilliant work *Máj*—a new poetical language regarded as a model by the following generations of Czech poets.

In the Bohemian Lands the classicist trend prevailed in the arts late in the eighteenth century. In painting, a transitional figure from Baroque to classicism was the distinguished portraitist, Jan Quirin Jahn (1739–1802). Karel Postl (1769–1818) introduced the typical classicist genre of panoramic landscape painting. Sculpture found application chiefly in rather diminutive sepulchral and other monuments, fountains, and small statues. Josef Malinský (1752–1827) transcended the standard classicism in his sensitivity to the idiosyncracies of the subjects of his statues, and Václav Prachner (1784–1832) did the same in the colossal proportions of his sculptures. The classicist break with the past was most evident in architecture. The plainness of the official utilitarian style was typified by the fortress of Josefov (Josefstadt, 1778). The more aesthetic, later Empire style shaped the *Stavovské Divadlo* (1783) in Prague, and left its imprint on such fashionable spas of northwest Bohemia as Mariánské Lázně (Marienbad) and Teplice (Teplitz). After the turn of the century it penetrated smaller towns as exemplified by classicist burgher houses in Blatná.

The sway of romanticism began in the 1830s. In painting, its main representatives were Antonín Mánes (1784–1843), with his idealized portrayals of historically significant landscapes, and Josef Navrátil (1798–1865), particularly effective in his depiction of actors and dramatic scenes from everyday life. In sculpture, romanticism revived earlier historical styles, particularly the Gothic, as reflected strikingly in the setting of the Prague monument to Francis I, created in 1844–46 by Josef Max. In architecture, a parallel trend led to the Gothicization of the Old Town city hall in Prague (1838–48), and to the rebuilding of the Hluboká castle in Tudor Gothic, begun in 1841.

The outstanding representatives of Czech classicist music worked abroad, in particular Jiří A. Benda (1722–95), composer of symphonies, piano and violin pieces, and operas at the Prussian royal court, and Josef Mysliveček (1737–81), who won fame in Italy as the "il divino Boemo" for his operas of fresh melodic quality. A late classicist composer in Bohemia, Jan V. Tomášek (1774–1850), was a versatile musician, noted for his programmatic piano pieces. Romanticist music, linked with the Czech national awakening, was pioneered by composers from the milieu of patriotic school teachers, typified by Jakub Jan Ryba (1765–

1815). The ranking early romanticist composer, František Škroup (1801–62), wrote the first opera in Czech, *Dráteník* (1826), and subsequently the national anthem (1834). The interest of the romanticist generation in Czech folk songs, manifest since the 1820s, culminated in the famous three-volume collection by Karel J. Erben, published in 1842–45.

THE SLOVAKS

A precursor of the Enlightenment in Slovak literature, the Franciscan Hugolín Gavlovič (1712–87) sought to inculcate basic social and cultural concepts in the minds of simple peasants through his poetical work of 17,000 verses, *Valaská Škola* (1755). Full-fledged Enlightenment inspired Jozef I. Bajza (1755–1836) to write the first Slovak novel, *René mládenca príhodi i skúsenosťi* (1783), combining the form of a travelogue with a moral critique of social conditions, while Juráj Fándly (1750–1811) satirized the life style of mendicant monks in his *Dúverna zmlúva* (1789). Late classicism, similar in its orientation to the Czech school of Puchmajer, blossomed in the first decade of the nineteenth century in Anacreontic poetry.[13]

The spirit of patriotic romanticism first sparkled in the poetical collection *Tatranská Múza*, by Pavel J. Šafárik (1795–1861), published in 1814. In 1824–32 Ján Kollár (1793–1852) composed his masterful apotheosis of Slavdom, *Slávy dcera*. He may be considered the early champion of humanitarian Panslavism following the pattern of Herder, but fully original in his literary creation. The preeminent writer of early Slovak romanticism—sometimes called "national classicism"—was, however, Ján Hollý (1785–1849), author of monumental epic poems based on Slovak history: *Svätopluk* (1833), *Cyrilometodiana* (1835), and *Sláv* (1839). The distinguished playwright of this generation, Ján Chalúpka (1791–1871), wrote comedies in the 1830s satirizing small-town life. The later romanticists, active in the 1840s and known as the school of Štúr, preferred the subjectivist medium of lyrical poetry to the more objectivist epos or drama. Andrej Sládkovič's (1820–72) *Marína* (1845), drawing parallels between love for a woman and the motherland, became the outstanding poem of Slovak romanticism. The first Slovak author of substantial belletristic prose, Ján Kalinčiak (1822–71), drew his themes from Slovak and other Slav history.

A regional school of painting developed in Slovakia in the eastern Spiš area in the late eighteenth century. Although supported by the mostly German burghers of the local towns, it made its imprint on the Slovak national culture as well. The early representatives of the Spiš

---

13. By Juraj Palkovič (1769–1850) and Bohuslav Tablic (1769–1832).

school[14] worked in the classicist style, though still with traces of the Baroque and Rococo. Subsequently the ranking member of the school, the portraitist Jozef Czauczik (1780–1857), ranged in his style from the Empire to Biedermeier and romanticism. Several artists, who like Karol Tibely (1813–1870) made their debuts in the full-fledged Biedermeier style of the 1830s, concentrated on landscapes, especially dramatic mountain sceneries of the Tatras. Another center of painting, but of a more cosmopolitan type, was Pozsony, which, as the seat of the Hungarian diet, attracted foreign artists to paint the deputies' portraits.[15]

The development of sculpture suffered from the characteristic diminution of the decorative element in classicist architecture. The two most notable sculptors from Slovakia became primarily identified with the broader Hungarian scene, but both produced major works in the Slovak area as well. Vavrinec Dunajský (1784–1833) created still partly Baroque statues in L'ubietová and Nitra, while Štefan Ferenczy (1792–1856) designed a remarkable classicist church altar in Tisovec (1825) and a monument in Dolná Krupá (1838).

In the first half of the nineteenth century, a new trend, the so-called neo-Hungarian style, deeply influenced Slovak folk music. Spreading into the countryside from the towns in the 1830s, its outstanding element was the *csárdás*. Efforts to collect folk songs intensified in the romanticist period, engaging the interests of both Šafárik and Kollár in the 1820s, and culminating in Kollár's two-volume *Národné zpiewanky* issued in 1834–35. While initially only the lyrics were published, attempts to record the musical notations were also made in the 1830s (by M. Szuchányi and Vladislav Füredy). Art music focused on the ecclesiastical field. Several composers, such as František Hrdina (1793–1866), wrote music in the style of the supranational Catholic adaptation of classicism and romanticism. Major literary figures, including Kollár, Michal Hodža, and Ján Chalúpka, participated in revising the authorized Protestant hymnal (1842). Slovak art music had not yet truly developed in the secular field. Authors of famous secular songs adopted preexisting melodies for their texts.[16]

THE CROATS

Croatian literature early reflected the critical spirit of the Enlightenment in the historical writings of Adam B. Krčelić (1715–78). A

14. In particular, Jozef Lerch (fl. 1782–1804) and Ján Jakub Stunder (1759–1818).
15. The leading artists representing successively the Baroque, the Empire, and the Biedermeier styles, were Achatius G. Rähmel (1732–1810), originally from Berlin, Jan Schauff (1757–1827) from Bohemia, and Ferdinand Lütgendorff (1785–1858) from Würzburg.
16. In particular, Samo Tomášik for his *Hej Slováci* (1834) and Janko Matúška for the stirring *Nad Tatrou sa blýska* (1844), destined to become the Slovak national anthem.

Franciscan from Dalmatia, Andrija Kačić Miošić (1704–60), exemplified the Enlightenment's interest in popular education in his widely read *Razgovor ugodni*, published in Venice in 1756. The famous *Satira* of Matija Reljković (1732–98) aimed, on the other hand, at influencing the upper classes by contrasting the advanced cultural and intellectual conditions of Germany with those of Slavonia, retarded by the legacy of Turkish domination. By the early nineteenth century Zagreb had supplanted Dubrovnik as the center of Croatian literature. Tituš Brezovački (1757–1808), writing in the Croatian capital, ridiculed his compatriots' prejudices and superstitions, particularly through his comedies, and the tradition of satirical writing was continued primarily by Toma Mikloušić (1767–1833).[17]

The rise of Croatian romanticist literature in the 1830s was closely associated with the Illyrian movement and the adoption of the *Štokavian* dialect as the literary language. Before midcentury, three poets magnificently expressed the new spirit. Ivan Mažuranić (1814–90) in his epic poem *Smrt Smailage Čengijića* (1846) fused the old Dubrovnik poetical tradition with the fresh national inspiration. Stanko Vraz (1810–51), a Slovene adherent of Illyrism, enriched Croatian literature with lyrical poetry celebrating the beauties of nature. Petar Preradović (1818–72), a translator of Byron and Manzoni, as well as author of patriotic, erotic, and meditative poetry, linked the Croatian with the broader European romanticism.

In Croatian art and architecture the Baroque yielded dominance to classicism only after the turn of the eighteenth century. The leading architect of the first half of the nineteenth century, Bartol Felbinger (1785–1871), Czech by origin but settled in Zagreb since 1809, designed classicist castles and palaces. He also built smaller townhouses in Zagreb in the Biedermeier style. Among the several painters active in Dalmatia, the most notable was Rafe Martinij (1771–1856), trained in Rome as a neoclassicist. Elsewhere in Croatia, Osijek developed into an art center of local significance. The founder of modern Croatian painting, Vjekoslav Karas (1821–58), though a neoclassicist by training, worked as a portraitist in the Biedermeier style in his native Karlovac.

The prominent Croatian classicist composer, Ivan M. Jarnović (1745–1804), wrote violin duos and concertos, as well as string quartets in the Mozartian style. He also enjoyed a European reputation as a violinist. The tradition of ecclesiastical music continued in Dalmatia,[18] while in secular music Dubrovnik in particular supported the work of Luka

17. A transitional figure, the classical scholar Matija P. Katančić (1750–1825), wrote his poems *Fructus auctumnales* in the neoclassicist style but with a preromanticist flavor of folk poetry.
18. Especially in the works of Julije Bajamonti (1744–1800) and Josip Raffaelli (1767–1843).

Sorkočević (1734–89) and his son Antun (1775–1841), composers of notable orchestral and chamber music. In conjunction with the Illyrian movement a national trend developed in Croatian music, especially in Zagreb, which had become the focus of Croatia's musical as well as literary life, particularly after the founding of the Musical Society in 1829. Most of the so-called Illyrian composers, including Josip Runjanin (1821–78), author of the national anthem, *Lijepa naša domovina*, were gifted amateurs, at best trained by the choirmaster of the local cathedral. An exception, Vatroslav Lisinski (1819–54), studied in Prague as well as Zagreb. In 1846 he composed the first Croatian opera, *Ljubav i zloba*, and his second opera, *Porin*, epitomized the Illyrian ideal of art music growing out of the national culture.

THE SLOVENES

A literary group, headed by two Augustinian monks, Marko Pohlin (1735–1801), author of the *Kraynska Grammatika* (1768), and Damascen Dev (1732–86), publisher of the almanac *Pisanice*, produced the first Slovene belles-lettres in the classicist style. Appearing from 1779 to 1781, *Pisanice*, contained epigrams, elegies, idylls, odes, and didactic-moralistic pieces with verses usually in alexandrine or hexameter. Another representative of the Enlightenment, Anton T. Linhart (1756–95), wrote the first modern Slovene plays as well as a pioneering history. A transitional figure was Valentin Vodnik (1758–1819), the leading Slovene poet of his period, whose two poetical collections still exuded the spirit of the Enlightenment, but with a distinct preromanticist flavor.

Early Slovene romanticism (1810–30) was intellectually dominated by the comparative linguist of international fame Jernej Kopitar (1780–1844), director of the National Library in Vienna, who insisted on strict moralism and local ethnic themes in Slovene literature. At the same time he emphasized in his lifework the relationship connecting Catholic Slavic peoples.[19] A new, cosmopolitan orientation was propagated in 1830–48 by France Prešeren (1800–1848), the preeminent Slovene poet of the nineteenth century, and by the literary critic Matija Čop (1797–1835). Advocating the style and vistas of European romanticism, they challenged Kopitar's restriction of literature to ethnic modes and themes. Prose and drama remained relatively underdeveloped. Janez Cigler (1792–1869), the most notable prose writer, perpetuated the old-fashioned stance of the first romanticist generation. Slovene romanticist literature was weakened by the Illyrian movement, above all by the defection of the gifted Stanko Vraz (1810–51) to Croatian belles-lettres.

---

19. Under Kopitar's influence, Urban Jarnik (1784–1844) from Carinthia, as well as other regional poets, eulogized the homeland, nature, and peasant folkways.

The Baroque was replaced as the dominant style of Slovene art and architecture in the late eighteenth century by classicism and in the first half of the nineteenth by Biedermeier and romanticism. Painting, especially portraiture, flourished, while sculpture and architecture suffered from a lack of demand for ecclesiastical structures and decorations. The leading Slovene classicist painter, Franc Kavčič (1762–1828), was active mostly in Vienna. Of the prominent Slovene romanticist portraitists, Josip Tominc (1790–1866) worked in Gorizia and Trieste from the 1820s; while Matevž Langus (1792–1855), a friend of Prešeren, and after him Miha Stroj (1803–71) painted mostly in Ljubljana. This artistic trio produced portraits of the outstanding personalities of the Slovene national awakening, as well as—in the case of Stroj—of the Croatian Illyrist leaders. Major romanticist landscape painters were Anton Karinger (1829–70) and Marko Pernhart (1824–71).

Despite late dominance of the Baroque in Slovene music, new styles began to emerge in the second half ot the eighteenth century as well. As early as the 1750s a preclassicist mass by Amandus Ivančič was performed in the Ljubljana cathedral. Before the turn of the century classicism prevailed entirely, promoted by the newly established Ljubljana Philharmonic Society (1794), and represented among other composers by Janez Krstnik Novak (1756–1833) and mainly abroad, by Franc Pollini (1762–1846). By the 1820s, preromanticist elements, especially echoes of folk melodies, were penetrating ecclesiastical music. The works of Jurij Mihevec (Micheuz, Micheaux, 1805–82) exemplified a transition from classicism to romanticism, which triumphed by midcentury particularly in the patriotically flavored vocal and instrumental compositions of Jurij Fleišman (1818–74) and Miroslav Vilhar (1818–71).

Realism and Modernism, 1848–1918

THE MAGYARS

The era of prosperity between the Austro-Hungarian Compromise of 1867 and World War I was particularly in its later decades a very rich and colorful age of Magyar literature and intellectual life. It began as an economic boom period and ended in tragedy but also in some respects with great achievements.

Ferenc Molnár (1878–1952) became a playwright of international fame. Not only elegant and entertaining but truly great was the poetry of Endre Ady (1877–1919), the intellectual leader of the *Nyugat* (West) Circle among young Magyar intellectuals and artists. Strongly influenced by French intellectual life, Ady started out as an impressionist.

His lifework is in a way supplemented by that of the eminent prose writer Zsigmond Móricz (1879–1942), author of powerful social novels and a masterful autobiography. The first writings of the distinguished literary essayist Lajos Hatvany (1880–1961) and György Lukács (1885–1971) were published before the end of World War I.

The representatives of the Nagybánya painting school were Pál Szinyei Merse (1845–1920) and József Rippl-Rónai (1861–1927). Károly Kernstok (1873–1940) became the leading expressionist painter who, unlike the impressionists, appealed to reason rather than feelings. Sculpture and architecture were influenced somewhat longer by the eclectic pseudo-historic style. The ostentatious, pseudo-Gothic parliament building by Emmerich Steindl (completed 1902) on the left bank of the Danube in Budapest is an example.

In music, however, the breakthough to the modern age was spectacular. It must suffice to mention such truly great figures as Béla Bartók (1881–1945) and Zoltán Kodály (1882–1967). Bartók created a unique synthesis between folk music and the modern style. At the same time he appealed in his orchestral music to the revolutionary tradition of Magyar liberalism. Kodály, like Bartók, a musicologist deeply interested in the ethnic roots of Magyar music, also became the composer of symphonies and choral works of wide national appeal.

Creative thinkers among Magyar humanists during the later part of this era were, among others, the sociologists Oscar Jászi (1875–1957) and Bódog Somló (1873–1920) and the cultural philosopher György Lukács. The historian Bálint Hóman exercised great influence in a more traditional sense. In the sciences, particularly biology and physics, Magyar contributions did not become famous throughout the world until the period between the world wars, although much groundwork had been laid before. Perhaps the most widely known Hungarian scientist before 1918, but certainly not the only outstanding one, was the gynecologist Ignaz Semmelweis (1818–65), who first used antiseptic methods in obstetrics, a monumental achievement for which he was honored only after his death.

THE CZECHS

The 1850s were a transitional period from romanticism to realism in Czech literature. Thus, Božena Němcová (1820–62), the preeminent Czech authoress of the nineteenth century, combined romantic patriotism with a realistic—though somewhat naïve—portrayal of contemporary rural life, epitomized in her novel *Babička*. The young generation of writers in two literary almanacs, *Lada Nióla* (1855) and *Máj* (1858), protested against the traditional patriotic norms. Its leader was the journalist and writer Jan Neruda (1834–91). The 1870s and 1880s witnessed creative tensions between two literary schools: the nationally focused *ruchovci* (named after the 1868 almanac *Ruch*) and the cosmopolitan *lumírovci* (rallied around the journal *Lumír*). Among the *ruchovci*, Svatopluk Čech (1846–1908) excelled by his patriotic and socially oriented poetry, often drawing on historical themes, and Alois Jirásek (1851–1930) by his novels combining inspired narrative with meticulous knowledge of Czech history. Within the cosmopolitan trend, the chief prose writer, though also a poet and dramatist, Julius Zeyer (1841–1901) frequently used as settings for his works the East Slavic or the Romance worlds, and his writings reflected mildly the pessimistic *fin de siècle*. The major poet among the cosmopolitans, Jaroslav Vrchlický (1853–1912), a devotee of the French and the Italian Renaissance among other wide-ranging interests, greatly enriched and perfected Czech poetical modes and language.

Modernism affected Czech literature in the 1890s. Under French literary influences, Jiří Karásek ze Lvovic (1871–1951) wrote brilliant poetry and prose in the decadent style and preached aesthetic escape from life and reality. The poet Otakar Březina (1868–1929) with striking symbolism undertook mystical probings of life and the cosmos. A realistic reaction to modernism developed at the turn of the century, partly under the magisterial influence of Thomas Masaryk. Thus Josef S. Machar (1864–1942) promoted radical democracy and anticlericalism in both prose and poetry, while Viktor Dyk (1877–1931) heaped scorn on the banality of the bourgeoisie, and Karel M. Čapek-Chod (1860–1927) excelled in naturalistic dissections of the mores of the Prague commercial and industrial elites.

In the 1850s and 1860s romanticism in Czech painting culminated in Josef Mánes (1820–71), who, influenced by Moravian and Slovak folklore, idealized the countryside and regional peasant types. A realistic countercurrent was represented particularly by Karel Purkyně (1834–68),[20] inspired by contemporary French styles. In the 1870s artistic activity intensified, giving rise to the first substantial generation of Czech artists. Initially linked by common work on the decoration of the National Theater, this group was destined to dominate Czech art for the rest of the century. Among its painters a dichotomy developed, reproducing the tension between the *ruchovci* and *lumírovci* in literature. The ranking representative of the national trend, Mikuláš Aleš (1852–1913), enhanced the Mánes tradition of folklorist themes and idealized peasantry. The cosmopolitans, drawing on West European styles, included the realistic painter of historical tableaux, Václav Brožík (1851–1901), and, in landscape painting, the realist Antonín Chitussi (1847–91). In

---

20. Son of the famous physiologist, Jan Purkyně (1787–1869).

the early twentieth century, two outstanding Czech modernist painters settled in France: Alfons Mucha (1860–1939), famous for his art nouveau illustrations and posters, and František Kupka (1871–1957), a practitioner of orphism, a variant of the cubist style. Within the Bohemian Lands the preeminent painter, Antonín Slavíček (1870–1910), was a master of impressionism. Václav Levý (1820–70) in Czech sculpture played a role analogous to Mánes's in Czech painting. His works though classical in form, were imbued by the warmth of romanticist inspiration. Josef V. Myslbek (1848–1922), a member of the generation of the National Theater, and the foremost Czech sculptor of the nineteenth century, fused a variety of styles—classicist, romanticist, and even Baroque—into a highly individual expression. Jan Štursa (1880–1925), the leading Czech sculptor next to Myslbek, after experimenting with impressionism and cubism, developed his own representational style in the early twentieth century.

Historical styles dominated Czech arthitecture into the second half of the nineteenth century. The interest in the neo-Gothic was further stimulated by the work of completing the cathedral in Prague from the 1860s to the 1880s. It was, however, the neo-Renaissance which scored the greatest successes, as exemplified in Antonín Barvitius' church of Saint Wenceslas in Prague-Smíchov (1881–85). The trend culminated in the work of Josef Zítek (1832–1909), whose masterpiece, the National Theater in Prague, was constructed in 1868–81. His pupil, Josef Schulz, was notably less successful as a designer of the National Museum (1884–91). The leading architect of the early twentieth century, Jan Kotěra (1871–1923), took a major part in the development of Czech cubism, which influenced West European architecture, especially French and Dutch, just before World War I.

After languishing in the 1850s, Czech musical life revived splendidly in the following decade, largely thanks to the genius of Bedřich Smetana (1824–84), creator of Czech national music and particularly famous for his operas (above all *The Bartered Bride* and *Dalibor*) and symphonic poems (the cycle *My Fatherland*). In the 1870s began the career of another outstanding composer, Antonín Dvořák (1841–1904), whose main strength lay in nonprogrammatic music—symphonies and chamber pieces. Against the nationalism of Smetana and Dvořák, the neoromanticist Zdeněk Fibich (1850–1900) exemplified cosmopolitanism in Czech music, especially in the opera. Realism found expression in the 1890s in the operas of Josef B. Foerster (1859–1951), and particularly in the composer of *Jenůfa*, Leoš Janáček (1854–1928), who subsequently embraced more radical orientations, such as expressionism. After 1900 Vítězslav Novák (1870–1949) passed from neoromanticism to impressionism. Other outstanding modernist composers were Josef Suk (1874–1935) and the young Jaromír Weinberger (1896–1967). Altogether Czech nineteenth- and early twentieth-century music, as represented especially by Smetana, Dvořák, and Janáček, reached the highest European level.

THE SLOVAKS

Older Slovak writers, mainly Andrej Sládkovič and Samo Chalúpka, continued to adhere to romanticism during the 1850s and 1860s. At the same time, realistic prose was emerging, especially in the works of Jonáš Zaborský (1812–76) depicting social relations in the countryside, and those of Ján Kalinčiak (1822–71), who—after his romanticist beginnings of the 1840s—adopted a realistic orientation, particularly in his social novel *Reštavrácia* (1859). Linking national with social motives, the realistic trend matured in the last third of the nineteenth century, culminating in the poetry of Pavel Országh Hviezdoslav (1849–1921) and the prose of Martin Kukučín (1860–1928). The twentieth century opened with the rise of modernism and the establishment of its own literary journal, *Prúdy*, in 1910. While the novelist Janko Jesenský (1874–1945) initially belonged to this group, Slovak modernism climaxed in the symbolist poetry of Ivan Krasko (1876–1958) and Vladimír Roy (1885–1936). Realism received fresh impetus before World War I from the works of Jozef Gregor Tajovský (1874–1940), who sharpened the element of social criticism by his concern with both rural and urban poverty.

In the 1850s the careers began of the first painters in the Slovak national style, Jozef B. Klemens (1817–83) and Peter Bohúň (1822–79). Both were trained in Prague and excelled more in portraiture than in landscape painting. Similarly a national style of sculpture emerged in the works of Ladislav Dunajský (1822–1904), offering—traces of classicism notwithstanding—largely realistic depictions. In the last third of the nineteenth century, Dominik Skutecký (1849–1921) and Ladislav Medňanský (1852–1919) focused on images of the local countryside and peasant folklore, but without a notable national inspiration. An overt striving for nationalism in art resumed in the 1890s, particularly with the figural paintings of Jozef Hanula (1863–1944) and the landscapes (mostly eastern Slovak) of Ľudevít Čordák (1864–1937). After the turn of the century, modernism was represented especially by the impressionist painter Peter J. Kern (1881–1963) and by Gustav Mallý (1879–1952), who from impressionist beginnings progressed to expressionism. In architecture, the talented Dušan Jurkovič (1868–1947) strove for a style using elements of Moravian and Slovak folk architecture.

The quickening of Slovak national life in the 1860s also revived musical activity, and minor composers produced nationalistic, often militant, songs.[21] A number of choral societies sprang up in the following decade, and their needs stimulated other composers, especially Štefan Fajnor (1844–1909), to adapt folk tunes and set Slovak poems to song in a folk style.

Also in the 1870s Ján Levoslav Bella (1843–1936) made the most promising start at creating original art music, both orchestral and chamber, with a national Slovak color. His emigration to Transylvania in 1881, however, severed his rapport with the Slovak national milieu. Thus, into the early twentieth century, Slovak national composers mainly supplied repertoires for the choral societies, and to some extent for churches. Among these patriotic artists was Viliam Figuš-Bystrý (1875–1937), who composed the first Slovak opera on the theme of Sládkovič's poem *Detvan*.[22]

THE CROATS

Romanticism endured in Croatian literature well into the second half of the nineteenth century. Under the Neo-Absolutism of the 1850s, several authors attempted to maintain the tradition of the Illyrian movement without, however, matching the brilliance of the previous decade. The most notable among them was Mirko Bogović (1816–93), a poet, playwright, and originator of the Croatian historical short story.[23] The freer atmosphere of the 1860s, and 1870s and the foundation of new cultural institutions—above all, the Yugoslav Academy (1867) and the Zagreb University (1874)—helped to intensify literary development, which became dominated by August Šenoa (1838–81), the author of perhaps the best historical and social novels of the century. An outstanding literary critic, he was also editor of the literary journal *Vijenac*, established in 1869.

During the fifteen years after Šenoa's death (1881–95), Croatian literature reached a state of maturity with not only a proliferation of writers but also an integration of literary efforts in the various parts of the Croatian territory into a single national literature. The dominant literary trend was realism, to which Šenoa's own work provided a transition from romanticism. Contemporary social problems were treated most successfully in the novels of Ante Kovačić (1854–89) and Vjenceslav Novak (1859–1905). Although prose overshadowed poetry, the realist period nevertheless produced in Silvije Strahimir Kranjčević (1865–1908) the most significant Croatian poet since Mažuranić.

---

21. A representative example of this genre is M. Chrástek's *Veniec národných piesní slovenských* (1863).

22. In this period, not Slovak but foreign composers—Vítězslav Novák and Béla Bartók—used Slovak folk melodies to inspire advanced forms of art music.

23. The career of the first major Croatian humorist writer, Janko Jurković (1827–1889), also began in this period.

Supplanting realism in the mid-1890s, the modernist movement in literature was particularly receptive to external stimuli, from both West European and Slavic countires. The Croatian *Moderna* encompassed a purely aesthetic (*l'art pour l'art*) trend, led by Milivoj Dežman-Ivanov (1873–1940), and a socially oriented current, indebted philosophically to Thomas Masaryk and championed by Milan Marjanović (1879–1955). Poetry once more became the leading medium of literary expression. Milan Begović (1876–1948) in a way epitomized in his *Knjiga Boccadoro* (1900) the new poetry, with its frank eroticism, arcadian perception of nature, and revolt against social conventions. Another important poet, Vladimir Vidrić (1875–1909), cast his essentially Dionysian inspiration into an externally classical mold. Croatian drama at last reached the highest artistic levels in the works of Ivo Vojnović (1857–1929), reflecting the influence of Ibsen, Maeterlinck, and, to some extent, D'Annunzio, especially in the masterpiece *Dubrovačka Trilogija*. The outstanding modernist prose writer, Antun G. Matoš (1873–1914), noted also for his brillant impressionist criticism, inherited Šenoa's mantle as the leading literary figure of Zagreb.

During the second half of the nineteenth century, Croatian artistic life—like literature and music earlier—increasingly centered in Zagreb. Though usually well trained abroad (in Italy, Germany, or Austria), the painters of this period were thwarted in their development by the mediocre artistic tastes at home. Thus the talented Nikola Mašić (1852–1902) was constrained to produce sterile academic tableaux with pseudo-folkloristic themes. The first notable sculptor of modern Croatia, Ivan Rendić (1849–1923), was trained in Italy, where academic realism had replaced the earlier classicism. After the turn of the century, modernist styles at least prevailed over formalistic academism. Painting was enriched by the art nouveau style of Mirko Rački (1879–) and the lyrical impressionism of Emanuel Vidović (1872–1953). Josip Račić (1885–1908) and Miroslav Kraljević (1885–1913) wished to reorient Croatian art from Vienna and Munich to Paris.[24] Destined for international fame, Ivan Meštrović (1883–1962) adhered to the nationalistic Medulić group, which sought sculptural subjects in national legends. The generation of artists maturing just before World War I, including Jerolim Miše (1890–1970), embraced the avant-garde currents of Europe from cubism to German expressionism.

Croatian architecture during the second half of the nineteenth century typically turned to the historical styles. The ranking architect, Hermann Bollé (1845–1926), undertook stylistic "purification" of older ed-

---

24. The influence of the Munich art school, however, was perpetuated above all by the postimpressionist painter and art critic Vladimir Becić (1886–1954).

ifices—among others, a re-gothicization of the Zagreb cathedral. In the early twentieth century, Viktor Kovačić (1874–1924) pioneered modernism in architecture.

After a decline dating to the era of Bach absolutism, musical life revived in Croatia in the 1870s, largely thanks to the vigorous leadership of Ivan Zajc (1831–1914), composer of operas and other vocal and instrumental music, who became director of the Musical Society's school in Zagreb in 1870. Trained in Italy and influenced by Verdi, he oriented other Croatian composers to his cosmopolitan or eclectic style. An outstanding member of this group, Djuro Eisenhuth (1841–91), was noted for his operas and short vocal pieces. Zajc's internationalism evoked a nationalist countercurrent in the early twentieth century. A transitional figure between cosmopolitanism and nationalism was Blagoje Bersa (1873–1934), whose exceptional talent raised Croatian instrumental music to the highest European standards. The national trend in Croatian music was pioneered by Antun Dobronić (1878–1955) in his operas and ballets, as well as chamber and vocal compositions.

THE SLOVENES

The task of national awakening continued to dominate the themes of Slovene literature from the 1850s through the 1870s. During this phase of "patriotic realism" the geographic focus of literary activity was not Ljubljana but first Klagenfurt, around the periodical *Glasnik slovenskega slovstva* (1854, 1858–68), and then Vienna, where the journal *Zvon* (1870, 1876–80) appeared. The editor of *Zvon*, Josip Stritar (1836–1923), was also a major poet. Among other writers of this era, Fran Levstik (1831–87), an outstanding belletrist and literary critic, looked toward the Slovene countryside for both literary themes and linguistic purity; while the Young Slovene leader, Josip Jurčič (1844–81), also an unusually versatile author, developed historical, folkloristic, and social themes in Slovene prose.

Slovene literature reached the stage of "critical realism" in the 1880s and 1890s, when the pursuit of national objectives was intertwined with social criticism. Such contemporary phenomena as the impact of capitalism on the peasantry and petty bourgeoisie and the confrontation between liberalism and clericalism were treated effectively in the novels of Janko Kersnik (1852–97) and Ivan Tavčar (1851–1923), also a prominent liberal politician. The leading literary journal from 1881, *Ljubljanski Zvon*, was guided by the author and literary theorist Fran Celestin (1843–95), who, affected by Russian realism, advanced the most cogent case for a social function of literature. Anton Aškerc (1856–1912) was the principal lyrical, epic, and dramatic poet in this period.

Opening Slovene literature to European-wide influences, the modernist era started in the mid-1890s when the control of *Ljubljanski Zvon* was assumed by a generation of young authors, initially devoted to naturalism. The brief naturalist phase, epitomized by the novel *V krvi* (1896) by Fran Govekar (1871–1949), was terminated by the younger generation's turn to decadence and symbolism under the spell of Baudelaire, Verlaine, and Maeterlinck. The transition was marked by the appearance in 1899 of Ivan Cankar's (1876–1918) *Erotika* and Oton Župančič's (1878–1949) *Čaša opojnosti*. Cankar during his literary career combined a radical subjectivism of artistic vision with a revolutionary and socialist faith. Župančič, a master of dynamic rhythm and metaphor, was to pass from his initial decadent preoccupation with sensualism to the earnest search for a purpose in human, social, and national existence.

While Slovene portraitists and landscape painters espoused romanticism into the third quarter of the nineteenth century, the seminal figure of Slovene art in Ljubljana was Janez Wolf (1825–84). He instructed the brothers Janez (1850–89) and Jurij Šubic (1855–90), both of whom subsequently won recognition in Austria, Bohemia, and Germany. Jurij Šubic passed from his initial romanticist idealism to realism.[25] In the 1890s Anton Ažbe (1862–1905), also a pupil of Wolf's, opened an art school in Munich and helped to inspire a group of impressionist painters, including Matija Jama (1872–1947) and Rihard Jakopič (1869–1943), in whose work Slovene painting attained European standards. In the early twentieth century an artist's group, *Vesna*, based in Vienna, championed a Slovene national art, often drawing on ethnic folklore, in opposition to the European orientation of Ažbe's school.[26]

After a lengthy stagnation, Slovene sculpture revived in the 1870s. Academically trained sculptors Ivan Zajec (1869–1952) and Franc Berneker (1874–1932) worked on monuments to national heroes. Increasing construction of churches and public edifices created additional demand for sculptural ornaments.[27] The architectural renaissance of the late nineteenth century depended initially on foreign masters, mainly from Vienna and Graz. Slovene architects began to participate in the mid-1890s, particularly with the rebuilding of Ljubljana, damaged by an earthquake in 1895. The most prominent among them was Maks Fabiani (1865–1962), a practitioner of art nouveau.

Romanticism flourished in Slovene music into the 1870s. While the early romanticists had concentrated on vocal music, their successors after

---

25. Another realist painter of the second half of the nineteenth century, Ivan Franke (1841–1927), moved in the direction of a national style.
26. The group included Hinko Smrekar (1883–1942) and Maksim Gaspari (1883–).
27. Thus Alojzij Gangl (1859–1935) created the decorative sculpture for the Ljubljana opera house.

midcentury, especially Benjamin Ipavec (1829–1908), and Anton Foerster (1837–1926), turned to more ambitious genres—chamber, symphonic, and operatic music. Around the turn of the century, the Slovene Theater of the Land (in 1892) and the Slovene Philharmonic (in 1908) augmented the institutional framework of musical life. After 1880, impressionism and neoromanticism prevailed, with Risto Savin (1859–1948) excelling in the opera and ballet, and Janko Ravnik (1891–) in vocal and piano pieces. Just before World War I, Marij Kogoj (1895–1956) introduced the expressionist style.[28]

28. A second generation of modernist composers included the young pioneer of atonality and absolute chromaticism in Slovene music, Slavko Osterc (1895–1941).

CHAPTER 7

Pattern of Spiritual National
Development, 1526–1918

In the first chapter of this study we attempted to generalize what the terms "East" and "West" stand for in the history of the Habsburg lands and whether concepts of political, administrative, and cultural affiliation common to all the Eastern Habsburg lands can be established. We have succeeded only in answering the simpler one of the two questions and have defined Eastern and Western concepts based on a combination of geographic and historical factors. We have failed, however, to trace a political, social, or cultural system common to all Eastern Habsburg peoples. On the contrary, we have assumed that while at least a limited kind of unity is characeristic of the Western Habsburg lands, precisely the contrary, diversity, is the most specific feature of the Eastern lands.

In our investigation of these issues we have considered West and East in terms of collective concepts of ethnic groups—Austro-Germans and Italians on one side, and Czechs, Slovaks, Slovenes, Croats, Serbs, Poles, Ruthenians, and also the non-Slavic peoples, the Magyars and Romanians, on the other. In doing so we have considered the geographic factor to be less important than the ethnic one, with all its implications, and have consequently perceived Czechs and Slovenes as Eastern peoples. This overall approach seemed reasonable, since we first had to analyze the problems of the individual ethnic group as of primordial importance. Having done so in chapters 2 through 6, we find it suggestive to look for a comparative pattern of national development of individual ethnic groups.

To what extent have certain challenges of a political, economic, and cultural nature influenced the growing national consciousness of these

groups? These challenges—to be sure, to a remarkably varying degree—are the issues common to all the Eastern peoples. Accordingly
we propose to confront the development of each Eastern Habsburg national group with the following broad historical issues: (1) the effect of
the Reformation and Counter Reformation and, in regard to the latter,
the whole Baroque era in the cultural field; (2) the impact of the Turkish occupation of Hungary on the Eastern Habsburg peoples who suffered either directly or indirectly from this long-lasting historical experience; (3) the Enlightenment, French Revolution, and Napoleonic
wars in their direct as well as indirect influence; (4) the influence of
the reactionary Restoration period after the Napoleonic wars until the
Revolution of 1848; and (5) the era of national unification of Germany
and Italy and the following period of European imperialism, including
the great showdown in World War I.

We will proceed in the following order: first the Czechs and their
closest ethnic relations, the Slovaks; then the South Slav peoples beginning with the westernmost, the Slovenes, followed by Croats and Serbs.
Thereupon the Poles and Ruthenians will be surveyed from the time
they were incorporated into the Habsburg empire in the late eighteenth
century. The discussion of Magyars and Romanians will follow.[1]

The Czech national identity was undoubtedly greatly furthered by
the Hussite religious and social revolts. It could be maintained in substance unimpaired throughout the whole sixteenth century and, in fact,
until the battle of the White Mountain of 1620, when Czech national
consciousness was humiliated and weakened for a time but by no means
destroyed. Two factors above all others prevented the complete destruction of the Czech nation in the darkest days of its history prior to
the German occupation of 1939. First, the Turkish occupation of Hungary, which lasted well into the 1680s, raised the importance of the
Lands of the Bohemian Crown for the Habsburg empire. This became
evident when at the beginning of the eighteenth century Emperor Charles
VI had to ask for approval of the new order of succession common to
all Habsburg lands—the Pragmatic Sanction—by the Bohemian estates,
their defeat in 1620 notwithstanding. Second, as will be remembered,
the new big estate owners in Bohemia who after 1620 had taken over
the domains of the former Protestant aristocracy were German, Italian,
or Spanish soldiers of fortune of minor noble rank. Within a century,

---

1. Due consideration will, of course, have to be given to the fact that Poles and Ruthenians are fully covered in volume VII of this series. In this volume on the Eastern
Habsburg lands only the Transcarpathian Ruthenians (Carpatho-Ukrainians) who were
settled in Hungary as early as the fourteenth century, long before the union of 1526,
and the Ruthenians of Bukovina are discussed. In this context it might be suggestive to
reiterate that the Magyars from the fourteenth to the beginning of the nineteenth century
are surveyed in volume V and the Romanians in volumes V and VIII, with the exception
of those in the Bukovina, who are discussed in this volume.

they had identified their interests with those of the Lands of the Bohemian Crown and its ancient traditions as represented by the old aristocracy humiliated after 1620. This transition satisfied at least Czech
conservatives. The full reawakening of the merely dormant Czech national spirit in the cultural field was from then on not far away and
was to be developed by ever widening strata of the population.

The political evolution of the Czech people in the Habsburg empire
is more difficult to trace than the national one, inasmuch as the eminent
position that the Czechs held among the Slavs who settled in the Western part of the Habsburg empire never found expression in specific
institutions in terms of autonomous rights granted to them. The fact
that the elected representatives of the Czech people played a most important role in Austria's parliamentary life after 1867 could not serve
as a substitute for the denial of autonomous rights comparable to those
granted to the Magyars and in a more limited way to Croats and Poles.

As to matters of administration, the Maria Theresan era meant a setback for Czech political objectives, since under the empress the re-
mainders of ancient states' rights in the Bohemian Lands were reduced
to insignificance, similar to the development in the Austrian Lands.[2]
This trend continued under Joseph II and was not reversed by his and
his brother Leopold II's lesser successors. The one major agency that
during part of Maria Theresa's reign took care of the Czech domestic
administration, the Austrian (Hereditary) and Bohemian Court Chancellery, was never entrusted with a specific Czech agenda. One cannot
absolve the Czech aristocracy from a share in the responsibility for the
reduction of Bohemian—and that meant in practice Czech—national
rights. Maria Theresa's and Joseph II's to a limited extent successful
efforts to emancipate the subject peasants or tenants were nowhere as
vehemently opposed as by the great nobles in Bohemia. In this narrow
attitude they followed a tradition that preceded the Thirty Years' War.
Quite apart from their concern for undiminished property rights, protection of peasant rights by the government meant to this elite a greater
interference of Vienna in Bohemian domestic affairs.

An increasingly important role was played throughout modern Czech
history by the major share of Bohemian industry and mining. Mercantilism, not introduced in the Habsburg lands until the second half of
the seventeenth century, would have been a complete failure without
the profits from Czech manufacturing and mining. It was mainly the
relatively advanced Czech industrialization that gave Austrian mercantilism a *raison d'être*. The fact that after the eighteenth century not less

2. Concerning the concept of historicopolitical entities (*historisch-politische Individual-
itäten*), that is, political units based on a historic political affiliation or a historic traditional
but not ethnic kind of nationalism, see Robert A. Kann, *The Multinational Empire*, 1:33–
38, and the literature quoted there.

than three-fifths of all Austrian Cisleithanian industrial establishments were situated in the three Lands of the Bohemian Crown was, of course, a consideration that had great influence on Austrian relations to Hungary, particularly after 1867. The protection of Austrian industrial interests, above all the forcing of exports of Austrian manufactured goods into Hungary, was a major issue that, even in times of most bitter conflict between Czechs and Germans on nationality questions in Bohemia, tied the interests of the Czechs to those of the former Hereditary Lands.

The interrelationship between the various phases of the history of the Habsburg empire and the history of the Czech people was most conspicuous in the cultural sphere. The golden age of Czech literature in the sixteenth and early seventeenth centuries was tied to the Czech Reformation, and so was the influence of the forced Czech intellectual emigration abroad on a Western Europe governed in general by less bigotted regimes than those in the Habsburg lands. The impact of the Enlightenment on the beginnings of the Slavic Renaissance among the Czechs is perhaps more obvious than that of the Restoration period on the historism of a Palacký or the romanticism of a Kollár, Hanka, or Čelakovský. There is no question that at the time of Dobrovský's death, almost two decades before the Revolution of 1848, Czech cultural and in particular literary development had passed the stage of mere linguistic rejuvenation, which remained characteristic of the cultural development of other Slav peoples who were more impeded in their development than the Czechs.

Among the Slovaks, the national evolution in terms of fully developed political consciousness took place much later than among the Czechs, with their independent, richly structured national past. A Magyar denationalization policy that offered the educated Slovak upper classes and the rich landowners an easy and rewarding way to Magyarization, and therewith a share in the privileges of the establishment, played an important role here.

The political evolution of the Slovaks not only as a people with a national identity of their own but also with claims to autonomy came fairly close to reality only during the Revolution of 1848 and then again in 1861 at the beginning of the era of reconciliation of the imperial government with Hungary. But in no way did this affect the administration of the Slovak territory as part of the Hungarian administrative system. Political and national evolution emerged only as a force to be reckoned with during the second half of World War I, and here the main impetus for political action came from abroad, especially from the United States.

Of considerable, not yet fully explored interest is the question why the fact that Slovak territory in the sixteenth and seventeenth centuries remained essentially free from Turkish occupation did not strengthen substantially the political or economic status of this ethnic group. Its copper and silver mines certainly were of great importance to the empty Habsburg treasury. Quite apart from the fact that, at least within living memory, the Slovaks had never represented a historic-political entity of their own, the answer could be, at least in part, that during the era of Turkish occupation of the bulk of Hungary, northwestern Hungary represented Hungary as whole to the Habsburgs, and the people in these territories were to them Hungarians, not Slovaks. The reduction to the status of a minority group only commenced with the conquest of Hungary by the imperial armies at the end of the seventeenth century. Therewith the Slovaks may have missed a great political chance, which did not recur until 1918.

While it is difficult to tie Slovak destiny to the great periods of historical change in the political field, it can be done far more easily in the cultural sphere. Here, as in other young national movements, religious affiliation played a dominant role for a long time. The impact of the Protestant Reformation on the cultural progress of the Slovaks, and thereby on the development of their national consciousness, was undoubtedly great. The same held true of the influence of the linguistic movement on the full development of a separate Slovak language in the late Enlightenment. It was helped along markedly by the patronage of the Catholic Church and Catholic scholarship, while the further literary evolution during the Slavic Renaissance moved in the direction of a Protestant-inspired Czech-Slovak linguistic union movement. The ideological Panslavism of Ján Kollár, whose romanticism was typical of the Restoration era, became an important contributing factor.

The Slovaks were not settled close to the main roads of political action in the Habsburg empire. Accordingly the chief political trends of modern history reached them more slowly than they did the nations with an independent national political history within the Austro-Hungarian monarchy. But in the end these currents could not bypass them.[3]

Slovene national identity was strongly tied to the later phases of the Protestant Reformation, in the second half of the sixteenth century. The setback in the era of the Counter Reformation was typical. Rather untypical, on the other hand, was the impact of the geographic location of the Slovene people on their national destiny. If the Slovak political evolution was impeded because the territory of the nation lay off the main roads of political action, almost the reverse was true of the Slovenes. Their territory lay across the main road from Vienna to the eastern shores of the Adriatic, with the principal seaport of the empire, Trieste, close by. The small Slovene wedge between the contiguous large German and Italian language areas, both of considerable political weight,

3. On the concept of nations with and without independent political national history in the Habsburg empire see Kann, *The Multinational Empire*, 1:43–47, 359–60.

greatly impeded the further political evolution of the Slovenes. It was hindered also because the Slovene settlements were spread over four Austrian crownlands—Styria, Carinthia, Carniola, and the Littoral. Only in one of them, Carniola, did they represent an absolute national majority.[4] In none did they ever achieve autonomous rights under the Habsburg scepter.

The political evolution of the Slovenes was nonetheless furthered by the Westernizing impact of the French occupation of the best part of Slovene territory from 1809 to 1813 and then again by the Revolution of 1848, in which the Slovenes, in view of their peculiar geographic position, developed the first national program of political organization on an ethnic basis within the Habsburg empire. Unionism, the notion of the union of the South Slav peoples of the Eastern and Western parts of the Habsburg empire in one joint, political entity, was initiated by the Greek-Orthodox Serbs. It developed somewhat later among the Roman Catholic Croats, followed within a few years by the likewise Catholic Slovenes.[5] The concept was not transformed into a genuine political program within the empire until the first decade of the twentieth century. Several factors account for this: the geographic location; the Catholic conservative orientation of the Croatian nation, which for a long time shrank from closer affiliation with the Greek-Orthodox Serbs; and the considerable political concessions promised to the Slovenes by the imperial government, even though they did not materialize.

The impact of broad historical events on the cultural development of the Slovene people was striking. It runs through the first Bible translations into the vernacular language in the sixteenth century, the influence of the Enlightenment, the experience of the French occupation, the concept of the cultural union of the Catholic Slavic movement, but above all the achievements of the great Slovene linguists, especially during the late Enlightenment and the Restoration era. Their work under Jernej Kopitar's commanding guidance gave the Slovenes, their small numbers and narrow territory notwithstanding, a leading position in the nineteenth-century phase of the Slavic Renaissance.

The Croats were far more directly influenced by the great historical

4. They had, however, a 5:3 majority in one of the three administrative subdivisions of the Littoral, namely Gorizia-Gradisca, but not in the Littoral as a whole.

5. In the context of this essay, "union" means primarily either the concept of trialistic empire to replace the dualistic Austro-Hungarian one or the less popular subtrialistic concept of a political union of the three South Slav peoples within the empire but subordinated and not coordinated with the dual states of Austria-Hungary.

A union concept that would comprise all Serbs, both within and outside the Habsburg empire, evolved only in the last pre-World War I decade. It would have given the Serbs leadership in a union of such kind outside the Habsburg empire and was therefore, before the outbreak of the war, not endorsed by the majority of the Croatian and Slovene populations, although undoubtedly it had the support of the radical activists in the Slovene and Croatian political camps.

experiences beyond the borders of the Habsburg monarchy than the Slovenes and Slovaks. Their national identity was fully established at the time they joined the union of the Hereditary Lands with those of the Hungarian and Bohemian crowns in 1527. The Reformation, and consequently also the Counter Reformation, had only a rather limited influence on the Croats in early modern history, but the fact that the nation remained undivided in a religious sense had a long-range effect on its future history. Of great and immediate significance was the Turkish occupation of Magyar Hungary, which spared, however, the western, most advanced part of Croatia. The results of this were complex. The establishment of military borders on Croatian soil as early as the sixteenth century, and lasting into the second half of the nineteenth, had two effects that somehow balanced each other. The military structure of the military borders tied the Croats to the emperor, the central administration in Vienna, and to the overall military establishment. In this respect the borders impeded political evolution of the whole Croatian nation toward the advancement of its autonomy. But at the same time the tie to Vienna strengthened Croatia's position against Magyar-dominated Hungary and therewith helped to prevent the Magyarization of the country. The radical Germanization efforts of Joseph II in Hungary, which strengthened nationalist Magyar tendencies mightily, led in turn to a clash between Magyar and Croatian nationalism which remained in substance unresolved to the end of the empire. The Westernization of Croatia, even more than that of the Slovene sister nation, was furthered by the French occupation of Napoleon's Western Croatian-Slovene Illyrian Kingdom. In this respect the promoters of the Napoleonic reforms unwittingly took up a tradition that had existed prior to the union of 1527 by way of the strong influence of Venetian Renaissance culture.

The Revolution of 1848, in which Croatia was strongly identified with the imperial cause, especially the imperial military one, did not help the Croatian national evolution, since anti-Magyar tendencies in Croatia were far too strongly penetrated by reactionary conservative tendencies. This is one of the reasons why Croatia's chances to achieve equality of political status with Hungary during the era of political reconciliation of the emperor with the Magyars, from 1860 to 1867, were to be disappointed.

Nevertheless, in the Hungaro-Croatian Compromise of 1868—a union between politically unequals—Croatia achieved relatively far-reaching autonomy in domestic matters. What perhaps more than anything else drove Croatia, with its Catholic and in part imperial tradition, increasingly into the arms of the union movement was the foolish policy of some Magyar or at least Magyar-selected governors (*bani*) that frequently favored the Serb radical minority against the Croatian majority.

The objective was obviously to weaken the union movement by driving a wedge between Croats and Serbs, of whom, up to the last years before the outbreak of World War I, the former appeared more dangerous to the government in Budapest than the Serb minority. The result of this policy was the reverse of what the Magyars had aspired to. In opposition to a divisive imperial policy, South Slav unionism grew steadily in strength, and the Serbs in Hungary proper and in Croatia, in close alliance with the Serbian government across the Danube and Sava rivers, assumed a clearly anti-Habsburg leadership of the union movement.

Was this development inevitable? In matters cultural, leaders of the Slavic Renaissance in Croatia, above all Ljudevit Gaj, were decidedly more proimperial than the leaders of the Slavic Renaissance among most other Slavic peoples in the Habsburg empire, bar the Slovenes. An arrangement with Bishop Josip Strossmayer, the great champion of South Slav cultural unionism under Croatian leadership in the second half of the nineteenth century, was certainly feasible. Even the movement generally referred to as the Croatian "Moderna" had no anti-Habsburg empire thrust. Yet Magyar intolerance alone could merely accelerate the disintegration process of the empire. It hardly changed the fact that national irredentists always prefer to rally around a brand of political activism centered abroad rather than at home. Such situations may in general be remedied only gradually, after a unification process has reached its goal. The Croatian case confirms this historical experience.

As to the most active element in this process, namely the Serbs, they achieved their political success in the Habsburg empire from a position of weakness—or perhaps more correctly, seeming weakness—than from strength. The limited territorial and cultural autonomy granted by Leopold I to the Hungarian Serbs meant to the imperial establishment first a genuine defense against the spirit of Magyar insurgency and in later generation a bulwark against overbearing aspirations of a Magyar-dominated Hungary. As noted, the intermittent Magyar support of the Serbs versus the Croats in Croatia-Slavonia, a typical *divide et impera* policy, was likewise meant to weaken the seemingly stronger national group by supporting the weaker one. The Serb position was greatly enhanced by the proclamation of the constitution of 1910 in Bosnia-Herzegovina, where the Serbs represented a relative majority of the population, although by that time the concept of a South Slav unionism within the confines of the Habsburg empire could be considered outdated. Serb national consciousness had preceded the union of 1526–27. It survived the empire.

In the Serb case this was more obvious in the political than in the cultural field. Largely owing to their limited numbers, their scattered settlements, and the relatively restricted range of Greek-Orthodoxy, the

Serbs (prior to the annexation of Bosnia-Herzevogina in 1908) did not play an important cultural role in the empire during the late Baroque era or in the Enlightenment. Romantic trends in the Slavic Renaissance had considerable influence, however, on the Serbs during the Restoration period. This influence continued to increase after 1848. Yet the successful aspirations of the Serbs to leadership in the South Slav union movement were anchored in political and not in cultural factors.

Two predominant issues determined the position of the Polish people within the Habsburg empire. The bulk of Polish territory under Habsburg rule was incorporated in 1772 as part of a nation ravaged by political disintegration from within and subject to attack from the outside. Polish national consciousness after the partitions could, however, never be questioned. The share of the Polish inheritance that became part of the Habsburg empire, namely Galicia, though with changing boundaries between 1772 and 1815, was never part of the cultural, historical, and subsequently industrial heartland of Poland. The one exception to this general statement was the republic of Cracow. Yet, an independent city state between 1815 and 1846, Cracow lost some of its significance as a cultural center after its incorporation into Austria.

The Poles had gained major, though only temporary economic concessions after their incorporation into the Habsburg empire during the reigns of Maria Theresa and Francis I (II). They also secured a measure of administrative autonomy in 1868, only a year after the conclusion of the Austro-Hungarian Compromise. In return, their representatives, the members of the middle and noble upper middle class, in substance the historic *Szlachta,* supported the Austrian Cisleithanian government to which they had been quite hostile prior to the Revolution of 1848. The Poles did so, to be sure, only as long as they believed the Habsburg empire was a viable state organization genuinely concerned with their interests. That meant roughly until the proclamation of a truncated Polish vassal state of the Central Powers in November 1916 and the subsequent steady decline of Austria's chances for survival.

The great cultural evolution of the Poles in the first decades of the nineteenth century occurred in substance outside the Habsburg monarchy, although it naturally had repercussions on Polish national feelings within the empire. It seems decisive that Polish allegiance to the Habsburgs rested on the fact that for almost a century, beginning with the suppression of the 1830–31 risings in Congress Poland and the concurrent Germanization policy in the east of Prussia, the Poles under Habsburg rule enjoyed increasingly a far better position than those in Prussia or Russia. The outlook for restoration of a genuine, free Poland, very different from the puppet state constituted by the Central Powers in the fall of 1916, made these previous comparative considerations completely irrelevant.

The Ruthenian national evolution in Austria was decidedly anchored in religious and linguistic movements. While the Transcarpathian Ruthenians in northern Hungary, settled there since late medieval times, had no opportunity to develop a national program of their own prior to the Revolution of 1848, the bulk of the Habsburg Ruthenian population, who came under the empire's rule after the partitions of Poland, could rely on government support of their religious and in some respects also their cultural wishes. Support of the Catholic Uniat Church against Greek Orthodoxy was in the interest of the government's anti-Panslavist policy but was also meant to be a check on Polish nationalist tendencies focused on the restoration of the Polish kingdom. The Ruthenian linguistic reform movement which followed the religious policy of the Enlightenment in the Restoration era was, however, at cross purposes with the government's ecclesiastic policy. The Ruthenians, whether liberal or conservative, rejected the notion agreeable to the government and to the Poles that the Cyrillic alphabet should be replaced by the Latin, and the liberals moreover considered the allegiance to Church Slavonic anachronistic.

By the time of the Slav Congress of June 1848 in Prague, the Ruthenians had developed a definite program for administrative separation of predominantly Ruthenian Eastern Galicia from Polish Western and Central Galicia. While the Poles remained masters in the crownland, some concessions in the field of language rights were eventually made to the Ruthenians. By 1907 their position in the *Reichsrat* in Vienna was considerably strengthened by the introduction of general, equal franchise and a distribution of parliamentary seats more favorable to them. Introduction of a new crownland constitution in the Bukovina, in 1910, further enhanced the Ruthenian position, and the introduction of a genuine national compromise between Poles and Ruthenians in Galicia was ready for enactment in 1914 when the outbreak of the war voided the fruition of all Ruthenian efforts.

Yet concessions came too late. The rift in Ruthenian political party life between conservatives and liberals, which roughly until the Slavic Congress of 1867 in Moscow was focused on domestic matters, gradually shifted to the sphere of foreign policy. The conservative Old Ruthenians continued not only to toe the Greek-Orthodox line, they also supported a pro-Russian, in part outright irredentist, foreign policy, whereas the majority of the more liberal Young Ruthenians took a no less irredentist pro-Ukrainian position that stood for union with their conationals across the Russian border.

Altogether it seems reasonable to conclude that the Ruthenian national and political evolution in the Habsburg empire—originally kindled by religious and linguistic issues, as is typical of many long-suppressed groups—revealed a great deal of consistency. The demands for autonomous political organization of the Austrian Ruthenians were initiated during the Enlightenment, articulated during the Restoration period, passionately raised in 1848, and continuously pressed forward in the period of national unification, though solved only after the dissolution of the empire.

From the standpoint of political status, the Magyars were the leading national group in the Eastern half of the Habsburg monarchy and, according to some historians, after 1867 the leading group in the whole empire. Their political evolution preceded by far the union of 1526. It suffered no major setback by the Reformation in Turkish-occupied Central Hungary and none in Turkish-controlled eastern Hungary including Transylvania. Magyar Hungary was all the more severely hurt by the Turkish occupation in socioeconomic respects, and in the cultural orbit as well by the Counter Reformation after liberation of Hungary by the imperial armies at the end of the seventeenth century. No question, the consequences of the Turkish occupation for the Magyars from the standpoint of isolation from Central and Western Europe were even more severe than the effects of the defeat of 1620 were for the Czechs. On the other hand, the restoration of Hungary in most—though not in all—respects to the status of 1526–27 by the peace of Szatmár in 1711 was far more successful than that of Bohemia.[6] Ecological influences, especially the lesser influence of the Germans in Hungary than in the Lands of the Bohemian Crown, may in part account for this. Another point in question was the Hungarian constitutional and administrative system. The estates and county institutions and the judicial system had proved to be stronger and more adjustable to preservation in the interest of the governing class than similar institutions in the Lands of the Bohemian Crown. Thus, while the Bohemian and Hungarian cases are comparable in regard to the effect of cultural delay brought about by external pressure, the institutional development differed. With the radical restriction of the estates system in the Maria Theresan and Josephin reform era, the Czechs lost further remnants of their political identity, although the simultaneous rise of their national consciousness compensated for this decline. Magyar-Hungarian political and national evolution survived in essence unchanged until 1849. After the Neo-Absolutist era, with its suppression of the Magyar revolutionary spirit of 1848–49, the Magyars' special status within the Habsburg empire reemerged enhanced and remained so unchanged during the entire era of the Compromise from 1867 to 1918; while the Czechs never, until 1918, regained fully what they had lost three centuries before.

6. The hereditary succession of the Habsburg dynasty had to be acknowledged and the nobility's right to armed resistance against violations of the constitution by the king had to be dropped according to the provisions of the diet (*Reichstag*) of Pozsony of 1687–88.

Economic interests, very naturally, played an important part in the process of forced Czech amalgamation with Austrian demands. As noted, the advanced industrialization of the Czechs did not conflict with the basic economic policies of Cisleithanian Austria. Czech manufactured and mining products, which had little competition within the borders of the Habsburg lands were an unchallengeable asset to Austria's economy. Agriculture in the Western Habsburg domains helped to keep production costs down.

The situation was different with Hungary. Tariffs between the Habsburg lands outside of Hungary had steadily declined ever since Maria Theresa's reign. Those between Hungary and the other Habsburg domains remained substantially unaffected by the new trend to more liberal trade policies. They were, however, not of unlimited duration. In the Neo-Absolutist era of Hungary's complete subjugation the customs lines between East and West were abolished and not reimposed again under the terms of the Austro-Hungarian Compromise of 1867. Now the customs union had to be renegotiated every ten years in protracted and cumbersome negotiations. As Austrian historians see it, the continuation of the customs union had to be paid for by further Austrian political concessions to the East. Yet the Hungarian position as represented by the Magyar government had its point too. By the mid-nineteenth century, Hungary had gradually begun to change from an—except for the mining industry—almost purely agrarian system into one in which industrialization began to gain gradually a significant share. To be sure, it was, to the end of the empire, not equal to the Austrian system. By and large in the Austrian economy, agriculture was still prevalent but industrialization was substantial. In Hungary the situation was not the reverse, as some experts see it; the difference was merely one of degree. Agriculture was dominant, but industrialization was not negligible and was steadily on the rise. It is thus understandable that the Hungarian government rejected Austrian wishes for a protective tariff policy that would have helped Austrian industry but not the weaker Hungarian industry. Hungary, on the other hand, was interested in a free trade policy that would have helped large agricultural exports. Yet the Hungarian government's simultaneous insistence on high protective tariffs against the import of Serbian agricultural products served the demands of the aristocratic Magyar large latifundia owners.

This aggravated not only the political crisis in relation to the Balkans but it ran counter to the interests of the major part of the Hungarian population, including the Magyars. All things considered, a free trade policy was perhaps the one factor in the Eastern Habsburg lands to which the agrarian interests of the middle and upper middle classes of all ethnic groups, in addition to those of the small peasants, could subscribe. But the shortcomings of this policy were obvious. It did not take care of the needs of the lower classes for essential industrial goods not yet produced in the East at moderate prices, and this was all the more unfortunate since the non-Magyar ethnic groups in Hungary represented an inordinately high share of the poorer population, including unskilled industrial labor.

In the cultural sphere, the great achievements of the Hungarian Renaissance in the Corvinian era preceded the union with the Bohemian and Austrian Hereditary Lands. At the time of the flowering of Baroque culture, Magyar Hungary still suffered from the Turkish occupation. To catch up fully was impossible, but undoubtedly late Baroque, in the fine arts as well as in literature and the humanities, was important in Hungarian cultural development. Western Enlightenment had an even stronger impact on Magyar destiny. The greatest advancement of Magyar Hungarian culture, especially literature, occurred during the so-called political reform era between 1815 and 1848, when Magyar political life was less restricted than in the Hereditary Lands and culture benefited from it. Such advancement could be impeded but not stopped by the victorious counterrevolution in 1849. In fact, cultural activities helped to serve now also as a substitute for political actions suppressed by the government. Further Magyar intellectual endeavors in the age of national unification and Great Power imperialism were characterized by far-reaching Westernization. Strong indigenous and very original cultural trends came to the fore again at the turn of the century. The strength of Magyar national consciousness remained, in any case, impervious to foreign influence.

Full national consciousness developed for the Romanians in Transylvania, as well as those in the Bukovina, only against great obstacles. In the Bukovina, national evolution was impeded by Turkish rule of much longer duration than even in Hungary; in Transylvania, where the Reformation made substantial progress in the sixteenth century and where Turkish overlordship interfered very little, Romanian national development was hampered by the interests of the three-nation state of Magyars, Szekels, and Saxons (Germans), to whose rule the Romanian peasant majority was subjected. There is the further fact that— somewhat like the position of the Poles in Galicia versus those in Russian Poland—the center of Romanian cultural life was anchored in the neighboring Danubian Principalities of Moldavia and Wallachia, just outside of Habsburg territory.

At the same time, the fact that Transylvania could retain her political identity, during the era of Turkish occupation of Hungary, was of at least indirect benefit to the Romanian unfree peasant population, insofar as it preserved the political framework within which these peasants could later make their political weight felt. This time began with the establishment of the Romanian Uniat Church in Transylvania at the very end of the era of Turkish occupation, in the late seventeenth century. It received strong impetus during the reign of Joseph II, who recognized for the first time limited Romanian political rights in response to the Magyar revolutionary risings against his reforms. The practical effect of the emperor's policy was of brief duration, but the demands for full equality of the Romanians did not disappear from the program of their nationalism.

Political and national evolution could not have succeeded if it had not coincided with the linguistic movement, which, as in the case of other oppressed Eastern national groups, evolved under ecclesiastic Uniat and Orthodox leadership. It subsequently spread, of course, into secular channels, although the Greek-Orthodox Bishop Şaguna still played an important role in the history of Romanian political nationalism in the first decade after the Revolution of 1848.

In administrative matters the success of Romanian nationalism in Habsburg-dominated Hungary was nil. Autonomous rights granted to the three-nation state by the intermittent establishment of a Transylvanian Court Chancellery did not accrue to the benefit of the Romanians.[7] Only in 1861 were they finally recognized as a fourth nation with equal rights in Transylvania. Inasmuch as Transylvania merged fully with Hungary in 1867, this meant in practice no rights at all. Yet all that time the "Gleichschaltung" under Magyar dominance could no longer suppress the force of Romanian nationalism which was now clearly oriented to the new Romanian national state beyond its borders. The religious problem—Uniat association with the Habsburg empire and Orthodox with tsarist Russia—had moved into the background. The question of alignment with Russia or of continuation of the affiliation with the German-Austrian-Italian Triple Alliance represented actually only one issue: which of the two affiliations was more likely to bring about national unification? Permanent collaboration with the Habsburg empire was unacceptable as long as it meant subjection of the large majority of the Romanians to Magyar rule. Consequently the limited concessions made to Romanian nationalism in the crownland constitution of the Bukovina of 1910 were welcome but of minor practical significance.

The Romanian national movement in the Habsburg empire started on its road to fulfillment of national objectives against very great odds. On the other hand, this process was less affected and impeded by countercurrents working against the dissolution process than those operative among the other ethnic groups surveyed in this chapter.

This brief survey does not encompass the evolution of the national groups within the pattern of national groups, with or without history,

7. With interruption from the end of the seventeenth century to the 1860s.

in the framework of the Habsburg empire.[8] While such a distinction is certainly arguable in terms of the political and social evolution of the individual ethnic groups, it would be artificial to acknowledge such differentiations within an East-West scheme in which the boundaries of the various ethnic groups overlap. The Eastern national groups—Czechs, Croats, Poles, and Magyars—would in that case form a rather artificial entity together with the Western Austro-Germans and Italians as historical nations against the five remaining Eastern national groups as nations without history. No organic pattern can be traced along such lines within the context of this particular study. Common historical experiences offer indeed a more reliable guide in perceiving joint trends of development.

In this sense the Reformation represented by and large an era in which the Eastern peoples—as noted with the major exception of the Czechs and perhaps also the minor one of the Slovenes—were at a disadvantage as against the Western. This meant not so much suppression as lack of opportunity to move forward. Progress flattened out on the road from West to East. The repressive era of the Counter Reformation hurt West and East alike, although, as mentioned before, not at the same time. The belated clearance of the Turks from Hungary exposed mainly the Magyars and in part the Croats for a longer time than other ethnic groups to a series of recessive historical setbacks. Added to this may be the fact that the richly creative cultural achievements of the Baroque age, which in many ways were corollaries of the Counter Reformation, could also enter Hungary only belatedly. True, it may be held that the Reformation could prosper east of the Tisza and in particular in Transylvania during that era because the Turks had little interest in taking sides in the religious conflict. Yet preservation of the Transylvanian three-nation state at the price of further suppression of the Romanian population offered meager compensation for cultural delay in consequence of the Turkish advance.

Exceptions in isolated areas notwithstanding, the overall effect of 150 years of Turkish occupation in the East was clearly that of isolation from the West and thus delay in further progress. Neither a declining Polish kingdom nor a still predominantly eastward, or rather inward, oriented Russia could offer fully compensatory values. The Turkish advance toward the West was indeed the major factor overshadowing all others that had shaped Eastern development different from Western, although naturally not all Eastern national groups suffered equally. The fact that those who suffered most, above all the Magyars, more than made up for their fall by their later rise indicates convincingly that the

8. Kann, *The Multinational Empire,* 1:38–47, 359–60.

political effect of historical experience may not nearly be as permanent as the long-range psychological impact.

Thus, generally speaking, the unifying bond in the early modern history of the Eastern peoples of the Habsburg empire from the end of the Reformation era to the end of the Turkish occupation of Hungary was cultural delay and increasing separation from the West. Obviously this does not preclude specific supreme achievements in various fields of human activity, but they could not blunt the overall negative impact of Turkish occupation and Counter Reformation.

In regard to the Enlightenment, the era of the French Revolution, the Napoleonic wars, and the romantic aspects of the Restoration era, which all were embodied in the Slavic Renaissance, we observe two great movements flowing in the same direction. One opens the gates wide for the Western influences of the Enlightenment, classicism, and romanticism.[9] Eastern isolation from the West had indeed ended. Even more important may be the other trend: national, cultural, and—more slowly—also political evolution in the form of independent cultural and political movements among all Eastern ethnic groups and within each one individually. Ideological trends within the Slavic Renaissance and various simultaneous aspects of Panslavism undoubtedly provided rich opportunities for cross-fertilization. Nor should we forget the influence from the East during the late Enlightenment and the Restoration period. Relatively limited prior to the later part of the nineteenth century, it nevertheless became strikingly apparent in late Polish culture, including the activities of the Polish exiles in France and increasingly those from Russia proper as well.

To be sure, the characteristic feature in the context of this study is not the movement of intellectual trends from East to West. What was decisive from the nineteenth century onward was the great opportunity for creative evolution of national cultural diversity among all Eastern peoples in the Habsburg realms, including Magyars and Romanians.

It is our contention that the main achievements of the Eastern peoples became even more distinct in the era of national unification and European imperialism from 1848 to 1918. Up to that time it may be argued whether, beginning with the Enlightenment, the Eastern peoples owed more to Eastern or Western influences. It might be fair to suggest that throughout the eighteenth century Western influences were clearly more prevalent, but in the nineteenth century and particularly from the Congress of Vienna to the Revolution of 1848, Eastern influences proved to be more vigorous and continued to be so. What char-

9. See Carleton J. H. Hayes, *The Evolution of Modern Nationalism* (New York: R. Smith, 1937), pp. 13–83.

acterizes the postrevolutionary era after 1848 is indeed the phenomenon that the East, which had by now come up fully to Western standards, had more to offer to the West than vice versa. This does not imply that Eastern cultural achievements had become greater than Western ones. Comparisons of that sort are sterile. What this statement does mean is something rather different. Well into the second half of the nineteenth century the West, its literary interests in certain aspects of Slavic Renaissance notwithstanding, was self-contained. It believed that it did not need any stimuli from outside. On the other hand, the East had to be willing and was indeed eager to familiarize itself with Western values. It was a natural consequence of this attitude that the standards of the East eventually caught up with those of the West. Impressionism, expressionism, functionalism, and other new concepts appeared in the East almost at the same time as in the West. On the other hand, the familiarity of the West with the evolution of the Slavic Renaissance had not gone beyond a small intellectual elite. Only in the late nineteenth century did the West begin to comprehend that developments in the East might mean more than stimuli for a small group of aesthetic connoisseurs. The whole political, social, and in part cultural evolution and revolution heading from the East thus hit the West with ever increasing force. For better or worse, but certainly for something very new and unexpected, the East in this last historical phase of its association with the Habsburg empire offered more challenges to the West than vice versa. This was indeed a kind of common bond of the Eastern peoples within the Habsburg empire until the very moment of its inevitable disintegration.

Bibliographic Essay

Significant literature in Western languages covering the topic of this volume is far more numerous in regard to Czechs and Magyars than to Croats, Slovaks, and Slovenes. Least rewarding is the literature on Ruthenians (West Ukrainians) and Serbs within the confines of the Habsburg empire. The situation is somewhat more favorable in regard to the Romanians. However, only the Romanians in the Bukovina are within the topical range of this volume.

In any case, the items listed here offer only a small selection of the literature in Western languages on all the national groups covered in this volume. Within this selection preference has been given to relatively recent publications in English, unless the particular significance of older works justifies their inclusion.

In each section an even more selective bibliography, in Slavic languages, and in Magyar and Romanian, on the history of particular nations follows the entries in Western languages. Additional references, particularly to literature on economic history, can be found in the footnotes of this volume.

THE HABSBURG EMPIRE

General History

R. A. Kann, *A History of the Habsburg Empire, 1526–1918* (2d ed.; Berkeley and Los Angeles: University of California Press, 1977) emphasizes nationality problems including their cultural aspects. Oscar Jászi, *The Dissolution of the Habsburg Monarchy* (Chicago: University of Chicago Press, 1929) offers a somewhat controversial but brilliant analysis of the long, drawn-out dissolution process of the empire. C. A. Macartney, *The Habsburg Empire, 1790–1918* (New York: Macmillan, 1969) does not discuss foreign policy and cultural developments, but accentuates institutional aspects. Karl and Mathilde Uhlirz, *Handbuch der Geschichte Österreichs und seiner Nachbarländer Böhmen und Ungarn*, vol. 1 (2d ed.; Graz and Cologne: Böhlau, 1964), covers the history of the Habsburg lands until 1526; its chief value lies in the excellent bibliography; the other volumes are outdated. Victor-L. Tapié, *The Rise and Fall of the Habsburg Monarchy* (New York: Praeger, 1971) is particularly strong on the Baroque period and on Czech history. On early modern Habsburg history see the work by R. J. W. Evans, *The Making of the Habsburg Monarchy, 1550–1700* (Oxford: Clarendon Press, 1979), with many references to Czech and Magyar sources. Adam Wandruszka, *Das Haus Habsburg* (Freiburg and Vienna: Herder, 1978; first pub. 1956) sketches interesting character portraits of the Habsburg rulers; an English version is also available, *The House of Habsburg* (Westport, Conn.: Greenwood, 1975). Erich Zöllner, *Geschichte Österreichs* (5th ed.; Vienna: Verlag für Geschichte und Politik, 1974) offers an effective survey. A survey study on the Slavs in general may be useful in terms of this volume; see Francis Dvornik, *The Slavs in European History and Civilization* (New Brunswick, N. J.: Rutgers University Press, 1962), a comprehensive treatment of the Slavic ethnic groups from the thirteenth into the eighteenth century.

Institutional History

Adam Wandruszka and Peter Urbanitsch, eds., *Die Habsburgermonarchie, 1848–1918,* is planned in 9 volumes as a collective history written by Western and Eastern scholars. So far 3 volumes have been published by the Akademie der Wissenschaften in Vienna: 1, *Die wirtschaftliche Entwicklung* (1973); 2, *Verwaltung und Rechtswesen* (1975); and 3 (in 2 parts), *Das Reich und die Völker* (1980). Many of the contributions are excellent.

Alfons Huber and Alfons Dopsch, *Österreichische Reichsgeschichte* (2d ed.; Vienna: F. Tempsky, 1901), though a brief work, is still an unsurpassed masterpiece. It is supplemented by Ernst C. Hellbling, *Österreichische Verfassungs- und Verwaltungsgeschichte* (Vienna: Springer, 1956), with the listing of modern literature. R. A. Kann, *The Multinational Empire: Nationalism and National Reform in the Habsburg Monarchy, 1848–1918* (4th reprint ed.; New York: Octagon, 1977) has also appeared in an enlarged, German edition, *Das Nationalitätenproblem der Habsburgermonarchie, 1848–1918* (Graz and Cologne: Böhlau, 1964), which covers the literature on the nationality problem of the Habsburg empire until 1964. Fran Zwitter, in collaboration with Jaroslav Šidak and Vaso Bogdanov, *Les problèmes nationaux dans la monarchie des Habsbourg* (Belgrade, 1960), discusses the nationality problems of the empire from a Marxian viewpoint.

Bibliography

Eric H. Boehm and others, *Austrian Historical Bibliography* (Santa Barbara: Clio Press, 1967) is an important bibliographical tool. Valuable bibliographical references are also to be found in *Austrian History Yearbook* (Houston: Rice University, 1965–), which includes many pertinent articles on the subject of this volume. Bibliographic guides on *East Central Europe* and *Southeastern Europe,* both edited by Paul L. Horecky and published by the University of Chicago Press in 1969, include not only general literature on the areas concerned but also entries on national groups covered in this volume, specifically the Croats,

Czechs, Magyars, Romanians, Serbs, Slovaks, and Slovenes. All nations of Eastern Europe, as well as the Soviet Union, are covered in the current annual *American Bibliography of Slavic and East European Studies* (*ABSEES*) for books and articles published since 1956 mostly in the United States and Canada.

THE MAGYARS

General History

C. A. Macartney, *Hungary: A Short History* (Edinburgh: University Press, 1962) is conservative in its approach. Ervin Pamlényi, ed., *A History of Hungary* (London: Collet's, 1975) is an important survey based on recent research, but slightly marred by the lack of bibliographic references to non-Magyar literature. Henrik Marczali, *Hungary in the Eighteenth Century* (Cambridge: University Press, 1910) is a significant work, as is the more recent treatment of this topic in Béla K. Király, *Hungary in the Late Eighteenth Century* (New York and London: Columbia University Press, 1969). Denis Sinor, *A History of Hungary* (London: Allen and Unwin, 1959) offers a brief introduction.

Bálint Hóman and Gyula Szekfű, *Magyar történet*, 5 vols. (7th ed.; Budapest: Magyar Egyetemi Nyomda, 1941–43), is the classical survey of Hungarian history in Magyar; although somewhat weak on the economic and social aspects, it includes excellent reviews of sources and annotated bibliographies; volumes 3–5 cover the period 1526–1918. Two comprehensive histories, written from the Marxian viewpoint, have been sponsored by the Historical Institute of the Hungarian Academy of Sciences: *Magyarország története*, 4 vols. (Budapest: Tankönyvkiadó, 1961–72), covers 1526–1918 in volumes 2–4; of the *Magyarország története tíz kötetben* (Budapest: Akadémiai Kiadó, 1976–), edited by Zsigmond P. Pach, volumes 5–8 have appeared by 1980, of which volumes 5–7 (in 6 parts) cover 1790–1918. T. M. Islamov, ed., *Istoriia Vengrii* (Moscow: Nauka, 1971–72), a 3-volume survey, presents a Soviet Marxian interpretation of the course of Hungary's history.

Institutions and Culture

Ákos Timon, *Ungarische Verfassungs- und Rechtsgeschichte* (2d ed.; Berlin: Puttkammer und Mühlbrecht, 1909), a standard work on constitutional, legal, and administrative history, supplements, for 1526–1608, Henrik Marczali's *Ungarische Verfassungsgeschichte* and *Ungarisches Verfassungsrecht*, published in Tübingen by J. C. B. Mohr, respectively in 1910 and 1911. Count Paul Teleki, *The Evolution of Hungary and Its Place in European History* (New York: Macmillan, 1923) presents a revisionist, conservative viewpoint but offers much significant socioeconomic material. Gyula Szekfű, *État et nation* (Paris: Presses universitaires de France, 1945) is significant on nationality problems as seen from the Magyar viewpoint. Erzsébet Andics, *Metternich und die Frage Ungarns* (Budapest: Akadémiai Kiadó, 1973), discusses Vienna's policy toward Hungary. For the late nineteenth century see Theodor Mayer, ed., *Der österreichisch-ungarische Ausgleich von*

1867: Seine Grundlagen und Auswirkungen (Munich: Oldenbourg, 1968) with emphasis on the Hungarian-Croatian interrelations, and Gustav Steinbach, *Die ungarischen Verfassungsgesetze* (3d ed.; Vienna: Manz, 1900). The achievements of the four great Magyars of the nineteenth century are treated in George Barany, *Stephen Széchenyi and the Awakening of Hungarian Nationalism, 1791–1841* (Princeton, N. J.: Princeton University Press, 1968); Istvan Deak, *The Lawful Revolution: Louis Kossuth and the Hungarians, 1848–1849* (New York: Columbia University Press, 1979); Béla K. Király, *Ferenc Deák* (Boston: Twayne, 1975); and Paul Böldy, *Joseph Eötvös and the Modernization of Hungary, 1840–1870* (Philadelphia: American Philosophical Society, 1972). Friedrich Gottas, *Ungarn im Zeitalter des Hochliberalismus: Studien zur Tisza-Ära, 1875–1890* (Vienna: Verlag der Österreichischen Akademie der Wissenschaften, 1976), studies the skewed modernization of Hungary during Kálmán Tisza's rule, and Zoltán Horváth, *Die Jahrhundertwende in Ungarn* (Neuwied am Rhein: Luchterhand, 1966) offers an interesting introduction to the intellectual revolution in the early twentieth century. Tibor Klaniczay, József Szauder, and Miklós Szabolcsi, *History of Hungarian Literature* (London: Collet's, 1964) presents a good survey of literature; Bence Szabolcsi, *A Concise History of Hungarian Music* (London: Barrie and Rockliff, 1964) one on music.

Zsigmond Pál Pach, *Nyugat-európai és magyarországi agrárfejlődés a XV–XVII században* (Budapest: Kossuth Könyvkiadó, 1963), analyzes the differences in socioeconomic development of Hungary and Western Europe in the early modern period. The organization and operations of the Hungarian Chamber are discussed exhaustively in István Nagy, *A Magyar Kamara, 1686–1848* (Budapest: Akadémiai Kiadó, 1971).

On constitutional and legal history of Hungary in Magyar see Ferenc Eckhart, *Magyar alkotmány- és jogtörténet* (Budapest: Politzer, 1946). Imre Lukinich, *A szatmári béke története és okirattára* (Budapest: Magyar Történelmi Társulat, 1925) deals with background of the peace of Szatmár on the basis of archival sources. Dezső Szabó, *A magyarországi urbérrendezés története Mária Terézia korában* (Budapest: Magyar Történelmi Társulat, 1933) offers an authoritative account, as well as documentation, of Maria Theresa's agrarian reforms in Hungary. A fundamental work on the Hungarian Revolution of 1848 is György Spira's *A magyar forradalom 1848–49-ben* (Budapest: Gondolat, 1959). A comprehensive political, social, and cultural history of the Neo-Absolutist period in Hungary is presented in the magisterial 4-volume work by Albert Berzeviczy, *Az abszolutizmus kora Magyarországon, 1849–1865* (Budapest: Franklin Társulat, 1922–37). Gusztáv Gratz, *A Dualizmus kora: Magyarország története, 1867–1918* (Budapest: Magyar Szemle Társaság, 1934), a reliable standard work in 2 volumes on the era of dualism, emphasizes political history. *Pintér Jenő magyar irodalomtörténete* (Budapest: Stephaneum, 1930–41) in 8 volumes covers all aspects of Hungarian literature; though weak on interpretation, it provides a wealth of factual information. István Sőter et al., eds., *A magyar irodalom története* (Budapest: Akadémiai Kiadó, 1964–66), in 6 volumes presents from the Marxian viewpoint a comprehensive history of Hungarian literature from the beginnings to the the post-World War II period. The predicament of the National Coalition parties in 1905–06 and Hungary's participation in World War I are explored respectively in István Dolmányos, *A koalíció az 1905–1906. évi kormányzati válság idején* (Budapest: Akadémiai Kiadó, 1976), and József Galántai, *Magyaror-szág az első világháborúban, 1914–1918* (Budapest: Akadémiai Kiadó, 1974).

Bibliography

Bibliographia Hungariae, 4 vols. in 1 (Berlin: De Gruyter, 1923–29), pertains to literature on the Magyars published abroad. Albert Tezla, *An Introductory Bibliography to the Study of Hungarian Literature* (Cambridge, Mass.: Harvard University Press, 1964) is useful mainly for reference works and literary history and criticism.

Domokos G. Kosáry, *Bevezetés a magyar történelem forrásaiba és irodalmába*, 3 vols. (Budapest; Közoktatásügyi Kiadóvállalat, 1951–54), covers historical sources and literature up to 1825. *Magyar történeti bibliográfia, 1825–1867* (Budapest: Akadémiai Kiadó, 1950–59), a collective work, sponsored by the Hungarian Academy of Sciences, continues in 4 volumes the comprehensive survey of Hungarian historical sources into the period of 1825–67. A lengthy bibliographic essay deals with Hungarian historical publications since World War II in *Études historiques hongroises 1980: Publiées a l'occasion du XVe Congrès international des sciences historiques par la Commission nationale des historiens hongrois* (Budapest: Akadémiai Kiadó, 1980), 2:613–808. See also Paul L. Horecky, *East Central Europe*, and *ABSEES*, listed earlier.

THE CZECHS

General History

Karl Bosl, ed., *Handbuch der Geschichte der bömischen Länder* (Stuttgart: A. Hiersemann, 1967–), so far 4 volumes have appeared with a fifth in preparation; this work presents the most detailed history of the Czech people in all its aspects in any foreign language; excellent bibliographic references are included. Ernest Denis, *Fin de l'Indépendance Bohême*, 2 vols. (Paris: A. Colin, 1890), and by the same author, *La Bohême depuis la Montagne Blanche*, 2 vols. (Paris: Leroux, 1903), are, except for the somewhat outdated source material, still significant works. Robert J. Kerner, ed., *Czechoslovakia* (Berkeley: University of California Press, 1940) includes a number of valuable essays on Czech political and institutional history. Robert J. Kerner, *Bohemia in the Eighteenth Century* (rev. ed. by Joseph Zacek; Orono, Maine: Academic International, 1969) is still useful. Hermann Münch, *Böhmische Tragödie* (Braunschweig: G. Westermann, 1949) and Elizabeth Wiskemann, *Czechs and Germans* (2d ed.; London: Macmillan, 1967) are excellent studies on German-Czech relations, as is Gary Cohen's more specialized *Politics of Ethnic Survival: Germans in Prague, 1861–1914* (Princeton, N. J.: Princeton University Press, 1981). Jan Opočenský, *The Collapse of the Austro-Hungarian Monarchy and the Rise of the Czechoslovak State* (Prague: Orbis, 1928) is a concise but excellent study. Robert W. Seton-Watson, *History of the Czechs and Slovaks* (London: Hutchinson, 1943), S. Harrison Thomson, *Czechoslovakia in European History* (2d ed.; Princeton, N.J.: Princeton University Press, 1953), and John F. N. Bradley, *Czechoslovakia: A Short History* (Edinburgh: University Press, 1971) are useful brief introductions to Czech history.

Přehled československých dějin 3 vols. in 4 (Prague: Nakl. Československé akademie věd, 1958–60), offers the fullest general treatment of early modern and modern Czech history available in Czech in a single work; written from a Marxian viewpoint it emphasizes the post-1848 era as well as social and economic developments (though politics and culture are also covered). A revised and updated version, *Přehled dějin Československa* (Prague: Academia), began to appear in 1980 under the general editorship of Jaroslav Purš and Miroslav Kropilák. Volume 1, part 2 (1982) treats the period 1526–1848. Josef Janáček, *České dějiny: Doba předbělohorská* (Prague: Academia, 1971) is designated as the first volume in a series covering Czech history since 1526.

Institutions and Culture

Kenneth J. Dillon, *King and Estates in the Bohemian Lands, 1526–1564* (Brussels: Les Éditions de la Librairie Encyclopédique, 1976), and Josef V. Polišenský and Frederick Snider, *War and Society in Europe, 1618–1648* (Cambridge and New York: Cambridge University Press, 1978), ably discuss important topics of Czech history. The same holds for Lawrence D. Orton, *The Prague Slav Congress of 1848* (New York: Columbia University Press, 1978), and Stanley Z. Pech, *The Czech Revolution of 1848* (Chapel Hill: University of North Carolina Press, 1969). Hans Raupach, *Der tschechische Frühnationalismus* (2d ed.; Darmstadt: Wissenschaftliche Buchgesellschaft, 1969) gives an adequate presentation. The topic is further explored in more specialized monographs: Stanley B. Kimball, *Czech Nationalism: A Study of the National Theatre Movement, 1845–83* (Urbana: University of Illinois Press, 1964) and Joseph F. Zacek, *Palacký: The Historian as Scholar and Nationalist* (The Hague: Mouton, 1970). Peter Brock and H. Gordon Skilling, eds., *The Czech Renascence of the Nineteenth Century* (Toronto: University of Toronto Press, 1970), Bruce M. Garver, *The Young Czech Party, 1874–1901, and the Emergence of a Multi-Party System* (New Haven, Conn.: Yale University Press, 1978), and Paul Vyšný, *Neo-Slavism and the Czechs, 1898–1914* (Cambridge: Cambridge University Press, 1977) are important contributions to social, political, and intellectual history. Count Francis H. Lützow, *A History of Bohemian Literature* (London: Heinemann, 1907) and Arne Novák, *Czech Literature* (Ann Arbor: Michigan Slavic Publications, 1976) offer brief introductory surveys. Hanuš Jelínek, *Histoire de la littérature tchèque*, 3 vols. (Paris: Editions du Sagittaire, 1930–35), is valuable. Miloslav Rechcígl, ed., *The Czechoslovak Contribution to World Culture* (The Hague: Mouton, 1964) is a truly comprehensive work on all aspects of Czech cultural and social history with an excellent bibliographic section: "Czechoslovakia and its Arts and Sciences."

Standard surveys of Czech constitutional and legal history are Jan Kapras, *Přehled právních dějin zemí České koruny* (5th ed.; Prague: Nakl. vlastním, 1935) and Bohumil Baxa, *Dějiny práva na území republiky Československé* (Brno: Právník, 1935). A fuller treatment from 1526 into the early nineteenth century is offered in volumes 2 and 3 of Jan Kapras, *Právní dějiny zemí koruny české* (Prague: Česká Grafická Unie, 1913–20); and a more recent interpretation of the period 1848–

1918 in vol. 1 of *Dejiny štátu a práva na území Československa v období kapitalizmu*, edited by Leonard Bianchi (Bratislava, SAV, 1971). On the evolution of the circuit (*kraj*) administration see Jaroslav Macek, *Krajská správa v českých zemích a její archivní fondy, 1605–1868* (Prague: Archivní správa Ministerstva vnitra, 1958). Bedřich Šindelář, *Vestfálský mír a česká otázka* (Prague: Academia, 1968) explores in detail the Bohemian aspects of the Thirty Years' War. Bedřich Slavík interprets afresh the intellectual origins of the Czech Enlightenment and national awakening in *Od Dobnera k Dobrovskému* (Prague: Vyšehrad, 1975). Antonín Okáč, *Český sněm a vláda před březnem 1848* (Prague: Zemský národní výbor, 1947) focuses on the Bohemian aristocratic opposition in the 1830s and 1840s. Karel Kosík, *Česká radikální demokracie* (Prague: Státní nakl. politické literatury, 1958) and Tomáš Vojtěch, *Mladočeši a boj o politickou moc v Čechách* (Prague: Academia, 1980) each deals with an important aspect of nineteenth-century Czech political thought and action, but Zdeněk V. Tobolka's *Politické dějiny československého národa*, 4 vols. (Prague: Československý kompas, 1932–37), is still the fundamental work on Czech politics from 1848 to 1918. Jan Mukařovský, ed., *Dějiny české literatury* (Prague: Československá akademie věd, 1959–) covers comprehensively, from the Marxian viewpoint, the history of Czech literature to the mid-nineteenth century in 3 volumes, and is especially valuable for its bibliographies.

Bibliography

Apart from the work mentioned above edited by M. Rechcígl, see Josef Macek, ed., *25 Ans d'Historiographie Tchécoslovaque, 1935–1960* (Prague: Československá akademie věd, 1960), and *Historiografie v Československu, 1970–1980* (Prague: Ústav československých a světových dějin ČSAV, 1980). The periodical *Bibliografie české historie* appeared from 1904 to 1941 as the basic bibliography for Czech history. Its successor since 1955 is the *Bibliografie dějin Československa* (Prague: Československá akademie věd). Rudolf Sturm, *Czechoslovakia: A Bibliographic Guide* (Washington, D. C.: Library of Congress, 1968) covers humanities and social sciences in Czech and Slovak, as well as in major Western languages. See also Paul L. Horecky, *East Central Europe*, and *ABSEES*, listed earlier.

THE SLOVAKS

General History

Robert W. Seton-Watson, *Racial Problems in Hungary* (London: Constable, 1908) is an old classic that first called the attention of the West to the treatment of non-Magyars in Magyar-dominated Hungary. On the same subject see also Ernest Denis, *La question d'Autriche: Les Slovaques* (Paris: Delagrave, 1917). Far more detailed is Lajos Gogolák, *Beiträge zur Geschichte des slowakischen Volkes* (Munich: Oldenbourg, 1963–72), which covers, in 3 volumes, Slovak history from 1526 until 1919.

František Bokes, *Dejiny Slovenska a Slovákov od najstarších čias po oslobodenie* (Bratislava: Slovenská akadémia vied a umení, 1946) is a standard general survey of Slovak history up to World War I. A collective work, sponsored by the Slovak Academy of Sciences, *Dejiny Slovenska* (Bratislava: Slovenká akadémia vied, 1961–68) offers a more detailed and up-to-date account of Slovakia's history to 1900 in the hitherto published 2 volumes. For the period since 1900 see L'ubomír Lipták's *Slovensko v 20. storočí* (Bratislava: VPL, 1968). Essays by leading historians freshly reinterpret the main eras of Slovak history in *Slováci a ich národný vývin* (Bratislava: Slovenská akadémia vied, 1969).

Institutions and Culture

On the Slovak national revival see the notable study by Peter Brock, *The Slovak National Awakening: An Essay on the Intellectual History of East Central Europe* (Toronto: University of Toronto Press, 1976). Helène Tourtzer, *Louis Štúr et l'idée de l'indépendance slovaque 1815–1856* (Paris: Cahors and Alençon, 1913) deals with the key Slovak figure of the nineteenth century.

Jozef Blaškovič, *Rimavská Sobota v čase osmanskotureckého panstva* (Bratislava: Obzor, 1974) is a well-documented case study of Turkish rule in Slovakia. For a seminal work on seventeenth-century Slovak intellectual history see Rudo Brtáň, *Barokový slavizmus* (Lipt. sv. Mikuláš; Tranoscius, 1939). Ján Hučko, *Sociálne zloženie a pôvod slovenskej inteligencie* (Bratislava: Veda, 1974) discusses the social basis of the Slovak national awakening. Imrich Sedlák, *Strieborný vek*, 2 vols. (Košice: Vychodoslovenké vydavateľstvo, 1970), elucidates the special character of the east Slovak national awakening in 1780–1848. A magisterial analysis and documentation of the 1848 revolution in Slovakia is Daniel Rapant's *Slovenské povstanie roku 1848–49: Dejiny a dokumenty*, 5 vols. in 13 parts (Bratislava: Slovenská akadémia vied, 1937–72). Pavla Vošahlíková *Slovenské politické směry v období přechodu k imperialismu* (Prague: Academia, 1979) and Milan Krajčovič, *Slovenská politika v Strednej Európe, 1890–1901: Spolupráca Slovákov, Rumunov a Srbov* (Bratislava: Slovenská akadémia vied, 1971) are important studies of Slovak politics in the late nineteenth century. Under the auspices of the Slovak Academy of Sciences, *Dejiny slovenskej literatúry* (Bratislava: Slovenská akadémia vied, 1958–) is designed as a comprehensive history of Slovak literature; so far 4 volumes have appeared.

Bibliography

See the bibliographies listed in the "Czechs" section. *Studia Historia Slovaca*, vol. 11 (1980), covers in detail Slovak historical publications issued in 1960–77. See also Paul L. Horecky, *East Central Europe*, and *ABSEES*, listed earlier.

The Croats

General History

Stanko Guldescu, *The Croatian-Slavonian Kingdom, 1526–1792* (The Hague: Mouton, 1970) is a solid brief introduction to Croatian history. The same holds for the conservative interpretation of Rudolf Kiszling, *Die Kroaten* (Graz and Cologne: Böhlaus Nachf., 1956). Vladimir Dedijer, Ivan Božić, Sima Ćirković, and Milorad Ekmečić survey in *History of Yugoslavia* (New York: McGraw-Hill, 1974) the history of the Croats, as well as of other nationalities of Yugoslavia, including the Slovenes, and the Serbs of Vojvodina and Bosnia-Herzegovina.

Historija naroda Jugoslavije (Zagreb: Školska knjiga, 1953–59), a massive collective work, includes coverage of the Croats (as well as Slovenes and the Serbs of Vojvodina) from the sixteenth through the eighteenth century in volume 2; it contains substantial bibliographies. Ferdinand Šišić, *Pregled povijesti hrvatskoga naroda* (3d ed.; Zagreb: Matica Hrvatska, 1962) covers the course of Croatian history in a single volume, while the same author's *Hrvatska povijest*, 3 vols. (Zagreb: Matica Hrvatska, 1906–13), offers a more detailed treatment of the period from 1526 to 1848 in volumes 2 and 3. Vjekoslav Klaić, *Povjest Hrvata od najstarijih vremena do svršetka XIX stoljeća*, 5 vols. (rev. ed.; Zagreb: Matica Hrvatska, 1972–73), deals with sixteenth-century Croatia in volume 5. Jaroslav Šidak, Mirjana Gross, Igor Karaman, and Dragovan Šepić in *Povijest hrvatskog naroda g. 1860–1914* (Zagreb: Školska knjiga, 1968) provide an authoritative account of Croatian politics in all Croat-inhabited territories, including Bosnia-Herzegovina.

Institutions and Culture

Francis H. Eterovich and Christopher Spalatin, eds., *Croatia: Land, People, Culture*, 2 vols. (Toronto: University of Toronto Press, 1964–70), offers much socioeconomic and cultural information. The problems of the military border are examined in two books by Gunther E. Rothenberg, *The Austrian Military Border in Croatia, 1522–1747* (Urbana: University of Illinois Press, 1960) and *The Military Border in Croatia, 1740–1881*, that is, until its abolition (Chicago: University of Chicago Press, 1966). On the anti-Turkish defense see also Nikolaus von Preradovich, *Des Kaisers Grenzer: 300 Jahre Türkenabwehr* (Vienna: Molden, 1970). Elinor M. Despalatović treats the political and social aspects of the Croatian national awakening in *Ljudevit Gaj and the Illyrian Movement* (New York: Columbia University Press, 1975). See further Zvane Črnja, *Cultural History of Croatia* (Zagreb: Office of Information, 1962) and Ante Kadić. *From Croatian Renaissance to Yugoslav Socialism: Essays* (The Hague: Mouton, 1969).

The standard general survey of Croatian constitutional and legal history is Ivan Beuc, *Provijest institucija državne vlasti u Hrvatskoj, 1527–1945* (Zagreb: Arhiv Hrvatske, 1969). Nada Klaić, *Društvena previranja i bune u Hrvatskoj u XVI i XVII stoljeću* (Belgrade: Nolit, 1976), critically reviews the manifestations of rural and urban social unrest in sixteenth- and seventeenth-century Croatia.

Vjekoslav Klaić discusses crucial issues of early modern Croatia's constitutional history in "Hrvatski sabori do godine 1790," *Zbornik matice hrvatske*, vol. 1 (1925). On Croatian participation in the Thirty Years' War see Ernest Bauer, *Hrvati u tridesetgodišnjem ratu* (Zagreb: Matica Hrvatska, 1941). Vaso Bogdanov, *Historija političkih stranaka u Hrvatskoj* (Zagreb: Novinarsko izdavačko poduzeće, 1958) exhaustively analyzes Croatian political parties of the nineteenth century. The Croatian national renaissance in Dalmatia and in Istria is treated respectively by Grga Novak, *Prošlost Dalmacije*, vol. 2 (Zagreb: Izd. Hrvatskog izda-

vačkog bibliografskog zavoda, 1944), and Božo Milanović, *Hrvatski narodni pre-
porod u Istri*, 2 vols., (Pazin: Istarsko književno društvo sv. Ćirila i Metoda, 1967–
73). A comprehensive history of Croatian literature is projected in 7 volumes:
Slavko Goldstein et al., eds. *Provijest hrvatske književnosti* (Zagreb: Liber Mladost,
1974–). Volumes 1–5 appeared in 1974–78, with volumes 3–5 covering the
eras from the Renaissance through the *Moderna*.

Bibliography

Regarding bibliographical information see the essay by Charles Jelavich, "The
Croatian Problem in the Habsburg Monarchy in the Nineteenth Century," with
many references to background literature, in *Austrian History Yearbook*, vol. 3
(1967), part 2. Michael B. Petrovich, *Yugoslavia: A Bibliographic Guide* (Washington, D. C.: Library of Congress, 1974) has substantial coverage of Croatian
affairs. See also Paul L. Horecky, *Southeastern Europe*, and *ABSEES*, listed earlier.

THE SLOVENES

General History

For a brief introduction see Dragotin Lončar, *The Slovenes: A Social History
from the Earliest Times to 1910* (Cleveland: American Jugoslav Printing and Publishing Co., 1939). On the late nineteenth and early twentieth centuries see the
useful study of Bogumil Vošnjak, *A Bulwark Against Germany* (London: Allen
and Unwin, 1917), and Carole Rogel, *The Slovenes and Yugoslavism, 1890–1914*
(New York: Columbia University Press, 1977). Politically motivated is Edward
Kardelj, *Die Vierteilung: Nationale Frage der Slowenen* (Vienna, Frankfurt, and
Zurich: Europa Verlag, 1971), abridged translation from the Slovene.

Bogo Grafenauer, *Zgodovina slovenskega naroda*, offers a standard treatment
of Slovene history for 1400–1848 in volumes 3–5; of these, volumes 3 and 4
were published (1956–61) by Kmečka knjiga and volume 5 (1974) by Državna
založba Slovenije, both in Ljubljana. Grafenauer's account is supplemented for
the period up to 1918 by Ferdo Gestrin and Vasilij Melik, *Slovenska zgodovina
od konca osemnajstega stoletja do 1918* (Ljubljana: Državna založba Slovenije, 1966).
A one-volume synthesis of Slovene history by major Slovene historians, including Gestrin, Grafenauer, and Melik, appeared in 1979 under the title *Zgodovina
Slovencev* (Ljubljana: Cankarjeva založba).

See also Vladimir Dedijer and others, *History of Yugoslavia*, as well as *Historija
naroda Jugoslavije*, vol. 2, both listed in the "Croats" section of this bibliography.

Institutions and Culture

Viktor Thiel, "Die innerösterreichische Zentralverwaltung, 1564–1749," *Ar-
chiv für österreichische Geschichte*, vols. 105 (1916) and 111 (1930), covers the central political and administrative agencies of Inner Austria, while August Dimitz,
Geschichte Krains von der ältesten Zeit bis auf das Jahr 1813, 2 vols. (Ljubljana: I.

v. Kleinmayr and F. Bamberg, 1874–76), does the same for Carniola. For literary history see Anton Slodnjak, *Geschichte der slowenischen Literatur* (Berlin: De Gruyter, 1958).

Metod Dolenc, *Pravna zgodovina za Slovensko ozemlje* (Ljubljana: Akademska založba, 1935) discusses comprehensively the history of law in the Slovene-inhabited territories. Mirko Rupel deals with the central figure of sixteenth-century Slovene Protestantism in *Primož Trubar: Življenje in delo* (Ljubljana: Mladinska knjiga, 1962). On the Slovene national awakening from the 1780s into the 1840s see Ivan Prijatelj, *Duševni profili slovenskih preporoditeljev* (Ljubljana: [Merkur], 1935). The same author treats political as well as cultural history of the later nineteenth century in his monumental *Slovenska kulturnopolitična in slovstvena zgodovina, 1848–1895*, 4 vols. (Ljubljana: Državna založba Slovenije, 1955–61). On the Slovenes in the Austrian Littoral until 1918 see the first part of *Istra i slovensko primorje* (Belgrade: Rad, 1952). A collective work, edited by Lino Legiša, *Zgodovina slovenskega slovstva*, 7 vols. (Ljubljana: Slovenska Matica, 1956–71), covers the entire history of Slovene literature. An 8-volume survey by a single author is Jože Pogačnik's *Zgodovina slovenskega slovstva* (Maribor: Založba Obzorja, 1968–1972); a one-volume summary is available under the same title (Maribor: Založba Obzorja, 1973).

Bibliography

A substantial bibliography is offered in Fran Zwitter et al., *Les problèmes nationaux dans la monarchie des Habsbourg* (Belgrade, 1960). See also Michael B. Petrovich's bibliography listed in the "Croats" section, and Paul L. Horecky, *Southeastern Europe*, and *ABSEES* noted earlier.

THE SERBS

General History

Two substantial works on Serbian history also offer information on the Serbs in the Habsburg empire: Josef K. Jireček, *Geschichte der Serben*, 2 vols. (Gotha: Perthes, 1911), of which a revised and enlarged Serbian edition, *Istorija Srba* (Belgrade: Naučna knjiga, 1952) appeared, and Michael B. Petrovich, *A History of Modern Serbia, 1804–1918*, 2 vols. (New York: Harcourt Brace Jovanovich, 1976). See also Vladimir Dedijer and others, *History of Yugoslavia*, as well as *Historija naroda Jugoslavije*, vol. 2, both listed in the "Croats" section. Projected in six volumes, *Istorija srpskog naroda* (Belgrade: Srpska književna zadruga), a collective work by leading Serbian historians under the direction of Radovan Samardžić, started appearing in 1981. Volume 5, part 2 (1981) includes coverage of the Serbs in Vojvodina, Dalmatia, and Croatia from 1804 to 1878.

Southern Hungary (Vojvodina)

For the history of Serbs in Hungary see two detailed older works, Johann H. Schwicker, *Politische Geschichte der Serben in Ungarn* (Budapest: Aigner, 1880) and by the same author, *Geschichte des Temeser Banats* (2d ed.; Budapest: Aigner, 1872). From a different viewpoint, less thorough and likewise somewhat antiquated, the subject is treated by Emile Picot, *Les Serbes de Hongrie* (Prague: Gregr and Dattel, 1873). Horst Haselsteiner discusses Serb political activities in Vojvodina from 1860 to 1867 in *Die Serben und der Ausgleich* (Vienna, Cologne, and Graz, Böhlau, 1976). Dušan Popović, *Srbi u Vojvodini* (Novi Sad: Matica srpska, 1957–63) is a 3-volume comprehensive history by the leading authority of the Serbs of southern Hungary to the mid-nineteenth century. Subsequent historical developments are treated in articles by Arpad Lebl, Stevan Mezei, and Kosta Milutinović in *Jugoslovenski narodi pred prvi svetski rat* (Belgrade: Naučno delo, 1967). A. Ivič, *Istorija Srba u Vojvodini od najstarijih vremena do osnivanja Potisko-Pomoriške granice, 1703* (Novi Sad: Matica srpska, 1929) covers exhaustively the origins of Serb colonization in Vojvodina.

Bosnia-Herzegovina

Regarding the Serbs in Bosnia-Herzegovina see Ferdinand Schmid, *Bosnien und die Herzegowina unter der Verwaltung Österreich-Ungarns* (Leipzig: Veit, 1914), a detailed but somewhat uncritical work. As background reading see also Ernest Bauer, *Zwischen Halbmond und Doppeladler* (Vienna and Munich: Herold, 1971). Vladislav Skarić, Osman Nuri-Hadžić, and Nikola Stojanović, *Bosna i Hercegovina pod austrougarskom upravom* (Belgrade: G. Kon, [1938]), published as volume 15 of *Srpski narod u XIX veku,* focuses on the Serbs, as well as the Moslems, of Bosnia-Herzegovina under Habsburg rule. Muhamed Hadžijahić, "Formiranje nacionalnih ideologija u Bosni i Hercegovini u XIX vijeku," *Jugoslovenski Istorijski Časopis,* 1970, no. 1/2, discusses perceptively special features of Serb nationalism in Bosnia-Herzegovina.

Bibliography

For bibliographic information see the essays by Wayne S. Vucinic and Dimitrije Djordjević in *Austrian History Yearbook,* vol. 3 (1967), part 2; and Joel M. Halpern, *Bibliography of English Language Sources on Yugoslavia* (2d ed.; Amherst, Mass.: Department of Anthropology, University of Massachusetts, 1969). See also Michael B. Petrovich's bibliography listed in the "Croats" section, and Paul L. Horecky, *Southeastern Europe,* and *ABSEES,* noted earlier.

THE RUTHENIANS

General History

Most information on the Ruthenians in Western languages has to be taken from sources that deal with general Ukrainian history. See Michael Hrushevsky, *A History of Ukraine* (New Haven, Conn.: Yale University Press, 1941) and by the same author, *The Historical Evolution of the Ukrainian Problem* (London: Garden City Press, 1915). See also Dmytro Doroshenko, *History of the Ukraine* (2d ed.; Edmonton, Alberta: Institute Press, 1941), and more recent, in German,

Borys Krupnyckyj, *Geschichte der Ukraine von den Anfängen bis zum Jahre 1917* (3d ed.; Wiesbaden: Harrassowitz, 1963). About the Ruthenians in Galicia see Ivan L. Rudnytsky, "The Ruthenians in Galicia under Austrian rule," *Austrian History Yearbook,* vol. 3 (1967), part 2.

Transcarpathia

There exist, however, two excellent modern monographs on Transcarpathian Ruthenians (or Carpatho-Ruthenians) by Ivan Žeguc, *Die nationalpolitischen Bestrebungen der Karpatho-Ruthenen, 1848–1918* (Wiesbaden: Harrassowitz, 1965) and Paul R. Magocsi, *The Shaping of a National Identity: Subcarpathian Rus', 1848–1948* (Cambridge, Mass.: Harvard University Press, 1978). An older, but still useful work is Hermann J. Bidermann, *Die ungarischen Ruthenen, ihr Wohngebiet, ihr Erwerb, und ihre Geschichte,* 2 vols. (Innsbruck: Wagner'schen Universitäts-Buchhandlung, 1862–67). From the Soviet Marxian viewpoint and with a heavy socioeconomic emphasis, Ivan G. Kolomiets, *Ocherki po istorii Zakarpat'ia* (Tomsk; Izd-vo Tomskogo Universiteta, 1953–59) offers the fullest account of the history of the Transcarpathian Ruthenians to the mid-nineteenth century, in 2 volumes. It is supplemented for the second half of the century by the same author's *Sotsial'no-ekonomicheskie otnosheniia i obshchestvennoe dvizhenie v Zakarpat'e vo vtoroi polovine XIX stoletiia* (Tomsk: Izd-vo Tomskogo Universiteta, 1961), also in 2 volumes.

Bukovina

On the Ruthenians in Bukovina see Traian Vǎleanu, "The Question of Bukovina—Then and Now," *Journal of Central European Affairs,* vol. 4 (1944–45). Though tendentious, I. M. Nowosiwsky, *Bukovianian Ukrainians: A Historical Background and Their Self-Determination in 1918* (New York: Association of Bukovinian Ukrainians, 1970) provides useful information. The same holds for the much more substantial collective work, edited by Denys Kvitkovs'kyi, ed., *Bukovyna: ii mynule i suchasne* (Paris and Philadelphia: Zelena Bukovyna, 1956).

Bibliography

For bibliographic information see Ivan Mirchuk, *Geschichte der ukrainischen Kultur* (Munich: Isar Verlag, 1957), and the periodical *Ukrainian Review* (London: Association of Ukrainians in Great Britain, 1954–). Magocsi's monograph includes an outstanding bibliography for Transcarpathian Ruthenians, while the work edited by Kvitkovs'kyi contains a wealth of bibliographic references for the Ruthenians of Bukovina. See also *ABSEES,* noted earlier.

THE ROMANIANS IN BUKOVINA

The Romanians until 1918 are covered in volumes V and VIII of this history, where the appropriate bibliographic information will be found.

On the Romanians in Bukovina see Dimitrie Drăghicescu, *Les problèmes na-tionaux de l'Autriche-Hongrie: Les Roumains (Transylvanie, Bucovine, Banat)* (Paris: Bossard, 1918); Ion Nistor, *Der nationale Kampf in der Bukowina* (Bucharest: C. Göbl, 1918); and Erich Prokopowitsch, *Die rumänische Nationalbewegung in der Bukowina und der Dako-Romanismus* (Graz and Cologne: Böhlaus Nachf., 1965), the best of these three useful studies. Vasile Curticăpeanu includes intellectual history of the Bukovinian Romanians in his *Die rumänische Kulturbewegung in der österreichisch-ungarischen Monarchie* (Bucharest: Verlag der Akademie der Sozialistischen Republik Rumäniens, 1966).

Mihail Kogălniceanu, *Răpirea Bucovinei* (Bucharest, 1875) gives an authoritative account of the circumstances of Bukovina's annexation by the Habsburg monarchy. Constantin Daicoviciu and Miron Constantinescu, eds., *Destrămarea monarhiei austro-ungare, 1900–1918* (Bucharest: Editura Academiei, 1964) analyzes the break-up of the Austro-Hungarian empire with special emphasis on developments in Bukovina, as well as Transylvania. Romanian nationalist activities in Bukovina during World War I are covered in Teodor Balan, *Suprimarea mişcărilor naţionale din Bucovina pe timpul războiului mondial, 1914–1918* (Cernăuţi: Editura autorului, 1923).

The book by Prokopowitsch provides substantial bibliographic information on the subject. See also Paul L. Horecky, *Southeastern Europe,* and *ABSEES,* noted earlier.

Index

This book is arranged basically according to eight national groups: Croats, Czechs, Magyars, Romanians (in Bukovina), Ruthenians (in Bukovina and Transcarpathia), Serbs, Slovaks, and Slovenes. Accordingly their names and those of their geographic areas are not used as primary headings in this index. The analytical table of contents should facilitate identification of subject matter pertaining to them.

The eight national groups, however, figure as subheadings under topical headings, and the following descriptors are used for their geographic areas:

Bohemian Lands: designate Bohemia, Moravia, and Austrian Silesia; until 1742 also the rest of Silesia; and until 1635, also Lower and Upper Lusatia

Bosnia-Herzegovina, Bukovina, Croatia, Dalmatia, and *Istria:* refer to the historico-administrative entities

Hungary: refers to the historico-administrative entity with special attention to the Magyar-inhabited area

Slovakia: refers to the Slovak-inhabited part of Hungary

Slovenia: subsumes Carniola, and the Slovene-inhabited areas of Carinthia, Gorizia, Istria, and Styria

Transcarpathia: refers to the Ruthenian-inhabited northeast Hungary, mainly the counties of Bereg, Máramaros, Ugocsa, and Ung

Vojvodina: subsumes Bačka and western Banat

Likewise, the relations of the eight national groups with each other, and with other national groups inhabiting their territories, are indexed and the national names are arranged in alphabetical order in the headings (e.g., *Czech-German relations*). Relations with nations in outside territories and countries are indexed under the name of that territory or country (e.g., *Germany: relations with Bohemian Lands*).

507

6198/001

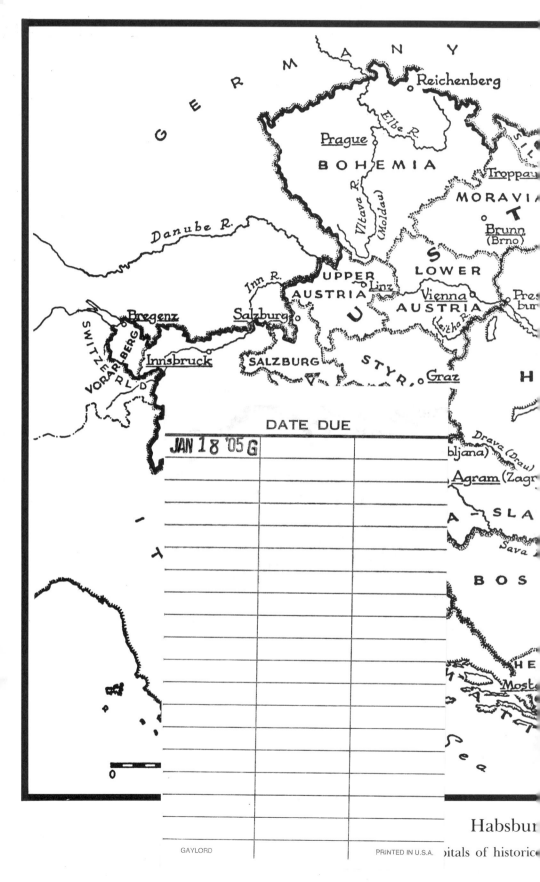

GERMANY

Reichenberg

Elbe R.

Prague

BOHEMIA

Vltava R. (Moldau)

Troppau

MORAVIA

Brunn (Brno)

Danube R.

Inn R.

UPPER AUSTRIA

Linz

LOWER

Vienna

AUSTRIA

Pres burg

Bregenz

Salzburg

Leitha R.

SWITZERLAND

VORARLBERG

Innsbruck

SALZBURG

STYR.

Graz

H

DATE DUE

JAN 18 '05 G

Drava (Drau) bljana)

Agram (Zagr

A - SLA

Sava

BOS

HE

Most

Sea

0

Habsbur

oitals of historic